The Hidden Epidemic

PCOS
polycystic ovary syndrome

The Hidden Epidemic

By Samuel S. Thatcher, M.D., Ph.D.

Perspectives Press

Indianapolis, Indiana

Perspectives Press
P.O. Box 90318
Indianapolis, IN 46290-0318
USA
(317)872-3055
http://www.perspectivespress.com

Cover design by Bookwrights

Manufactured in the United States of America

Hardcover ISBN 0-944934-25-0

The information contained in this book is meant as an overview of the subject. Its purpose is to improve awareness and understanding of a medical condition that is not well defined. It is meant to stimulate interest and thought, but not to dictate, or even guide, medical treatment. There may be many equally good strategies for evaluation and therapy. Each patient is unique and should be individually evaluated and treated. Every attempt has been made to assure that the material is correct, but there remains the possibility of errors for which the author or publisher cannot be held responsible.

Library of Congress Cataloging-in-Publication Data:

Thatcher, Samuel S.
   PCOS : the hidden epidemic / by Samuel S. Thatcher.
      p. cm.
   Includes bibliographical references and index.
   ISBN 0-944934-25-0 (hardcover : alk. paper) --

   1. Stein-Leventhal syndrome -- Popular works. 2. Consumer education.

RG480.S7 T48 2000
618.1'1--dc21

                                                    00-037316

This book is dedicated to my patients.

It is easy to underestimate the number of individuals whom it takes to move a book from conception to delivery, and it is easy to see why there is a long list of acknowledgements accompanying each such effort. What started as a personal pursuit, quickly became a group effort. Every member of the staff at the Center for Applied Reproductive Science (CARS) has contributed to the effort, some directly, while others had to endure the process. My heart-felt appreciation is offered to the following individuals, each of whom in his or her own way has made a special contribution:

Drs. Joe Kennedy and *Steve Sawin*, my practice partners.

Lisa Buchanan, the CARS information officer, for her research and writing support.

Luann Johnson, for her tireless coordination of the project and for her preparation of the advocacy chapter.

Melissa Himelein, who addressed perhaps the most important issue of PCOS, body image, and has changed my own image of obesity management.

Frankie Ramsey for his computer expertise, and who, along with *Katie Williams,* helped in the preparation of illustrations.

Brenda Bryan, CARS nutritionist, for her kind review of Chapter 8 and *Carol Fenwick,* our consulting nutritionist and exercise physiologist at CARS Asheville, for her incisive and insightful discussions on lifestyle management.

Lesa Childers, who has been a reckoning force in increasing awareness and support for PCOS.

Paula Puffer specifically for her contributions to the resource chapter, and who, with *Kristin Rencher* and *Christine Gray DeZarn* and the Board of Directors of the *PolyCystic Ovarian Syndrome Association* offered their help, not only for this book, but more importantly for bringing PCOS into focus for countless women and health care professionals.

Bec Waddell, monitor of the INCIID PCOS, bulletin board for her careful review.

Theresa Grant at INCIID to whom I will be forever grateful for introducing me to my editor and publisher at Perspectives Press, *Pat Johnston*, who, with first-hand knowledge of PCOS, clear vision, and great skill, molded the final product. A better advocate for us all could never be found.

... and to my wife, Nel, who has always kept a fire in the hearth and a candle in the window.

S. S. T.
July, 2000
Johnson City, Tennessee

Table of Contents

Why This Book?
An Introduction

It isn't often that the publisher of a book writes its introduction—let alone that that publisher also provides its first anecdote. But let me share with you a story...

> By the time I was 19 and had just become engaged to the man I would soon marry, I knew instinctively that the irregular and very painful and heavy menstrual periods of my teen years must mean that something was wrong. I insisted that my fiance and I talk about what it might mean if we couldn't have a baby. We agreed that adoption would be a good way to form a family. Having had that talk and come to that decision still did not prepare me, though, for the pain and isolation of our infertility.
>
> Four years later, while Neil Armstrong walked on the moon, I was not delivering the baby I had been diagnosed six months before to have been pregnant with, but was instead recovering from the major surgery that would wedge both ovaries and leave me with only one fallopian tube, would give a name to my "female problems"—Stein Leventhal Syndrome—would label me "fertility impaired," and would start me down the path to my life's work as an infertility and adoption educator.
>
> Was I "lucky" to have found my life's mission in that way? Was I "luckier" than most PCOS patients to have relatively few skin and hair problems? Was I "luckier" that my tendency to gain weight so much more easily than my peers responded "well" for many years to my bouts of severe fasting, keeping me "voluptuous" rather than "fat?" until my 40s?
>
> If "luckier" means finding my way to the perfect children whom I was meant to parent rather than to the children I expected to deliver by easing me toward adoption, yes, I agree! I was lucky.
>
> But since those "missing symptoms" tended to make me appear "normal enough" to be unalarming to my doctors, who then missed life-threatening connections between my long-ago Stein-Leventhal diagnosis, an aunt with the same diagnosis thirty years before, a family full of overweight people, and a father who died at age 56 of type 2 diabetes-related heart problems, at age 54 I don't count myself as entirely "lucky."

Can it really be, given that Stein Leventhal Syndrome has been being diagnosed for over 60 years, that only now dermatologists and internists and gynecologists and nutritionists are putting the pieces of this puzzle together to begin to save the lives of women? Sad, perhaps, but true. It was the magazine articles about Syndrome X, CHAOS Syndrome, etc. half a dozen years ago and subsequent articles about Insulin Resistance that woke me up and made me insistent that my own internist learn more about these connections she (and most of her peers) had heard little to nothing about. For a while more it will take this kind of informed and proactive consumer stance in order for women with PCOS to get the care they deserve.

When Sam Thatcher called me one spring morning in 2000 and proposed to me the book you are now reading, as a woman with PCOS I knew what the acquisitions editor at the larger publisher he had approached about it didn't know: that while PCOS may be a "niche" subject, its niche is far from small. As an infertility and adoption educator and a consumer advocate of 20+ years experience, I knew something else that that large publisher's acquisitions editor didn't know: that the audience for an early 21st century book on PCOS is larger than just women diagnosed with PCOS. It includes family members, physicians, nutritionists, nurses, technicians, physical trainers, mental health professionals and more—all of whom need the same level of information. The larger publisher had told Sam that in order to sell, self-help books on health topics need to be written on an eighth grade reading level. That didn't seem right to Sam, who commented, "If that's the case, then the average book buyer is not as smart as my patients seem to be." As an experienced consumer advocate I agreed with Sam that this was not a book that needed to be "dumbed down" in order to meet its audience's needs.

There was one very important reason for Sam Thatcher to write this book and for Perspectives Press to publish it: it was needed. Once begun, there was almost no stopping it. The manuscript that was expected to be perhaps 350 pages long grew to become almost 500 pages in length because there was no way to create a book respectful of the consumer's need for a reference tool—a comprehensive look into the multiple facets of PCOS—without its being this long. The result was a book that could also serve as a topic review for the health care professionals who are its secondary audience.

No matter which hat I put on—my hat as a woman with PCOS, my hat as a consumer educator and advocate, my hat as a publisher—I find myself more than pleased with the final result of this author's labors. Sam Thatcher cuts no slack. In *PCOS: The Hidden Epidemic* Dr. Thatcher says that PCOS is real; PCOS is forever; and PCOS can have life-threatening consequences. "It is not nearly so important that the label of PCOS is applied," Dr. Thatcher wrote in his book proposal, "but that the association of the signs, symptoms, and medical risks is made. The diagnosis of PCOS carries with it not only an obligation for understanding, but also an obligation for present and future health risk management."

With the passion that only an advocate can muster, Sam Thatcher asserts that women with PCOS **deserve** (note the emphasis—it was deliberate) to have information, support, attention, and adequate medical care. He's taken a giant step forward with the information gathered here in *PCOS: The Hidden Epidemic*, making it easier for women with PCOS to begin to take charge of themselves, their medical condition, their care, and their lives! Perspectives Press is proud to be supporting that.

Patricia Irwin Johnston, M.S.
infertility and adoption educator, consumer advocate, and author
Taking Charge of Infertility
Understanding Infertility: Insights for Family and Friends
Launching a Baby's Adoption

What Is It?
Definition and History

> "I got my period at thirteen just like my friends did, but after about two years, I started having heavy bleeding and cramping every month, and then my periods became irregular. I would have one and then not have another for two or three months. My mother talked to her doctor about it and he said it was normal for a teenage girl to experience irregularities in her menstrual cycle and that I was young and didn't need to worry about it. Not too long after my period started, I began to grow excessive hair in places that were very embarrassing to me. I gained weight that I have never been able to get off. In college, I had to get a physical and I told the doctor I hadn't had a regular period in two years and he started me on birth control pills. The pills helped to regulate my periods. My last year of college, I got married and soon after I got off the pill and we started trying to get pregnant. We tried for several years and I just decided that I was too stressed and we should wait longer. We tried again when I was in my early thirties, but with no success. Now, I was over-weight, had this excessive hair to deal with, and couldn't conceive a child. That's when we ended up in the repro-ductive endocrinologist's office. Finally after years of doc-tors telling me I could lose weight if I just tried or that I couldn't have a baby because I was too stressed or to go back and try electrolysis again for the hair growth, some-one gave my problems a name–PCOS. I wasn't crazy. It wasn't all in my head. I had a real medical condition with a real name. For the first time I felt like there was hope. Even if I couldn't get pregnant, someone knew what was happening with my body."

This patient thought she was crazy, but of course you and I know that she was not. Her story is not uncommon among PCOS patients. There seemed to be no help and little hope.

What is PCOS?

Chances are that, for many of those reading this book, the term PCOS was unfamiliar to you just several days to several weeks ago. You may recently have been given the diagnosis by a physician. You may have read an article mentioning it in a women's magazine. You may have been surfing the Web. Something struck a bell for you, and now you are trying to find out more.

Unfortunately, despite the fact that they may have been living with PCOS all of their lives, many readers of this book will be in this situation of never having heard of it before because of failings in our health care providing systems. Whether you first encountered PCOS at your doctor's office or on the Internet, once you become aware that the syndrome exists, you are likely to find that it is like taking off blinders. Quite likely you will see the signs and hear the symptoms of PCOS everywhere—in family members, among co-workers. PCOS may seem ubiquitous! But what is it?

Perhaps it is fitting that we start with the most difficult question of this book—its definition. One presenter at a medical conference applied a familiar cliche to PCOS, "I can't define it, but I know it when I see it." In some way or the other, every definition of PCOS is still lacking. It is clear that what we call polycystic ovarian syndrome (PCOS) is a complex hormonal disturbance that affects the entire body and has numerous implications for general health and well-being. It is also clear that PCOS is not a new problem. But, for far too long, it has been under-diagnosed and under-treated. Health care providers often have concerned themselves with a single symptom while ignoring the larger spectrum of problems that make up what PCOS is. It seems that health care providers like me are also awakening to the complexity of PCOS. This new awareness is due in no small part to the demands of our patients, but it is also due to new understanding and treatment strategies. Therapies that were not available only a few years ago are now becoming commonplace. These are exciting times, and a definitive answer as to the cause(s) of PCOS could be near at hand. Soon, the definition of PCOS is likely to become more precise.

What's the history of PCOS?

The earliest description of polycystic ovaries dates to 1845, when "sclerocystic" changes of the ovary were described in a French manuscript. The term *sclerocystic* refers to the typical physical appearance of the PCOS ovary, characterized by a tough, thickened, shiny white covering, overlying a layer of many (poly) small cysts just under the ovarian surface. This is still the description used by pathologists. Soon after 1900, there were several isolated reports recounting cystic changes of the ovary and treatment by removal of a portion of the ovary, a procedure called a wedge resection. Still, the connection between the polycystic ovary and a larger syndrome (PCOS) had not been made. As you will learn, PCOS affects much more than the ovary, and the syndrome is much more complicated than just an ovary filled with multiple small cysts.

In 1935, doctors Stein and Leventhal reported an association of three problems: 1) excessive male-pattern hair growth (hirsutism), 2) obesity and 3) menstrual cycle disturbances leading to infertility. This now classic triad of problems was found in association with enlarged sclerocystic ovaries containing many small cysts. Because of the appearance of the ovaries in these individuals, they designated this condition polycystic ovarian disease.

A disease or syndrome?

PCOS has often since been referred to as Stein-Leventhal syndrome. The earlier term, disease, is not quite correct. A disease is a specific and constant set of symptoms and physical findings. Even in this first report, not all of the patients investigated had all three of the identified problems. The term disease now has been abandoned in describing PCOS in favor of the term syndrome, which is defined as a grouping of symptoms, including both physical and laboratory findings. It must be realized that the term syndrome still might eventually be found to be too restrictive and that this condition is broad spectrum with a vast diversity among patients.

At a 1990 National Institutes of Health (NIH) conference that brought together a wide range of PCOS experts, a consensus was reached that the two consistent components of PCOS, therefore providing a definition, were hyperandrogenism (elevated male hormones) and chronic lack of ovulation. With all due respect to this elite group, their definition also poses problems, because it underestimates the possible long-term metabolic consequences of PCOS. Individuals with PCOS who may not be infertile because they have occasional, if not normal and regular, ovulation may still have obesity, excessive hair growth, and a propensity to develop diabetes.

PCOS is like the classic story of a number of blind men, each able to touch just one part, trying to describe what an elephant must look like.

What are PCOS' signs and symptoms?

In medical parlance signs are characteristics of a disease that can be physically seen and recorded while symptoms are the complaints which may, or may not, be seen. For example, a fever measured on a thermometer is a sign, while feeling warm is a symptom. The most common signs of PCOS are obesity, hirsutism, and lack of timely ovulation. Over 95% of women who have all three of the classic signs of obesity, excessive hair growth, and infertility and/or irregular periods have PCOS. Yet, some women may have none of these findings and still have disordered hormone production and metabolism, symptoms which are not visible as signs.

Not all PCOS patients are obese. Balen and his colleagues in Britain reported that 38% of 1741 women they reviewed who had polycystic ovaries on ultrasound scan were also obese. It is not known what percentage of obese women have PCOS, but it is certainly less than 50%. Many with PCOS may maintain a near normal weight, though often only with a great effort, so that if they were not conscientious about their eating patterns, they would weigh much more. There is also a distinct group of thin PCOS patients who may have even more firmly entrenched hormonal and fertility problems than do many obese patients.

Not all patients are excessively hairy (hirsute), but many may have other skin problems, such as acne. Some patients with abnormal hair growth have been given told that their hirsutism is idiopathic, meaning having no known cause. On closer examination by a physician aware of PCOS, most such individuals with an increase in body hair growth will be found to have subtle abnormalities of their hormones or, upon ultrasound, will be found to have polycystic ovaries.

By definition, PCOS must be associated with either relative or absolute changes in hormone levels. Hormones are chemical messengers that are released into the bloodstream in very small quantities, creating dramatic effects throughout the body. Specifically, PCOS is characterized by elevated levels of male hormones (hyperandrogenism). Sometimes these changes may be so subtle that standard laboratory testing may still be reported as normal and there may be no outward physical signs of the disturbance. In some patients there may be few outward signs of hormonal alterations, although laboratory determinations are markedly abnormal, and in others there may be marked physical signs with apparently normal laboratory testing. Regardless, in such patients there is still a hormonal disturbance in either the signaling or receiving systems.

Not all PCOS patients are infertile, but PCOS is probably the single most common cause of menstrual cycle disturbance and infertility due to lack of ovulation (anovulation). Often a previously unexpected diagnosis of PCOS is made during an evaluation for infertility. At the same time, some women with PCOS may be outwardly fertile, but this may be due to an early start at a family at a time before PCOS was fully developed, or to a chance ovulation with a super-fertile male partner, or simply that some women with PCOS still ovulate relatively regularly.

How common is PCOS?

PCOS is the most common hormonal disturbance among pre-menopausal women. Certainly, PCOS is a leading cause of infertility due to lack of ovulation. Depending on how the disorder is defined, at least 5% of all women of reproductive age have some characteristic of PCOS. PCOS has no respect for race or nationality, although the physical manifestations may vary among ethnic groups. For example, Asian women are less likely to have excessive hair growth than are women of Western European origin.

Some researchers make the distinction between "PCO-appearing" ovaries on ultrasound and "true" PCOS. With pelvic ultrasound it has been found that approximately 20-30% of women of reproductive age will have polycystic-appearing ovaries, some despite proven fertility and lack of other characteristic findings. (See figure 1-3)

Why do women with PCOS seek medical care?

There are three broad reasons why PCOS patients seek medical care:

- They are having menstrual cycle disturbance and/or infertility.
- They are concerned about physical appearance because of obesity

and/or excessive hair growth.
- They are experiencing metabolic derangements, including abnormalities in blood fat *(lipid)* levels, insulin/glucose (sugar) levels, and elevated blood pressure *(hypertension)*.

Often gynecologists, the health care providers to whom many women turn for help, have concerned themselves with only the first of these complaints and have been relatively insensitive to the latter two. Internists may focus only on the metabolic problem without concern for the specific hormonal problems. Dermatologists may have dealt only with the surface problems. Generalists have often failed to make, or to understand, the relationship between the different faces of PCOS. A more holistic approach to PCOS is certainly warranted and can have a significant effect in altering quality of life and long-term health consequences.

Why didn't my doctor tell me what was wrong?

It is a sad reflection on the medical profession, but we have not done a very good job of helping PCOS patients. We have been able to help some women establish a pregnancy with fertility drugs, others to gain some semblance of normal menstrual cycles with birth control pills, and still others to adequately control hypertension. But too often there has been a failure to see the big picture—the full polycystic ovarian syndrome that produces the symptom being reported and treated.

The average medical visit lasts about fifteen minutes, during which time a history must be taken, an exam performed and a treatment plan given. If the symptoms were described and PCOS was given as a possible answer as part of a multiple-choice test, most physicians would probably answer correctly that the patient has PCOS. Unfortunately, in most busy practices, there isn't the time for the detailed history that needs to be taken and the thorough discussion that must follow in order for the typical physician to suspect and diagnose PCOS. This is a fact, but it is not an excuse. Most physicians have heard of PCOS, but, because of the very recent advances in PCOS, few physicians fully understand its full spectrum and implications. The physician you saw was probably more task-oriented, trying to exclude pathology of an immediate health threat and prescribing a precise therapy for the specific problems that caused the appointment to be made. For example, a patient seen for lack of a period *(amenorrhea)* is given something to "bring on a period." In other words, your physican was so intent upon looking at the condition of the "tree" that you presented to him that he did not step back to examine the condition of the forest.

A combination of growing awareness and patient demand is leading to increased knowledge, proper identification and management of the presenting problems, and long-term health maintenance. Still, it is quite possible that the medical and research communities are only at the tip of the iceberg in understanding PCOS. To this end, some physicians are now specializing in evaluation and treatment of PCOS, and PCOS centers specializing in a multidisciplinary approach are beginning to appear. (See Chapter 18).

Is there a common ground with PCOS?

Let's first look at several characteristics that individuals with PCOS tend to share—what joins, not separates.

Follicles, consisting of the egg and surrounding supportive cells, are the major functional units of the ovary. The polycystic ovary is filled with increased numbers of pea-sized cysts that form from arrested follicular development, which results in lack of ovulation. The small cysts of PCOS produce relatively large amounts of androgens (male hormones). It is debated as to whether PCOS arises as a metabolic effect of the follicle, a disorder of the ovarian regulatory mechanism involved in the brain and pituitary gland, or from sources outside the ovary. (See Chapter 2).

An important observation has been that surgical removal of a portion of the ovary can restore regular periods and fertility in some women. For this reason, it has been suggested that the ovary is the origin of the abnormality. Direct measurement of androgens from the bloodstream may or may not be abnormal, but the side effects of hyperandrogenism are present. Clearly this leads to skin problems (see Chapter 7), but it can also create a greater risk of abnormal levels of lipids in the blood. In the ovary (see Chapter 2), increased androgens are produced in the smaller size follicle cysts that characterize PCOS.

Most recently, abnormalities of insulin and sugar metabolism have also been linked to the central problem of PCOS (see Chapter 9).

We also know that PCOS is inherited (see a full explanation in Chapter 3). For the near future, this also means that a cure is unlikely. At present we must settle for trying to control, or better yet, to correct the symptoms rather than to cure the condition.

PCOS has its roots based in genetic predisposition and the alteration of several basic metabolic pathways. This leads to a constellation of signs and symptoms which are collectively known as PCOS.

Figure 1-1 PCOS Origins & Effects

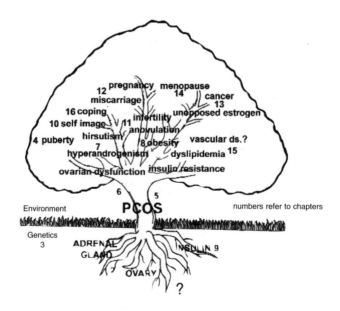

What's in a name anyway?

How all this fits together is really unknown. Is there only one cause, or are there many? Present research is unraveling the mysteries of this disorder. Important lines of evidence are emerging and offer clues about a central mechanism. But, will there be only one central cause found? An important principle of medicine is that we always first attempt to link all physical complaints and clinical findings into a single disorder. Although thus far we have not been able to do this with PCOS, it does not mean that we cannot do so in the near future. For the present, PCOS remains a "final common pathway" of a variety of disorders. The diagnosis of PCOS remains principally one of exclusion. That is, PCOS is what is left when all other possible explanations are excluded. Other problems that share characteristics of PCOS are presented in Chapter 15. At present, PCOS can be a sign/symptom of a variety of problems; much like a fever is a consequence of a number of diseases, but, in short, the cause of PCOS is unknown.

Problems remain with the term PCOS itself. The ovaries may, or may not, be the primary source of the disorder. This may be one reason why polycystic *ovary* syndrome is preferred over the often used term polycystic *ovarian* syndrome. The ovary remains the axle on which the PCOS wheel turns, but it may not be exclusively an "ovarian" syndrome (though, in the final analysis, I can't believe that it matters whether the term *ovary* or *ovarian* is used!)

Can PCOS exist in the absence of the ovaries? This philosophical question is addressed in Chapters 14 and 15. The fact that the small cysts of PCOS are not truly cysts, but are disordered follicles, lead Dr. Walter Futterweit to suggest in his extensive 1984 monograph on the subject that the disorder be called *polyfollicullar* ovarian disease. To call PCOS *hyperandrogenic chronic anovulation* may be correct in many ways, but in addition to being too restrictive, it is a mouthful of medical terms. A number of other suggestions for renaming PCOS have been made, but none has gained acceptance by anyone except its own author.

Figure 1-2 PCOS Vicious Circle

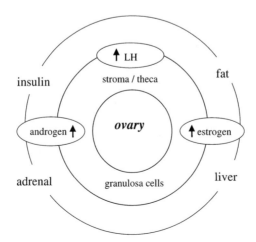

Since the designation of PCOS is so well entrenched in the literature and medical practice and no better name has emerged, it seems as if the term is here to stay. It is much less important what the disorder is called than that it is appropriately recognized and treated.

However, since the designation of PCOS is so well entrenched in the literature and medical practice and no better name has emerged, it seems as if the term is here to stay. It is much less important what the disorder is called than that it is appropriately recognized and treated.

This condition about which we know more and more remains difficult to pin down. We may well find that despite what we know now, the next decade will teach us that we really know little at all about the spectrum of symptoms we now call PCOS. For now, however, we can offer offers a working statistical profile for PCOS presented in the table below:

Figure 1-3 PCOS Balance

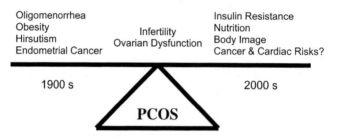

A Year 2000 Statistical Profile of PCOS

- 20-30% of all women have PCO changes evident on ultrasound
- 5-10% of all women have elevated androgens and chronic anovulation
- 90% plus of PCOS patients show PCO on ultrasound
- 40-60% of PCOS patients have weight/obesity problems
- 60-90% of PCOS patients have skin and/or hair problems
- 50-90% of those with PCOS have abnormal ovulation patterns
- 40-80% of those with PCOS have a fertility impairment
- 40-80% of those with PCOS demonstrate insulin resistance
- 40% of those with PCOS develope type 2 diabetes by age 40

Let's move on

I hope that this chapter has set the stage. I know that you may continue to feel confused and that you don't understand it all. None of us do. In each of the next chapters a specific area of PCOS has been identified and is explored in greater depth. After reading the rest of this book you should have more answers than questions, or at least your questions will be the right ones and the ones with which even the medical community struggles. It is my hope that the following chapters will give you insight into the present level of understanding of this important problem, the capacity to evaluate treatment options available, and the reassurance that you are not alone in the fight.

How Does It Work?
Biology of the Female
Reproductive System

Claude Bernard, a French physiologist of the 19th century, proposed that we live in two environments, the external world that surrounds our body and a more important internal milieu. The cells of the body are bathed in a primordial sea, and our increasing freedom from the external world and a capacity for independent life comes from our capacity to protect and maintain a constancy in our internal environment—the concept of homeostasis. A vital function of every organism is the protection and harmony of its own internal environment.

Let me warn you from the start that this chapter is complicated. Together we will have to wade through the thick and into the deep. To understand PCOS, a basic understanding of reproductive endocrinology is essential. This chapter will provide the framework of how the female reproductive system works and what goes wrong with how it works in women with PCOS. You may need to use this chapter several times as a refresher course while your understanding of PCOS increases.

What does the endocrine system do?

To keep in internal balance and to allow communication with the outside world, the body utilizes three entwined communication networks: the nervous system, the immune system, and the endocrine system. The field of endocrinology is concerned with the last of these three: understanding where, how, and why hormones are produced. Hormones are minute chemical messages carried by the bloodstream in order to relay information from one part of the body to distant sites. One hormone can cause various effects depending on three things: which type of cell or tissue it is acting upon, the sex of the individual, and the stage in the individual's life cycle. Male hormones, for example, can increase muscle mass in the male, or they can cause unwanted hair growth in the female, and they can increase the risk of heart disease, or they can improve libido. One bodily function may have an exhaustive list of hormonal regulators. Ovulation is controlled by pituitary hormones, steroids, prostaglandins and numerous growth factors. Certain organs have as their chief function hormone production. For example, the pancreas produces insulin and the thyroid gland produces thyroid hormone. Many other organs, such as the liver and kidneys, produce hormones as one of their several functions. Virtually every cell, tissue, and organ in the human body responds to hormonal signals coming from an adjacent cell or one in a very different area of the body.

The domains of hormonal function are indistinguishable from the basic functions of an individual cell, or an entire organism. From a scientist's point of view, a fascination of PCOS is its intimate relationship with each of these areas:

- Maintenance of the internal environment
- Growth and development
- Production, storage, and utilization of energy
- Reproduction

How do hormones work?

Hormones work by attaching, or *binding*, to a *receptor* on a *target cell*. When a hormone binds to the receptor cell, it causes the cell to perform a specific function. To use an analogy to help to visualize how hormones work, you might think of a key being placed into a lock and turned, thus opening a door. A hormone is like a key that turns in the receptor lock on the door to open cell function. Not all cells have receptors to all hormones. Most cells have receptors to insulin, few cells have receptors to a hormone like progesterone. The type of receptors a cell has is an important factor in what role the cell performs in the maintenance of a healthy body.

Figure 2-1 Receptors

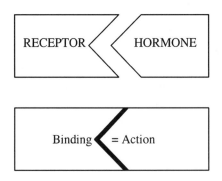

All hormones have the essential capacity to control their own pro-
mechanism is that of thyroid hormone. Thyroxine (thyroid hormone) is
released by the thyroid gland under the influence of thyroid stimulating hormone (TSH) produced in the pituitary gland. When thyroid hormone falls,
TSH rises to compensate. When thyroid hormone rises, TSH falls. This is
called negative feedback and is the yin and yang of endocrinology that keeps
the body in balance. Positive feedback systems also exist where an increase in
hormone A results in an increase in hormone B. Most endocrine dysfunction
has its origin in altered feedback mechanisms and PCOS is no exception.

Almost all hormones are secreted in short bursts called *pulses*. These
pulses also vary by different stages of the menstrual, wake-sleep, light-dark, or
feed-starve cycles. These rhythms, together called the body's *biorhythms*, may
vary in minutes, hours, days, months or seasons. Most are aware that female
roommates or family members will often synchronize their menstrual cycles.
Most biorhythms originate in an area of the brain called the hypothalamus, the
body's pacemaker.

What does the ovary do?

The female *ovary* and the male *testis,* collectively known as the
gonads, are very active members of the endocrine orchestra and are the central figures of reproductive endocrinology. The ovaries and testes are similar to
one another, in that each has two closely intertwined functions: as the storehouse of the germ cells (eggs or sperm) and as the primary source of sex hormones.

Each egg or sperm is the cellular messenger of heredity. Sperm and
eggs carry the genetic code (DNA) of female and male partners from one generation to the next. Hormones are intimately involved in germ cell growth, as
well as producing the separation of what is male and female. Both the testis
and ovary are controlled and stimulated by the same two pituitary hormones
called *gonadotropins* (trop=make grow) to make the sex hormones—estrogens, progestins, and androgens. While males and females have the same hormones, they are produced in different amounts. Those with PCOS should not
be alarmed if told that your male hormones are elevated; be assured that you
are completely female.

What's in an ovary?

An easy question? Not really. The structure (*anatomy*) and function
(*physiology*) of an ovary is complex.

The ovaries, one on each side of the pelvis, are attached at one end
to the side of the pelvic bone by a fold of tissue that carries the blood vessels
and nerves. On the other end they are attached to the uterus by the ovarian
ligament. While the testes must be outside the body and at a lower temperature to function properly, the ovaries do not have the same sensitivity to heat
and are located deep in the pelvis. Although much more difficult to reach than
the testes, the ovaries have the same rich nerve supply as the testes, which

accounts for the pain some women experience when certain positions during intercourse cause mild trauma. Much more so than the testes, the ovaries are constantly remodeling themselves, changing shape and changing the pattern of hormones produced. The size of the ovary depends on the stage of the menstrual cycle. Early in the menstrual cycle, an ovary is about the size of a walnut, one half to three quarters the size of a testicle. The size of an ovary doubles as the follicle(s) develop and ovulation nears.

Draping over the ovaries are the fallopian tubes. Their position ensures a maximum chance that an egg will be captured as it is released from the ovary at ovulation.

Figure 2-2 Gross Anatomy

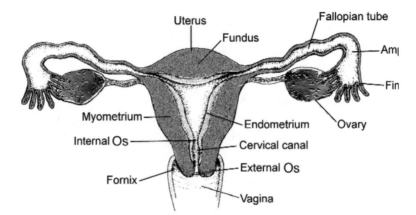

The ovary is comprised of four major specific types of cells or tissues, each with a different specific function:

- Oocytes (eggs)
- Granulosa cells (follicle cells that support the oocytes)
- Stroma (the "stuffing" of the ovary that surrounds the follicles)
- Germinal epithelium (the surface of the ovary)

First the egg

The two million oocytes present at birth are a woman's entire life supply. No new eggs will ever be produced, and no method has ever been devised that will stop the steady decline. By the time menstruation starts during puberty, the number of eggs has already been reduced to tens of thousands. Menopause occurs when the egg and follicle store becomes too small to support normal ovarian function. This is a very different situation from the male who continues to produce millions of sperm daily until very old age.

Most eggs are never ovulated; many ovulated eggs do not fertilize; many fertilized eggs do not become embryos and implant into the uterus; and many implantations are lost in the early weeks of pregnancy. The number of ovulations in a woman's lifetime ranges from zero in some PCOS patients to a maximum of about 400 when there has been no intervening birth control pill use or pregnancy. Over 99.9% of all follicles will degenerate by a precisely pro-

grammed process called *atresia*. Since most eggs never mature, there is an
inherent inefficiency naturally present in the ovary that is made much worse
by PCOS.

Then the follicle

Each egg is primitive in its metabolic machinery and must rely on its
supportive surrounding follicle for nutrition and growth. There is a close sym-
biotic relationship between the egg and follicle. Each follicle cell sends and
receives minute chemical messages that affect its own function, a type of communication called *autocrine*. Signals are also sent to closely neighboring cells
through *paracrine* communication. A precise synchrony of these cells is essential in order to produce a follicle capable of ovulating a healthy egg. Disorders
of these very basic communication systems may be at the root of PCOS.

Figure 2-3 The "Crine" Systems

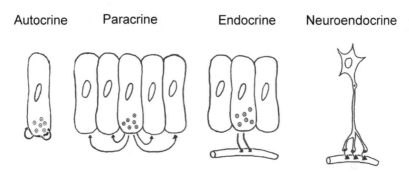

Autocrine   Paracrine   Endocrine   Neuroendocrine

Because of their granular appearance when viewed through the
microscope, follicle cells are called *granulosa cells*. Each oocyte begins its
development with only a small single rim of granulosa cells. Follicle growth
occurs as a consequence of the rapid multiplication of granulosa cells. As the
follicle grows, a cavity, or *antrum,* is formed in its central portion. With
antrum formation, granulosa cells take on different functions depending on
where they are located within the follicle. The follicle cells most intimately
involved with the oocyte are the *cumulus cells*, referring to their cloud-like
appearance around the oocyte. These cells are the umbilical cord of the
oocyte, supplying the egg with basic nutrients. The cells along the inside of the
follicle wall are called *mural granulosa cells* and are the principal cells of
estrogen production.

Figure 2-4 Follicle Anatomy

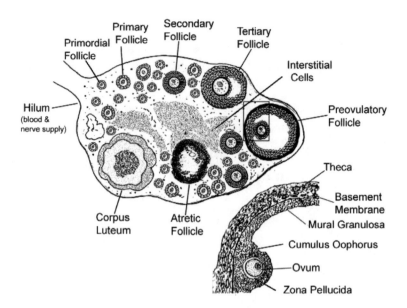

The egg is smaller than a pinhead and changes little during follicle growth. But granulosa cells proliferate and fluid increases in the antral cavity, so that the follicle that once was microscopic in size grows to silver dollar size (20-25 mm) just before *ovulation*. Ovulation is a precisely ordered process of separation of the follicle wall and release of the egg.

Controlled by the stroma

The layer of cells immediately surrounding the outside of the follicle is called the *theca (theca*=sheath) cells. The theca forms an important component of the body's endocrine network, receiving messages through its intimate relations with the ovarian blood supply. Granulosa cells do not have a direct blood supply and must receive their endocrine directions either from the rich plexus of very small blood vessels in the theca or from the theca cells themselves. Theca cells have their origin from the ovarian stroma. *Stroma* is a generic term used to describe the filler substance, the connective tissues that fill the interstitial spaces, of various organs. Far from just fluff, the stroma of all organs have important roles, but stroma of the adrenal glands, testes and ovaries have an additional specialized function of steroid hormone production. The stroma is also laden with *interstitial cells* that are very similar to theca cells in their capacity to produce androgens. The greater the amount of stroma and interstitial cells, the more androgen production. Since PCOS patients do indeed have more stroma and interstitial cells, this explains the usually elevated androgen levels of PCOS patients.

Covered by the germinal epithelium

The surface of the ovary is called the *germinal epithelium*, so-named because it was once thought that the germ cells (oocytes) had their origins here. This is now known not to be the case. The germinal epithelium is more richly endowed with receptors for estrogen than any other ovarian component. A combination of estrogen stimulation and remodeling after ovulation is thought to be the reason that the vast majority of ovarian cancers arise from the ovarian surface. (See Chapter 13). This also may be one explanation for why the ovarian surface is the most common site of endometriosis. (See Chapter 15).

How does the structure of the ovary differ in PCOS?

The polycystic ovary is generally one and a half to three times the size of a normal ovary. It is often more rounded, with a smooth, white, glistening surface that does not show the war-torn scars which are signs of previous ovulations. In some cases, the term *sclerocystic* has been used to describe both the cystic appearances of the ovary and the thickened pearly white (sclerotic) surface. Although the abnormal surface has been hypothesized as a block to ovulation, this seems doubtful. Why the ovarian surface (capsule) of the ovary is thickened in PCOS is not known. The capsule of the testis is much thicker than the ovary, so this thickening may be related to androgen stimulation .

Follicles of the polycystic ovary do not fully mature and are arrested in their development at about pea size or smaller (4 to 12 mm). It is from this large number of arrested follicles that the term *polycystic ovaries* arises. These follicles may have a mildly disordered granulosa cell layer, but even more pronounced is an overly thickened thecal investment. There is also an increase in the amount of tissue around and between the follicles *(stromal hypertrophy)*. The stroma actively produces androgens and is called *the interstitial gland*. In some cases of PCOS, the multifollicular ovary predominates, while in others there is more stroma than follicles. In some cases, there are few follicles and stromal cells fill the vast portion of the ovary. This condition has been called *hyperthecosis* and is thought by some to be a different disease process. Regardless of the relative amounts of small follicles or stroma, all are probably variants of PCOS. Cases where stroma predominates may be at a greater risk for insulin resistance. (See Chapter 9).

Figure 2-5 The Polycystic Ovary

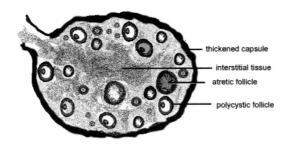

thickened capsule

interstitial tissue

atretic follicle

polycystic follicle

When stimulated by fertility drugs, eggs from the follicles of polycystic ovaries fertilize less well for in vitro fertilization and there is a slightly increased chance of miscarriage in resulting pregnancies. It is not known whether the lessened quality of oocytes from polycystic ovaries is due to an inherent defect in the egg itself, or to disordered follicle development. However, the latter is much more likely.

What's a cyst?

A cyst is a fluid-filled structure consisting of a wall and a cavity. For descriptive purposes, think of a cyst as being similar to a balloon filled with water. Cysts come in all types and sizes. The ovary is by nature cystic. Cysts are not necessarily abnormal and certainly all cysts are not pathologic. Cysts are described by what cell type make up the wall, or the type of fluid the cyst contains. The cyst may contain only clear fluid, blood, pus, or endometriotic fluid. Ovarian cysts may be malignant, but this is rare in women under age 40. Benign cysts far outnumber cancerous cysts at any age.

Much can be determined about the character of cysts through an ultrasound scan and this represents the primary means of diagnosis. Cysts that have a thin wall and contain only clear fluid, often called "simple" cysts, are very common in women of all ages. This type of cyst almost never represents a serious problem, although it can be painful. Simple cysts most often result from a follicle that has grown, but failed to ovulate (*follicle or follicular cyst*). *Luteal cysts* form after ovulation and often contain a small area of entrapped blood. Luteal cysts are common during pregnancy and do not usually indicate a problem with progesterone production. Collectively, luteal and follicular cysts are known as *functional cysts* (perhaps more appropriately dysfunctional cysts) because they arise as by-products of the everyday functions of the ovary. These cysts will always resolve over time, but this may take one to three months. Ovarian cysts that are over about two inches in diameter (5 cm) and do not disappear in two to three months should be further evaluated.

The cysts of PCOS are small functional follicular cysts. They are never malignant. These cysts arise from follicles that are arrested in their development, neither advancing toward ovulation, nor quickly resolving. It is not known how long a single PCOS cyst remains in the ovary, but there is a gradual death and replenishment, suggesting an ongoing process. At this early stage of follicle development, follicles produce more male than female hormones. These cysts alter the normal cyclic ebb and flow of ovarian function, creating a kind of "log jam" or "gridlock." They are central in what PCOS is, as these cystic follicles have been blocked from their normal growth by whatever causes PCOS.

Some women will have an increase in follicles over 10 mm, but under about 15 mm. This has been called the *multicystic* ovary in contrast to the polycystic ovary. In my experience, individuals with multicystic ovaries usually are different from those with PCOS. These women tend to be taller and thinner and often have had large cyst formation after using clomiphene. This could be a completely different form of ovarian dysfunction, although the disorder is poorly characterized at present.

The menstrual cycle: hormones from heaven or from hell?

Knowledge of how the *menstrual cycle* works is critical to understanding female endocrinology. A menstrual cycle begins on the first day (*day 1*) of bleeding (*menstruation*) and lasts until the day before the next day one of bleeding. Regular periods (*menses*) are a sign of normal function of the ovary, the uterus, and their regulating mechanisms. Various studies have shown that the average and most common menstrual cycle length is 28 days. Although reassuring, the perfect 28-day cycle does not guarantee ovulation has occurred. While some women have cycles that are exactly 28 days every month, most will vary a day or two. Few women escape the occasional irregular, or anovulatory, cycle. It is only when irregular cycles become a way of life that they gain real importance in health and fertility. Routine cycle length of over 35 days occurs in only about 1% of women. Most will have PCOS.

Cycles longer than 32 days and shorter than 26 days have a much higher likelihood of *anovulation* (lack of ovulation). Cycles in which ovulation occurs after cycle day 14 have greater chances of producing an egg of lesser quality, a decreased chance of pregnancy, and an increased risk of miscarriage.

Frequently women with PCOS experience *oligomenhorrhea*, menstrual cycles that last over 35 days, (*oligo*=few, *menorrhea*=monthly flow). Some with PCOS have no periods at all, This is called *amenorrhea* (*a*= no). Not all women with PCOS have irregular periods, but this is often an obvious reason that medical help is sought. Most, but not all, women who do not have periods on their own will have *withdrawal bleeding* when medications are given to induce a period.

Important note: If your cycles are over 35 days long, do not waste time using methods to determine whether you are ovulating. Even if you are ovulating, it is delayed and associated with difficulty establishing and keeping a pregnancy. (Further information about ovulation detection and treatment of infertility is available in Chapter 11).

What would it be like if your cycles were normal?

As a basis for understanding how all this can go astray with PCOS, it is essential to understand the basics of how the ovary works—the normal ovarian cycle. Using this information as a template we can then add the possible causes of PCOS.

There are four major hormones of the ovarian cycle. Two of them, *follicle stimulating hormone* (FSH) and *luteinizing hormone* (LH), are called *gonadotropins*. Both LH and FSH are made and secreted by the pituitary gland. The other two, *estradiol* (E_2) and *progesterone* (P_4), are steroid hormones made and secreted by the ovary.

In a normal cycle, FSH stimulates the growth of follicles; growing follicles make E_2; rising E_2 levels facilitate LH release; LH results in ovulation and P_4 production. When no pregnancy occurs, P_4 levels drop, a period (menses) ensues and the cycle restarts. Also, as P_4 is falling toward the end of one cycle, FSH starts to rise in preparation for the next. This sketch remains the basis of our understanding of female endocrinology, regardless of how sophisticated and scientific the discussion may become. Now, let's retrace the steps in more detail, with special reference to what goes wrong in PCOS.

Figure 2-6 Hormone Cycle

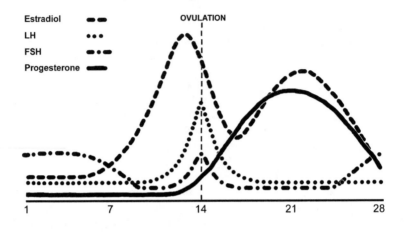

Folliculogenesis and the follicular phase

The ovaries are constantly bubbling with small growing follicles emerging from a resting pool. Follicle growth and development, called *folliculogenesis,* starts before birth and continues until after menopause, but the complete cycle of normal follicular development and ovulation does not begin until late puberty and usually ends several years before menopause. Menopause occurs when the follicle pool is nearing exhaustion. Although early follicle growth may occur, there is no ovulation. Follicle growth requires FSH. Before the onset of puberty (discussed in Chapter 4) follicles grow, but they degenerate because of a lack of FSH to sustain their growth. With menopause the FSH reaches high levels in an attempt to keep the ovary functioning, but there are just too few follicles to mount a good try. An FSH level above 10 IU/L on cycle day 2-3 is cause for concern, as it is associated with decreased fertility. The major shift and rapid decline in fertility appears to occur between ages 37-38 when follicle number reaches about 25,000. Interestingly, as the follicle number declines, the PCOS ovary may start to normalize. This might be a time of more regular cycles and increased fertility in those with PCOS.

In its early stages, follicle growth is slow. In fact, follicular growth takes much longer than was once thought. Nearly a hundred days of development, over three menstrual cycles, are required before the follicle is competent to ovulate. It is not known what calls for follicles to leave the *resting pool,* but once the march is started it will continue until the follicle ovulates or becomes *atretic* (dies). For their first 85 days, growing follicles are thought not to be particularly responsive to FSH. The capacity to respond to FSH is acquired only in the last two to three weeks before ovulation. This corresponds to the time when most follicle growth occurs.

Here a shortcoming in use of fertility drugs becomes evident. All fertility drugs are given in the last two weeks before ovulation. All probably work in only one cycle. In women with PCOS, follicles and their oocytes will have been in an abnormal ovarian environment for at least two of their three months of development. This may partly explain why egg quality may be sub-optimal in PCOS patients using fertility drugs. A holdover effect from fertility drug use could also explain why some women become pregnant in the first month or two after stopping fertility drug treatment.

Figure 2-7 Stages of Follicular Growth

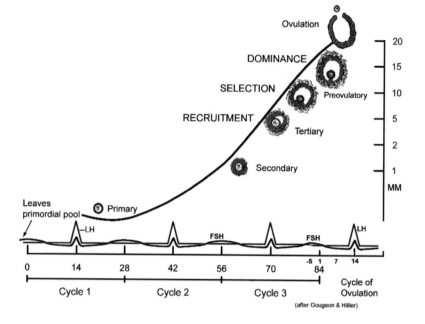

(after Gougeon & Hillier)

With the demise of the corpus luteum, FSH levels start to rise. Until this point, granulosa cells have slowly proliferated, small spaces have developed between the innermost granulosa cells and these spaces have coalesced to form a small fluid-filled cavity called the *antrum*. If the follicle is on time and healthy, it will become one of a group (collectively called a *cohort*) of two to twenty small antral follicles which are said to be *recruited* and given the possibility of greatness in ovulation. These follicles range from 2-5 mm in diameter, and while similar, are not identical. These differences may later translate into variation in oocyte quality. The follicle may have the capacity to control its own destiny through production and response to paracrine and autocrine signals from various potent regulators called *growth factors*. The follicle has an interesting talent of responding to FSH and in so doing increases its own responsiveness to FSH. This may be modulated by growth factors. At the same time, the theca develops its capacity to respond to gonadotropins and produce androgens. It is around this time in development when PCOS rears its ugly head. These small follicles normally produce more androgen than estrogen and it is here that things get stuck.

Intrafollicular Growth and Regulatory Factors—
the "fine tuners" of ovarian function (partial listing)

- Inhibin—decreases FSH release from pituitary
- Activin—enhances FSH action on aromatase, increases FSH and LH receptors, prevents premature luteinization
- Follistatin —opposes action of activin
- Oocyte maturation inhibitor (OMI)—prevents maturation of the egg until after LH surge
- Insulin-like growth factors (IGFs)—enhance gonadotropin stimulation and actions
- Insulin like growth factor binding proteins (IGFBP)—oppose action of IGFs
- Vascular endothelial growth factor (VEGF)—promotes vascular permeability
- Interleukins (ILs)—"cytokines" — have a role in ovulation, and cell proliferation
- Tumor necrosis factor (TNF)—possibly involved in follicular atresia and insulin resistance

Under the stimulus of FSH, the follicle cells rapidly multiply and the antrum enlarges. Only one to several of the follicles recruited will be *selected* to produce *estradiol* (E_2) (*estr*=frenzy). The selection process usually occurs cycle day 4-7, when the follicle is about 10 mm in diameter. From this group a single preovulatory, or *Graafian*, follicle emerges and takes control of its own destiny. Estradiol production rapidly increases. Estradiol is formed from testosterone by a special enzyme called *aromatase,* which is present only in granulosa cells. Aromatase in the granulosa cells is fed by the androgens produced in the follicle's surrounding thecal cells. As such, estradiol production becomes a marker of follicular growth and is commonly measured to assess the success of stimulation with fertility drugs.

As the follicle grows, it also makes an increasing amount of growth factor *inhibin,* which is the body's signal to reduce the FSH stimulation from the pituitary gland.

Figure 2-8 2 Cell - 2 Gonadotropin

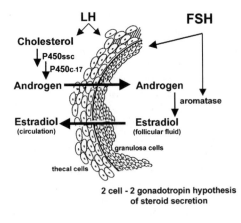

2 cell - 2 gonadotropin hypothesis of steroid secretion

In a normal ovulatory cycle, one follicle will achieve *dominance* over all others and in doing so causes its competitors to start to degenerate. Dominance is achieved when the follicle reaches about 10 mm in diameter. It is unclear whether it is the fastest growing follicle, the one that produces the first or most estradiol, or some undiscovered factor that enables dominance. In fact these are not mutually exclusive and may be the same. The dominant follicle rapidly increases its estradiol production, accumulation of follicular fluid, and receptors for luteinizing hormone, becoming the chosen preovulatory follicle. It stands in wait for the LH surge.

The LH surge

Typically, LH levels are low, except at the time of the LH surge. On day 13-14 of the idealized cycle there is a sudden release of luteinizing hormone, the *LH surge*. In British women, most LH surges begin between midnight and 8 a.m. There is some evidence that in the spring ovulation occurs mostly in the morning and in the afternoon/evening in fall and winter. I have not been impressed that American women are quite so predictable. There is a major gap in our understanding of what causes the LH surge to occur. Whether it is estrogen that promotes LH release, or some factor produced by the ovary paralleling estrogen production is not known. We also don't know why some women will have an early surge when follicles are still immature, or why others with normal-appearing pre-ovulatory follicle development fail to surge.

The LH surge has three functions:
- Resumption of meiosis (rearranging chromosomes)
- Promotion of ovulation (follicle wall changes)
- Luteinization (starting progesterone production)

Prior to the LH surge, the oocyte has been in an arrested stage of development since before birth. This means that for between fifteen and forty years the oocyte has been awaiting this LH signal to start rearranging its chromosomes to prepare properly for meeting with a sperm. During this time, changes can occur in the DNA of the oocyte that might make this meeting less than blissful. Certainly this form of aging is one cause of decreased fertility, increased risk of miscarriage, and birth defects seen in the later reproductive years.

Ovulation

Ovulation is a precisely orchestrated process in which the follicle wall dissolves and the oocyte, with its supportive cumulus cells, is released. It would be easy to imagine ovulation as being much like a volcano eruption, but instead the process appears to be well ordered and determined by a precise sequence of events in the follicle wall. Given this complexity, it is easy to see why disorders of ovulation are common. Ovulation shares many characteristics with inflammation, and requires prostaglandins, cytokines, and various substances associated with the immune response, as well as various other substances. It has been reported that large quantities of non-steroidal anti-inflammatory drugs, for example aspirin and ibuprofen, can block ovulation, but some believe that small amounts may improve blood flow to the follicle and enhance the health of the follicle.

Ovulation will not occur in the absence of the LH surge, nor does an LH surge equal ovulation. Sometimes there is either an inadequate amount of LH or an altered capacity of the follicle to respond to LH. If the preovulatory follicle has been ill prepared to respond to the LH surge, it can become a follicular cyst, or, if recurrent, it becomes *luteinized unruptured follicle syndrome* (LUF).

Ovulation is thought to occur about 24 hours after the peak of the LH surge, or 36 to 48 hours after surge onset. The measurement of LH surge is the basis of the ovulation predictor kits that are commonly recommended as an aid for timing sexual intercourse. LH testing may be unreliable in some with PCOS because of the continuously high levels of LH.

Often, ovulation alternates between the right and left ovary. Alternating right and left sided pelvic pain at mid-cycle may be an indication of ovulation. Sometimes the pain can be felt only on one side, or not at all. It is not known whether this pain, called *mittleschmerz*, is caused by the large preovulatory follicle, its rupture, or irritation from the fluid in the pelvis after ovulation. It is unclear why some with PCOS continue to report this mid-cycle pain despite lack of ovulation.

The luteal phase

The third role of the LH surge is to perform that function for which it is named—*luteinization*. Luteinization is the process whereby the follicle is converted into the corpus luteum (*corpus* = body; *lute* = yellow). The follicle which has produced large quantities of estrogen converts to producing both estrogen and most importantly, progesterone (*pro* = for; *gest* = pregnancy. The corpus luteum forms as the follicle fills in with a proliferation of the luteinized granulosa cells, theca cells and blood vessels of the ruptured follicle wall. The corpus luteum is 1 to 1.5 inches (20-35mm) in diameter and can be seen on ultrasound, but not so clearly as the follicle. Occasionally some cystic areas might remain, but are of no significance.

The corpus luteum has a finite life span of ten to fourteen days and is more predictable than the process of follicle growth. That is, if the cycle is 32 days, ovulation will not occur until days 17 to19. If implantation, which is usually about six to ten days after ovulation, does not occur, progesterone levels fall and menstruation results.

Let's review. The ovarian cycle is divided into two major sections. The first, the follicular phase, lasts from the onset of bleeding until ovulation. Two hormones of the follicular phase are FSH and estrogen. The second phase, the luteal phase, lasts from ovulation until the next bleeding begins, and is characterized by LH and progesterone.

Is my progesterone level too low?

There is no more common question or area of ovarian function that is more misunderstood than that of progesterone levels. This topic is also presented in Chapter 11. Progesterone is a reasonable marker of ovulation and later serves as an indication of a healthy pregnancy, but as often as not progesterone level test results are misinterpreted.

Possible causes of low progesterone include:
- Improper timing of the test
- Delayed ovulation
- Lack of ovulation
- Low point of hormone pulse

The luteal phase, and thus luteal function, is considered inadequate if luteal phase length is shorter than ten days, or if the progesterone level is low. Progesterone is measured six to eight days after ovulation, at the time of its maximum production. Proper timing of the blood test is critical. The timing of the blood test for progesterone in PCOS is completely unreliable unless the time of ovulation is known. If ovulation does not occur or is delayed, the progesterone level will be low. It is ovulation that is most often the problem, not progesterone. Luteal phase defects are almost always a sign of a defective follicular development, rather than a problem with the luteal phase itself. Supplementation with progesterone does not address the real problem; it may increase the progesterone level but that increase is only cosmetic for the cycle in question. It is true that progesterone can be used to help regulate menstruation and perhaps enable development of healthier follicles in subsequent cycles. However the data demonstrating whether or not progesterone use prevents miscarriage is far less clear.

Mid-luteal Progesterone Levels
(seven days after ovulation)

- Less than 10 ng/ml— probably not ovulatory
- 10-20 ng/ml— equivocal for ovulation
- the closer to 20 the more likely ovulation has occurred,
- the closer to 10 the less likely
- over 20 ng/ml—probably ovulatory

So what controls the ovary?

Easy to this point—right!? So let's move up the ladder.

The hypothalamic-pituitary-ovarian axis (HPO) is the invisible wiring system that relates the ovary to the other components of the endocrine system and reproduction with the body's internal and external environment. The field of neuroendocrinology is concerned with how the endocrine system is related to the nervous system and the brain.

At the base of the brain is the hypothalamus. The hypothalamus is the major switching station for endocrine activity, as well as that part of the brain concerned with regulating survival functions—temperature control, appetite, growth, metabolism, salt and water regulation. It receives signals from the outside world such as light, darkness, odor, and stress and from the internal systems of the body, notably the ovary. Numerous neurotransmitters, such as dopamine, adrenaline, and serotonin, all interact at the level of the hypothalamus. Signals coming from many directions are converted into a single signal for gonadotropin release, which is gonadotropin-releasing hormone (GnRH). A Nobel Prize was awarded for figuring out the system and synthesizing this really rather simple hormone.

GnRH release occurs in pulses that vary in amplitude and frequency, depending on the stage of the menstrual cycle. The pulse generator is clearly disturbed in PCOS, with alteration in both frequency and amplitude of GnRH secretion. There are no routine tests to specifically determine hypothalamic function, but its actions are indirectly seen in almost everything hormonal.

The *pituitary gland* is not much larger than a pea, and at dime-size it is considered enlarged. It is located under the hypothalamus and just above the roof of the mouth in a bony valley of the skull called the *sella turcica*. The pituitary is a signal converter that changes hypothalamic signals into gonadotropin (FSH and LH) release. It also manages the thyroid and adrenal glands, so it is not surprising to see an overlap in disorders involving the glands acted upon by the pituitary.

Figure 2-9 HPO Axis

HYPOTHALAMIC - PITUITARY - OVARIAN AXIS

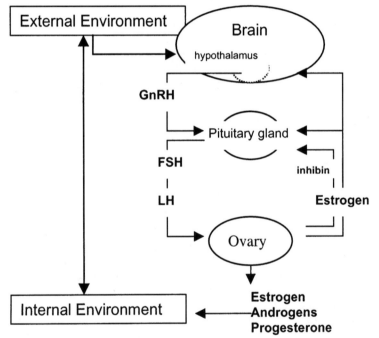

How does the *function* of the ovary in PCOS differ?

Some investigators have suggested that alterations in GnRH pulse generator and gonadotropin release are the primary abnormality in PCOS. Alterations in the HPO axis clearly exist, but it is more likely that the ovary leads rather than follows in this vicious circle.

- PCOS may be a primary disorder of the HPO signaling gonadotropin production and release
- PCOS may be caused by problems with hormone receptors (hormone action)
- PCOS may indicate dysfunctional enzyme function (altered steroid production)
- PCOS may result from problems with growth factors (paracrine and autocrine regulation)
- PCOS may originate from insulin and insulin resistance

PCOS is characterized by increased levels of LH. LH stimulates the theca and interstitial cells to produce androgens. These elevated androgens have been hypothesized to block further follicular development and cause the follicles to slowly degenerate. At the same time, the constant low levels of estrogen in PCOS have been thought to be the source of the persistent LH elevation.

It is around the time that the follicle starts to produce androgens and estradiol that the system seems to fail. It has been suggested that the follicles of PCOS ovaries might be lacking in receptors that would allow response to FSH, but this theory has fallen into disfavor. If this happens, it is secondary to already altered follicle health.

Enzymes are proteins that catalyze (control by speeding up or slowing down) biochemical reactions. Many different enzymes are necessary for the production of the different steroid hormones that are produced by the ovary. Probably each of these enzymes has been examined for clues as to the origin of PCOS. Most have been excluded, but several candidates remain.

For example, it has been postulated that a disorder in *aromatase* (P450arom), the enzyme that facilitates the interconversion of testosterone to estradiol, is the underlying cause of PCOS. While this has not been totally excluded, it does not seem to answer enough questions. It was proposed that a defect in the enzyme *17-hydroxylase* (P450c17) may be responsible for both the block in follicle development and the abnormal hormonal production that follows. Enthusiasm has waned with additional genetic studies. Another candidate is the enzyme that prepares the cholesterol molecule used in making sex steroids, *cholesterol side chain cleavage enzyme* (P450scc). This enzyme is presently a forerunner in the race to determine a cause for PCOS.

Growth factors are substances that alter the growth and differentiation of cells and were the forerunners of hormones in our evolutionary development. They act locally, in both autocrine and paracrine pathways, but influence global function of the body. Some growth factors native to the ovary include substances very similar to insulin, *insulin-like growth factors* (IGFs) and their binding proteins (IGF-BP) and others closely related to the immune system. We are just beginning to uncover how and which growth factors are involved in folliculogenesis. An increasing number of scientists believe that PCOS may have its origin in an inherited alteration in the production of specific growth factors.

A recent exciting and compelling candidate for a (the) cause of PCOS was a growth factor produced by the granulosa cells called *follistatin*. Follistatin reduces the follicle's response to FSH and is a logical place for a block in folliculogenesis to occur. It was thought that follistatin may be the common link between the ovary and insulin resistance, as well as being involved in the reported enzymatic alterations of the polycystic ovary. Unfortunately, this candidate, like many others, failed under closer scrutiny. The role of growth factors and paracrine regulation is still a productive area of research. (See Chapter 3).

There are many that are skeptical that a single cause of PCOS will ever be found.

How is the uterus involved?

The uterus is universally described as being the size and shape of a pear. After a delivery, the uterus, now said to be *multiparous*, is usually about 50% larger than the nulliparous uterus of a woman who has never given birth. The two major divisions of the uterus are the *corpus* (body) and the *cervix* (Latin for *neck*). The upper body of the uterus has an inner lining, the endometrium (*endo* = inside, *metr* = uterus), that undergoes considerable remodeling each month under the influence of ovarian hormones. It is sur-

Figure 2-10 Ultrasound of Uterus

ENDOMETRIAL GRADING

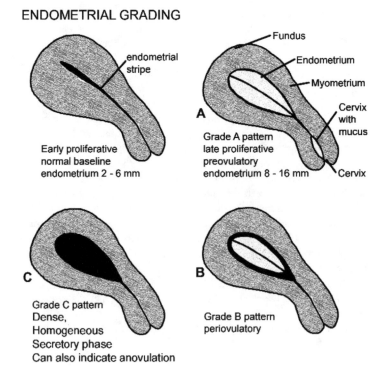

endometrial stripe

Early proliferative
normal baseline
endometrium 2 - 6 mm

Fundus

Endometrium

Myometrium

Cervix with mucus

A

Grade A pattern
late proliferative
preovulatory
endometrium 8 - 16 mm

Cervix

C

Grade C pattern
Dense,
Homogeneous
Secretory phase
Can also indicate anovulation

B

Grade B pattern
periovulatory

rounded by a dense muscular layer, the *myometrium* (*myo* = muscle) whose contractions are responsible for menstrual cramps and whose rhythmic contractions force the baby through the birth canal. After about nine weeks, the pregnancy itself takes control of uterine function, but until then the uterus takes its orders from the ovary. The lowest portion of the uterus, the cervix, serves as its gateway and reservoir for sperm. Cervical mucus is important for sperm survival and transport. Except around the time of ovulation when the estrogen level is high, cervical mucus is quite hostile to sperm.

The embryo is transported through the fallopian tubes and enters the uterus on about the fourth day after fertilization. It should take up residence here until the forceful muscle of the uterine wall begins to contract and labor starts.

Most bleeding problems, whether too much or too little, are a result of alteration in the effects of ovarian hormones on the endometrium. It is not surprising that the loss of cyclic ovarian function and resulting abnormal hormonal environment causes bleeding problems. The uterine cycle is a mirror of the ovary's endocrine activity. Its proper function is intimately related to normal ovarian function.

My uterus is tipped. Is this important?

The uterus is commonly tilted toward the front of the body (*anteverted*), but in 20–30% of women, the uterus is positioned toward the backbone, or *retroverted*. There may be more back pain with a retroverted uterus and some have thought that there is a greater chance of endometriosis, but neither theory has been proven. Overall, there is one most common position for the uterus, but there are many normal positions. The position of the uterus has little to do with its functioning, but it is surprising how many women are made to worry that something is wrong after having been told that their uterus is "tipped". My theory is that women are intently focused on every word their gynecologist utters during a pelvic exam (hardly time to tell a joke), so the casual muttering used to remember the position of the uterus in order to record this time-honored but largely unimportant piece of information on the exam form is forever recorded in the patient's memory.

How does the uterus work?

When the gynecologist asks, "What day is it?" the answer is neither "Monday" nor "October 31st." Rather, the desired response is the day of the menstrual cycle. The first day of bleeding is designated as Day 1. "Day 1" is sometimes difficult to tell because of the spotting that is often seen before a heavy flow starts. To add to the confusion, different physicians and clinics may designate different days as Day 1. Usually there are two or three days of relatively heavy bleeding during menstruation, with two to four days of lighter flow.

There are three phases of uterine development:
• Menstrual phase
• Proliferative phase
• Secretory phase

The menstrual and proliferative phases of the uterus roughly correspond to the follicular phase of the ovary, and the secretory phase corresponds to the luteal phase.

Menstrual phase

Menstruation is defined as the periodic bleeding associated with the loss of the endometrium. Menstruation occurs as a consequence of the regression of the corpus luteum and a fall in progesterone production that occurs when a pregnancy is not established. The menstrual fluid is a mixture of uterine lining, tissue fluid and blood. Actual blood loss varies in amount with one-half to ten ounces (averaging four to five ounces) considered normal. To give an idea of how much this entails, a sanitary pad or tampon holds about one ounce. Typically, the amount of flow remains relatively constant from month to month. Either heavier or lighter flow can be a sign of ovulation failure. If a tampon alone is adequate protection, there is usually not a serious problem. Abnormally heavy bleeding, called *menorrhagia*, is of more medical concern than is very light flow. Very heavy periods increase the risk of anemia or can be sign of structural problems like uterine polyps and fibroids. Structural problems are usually easily identified by ultrasound evaluation.

Menstruation is caused by the periodic dilation and contraction of small blood vessels surrounding the endometrium. As the blood flow is started and stopped, there is a flushing effect on the uterine lining. *Prostaglandins* are hormones produced in the uterus that not only regulate blood flow, but also cause muscle contraction. Prostaglandins are the major source of menstrual pain. Sometimes more painful periods mean a greater chance of ovulation. Likewise, more prostaglandin is released with endometriosis. Moderately painful periods may be either a good or bad symptom. Particularly painful periods, *dysmenorrhea,* can be an indication of endometriosis (see Chapter 13). Prostaglandins are reduced with the use of the non-steroidal anti-inflammatory drugs such as aspirin, ibuprofen, naprosyn and others.

It would seem that the menstrual phase would be a time when there was a lot happening in the pelvis, but this is not true. On cycle day 2 or 3, both hormonally and anatomically the reproductive system has reached the "baseline." This is the time when the most accurate hormone testing can be performed. It is also the optimal time for a screening ultrasound or *baseline scan*. The endometrium should be thin and the ovaries quiet, without evidence of cysts.

Proliferative phase

With increasing production of estradiol from the growing follicles, endometrial cells multiply. Logically, this cell proliferation is called the proliferative phase. As the endometrium thickens, bleeding stops. The proliferative phase lasts until the ovary produces progesterone, or a synthetic progestin (see Chapter 17) is given to induce a period. If there is a low level of progesterone production, as seen in those who do not ovulate, there is continued estrogen production and endometrial proliferation.

Secretory phase

With the production of progesterone from the corpus luteum, the endometrium is converted into a very lush environment in preparation for implantation. Endometrial glands produce a nutritive secretion and logically this is called the secretory phase. If a pregnancy occurs it sends the signal human chorionic gonadotropin (HCG) to the ovary to continue progesterone production and maintain the favorable lining. If no pregnancy occurs, progesterone falls, the endometrium starts to breakdown and the cycle starts over.

Do I need to have regular periods?

If ovulation is not occurring regularly and in the absence of cyclic progesterone, the endometrium becomes overly lush. In this situation of *unopposed estrogen* there is an over growth of the endometrium. The endometrium can be likened to a full bucket to which more keeps being added causing it to overflow. This bleeding is not truly menstruation, but is more appropriately called *dysfunctional uterine bleeding* (DUB). Left unchecked, it is thought that the initial normal cells become progressively deranged, leading to *hyperplasia* and, very rarely, to cancer in women under age 40 (see Chapter 13). Sometimes a dilation and curettage (D&C) may be necessary, if bleeding cannot be first controlled medically. Diagnosis of DUB can be made by ultrasound or endometrial biopsy. Ultrasound is generally more appropriate, more diagnostic, and much less painful than a biopsy of the endometrium. Ultrasound scan shows a very thickened lining. Since this is a medical problem, the best solution is usually related to medications for treatment. This treatment involves use of progesterone or progestins (see Chapter 17) to mature and then cause a more complete sloughing of the uterine lining. It is not the progestin but its withdrawal that causes

Figure 2-11 Menstrual Cycle

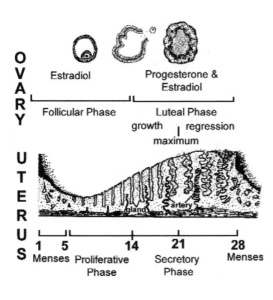

the bleeding. In another case there may be insufficient hormones to stabilize the lining, which is abnormally thin on ultrasound. This situation may require administration of estrogens to stimulate the lining growth before progestins are used.

Just the facts Ma'am

This chapter may very well have seemed complex—even daunting. As we said at its beginning, it may be useful to refer back to it as you learn more and more about PCOS. But before we proceed with a closer look inside the problem of PCOS, let's list several facts about PCOS that we know with certainty to be true.

- PCOS is associated with disordered ovarian function that results in the failure of a follicle to mature and become capable of ovulating a 'good' egg. This is called *chronic anovulation.*
- With PCOS, follicles are arrested at the stage where they produce relatively more testosterone than estradiol, resulting in *hyperandrogenism.*
- The disordered hormone production of PCOS feeds on itself and further disrupts the ovary and the entire body's metabolism, which is why PCOS is a *panendocrinopathy,* a disturbance of the entire endocrine system.

The origin of the block to proper ovarian function is not known. It may, or may not, arise within the ovary itself. (This is further discussed in Chapter 3).

How Did I Get It?
The Genetics of PCOS

"My aunt is polycystic"

"My husband's grandmother only had one child and then had two miscarriages. She was a large woman and is remembered for her moodiness."

"My dad is 55 and was just told he was a borderline diabetic, but they told him he could control it with diet."

In my native East Tennessee home it is said that our family tree doesn't have all that many branches. If PCOS is a genetic condition, it is one gene that we surely have in our shallow pool. As I began to practice reproductive endocrinology here, I was impressed with the large number of women who truly had all the characteristics of PCOS. In talking with colleagues across the country, I became aware of anecdotal evidence that suggests that there may be a number of areas in the country where there are clusters of PCOS. Then again, this could instead be an example of the well-known fact that when one's level of awareness is increased about a particular issue, one suspects that the problem is everywhere.

PCOS has always been and remains the single most common diagnosis at the Center for Applied Reproductive Science. This was true even before we became a referral center that specialized in the disorder. Although I had long been interested in genetics and ovarian function, it was more my patient population and their needs than my academic career that stimulated such an interest. In taking family histories I began to see a pattern, but it was not until the insulin/metabolic-syndrome/PCOS connection came into full light that I really began to appreciate the impact of genetics.

Nature versus nurture?

For centuries, experts in the studies of philosophy, science and medicine have pondered the question of how much of who we are is inherited and how much is due to environment. There is no medical issue that begs the answer of this question more than does PCOS. Far be it from me to suppose that I can answer this question in the next few pages. PCOS as a genetic trait is not as straightforward as having brown or blue eyes. What we inherit in PCOS and many other genetic problems is not the disorder itself, but a predisposition, or tendency, for its development. Under the right (or perhaps I should say wrong) conditions, PCOS emerges. For example, an individual may have quite severe insulin resistance, weigh 220 pounds and may not be having periods. With a weight loss to 180 pounds, menses becomes normal and a pregnancy occurs. Is she still insulin resistant? Yes. Will she develop type 2 diabetes? Maybe not, if her weight stays down; maybe so, if her weight increases. Does she have the gene for insulin resistance? Yes. She does.

A Genetics Primer

Most of us have had some education pertaining to genetics, perhaps in a school science class. This experience may have been long ago and may be quite dim, so let us review a few central points on which the field of genetics is based. I consider that an understanding of the terminology is essential to understanding the mechanisms of PCOS. Still, some readers may want to skip through this section to the material directly related to PCOS.

What is a gene?

A gene is the basic unit of heredity. Genes are bits of DNA that direct the reproduction, growth and function of cells. Some genes are structural and code for the construction of the body's building blocks. Other genes are regulatory and act to promote or suppress the function of the structural genes.

How is genetic information stored?

Genetic material is stored in the nucleus of the cell as deoxyribonucleic acid (DNA). What makes each bit of DNA unique is how its four different chemical constituents, called bases and designated A, T, C, G, are lined up like vertebrae along a backbone of a structural sugar, deoxyribose. One piece of the code may read ACTGCGCGG, and code for one piece of genetic information, while another may read CGCGTTAAA and code for an entirely different piece of information. Compared to the Morse code that has two types of signals, dots and dashes, the genetic code has four signals, ATCG. These bases can be thought of as letters that run together to form words. The words are put together to form sentences that express a complete thought. This complete thought is a gene.

Genes are packaged into discrete chromosomes. Think of all the genetic material recorded together as one great book that holds all the information about how the body works. The book is divided into chapters called chromosomes. While each chapter may stand alone and contain a specific amount of information, the chapters are also interrelated, so that the entire story can be told. Just as in this book, a bit of information in one chapter, gene A, may require information in a second chapter, gene B, before there can be an understanding and the scholarly activity of the body's functions can be accomplished.

The human has 46 chromosomes, 23 pairs. Two are the sex chromosomes, X and Y, and the other pairs are called autosomes and are numbered from one to twenty-two based on their size. A female has two X chromosomes (XX) and the male has one X and one Y chromosome (XY). When a gene is located on either the X or Y chromosome, it is said to be sex-linked. Since there are two chromosomes, one from each parent, there are two different genes or alleles located at the corresponding sites *(loci)* on each member of the chromosome pair.

As one cell divides to form two cells, the DNA in the chromosome doubles *(replicates)* so that exact DNA copies are made and then halved. This process is called *mitosis* and is the normal mechanism through which there is cellular growth and maintenance. Each cell makes a cell just like itself. In essence, it clones itself.

Sexual reproduction is the source of human variety and our unique individualism. A special process called *meiosis* occurs in reproduction, during which time the DNA material is halved and then halved again. This allows a reduction in genetic material so that we do not have twice the normal amount. Each of the two chromosomes from each of the two parents results in four different alleles (genes), so that sixteen different combinations are possible for a single gene. It can easily be seen how four different copies of the supposed 60,000 genes permit the endless diversity that makes each of us unique. Two more important terms are *phenotype,* referring to how we look or act, and *genotype*, referring to our genetic potential. More about this later.

How are genes inherited?

There are two basic ways in which genes are expressed: *dominant* or *recessive*. This concept is the basis of Mendelian genetics, after the classic studies of peas by the monk Gregor Mendel. While eye color is a trait and not strictly a single gene, it serves to illustrate the concept of dominant versus recessive genes. Brown eyes are dominant. Babies born from two brown-eyed parents will always have brown eyes if the brown-eyed gene is passed on by either of the two parents. (Remember each parent has two copies of the gene, but passes only one). The trait for blue eyes is recessive, so a brown-eyed individual may carry one gene for blue eyes and a blue-eyed baby may result if this individual has a child with another brown-eyed person who also carries a blue eye gene. Although the phenotype (actual appearance) of either or both parents may be for brown eyes, these same individuals may carry a recessive blue eye gene and have the genotype (potential) of both brown and blue. Two blue-eyed parents cannot have a brown-eyed child.

The chart below graphically illustrates the different possibilities of how the genes can be sorted. The dominant gene is in capital letters and the recessive in small. So two genotypes (BB or Bb) may yield the same pheno-type, brown eyes. Since blue eyes are recessive, only one genotype is possible (bb).

Individuals that "carry" a recessive trait are said to be *heterozygous* (Bb) compared to the *homozygous* person who has either the (BB), or (bb) genotypes. The presence of recessive traits is one mechanism by which genetics can skip a generation. The heterozygous gene is there in the gene pool, but its expression skips a generation, perhaps several.

It seems easy, doesn't it? Now it gets much more complicated even in this, the simplest of models. As above, one gene for eye color gives three possible genotypes (BB, Bb, bb). If there were two genes, the possibilities would be AABB, AaBB, AaBb, Aabb, aaBB, aaBb, aabb. Consider the number of traits (signs or symptoms) found in women with PCOS. The possibilities for genetic variation and expression become mind-boggling.

What about hazel eyes? Obviously the system is not as simple as presented above. If we use the brown and blue eye analogy with PCOS, some will have brown, some blue and most will have hazel eyes. Genes do not blend, so there must be other factors or a series of genes that will control how genes express themselves. While genes do not mix like paint colors, there is a special type of blending based on the vast hierarchy of factors controlling gene expression. Most genes are *linked* together to perform their function. Gene A may be linked to gene B and each may be inherited separately. A second twist on this occurs

		Female Eye Color	
		BROWN	BLUE
Male Eye Color	B R O W N	Brown (BB)	brown (blue carrier) (Bb)
	B L U E	brown (blue carrier) (Bb)	Blue (BB)

with the example of gene *penetrance*. Some genes are more or less forceful in their expression. A gene's capacity to express itself may be limited under some circumstances. In the next generation this suppression may be lifted and the expression of the gene is much more clearly seen. This is yet another example of how a trait may be dormant for several generations only to become visible again under the proper circumstances. This is similar to a weed seed that has lain dormant for years and is brought to the surface by plowing the garden.

To show really how complex PCOS is, we can think about the eye color analogy once again. In the simplest situation, only a few with PCOS would have brown or blue eyes, almost all would have the most common hazel. In reality, the genetics of PCOS may be closer to the situation of an inborn mechanism for our eyes to change from brown to blue or to become blue when we put on a blue suit.

How are diseases and disorders inherited?

There are several distinct ways in which diseases and disorders can be inherited:

One way is through **alterations in number or structures of chromosomes.** An unfortunately common example of this is Down syndrome where there is a failure of a chromosome to separate normally at meiosis, resulting in an extra 21st chromosome (trisomy 21). Structural abnormalities are a common cause of miscarriage. The field of study that investigates chromosomal alterations is called *cytogenetics.*

Some diseases are the result of an **abnormality or alteration of a single gene.** Using the example above of the genetic code, a single base substitution, for example an A is changed to T, would result in a misspelled word. This misspelled word is called a *mutation.* A single letter can change the meaning of a word. Alteration of a single word may change the meaning of a sentence or make it unreadable. There are several forms of severe insulin resistance that are known to arise from a *point* (letter) mutation. Techniques ("spell checkers") are now available to locate these mistakes. The dictionary has almost been compiled (see Human Genome Project below) that will allow the misspelled words to be looked up. The branch of genetics that alterations in DNA and genetic expression is *molecular genetics*, or molecular biology

Some genetic inheritances come as a result of **cumulative effects of interacting genes** (several = *oligogenic*) (many = *polygenic, multigenic*). It is thought that PCOS falls into either this or the next category. We know that PCOS is not due to a chromosomal abnormality. It also seems unlikely that it is a single gene. More likely, several genes seem to be working together to produce the spectrum of PCOS.

Still other genetic problems are a result of a **combination of genetic inheritance and environment (multifactorial)**. Most diseases are far too complex to be explained by the above four processes. A multifactorial origin takes into account environmental factors that can mold the genetic factors. Weight is in part genetic and in part environmental. Genetics does not make the car turn into a Kentucky Fried Chicken drive through, but it could influence our desire to do so. The more we know about genetics the less it seems that we are in control of who we are.

The Human Genome Project

As this book is in final stages of preparation, it was announced that the entire genetic composition (genome) of the fruit fly had been unraveled. This was no small task and represents the first time that any animal species has had its entire genetic code deciphered. This was accomplished through a combination of the use of high-speed computers and modern molecular biology. In 1990 the Human Genome Project began with the goal to sequence and determine the DNA make-up of the human genetic code. This project is a collaborated effort between many laboratories, each given a small piece of the puzzle to solve. By 2005 it is predicted that the project will be complete. The leaders are proud that the HGP is one of the only government programs, ever, that is ahead of schedule and under budget. The HGP will enable researchers to have a blueprint on which to evaluate human disease. In the near future we may well have the knowledge we need to more specifically identify the genetic factors comprising PCOS. This scientific achievement of the HGP eclipses that of putting a man on the moon and may represent the most important scientific advance thus far. You can visit the project at www.ornl.gov/techresources/human_genome/publicat/publications.html. The HGP is not only a great work of human understanding, it has great commercial appeal as well. Understanding only a very small area of the human genome could be translated into development of new drugs worth millions. As can be imagined, a very competitive spirit is quickly emerging between government and private enterprise and about control of information and its translation into new technology. The race is on.

Why are genetics studies in PCOS so difficult?

The genetics of PCOS, like the disorder itself, are not black or white, but very much on the gray scale. There are reasons why the genetics are so complicated.

- Lack of a universally accepted diagnosis of PCOS.
- Outward appearance (phenotype) can be vastly different despite similar genetic constitutions (genotype).
- PCOS patients often come from small families with a limited number of sisters and brothers (sibs) to compare.
- We are not sure what PCOS looks like in the male.
- There has been no specific genetic marker for PCOS.
- Problems in collection of family histories.

This last point is best illustrated by the studies of Dr. Azziz in Birmingham, who found a marked difference between collected history and actual history of family members. Often a PCOS patient gave incorrect information about her sisters, whom she thought she knew well. In a different study of hirsute women, almost half reported a normal menstrual history, but on closer examination it became clear that almost half of those did not ovulate. It is very important to obtain a complete and accurate family history.

It is surprising how few truly know their family's past history. In the case of infertility alone, a patient will relate that there was a spacing of five years between herself and her brother. If this was unplanned, this indicates quite significant infertility; it just wasn't mentioned or perhaps was left untreated. However, some fertile parents may have deliberately planned such spacing between their children. Still other parents may have found their family planning interrupted by other factors—such as a war which kept fertile partners apart from one another. I must confess that I am as bad as any when it comes to having accurate information about my parents' fertility. I have one sibling—a brother five years younger than myself—and I always assumed that that was because my folks only had sex twice in their relationship. Specifically ask family members about age at start of menstrual cycles, infertility, pregnancy loss, diabetes, heart disease and cancer.

Is PCOS an alteration of one, a few, or many genes?

If this were an easy question, the experts would have figured it out by now. The fact that there hasn't been a single gene isolated as the cause of PCOS suggests that the answer involves more than one gene. As 1999 came to a close, it was thought that the research consortium of Drs. Dunaif, Strauss and Legro had found the key. They proposed that the gene associated with follistatin, a regulatory protein made in the granulosa cells of follicles, tied together all the loose ends. The search for the prize was over; the package just needed a little tidying. As the year 2000 began, it was found that in fact follistatin may be involved but it is not the Holy Grail of PCOS. This same group has now hypothesized single gene defects associated with the insulin receptor gene. Obviously we thought we were further along than we actually are.

One of the earliest concepts of genetics was the "one gene, one enzyme" theory. Enzymes are the control points for most bodily functions. Enzymes in the ovary involved with steroid production, action, and metabolism would seem perfect targets as the origin of PCOS. As such the genes that control production of enzymes are an active area of study. Most of the enzymes have a common processing system called the cytochrome P450 pathway. The following genes coding for enzymes of the cytochrome P450 system are candidates:

enzyme	gene	status
cholesterol side chain cleavage	(CYP11a)	still a contender
17-hydroxylase / 17,20 lyase	(CYP17)	losing favor
aromatase	(CYP19)	probably uncommon

None of these enzymes appear to be specifically related to insulin and insulin action, so we must hypothesize a second gene or set of genes related to either insulin production and secretion for the pancreas (the *insulin gene*) or genes related to the uptake of insulin by the cell (*insulin receptor gene*). It appears unlikely that the gene coding for the insulin receptor itself is involved as a primary cause of PCOS. Steve Franks, one of Britain's leading PCOS experts, and his colleagues have favored the former possibility of abnormality in the regions of DNA around the insulin gene to be much more likely.

While it may not be the insulin receptor itself, it may be an event—*serine-threonine phoshorylation*—that occurs after the receptor is activated (*post receptor signaling*) that is central to the development of PCOS. The attractiveness of this proposal is increased by the possibility that this same process could account for an abnormality in the CYP17 gene, thus providing a unified theory of insulin resistance and ovarian dysfunction.

It seems PCOS may be just too complex to have a single gene as its origin. It is difficult to explain insulin resistance and at the same time the arrested follicular development, hyperandrogenism and adrenal involvement with a single mechanism. Professor Franks has proposed an oligogenic (few genes) origin of PCOS, although he is quick to point out that there may be only one dominant gene in a specific family grouping responsible for PCOS. This seems to make a lot of sense and better explains the vast divergence of physical and laboratory findings.

So, if we assume that there can be several genes that cause PCOS, a possible scenario might be that Family A will be Type A PCOS. Family B may have Type B PCOS. The resulting offspring from the union of the families may have either Type A PCOS, Type B PCOS or maybe Type C PCOS, which could be a combination of both A and B. The Type C could be a double dose and worse than either Type A or B. A second scenario is that Family A carries the lock, while family B carries the key. Their resulting children inheriting both lock and key, open the door and PCOS comes out. I tend to favor the first possibility in that there seem to be several major branches of the PCOS tree.

In my view, after observing family history and characteristics of individual patients, it seems that there may be four individual pathways. One is mostly related to the specific ovarian defect, a second related to insulin resistance, the third is of adrenal origin, and a fourth the ubiquitous "other" category, accounting for various problems that cause the *appearance* of PCOS without actually *being* PCOS.

The "nickel bag" concept

Despite a genetic basis, there may be more to PCOS than just one or even several "bad" genes. In the genetics jargon this may go by many names with slightly different definitions such as multifactorial, incomplete penetrance, or transmission disequilibrium. Basically, there are both genetic and acquired (environmental) factors that combine to form a threshold. A list of the genetic factors can include all of the above errors in steroid and insulin processing plus the genetic predisposition for obesity, abdominal fat, appetite, and energy expenditure. The environmental factors can include diet, activity, stress, psychological conditioning, and age. In some cases, genetics alone may be sufficient to cause PCOS, while in others there must be additive effects of the environment to cross the threshold.

In my early elementary school days, we could buy a bag of assorted candy for a nickel. Five cents was the *threshold*. I know this nickel bag concept connotation has a very different association now, but anyway, this bag had several different types of candy. Some types might cost two cents and others were two for a penny. It still cost a nickel for the bag, and you never knew exactly what you were going to find in the bag. Sometimes the clerk would put in three pieces of the same kind of candy, which might be analogous to our having a very strong helping of one of the genes of insulin resistance or steroid metabolism. In the PCOS bag there might be a penny's worth of insulin resistance, a penny each for two different ovarian enzymes, a penny of fat and a penny of inactivity. The bag is now full.

What is the pattern of inheritance in PCOS?

We know that there are three major modes of inheritance: dominant, recessive, and sex-linked. There have been about ten studies on a total of about 1500 families with PCOS in which the question of mode of inheritance has been specifically addressed. The majority of studies have concluded that the primary method of gene expression for PCOS is through an *autosomal dominant* pattern. This means that 50% of offspring will have the disorder if one parent carries the PCOS gene and 75% will have it if both mom and dad carry the gene.

Does PCOS run in my family?

Probably. In the appendix is a sample family tree, or as geneticists refer to it, a pedigree. Geneticists use a pedigree, or a family tree, to both record family history and to establish what form of inheritance is operating. Completion of this form may be very helpful in your investigation into PCOS, and if not directly helpful, it should at least be an interesting exercise to perform for an insight into who you are genetically. Sometimes this can be a scary exercise, but by identifying specific family traits, you may alter your disease risk factors. This gives new meaning to genealogy research.

Did I get PCOS from my mom's or my dad's side?

It seems that PCOS can be just as easily passed down from either the female or male parent's gene pool. It is generally thought that about one third of PCOS is from the maternal side, one third from the paternal side and about one third combined.

Is obesity inherited?

Yes. Is there a single fat gene? Probably not. There have been as many as seventy different genes thought to have an effect on obesity. Obesity is a component of at least one half of PCOS patients. Like PCOS, there is a strong hereditary component to obesity. What is now a genetic burden was once our greatest capacity to survive. No less a genetic luminary than Charles Darwin commented on the relationship of genetics, survival and fat. He recorded that domestic animals are fatter and reproduce earlier than those in the wild. He hypothesized fertility was directly related to the amount of food available. The capacity of a species to reproduce is directly related to nutritional status. It is still possible that the gene that allowed us to prosper now may place us at a distinct evolutionary disadvantage.

The traditional example of a genetic advantage gone astray is that of the Pima Indians. A hundred years ago the tribe existed at a semi-starvation level. Food was scarce and the capacity to store fat was equal to the survival rate. Their diet consisted of no more than 15% fat. Now, consuming a typical Western diet, over 50 % of the Pima population are obese by the age of 30. Weights of over 300 pounds are commonplace. It is possible that some native tribes no longer exist because they lack this genetic advantage of survival by storage of fat. This has been referred to as the *thrifty gene* concept of find food, eat food, store food, as a guard against the uncertainty of food no longer existing. The thrifty gene may be a close relative to the gene(s) of insulin resistance. Insulin resistance increases as weight increases, and there is a clear genetic basis for insulin resistance.

That there is a genetic component of obesity is shown by a classic experiment where normal weight volunteers were paid to consume food in excess of their caloric needs. Their weight rose rapidly at first, then reached a plateau at which no more weight was gained. When the study was over and participants resumed their usual diet, weight was lost and their pre-study weight re-established.

A classic way to study disease patterns is by comparing identical and non-identical twins. Identical twins, even when living completely separated lives, tend to have the same body weight and body habits, while non-identical or fraternal twins vary markedly even when they have a very similar lifestyle.

It may be related to inherited composition of the satiety center in the brain or genes that control metabolism.

Leptin—*the* fat gene?

There is intense excitement over the *ob* gene, which is lacking in the *ob* strain of mice. These animals gain an excessive amount of weight when overfed. This missing *ob* gene is the signal for fat cells to make *leptin*. First identified in 1994, leptin may be the elusive signal to the hypothalamus controlling fat stores. It may be the way fat communicates with the hunger and satiety centers of the brain. The absence of leptin would send the signal to eat, to recharge fat stores. Obesity, then, may be the result of an improperly sent or received signal. Discoveries about leptin may be among the greatest advances in understanding fat metabolism in the last fifty years. Virtually every endocrinology journal has a couple of articles about leptin research each month. The relationship between leptin and PCOS is under active investigation.

At first, it was thought that the answer to human obesity had been found. Too bad, but leptin has fallen short of expectations. In the human, the *Lep gene,* equivalent to the *ob* gene in mice, is found lacking in only very small group of individuals. The chromosomal site (locus) that controls leptin action is closely related to the site of at least one gene of insulin resistance. Obese individuals have much higher levels of leptin. Weight loss lowers leptin. It has been hypothesized that a genetic mutation results in *leptin resistance* in a manner similar to insulin resistance. This implies that the leptin signal is distorted and for obese individuals food always has the green light to be eaten either because it looks/tastes good or the body perceives hunger in the presence of fullness.

The reports linking PCOS and leptin presently are inconsistent and there is still work to be done. It's possible that there will be leptin-altering drugs to rival the insulin-altering drugs. The sleuths are on the path.

Can males have PCOS?

While some believe that PCOS has an X-linked inheritance and would be manifested in males, this seems unlikely. We know that the PCOS "gene" can be passed down through the male side of the family with equal ease as through the female side. One would think it impossible that males could escape some evidence of PCOS. There must be PCOS in the male genotype (potential for expression) to justify the pattern of inheritance in the female.

Obviously, there are problems in making the diagnosis of PCOS in males. Certainly, men do not have ovaries and do not have periods. What would be considered hirsutism in the female is the normal hair distribution in the male. Still, is there an physical or behavioral expression (phenotype) of the PCOS genotype?

Four different findings have been suggested as a pattern of symptoms that, found together, may represent the male counterpart of PCOS.

· **Increased hair growth "pilosity":** Certainly some men are hairier than others and at least one investigator has suggested an increased number of hair follicles are present in the males of PCOS families. Measurement is difficult, but not out of the question. This finding needs confirmation.

· **Oligospermia and decreased midline hair:** Again suggested but not proven that men of PCOS families have lowered sperm counts. It should be an easy question. The genetics of males with decreased sperm counts are being closely scrutinized. It is known that an abnormality exists on the Y chromosome that results in severely reduced sperm numbers and that this alteration can be transferred from father to son. Other studies have not shown any alteration of fertility or gonadotropin levels in brothers of women with PCOS. The association of male infertility with PCOS remains weak, but worthy of study.

   • **Premature balding:** This has been suggested in more than one study. A thorough study by Dr. Legro at Penn State University in Hershey has not substantiated the balding issue. In fact, he found that premature balding was less often seen in family members of PCOS. Still, look back through your family tree to see if there is any evidence. Male pattern balding is certainly genetic and related to androgens.

   • **Insulin resistance:** In 1971 Dr. Givens first suggested the possibility of insulin resistance in the male when there is a family history of PCOS. He also believed that much of PCOS was passed down through the paternal side of the family. Insulin resistance is inherited and Dr. Legros has put forward *insulin resistance* as the male phenotype of PCOS. He has added to it the catchy phrase, "HIR in HIM." In addition to insulin resistance, his group also found increases in triglycerides and DHEAS in brothers of PCOS patients.

   So what do we know? The top two choices listed above are shaky, the third is disputed. The insulin resistance issue and probably obesity are almost sure things. It is surprising how many women being treated for PCOS have a history of type 2 diabetes in their family. They frequently report borderline diabetes in either their father or mother. More often patients report diabetes in their grandparents who may now just be old enough for the overt signs of the disease. These signs and symptoms clearly linking some aspects of PCOS to male relatives are yet another argument against the appropriateness of the current label for this spectrum we now call PCOS.

Why miscarriage?

   A strong relationship exists between miscarriage, multiple miscarriages and PCOS. The most likely cause of pregnancy loss is hormonal, but an altered hormonal environment increases the risk of genetic mistakes.

   Before birth, the chromosomes of the egg are arrested in their process of division and are not activated until the LH surge immediately preceding ovulation. During this span of 15 to 45 years, chromosomes become progressively less able to undergo normal division. When an unequal division of the chromosomes occurs it is called *aneuploidy*. The most common group of aneuploidy is the *trisomies*, a situation with one additional chromosome, 47 instead of 46. The most common of the trisomies is trisomy 21 (Down syndrome), which involves three instead of two chromosome 21. This disorder is of particular importance because it is one of the only aneuploidies compatible with life outside the uterus. There also seems to be something about the 21st chromosome that makes it particularly susceptible to the lack of separation (*non-dysjunction*).

   Other types of chromosomal disorders include *deletions*, where only a part of the chromosome is lost, *additions* where a part is gained, and *translocations* where one part of a chromosome is transferred to a different location. These may have no effect whatsoever, or if serious enough, may cause a spontaneous pregnancy loss. Structural abnormalities of chromosomes are determined by a karyotype. A *kary-*

otype is a method where a sample of cells from a pregnancy or from blood of the parents is analyzed for the physical configuration of the chromosomes.

Risk of Chromosomal Disorders at Birth

(approximated from several sources)

age	Trisomy 21 (Down syndrome)	all chromosomal disorders
25	1 / 1250	1 / 500
30	1 / 1000	1 / 400
35	1 / 400	1 / 200
40	1 / 100	1 / 60
45	1 / 30	1 / 20

If only for a few "good eggs."

The major cause for pregnancy loss is poor egg quality. Clearly, the chance of chromosomal abnormalities increases with age. After many years of chromosomes in a resting phase, they are more likely to stick together during cell division. Those with PCOS are not immune to the effects of aging. In fact, in younger women with PCOS, there is another type of aging that has a similar influence on egg quality – delayed ovulation. A very precise synchrony is mandated for production of a healthy egg. Once the oocyte begins its development, events must be timely. Timing is everything. We know that the oocyte that is ovulated past day 14 is much more likely to be defective. Delayed ovulation occurs often in PCOS, virtually every time the cycle length is over thirty days. Not all eggs subjected to intra-follicular aging are defective, but statistically the risk is higher.

A third origin of miscarriage in women with PCOS is involved with the very nature of PCOS itself. We know from our experience with in vitro fertilization that there are many more follicles than good eggs and more good eggs than good embryos. A completely different type of genetics may result in an inherited defect in the metabolic machinery so that an abnormal hormonal environment is created for the egg. We know that androgen reduces egg quality, but how this happens is not known. We know that women with elevated LH levels have an increased risk of miscarriage, but again the mechanism is not known. The egg itself probably starts its course as normal, but iss adversely affected during its development by an altered ovarian and/or follicular environment. Development may be altered at one of many stages: ovulation, fertilization, implantation, or pregnancy viability.

In the end, it's about the beginning.

Whether we are shy or outgoing, succeed or fail in our profession, die of cancer or heart disease may be solely determined by the genetic combination that occurs at conception. Accidents are the only major cause of death that are not genetically controlled to some degree. Interesting preliminary reports suggest that there may even be an accident-prone personality, or at least one that will take more risks, that is genetically determined. Each of the major signs and symptoms of PCOS has a genetic basis—obesity, ovarian dysfunction, manifestations of hyperandrogenism, insulin resistance. Our first goal will be to identify and understand the genetic mechanisms of health and disease. A natural progression will lead to designer drugs to overcome the problem. Finally, the ability to alter or select the genetic make-up of our offspring is almost too large an issue to ponder.

When Does It Start?
Before Birth through
Teen Years

"I was lucky and was able to conceive a child when I was younger. I have had so many problems since then. Will my daughter have PCOS? How can I begin to help her?"

Often there are two individuals, a teen and her mom, at the initial consultation. Most health professionals are more comfortable dealing with the older of the two, who is often the more outspoken and leads the conversation. It is even more likely that it is the mom who is reading this chapter for her daughter, rather than the teen herself. The concern for one's offspring never stops. Neither mom nor daughter is all that comfortable with this coming of age of the reproductive system. Each would probably prefer that the teen be seen separately, but a strong common bond has brought them into the physician's office.

To start, we have a problem of terminology. What is the female called in the years around puberty, ages eight to eighteen? The term *girl* is too diminutive and seems to represent a position of less stature. The term *young woman* has some of the same problems and can even sound scolding. Should a menopausal woman be referred to formally as an *old woman*? *Adolescent* seems pejorative and even carries a negative connotation, as if bad behavior could be expected. To consider that this individual has identical health concerns to another ten years older is also incorrect. Surely, this is a formative time. A time when individual identity is solidified. A time when the foundation for future health and well-being is laid. For the purpose of this presentation, *teen* seems to be a safe enough description, knowing that some will be just shy of this age.

. **A most common case**

When asked if there is a particular pattern to the first signs of PCOS, my answer is yes, *but*. There are still many variations of the PCOS theme. A typical scenario that is repeated time and again follows.

The onset of puberty with breast and pubic hair development normally occurs between ages nine to eleven, with periods starting at the typical age of twelve to thirteen years. Some with PCOS start menstruating earlier, while a few make their debut with a gynecologist around age 16 for never having had a period. Most commonly, there are no problems with the onset of menses. Usually, menstrual cycles are at first regular, or slightly farther apart. By high school, cycles start to lengthen and become increasingly erratic. When bleeding occurs, it can be heavy and painful. Frequently this results in a prescription for oral contraceptives (OCs) and ibuprofen. "The pill" usually regulates the menstrual cycle, giving the false impression that all is well. All the while PCOS is percolating under the surface.

As the teen years progress, signs of PCOS such as skin and weight problems rear their ugly heads. Those with PCOS often weigh slightly more than their peers despite sports and a similar diet. Some will easily establish a pregnancy in the late teens or early twenties. OCs may even increase the chance of pregnancy by suppressing abnormal hormonal production.

The next big visit to the gynecologist occurs in the early twenties when either the erratic bleeding pattern has become unmanageable, or a pregnancy is desired. A marriage has often intervened and weight has risen significantly. For the first time some will hear of PCOS, for others it still may be years away.

Although how and when PCOS emerges is variable, the fact is that the majority of PCOS is genetically programmed and unavoidable. Most cases of PCOS are evident in the teen years and should not be difficult to diagnose. PCOS in many ways is a caricature of puberty; the characteristics of puberty are over exaggerated, possibly "persistent". Early recognition of PCOS can lead to early treatment; early treatment improves body image and future health.

How does it all start—brain sex?

As a pregnancy finishes the first trimester, or by twelve weeks gestation, there is the first pulsatile secretion of luteinizing hormone (LH) and follicle stimulating hormone (FSH) from the fetal pituitary gland. By the time the pregnancy has reached mid-gestation, about twenty weeks, there is a maturation of the feedback mechanism between the ovary and the hypothalamus. A preferential secretion of FSH over LH begins that is distinctly different from what is going on in the male fetus and this FSH/LH difference will continue throughout the reproductive life span.

The height (amplitude) and frequency of FSH pulses are greater and occur earlier in females and LH is greater in males. Variation in frequency of LH alters the ratio of LH/FSH secreted. In the natural process of feedback, estrogen should reduce LH release from the pituitary gland, but we know that in females it does the opposite: estrogen stimulates LH release. This seems to be a characteristic of the female sex of most species studied. It is thought that how the brain responds to estrogen is determined at a *critical period* during prenatal development. Certain behaviors and conditions such as dyslexia, left-handedness, and mathematical ability appear to occur very early and are gender-related. Despite a constant search, no specific differences have been related to sexual preference or gender.

From research in animal models of PCOS, we know that if the brain is exposed to androgens during the critical period of development, future menstrual cyclicity will be lost. It seems that PCOS patients share some characteristics of those who have experienced prenatal androgen exposure. Instead of developing the typical cyclic (*phasic*) pattern of alteration in LH and FSH secretion, female fetuses with PCOS experience a constant minimally changing (*tonic*) pattern that characterizes PCOS, the origin of which remains unknown.

After delivery and separation from the high maternal steroid levels during pregnancy, there is a transient activity of the LH pulse generator that then becomes dormant during childhood. For unknown reasons, the brain, pituitary gland and ovaries all remain quiet during childhood, despite a capacity to respond if given a hormone challenge. This situation defies the normal feedback mechanisms of the endocrine system and has puzzled researchers. While it cannot be explained, it can be labeled. The phenomenon that keeps gonadotropin secretion and steroid production of the ovary at low levels has been called the *gonadostat*. The initial trigger for puberty is not known with certainty, but it seems that there is an overall realization of the body that it is now gaining the capacity to reproduce. Stress of any form can send the signal that reproduction would not be in that individual's best interest and delay puberty.

To use an automotive analogy, one might think of puberty like this... as the foot is taken off the brake (*gonadostat*), the accelerator (*pulse generator*) is slowly advanced, and the car goes forward (the LH pulse frequency increases). The first changes in puberty occur during sleep, when pulses increase in amplitude and frequency. The ovary, which has been at a slow idle, receives the stimulus to initiate coordinated follicle development. There will be many months of "running at the hill" before the necessary speed is gained to get over the top—that is, for ovulation to occur. During puberty the ovarian volume increases by ten times. The multicystic or polycystic appearance of ovaries in puberty is typical. Indeed, it may be that all pubertal females have PCOS as a stage of normal development, but that it is transient in most.

There is some innate sense of metabolic balance that is critical for puberty to occur. Puberty may represent only the rapid rise portion of a normal growth curve that at first is slow, then rapidly increases, only to slow once again at maturity. There may be no magic, no unique mechanisms; just a slow programmed rise in body growth. Obviously, our understanding of puberty remains primitive.

What is puberty?

Puberty is defined as the time when the capacity to reproduce is acquired. The human is one of the most sexually endowed of all species. There is virtually no part of our physical or mental being that does not show variation between the sexes (*sexual dimorphism*). Although there are hints of male and female differences throughout childhood, it is at puberty that the body and sexual image undergo the most change. Puberty represents the coming of age of the hypothalamic-pituitary-ovarian-adrenal (HPOA) axis.

Puberty is a continuum that integrates genetics and environmental factors such as geographic location, exposure to light, nutrition, weight, exercise, and general overall health. During puberty there are several simultaneous processes at work. Once puberty starts, it marches through an ordered series of events under the control of different, but interrelated hormonal mechanisms. The earliest stages of puberty are not physically noticeable and start several years before outward signs. The physical herald of puberty is development of the secondary sexual characteristics including altered body form, sexual hair growth, and breast development. The central event of female puberty is menstruation.

Advanced and delayed puberty are often associated with distorted body

Facts about Puberty

- Total pubertal changes take an average of 4.2 years (1.5-6.0).
- By age 13 only 4 of 1000 teens lack some sort of evidence of sexual development.
- If there has been no evidence of sexual maturation by age 13, help should be sought.
- Delayed puberty is the absence of sexual characteristics by age 13 or menarche by age 16. Precocious puberty is defined as sexual characteristics before age 8.
- Living closer to the equator, at lower altitudes, or in rural areas are all associated with an earlier puberty. It is possible that later puberty occurs in more technologically advanced societies.
- Those who are mildly overweight have earlier puberty. Obese and thin women have later.
- Two hundred years ago, we were 25% shorter and reached a stable height in our early 20s, rather than at age 17-18.
- Over 95% of height is reached at menarche.
- Breast development begins at around age 10 and precedes menarche by 2.5 years.
- The average age of menarche in the US is 12.8 years for white females and about 6 months earlier for Afro-American females.
- Anovulatory cycles are common before age twenty.

image and the anxiety of not conforming to peers. PCOS is more often associated with early puberty, although menses may be delayed in some patients with PCOS. Early maturation of sexual characteristics is more likely associated with problems of social adjustment. This is in part due to the increased interest gained from older admirers. Sexual and emotional development may not coincide.

How is puberty measured?

It is important in the evaluation of possible abnormal pubertal development to know what normal is. A staging system of breast and pubic hair growth was developed by Tanner in England and has been variously modified by others. It serves as a worldwide benchmark to assess pubertal milestones. Breast and pubic hair development are classified as stage 1 (prepubertal) to stage 5 (adult). This staging represents a clinical guide only and there is considerable variation within the limits of normal. Development appears to occur at slightly different ages in countries and among different races in the same country. The following data is presented for American white females.

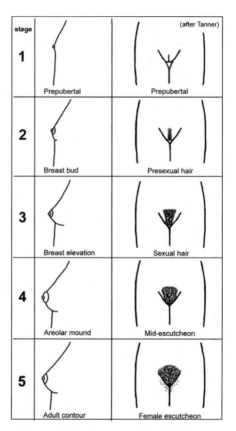

Figure 4-1 Stages of Development

Figure 4-2 Average Age and Stages of Female Sexual Development

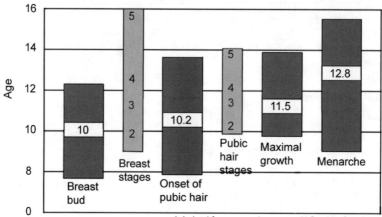

* derived from several sources , U.S. white females

What is the first sign of puberty?

Breast development—thelarche

The first noticeable sign of puberty in females is usually the initiation of breast development *(thelarche)*. The development of the breasts is primarily under the control of estrogens secreted by the ovary. Initial development may occur in one breast only for several months. Even in adults, it is more usual than unusual for breasts to be of different sizes. Staging does not depend on size or shape, both of which are related more to genetic and nutritional factors.

The information included here is taken from a study sponsored by the American Association of Pediatrics compiled by Herman-Giddens and colleagues on 17,070 office patients between ages 3 and 30. While it may be the most reliable study to date on early pubertal development, it may also distort data because it used the cut-off age of 13, thus adding the early bloomers and leaving out the late ones. In this study, thelarche occurred at an average age of 9.96 years in European Americans and 8.87 years in African Americans. At stage 2 of development, the height and diameter of the nipple changes from the prepubertal size of about 2.9 mm to 3.3 mm. This change may be somewhat difficult to distinguish, even by an experienced observer, because

Stages of Puberty
• Breast development (thelarche)
• Sexual hair (adrenarche)
• Accelerated growth (growth spurt)
• Menstruation (menarche)

of varying amounts of fat. That does not mean a mom cannot tell. Most reach developmental stage 3 at 11 to 12 years. The nipple has continued to enlarge slightly and breast development should be clearly evident. Stage 4 is characterized by a well-developed mound of tissue immediately underneath the nipple. Growth between stages 4 and the adult stage 5 is the most variable.

What if the breasts are not developing?

Breast development requires both estrogen, signifying initiation of ovarian function, and receptors in breast tissue for estrogen. The breasts differ somewhat in receptor number accounting for one breast larger than the other in most women. Since receptor number cannot be changed, it is also the reason that using supplemental hormones will not increase breast size. Final breast size is genetically determined (constitutional) and partly due to body weight. Taller, thinner, or especially aggressively athletic teens may have delayed breast development.

If there is failure of breast development by age 13 and especially if there is short stature, FSH levels should be drawn to exclude abnormalities in ovarian development (ovarian dysgenesis). *Ovarian dysgenesis* is a genetic abnormality where the ovary does not properly form and is doomed to failure before it has a good chance to start. FSH is unmistakably elevated in this condition. Low and normal FSH levels are reassuring that the ovary is normal, but still dormant. Often application of "tincture of time," otherwise known as a wait-and-see approach, is best.

When is pubic hair evident?
Sexual hair growth—adrenarche

About two years prior to any physical sign of puberty there begins a slow increase in dehydroepiandrosterone sulfate (DHEAS). The physiologic trigger for this rise is unknown. The emergence of pubic hair is called the *adrenarche*, or *pubarche*. Facial, axillary (arm pit) and genital hair growth are all secondary sexual characteristics under the influence of androgens derived from the adrenal glands. (See Chapter 7). The hallmark of adrenarche is development of pubic hair with axillary hair about two years later. Usually adrenarche follows thelarche within about six months. It is relatively common for the adrenarche to precede thelarche. Onset of axillary hair occurs at 11.8 years while acne occurs at an average age of 12.2 years. In some, acne may be the first sign of puberty. These events are followed by the growth spurt, which should begin about two years after the appearance of pubic hair. The pubic hair stage roughly corresponds to the breast development stage; that is, stage 3 breast will correspond to stage 3 pubic hair.

The adrenarche is the province of the adrenal gland alone and is dissociated from ovarian or menstrual functions. Adrenal androgens do not limit the development of puberty. Even those patients that make pathologic amounts of adrenal androgens have the onset of menses at the appropriate age, as do those with low levels of adrenal androgens. It also appears that the adrenal androgens are not responsible for the growth spurt in either males or females.

Normal height and breast development, but absence or markedly decreased pubic and axillary hair may be due to a disorder of *androgen insensitivity*. The essential diagnostic test for this disorder is a testosterone level and if elevated, a genetic karyotype.

What is too young for hair growth?

Precocious pubarche (PP) is defined as appearance of pubic and/or axillary hair before age 8. PP is five times more common in females than males. Several studies have addressed the issue of whether or not PP can lead to adult hirsutism or PCOS. There is mounting evidence that PP may be a manifestation of PCOS. Young females with precocious pubarche already have insulin resistance.

PP before age 8 is not rare, nor is it usually of medical consequence. It is of greater concern when there is associated breast development and especially menstruation. This is referred to as precocious puberty and always warrants an early evaluation and possible therapy to prevent stunted growth. Depending on the clinical circumstance, evaluation may include testing for 17-hydroxyprogesterone to exclude an occult form of congenital adrenal hyperplasia, determination of bone age and a challenge with gonadotropin releasing hormone analog.

Isn't acne just a part of growing up?

Yes and no. Virtually no teen escapes oily skin any more than the development of pubic hair. No teen should suffer the permanently scarring forms of acne that have plagued earlier generations. While any acne can be disturbing to a teen, severe acne is a lifelong stigma. There is evidence that the severe forms of acne are inherited and an early intervention may be needed.

Acne may be the first sign of puberty in females, preceding either breast or pubic hair development. Acne at an early age is a signal that worse may be coming. The most severe forms of acne occur in males and no male is completely immune. Dermatology consultation should be considered early if severe development of acne occurs later on in puberty.

Why are males taller than females?

The growth spurt

Although increased rate of growth occurs before other evidence of puberty, it is not nearly so detectable as breast budding. A very rapid increase in height, called the growth spurt, occurs at age 11 or 12, or about two years after breast budding and about one year prior to menarche. The growth spurt occurs between developmental stages 2 and 3.

Males reach their stage of maximum growth about two years later than do females. This delay in the growth spurt in part explains the differences in final height of about 12 cm (2 ½ - 4½ "). The average height for females is 163 cm. Over 95% of adult height is reached at menarche, after which only one to two additional inches is usually gained. The mechanisms controlling growth may be even more complicated than those of controlling gonadal or adrenal development and involve growth hormone, thyroid hormone and insulin like growth factors, as well as gonadal steroids. The adrenal gland has little impact on growth. An X-ray of the left hand and wrist is used to determine bone age and assess of growth potential. All parents of children whose growth pattern is quicker or slower than other children of the same age should at least ask the question of their physician, "Is this all right?"

Why is calcium so important?

Bone mass and therefore bone density is related to genetics and over-laid by lifelong hormone status. Almost all of the bone in the hip and spine is present before age twenty. While bone loss begins before age thirty, the initial loss is slow until the perimenopausal years, when there is a rapid acceleration of loss. Bone formation and therefore bone density is related to calcium intake in childhood and the early teen years. Calcium intake should be 1500 mg daily. The usual diet of teens may contain no more than 500 to 1000 mg daily calcium (one cup of milk, fortified juice or 1 oz. of cheese has about 300 mg of calcium). More bone = less osteoporosis, a simple equation.

"Fight versus fertile?"

After the growth spurt comes the "strength spurt." Mature men have one and a half times the muscle mass of women. Muscle mass and storage of intra-abdominal fat (a.k.a. the beer belly) is under the influence of testosterone. Pubertal females gain fat in the hips while the waist stays the same. Mature women have twice the body fat of men.

Is there a connection between weight and puberty?

Both weight and percentage of body fat are thought to be important for onset and maintenance of reproductive function. Just as birth was a search for new nutrient sources, development of sexual maturity has to wait until there are adequate resources to share. In the body's infinite wisdom, it has an internal scale relating nutritional balance and reproductive performance. If there are too few metabolic stores, menses are erratic and reproduction less successful. It is a natural protective mechanism. The reverse may be true with excessive stores. The body once again falls from a metabolic equilibrium and reproduction fails.

Landmark studies by Frisch showed that there had to be a "critical," "invariant" weight of about 106 pounds (48 kg) for the initiation of puberty. This "critical weight" theory has been called into question when it was found that the weight was coincident with, and did not predate puberty. Frisch believed that body fat of 22% was necessary at age sixteen to maintain normal menstruation. Frisch's findings are still valid as observations, but not as an explanation on the cause of puberty.

More recently, added emphasis has been placed on nutrition, percentage of fat, and a shift in body composition from about 15% to 25% fat. As the weight increases, so does the percentage of body fat. A normal mature female has about 52% water and 37% fat. Modestly overweight teens have an earlier menarche, while obese teens and their thin athletic counterparts have delayed or erratic menses. Young diabetics have a later menarche. Clearly some factor that regulates energy is critical.

There is a search for some communication mechanism between fat and the brain that is responsible for normal reproductive processes. Recent research has put forward leptin as a leading candidate for this role as an ovarian regulator. The leptin level is related to the amount of body fat, but it may be another association rather than etiology and more proof is needed. (See Chapter 8 for a discussion on leptin).

At what age do periods start?

Menarche

In the United States, the age of first menses (*menarche*) had decreased two to three months per decade in the 200 years before 1950. Children have been raised in relative affluence and good nutrition over the last fifty years and there has been no further decline in the age of puberty. There is some evidence that puberty may be occurring slightly later. This upward trend could either be a result of deterioration in our environment, eating habits, or perhaps the body's wisdom on reproduction before societal maturity. The average age of menarche in the U.S. is 12.8 years for European American females and about six months earlier for African American females. This difference is regardless of socioeconomic factors, but it is noted that mothers of these teens weigh about 20% more than their counterparts. There is relatively good correlation of menarche between mothers and sisters. As many as 50% of teens are still erratic in ovulation four years after menarche. Luckily, the early teen years are a time of relative infertility.

Is it just a stage to grow out of?

A particularly useful study has been published by van Hooff and colleagues studying Dutch schoolgirls ages 14 to 16. One importance of this study is that information was not gathered from teens seeking medical care, but from surveys in the schools. The vast majority had not consulted a physician about period problems. The investigators found the characteristics of obesity and skin problems could not reliably predict those with hormonal disturbances, but nearly 60% of those who had menstruated no more frequently than between 42 and 180 days had endocrine signs of PCOS. Those with irregular cycles, that is, they were variable in length between 22 and 41 days, showed a progressive normalization of bleeding patterns over time, but those with oligomenorrhea did not improve, and this pattern continued into adulthood. Physicians tend to reassure teens that their menstrual pattern will correct itself, which, for patients with still-unrecognized PCOS is both inaccurate and inappropriate information. This study clearly shows that this was not just a stage, but a warning sign of PCOS.

What can menstrual pain and bleeding tell us?

Periods after ovulation are more regular and usually moderately painful. Ovulatory cycles are usually associated with three to seven days of bleeding. No more than two or three of these days of bleeding should be heavy. Light and painless menses are more often associated with lack of ovulation. If there is a prolonged time between periods, the resulting menses are more likely long, heavy, and painful. Prolonged heavy, painful periods can be either ovulatory or anovulatory, but should be investigated whether cycles are regular or not. It is unproven that teens with painful periods have a greater chance of endometriosis in the future, but it is surprising how many women with endometriosis had painful periods from the start. It is not uncommon for school days to be missed and activities restricted due to dysmenorrhea (painful menstruation). There is a reasonable chance that this can be avoided.

Painful periods, like irregular periods, are good reasons to consider oral contraceptives. Most users have less pain, less bleeding and more timely bleeding. OCs should be prescribed along with prescription strength non-steroidal anti-inflammatory drugs such as Naprosyn™ and Ibuprofen™. In some cases aspirin or a combination preparation like Midol™ or Pamprin™ can suffice and should be tried first. There is no reason why this kind of suffering should not be reduced.

A word of caution is in order. Very heavy and prolonged menstrual bleeding can be a sign of several serious blood clotting disorders. If there has been a history of easy bruising and "free bleeding" with minor injury, this should be brought to the attention of a physician. Serious problems are usually easily diagnosed once aware that a problem might exist.

No period?

If there has ever been menstrual bleeding, regardless of how much, there is a reassurance that this much is normal. If menses subsequently stop, this is called *secondary amenorrhea*, as opposed to *primary amenorrhea* where there has never been a menses. The experts now say that we should not use the terms *primary* and *secondary amenorrhea*, because the causes can be overlapping, specifically with PCOS. I still believe that these terms have utility, because even one episode of bleeding ensures that many things are right and excludes a structural problem.

If there has been timely breast and pubic hair development and all is normal in every way except menses, there is concern about lack of development or obstruction of the pathway that allows blood to escape (the outflow tract). These problems usually date from the embryonic stages of development (congenital). While rare, complete absence of periods due to absence of the uterus is the second most common *pathologic* cause, after ovarian dysgenesis, of primary amenorrhea. This condition can usually be determined by ultrasound. Another even rarer cause of primary amenorrhea is an imperforate hymen. There is normal menstruation, but the blood cannot escape through the thickened hymen, which completely blocks the vaginal opening. These individuals usually present with pelvic pain and the diagnosis is quite evident upon physical examination.

Much, much more common causes of amenorrhea are two other groups of disorders that have normal anatomy, but their origin is in abnormal communication between the hypothalamus, pituitary, and ovary, the HPO axis. In this we fall back to the basic endocrine question—is there too much or too little?

On the too-little side, teens tend to be thinner and taller. These teens tend to be athletic, and eating disorders are common among them, sometimes in part due to a desire to maintain thinness. In this group there is usually a slowing of all signs of puberty, not just menstruation. After exclusion of more serious problems, many times it is best to just wait. Postponement can be a therapy itself, but should be administered like other therapy; that is, under close guidance and frequent reassessment.

On the too-much side, most teens are heavier and possibly all of the stages of puberty have occurred except menses. In the very obese, puberty can be delayed by suppression similar to the overly thin. However, the more common problem is the modestly to moderately overweight teen who is otherwise normal except possibly for a little increase in acne or hair growth but a period just hasn't occurred. There is an excellent possibility that this individual has PCOS. Still, PCOS remains a diagnosis of exclusion.

Some recommend proceeding directly to a *progestin challenge*. A common regimen is medroxyprogesterone acetate (Provera) 10 mg for ten days after which there should be "withdrawal bleeding." Personally, I usually first like to perform basic endocrine testing that will include estradiol, thyroid stimulating hormone, prolactin, follicle stimulating hormone and luteinizing hormone, possibly DHEAS and testosterone if there is much excessive hair growth. Routinely, despite the wish to deny the possibility, a pregnancy test is performed before extensive testing. Most diagnoses will be made or excluded by these tests. If the estradiol level is low there may need to be estrogen added to the progestin regimen to initiate a period. Any teen with an elevated FSH level or lack of sexual development and menses by age 16 should have a chromosomal mapping (karyotype) performed.

Where do we go from here? It depends on a number of factors. This is a time to discuss general health concerns and develop a plan. Often this plan will include oral contraceptives for menstrual cycle regulation.

Does puberty differ in PCOS?

Most PCOS patients undergo a particularly normally timed puberty. Breast and hair development corresponds to others of the same age, or is earlier. However, there are notable exceptions. Some have a delayed menarche and never establish a normal menstrual cycle. This group does not have the typical delayed puberty because all other features—including breast, pubic hair and height—have occurred in a timely fashion. Girls with PCOS have the same mechanisms at work which prevent their older counterparts from having regular menses.

Persistent puberty as the cause of PCOS?

PCOS and puberty have many common characteristics. The major difference is that puberty is a transient. While the causes of PCOS are most often inherited, it is during puberty that they become manifest. It has been theorized that the PCOS is result of a state of "persistent" puberty. The exaggerated adrenarche hypothesis holds that early elevations of adrenal androgens cause an increase in formation of estrogen in fat. This acyclic weak estrogen is enough to increase LH from the pituitary in a constant (tonic) positive feedback system, rather than cyclic (phasic) and negative feedback fashion. Elevated LH causes stimulation of increased ovarian androgens, leading to more raw materials for androgen and estrogen production; thus, there is potentiation and preservation of this abnormal system. ($\uparrow$androgen = $\uparrow$estrogen = $\uparrow$LH = $\uparrow$androgen = PCOS). This is further heightened if there is insulin resistance that both adds to fat formation and androgen production. The problem is not in the brain or in the pituitary, but in the signals they are receiving. This theory is now considered an observation rather than a cause, but it still helps explain how the system works.

When should help be sought?

Basically, seek help when you want an answer. Puberty is a progressive and orderly march. When any event falls out of line, questions should be asked. This may be early hair growth, or no period eighteen months after breast and pubic hair development. Evaluation should also be initiated if there is excessive acne or abnormal hair growth. Help should be sought if, six months after they start, menses are very frequent, excessive, or far apart. Sometimes a word of reassurance from a physician is all that is needed. Still, be aware that too often the early signs of PCOS are passed off too lightly. If a concern continues, or if you feel that it was not completely addressed, ask again. A delay in diagnosis rarely is medically serious, but it does mean dealing with the symptoms for a longer time. An early start with control measures for PCOS can make a difference. It seems probable that early intervention will not alter fertility or even long-term health, but self-image and quality of life can be improved.

Which physician takes care of teens with PCOS?

Too young for old and too old for young. In the perfect world, the family physician, an expert on the life cycle, is both a pediatrician and a gerontologist and is well versed in the transitions of life. There are also specialists in adolescent medicine. Unfortunately the generalists are too busy and the specialists are too few. The teen years are a time of relatively good health with very few health concerns or events, other than the occasional accident. Visits to the doctor are few and far between. Therefore, the pediatrician may be uninvolved. Gynecologists and internists are generally uncomfortable dealing with early teens. After having said this, the most important physician in this evaluation is one with whom a dialogue can be established. This may be a gynecologist, a reproductive, pediatric, or medical endocrinologist, or the local family practitioner. It is not too early to teach health consumerism.

Is a physical (pelvic) examination always necessary?

Perhaps it is reasonable to ask before the visit what is to be expected. In almost all cases the first visit should be an introduction and time of communication to set up trust and a plan. In my first few sentences I try to relay that no examination will be done on that day. There always seems to be relief. Still, the circumstances must dictate the content of the first visit. In assessing breast development and hair growth, a physical exam can be of use, but most of the signs are clearly obvious and the history is clear. In cases of acute pain or excessive bleeding, examination is much more likely.

More important than the exam is blood testing. (See Chapter 5), which is often performed at a return visit, perhaps for that purpose only. Ultrasound scan can also be very valuable. Vaginal ultrasound is better for evaluation of the pelvic anatomy and can usually be performed with relative comfort on anyone who uses tampons. Abdominal ultrasound requires a full bladder to serve as a window through which the uterus and ovaries can be seen. Most information about pelvic pathology can be obtained by ultrasound scanning. Pelvic anatomy is often more difficult and embarrassing, but also more important if there has never been a period.

Are the tests for PCOS the same in teens?

Generally, yes. Don't worry. Don't postpone. Ask! PCOS is called a diagnosis of exclusion, indicating that it is what remains after all other causes for symptoms have been removed. There are other, and in some cases more serious, diseases that can be mistaken for PCOS. On the first evaluation, I tend to be relatively broad in scope. (See Chapter 5). Sometimes there are surprises. Teens who have never had a period may require slightly different testing than those who have had periods and then stopped or those who have infrequent periods. A correct first diagnosis is very important. The problem arises as to when to seek help.

What are the chances of infertility?

In reviewing patient records, many with PCOS seem to have established a pregnancy in their late teens only to be infertile at a later date. A common scenario is this: "My mom quickly became pregnant with me; she wasn't even trying. She was nineteen. My brother was then born soon after." Her mom had not been labeled as infertile, nor was she said to have PCOS. Although no contraception was ever used, in retrospect, she had all the classic symptoms of PCOS.

Early fertility followed by risk of subsequent infertility is is hardly a recommendation for attempting a pregnancy in the teenage years. Teens that have periods over 35 days apart are less likely to ovulate and have decreased present and future fertility. No one with PCOS should take it for granted that they are either fertile or infertile. Most (80–90%) with PCOS will achieve a pregnancy. It is just unknown in advance how tough the path might be.

Is contraception necessary?

Frequently, I see women who have thought they could not become pregnant and have even been told that they will never have a child. That phrase "You will never be pregnant" sometimes seems to work better than fertility drugs. Whether the physician was trying to protect the patients from later disappointment, or had some form of higher wisdom, is a mystery. It is surprising both how much and how little it sometimes takes to achieve a pregnancy. Many think that a pregnancy is not possible because of their erratic periods. PCOS should not be used as contraception. Reliable contraception is needed for the sexually active female both to prevent pregnancy and to protect against sexually transmitted diseases. Oral contraceptives are not protective against AIDS and venereal disease.

Why use the Pill?

Once the diagnosis of PCOS has been made, we must turn to treatment. Generally this is easy and almost always the answer is oral contraceptives (OCs). This can be equally hard to accept by mom, dad and the teen. Some teens would rather have the pill on the breakfast table, while to others their reproductive health is a very private issue. A review of oral contraceptives is given in Chapter 17. Their positive health benefits for PCOS patients far outweigh the negative. To have a precisely timed menses with less pain and bleeding is very desirable. There is the additional benefit of control of skin problems. OCs should be started after an induction of the first menses. If progestin alone is not adequate then a combination of estrogen and progestin can be used. There should be no problem with even very long term use of OCs. It is very doubtful that teens believe that the pill is a license for sexual intercourse. So what to do? If the diagnosis of PCOS is in question, the reader is referred to Chapter 5.

When is too young for oral contraceptives?

There has been concern that use of oral contraceptives may cause a premature closure of the epiphyses plates of bone and therefore limit adult height. This remains speculative, but it is known that over 95% of height is reached by menarche. This would indicate the OCs could be used at anytime thereafter. Some have suggested a waiting period of two years after onset of menses, but this seems unfounded. However, since it is unclear what the menses pattern will be, it would be wise to wait until this has been established. An adage may be that if the teen has matured to the stage of having periods, then there should be no problem in OCs for control of bleeding. My answer to "When should OCs be started?" is "When they are needed."

Too young for insulin-altering drugs?

There have been several studies using metformin in teens. There would appear to be no contraindication for their use and the therapeutic effects are likely to be the same regardless of age. The reason to use these agents would be the same as their use with their older counterparts and is more thoroughly discussed in Chapters 9 and 16. Once again, starting the medication is easier than knowing when to stop. There should be a definite therapeutic objective in place before the medication is started.

Why is puberty so hard?

One explanation as to the reason we are born is that the fetus has exceeded the size and metabolic capacity of the mother to nourish the pregnancy. There must be an escape from the confines of a relatively small pelvic cavity. Any bigger and we just wouldn't fit. At birth we are in many ways still in a primitive developmental stage. We face a long and tedious journey to full maturation. We can only philosophize about the length of the expedition to societal maturity. Our capacity to survive as a species involves development of complex communication and interactive skills. If we developed much faster sexually we would be ill prepared to care for the young that are produced because of our complex social structure. Some have attributed our very success as a species to this prolonged period of social development and reproductive competence.

In primitive societies, puberty is greeted with celebration. Multi-layered stresses and complex adjustments characterize modern society's view on puberty. During puberty there is the emergence of abstract thinking, perspective, introspection, sexual identity, autonomy, and coping strategies. There is a move from the sheltered family environment and school classroom into world citizenship. One can only hypothesize what changes will be needed in the future to travel the information highway. Conflict arises from the competition in thought and position. Since the world is hardly harmonious, easing into it cannot be either. Generally there are good adaptations. Stormy teen years will often lead to a stormy adulthood.

Puberty is a continuous adaptive phase and not as explosive as many with teenagers might imagine. When we compare puberty to the adaptation that must take place with the first breath of air in the delivery room, the life of a newborn, a toddler or a first year college student, it isn't so dramatic. Most females start with a negative self-image at puberty. This is amplified by the typical PCOS characteristics of skin, weight and period problems.

Do I Have It?
Diagnostic Testing

"I'm a teacher, and one of the girls in my high school classroom was gaining weight and developing excessive body hair. One day when we were talking after class, I felt open enough to ask her if she ever had problems with an irregular period. She looked really surprised and told me that her mother wanted to take her to the doctor, because she was only having a period every three months and each time was very painful. I called her mother and told her about PCOS. The girl went to a specialist who diagnosed her with PCOS."

Despite how easy the diagnosis of PCOS may seem, the clinician must also be ever vigilant about the PCOS "look alikes." It is surprising how often health care providers miss it.

How is the diagnosis made?

Every individual with PCOS deserves a thorough evaluation to confirm the diagnosis, exclude other diagnoses, establish a baseline on which to evaluate change over time, identify potentially serious health risks, and direct therapy. The place to start in any medical evaluation is a complete past medical history. In no other disorder is this more important than PCOS. Often the diagnosis of PCOS becomes highly probable from past medical history alone. A template for recording, or at least organizing your thoughts about what may be asked is provided in the appendix. Having a chance to think about the answers may shorten the history-taking portion of the consultation and allow more time to talk about what's wrong and what can be done.

There are three major ways to make the diagnosis of PCOS:

- **Clinical findings:** These include confirming menstrual disturbances, hair and skin problems, and obesity. Menstrual cycle disturbances have been explained in Chapter 2, while Chapter 7 is devoted to skin problems and Chapter 8 to difficulty in maintaining weight.
- **Laboratory testing:** An explanation of the commonly used and recommended tests is given below.
- **Ultrasound scan:** Transvaginal ultrasound is the most powerful diagnostic imaging tool for the evaluation of PCOS. This painless, quick, safe, and relatively inexpensive technique allows the observer a window through which to evaluate the structure of the uterus and ovaries. The polycystic ovary has a particular appearance on ultrasound, which is described below. PCOS also may be associated with abnormalities of the uterine lining (endometrium), which is easily diagnosed by ultrasound.

Most individuals will have abnormalities in all three diagnostic areas, though some will have identifiable results in two areas and a few in only one diagnostic area. Some may argue that findings in a single diagnostic category should not constitute PCOS, but until we have PCOS better characterized, or find a different diagnosis, PCOS represents an identifiable unifying diagnosis that should remain. The most minor of apparent problems may have significant implications for future general health and well-being.

What should be checked at physical examinations?

The major physical findings in PCOS of weight and skin problems are usually and unfortunately too obvious to most. The physical examination may be postponed to a later visit. Still, a physical examination can help quantify these changes and possibly discover some additional associations. The list below is not all-inclusive, but illustrates areas of special attention for diagnosing PCOS.

- Vital signs: weight, height, body mass index (BMI), waist-hip ratio, blood pressure and pulse
- Skin: degree of hirsutism, acne, discoloration
- Thyroid: fullness, mass
- Breast: development, mass, discharge
- Genitalia: size of clitoris, health of vaginal lining, cervical discharge
- Size and position of uterus, consistency, tenderness
- Size and tenderness of ovaries

What else could it be?

The diagnosis of PCOS is what's remaining after all of the other possibilities have been removed. This is a so-called *diagnosis of exclusion*. While much less common, or even rare, several serious diseases with the same gen-

eral symptoms can masquerade as PCOS, especially those that cause an elevation in male sex hormones (hyperandrogenism). Fortunately, the more serious disorders are easily separated when the physician is aware of their possibility. A key point in the history, and one that is especially important in the
exclusion of more serious problems, is the speed of symptom progression. The
more dangerous problems are usually of more rapid onset and do not tend to
occur in other family members.

PCOS is associated with chronic, but no more than moderate, elevations in the male hormones. While there may be excessive hair growth and
other skin changes, these are quite different from a much more ominous condition known as *virilization*. Virilization is a condition where male sexual characteristics become prominent. Characteristics include deepening of voice, balding, increased muscle bulk, increased size of the clitoris, and marked hirsutism.
It is rare, but not impossible, for the individual with PCOS to be virilized.
Virilization always warrants immediate attention and thorough evaluation.

Some of the less common diseases that have findings similar to those
of PCOS include other disorders of the endocrine system, such as an overactive thyroid (hyperthyroidism) and under-active thyroid (hypothyroidism),
excessive production of the hormone prolactin (hyperprolactinemia), excessive
production of the adrenal hormone cortisol (Cushing's syndrome), and the
presence of pituitary, adrenal and ovarian tumors. Thyroid disease and hyperprolactinemia are easily excluded by measurement of the thyroid stimulating
hormone and prolactin. The following paragraphs describe some of the more
common diagnostic findings that may be confused with PCOS.

Congenital adrenal hyperplasia (CAH) results from an inherited
enzyme deficiency that partially or fully blocks the normal metabolic pathway
of adrenal steroid hormone production. While adrenal steroids may be only
weak androgens, their abundance in CAH leads to signs and symptoms of
hyperandrogenism, which are often the same as PCOS. There are several
types of CAH depending on which adrenal enzyme is involved. The most common type of CAH *is 21-hydroxylase deficiency*. In its *classic form*, 21-
hydroxylase deficiency is usually recognized at birth by more male-appearing
external sexual organs in a female newborn. This form of CAH can have fatal
consequences if not monitored properly. A milder form of 21-hydroxylase deficiency, called *late onset, acquired*, or *occult*, may go unrecognized until after
puberty, when females develop the same problems as do PCOS patients. The
prevalence of the 21-hydroxylase deficiency depends on the particular patient
population and the aggressiveness of diagnostic testing. Testing for 21-hydrox-
ylase deficiency involves measurement of 17-hydroxyprogesterone. This test
can even be used on amniotic fluid for prenatal diagnosis.

Cushing's syndrome is a disorder characterized by very high levels
of the adrenal hormone, cortisol. Cushing's syndrome shares some symptoms
of PCOS, including obesity, hypertension, and possibly hyperandrogenism.
Cushing's syndrome is usually obvious through history and physical examination. The diagnosis is confirmed by measurement of cortisol (see below).

Other causes. Young physicians are taught to think of horses, not
zebras, when galloping hoofs are heard—that is unless they live in Africa—and
yet too often doctors have wasted time looking for the much rarer problem

rather than making the obvious diagnosis of PCOS. There is a relatively long list of very uncommon disorders that have been associated with hyperandrogenism and polycystic ovaries. Tumors do occur and can be dangerous, but their rarity, relatively rapid onset, and severity of symptoms make them difficult to miss.

An uncommon cause of PCOS, which would be missed if the association were not known, is the use of valproic acid (Depakote™) for control of seizure activity. If you are on seizure medication, be certain that your physician is aware of this association!

Are there blood tests for PCOS?

Perhaps someday, if a more precise cause of PCOS can be identified, there will be a single test that will give a definite positive or negative diagnosis. Until then, we rely on a panel of tests that are indirect measurements and serve to evaluate the different known associations of PCOS.

Even among those who are supposedly in the know, there is wide opinion as to what test to use to evaluate PCOS. Some physicians, at a loss as to what blood tests in the vast array of possibilities should be ordered, select tests almost at random, adding considerable expense to an investigation. Additionally, too often when test results are returned to the patient, they are accompanied by little explanation. An individual familiar with the specific test interpretation, as well as with PCOS, best interprets laboratory test results.

What does an abnormal test value mean?

Virtually all patients with PCOS will have at least some subtle laboratory abnormalities. The reported results may be on the upper limits of the normal range, showing only a tendency rather than a discrete abnormality. Often a pattern will emerge only after considering a group of tests together, rather than as a result of a single test value. The marginally elevated test is almost always dysfunctional, rather than pathologic. The term *dysfunctional* is used to indicate a disordered physiology, while *pathologic* is usually attached to disease.

Subtle abnormalities may point toward dysfunction in the control mechanisms of the hypothalamus, pituitary, ovary and adrenal (HPOA) axis. Different from PCOS, serious pathology in this axis is more likely seen as a marked elevation, or suppression, of a single test. Any level that is twice the upper, or one half lower, normal limits is particularly important and may indicate a serious problem.

As a general rule, if the test result is not in keeping with clinical findings and the patient's history, it may be wrong. This may be due to lab error, improperly timed specimen collection, or unexplainable chance occurrence. Hormonal evaluation in patients using an oral contraceptive will often give misleading results with suppression of low level gonadotropin, ovarian steroid and SHBG levels.

While a thorough evaluation is important, repeated blood testing for the same hormones could be questioned, especially when a specific reason to do so is not given. Abnormal tests should be repeated for confirmation. Likewise, if the test is unexpectedly normal, a repeat should be considered.

Diagnosis

71

So, what is normal?

Normal is a statistical term that in the simplest definition means like every one else, or average. *Range* is the span from the highest to lowest level. In evaluating laboratory tests a *normal range* is given that indicates the limits in which the sample would be considered not different from the rest of the population. In most studies, the normal range is quoted with a 95% *confidence interval* (p≤ 0.5). This means that 95% of "normal" individuals will fall within these limits, but also that 2.5% of "normal" individuals will have a level higher and 2.5% a lower value than the normal range by chance alone. The farther away a value is from the normal range, the greater likelihood that it is abnormal. Two terms that are commonly used in hormonal testing are sensitivity and specificity. Sensitivity gives an indication about how likely the test is to give a true answer; that is, to pick up a problem that truly exists. Some tests may be

---

**Sources of
Lab Test Variation**

- Inappropriate normal range
- Sensitivity and specificity
- Reproducibility and accuracy
- Pulsatility of hormone release
- Sample processing
- Day of cycle,
- Time of day
- Fasting, non-fasting

---

very sensitive; that is, the false negative rate is very low, but the false positive rate may be quite high. Specificity refers to the ability of a test to determine only the abnormality that is being investigated. The false negative rate may be high but the false positive low. Obviously, there are few perfect tests, and none for the diagnosis of PCOS that combine a high sensitivity and high specificity.

Several problems remain with interpretation of what is considered "normal." The first problem is that if the original normal range inadvertently included PCOS patients, that is, if the normal range also had abnormal values, then the range would be skewed toward the high side and the abnormalities of PCOS might not be noted. There is the additional problems related to the pulsatility of hormone release. For example an LH or progesterone level repeated after 30 minutes would have a different level. One may be normal, the other abnormal. There are also variations in the assay techniques. The same sample run twice can give slightly different values due to assay (*reproducibility*) and technician (*accuracy*) variation. Hormones can be somewhat fragile, so there can be some degree of alteration concerning how the sample is stored and processed. Lab values can also vary by time of day, stage of the cycle, and whether fasting or non-fasting. The take home lesson is that lab tests are only a tool to be used in arriving at a diagnosis. Abnormal levels should be repeated and normal levels still do not completely exclude a problem. So you see, it isn't quite as easy as going to the doctor's office for a blood test to see if you have it.

When is the best time for hormone testing?

As a rule, endocrine testing other than pregnancy testing is best performed in the morning, soon after a spontaneous or induced menses. The days around ovulation or mid-cycle should be avoided. Glucose and lipid evaluation should be in the morning after fasting (no food or drink or anything by mouth after midnight the previous night).

Which blood test?

There have been a large number of tests and procedures used in the past for evaluation of PCOS. Listed below is a relatively exhaustive list including most tests available in present reference laboratories. There may be other tests performed on an experimental basis. All tests may not be useful in all individuals. *Normal levels will not be given because of the marked variations between laboratories and techniques.* Each laboratory report is required to include the normal range, but skill is still needed in interpretation.

Androstenedione: Androstenedione may be the steroid most often elevated in the PCOS patient. However, its lack of specificity in determining the source of hyperandrogenism, or modifying its treatment, probably make measurement of this hormone unnecessary. Androstenedione is almost totally and equally produced from the adrenal gland and ovary. It is the precursor hormone for many of the other steroid hormones.

Cortisol: Cortisol is an adrenal steroid hormone that is essential for a number of complex body functions. Its deficiency is known as Addison's disease, which has little in common with PCOS, and its excess is known as Cushing's syndrome, which has several characteristics of PCOS (see above). A random measurement of the blood cortisol is of little use. Instead, a diagnosis should be made by 24-hour collection of urine, from which the total amount of cortisol production is determined (urinary free cortisol, UFC). A second method of evaluation is the overnight dexamethasone suppression test. This test is simple to perform and involves taking a 1 mg. dexamethasone pill at 10:00 p.m., followed by a blood test for cortisol early the next morning. Dexamethasone is a very potent inhibitor of adrenal hormone production. Usually the suppression is quite obvious, but obese patients can have incomplete suppression. There is controversy surrounding the issue of which screening test is best. If one test produces positive results, then both tests should be performed. If both are abnormal, further investigation is certainly warranted, including a direct measurement of the pituitary hormone, adrenocorticotrophic hormone (ACTH). Routine use of cortisol determination is not warranted in evaluation of PCOS.

Dehydroepiandrosterone (DHEA, DHA) and dehydroepiandrosterone sulfate (DHEAS) are relatively weak androgens and are almost exclusively of adrenal origin. Although produced in relatively large amounts, they have little potency. They can be converted in the ovary and peripheral sites into more potent androgens. Adrenal tumors often produce very large amounts of DHEAS and are seldom associated with only modest elevations. A DHEAS measurement can be used to determine whether there is an adrenal component to PCOS and whether the patient may benefit from a trial of low dose corticosteroids. Women with 21-hydroxylase deficiency

(described below) may or may not have an elevated DHEAS. Although measurement of DHEAS is considered the "gold standard," 11ß-hydroxyan-
drostenedione (11-ß) has been proposed as a superior marker for adrenal
hyperandrogenism. There can be lack of correlation between 11ß and DHEAS
secretion, and either androgen can be over-secreted. It is preferable to measure
both markers, but the availability of the 11ß assay is very limited and its measurement is not common practice.

  Estradiol: estradiol (E2): see *estrogens* below.

  Estrogens: The reproductive hormones are divided by structure and
function into three major classes: estrogens, androgens and progestins. Men
produce only small amounts of estrogen but large amounts of androgens, principally testosterone. Women produce large amounts of estrogens and much
less testosterone. However, complicating the matter is the fact that all estrogens are made from androgens, so androgens are vital for normal hormonal
function in women. Men do not usually have to worry about estrogen excess
because they lack the enzyme that converts androgens to estrogens.
(Testosterone metabolism is discussed in detail in Chapter 7).

  There are three major estrogens produced in the human female: estriol, estradiol, and estrone. Estriol (E3) is made from the placenta and is important only in pregnancy. Estradiol (E2) is the most potent and main estrogen in
reproductive age women. Estradiol is almost exclusively produced from the
developing follicles of the ovary and can be used as a marker of follicular
growth during drug therapy for infertility. Sometimes an estradiol measurement is made when there is a concern about estrogen deficiency when menstruation is not occurring. Estrone (E1) is the major by-product of estradiol as
it is cleared from the circulation. It can also be produced in tissues outside the
ovary—especially in the liver, fat, muscle and other tissues—in a process called
peripheral conversion. Estrone is also the most common estrogen produced
after menopause and is used in some hormone replacement preparations.
Estrone is much weaker than estradiol in all of its actions. Usually there is little need to measure estradiol or estrone in a general evaluation of PCOS. All
estrogens have the capacity to induce endometrial development.

  Estrone (E1): see *estrogens* above.

  Follicle stimulating hormone (FSH): FSH is one of the two
gonadotropins produced by the pituitary gland (the other luteinizing hormone
is presented below). FSH is aptly named because it does what it says, it stimulates follicles of the ovary to grow. (See a full description of FSH and its function in Chapter 2). There are two reasons to measure the FSH level. The first
is to exclude an occult failing ovary in women with menstrual cycle abnormalities. FSH is an excellent marker of the store of follicles and, therefore, of eggs
remaining in the ovary. As menopause nears, FSH levels start to rise, which is
the body's attempt to maintain its normal function of ovulation. In most laboratories, levels over 10 are very concerning if fertility is desired. It is important
not to miss this diagnosis in therapy planning. The second reason to measure
FSH is to evaluate the LH:FSH ratio, which is an excellent marker for PCOS.

  17-hydroxyprogesterone (17-OHP4): 17-OHP4 is a hormone
produced by the corpus luteum and by the adrenal gland. 17-OHP4 measures

pregnancy well-being, but its most common use is in evaluating 21-hydroxylase deficiency, a form of congenital adrenal hyperplasia. A clinical picture virtually identical to PCOS can be caused by an isolated, inherited disorder of the adrenal glands, congenital adrenal hyperplasia, in which an enzyme responsible for inter-conversion of steroids, 21-hydroxylase, is missing, or present in a small amount. The result is a build-up of 17-OHP4, which is a weak androgen and thus, PCOS findings. A measurement drawn at 8-9 a.m. in a fasting state during the follicular phase will identify most cases of 21-hydroxylase deficiency. Levels should be over twice the normal range. If a question about this disorder remains, a small dose of the pituitary hormone that stimulates the adrenal gland, ACTH, is given by an intravenous injection, with a comparison made of 17-OHP4 before and 30 to 60 minutes after the injection. Because of the enzyme block, ACTH causes a marked exaggeration of the 17-OHP4 level. This is called an ACTH, or Cortrosyn™, stimulation test.

I was recently in a meeting of endocrinologists when a heated argument occurred as to whether this hormone should be routinely checked. In my patients, it seems that it is a very rare finding indeed. In other centers, several of the PCOS patients carry the CAH gene. One could argue either for or against routine testing.

Luteinizing hormone (LH): LH and FSH are the two gonadotropins produced by the pituitary gland that control ovarian function. (See Chapter 2). LH is indispensable for ovulation and its measurement serves as a basis for the ovulation predictor kits available at pharmacies. Except at ovulation, LH levels are low and lower than FSH.

There is controversy over the measurement of LH as a part of the diagnostic evaluation of PCOS. I am strongly entrenched in the camp that measures the LH:FSH ratio. Increased LH is related to, if not diagnostic of, PCOS. Not all PCOS patients, especially those with high insulin levels, have an elevation in LH. In fact, PCOS patients that have normal LH levels may be more likely to fall into the high insulin group, or high adrenal hormone group. Some PCOS patients, especially those markedly obese, may have gonadotropin levels that are suppressed, rather than elevated. Still, LH measurement may be useful in sorting out the underlying direction PCOS has taken.

Traditionally the diagnosis of PCOS has been made when the LH:FSH ratio is over 3. A relatively recent change in the type of assay used to measure LH has resulted in lower reported LH levels. If LH is higher than FSH in the early part of the menstrual cycle, PCOS should be suspected. The alteration in the LH:FSH ratio is more likely to be evident before, rather than after, a progestin challenge.

Prolactin: Prolactin is a pituitary gland hormone that assists in milk production for breast feeding *(lactation)*. The hormone is, by necessity, elevated in pregnancy and during breastfeeding. Prolactin suppresses ovulation and is one of the reasons why breastfeeding women are relatively infertile. Prolactin levels may be elevated outside these times. Potential functional causes of mildly elevated prolactin levels are drug use, anesthesia, stress, blood drawing, recent breast stimulation, breast examination, and blood sampling around the time of ovulation. Patients with more than marginally elevated pro-

lactin levels on repeat examination should be referred for *magnetic resonance*
imaging (MRI) to rule out more problematic causes of elevated prolactin.

Breast secretions (*galactorrhea*), for example, may be no more than a drop of greenish secretion, often from both breasts. It is more commonly seen after breast massage. Galactorrhea rarely is associated with breast cancer, but should always be investigated.

Galactorrhea often indicates *hyperprolactinemia*, which is a relatively frequent cause of infertility and menstrual cycle disturbance. Hyperprolactinemia has been associated with increased production of DHEAS, which is reversed after treatment with prolactin lowering agents. Hyperprolactinemia can be a sign of a prolactin-producing pituitary gland tumor (*prolactinoma*). These are benign and usually easily treated with medications such as bromocriptine (Parlodel) or cabergoline (Dostinex) with restoration of normal periods and fertility, though surgery may be indicated in more resistant cases. Less often, hyperprolactinemia may be an indication of other structural abnormalities of the brain. It is often found with hypothyroidism, and a TSH level should be obtained to exclude thyroid disease.

It is still not clear that the findings of PCOS and hyperprolactinemia, both relatively common disorders, are not coincidental. There is no evidence that prolactin lowering agents have a role in treatment of PCOS, although there are antidotal reports of successful use.

Sex hormone binding globulin (SHBG): SHBG is not a hormone, but it is included here because its measurement may be important in interpretation of sex hormone levels. SHBG is a protein that attaches to estrogens and androgens, and aids in the transport through the blood stream. Only a "free" or unbound hormone is capable of carrying out its designated duty. Therefore, the ratio of free to bound hormones becomes important in assessing hormone action. Estrogen causes a rise in SHBG and is one of the beneficial actions of birth control pills. Androgens cause SHBG to fall. A lower level of SHBG translates into increased amounts of active available free androgen. A low level of SHBG is a relatively good indicator of insulin resistance. Age, weight, diet, and steroid and thyroid hormone levels all affect the concentration of SHBG. Hypothyroidism is associated with a decrease in SHBG. There is an inverse correlation between body mass and SHBG in women, but not men. Women with high waist-hip ratios have lower SHBG, possibly relating to correlation with hyperinsulinemia.

Testosterone: Though known widely as a male hormone, testosterone is an essential female hormone. However, in excess it can have profound effects on the skin and possibly cardiovascular risks (see Chapters 7 and 9). In women, over 75% of testosterone circulating in the bloodstream is derived from conversion of other steroid hormones by the liver and skin. The remainder comes equally from the adrenal gland and ovary. Problems with testosterone can arise either from the ovary and adrenal glands or from other organs known collectively as peripheral conversion.

To exert its effects, testosterone must be "free" from the carrier proteins (SHBG and albumin) to which it is bound as it circulates through the blood stream. Either free or total testosterone can be measured, and, theoretically, measurement of the free form would be better. Unfortunately, the assays for free testosterone are more expensive and less reliable than are those for total testosterone. SHBG and total testosterone measurements are sometimes combined to calculate the "*Free Androgen Index*" (FAI) and to approximate the amount of free testosterone available. Marked elevation of either free or total hormone is equally worrisome and warrants complete investigation.

Thyroid stimulating hormone (TSH): Thyroid disease is quite common in PCOS. TSH is the single most important measurement of thyroid function. The tests for TSH are now widely available and this measurement is usually all that is necessary to screen for both *hyperthyroidism* (overactive) and *hypothyroidism* (underactive). (See Chapter 9) If the TSH level is abnormal, the test should be repeated, together with a test for thyroid hormone, specifically free thyroxine (free T4). A low TSH with a high free thyroxine indicates hyperthyroidism. A low TSH and low free thyroxine indicates the relatively uncommon disorder of central suppression. An elevated TSH level almost always suggests hypothyroidism. Two symptoms of hypothyroidism, weight gain and irregular periods, are also common complaints of those with PCOS. There is no clinical utility in the "thyroid panel," and this test should be abandoned. TSH is the method of choice to monitor thyroid replacement therapy. It should be noted that there is a four to six week period necessary for equilibrium to be reached. Replacement therapy should be increased or decreased to keep TSH levels firmly in the mid-normal range. Often there is a noticeable difference with even minute changes in therapy. It is recommended that the same brand name therapy always be used. If you are taking thyroid supplements, you must have routine TSH testing, as too much thyroid hormone can significantly increase the risk for osteoporosis and heart disease.

What about the insulin / PCOS connection?

Every evaluation for PCOS should include a determination of insulin resistance and exclude diabetes. Since this is a relatively new association, it is often omitted in the PCOS evaluation. Some of the recommended tests described below are very simple and can be performed in any doctor's office, while others may be performed only in research centers.

C-reactive protein: This is protein that circulates in the blood and is a marker for inflammation. A specialized sensitive assay for C-reactive protein is increasingly used as an indicator of the propensity to develop vascular disease. This protein is elevated in diabetes, but this information is still of questionable use in younger PCOS patients.

Glucose and glucose tolerance testing (GTT): The glucose levels in the blood constantly change in response to food intake and the body's use. (See Chapter 9) The most reliable glucose determination is made in early morning after not taking anything by mouth after midnight the night before the test. The American Diabetes Association (ADA) has designated individuals with fasting glucose levels over 126 mg/dl as diabetic. A new category is used to describe individuals with fasting levels 110-126 mg/dl as having impaired glucose tolerance. Type 1 diabetics are individuals who produce low amounts of insulin and were previously referred to as insulin dependent diabetics (IDDM). *Type 2 diabetes* replaces the older terminology of *late* or *adult onset* to describe *insulin resistance* that has resulted in elevated glucose levels in the face of high insulin levels. No distinction is made for whether insulin is being used in treatment.

The oral GTT was developed as a method to measure insulin resistance and impaired glucose tolerance. If there is obesity, a family history of diabetes, or other risk factors, a GTT should be considered in the PCOS evaluation. In PCOS patients, it is probably better to ask Why not, rather than Why do the test. The oral GTT is performed by a blood sample for glucose, followed by a glucose drink and an additional glucose determination at various times after the drink is consumed. The ADA recommends a two-hour screening after a 75-gram glucose intake as definitive testing, but a one-hour 50-gram glucose test is used in most obstetric practices and probably will identify the same individuals. For the test to have the greatest predictive capacity, it is suggested that a diet rich in carbohydrates be consumed for several days before the test. A glucose level of less than 140 mg/dl after a 2-hour test is normal, a level of 140-199 is impaired glucose tolerance, and a diagnosis of diabetes is made when the level is over 200. More information – especially with PCOS – can be obtained by measuring the blood level of insulin and glucose. The ratio of glucose to insulin has been used as a measurement of insulin resistance. There are also several more complicated tests that more precisely determine the degree of insulin resistance such as the *euglycemic clamp* discussed in Chapter 9.

Hemoglobin HbA1c: This blood test is a unique marker of how well diabetes is controlled. There is usually no reason to measure this in a PCOS patient unless diabetes is confirmed.

Insulin: Insulin is a hormone produced by the pancreas that regulates metabolism of glucose, the essential sugar of energy. The body constantly needs glucose, but most of us are not constantly eating, nor can we handle the large glucose surge that occurs after meals in the absence of insulin. The role of insulin is to ensure a steady glucose supply. There is a strong association between PCOS and higher than normal insulin levels (*insulin resistance*). (See Chapter 9 for a more complete explanation). Insulin resistance may be present in advance of or without elevated glucose levels. Insulin levels should be obtained fasting and possibly after a glucose challenge (see above). What constitutes a normal insulin level has not been satisfactorily determined. Usually levels above 20 are associated with insulin resistance and levels under 10 are normal. We use 14 uU/ml as a cut off point of normal.

Is hormonal testing all that is necessary?

Several tests that measure chemicals other than hormones can also be useful in the diagnosis of polycystic ovarian syndrome.

Comprehensive biochemical profile: This is the designation for a group (panel) of blood tests that evaluate the body's overall metabolism, salt and fluid balance. Various electrolytes (salts), fats, glucose and liver enzymes are measured. Overall these tests are used to evaluate the function of the liver and kidney. Some therapies used to control PCOS potentially have adverse effects and their use needs to be monitored periodically. This is a relatively inexpensive test obtained from a single blood sample. It is best to obtain this after fasting.

Lipid panel: The panel includes tests that measure the concentration of cholesterol, triglyceride, and relative concentration in lipoproteins (the good and bad cholesterol). This is a useful test for the general evaluation of health risks in all women, but it is of special importance in PCOS. Individuals with PCOS have a distinct tendency toward lipid abnormalities. When abnormalities are found, treatment can be prescribed which may significantly alter the risk of heart attack and stroke. The various lipids and their importance are discussed in Chapter 8.

Should I have an ultrasound scan?

Yes, sonography of the pelvis by individuals experienced in evaluating ovarian and endometrial function is warranted in every initial PCOS evaluation. Simple and important information could be missed were this scan not performed. Not only can the ovaries be evaluated for PCOS and other pathology, using ultrasound, but the uterus can also be examined for pathology. Even the best gynecologists miss important pathology by only performing a bimanual pelvic exam. Ultrasound is especially helpful in women who are overweight.

Ultrasound interpretation is based on evaluating the different densities of tissues. High frequency sound waves are used painlessly, safely, and without radiation to view the internal portions of the body. In order for the pelvic organs to be seen properly, the bladder must be full. A full bladder allows a "window" between the abdominal wall and pelvic organs to allow better visualization. Sound waves are sent from an instrument called a *transducer*. The sound passes through each type of tissue with different degrees of difficulty. Bone reflects sound waves and is seen as bright white on the ultrasound screen (*echodense*). Sound waves easily pass through water and this image is black on the screen (*echolucent*). Transvaginal ultrasound is preferable to abdominal ultrasound in the evaluation of the ovaries and uterus. The transducer, which is less than an inch in diameter, is placed into the vagina. Here, it is adjacent to the ovaries and uterus. Abdominal ultrasound is preferable to view pregnancies after about 8 weeks, and may sometimes aid in the investigation of pelvic pathology, such as a very enlarged uterus or ovary.

Ultrasound is a powerful tool for examining the ovary. With ultrasound, the number and size of follicles can be determined. The preovulatory follicle of a natural cycle is usually ovulated at about 20-23 mm. With clomiphene therapy the follicles may grow larger, around 24-30 mm. While on gonadotropins they are smaller, about 18-22 mm at time of ovulation. To trigger ovulation, HCg is usually given when follicles are 1-3 mm smaller than ovulatory size. The finding of greater than eight to ten cystic structures, smaller than 10 mm in either ovary meets the generally established ultrasound criteria of polycystic ovaries.

Figure 5-1 Scan of Ovaries

Diagnosis

79

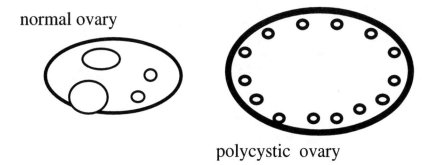

normal ovary

polycystic ovary

Often cysts of PCOS are located in a peripheral subcortical ring lead-ing to the reference of a "string of pearls." The PCOS ovaries are typically 150% to 300% of normal size. In some cases, the ovary is virtually filled with small cysts. In other cases, it is heterogeneously dense with hardly detectable microcystic changes. It must be remembered that any situation that causes an elevation in male hormone levels may result in polycystic ovaries on ultra-sound. Diffusely enlarged ovaries are consistent with the diagnosis of *hyper-thecosis*, which is probably a less common variant in the PCOS spectrum and possibly more likely associated with insulin resistance.

Much has been made about whether the polycystic ovary is the same as PCOS. As James Givens, a well-known PCOS investigator, has summed up the situation, the polycystic ovary is a sign and "not a diagnosis." A specific designation of the "PCO-appearing" ovary has been suggested but seems con-fusing. Either the ovary is polycystic or it is not. If the ovary is polycystic, there is a greater likelihood of PCOS. Rarely, it may be possible to have PCOS with-out polycystic ovaries, but this would very much go against the original defin-ition of PCOS. When large groups of women from the general population were examined for the prevalence of polycystic ovaries, it was found that 20-30% of all women examined by ultrasound had polycystic ovaries. While some were fertile and had regular menstrual cycles, a large percentage had alterations in the hormonal levels or menstrual cycle. The importance of ultrasound findings of PCOS without other problems is not known

There seems to be a specific group of women who have a greater number of larger follicles than those usually seen with PCOS. The ovaries do not have the appearance typical of polycystic ovaries. These women seem to have little in common with women with PCOS, except their infertility. The case of these multicystic ovaries may be a subtle enzyme abnormality respon-sible for follicle growth. They also seem particularly resistant to clomiphene therapy.

Ultrasound also gives information on the status of the lining of the uterus, called the endometrium. On an ultrasound, this is referred to as the endometrial stripe. An evaluation of the endometrium is useful in all women with irregular periods. There are two abnormal conditions, too much and too little. Either is possible with PCOS. In the scenario of too much, the endometrium may be overly thickened, called an *overgrowth*. In this case, there is abnormal bleeding, causing the uterus to overflow. In more extreme cases, this can be related to the pathologic condition of endometrial hyperplasia, and in rare cases, endometrial cancer. Biopsy of the lining usually is not suggested until the lining remains thickened after medical therapy to regulate bleeding. In other situations of irregular bleeding, the lining may be abnormally thin and require additional hormonal support either to prevent too frequent bleeding, or to allow proper development for bleeding to occur. (See figure 2-10).

During the twenty-five years of clinical use in reproductive medicine, ultrasound has not been known to cause harm to any patient.

Is there a recommendation about which tests are best?

This is a tough topic, but, as is probably clear to most readers by now, it is my belief that one properly timed and comprehensive evaluation is worthwhile. Some believe that it is not cost effective when the diagnosis is already known. I wish I had the degree of clinical certainty to always be right with my diagnoses. There are surprises every day. The cost of a full battery of blood tests is probably $200-600, and in today's medical market, this is not very expensive. Some would argue that it would not change therapy. This is certainly not the case today. Especially if high levels of insulin are found and fertility is desired, it may be preferable to use insulin lowering agents before more traditional, but also much more aggressive, fertility therapy.

At the Center for Applied Reproductive Science, our basic evaluation performed two to three days after a period starts (cycle days 2-4) includes these laboratory and clinical tests:

- Fasting comprehensive biochemical and lipid panel
- Two hour GTT with insulin levels
- LH:FSH
- Total testosterone
- DHEAS
- SHBG
- Prolactin
- TSH
- Transvaginal ultrasound

We have found this combination of tests, in addition to a physical exam, to provide an excellent screening to evaluate both general health status and the various facets of PCOS in our patients.

Who Treats PCOS?
Getting the Care
You Deserve

with Lesa Childers[1]

As the Coordinator of the WNC PCOSupport Chapter, it is not unusual for me to be contacted by women with PCOS to discuss doctor frustrations and to ask for physician referrals. One woman recounted this very distressing episode during her last visit with her OB/GYN, "As a matter of fact, I knew about PCOS at that time and after asking him if I might have it, he replied that he didn't even consider PCOS to be an actual medical condition. He seems to think it is a group of symptoms of infertility that some doctors like to call PCOS." As a result of this interaction and countless similar others, I have come to realize that finding a doctor that is knowledgeable and willing to treat the disorder may be the greatest challenge faced by women with PCOS.

In today's rapidly changing medical environment, finding a health care provider can be a daunting and frustrating experience. At present there is a trend away from small private practices toward large health organizations, an increase in the influence of managed care on decision making for doctors and patients, and a dramatic rise in malpractice litigation. All of this has resulted in a general climate of mistrust and alienation between patients and their doctors. Choosing healthcare provider that can give you the care you deserve is a chore.

[1] **Lesa Childers,** *B.S. was responsible for the primary development of this chapter. She is a PCOSA Chapter Development Coordinator and local organizer of Western North Carolina PCOSupport. She received the Founder's Award for her volunteer efforts with the PCOSA and is widely recognized as a leader in PCOS-related educational efforts. Having dealt with PCOS and infertility for many years, she has a deep understanding of the frustrations involved with seeking information and care. Lesa is employed as a social worker at a mental health agency and is the proud parent of two daughters.*

How do I find a physician?

The difficulty of diagnosing PCOS has been discussed earlier. Because the symptoms and physical findings vary and because not every patient presents with the same symptoms, the diagnosis of PCOS is often missed. Only in the last few years has medical research been able to make connections between a metabolic endocrine disorder and disturbances in multiple body systems. PCOS is challenging to physicians trained to diagnose and treat specific, well-defined diseases. PCOS patients enter the physician's office often with a collection of vague symptoms. Even when diagnosed the lack of curative treatments for PCOS is frustrating. Although all the dots are there, not every physician is able to connect all dots that form the image of polycystic ovary symdrome.

A woman may begin to experience some symptoms of PCOS at a very young age. She may have been overweight as a young child and the pediatrician may have told her mother to simply watch her diet. In her teens, she may have sought medical help for acne or excessive facial hair and her dermatologist offered creams or electrolysis as treatment. In her twenties, perhaps still overweight, she may have sought help from her gynecologist for irregular periods and been given a package of birth control pills. In her thirties, an inability to conceive may have sent her to a fertility specialist where she was given medication to control ovulation. Unfortunately, our culture often discriminates against overweight women. It is a sad fact that many physicians are also prejudiced against these women, assuming them to be lazy or lacking self discipline. These doctors often dismiss these patients, telling them to simply go home and lose some weight.

Years of seeing one doctor after another while her symptoms often compound rather than subside is disheartening. There is the perception and often the reality that valuable time has been lost while going from one doctor to another. Self esteem may drop as weight and frustration rise. Blood tests or ultrasounds that would lead to a definitive diagnosis of PCOS are not done. The bottom line is that each of these medical specialists has treated a small aspect of the problem, but none has put all the pieces of the puzzle together as PCOS.

Physicians should not consider themselves, nor should their patients consider them to be infallible. Patients must ask questions and communicate honestly with their physicians. Confidence in the capacity to live better with a chronic condition is one of the greatest tools in the struggle with PCOS. There may need to be an extensive search to find a doctor that is truly knowledgeable about PCOS. This physician may be a primary care provider, but more often will be a gynecologist, endocrinologist, or reproductive endocrinologist who has experience treating PCOS and is well informed about new research areas.

For women with PCOS, the decision about whom to choose to provide medical care is critical both to present physical wellness and long-term quality of health. Seeking a doctor who has a strong base of knowledge about PCOS and who understands present treatment is quite a challenge. Many doctors simply do not have the time to keep up with the latest research about the syndrome, especially, if they are in a practice where they do not see large numbers of patients with PCOS. And some doctors, unfortunately, just aren't interested in gaining further knowledge or offering new treatment options. Furthermore, managed care/insurance providers have a strong influence on what direction many women take in getting care. For these reasons, the key to being a smart consumer is to become as educated as possible about PCOS, and to gain a good understanding of the arena in which you are seeking care.

Being a passive or non-participatory patient doesn't work with PCOS. In the hands of a less than knowledgeable or disinterested care provider, there can be an escalation of symptoms resulting in the development of diseases such as endometrial cancer, diabetes or possibly heart disease. Finding quality care is imperative for all women with the disorder.

What are the choices?

There are many different types of doctors and understanding their roles in the provision of health care can sometimes be confusing. We will discuss the types that generally end up caring for women with PCOS in this section.

Board Eligible/Board Certified

In the past some physicians did a year or so of medicine after medical school and hung out their shingle as a general practitioner (GP). That designation has stuck, although even the traditional GP is now usually Board Certified in Family Medicine. Each specialty has it own "board" that individually tests applicants and ensures a high standard of competence. Some Boards have both written and oral exams while others only written. When an individual has completed a certified residency program, he/she usually becomes Board eligible.

After a year or so of practice the final Board examination is taken in order to become "Board Certified." Testing is comprehensive and quite a few fail, at least on their first attempt. Many of the boards also have subspecialty examinations, for example endocrinology (internal medicine), pediatric endocrinology (pediatrics) and reproductive endocrinology (obstetrics and gynecology). They require an additional two to three years of specialized training after residency.

Primary Care Physicians (PCP)

These physicians are sometimes referred to as the "family doctor" or "GP" by their patients and can handle the majority of medical problems that may develop over the ages. An essential part of their job is knowing to what specialist and when to refer for evaluation. As generally stated in the medical community "triage is everything."

Obstetricians/Gynecologists (OB/GYN)

Doctors in this field specialize in treatment of disorders of the female reproductive tract and in the care of women throughout pregnancy. Some women choose these physicians as their PCP, especially during the reproductive years. All gynecologists have had basic training in PCOS, but too often tend to concentrate on only isolated symptoms such as menstrual irregularity. While the gynecologists may be the first consult, they may not be the best final destination for those with PCOS.

Endocrinologists

This medical discipline deals specifically with the broad scope of diseases of the hormone producing organs and hormonal imbalances. Diabetes and thyroid disease are disorders frequently treated by these doctors. Their medical training began with a residency in internal medicine followed by at least two years sub-specialty training in endocrinology. They are certified by the American Board of Internal Medicine. Many with PCOS have had their diagnosis confirmed by an endocrinologist as the result of a referral by a primary care physician or their Ob/Gyn in response to symptoms of obesity or insulin resistance. They may continue to seek treatment through this doctor, particularly if they are not necessarily interested in becoming pregnant or are post-menopausal. The endocrinologist may be much more medically oriented than the gynecologist, or reproductive endocrinologist.

Reproductive Endocrinologists (RE)

Physicians in this field are sub-specialists who have completed a residency in obstetrics and gynecology and are certified by the American Board of Obstetrics and Gynecology. In addition, they have received at least two years of specialized training in medical and surgical problems as they effect the reproductive hormones, reproductive organs and fertility in both women and men. Most of the time, couples find themselves seeking help from a RE when infertility treatment has been previously unsuccessful. REs practice more aggressive methods of treatment such as intensive drug therapy, surgery or assisted reproduction (for example, in vitro fertilization). While not all REs are interested in treating PCOS in women not seeking pregnancy, all have received training in this area.

Dermatologists

These doctors specialize in treatment of skin related conditions. Women with PCOS will many times find themselves seeking help from these professionals for hirsutism and/or acne. Sometimes these physicians see the women troubled by the cosmetic effects of PCOS before the diagnosis of PCOS has been made. Most concentrate on skin problems and less on the hormonal alterations that caused the skin problems. They provide a very important portion of the treatment related to excess hair and acne.

Any of the above physicians could be the first to make the diagnosis of Polycystic Ovary Syndrome and any can administer treatment. All have their individual strengths and weaknesses. Women with PCOS will have different needs throughout the span of their lifetime and may need to seek treatment with several different types of physicians. For instance, a young woman not interested in pregnancy may receive appropriate treatment from her family practitioner or gynecologist. On the other hand, a reproductive endocrinologist would probably best serve a woman dealing with longstanding infertility. Other issues related to the development of insulin resistance or diabetes may need to be treated by an endocrinologist. Most important in decision making is finding a physician who is PCOS-knowledgeable and interested in providing quality treatment.

Another factor in making the choice of a physician is the variety of practice types available. Although on a decrease, some doctors practice in a solo or small group environment. If seeing the same doctor routinely is important to a woman, then this type of practice will be her best choice. Other doctors are involved in a large specialty group. Women who are comfortable seeing different doctors for treatment may choose this type of practice. There is also the option in some areas of a multi-specialty practice, meaning a group containing a range of specialists in one practice, such as primary care physicians, surgeons and radiologists. Some hospitals also have clinics in which different types of physicians may practice.

When beginning a "doctor search" a woman should consider what type of relationship with which she is most comfortable. Traditionally, patients and doctors have had paternal relationships, the patient submitting to the doctor's authority and expertise. Though paternal relationships are becoming less frequent, this type of relationship usually develops when a patient is intimidated by her doctor or in awe of his expertise. Some patients develop adversarial relationships with their caregivers meaning they develop an "us against them" attitude. This environment can be created when a need is felt to blame someone for treatment failure or when treatment options are not discussed or negotiated. In most cases, both of these types of relationship compromise care and frequently result in failure.

Mutual respect and courtesy is fundamental in all successful relationships. The best outcomes are realized when a partnership is formed in a collegial relationship. The physician recognizes that the woman is the most expert in evaluating her own body. The physician serves in the role of teacher, counselor and technician. The woman is an active participant in her own care. Through an open dialog patients learn the medical basis of their problems and about treatment options. Each member of the partnership respects the other's expertise, and the phrase, "I disagree," from either side is not met with contempt. Trust is essential and paramount and is built from mutual respect. Mutual respect is the key to long term success.

How do I make a choice?

Step 1—Become an Educated Consumer

It is imperative that women with PCOS gain as much understanding of the disorder as possible. This is important for several reasons. First, understanding the disorder makes a woman aware of what kind of treatment she may need in relation to her symptoms, which could affect what type of physician she chooses to see. Second, being knowledgeable about PCOS helps a woman to recognize others who are also knowledgeable. Since we have already established that most physicians are not PCOS experts, this could be very important in decision-making.

Realization of the broad spectrum of PCOS is relatively new. There are a vast and fast growing number of resources. These could include books and articles, visiting PCOS and related Web sites, and joining support groups to learn and share with others. (See Chapter 18).

Step 2—Narrow the Field of Choices

Doctor shopping can be hard work. To find the right fit of comfort, durability and expertise is no short task. There are several ways to seek out good referrals.

Ask your family doctor. Find out if they have a specialist to whom they frequently refer women with PCOS. If so, ask them why they trust this particular physician for PCOS care and what kind of feedback they have received from other patients who have gone there. Listen for the referring physician to tell you something about the doctor beyond credentials.

Search through consumer and professional organizations on the Internet. PCOS is most often best understood by reproductive endocrinologists and endocrinologists. National infertility consumer organizations such as RESOLVE (www.resolve.org) and the American Infertility Association (www.americaninfertilityassociation.org) and International Council for Infertility Information Dissemination (www.inciid.org) can provide you with referrals to reproductive endocrinologists and gynecologists. Most REs and gynecologists interested in PCOS belong to the American Society for Reproductive Medicine (www.asrm.org). Most endocrinologists belong to the Endocrine Society or the Association of Clinical Endocrinologists (http://www.aace.com). By far the most specific Web site is that of Polycystic Ovarian Syndrome Association (www.PCOSupport.org). Their physician directory is still limited, but it crosses the boundaries of all specialties. When visiting an individual medical practice's Web site, notice what is listed as areas of specialties. For instance, some REs want to primarily focus on infertility patients and especially assisted reproduction, others welcome non-infertility patients.

Log on to a chat room and ask if anyone has information about physicians in your area. Remember, a glowing testimonial is not always an indicator of expertise.

Ask others with PCOS about their care. You may have a family member or friend who is dealing with PCOS and has an established relationship with a physician. Inquire about how the care is going and if they would recommend their doctor to others.

Join or attend a meeting of a local support group such as PCOSupport or RESOLVE to gain information of what and how physicians in your are addressing PCOS.

Contact major hospitals in your area. They often have a physician referral service. Ask for a recommendation of one or more doctors who treat women with PCOS. If you are met by an unknowing pause, ask for local REs and endocrinologists.

Contact your regional medical school Department of Obstetrics and Gynecology Division of Reproductive Endocrinology and Internal Medicine Division of Endocrinology.

Use insurance provider lists. It is a fact of life that your choices might be limited by third party payers. You may have a major expense if an "out of network" physician is chosen.

Use the Yellow Pages. Letting you fingers do the walking is a starting point, but only that. It tells you who is out there. The size of the advertisement and its attractiveness is hardly a recommendation about care.

Step 3—Make Contact

Based on the results of your search, you may have the name of one or a list of several doctors who are candidates to become your healthcare provider. Do not make the assumption that a local physician cannot be extremely knowledgeable about PCOS, or that travel to a major national medical center is necessary.

Next, the plan of action should involve making telephone contact with the practices that you have designated as possibilities. Ask to speak with a nurse to discuss some basics about how PCOS treatment is handled by that particular doctor. If there is no protocol or you get the sense from staff that they don't know what you are talking about, consider this as a red flag. There is reason to believe that PCOS is not a specialty in that practice.

Of course, each patient will have her own specialized needs and concerns. However, below are lists of possible questions. You might want to add more of your own. Try to make your call conversational, not a drill. The office staff is not on trial. Initially, consider it more of a first date than a marriage proposal.

Practice-Specific Questions

- What kinds of services are offered?
- Is my physician Board Certified, Board eligible?
- At what institution was his/her specialty training?
- How many patients are usually seen in a day and how long is an average visit?
- Will I see a physician at each visit?
- Will I see the same physician each time?
- If I call, how quickly will I be called back?
- Is it always necessary for an office visit to offer advice?
- How are patient needs handled after hours?
- How are needs handled on weekends and holidays? (especially important for infertility problems)
- Do I need a physician referral to be seen?
- What is the cost of an average first and return visit?
- Is the practice a "participating provider" with your insurance plan?
- Will the office accept assignment (directly bill the insurance company)?
- Are there payment plans?

The answers to the questions above will give you an overall impression of how the office is run. Ask if you need a referral from your PCP, a "network physician", or other physician. These are very important factors for avoiding a potentially uncomfortable situation.

PCOS-Specific Questions

- How many POCS patients are being actively treated by the practice?
- What ancillary services are available? (nutritionist, exercise physiologist, psychologist, endocrine lab, ultrasound, hair removal systems)?
- Do many patients receive insulin-altering drugs like metformin?
- Is clinical or basic research performed in conjunction with your office on PCOS?
- If also for fertility, does your center perform laparoscopy, gonadotropin injections, assisted reproduction including in vitro fertilization, and sperm injection?

Based on your telephone contacts, make an appointment. You do not necessarily need to visit several practices unless your first choice just doesn't seem to be the right fit. Trust your instinct.

Step 4—Prepare for the Visit

As pointed out earlier in this chapter, the best way to get quality care is to become a "PCOS expert." Although you clearly know more about yourself, never assume that you know more than your physician about PCOS. You may enter his / her office armed with misinformation: there is a lot of it out there as well. ANY PHYSICIAN WORTH SEEING APPRECIATES AN INFORMED PATIENT. Regardless, you will have a limited amount of time on your first visit. Having your complete past history recorded in a timeline of pertinent events and records from your previous evaluations can save important time to use in other areas of discussion.

Preparation for your visit should include obtaining copies of all relevant medical records for review with the new doctor. Sometimes patients are responsible for this and sometimes the practice will ask you to sign a release so that they may request them from your previous care providers. It is imperative that you

---

**Take with You
to Your First Visit**

- Timeline (date of first symptoms until present) of problems.
- Records from previous evaluations and therapy.
- Names and addresses of health care providers to whom results of consultation should be sent.
- PCOS history template from back of this book.
- List of questions to be answered
- Something to read or work on. It can be a time to catch-up. Good and bad physicians alike often run behind schedule.
- If infertility is an issue, remember that it takes two. Take him as well.

have those to present to the doctor at this initial consultation. He or she will need them to plot a history of your symptom path and this also may reduce the need for additional testing.

Offer the information to the receptionist or nurse before your contact. Often this will allow the physicians to prepare their time with you as well. The history template provided in the appendix will anticipate most every question on medical history as it relates to PCOS. You might want to photocopy, complete and provide it to your physician with your other records. You do not need to provide questions for your physician in advance, but do have them written beforehand.

Step 5–The Interview Process

You have done all of the preliminary work and are ready to meet with your potential health care provider.

When meeting with the doctor for the first time, remember that you will not get all of the answers you want in one visit. Use this visit to get a good feeling for whether or not you will be comfortable with this person and this staff as your care providers. Learn as much as you can and take notice of how you are treated when questions are asked.

An initial consultation usually consists of the following:
- A discussion of why you are visiting or what are your needs.
- A review of diagnosis/medical records/concerns.
- Questions session.
- Discussion of possible treatments.

Listen carefully and notice body language during this interaction. If you have questions written down, as previously suggested, take notes when needed. These notes could consist of answers given to you verbally by the doctor or your impressions about certain answers.

PCOS Questions for Your Physician

- What are the "causes" of PCOS? (All would be speculative).
- Do you have a standard treatment for PCOS patients?
  (The answer should be "No.")
- Do you prescribe insulin-sensitizing agents and what are your thoughts on their use? (The answer should be positive).
- What are my individual health risks for the future?
- Do you ever make referrals outside of your practice for problems such as hirsutism or acne?
- What are your feelings about nutrition and exercise related to PCOS?

Step 6—Process the Outcome of the Initial Meeting

Following your initial visit take some time to process. You may do this alone or discuss your impressions of the visit with someone else (especially if that person was a part of the visit). You may do so by asking yourself some simple questions:

Evaluate the "feel" of the office.

- How was I greeted?
- Did I sense a warm, comfortable atmosphere or a cold, indifferent setting?
- How many people are still waiting to see the doctor? Do they seem like me?
- What kind of magazines and books are lying in the lobby?
- Was the exam room private? Comfortable (as possible)? Supplied?
- How do I feel about billing/insurance policies?
- Did I feel welcome and cared for?

Form an impression of the support staff.

- Were they professional? Are they happy being there?
- Was there adequate staff? Did they seem to know the job?
- Was their speech and body language warm and friendly or cold and aloof?
- Was the staff responsive? Did they treat me as an individual?
- Did they have a positive attitude about my visit? Did they want me back?
- Did I feel welcome and well cared for?

Consider the circumstances of your meeting with the doctor.

- Where does the doctor meet with me...in his office or in an exam room?
- Was I greeted appropriately? Eye contact?
- Is there genuine interest in the practice of medicine
- Is the evaluation rushed? Is the doctor preoccupied?
- Did the doctor seem knowledgeable about PCOS?
- Were my questions answered in a satisfactory manner?
- Was communication effective, thorough and comfortable?
- Did the doctor treat me as an individual?
- Are we compatible?
- Do I feel welcome and well cared for?

Step 7—Make a Decision!

Congratulations! As a well-prepared and educated consumer, you should have gathered enough information to enable you to make a decision with which you can be comfortable. Is the healthcare provider for you? No practice is perfect and many will fall down with the above scrutiny. Don't settle for second rate care. However, if the above score is low, save yourself and the physician the agony of a relationship gone wrong. If for some reason you chose not to have this person provide for your care, all is not lost, as you now have a clearer idea for future interviews of what you expect from a doctor and have made an informed decision.

How do I build a good relationship for long-term success?

Successful long-term doctor/patient relationships are built on several very important factors. The doctor, the medical staff, and the patient share in the responsibility for keeping the relationship flowing positively. Understanding that each partner has certain needs and limitations is key.

Responsibilities of Patients to their Physicians:

- Treat your doctor with respect and courtesy.
- Be punctual for visits.
- Be friendly and polite.
- Be a good listener and don't interrupt when he is explaining something of concern.
- Clearly state your concerns.
- Understand that the doctor's time is valuable and do not expect extended amounts of small talk or chatting.
- Understand that your doctor has a personal life, just as you do. Use discretion in making contact outside of normal office hours.
- Be honest and clear during visits. It important that you state your needs honestly and clearly during visits. Answer your doctor's questions truthfully. He/she may not be able to offer the correct treatment otherwise. The doctor is dependent on what you tell him in suggesting a direction for treatment.
- Share responsibility for decisions. It is your responsibility to be knowledgeable enough to make a decision about a treatment option. While your doctor should explain thoroughly all options, you have the responsibility of asking questions and making final decisions about your care.
- Participate in the agreed upon treatment plan. Once a path of treatment has been mutually decided upon, it is your responsibility to fully comply with instructions.
- Be a responsible consumer—pay your bill. You are responsible for paying for services in a timely manner. This helps keep healthcare costs down for everyone. If a problem develops, speak to the doctor or accounts representative about it. Usually a plan of payment can be worked out.
- Maintain a healthy lifestyle. Decisions we make on a daily basis could affect our overall health for years to come. It is our responsibility to recognize that healthy diet and exercise could be the key to PCOS treatment. It is not unreasonable for your doctor to ask that you consider a change in lifestyle, if it is going to seriously affect your treatment. There is not a magic pill for PCOS.
- Let the practice know of your dissatisfaction.

Finally, it is important that patients *have reasonable expectations* of the relationship between doctors and their patients. It is unreasonable, for example, to expect your doctor to be able to speak with you by phone every time you call. He may be the only physician you see, but you are not the only patient he sees and he cannot be expected to interrupt the care of other patients to take incoming calls scattered throughout the day. Additionally, a call to your doctor after hours, when he does not have your chart in front of him, could result in your not receiving adequate advice. No physician can remember every detail of each patient's case and care without available files.

Responsibilities of Doctors to their Patients:

- Treat patients with respect and kindness.
  - Use good manners.
  - Doctors should value you as a person and treat you accordingly.
- Physicians should listen to your concerns and respond.
- It is important to treat the whole person, not just the body.
- Promote hope, when hope exists.
- Medical staff should not keep patients waiting, unless absolutely necessary—everyone's time is valuable.
- Provide reasonable care and skill. Ethically, doctors have a responsibility to provide reasonable care and skill when treating patients. Each medical arena has "standards of care" which knowledgeable physicians are expected to meet or exceed. Being honest about treatment options and outcomes is a part of reasonable care.
- Provide adequate time for care. Although it can be very difficult, doctors should allow an adequate amount of time to fully examine, diagnose and discuss patient concerns during visits.
- Respect a patient's right to choose a treatment path. Ultimately, the choice of treatment remains in the hands of the patient after a thorough explanation of options by the physician.
- The doctor should state clearly his recommendations and concerns with each option, then allow the patient to decide what direction to head.
- Be knowledgeable. Doctors have the duty to keep current on new medical information. This is especially important for treating women with PCOS, as treatment options are changing and broadening through research.
- Maintain confidentiality. Doctors have a responsibility to keep all information shared with them in the course of treatment confidential. Medical records are also confidential and should never shared without consent.

The Role of the Staff

Do not underestimate the input of the entire office staff in your plan with your physician. Whether nursing, technical, or clerical, these people do not have menial positions and you should not minimize their importance in your care. The receptionist who works you in at the last minute for an appoint-

your care. The receptionist who works you in at the last minute for an appointment, the billing representative who files your insurance, the laboratory staff,
the nurses, each is professional in their own right and should be treated as
such. Cultivating a good relationship with the office support staff can go a long
way toward facilitating your care.

What if a question arises?

At each visit you should be given adequate time to properly ask and
have your questions answered. Bring your list with you.

Questions about treatment protocol,about side effects of medications,
etc., may arise outside office visits, of course. Questions should be encouraged
and you should feel free to call with them. It is also very reasonable to expect
that any question that arises be handled quickly and efficiently. This usually
means that you should get an answer before the end of the working day in
which the call was placed, unless you have been told otherwise. If not place
your call again the following morning. If it is an emergency ask that the physician be contacted immediately. An answer about how to proceed should be
immediately forthcoming. This is an expectation of good care on the part of
both patient and physician.

In this age of e-mail and fax, many patients erroneously assume that
they should be able to question their doctor electronically and get answers
without making another trip to the office. However, it is not in the best interest of patients for doctors to practice medicine online. Faxes and e-mails are
not always confidential and your concerns cannot always be addressed fully. In
the future there may be much more interaction over the Internet and there are
the rare exceptions to the above statements which probably more reflects on
interest in the Internet than professional policy.

Telephone calls asking to speak to the doctor directly can interrupt
patient care. "Just a quick question" often results in an hour-long phone consult. This forces other patients who had scheduled appointments to be
delayed. Some doctors return telephone calls during a specified time. Others
rarely communicate except by direct contact. In cases of long distance care, it
may be possible to set up a phone consultation just as you would an office visit,
but expect to pay for this service.

You selected your doctor and his office for their skill and expertise.
You are paying for his best care. In most medical practices staff members will
take your incoming calls and transmit your questions to the doctor for
response. If your questions or concerns are not addressed adequately by the
staff, it is not unreasonable to schedule a separate visit for a consultation with
the physician to address these concerns. Sometimes there is no substitute for
a sit down face to face talk with your physician.

Communication is critical. If it is not occurring, first let the physician
know. If it continues, consider a change.

What about test results?

Some appointment visits will be for specific procedures such as lab
testing or ultrasound. The reason for the test should have been explained in

advance. The nurse or technician may give you general information about why the test is performed, but you should limit the "ifs". Ask when the results will be available. Remember it may take hours to days to get the results depending on the test. Usually the physician's office will call you with results that need an immediate attention. Ask whether you should call or you will be called for routine testing. When the test returns the answer to questions may be simple and the nursing or technical staff able to answer many of your questions. Normal probably means normal, but still discuss the results with your physician at your next meeting. You should be told the results of all testing and the pertinence to your diagnosis and therapy.

How do I make the most of my medical care?

Once a doctor is selected, you must be proactive. This is accomplished in a variety of ways:

Make a plan.

After making the decision to seek medical care and choosing a physician, it is important to establish a plan regarding your care. Discuss the plan frequently and keep communication open along the way. This not only promotes better doctor-patient relationships and reduces the possibility of miscommunication, but by being proactive in your care, you maintain a sense of control, which can reduce stress. For women who daily face a body that seems out of control to them, having a plan is comforting. At every step in the plan, it is important to equip yourself with as much support and education as possible. Any good plan made for any purpose is meant to be flexible and constantly under evaluation, so plans should be frequently reassessed.

Make sure you understand what you are told.

"Tell me that again" or "I don't understand" are completely acceptable statements. Do not sit idly nodding approvingly when you haven't a clue what the doctor just said. A major part of your plan with your doctor will include a discussion of medications. Medications such as metformin, used to treat insulin resistance or spironolactone for hirsutism, as well as drugs used to treat associated infertility may have side effects. Be sure that you understand why your doctor is prescribing a specific medicine for you, when and how to take the medicine, and what any possible side effects might be. Repeat the instructions you are given concerning any medication to be sure that you have understood correctly.

Enlist help.

For some it is impractical or too personal to share their medial condition with others no matter how close. Others find it helpful if a friend, relative or partner accompanies them to visits. Sometimes the amount of information given out can seem overwhelming and the more "listening ears" that are present, the better off you are. What you may miss your partner will remember and vice versa.

Including your partner in this planning process is of course essential if you are being treated for infertility (see Chapter 11), but PCOS patients working on other related issues can also find it especially helpful to bring their major source of support, their partner, onto the team.

Evaluate your commitment

Be especially clear on the number of visits you will be required to make to the office. Often this varies with treatment protocol, but it is important for you to have a general idea so that you may schedule your time off from work or class. This information can be especially important for those who must travel long distances to reach the offices of a physician who is well informed about PCOS issues.

Keep a journal

This need not be a major ordeal. You may want to record your personal experiences as a diary, but this is a specific, brief record of dates of visits, medication starts and stops, changes in the way you feel, important test results. It is possible that your medical records may be more informative and certainly easier to access in the future. If you change practices ask for a copy of your medical records. You have freedom of access to these. Make a copy to take to your next physician and always keep a copy for yourself.

What if a disagreement arises?

Your relationship with your doctor will probably be like all other long standing relationships in life—there will be times of good communication and understanding and there will be times of disagreement or miscommunication. Usually it is far better to work through these times than to just give up and move on. In order to avoid an escalation of feelings or a break in the relationship, a few steps toward resolving the issue may be necessary.

First, talk with your physician about your concerns, either during a regularly scheduled visit or in a visit specifically for this purpose. Always practice good communication skills by making eye contact, speaking clearly, stating exactly what your concerns are and listening carefully to responses. Following a thorough statement of the problem and discussion of possible resolutions, mutually decide on a plan of correction, if possible. Sometimes it is acceptable to agree to disagree on certain matters.

Unfortunately, there are times in relationships when it is better for both parties to move on. The decision to seek care elsewhere is usually not easy and should always be the last resort. Times when this is appropriate could include serious personality conflicts, loss of trust, deciding that this is not the best person to treat your illness, scheduling problems that can't be resolved, when you move to a new location and when a doctor leaves or retires. Once you have decided to change, inform your present doctor, and have your medical records forwarded to your new provider of care. When either patient of physician loses trust, it is better to change.

How do I navigate the insurance maze?

A woman's health care needs are quite different from a man's. According to the book *Our Bodies, Ourselves*, a woman is two to three times more likely to interact with the medical care system than a man. Not only do women enter the system on their own behalf but they also spend a great deal of time, energy, and money on the health needs of others. Studies indicate that women are often over-treated, or under-treated depending on their insurance status, income, age, and race. They have not been adequately represented in research studies or clinical trials. This has led to a series of research trials on women's health issues conducted by the National Institutes of Health as well as passage of the Women's Health Equity Act of 1992. However, neither of these events has led to reform of the "system" in areas crucial to midlife and older women. Many women are either uninsured or underinsured because of their employment history in the paid workforce. They lack the means to obtain good health care over a long period of time.

PCOS patients sometimes have an easier time getting coverage for their treatment than do others who don't have PCOS. Whether or not a woman is trying to get pregnant, many laboratory and ultrasound charges are often covered under a diagnosis code for PCOS. On the other hand, many older women have trouble getting anything covered under PCOS diagnosis because it is seen as a fertility issue and nothing more. Insurance companies need to be aware that PCOS has serious ramifications in the areas of diabetes, cardiovascular health, and cancer. Treating PCOS can go a long way toward preventing these diseases or minimizing the expense associated with treating these diseases over a long period of time.

There are many areas of reform in progress in the health insurance industry at the federal and state levels. Fee for service as well as managed care providers are working to offer a better series of packages and options for the benefit of consumer, provider, and insurer. It is not an easy task. In the mean time, there are no real standards for coverage of infertility or PCOS in the health care industry. No two-health plans are exactly alike. The person sitting next to you at work may not have the same coverage as you even though you work for the same employer. According to RESOLVE, you must be your own advocate for coverage. You must learn your policy inside and out, and especially in regard to what is included as well as excluded. Some plans will pay for diagnosis but no treatment. Others will cover medications but no procedures. Still others will pay a lump sum to be used however the patient and physician desire. Other plans will not cover any aspect. It is your responsibility, not your doctor's, to know what your plan covers.

It is an unfortunate reality that many women are forced to base decisions about the kind of care they receive on what their insurance company allows. Most people simply can not afford to work outside of that system unless absolutely necessary. Unfortunately, many insurance companies don't cover certain types of treatment, such as those for infertility. Therefore, this forces the woman to pay out of pocket for all treatment or not seek treatment at all. Even those women who aren't seeking infertility treatments, but seek care from doctors who specialize in that area such as a reproductive endocrinologist can receive denial or questions about necessity of care from some insurance companies. It can all become very frustrating and very discouraging.

Education, once again, is the key to gaining success in this arena. Understanding how your personal insurance works, as well as what other kinds of plans are available will aid in your goal of becoming a smart healthcare consumer. Also, if your insurance coverage is a part of your benefits package with your employer, find out who your benefits/insurance coordinator is within the human resources department. Usually part of this person's position is keeping you informed as to coverage and advocating for you with the insurance company. This person could be very important to you if problems arise.

Managed care is a term to describe a system that combines healthcare coverage with delivery of healthcare for a prepaid premium. Managed care companies have contracts with doctors and hospitals that have set policies as to what they can or can't do. An authorization process limits access to specialists, cuts down on self-defined unnecessary procedures and limits money spent on prescription medications. The managed care companies use several methods to reduce costs including emphasizing preventative care, using primary care physicians as "coordinators" of patient care, limiting choices of doctors and facilities to those within the contract, limiting hospital admissions and duration of stay, monitoring prescriptions of medications, and using a utilization committee to decide whether or not procedures are necessary. While attempting to lower healthcare costs, this system can be difficult to work within and can compromise care. Women facing a lifetime battle with PCOS may find that the managed care companies do not feel a specialist is necessary to monitor her condition indefinitely. Some women have had to make the decision to choose a doctor not covered by her plan and pay for services rather than accept a lower level of care than needed.

There are four basic types of insurance. These are *fee-for-service* or *unmanaged care, preferred provider organizations, health maintenance organizations* and *independent practice association.* Who bears the risk of incurring costs and who decides what treatments are necessary determine the differences in these types of coverage. Below is a description of each:

Fee-for-Service

Most patients are familiar with this coverage as it is the unmanaged traditional type that approximately half of all insured Americans currently use. In this system the patient can choose who her healthcare provider is with little interference from the insurance company. She gets the care that the doctors deem necessary and the insurer reimburses at a preset rate (this is often 80%). The patient pays the portion not covered by the insurance company. Doctors can spend, as much time as needed to treat the patient, order tests as they wish, and write prescriptions for drugs they feel necessary. Because for many decades under these plans there were no incentives to contain costs, and the price for healthcare grew steadily. As a result, the insurance companies increased premiums and the number of uninsured persons expanded greatly. Today, most fee-for-service companies include some managed care elements. These can include pre-authorization for surgeries, pre-certification, utilization reviews and restrictions on covered prescriptions.

Preferred Provider Organizations (PPO)

This type of health insurance is characterized by a managed care organization contracting with private practice physicians to provide medical care for those insured. In exchange for increased patient volume, the physicians agree to have their work controlled and to accept a decrease in usual fees. The organization then steers patients to these practices. But if the patient chooses to go out of the network they may do so at a lower rate of reimbursement. Services and coverage vary greatly from one PPO to another.

Health Maintenance Organizations (HMO)

HMO's are companies that provide healthcare for a prepaid premium, often by hiring their own doctors, whose salaries are often based on how effectively they keep costs down. These insurers are often for-profit corporations that try to provide cost-effective health care by limiting service and encouraging preventative medicine. While there is usually not a deductible for patients to meet with these services, there is usually a co-payment for doctor visits and medications. Primary care physicians are used as care coordination of patient care and must make referrals to specialists before a patient can be covered under the plan.

Independent Practice Associations (IPA)

An IPA is a group of private practice physicians who form an association that contracts with various HMOs. The physicians are not compensated for the actual medical care given, but accept a set monthly fee per patient in exchange for providing all care for HMO members. In this plan all the risk moves from the insurers to the doctors. These flat fee systems encouraged doctors to see as many healthy patients as possible because they can not benefit financially from treating patients with complicated or time consuming illnesses.

Tips for Insurance Success

- **Do your homework.** Learn as much as possible about what plans are available. Find out about how the plan works, how do you access specialists, what treatments are not covered, etc. Compare premium costs to covered services. It will do no good to get a low premium if the care you need is not covered by the insurance.
- **Be knowledgeable about local health care options**. If you are required to have a primary care physician to coordinate your care, then choose one who will support your desire to find the best care possible for PCOS. It may be that the PCP is capable of treating you effectively, but if not, make sure he will refer you to a specialist to provide that much needed care. Interview your PCP in a similar fashion as you would interview a PCOS or fertility specialist. Know that he is the key to a higher lever of care and thus is a very important part of your healthcare team. Choose, choosing a doctor with knowledgeable insurance staff who will advocate for your needs.
- **Understand the appeals process**. Know how to file an appeal if coverage of care is denied. If you feel that care should be covered, take the time to officially discuss this with your insurer. They may revoke the denial or consider a policy change.
- **Use your insurance wisely**. Do not seek unnecessary treatment or abuse your coverage. This just raises the premiums for everybody, including yourself!

Women Don't Shave!
Hair and Skin Problems

*"I tried electrolysis, but the hair just kept grow-
ing back. I was told that I was abnormal. Now I have
to shave twice-a-day and use cake make-up."*

*"I feel like a freak. The excessive hair problem start-
ed when I was in high school and it was so embarrassing
for me. I am constantly wondering if people are staring at
me."*

Whether we like it or not, our hair, skin and basic body shapes are the
first impressions we make on those we meet. Our western hemisphere, 21st
century view of female beauty does not include facial hair and acne. While of
no specific health risk, skin problems profoundly affect self-image. Having to
deal with these skin problems that accompany PCOS can lower self-esteem
and affect the way we approach others. This can have a lasting impact.

Sexual hair growth is under the control of androgens. As already
pointed out, a hallmark of PCOS is abnormally high androgen levels (*hyperandrogenism*). The skin manifestations associated with PCOS are at least as
common as menstrual cycle irregularity or obesity. While there are no perfect
treatments for these problems, active management can result in significant
improvements.

Why do we have hair anyway?

Although our hair once served humans for protection and temperature regulation, we have long passed this stage in our evolutionary growth.
Now, hair has purely sexual and social roles. Think about the billions of dollars
spent on cosmetics and hair products used to enhance our sexuality. Think
about those poor men who buy hair to glue to the top of their balding heads.
Is it any surprise then, that women consider male pattern hair growth, *hirsutism*, to be such a problem?

The primary sexual characteristics are the genitalia. We keep this area of our bodies reasonably well covered and strongly rely on the secondary sexual characteristics for gender identity. Secondary sexual characteristics develop during puberty as a cardinal sign of the reproductive system's coming of age. These alterations in body appearance help define culturally what is male and female. Examples of female secondary sexual characteristics include body shape and breast development, while male secondary sexual characteristics include increased muscle mass, a deeper voice and a characteristic pattern of hair growth.

Androgens are hormones that define male sexual characteristics. Both men and women have androgens, but their concentration is lower in women. In fact, androgens are the hormonal precursors from which all estrogens are made. The skin is highly responsive to very small differences in androgen production. Specific areas of the skin, particularly along the midline of the body, are much more susceptible to androgens. The trouble spots include the face, nape of the neck, mid chest, lower abdomen, thighs and lower back. On the face, the upper lip is not nearly so sensitive to male hormones as are the chin and the area under the jaw. On the chest and abdomen, higher androgen effect is demonstrated by more hair growth spreading to the right and left of the midline. The arms and legs are less susceptible to androgens. Women with very small androgen elevations may experience problems with hair growth, but this does not mean that such women are not fully female. Women with PCOS are fully female.

Excessive hair growth is only one of the skin problems associated with androgen excess. Additional manifestations of hyperandrogenism, though present, are often dismissed or may not be recorded in the physician's evaluation. These signs include acne, seborrhea, balding, hidradenitis suppurativa (inflammation of the apocrine glands in the armpit and groin), dandruff and acanthosis nigricans, which will be presented later.

Biology of Skin

There are three types of hair on the human body: *lanuago, vellus* and *terminal*. Each hair is produced by a hair follicle and, depending on its programming, a single follicle probably can produce all three types of hair. Lanugo, commonly shed soon after birth, is prominent in preterm infants. Vellus hair, which is fine and unpigmented, is usually seen on the face and forearms and replaces lanuago hair. Terminal hair is coarser, is usually pigmented and is limited to areas of the scalp, around the eyes and, after puberty, the secondary sexual sites.

The hair follicle has an expanded base enclosing the *dermal papilla*. The cells of the dermal papillae are the control center for hair growth. Melanocytes located around the hair follicle transfer *melanin* to growing hair. Melanin is the natural dye responsible for hair and skin color. Melanin has a role of protecting the skin against the sun. The more melanin, the darker the skin.

Associated with each hair follicle there is a small *sebaceous gland* that produces *sebum*. Sebum is an oily substance that has an evolutionary role

of protecting and waterproofing the hair. Together, the hair follicle and sebaceous gland are known as the *pilosebaceous unit (PSU)*. (See Figure 7-1)
Sweat glands are also scattered through the skin in order to help maintain the
proper body temperature.

Figure 7-1 Growth of Hair Follicles

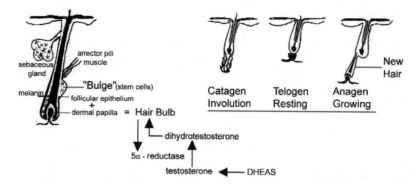

Specialized sweat glands called *apocrine* glands are associated with areas of sexual hair growth. The secretion from these glands is the strong sexual attractant *pheromone* in some species, but the role is thought to be not so clearly pronounced in the human. It is hypothesized that hair may have a role in spreading scent from the apocrine secretion gland. These glands, relatively inactive prior to puberty, are found around the moustache, sideburns, neck, lower back, mid-chest, breasts, and lower abdomen, but by far the highest concentration are in the arm pits (axillae) and around the genitalia and groin area. Under the influence of androgen at puberty, both boys and girls, experience a growth of axillary and pubic hair, an increase in apocrine gland secretion and an increase in body odor.

How does hair grow?

There is no new growth of hair follicles after birth, although there is a continuous activation and cycling of hair growth. The determination of hair growth pattern depends on the body site, skin sensitivity, and the amount of circulating androgens. Androgens are clearly the driving force for hair growth.

The life cycle of hair has three phases. The first is the *anagen* (growth) phase, which is followed by a short transitional phase of several days called the *catagen* phase and then the *telogen* phase (resting). At the end of the telogen phase the hair falls out and is replaced by new anagen phase hair. When plucked, the growing anagen hair will have an obvious epidermal root sheath. The same hair follicle may produce a hair of a different color or texture, depending on its hormonal programming. The length of the anagen phase determines how long a hair will be. Each region of the body has hairs that differ in the length of the anagen phase. The anagen phase of the scalp is about three years, while typical body hair's anagen phase is about five months. Hair from one site will retain the same characteristics as the hair from the site of transfer. This fact forms the basis of the hair transplant therapy.

How do hormones affect the skin?

Although not usually appreciated as such, the skin is an endocrine organ. It has the capacity to respond to hormonal signals and to convert steroid hormones into very potent androgens with specific activity on the hair follicle.

You will recall from an earlier chapter our description of hormones and their receptors as being analogous to a key operating a lock. Hormones work by binding to a receptor, thus "unlocking" a specialized activity. Therefore, the actions of a hormone are not only due to the amount of hormone (number of keys), but also to the number of receptors (locks). The amount of hormone produced is determined by whether the individual is male or female and the overall endocrine environment. The number of hormone receptors is a function of an individual's sex, and also of their genetic predisposition, which has been passed down from their mother and father.

There is an absolute requirement of androgen for hair growth. While the principle androgen of the body is testosterone, there are other weaker androgens produced by the ovary and adrenal glands that can bind to the androgen receptor. The hair follicle is unique, in that testosterone itself is not active androgen. Testosterone must be converted to *dihydrotestosterone (DHT)* by the enzyme *5 alpha-reductase* in order to exert its effect. Only sexual hair follicles contain the necessary enzyme converting capacity in the hair follicles. It is interesting that the hair follicle also contains aromatase, which can convert androgens to estrogen and may serve as a somewhat protective mechanism against hyperandrogenism.

How do hormones cause hirsutism?

There are three different mechanisms by which hormones can alter the skin.

- Increased concentrations of male hormones (hyperandrogenism)
- Increased numbers of androgen receptors
- Altered conversion of hormones by the hair follicle.

The problem most PCOS patients have is the easiest to explain of these three mechanisims. It is simply either an absolute or a relative increase in androgens circulating in the blood. Often androgen levels may be altered enough to cause quite pronounced hirsutism, while the levels of androgens in the blood remain in what is considered the normal range.

Elevated androgen levels may be only a part of the problem. For androgens to have an effect on the skin, they must bind together with an androgen receptor in the skin. There is a vast difference between individuals with respect to the number of androgen receptors in their skin, and even between specific areas of one person's skin, and therefore, their sensitivity to androgen stimulation. The number of androgen receptors varies among ethnic groups and among individuals. A fair skinned individual of Scandinavian origin may have little excess hair growth despite high levels of androgens, because androgen receptors are present in relatively low numbers. An individual of Mediterranean descent may get only a small "whiff" of extra androgen and become quite hairy (*hirsute*). European women with PCOS are likely to be hairier than their Asian, African, and Native American counterparts.

The third requirement for androgen action in the skin, the conversion of testosterone to DHT by 5 alpha-reductase, has a much weaker, but not impossible link with excessive hair growth and is probably less important in the syndrome called PCOS.

Why is my skin more oily at different times of the month?

Even among women with regular menstrual cycles and ovulation, many have skin problems that wax and wane. In regularly cycling women, the second half of the menstrual cycle is characterized by increased progesterone levels. Progesterone is a weak androgen and may create a situation of relative hyperandrogenism leading to increased oiliness of the skin and acne. Also consider that during menstruation estrogen levels are low, creating a situation of relative *hypoestrogenism,* or relative *hyperandrognism.* Even though androgen levels are not elevated out of the ordinary, the protective effect of estrogen has been removed during this period, resulting in relative hyperandrogenism. Among normally cycling women, neither of these brief periods lasts long enough to cause unwanted hair growth.

When is hair growth excessive?

Hirsutism is defined as male pattern hair growth in a female who has an increase in amount and/or coarseness of hair. Some women (and men) are just hairier all over their bodies than are others. The excessive growth of non-sexual hair is called *hypertrichosis,* and while it may cause a problem with body image, it is not associated with hyperandrogenism.

A situation of *relative hyperandrogenism* occurs in the life phase called perimenopause (nearing menopause) when estrogen levels become chronically low. Although androgen levels are also low, their reduction is less than that of estrogen. The inhibitory effects of estrogen may lose out to the stimulatory effects of androgens. The relative hyperandrogenism may then be sufficient to cause the modest increases in facial hair that some women report.

A faint mustache is quite common and may be more related to a family trait and/or ethnic group than to a hormonal imbalance. As androgens increase, however, the coarseness and color of the hairs of the upper lip increase toward the mid-line. You may have noticed that seldom in women with excessive hair growth is the hair worn up on the head. Hairstyle is often changed to conceal the lower hair of the neck and the start of sideburns. A non-prejudicial question I usually ask my patients is, "How much hair do you have between the umbilicus and pubic hairline?" Often this is a good clinical indicator of the overall amount of hirsutism. Other areas of male pattern hair growth include sideburns, lower neck, lower back and inner thighs.

Many women worry about the "stray" hair on the breasts. Virtually all women have these, especially around the nipples. Of more concern is coarse hair in the middle of the chest, often indicating excessive androgen.

Hair is much like weight—when it comes to identifying it as problematic, every other woman seems to have less of a problem. Virtually all authors on the subject comment on Western society's preoccupation with the pattern of female hair growth. Generally, an excess of hair growth is overestimated by the concerned woman and underestimated by her physician. Regardless of the origin of the concern, it is a concern.

Can hirsutism be quantified?

In many ways this correlates with abnormal bleeding, and what the patient is often saying is that there has been a change. Often this is physiological and/or dysfunctional change, but seldom is it pathologic.

There have been several attempts to quantify hirsutism. The most widely used method is the *Ferriman-Gallwey scoring system* that examines eight different sites on the body and scores the amount of hair growth on a scale of 1 to 4. A total score greater than 8 is considered hirsutism.

Is there hirsutism without a cause ?

The term *idiopathic* means unexplained, and *idiopathic hirsutism* is probably a useless term, but it continues to be used in medical reports. Often this designation means that no one looked hard enough, while other times it represents a minor hormonal imbalance not sufficient to tip the scales of the endocrine laboratory. Most patients with hirsutism will have minor abnormalities of endocrine testing, if they are aggressively evaluated. Hirsutism is always a result of an alteration in either amount or receptivity of androgen. Most importantly, treatment for idiopathic hirsutism is not different.

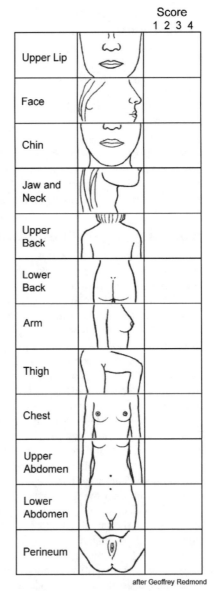

Score
1 2 3 4

Upper Lip

Face

Chin

Jaw and Neck

Upper Back

Lower Back

Arm

Thigh

Chest

Upper Abdomen

Lower Abdomen

Perineum

after Geoffrey Redmond

Figure 7-2 Hirsutism Score

How do I get rid of that unwanted hair?

There are numerous remedies used and countless money spent on treatment of unwanted hair. The two ways that hair is removed are by the removal of the hair shaft (*depilation*) and by removal of the hair from its root, (*epilation*). Epilation, which is accompanied by destruction of the dermal bulb, has the potential to permanently remove hair and it is possible only through laser or electrolysis therapy.

Is bleaching a problem?

No. I see few patients with excessive hair growth who don't use some form of bleaching. Bleaching is a good first line therapy when there is only a spotty or modest increase in hair. The most commonly treated area is the upper lip. There is a vast line of bleaching agents, most of which employ a weak solution of hydrogen peroxide as the active ingredient. These agents are inexpensive, safe, and easy to use, but must be applied often.

> **Hair Removal Methods**
> - Bleaching (cover up)
> - Depilation (removal of the hair shaft) by
>   - Shaving
>   - Creams
> - Epilation (destruction or removal of hair from its root) by
>   - Plucking
>   - Waxing
>   - Sugaring
>   - Electrolysis
>   - Laser

Does shaving cause hair to grow faster?

No. Despite the common belief, shaving does not affect the rate of hair growth. Shaving does blunt the tip of the hair, causing it to feel coarser and thicker. Shaving is not as terrible a solution as it might seem to some, though it certainly carries negative connotations associated with manliness. The major potential side effect of regular shaving of unwanted hair is an irritation of the skin called *pseudofolliculitis*.

Does plucking make two hairs grow back?

No. However, repeated plucking may cause permanent damage to the hair follicle, leading to finer hair, thus delaying the inevitable regrowth of a single hair from the hair follicles. Electronic tweezers are just a sophisticated means of plucking and offer no advantage to manual tweezers. Waxing is simply an alternative to plucking whereby larger groups of hairs are removed at once. *Sugaring* is similar to waxing, and while very inexpensive, may not work as well. Sugar and water are mixed into a paste, layered on to skin, covered with a cloth and left to dry. When the cloth is removed, so are some of the hairs. Side effects of plucking or waxing may include inflammation, darkened discoloration (hyperpigmentation), and even scarring.

What about hair removal creams?

One of the most noxious remembered smells of my youth was that emanating from the bathroom as my mom used a hair removal cream. I hope they have improved. Chemical depilatories are relatively simple to use, inexpensive and less painful than plucking. They work by removing hair through a chemical reaction that causes hair protein to dissolve (creating the smell!) Since there is some destruction of the lower hair shaft, regrowth of hair after use of a depilatory may be slower. The skin is not totally immune from this chemical reaction and irritation is common, especially on more delicate facial skin.

How does electrolysis work?

In the most general sense, electrolysis is the removal of hair by means of passing an electric current through the hair shaft, destroying the shaft. There are three general forms of electrolysis, *galvanic* using a direct current, *thermolysis* using alternating current, or a blend of the two. Galvanic electrolysis is a more traditional approach, more time consuming and less likely to be permanent. Here, an electric current converts the water and a salt associated with the hair shaft into minute amounts of lye (sodium hydroxide) which then dissolves the hair follicle. While more precise than thermolysis, in most ways galvanic electrolysis is similar to the depilatory creams. Thermolytic electrolysis uses heat rather than a chemical reaction and is more likely to destroy the dermal papillae from which the hair grows, resulting in permanent hair removal.

A drawback of both therapies is that each individual hair follicle must be treated. The procedure is time consuming and costly compared to more temporary hair removal methods. Sometimes patients are asked to shave between treatments and to allow the hairs to grow back for several days so that only the anagen hairs will be visible and the treatment more effective. The amount of discomfort reported by those who have undergone the procedure is variable and can depend on the skill of the operator. Special anesthetic creams have made the procedure more tolerable. It is critical that certified electrologists be used. Inexperienced operators can increase the amount of pain, risk of infection and scarring, as well as being less effective. Many states have a certification program. Complete removal of facial hair can require multiple visits and even take several years. Prior control of PCOS aids the process.

How does laser therapy compare?

Current methods of laser hair removal are based on the principle that the melanin, the dark skin pigment that is responsible for hair color, absorbs the laser beam much like dark clothes absorb the sun's rays. Melanin is in the highest concentration in the hair bulb, the site of hair growth. By permanently damaging the hair bulb, regrowth of hair can be prevented. The laser beam is a highly focused ray of light that generates a large amount of energy in a very small space and results in destruction of the hair shaft. This gives the laser the theoretical advantage of permanent hair removal. While hair is destroyed, the skin, which has much less melanin, remains relatively undamaged. Patients with dark hair, which feels most worrisome, have better chances of treatment success using laser therapy than do those with light hair.

Lasers (Light Amplification by Stimulated Emission of Radiation) work by passage of an electric current through a "medium" that emits the beam at a specific wavelength. The beam is then concentrated by use of mirrors. Lasers are usually named by the medium through which the current is passed. The most common lasers used for hair removal either use a ruby (aluminum oxide) or a synthetic crystal (alexandrite). The medium does not have to be a crystal; it can be a gas like carbon dioxide (CO_2). The CO_2 laser is the most commonly used laser for gynecologic surgery, but it is poor for hair removal.

Before laser therapy, it is usually suggested that hair be allowed to grow to permit the best target. Laser therapy is less painful and fewer visits are required compared with electrolysis. There is usually a mild tingling sensation of the skin and temporary redness. Since areas of skin rather than individual hairs are treated, the procedure is quicker than electrolysis. Most who have used laser therapy prefer it to electrolysis. Some women have had truly excellent success and report a major change in the way they view themselves. Other women have not been quite so lucky. With both laser and electrolysis there will be a continued transformation from the villus to terminal hair. This becomes progressively less problematic as more hair follicles are destroyed. A lack of complete hair removal should not indicate a failure of therapy, however.

Laser therapy shows great promise. At least one laser, the Epilaser, has received FDA approval as a permanent hair removal method.

So why doesn't everyone use laser therapy?

Laser therapy is relatively new and many either do not know about the therapy or do not appreciate how effective it can be. The big drawback is the cost of the laser equipment, which is passed on to the consumer. Treatments run between $100 and $500 each, and at least two and as many as eight treatments may be necessary. Usually there are several closely spaced treatments followed by others that are spread out over many months.

Unfortunately, laser therapy has some problems resulting from the commercial promotion of the therapy both by the laser companies and the physicians. Lasers can be promoted as a get rich quick scheme and have been peddled to centers unskilled in patient evaluation and laser use. Some companies have promoted fixed pricing at inflated levels. Additionally, there are laser companies that have a "gag clause" preventing physicians from publicizing their cumulative results. Consumers considering laser treatment should exercise caution and careful judgment in choosing a service provider. Make sure a reputable experienced practice, usually a dermatologist that is routinely performing the procedure, is consulted. Ask about their center's success rates, costs, number of treatments expected, and chances of permanent hair removal.

Is there a pill?

There is no medication in the United States that has been approved for the treatment of hirsutism. The single most effective medical therapy for the skin problems associated with hyperandrogenism is not a pill, but The Pill. Oral contraceptives (OCs) have several positive actions on reduction of acne and excessive hair growth. They reduce the level of luteinizing hormone by directly suppressing LH release from the pituitary gland. A second mechanism of their action is to increase the concentration of steroid binding globulin, SHBG. SHBG acts as a sponge, soaking up free testosterone and removing it from circulation. Less LH results in less androgen production; less circulating androgen means less androgen action. With oral contraceptive use, there are other health benefits for PCOS patients, including menstrual cycle regulation, less functional cyst formation, less risk of overgrowth of the uterine lining, less risk of ovarian cancer, less endometriosis, less blood loss, and diminished pain with periods.

Picking the right OC can be trial and error. The Pill is much like a pair of shoes; they all have the same purpose, but each fits differently. A more thorough presentation of oral contraceptives is presented in Chapter 17.

Are there other medications besides OCs?

There are several drugs that are used for conditions other than excessive hair growth that have the capacity to block the production of androgens or inhibit their action. These are called antiandrogens. All of these are potential teratogens, meaning that they could cause birth defects. For this reason, anti-androgens should only be used by women not trying to be become pregnant and birth control should be used while taking these medications. Several studies have shown equal effectiveness of spironolactone, flutamide and finasteride, but they vary in cost, in side effects, and in potential toxicity.

Oral Agents for Hirsutism	
• Oral contraceptives	• Finasteride
• Spironolactone	• Ketoconazole
• Cyproterone acetate	(no longer used)
(outside U.S.)	• Cimetidine
• Flutamide	(not shown effective)

Spironolactone (Aldactone™) is a diuretic used to treat hypertension. It has an idiosyncratic action as an anti-androgen and can reduce excessive hair growth by blocking the effects of androgen. It is the most widely prescribed anti-androgen in the United States. At high doses, spironolactone also blocks the metabolic pathway which affects the capacity of ovary and adrenal gland to make androgens. It also alters the conversion of testosterone to dihydrotestosterone (DHT) by 5 alpha-reductase enzyme.

Some patients have a surprisingly good response to this therapy, while others seem completely resistant. In some cases, especially when OCs cannot be used, spironolactone may represent first line therapy. The effects of OC's may be additive, as well as reducing a tendency of irregular bleeding which sometimes complicates the use of spironolactone. Although an adverse side effect of spironolactone use may be high levels of potassium in the blood (*hyperkalemia*), this is rarely seen in young healthy women. Because spironolactone is metabolized in the liver, baseline liver function testing should be performed. The most common side-effects are nausea and indigestion with some patients reporting increased fatigue.

Cyproterone acetate (CA) is a potent anti-androgen and weak progestin. CA is currently available only outside the United States. Its effectiveness in treatment of hirsutism is well substantiated. Most patients will report decreased hair growth and some patients may become amenorrheic. While CA is usually well tolerated, its cortisone-like activity may cause weight gain. CA has also been compounded with ethinyl estradiol and marketed as an oral contraceptive, Diane™. The usefulness of Diane™ in the treatment of hirsutism has been questioned, but it may help to control hair growth. Drug-induced hepatitis has been reported and it is prudent to monitor liver function.

Flutamide is a non-steroidal anti-androgen indicated for treatment of prostatic cancer. Its action is similar to spironolactone and cyproterone acetate, in that androgen action is reversibly blocked at the androgen receptor. Flutamide is theoretically superior to cyproterone acetate due to its absence of steroid-like activity and superior to spironolactone because of its lack of alteration in kidney function. A majority of patients report the side effect of dry skin. Less common side effects are hot flushes, increased appetite, headache, fatigue, and nausea. It is metabolized by the liver, and fatal liver toxicity has been reported. The incidence of side effects and toxicity is disputed.

Finasteride is not a true anti-androgen, but since it is an alternative to anti-androgen therapy, it is described here. Finasteride is an inhibitor of 5-alpha-reductase activity and was initially indicated for use in the management of benign prostatic hypertrophy. Now it has been approved and received the most publicity for its capacity to thwart male pattern baldness in some men. This effect has not been substantiated in women. It acts at the point of production of the active skin androgen dihydrotestosterone, so finasteride shows promise in the treatment of hirsutism. The safety profile and tolerance appears to be very good. Despite the pregnancy warning and high cost, the theoretical advantages and excellent tolerance may make this a drug to consider.

GnRH Analogs GnRH analogs work by blocking gonadotropin releasing hormone (GnRH), subsequently LH release, and follicle growth. Both estrogen and androgen production are then markedly reduced. There are three agonists used in the United States: Lupron™, Zoladex™ and Synarel™. Their action is identical, but they differ in route of administration—monthly to tri-monthly injection, implant, or daily nasal spray. The side effects are those of menopause, including hot flushes and reversible reduction in bone density. Adrenal androgen production is unaffected. While quite a good therapy for suppression of the ovary and its abnormal hormonal production of PCOS, the high cost and undesirable side effects limit GnRH use. The side effects can be markedly reduced when estrogen and progestins, either separately, or in combination as an oral contraceptive are given in addition to the analog. This "add back" therapy offers additional advantages of increasing SHBG, reducing the risk of osteoporosis and symptoms of menopause. A great disadvantage remains in the high cost of this regimen.

Vaniqua™ Vaniqua is a prescription cream that appears to slow facial hair growth in 70% of users. The medication is applied to the face twice per day in the same manner as moisturizer and works by blocking 5 alpha-reductase. Hair growth will resume, if not used regularly. It is expected to receive FDA approval during the summer of 2000, and be released by Gillette and Bristol-Myers Squibb in the fall.

How is acne related to PCOS?

Acne is the most common skin disorder of all. Acne, in medical terminology *acne vulgaris*, rapidly occurs as androgen levels rise. It provides an earlier indication of hyperandrogenism than does abnormal hair growth. Almost every teenager will have some acne as a result of the emergence of sex hormone production. It is not unusual to see a 30-year-old with light acne due to PCOS. Contrary to popular belief, acne is not related to the type of food one eats.

Androgens increase *sebum*, which is a combination of skin oils and old skin tissue. Increased sebum causes the plugging of skin pores. Bacteria that thrive on sebum are increased, resulting in inflammation. The inflamed skin pore is called a *comedone*. Closed comedones are "whiteheads," while "blackheads" are open comedones. The black color does not come from dirt, but from the breakdown of keratin, a natural skin product. *Papules*, an elevated reddened area, and small pus-filled pimples (pustules) can form inflammation. This lasts from one to four days. The most severe cases of acne can result in nodules that increase the risk of permanent scarring.

Acne occurs in the *pilosebaceous unit*, which consists of a sebaceous gland and a hair follicle. The product of the sebaceous gland is sebum. Maximum sebum production occurs between ages sixteen and twenty. A special form of bacteria resides in the sebaceous gland, which initiates an inflammatory reaction and white blood cells enter the area, kill the bacteria and cause the release of enzymes.

Between 30% and 50% of acne patients show no detectable hormonal imbalance, but the remaining will have at least one abnormal lab value. There seems to be a similarity between hormonal findings in patients with hirsutism and those with acne, suggesting the difference may be in hair follicle number of the skin. An interesting finding was that women with acne were twice as likely to indicate PCO on ultrasound. However, more study is needed to clarify this association.

There is no reason for the scarring acne of twenty years ago. Antibiotics and local cleansing agents can do much to control acne. Topical medications with erythromycin and benzoyl peroxide seem safe. Tetracycline, on the other hand, can affect fetal bone and tooth growth and should be avoided. The use of isotretinoin (retinoic acid), a derivative of vitamin A, can markedly reduce sebum production. Retinoic acid is one of the few drugs that the FDA classifies as category X, indicating that it has definitely been shown to cause birth defects. For this reason, when using this drug, patients should use <u>two</u> methods of birth control in order to be especially careful to prevent pregnancy.

Oral contraceptives can be of benefit in preventing acne as well. There is only a single oral contraceptive, Ortho Tri-Cyclen™, that has been approved by the FDA for treatment of acne, but others, especially those containing desogestrel, should be equally effective.

Dandruff—A hormonal disorder?

A particularly common skin condition and one not usually associated with hormonal alterations is dandruff. Contrary to what is generally believed, dandruff is caused by oily, not dry skin, and is a variety of *seborrheic dermatitis.* Increased male hormone levels also cause seborrhea.

I'm losing my hair, what can I do?

Hair loss, *androgenic alopecia,* can be as troubling as excessive hair growth. Men spend millions of dollars on attempts to prevent hair loss. At least for them, hair loss can be considered manly because of the relationship with male hormones. It is a paradox that the same hormones that initiate and sustain hair growth also cause baldness.

For women, hair loss and balding are extremely distressing. While there seems to be a strong genetic factor, the principle mechanism of most cases of hair loss is hormonal. Women may get a double dose when there is a genetic predisposition toward balding, as well as an increase in androgens. Usually hair shedding occurs before thinning. While androgenic alopecia is the major cause of female hair loss, other causes of hair loss, such as thyroid disease, anemia, pregnancy, a variety of drugs, diet, and illness, should be excluded. This hair loss may be temporary and reversible if the problem is identified and corrected. Alopecia is not necessarily a sign of androgen excess, but androgen excess is present in about 40% of cases and should be excluded. Alopecia may also occur with low levels of estrogen and the relative hyperandrogenism that occurs around menopause. Hair loss can be worsened by *traction alopecia,* caused by easy pulling of the hair by any means (ponytails, hairbands, nervous pulling of the hair, excessive brushing, styling, or blow-drying). Coloring the hair and shampoos do not seem to make a difference.

A scalp hair lives between two and five years. We naturally lose about 75 hairs a day from our estimated 100,000 to 150,000 hair follicles. It will take a loss of as much as 50% of scalp hair before the casual observer will notice a difference.

Figure 7-3 Thinning Hair

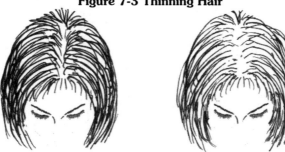

Hairs from men's balding scalps have higher levels of receptors for androgens, and higher levels of the enzyme 5-alpha reductase to convert testosterone to the active skin androgen, dihydrotestosterone (DHT) (see above). The most androgen sensitive area of the scalp is the vertex, which is the highest point of the head. The frontal hairline is usually preserved as there is thinning on top. Frontal balding and anterior hairline recession are seen only in the more severe cases of androgen excess.

We are constantly being bombarded with television advertisements about hair loss in men. While it is not promoted as such, it would seem reasonable to assume that the drugs would also be equally effective in women. Not true. It makes sense; it just does not work. An excellent candidate would appear to be finasteride (Proscar™), with the potent blocker of 5 alpha-reductase, which, as mentioned above, is used to reduce prostate size. There are two forms of the enzyme (I and II) and the finasteride is more effective on the prostate (form II) of the enzyme than that of the skin (form I). Recently the makers of finasteride conducted a study in androgenic alopecia and found the drug ineffective in postmenopausal women with hair loss, despite its effectiveness in men. Minoxidil (Rogaine™), which causes dilation of scalp blood vessels, has also been tried. With minoxidil, there has been a slowing of hair loss in some women. Long-term use is necessary because of a rebound of accelerated hair loss when the drug is stopped. Oral contraceptives alone, especially those of lower androgenic potential, or when used with spironolactone, may be of help. Treatment is often unsatisfactory. Hair transplants may be used for women as well as for men.

As can be an imagined, the mechanism for hair growth (and loss) has been extensively studied, but no unified theory or treatment has emerged.

I didn't always have these skin tags.

Skin tags (*acrochordons*) are small benign skin lesions that increase in frequency with age. They are also more common with obesity and insulin resistance. They can be raised or stalked, smooth or rough, flesh-colored or darker than surrounding skin. The most common places for skin tags are the eyelids, neck, armpits, upper chest and groin. They can be easily removed by a physician using cautery (burning), freezing (cryotherapy), laser, or excision with a scalpel. Often pulling or cutting them off at home results in incomplete removal, they grow back, and bleeding can be quite heavy considering their size. Some have used a thin thread to tie off the tag. There is a small risk of infection that is probably increased by home removal. There is no need for removal unless unsightly or irritating.

What is acanthosis nigricans?

Acanthosis nigricans (AN) is usually described as velvety, raised, pigmented skin changes, most often seen on the back of the neck, axillae, and beneath the breasts. AN is often seen in association with skin tags. Possibly the best description is that it looks like the affected area is 'dirty' and would benefit from scrubbing. Obviously this is not the case.

Ovaries in these individuals with AN tend to be larger with less cystic change. A search for acanthosis nigricans should be a part of every physical exam of the PCOS patient. AN should always alert the clinician to a risk of diabetes, major lipid abnormalities, and hypertension. Although much less common, it may also be a warning signal of cancer.

Acanthosis can resolve with weight loss, but not necessarily because insulin is lowered. A strong association exists between AN and insulin resistance. The grouping of hirsutism, acanthosis nigricans, and insulin resistance has been referred to as HAIRAN syndrome (hyperandrogenic-insulin resistant-acanthosis nigricans syndrome), but this is likely a more severe variant of PCOS rather than a discrete disease.

What are these sores?

Hidradenitis suppurativa is severe chronic inflammation of the apocrine glands of the armpit (*axilla*) and groin region. Mild cases of hidradenitis are relatively common and appear much like several small "boils" that are reddened, hardened and contain pus. They may appear much like an infected hair follicle, which in reality is close to the truth. Applications of warm wet compresses can offer some relief. Because this disorder is hormone-related, oral contraceptives and anti-androgens may be used with some success. The severe infections, which sometimes occur, are very difficult to treat and surgical excision may be necessary.

What's on the horizon?

Most often the skin problems associated with PCOS are of little medical consequence. Nevertheless, they are very important to the way we see ourselves and unfortunately, to the way others view (judge) us. Laser therapy can make a real difference. At last it is completely removed from the world of "used car salesmanship" and considered non-elective therapy by insurance carriers. There is still much to be done in the field of medical therapy, but drug development is hampered by the possibility of inadvertent exposure to these drugs during pregnancy, a risk that many pharmaceutical firms are unwilling to take. At some point in the future it may become possible to directly alter the genetic programming of skin or its capacity to respond adversely to its hormonal stimulation.

Designer OCs will be progressively available. An OC with a progestin component that has minimal mineralocorticoid and anti-androgenic qualities, *drospirenome,* may be available soon. This could not only lessen hair growth, but improved the side effects of fluid retention and hypertension and headache that may accompany OC use. Other drugs that specifically block 5 alpha-reductase are also in development.

Fat for Life?
It's Not Just a Matter
of Self-Control

*"For years, I tried every diet ever invented and worked
out more than any person should ever have to and I still
could not get my weight off."*

I have a confession. In my first year or so of reproductive medicine practice, I often refused therapy to excessively overweight patients. I thought this was in their best interest and that my insistence would force the issue of weight loss. Not only was this a bigoted approach, it wasn't very successful.

I remember well one patient who, after having listened to my plea about weight loss, agreed that it was a good idea, although she had also been offered immediate therapy. We expectantly watched and waited while her weight fell pound after pound from about 230 to 180 pounds. We then decided that it was time for therapy for ovulation induction. She didn't get pregnant, and I never saw her again. I later heard that she had gained back the weight she had previously lost and was ashamed to return to see me.

My intentions were honorable, but I still feel that I did this patient a disservice. For a number of years, I continued to talk about weight management, but very half-heartedly. Since there did not seem to be any chance of improving the weight situation, the goal became to override PCOS with fertility drugs. Now I feel that I have done my PCOS patients an additional disservice. My early PCOS patients did not receive the full medical and metabolic evaluation they warranted or deserved. I missed several cases of overt diabetes, and I believe that I subjected the pregnancies of those women to more risks than were necessary.

In the last few years, my own thoughts about fertility and PCOS have changed dramatically. My eyes and my mind have been opened to establishing the best health and trying new interventions to treat, not necessarily overpower, the underlying causes of PCOS. The concept of ***metabolic balance*** has emerged. Metabolic balance involves, in part, healthy eating, healthy activity, stress management through adaptive coping skills, and normalizing of metabolic parameters such as lipid and insulin levels. It involves taking an *individualized* approach to lifestyle changes that will promote maximum health and well-being.

Figure 8-1 Metabolic Equilibrium

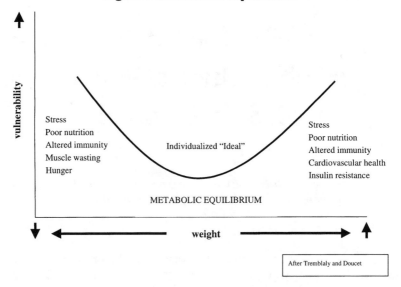

Stress
Poor nutrition
Altered immunity
Muscle wasting
Hunger

Individualized "Ideal"

Stress
Poor nutrition
Altered immunity
Cardiovascular health
Insulin resistance

METABOLIC EQUILIBRIUM

weight

After Tremblaly and Doucet

Only now is this puzzle of what makes each of us both unique and related beginning to be pieced together with new techniques in genetics and molecular biology; the future is exciting. We are on the threshold of understanding obesity, thus offering new hope. This chapter will present definitions and measurements of obesity, its health consequences, and therapeutic options, offering new help.

The unfairness of it all.

Some individuals consume large quantities of food and never seem to gain weight, while others work hard to stay simply "fat," as opposed to severely obese. When seeking medical help for any number of medical reasons, much too often the obese patient has been told to "eat less" and "exercise more." Unfortunately, many obese patients, and possibly their serious medical problems, are dismissed with the remark, "If you would only lose weight," and perhaps the unspoken thought, "If she only had self-control." This approach is obscene.

Over the years I have listened to numerous "experts" (who by the way, never seem to have a weight problem) oversimplifying the problem of obesity with a more refined, but similar, philosophy. Repeatedly, it is stated that weight is gained when calories taken in exceed calories used, and reducing calorie intake to less than calories used results in weight loss. Of course, this must be true, but equally valid must be subtle innate difference(s) in the way each of us utilizes calories.

In this difference, hangs the tale. A patient came to me for a PCOS consultation. She was an exercise physiologist and had spent her life practicing what she preached. During college, she watched as her body started to change. Her friends and colleagues looked askance that she would let herself gain weight and outwardly seem unfit. How could she be so out of shape? She was one of the most motivated and informed individuals I have met. She had the perfect diet and exercise pattern, but she was still "plump." She had PCOS.

Another example that illustrates this point occurred when I was taken, with some reluctance on my part, to a local dance recital. All of the dancers were "professional amateurs." I know that members of the troupe had an excellent pattern of exercise and probably their eating patterns were more similar than different. Still, each member of the troupe varied dramatically in body shape. There were thin dancers, medium size ones, and even a couple that most would say needed to lose a few pounds. Why such a difference? There has to be much more to obesity, especially obesity in PCOS, than diet, exercise, and eating habits.

Body image = Self image?

Among American women thinness symbolizes success, control and attractiveness. Perhaps this is why an estimated 50% of women are trying to lose weight. The idealized body of today's fashion model would have had very little selective advantage for survival in millennia past, though neither would obesity. When the perception of the ideal human form became so skinny is unclear. Obviously, the classical painters didn't view the female figure as thin, but illustrated beauty as full figured, relatively mature, female form. A larger body size has been viewed as a sign of success and elevated social status. In some Puerto Rican communities, weight gain after marriage is a sign the husband is a good provider.

What has caused the change in the present Western idea of the perfect form is unclear. Obesity has negative connotations and downright discrimination exists about severe obesity. Children comparing silhouettes of obese versus thinner peers associated the obese silhouette more often with the characteristics lazy, dirty, stupid, ugly, liar and cheat. Studies have shown that obese individuals complete fewer years of school, have decreased entry rates into prestigious institutions and are less likely to enter professions judged to be desirable. These negative stereotypes extend deeply into the medical profession, where little attention has been directed to understanding the psychosocial burden of obesity.

It's a shame that obesity is such a socially acceptable form of bigotry.

What is obesity?

Obesity is an excessive storage of body fat. Implied in the definition is that the fat stores are high enough to impair present health or to put the individual at higher risk for future health impairment. It is not just being "a few pounds overweight." Metabolically, obesity is a result of a long-term positive energy balance. It may be possible to be fat and fit, but obesity is clearly linked to multiple medical problems. The obese individual with PCOS is at a greater risk for health problems than is the obese individual without PCOS. Almost 100 million Americans are overweight (a body mass index, or BMI, over 25), or obese (BMI over 30).

Obesity should be considered a legitimate, chronic, lifelong disorder and approached as such. It would be ridiculous to treat an individual with elevated blood pressure for one month and after it returns to normal stop therapy. Obesity, like hypertension, is a sign of a much broader based physiologic alteration.

Which came first?

Whether obesity is a cause of PCOS, a result of PCOS, or completely independent of PCOS has not been fully explained. However, there is an unmistakable association between obesity and PCOS. Most develop the signs and symptoms of PCOS before weight gain. Many obese women do not have PCOS and not all with PCOS are obese. Certainly, many metabolic derangements improve with weight loss, but PCOS is not "cured" by weight reduction. Obesity can be considered similar to a fever. At low elevations, fever makes you feel bad, while at high levels it can kill. Fever is not the cause of disease, but a consequence of the disease process. We treat the fever while treating the disease. Obesity is treated while treating PCOS.

Why is obesity?

The body keeps only about 300 calories available for immediate use, but an individual of normal weight may survive total starvation for up to two months. Fat is our long-term energy storage warehouse. Through much of our human history, weight gain and the capacity to store energy was a major survival factor against cold and famine. Energy supply and energy stores are also closely allied with reproduction. There is no evolutionary advantage of reproducing when childbearing would place both mother and child in danger. There must be an innate protective mechanism to ensure the survival of both or the reproductive process fails. In some African communities, "fattening" huts are provided for the "elite" girls during puberty to ensure weight gain and normal menstruation.

For most, food is now a plentiful resource. However, our 21st century diets have increased in calories, are high in fat; they are *energy dense*. At the same time, our caloric expenditure has slowed. Interestingly, the formerly adaptive genetic predisposition to store fat that once permitted survival and reproduction now places humans at an increased risk for morbidity (illness) and mortality (death).

Some humans have always been heavier than have others (see also the discussion of genetics in Chapter 3). Whether this is a normal adaptive mechanism especially important in individuals such as the Northern

Europeans, or a pathologic exaggeration of a normal mechanism is not known. It has been suggested that obesity and eating behavior is an evolutionary advantage operating in a "toxic environment" of unlimited food and low energy expenditure. Certainly, obesity has been around for a long time. Evidence of obese women has been found in Stone Age archeological sites across Europe.

A woman of the 19th century who was working in the fields and chopping wood while breastfeeding may have weighed 180 pounds. Little could be done that could either improve her diet or exercise pattern. However, by today's medical classification she would be considered obese by modern standards, yet in excellent health. This 19th century woman's genetic background had programmed her to weigh no less. In the 21st century, this same woman's genetic descendant, working at her desk, driving her minivan, and attending a fertility clinic might weigh 230 pounds. (Consider 180 pounds genetic, 15 pounds environmental conditioning, 15 pounds inactivity, and 20 pounds just plain improper eating). She has the same genetic make-up, but is in a very different environment from her ancestors – so much so that she is now at considerable health risk. The point is that our genes determine our potential, but our environment realizes it. Some of us are over achievers.

Weight changes of the world population over the last 50 years have been much too dramatic to suggest genetic cause. In the United States in 1960, 15% of the female population was considered obese. In 1990, the prevalence of obesity had risen to 25%. Obesity has become a major world epidemic, in part a response to today's sedentary lifestyles and also to dietary indiscretion.

How do we get fat?

Weight gain occurs when the additions to a body's energy account (measured in the currency of calories) are greater than the withdrawals. The bottom line of a person's energy account is not usually affected by small daily petty cash transactions as long as there are both credits and debits. Only when there is a series of frequent withdrawals (negative energy balance) or a pattern of ongoing deposits (positive energy balance) daily over a period of time does a change in the account (weight) balance occur. Persistent small additions to the energy ledger can be translated into very large differences in worth (weight) over the long-term. Think of fat as your retirement account. Each week a small deposit is made. Soon your interest is compounded and the account swells. Unlike a bank account, deposits to the body's fat stores are easier to make than are withdrawals.

Some suggest that obesity is a consequence of overeating, while others argue that types of food consumed causes weight gain, and still others think obesity is the result of a genetic predisposition. While obesity is due to a positive energy balance, what causes it is different in each individual. The great misconceptions are that obesity is due *only* to lack of self-control, or *only* to overindulgence, or *only* to lack of exercise.

Although major life changes can result in large weight changes, weight gain is generally slow. A pound of fat consists of 3500 calories. Just 100 extra calories a day can cause a pound per month increase in weight; that's twelve pounds in a year. This same holds for weight loss. A hundred calories a day less—that's half of a can of a soft drink—is a pound a month loss.

I used to be thin!?

Many with PCOS have had a weight problem their entire life, but for others, weight gain seemed sudden. Here science and perception seem to differ. No life stage can account for major shifts in weight. Whether you believe it or not significant weight gain rarely is due to age, medication use, or disease. At certain times in life we are more prone to weight gain, but these are likely related to social changes in diet and activity, rather than to hormones and changes in metabolism.

We have all noticed the chubby kid in puberty grow lean with the growth spurt. Overweight children sometimes become lean adults, but too often the reverse is true. A major weight shift is often associated with marriage, which usually brings with it dramatic changes in eating and activity patterns. Exercise may decrease while at the same time meals become more regular, if not larger. A common belief is that weight increases with each pregnancy. While fat storage in the gynoid pattern of hips and thighs is promoted during pregnancy, an increase of more than two to three pounds cannot be blamed on pregnancy alone. The reproductive years are the times of greatest weight gain and for reasons discussed above. Usually there is a gradual increase starting in the late teens or early twenties through the forties. Most believe that menopause causes weight gain, but there is no scientific support for this. In fact, weight tends to be a gradually lost starting in the fifties.

How is obesity measured?

Few individuals are the weight they want to be. The self-image of fat may exist, but this can be very different from obesity. The bathroom scale is not necessarily the best judge of obesity, nor is obesity alone may the best predictor of health risk. Still, we need measurements to assess therapy and help evaluate risks.

The first attempt to determine what constitutes "normal" weight was devised by insurance firms at the turn of the 20th century, using height and weight for a two-dimensional estimate of health risk. From this came the concept of the *ideal body weight* (IBW). These charts may contain significant bias, and their validity concerning good health can be questioned. To consider IBW as either a possible, or mandatory, target is unrealistic for many women with PCOS. One may be very healthy at weights much higher than the IBW.

IBW = 100 lbs. for the first 5 feet and 5 lbs. for each additional inch of height
(Add 10% for large frame and subtract 10% for small frame)
(Men 106 lbs. for the first 5 feet and 6 lbs. for each additional inch of height)

Example at 5 ft. 4 in. IBW = 100 +20
IBW = 120 pounds (±10% =108-132 lbs).

A second formula has been derived for obese individuals to account for the increased muscle mass that supports the extra weight.

IBW = (Actual weight - IBW) X (0.25) + IBW

Example at 5 ft. 4 in. and 180 pounds = (180-120)(0.25) = 15+120
IBW = 135 pounds (±10% =120-150 lbs).

Body mass index (BMI) is a simple method to evaluate the body in three dimensions rather than two. BMI is calculated by weight in kilograms (kg) (1 kg = 2.2 pounds) divided by the square of the height in meters (m) (1 m = 39.4 inches). (See BMI calculation chart listed in pounds and inches in appendix).

BMI = *Weight* in kg. = (1 kg. = 2.2 lbs). divided by *Height* in meters x height in meters (1 m. = 39.36 inches)

Example at 90 Kg (203 lbs). and $1.75m^2$ (5 ft. 6 in). = 90/ (1.75 X 1.75)
BMI = 30

Generally, a BMI above 28 in both men and women defines obesity. In the U.S. National Health and Nutrition Survey, 85% of men and women fall below a BMI of 28. The world standard for obesity has been set at a BMI of 30. A problem with BMI measurement is that there is no differentiation of muscle and fat, and the measure does not take into account fat distribution or frame size. (See appendix for BMI Chart)

Risk for Chronic Health Problems Related to BMI		
BMI	Description	Medical Risk
Under 18.5	"Underweight"	Variable
18.5 – 24.9	"Healthy"	Very low
25 – 30	"Overweight"	Low
31 – 35	"Obese"	Moderate
36 – 40	"Obese"	High
Over 40	"Morbidly obese"	Very high

Neither weight nor BMI is an absolute measure of the amount of fat, which is the real issue under consideration. In adult men of average weight, the percentage of body fat is 15-29%. A woman, who has less muscle mass, is 25-30% fat. An estimate of body fat can be made by the following formula:

% Fat = 1.2 (BMI) + 0.23 (age) -10.8 (gender)* – 5.4
*gender = 1 for males or 0 for females

Example:
A woman age 30 with a BMI of 30 = (1.2(30)) + (0.23 (30)) – (0) – (5.4)
= (36 + 6.9 – 5.4)
% Fat = 37.5

With a BMI of 25 the same individual would have 31% body fat.

It may be surprising to know that women in the United States are not considered to have the highest prevalence of obesity. The eastern European countries, including Russia, Germany and Poland have a higher average BMI. BMI also varies among a country's population and is related to socioeconomic status, but exactly how it is related is unclear. Cross-culturally, women have an average of 38% body fat. Increase in food availability and decrease in exercise are among the factors responsible for the rapidly increasing BMI of the world's population. The problem is reaching epidemic proportions.

Is all obesity the same?

The region of the body in which the majority of fat is located distinguishes two distinct types of obesity. When there is an increased amount of fat located inside the abdomen around the internal organs (visceral fat) and in the upper half of the body, it is called an *android* pattern of obesity. Obesity mostly confined to the hips, legs and the lower body is called *gynoid* obesity. This dichotomy is also referred to as *centripetal* (central) obesity, versus *peripheral* (all round) obesity; or, as an apple or pear.

Figure 8-2 Types of Obesity

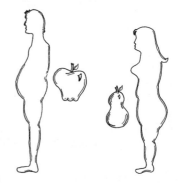

The easiest relatively reliable method of body distribution can be calculated as the *waist-hip ratio* (WHR). To calculate a WHR, place a measuring tape around the widest part of the hips and then around the narrowest portion of the waist, as a seamstress would do.

WHR = the waist measurement divided by the hip measurement of the waist.
Example WHR = 32 / 48 = 0 .67

A ratio of over 1 in men and over 0.85 in women identifies individuals with increased abdominal fat accumulation. Obese individuals with a ratio of less than 0.75 suggests gynoid obesity. Men and women with a waist diameter of over 39 inches are thought to be at increased risk.

This immediately emphasizes a sexual division of obesity and a relationship of androgens. (Figure 8-2) Android obesity carries a significantly greater risk of raised blood pressure (hypertension), abnormalities in blood lipids, and diabetes. There is some degree of population variation in WHR. Black women have been reported to be at less risk of cardiac disease and diabetes than are white women with the same WHR. Men and women of the same WHR have approximately the same risk of coronary artery disease.

Other anthropometric measurements have been used, such as skin fold thickness to identify medical risks. These are indirect measurements of visceral fat, which is best measured by magnetic resonance imaging (MRI). Body density can be measured by DEXA scan in a manner similar to that used for bone density.

What are the medical consequences of obesity?

My experience as a physician has included only one death due to an ectopic (tubal) pregnancy. I was a medical student at a time before rapid pregnancy tests and ultrasound were available when a gravely ill and very obese 35-year-old woman was admitted to the intensive care unit. It was not clear why she was spontaneously bleeding, only that the capacity for her blood to clot had been exhausted. After about twelve hours of valiant attempts to stop the bleeding she died. At autopsy it was discovered that she had a ruptured ectopic pregnancy. This was a needless death. Deep seated bias in the medical community, reluctance by some with obesity to seek medical care, and decreased efficiency of diagnostic techniques produce suboptimal care for obese patients. This may explain why the death rate from appendicitis in obese patients is twice that of non-obese patients.

Not until insurance companies started to analyze why people live longer (we know the motive here) did the relationship between obesity and increased death rate become so obvious.

- Overweight adults are three times more likely to have hypertension. One half of hypertension in the U.S. is related solely to obesity. A 1% decrease in weight is reported to cause a 1 mm Hg fall in systolic blood pressure and a 2 mm Hg decrease in diastolic pressure.
- Individuals with a BMI over 28 have a sixteen times increased risk of developing diabetes, About 90% of type 2 diabetes is weight related.
- A ten-fold increase in gallstones is reported in individuals with a BMI over 28.
- Weight related medical conditions are the second leading cause of death. In fact, there are an estimated 300,000 obesity-related deaths annually.

    Further studies demonstrate that health problems related to obesity touch not just the individual and her immediate family, but his employers and coworkers, as well. For example:
- In 1990, a U.S. study estimated that direct health costs of patients with BMIs greater than 29 represented nearly 7% of all direct health costs, the equivalent of over 50 billion dollars. The total cost is significantly higher.
- Over 502 million workdays are estimated to be lost due to health problems associated with obesity, and obesity increases the risk of a wide range of disease processes.

If one looks at the health costs of obesity, it's easy to see why physicians are so forceful about weight loss. Physicians, as well as health care providers in general, see these facts, but they fail in understanding the complexities underlying the causes of obesity and the difficulties in treating it. Our patients need our support for change, not blame for the past.

Skin	**Kidney**
Striae	Protein in urine
Acanthosis nigricans	Renal vein thrombosis
Increase hair growth /loss	**Bones, joints and muscle**
Heart	Chronic back pain
Myocardial infarction (heart attach)	Osteoarthritis
Sudden death (ventricular arrhythmia)	Rheumatoid arthritis
Coronary artery disease	Gout
Heart enlargement	Bone spurs
Angina pectoris	**Neoplasia** (women):
Congestive heart failure	Cancer of endometrium, breast, cervix,
Vascular system	ovary, gallbladder, and bile passages
Hypertension	**Reproductive and sexual function**
Stroke (cerebrovascular accident)	Obstetrics
Fluid retention (feet swelling)	toxemia, hypertension
Varicose veins, hemorrhoids	diabetes mellitus
Blood clots (thromboembolism)	prolonged labor, cesarean section
Respiratory system	excessive bleeding
Sleep apnea	growth retardation
Too many red blood cells (polycythemia)	death
Gastrointestinal system	Gynecology
Gallstones and gall bladder disease	irregular menstruation
Fatty liver	reduced fertility
Gastroesophageal reflux	uterine fibroids
Hormonal and metabolic functions	Decreased libido
Polycystic ovarian syndrome	Decreased orgasm
Diabetes mellitus	**Miscellaneous**
Hyperinsulinemia	Increased surgical / anesthetic risks
Gout (hyperuricemia)	Accident proneness
High cholesterol and blood lipids	Interference with diagnosis

What controls our eating behavior?

In 1940, the hypothalamus was established as the appetite control center. In rats, when the ventromedial nucleus (VMH), of the hypothalamus was experimentally altered, a loss of satiety (the sensation of being full or satisfied) was observed. When an adjacent area, the lateral hypothalamus, was altered, hyperphagia (overeating) occurred. This led to the "dual center" theory, with the VMH as the *satiety center* and the lateral hypothalamus as the *hunger center*. The implication of this theory is that an imbalance could lead to eating in the presence of fullness. Overeating could be caused by heightened sensations traveling from the brain to the hypothalamus after viewing very appealing food to send the message—"There's always room for dessert."

The VMH of the hypothalamus, which controls energy expenditures, is adjacent to the *arcuate nucleus*, which is the pulse generator for hormones that control reproductive function. How the body and brain send signals (neurotransmitters) to the VMH remains a hot bed of research. The VMH may be the site of action of appetite suppressants such as amphetamines, and so has become the target for new anti-obesity drugs that inhibit the uptake of serotonin. Some individuals may be programmed to eat too much, while others may have an abnormality in metabolism resulting in altered signals to the

VMH. Additional areas of research including insulin resistance and the obesity gene are presented in Chapter 3.

Why do some gain weight and others lose on the same diet?

A longstanding issue among scientists and clinicians is the relative contribution of genetics (inheritance) versus environment (acquired) in the origin of obesity. Obesity is commonly recognized as a *multifactorial* disease. Many similarities are found between obesity and PCOS.

It is all too obvious that for some, gaining weight is easy while weight loss is a struggle. Still, it is well substantiated that all will lose weight if the caloric intake falls below 1200 kcal a day. However, this may be at the expense of muscle, making the value of such an approach highly questionable.

Obesity results from a positive energy balance, and eating habits (food intake) can be learned and unlearned. A clear inherited susceptibility exists toward a positive energy balance. Overall, 25-40% of BMI and 50% of fat distribution is under genetic control and thus inherited and beyond our control. There is both a genetic basis for obesity as well as a genetic basis for weight gain, and these are not necessarily the same. In one study, a high fat diet produced weight gain only in obese subjects who had obese parents. The old theories that "fat people just eat too much," are falling by the wayside.

What makes us <u>over</u>eat?

Food tastes good. While sugars are pleasing to the palate, their consumption leads to appetite suppression, hypoglycemia, and then an increase in appetite. Sugars have an addictive effect. A preference for sweet and fat mixtures has been observed in obese women. Fat tastes good. In fact, fat tastes best. Fat has a delightful feel in the mouth and is considered the most pleasurable of all foods. Commercial food producers, especially those in the fast food industry, have not been beyond capitalizing on this phenomenon. Fast food is addictive. The energy dense fat-carbohydrate mix of fast food is guaranteed to have you queuing up for more special sauce.

Availability. We no longer have to hunt or gather our food because a pizza is only a phone call away. There are massive repositories called supermarkets, which contain every imaginable food item, not to mention the "all you can eat mega bar" at a local steak house. The fridge is the greatest place in the house, except maybe the bedroom or TV room. Why shouldn't we indulge in something so pleasurable and so easy?

Differences in perception. A study was performed in

Reasons We Overeat

- Enjoyable tastes, aromas and textures
- Availability
- Perception and sensitivity
- Social and environmental cues
- Altered energy balance regulation
- Food as a coping mechanism

which obese and thin individuals were placed alone in a room with a chair, a table, a lamp and a picture on the wall. After a few minutes, they were escorted into another room and asked to describe the contents of the first room. Thin individuals responded directly and without embellishment about what they saw: a chair, a table, a desk, etc. Their heavier counterparts were more likely to reply in much more detail: an oak chair with a forest green leather seat, a brass lamp with a beige textured shade, a landscape print of the mountains, and so on. Maybe obese individuals are more sensitive to environmental cues and to the art of food than are their thinner counterparts. Obese individuals may truly enjoy food more. It may be true that some live to eat, while others eat to live.

Social and environmental cues. It has been suggested that obesity originates with overfeeding in infancy, although support for this hypothesis is weak. Certainly our dietary training begins at an early age. Cues to eat are many and varied. We are often placed in environments where we eat by habit or for social acceptance. Environmental conditioning can be unlearned. (See behavioral modification below).

Disorders in regulation of energy balance. Overeating may be due to a defective mechanism in the body's recognition or utilization of energy stores. This could be a genetic or acquired defect of the hunger and satiety control centers in the hypothalamus. Alternatively, the control mechanisms may also be disrupted by controllable metabolic conditions such as hyperinsulinemia, hyperglycemia, or hyperlipidemia.

It may be much simpler than this. Too long between meals and hunger can result in overeating. A very common problem is that very little is eaten throughout the day, then the feed bag is tied on at night. Not only must meals be frequent, there must be balanced allocation of fat, protein and carbohydrates as described later.

Food as comfort. Most people have that special food that is saved for special times. Most comfort foods are very energy dense. While they give a temporary pleasurable feeling of satiety, the rebound on the body can be substantial. It seems that a coping system so widely used with good feelings would have a better justification by the body.

How are calories used?

Energy funds are required for every business transaction of the body. Using our bank account analogy above and the chart of accounts in figure 8-3, we can easily see that our discretionary funds, those available by increasing our physical activity, make up a small percentage of the total.

The body uses energy in three ways:

Resting metabolic rate (RMR) RMR is the energy necessary for the basic operations of the body's business, for example, respiration, mental activity, etc. RMR is by far the largest drain on the body's energy resources. The RMR accounts for about 50% of total calories used per day. Individuals at the same weight but different body compositions will have different RMRs. Although pound for pound muscle may have a higher RMR, an obese person will have a total RMR that exceeds that of the thinner individual.

Figure 8-3 Energy Expenditure

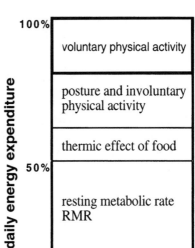

RMR is age related. Some decline is due to loss of muscle mass due to inactivity, but the younger can handle energy dense foods and more food at single settings. They tend to store more energy as glycogen and less as fat. It could be that the RMR, which may be genetically determined, is both the principle alteration in women with PCOS and the factor hardest to change.

Thermic effect of food (TEF) TEF is the dietary energy used in the consumption of food. The body is not the perfect machine. It takes energy to make energy. The body can lose weight merely by the consumption of food. Foods vary in energy required for their breakdown. Solids require more energy to consume than do liquids. Large meals use more energy than do small ones. Non-dieting obese individuals may have an elevated TEF, but this is offset by a decrease in physical activity. In obese individuals calorie reduction is accompanied by TEF reduction. This may be partly responsible for the poor weight loss they report, despite caloric restriction.

Fat takes very little, carbohydrates require an intermediate amount, and proteins use the highest amount of energy to be metabolized. Triglycerides require the least energy. Saturated animal fats are utilized with less energy than are unsaturated animal fats. For example, the body uses more energy to process and utilize beans than it does to process and use french fries. Processed food typically needs less energy than do raw foods. One report states that fructose, the sugar of fruits, while containing the same calories as glucose, requires more energy for its breakdown. This effect is less obvious when fructose and glucose are consumed as parts of a mixed meal. Although this is an unsubstantiated scientific finding, it is considered gospel in some popular diet plans.

Armed with the concept of TEF, many "diet spinners" have attempted to sell the concept that one food will "burn," "bust," or "block" another type of food. The scientific evidence is just not there. Since the amount of the total body expenditure for TEF is only about 10%, it is unlikely that major alteration can be made. The concept should not be completely dismissed: increasing foods that cause a higher TEF will help in weight control.

Physical activity Exercise is the third way that the body utilizes energy. This expense account might be called the discretionary fund. It is relatively small compared to the BMR, and although the voluntary amount of physical activity is small, it is an aspect that we can control. Or can we?

Clearly an association exists between body mass index and physical activity—with the exception of trained athletes, the higher the BMI, the lower the physical activity. What is less clear is whether obesity causes a decrease in activity or is a result of it. The number of cars per household and the number of hours spent viewing television are related to weight gain. However, selling a car hardly ever results in weight loss. How great it would be if it were only that simple.

The amount of energy expended depends on the type and duration of the exercise, as well as on the exerciser. After vigorous exercise, the metabolic rate remains elevated. An additional 200-kcal loss can be earned by two hours of strenuous exercise. Exercise can be in the form of strength, flexibility, and aerobic cardiac conditioning. Best health can be achieved with a combination of all three, but anaerobic exercise is the most efficient method of burning calories.

Exercise—How long, how often, how hard?

If you are exercising on your own, start slow and continue often. If exercise is new to you, it's best to seek professional advice or to join a group. Smokers often say, "Quitting is easy. I've done it a thousand times." The same can be said for exercise programs. Supervised group activity has substantial benefits, but the dropout rate is high after several months. That's okay, if you continue to exercise at home. Home-based, self–supervised activities are more often continued than is participation in organized classes. Compliance is further improved when the exercise is low intensity and the exerciser periodically checks with an exercise professional for progress checks. Social support, especially from a mate and family members is critical. Often they could benefit from a little extra activity as well. Your plan—a plan for life—has to be comfortable to you.

Some good news for those exercising to reduce is that while an individual at 130 pounds will use only 70 calories by walking a mile, at 220 pounds the loss will be 115 kcal. Additionally, changing from walking to running only increases the energy loss by about 50% but may cause knee and back problems. Walk, and walk fast, but don't run.

In discussing this issue with a recent patient, she told me that she lived a half-mile from her mailbox. My suggestion was that every day for the rest of life that she would commit to walking for the mail. This is a readily identifiable objective that could easily become an enjoyable routine.

Do I have to exercise?

Evidence is increasing that losing weight takes less total activity at a less strenuous level than previously thought. The key is low intensity and prolonged activity. It can be hard to find enough leisure time for this activity. Try to incorporate increased physical activity into everyday life. Just rising from a sitting to standing position can have significant impact on weight if repetitively performed. Just being "up and about" uses twice the number of calories as sitting. Just as dieting can be excessive, so can exercise, and it can end up as a detriment to health and well-being.

Tips for the Non-Exerciser
- Move, except to the kitchen during TV commercials.
- Take a distant parking place, which also may save your car from bangs.
- Take the stairs.
- Plant a garden.
- Walk around the yard after dinner, stop to smell the flowers, or pull a weed.
- Look for a hobby that requires standing or an increased activity over just sitting.
- Walk while on the phone.
- Walk in the mall and shop. (Shop doesn't mean buy).
- Baby-sit.
- Walk to see an office colleague or neighbor instead of phoning.

Physical activity has a number of positive health benefits regardless of BMI and age.

Benefits of Exercise
- High levels of physical activity protect against obesity.
- Endurance exercise without dieting results in moderate fat and weight loss.
- Regular exercise is a good predictor of long-term weight control.
- Energy expenditures are increased after the exercise, resulting in additional calories used.
- Exercise is partially protective against risks of smoking.
- Physical activity reduces medical complications of hypertension, diabetes, and cancer.
- Quality of sleep is improved after exercise.
- Exercise increases sexual appetite (libido) and performance.
- Exercise increases endorphins, the "feel good" hormones.
- Increased physical activity reduces premenstrual syndrome.
- Exercise helps the pain of endometriosis.
- Exercise increases high-density lipoproteins (HDL), and good cholesterol.
- Exercise reduces bone loss.
- Physical activity improves self-image.
- Mild depression is lessened, possibly leading to less eating.

Does increased physical activity stimulate appetite?

No. When overweight individuals increase their activity, energy intake does not increase. The same is not true for persons of normal weight, who tend to compensate for energy loss due to exercise by eating more. Increase in activity results in greater weight loss than dieting alone. Individuals who exercise have been shown to be more compliant with calorie restriction.

Should I diet?

This is the central issue of this chapter. To some it is the central theme of their life. In the above sections a strong case was made for the negative medical consequences of obesity. An equally strong case can be made for the non-diet approach that involves increase in physical activity and behavioral modification. Still this approach involves healthy eating which for most with a weight problem is the same as dieting. Very quickly we can get tied up in semantics. To appease all let's say that we are "fighting for fitness" or if you like, attempting to reach a "metabolic harmony". To establish a common starting point, let's make several general assumptions about dieting:

Weight loss diets
- Make you hungry
- Focus on food
- If rigorously followed, will result in some weight loss
- Are temporary
- Result in rebound weight gain
- And in the end, FAIL

In conclusion, "DIETS" DON'T WORK. Now that we are straight on the crucial point, let's start building.

To lose weight?

Perhaps it seems hypocritical to discuss weight loss now. I know that there is a fine line between good nutrition and weight loss, a line that will be pushed in the remainder of this chapter. Still for many, establishing a plan for good nutrition will be synonymous with weight loss and is the most easily qualified and identifiable outcome of nutrition intervention.

Is it good nutrition or dieting?

Diets and dieting have unfortunate connotations. We all have a diet. It's just that for some of us our diet is poor. The shift should be away from a goal of dieting for weight loss and toward adopting an eating plan based on good nutrition. True, for many, good nutrition will promote weight loss, but it does much more: Good nutrition fosters good health. The American Dietetic Association and the American College of Sports Medicine support this stance. The thin PCOS patient may benefit from good nutrition just as much as the obese. Alteration in diet should be only one part of the foundation of good health. Also included should be physical activity, alteration in substance abuse and mental health. It's all connected. The major parameter of success is not weight loss, but reduction in disease risk.

Behavior modification

Along with the desire to reproduce, to sleep and to avoid pain, eating is one of our primal driving forces. Many obese individuals are obsessed with food. They eat to relax, eat for comfort, and eat to celebrate. The next helping of food is thought about before the last bite is finished. They are also obsessed with weight loss. There is an estimated $33 billion annually spent on weight loss.

Our present cultural factors also are very strong in influencing food choices. We live in an environment of low energy and high food availability. Individual lifestyles make it much easier to "grab a burger." The power lunch, or office workers ordering out, can force one into a diet that might not ordinarily be chosen. Kids are encouraged, not discouraged, into bad eating habits by being told to "eat your spinach and then you can have dessert," or "if you do your homework, we will go to McDonald's." We also value food as a social ritual to express a relationship, or to celebrate an occasion.

Figure 8-5 Behavior

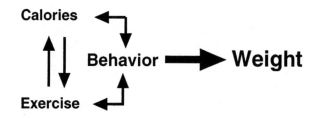

It is a disappointing fact that most dieters return to their previous weight within five years, regardless of the diet plan used. *It is behavior modification that will determine whether weight loss can be sustained.* Plan to be one of those who will beat the odds. To do this requires a reengineering in the way we think about food, the way we eat, and the way we spend our time not eating. Some behavior changes are associated with altering calorie intake, while other behavior changes involve how we use the calories. It might be easier than you think. Behavior can be <u>unlearned</u>.

25 Tips to Healthy Eating
- Be aware of how you are presently eating.
- Shop for food from a list and shop after meals.
- Understand good nutrition, read labels.
- Drive by, not through, "fast food" restaurants.
- Watch ready-to-eat foods, some are incredibly caloric.
- Decrease energy dense foods.
- Remember, the diet section of the market is the produce counter.
- Set a realistic caloric intake for yourself.
- Understand your calorie needs and use—then stop counting calories.
- Schedule meals, don't get so hungry that you must eat.
- Reduce non-hunger eating, and learn to decline the offer of food.
- Don't go to parties hungry, avoid grazing.
- Be aware that you are eating; limit eating while working or watching TV.
- Eat three balanced meals; plan snacks.

- Fill, but don't heap one plate; don't take seconds; leave
  a small portion.
- Eat slowly; stop and wait for a fullness; avoid over fullness.
- Keep serving dishes off the table; use smaller dishes.
- Don't cook too much, and don't save leftovers.
- Save a salad for the end of the meal to top you up.
- Don't eat after 8 PM, one <u>small</u> snack is OK.
- Drink at least eight glasses of water a day.
- Make small changes.
- Keep a food diary; write a cookbook.
- Accept a set back; have an occasional binge and really enjoy it.
- Work with a coach, especially a skilled nutritionist.

How do I start?

Self-assessment is the first step. It is always surprising how many will say that they are desperate to lose weight. "Doctor I will do anything." In reality, they will do very little, or they start too aggressively and quickly become discouraged and stop. Truly decide that this will be "the first day for the rest of your life." The aim of intervention is to produce long-term lifestyle changes to optimize health and self-image. This is a tall order, so that's the reason it takes so much education and planning. To be sustainable, your plan has to be realistic, easy, relatively quickly rewarding, and in keeping with your lifestyle. There will be slips; get back up and back on track. Remember that you are in it for the long run.

There are two levels to a good plan—corrective and maintenance. In the corrective portion, more attention must be paid to each of the areas of weight loss, physical activity and self-image. See the "How do I do it?" at the end of the chapter

Weight Loss Facts
- There is no magic diet, pill, or exercise program that
  cures obesity.
- Obesity kills. The chance of an adverse health event
  increases with BMI. View weight loss as a necessary
  life-saving measure.
- The adverse health consequences of obesity are additive and
  may not be fully reversible.
- You, not your health care professional, are responsible for
  the change.
- To lose weight takes more than the wish to do so.
- To keep weight off is harder than losing weight.
- Set realistic goals.
- Every day for your entire life will be a renewed struggle. It
  does get easier with time.
- Since it took years to put on the weight, it may take years to
  take it off.
- Weight starts to fall after age 50.

Will I ever be my ideal weight?

Forget about the ideal body weight! I know this is heresy, but in PCOS patients, normal weight and the body weight that insurance and American culture has mandated as ideal will never be the same. A goal to reach such a weight is doomed to fail from the start. Furthermore, for physicians to try to impose these restrictions is disheartening, if not punitive. It is necessary and it is time, for every woman with PCOS who is reading this book to make the best out of a bad turn of fate!

Strive for *metabolic fitness*. Rather than seeking an "ideal" weight, a more realistic final expectation is to break and maintain weight under 200 pounds, or to achieve a 20% weight reduction, whichever is the greater loss. With a 10% weight reduction, there has been shown to be a marked improvement in blood glucose, lipid levels, hypertension, and menstrual function. In fact, a reasonable goal may be to consider that it may take the same number of years to return to a target weight as it did to gain from the target to the present weight.

Do not expect overnight success with weight loss. Often fat loss may be noticed less on the bathroom scales and more in the compliments of those around you. Fat loss may be disguised by weight distribution. Pounds may go quickly, they may go slowly, but they will go. Even if weight is not lost, be comfortable that you have moved toward metabolic fitness. Work on yourself to feel good (well), about the work on yourself.

Are all foods created equal?

Certainly, a calorie is a calorie; it doesn't matter how you get it. Foods differ in their *density* of calories. Fat has nine calories per gram as opposed to protein and carbohydrates, which have four calories in each gram. Fatty foods are very *energy dense*. Studies have shown that as fat increases so does calorie consumption. Too much fat, or too many calories causes be a marked insulin release and post meal depression. Too little and you remain hungry.

The book *Sugar Busters* has popularized a concept of glycemic index and to a lesser extent *The Zone* presents the same concept. The glycemic index is a measure of how high blood sugar rises in response to given amounts of various foods. This is based on relatively shaky ground and differences may be trivial. For instance it is now known that simple sugars (sucrose) stimulate the same changes in blood sugars as complex sugars (starches). It seems that insulin response is based more on total calories consumed than on the glycemic index of a particular food. So enjoy your baked potato— just limit the sour cream, butter, bacon bits, and cheddar cheese.

A balanced diet of vegetables, fruits, whole grains, beans, potatoes, pasta, modest amounts of lower fat dairy products, chicken, and lean meat still offer the greatest variety and so tends to be the overall favorite.

How many calories?

The daily caloric need is estimated to be about 12-15 kcal per pound depending on activity level. At a weight of 200 pounds, 2400 - 3000 calories are used maintaining this weight. Theoretically, if there is a reduction to 2000 calories a day, 1-2 pounds will be lost a week. Remember that there is 3500 kcal in a pound of fat. Beware: Theory and truth often differ.

The American Dietetic Association recommends a calorie level of no less than ten times your desired weight. This translates into getting at least 1400 calories a day, regardless. Calorie intake should be 1800 to 2200 kcal per day, depending on previous intake. If a balanced diet is maintained, calories are consistently restricted by 200-500 kcal/day, and exercise is modestly increased, weight will be lost.

Very low calorie diets don't work.

Health care providers and hospitals were quick to get on the wagon of the moderate and severe calorie restriction diets. They appeared to work and were a sizable source of previously untapped income. Then came the bad news. They really didn't work. The two and five year success was miserable. In 1990, a U.S. House of Representatives subcommittee—the same one that sent legislation about reporting success rates for in vitro fertilization centers—charged the weight loss industry with fraudulent advertising after they failed to demonstrate long-term weight loss in their clients.

There are still scattered plans around. You can always tell by impressive, friendly advertising and high expense of the program, especially the meals. Most follow a 1000-1200 kcal a day diet. These diets can produce a 10-15% weight loss in 10-20 weeks, but unless there is a maintenance program, such as the above modest caloric restricting, the weight is easily gained back, producing a yo-yo effect. These approaches may be worse for fertility than obesity is!

Very low calorie diets have been associated with thinning of skin, hair loss, and cold intolerance. In diets where the protein was derived from gelatin or collagen, deaths have occurred. If a protein source such as egg albumin or milk-soy is used, the diet appears safe for most. Diets under 800 kcal a day or long-term fasts are clearly dangerous.

Millions of book buyers can't be wrong—can they?

The first diet book was published before 1900. Since then, over 25,000 different diets have been created. These diets claim a "new secret", less hunger, more calories burned, and more weight lost. Incredibly, most of them use the term "easy." Few meet scientific scrutiny, although they typically claim they are based on scientific principle. Still, there must be something positive about any diet plan that is responsible for the selling of several million copies and a place on the New York Times Best Seller list for weeks. Are we really that gullible? The perfect diet may still be out there, but if it is, it hasn't been found. Meanwhile, weight loss is not easy and no "fad" diet has ever totally met its claims.

First let's look at what diet plans tend to have in common.

- *All "popular" weight loss diets involve restriction of calories as their primary method of action,* even if they say they don't. Most vary between 1400 and 1800 kcal per day. Virtually all-obese individuals will lose weight on this regimen.
- No diet has stood up to intense scientific scrutiny in controlled trials and there has been no head to head comparison as to which may be best.
- All are touted as "breakthroughs"; all are self-serving with glowing reviews of their own success.
- Some of the menu plans are very clever and rival the gourmet cookbooks. The menu ideas are sometimes the best part of the book.

How do the diet plans (books) compare?

American Diabetic Association: Year 2000 Nutrition Recommendations for Individuals with Diabetes.

Type: Balanced non-diet focused calorie intake.

Premise: Based on U.S. Government guidelines and six food groups. Uses exchange portions.

Method: 10%-20% protein, less than 10% saturated fat and less than 10 % from polyunsaturated fat. This leaves 60-70% to be divided between monounsaturated fats and carbohydrates. No differences in blood sugars are found when simple sugars (sucrose) are compared with complex carbohydrates (starches) such as potatoes and pasta. For weight loss, the ADA recommends a daily reduction of 250-500 calories from calculated food intake history. Individual foods are neither good nor bad and all foods can fit. They recognize that many are refractory to weight loss.

My take: It would be trendy to say the establishment is wrong; they often are. It would be foolish and insulting not to listen to such a large and respected organization as the ADA. There is no dietary plan that is more broadly adopted than the ADA's. This is a good place to start and I suggest a little heavier on the fruit and vegetable side with decrease in energy-dense foods.

Atkins Diet: *Dr. Atkins' New Diet Revolution* by Robert Atkins.

Type: Very low carbohydrates, high fat, high protein.

Premise: Obesity occurs because of a metabolic imbalance, not overeating. Carbohydrates alone cause obesity. Claims not to be calorie restrictive.

Method: Minimal carbohydrates. The objective is ketosis.

My take: Ketosis is bad and this diet is even worse. It seems to work and many lose weight, but it seems the very antithesis of health. Although it states that it is not calorie restrictive, it is. Long term use would seem difficult. It would not seem to be a good plan for PCOS and cannot be used when planning for pregnancy.

Carbohydrate Addicts Diet: *The Carbohydrate Addict's LifeSpan Program: A Personalized Plan for Becoming Slim, Fit and Healthy in Your 40s, 50s, 60s and Beyond* by Drs. Richard and Rachael Heller.

> Type: Low carbohydrate
>
> Premise: Carbohydrates boost insulin that causes weight gain.
>
> Method: Eating two low-carbohydrate meals and one "reward" meal per day.
>
> My take: Advice is inconsistent. Food restriction can lead people to binge eating.

Choose to Lose: Dr. Ron Gor and Nancy Gor.

Pritikin Principle: by Robert Pritikin.

Eat More, Weigh Less: by Dean Ornish.

> Type: Low fat (about 10-20 g) High in carbohydrates.
>
> Premise: Cutting fat is the key to weight loss.
>
> Method: Stingy with fats. Shift away from energy dense foods. Increase fiber.
>
> My take: Quite healthy. Especially good for individuals with elevated lipids. Unclear whether increased carbohydrates may increase insulin. The Gors are especially generous with calories, about 2200 daily. Ornish stresses lifestyle changes including exercise and meditation

The Insulin Control Diet: *The Type 2 Diabetes Diet Book: The Insulin Control Diet: Your Fat Can Make You Thin,* by Calvin Ezrin, MD, and Robert E. Kowalski.

> Type: Low carbohydrate, low protein, very low calorie.
>
> Premise: Decrease insulin, lose fat.
>
> Method: Eating one or two low-carbohydrate meals and one "reward" meal per day.
>
> My take: About 650 calories daily for women. Much too low in this diet. Cannot be recommended for pregnancy or long term use. Rebound weight gain likely.

Protein Power: *Protein Power: The High-Protein/Low Carbohydrate Way to Lose Weight, Feel Fit, and Boost Your Health—In Just Weeks!* by Michael R. Eades, MD, and Mary Dan Eades, MD.

> Type: Low carbohydrate.
>
> Premise: Discusses hunter-gatherers eating fish, meat, berries, fruits and vegetables, and limiting what early humans never knew existed—grains, refined sugars, and other concentrated starches.
>
> Method: Eating one or two low-carbohydrate meals and one "reward" meal per day.
>
> My take: High in fat. In some ways more like the Atkins diet with more fruits and vegetables.

Slim-fast™:

      Type: Meal replacement balanced calorie restriction.

      Premise: Limiting calories in one or two meals daily with a "sensible" third will provide good nutrition while reducing total calories intake.

      Method: Well formulated, balanced nutrition "meal in a can" for about 220 calories.

      My take: I like SlimFast™ and think it is a healthy alternative. The benefits include not having to think about what to have for lunch or breakfast, its cheap, it's easy, it's relatively filling, and several hundred calories can be saved each day by making a single lunch substitute. Try different brands and flavors to suit your preference. This approach can be combined with almost any other diet or maintenance program. It is difficult to have any meal for 200-250 calories and certainly beats two donuts.

Sugar Busters: *Sugar Busters! Cut Sugar to Trim Fat* by H. Leighton Steward et al.

      Type: Calorie restrictive, low carbohydrate (40%), fat (30%) protein (30%).

      Premise: Sugar is toxic. Obesity is from insulin overload. Certain foods have high glycemic index.

      Method: Good and bad foods based on glycemic index. Vegetables, fruit and grains are stressed.

      My take: Goes off on several tangents, lacks scientific credibility for many of its concepts. A little higher on fats. Limits many really good foods like carrots, bananas, pasta and white potatoes without substantiation. I believe they can be added back without seriously compromising many of the book's principles. Reasonably good diet for insulin resistance. Completely satisfactory for pregnancy planning. I like this diet because it stresses good dietary practices, a life long commitment, (and possibly, because of its Southern food).

Volumetrics: by Barbara Rolls and Robert Barnett.

      Type: Lower fat, balanced calorie restriction.

      Premise: Eat less, eat better.

      Method: Lower calorie dense foods, calorie reduction, decrease energy dense foods, and increase bulk.

      My take: Balanced.

The Zone: *A Week in the Zone* and others by Barry Sears.

      Type: calorie restrictive, low carbohydrate (40%), fat (30%) protein (30%)

      Premise: Carbohydrates cause obesity. Don't count calories, count protein.

Methods: Also uses glycemic index. Advises against typical ADA food pyramid and stresses vegetables and fruit. Fat is reduced, grains are unnatural foods for humans and should be limited. Eating the right foods puts one into the right insulin zone. (10g of fat, 20g of protein and 30g of carbohydrates at each meal).

My take: Easy to read and comprehensive, balanced diet plan. Smacks of a real diet with significant calorie restriction. Tries to scientifically justify what amounts to a low calorie diet. If you lose weight on this diet, it is not because the ideal mix has been reached, it is because calories have been cut in half, and that should work well. I can't imagine a life in the "Zone" for most. Unconventional to mention ecosanoids, which I agree are derived from fatty acids and are the basic backbone of some hormones, though I never thought these had very much to do with dieting metabolism. Just OK for pregnancy planning and would need more calories during pregnancy.

Low fat diet or low carbohydrate?

It really might not matter. The issue is not low fat or low carbohydrates, just low. The problem remains finding a nutrition plan that reduces calories without hunger, improves nutrition and is satisfying, and can be maintained tomorrow. The search is why millions of diet books are sold.

Because of their diuretic effect, low carbohydrate diets can cause an initially speedy loss of weight. The increase in ketones produced when stored fat is burned causes an increase in urination and salt loss. Also, low carbohydrate diets deplete glycogen stores–with each molecule of glycogen lost, three molecules of water are lost. Return to eating carbohydrates and the water weight comes back. Although low-fat diets have not clearly been shown to be superior to diets that simply reduce calories, they offer potential benefits to cardiovascular health and are recommended for individuals abnormal lipid levels. A 10% reduction of fat can translate into a 10-15 pound weight loss over a year. Many complain of hunger on low fat diets. High fat diets probably cause people to eat more calories, high protein diets less. Most would agree to reduce energy dense foods. Keep in mind that fat, protein, and carbohydrates have separate roles in metabolism and each is an important building block of sound nutrition.

Should I take vitamins, supplements?

In a balanced diet additional vitamin supplementation is unnecessary. They are necessary in diets that do not connote relatively large amounts of fruits and vegetables. The ADA reports that there is no known benefit from chromium replacement. Magnesium deficiency appears related to insulin resistance, carbohydrate intolerance and hypertension. It is rare to have a low magnesium level and replacement is not recommended. All women contemplating pregnancy should be taking an additional supplement of at least 400 mcg. of folic acid daily. Folic acid supplementation may have a positive benefit on PCOS and I often suggest use of 1 mg daily. Many women are iron deficient. Supplementation may be necessary. There may be a theoretical, but unproven, benefit of adding antioxidant, vitamin E.

What about fiber?

Fiber rich foods are less energy dense. High fiber diets are effective in the short term, but long-term compliance is a problem with some due to gastrointestinal disturbances including gas and loose frequent stools. Fiber can lower lipids, and reduce the risk of colon cancer. Fiber is of questionable benefit in reduction of blood glucose. Higher fiber intake is not mutually exclusive of other diet types. Many consume only 10-12 grams of fiber daily, while recommended amount is 25-30 grams daily. Additional fluid is needed for effectiveness of extra fiber.

Should calories be counted?

The answer to this question is yes, then no. Calories are a useful tool for education and training. Persistent counting of calories, however, is like infertility patients who continue to chart the temperature in search of ovulation. Calorie counting calls attention to the food and weight. Most calorie counters tend to alternate between denial and guilt. Calorie counting and hunger seem to be closely related. Watch portion size and hunger cues instead.

Are there really "diet" foods?

Many people use the new required nutrition information labels on food packaging to make decisions about which foods to purchase and use. This is helpful, but only if you are knowledgeable about what the terms on the labels mean.

Beware of all processed foods. The front of food containers may not give the whole truth, so look for the required nutritional information section on the back or side and read it carefully!

Common Labeling Misrepresentations

Foods labeled as *fat free* and *low fat* are not the same as *low calorie*. In these foods, carbohydrates replace fat. Low fat products may be very caloric. Read labels!

Beware products labeled *lyte, light* and *lite*. Some of the sugar may have been removed, but composition of these products varies greatly. Often these terms mean light in color or consistency. All oils have 14 g of fat per tablespoon.

Used as part of a low calorie diet. Any food can be a part of a low calorie diet. A chocolate sundae can be a part of a diet, as long as an appropriate adjustment is made in other foods.

Low cholesterol does not mean *low fat*. Polyunsaturated oil may have fats that are preferable, but the calories will be the same as other fats.

I want a new drug!

So do we all. When I was a young teen in the days of Dr. Feelgood, my dad had been prescribed amphetamines for weight loss. When he asked if his son could also use the medications, the physician replied, "Sure." For four days I didn't eat and for four nights I didn't sleep. My dad and I had a bonding experience as we spent the night hours talking incessantly about endless subjects. I lost about twenty pounds, and when I came down, it was horrible. Now, you might be able to obtain a similar experience through a street vendor. Many states prohibit the dispensing of amphetamines (dextroamphetamine, metamphetamine) and rightly so. Additionally, the FDA has banned over 100 ingredients from consideration as "diet products." These include caffeine, alcohol, dextrose and guar gum. The FDA is attempting to remove the following devices from the market. These devices range from ineffective to dangerous:

- Electrical muscle stimulators
- Sunglasses that purport curbing the desire to eat
- "Magic" earrings that are customized to fit and reported to stimulate acupuncture sites.

The FDA also warns consumers to immediately question any drug, product or service that has claims containing the following words:

ancient	amazing	breakthrough
easy	effortless	exotic
exclusive	guaranteed	magic
miracle	miraculous	mysterious
never before	new discovery	secret

Beware and avoid the following "weight loss wonders:"

- Benzocaine (Slim-Mints™, Diet Ayds™) these agents contain a local anesthetic and alter taste perception
- Diet patches
- Fat-blockers that absorb fat and mechanically interfere with absorption
- Starch-blockers that impede starch digestion and can cause gastrointestinal side-effects
- "Magnet" diet pills that "flush out fat"
- Bulk fillers that are fiber based and absorb fluid and give the feeling of fullness
- Guar gum (Cal-Ban™) is a complex sugar that absorbs water and has caused intestinal obstruction
- Glucomannan the "weight loss secret of the Orient"
- Spirulina, an algae that has been proven ineffective

A clinically useful drug for obesity treatment should have the following characteristics:

- Demonstrated effect on reducing weight and weight-dependent disease
- Tolerable and/or transient side-effects
- No addictive properties
- Maintained efficacy when used long-term
- No major problems after years of administration
- Known mechanisms of action(s)
- Reasonable cost

No currently available agents meet these criteria. Fat melting pills don't exist (yet).. If the medication is ever developed, it will be worth millions or billions of dollars to the pharmaceutical industry. It is unlikely that it will be purchased through a television advertisement "not available in stores." It is unlikely that it will be available in health food stores.

Some would question whether medication use should ever be used. I'll not go quite that far, but it is not primary therapy and should probably be limited to the initial stages of therapy. Pharmacological therapy can be very useful and can give an extra push to the effort of weight loss. Drug therapy may be considered part of a long-term management strategy for obesity. But drug therapy, like diet and exercise, must be individualized. It should be used in conjunction with diet and lifestyle management, and should only be used under medical supervision. Most consider maximum weight loss will be 10-20%. There are only two drugs that consistently have been shown to cause long-term weight loss, sibutramine (Meridia^{TM}) and orlistat (Xenical^{TM}) (see Chapter 17).

Bottom line, **unless there are also lifestyle changes**, my advice would be don't bother with weight loss drugs.

Should surgery be considered?

Gastric stapling is an effective way of markedly reducing weight in the severely obese (BMI ≥35). Surgical treatment has been effective in permanent weight loss and is estimated after four years to be less expensive than other treatments. Substantial weight loss of more than 20 kg. generally occurs within twelve months of the operation, although some weight is regained within five to fifteen years. Some studies indicate that surgery may prevent progression of impaired glucose tolerance to type 2 diabetes and lessen the risk of other obesity-related diseases. Quality of life measures, including employability, median wage, sick days, social interaction, mobility, self-image, assertiveness and depression are also improved in the majority of patients after anti-obesity surgery.

On the negative side, this is a very drastic step and should be taken only after all of the more conservative measures have failed. In general, most PCOS patients should not use, and do not qualify for this therapy. It may be an inappropriate therapy for PCOS, but this has not been evaluated. Dramatic weight losses can have an adverse effect on fertility.

The effectiveness of surgery is in either markedly reducing the size of the stomach's capacity, gastric plication, or causing a malabsorption of food. "Dumping syndrome," which is characterized by diarrhea after eating, is common. Regardless, the physiologic outcome is unnatural. The surgery itself carries a high risk. Laparoscopic techniques are increasingly used, which may be less aggressive and associated with less risk. Individuals considering surgery should be completely informed, highly motivated, and in otherwise excellent health. Only surgeons who are well experienced with the procedures, and have previous good success rates should perform surgery.

Liposuction?

Liposuction should be considered for cosmetic purposes only. It is hardly an easy, quick fix.

Alternative medicine?

A number of non-conventional therapies have been promoted as effective in the management of weight, but there is very little objective research to substantiate these claims. (See Chapter 17). Uncontrolled trials of acupuncture and yoga have shown a beneficial effect in assisting weight loss, and some contend that support from psychoanalysts can produce favorable weight loss and weight maintenance in their patients. There is no evidence that hypnotherapy is any more effective in the long-term than the usual diet and behavior modification programs. However, hypnosis may improve self-image, and possibly help patients adhere to a prescribed diet.

Are there problems associated with weight loss?

Losing weight does not always produce only good effects. A 10-20 pound weight loss has been associated with nearly a 50% increase in the risk of gall bladder disease. Bone density is typically increased in obese patients and reduced after weight loss. Cycles of weight loss and gain can increase cardiovascular morbidity and mortality. Fertility may be hampered by the stress of weight loss. Self-esteem takes a dive when weight is gained back. A greater loss of control is also experienced when weight is regained.

How do I do it?

First, you *don't do it alone!* Second, *only you can do it.* Establishing a new healthy eating and exercise plan—one designed to produce metabolic balance—is a five-step process.

Step 1: Pre-evaluation

Medical assessment. To be told by a health professional to go home and lose weight is completely unacceptable. If this is suggested to you, seek another physician. The physician is usually the entry point into medical care. He or she is usually the chief operations officer who can help evaluate medical status and expedite intervention. There should be frank informed discussion and mutually agreed upon assessment of where you are, where you should be and how to get there.

Evaluation should include:

Complete medical history with emphasis on weight gain pattern, exclusion of coexisting medical problems, family history of weight, hormonal/fertility problems, and medical illnesses.

Physical examination noting BMI, WHR, blood pressure.

Laboratory evaluation of blood chemistries for fasting, and probably stimulated glucose/insulin levels, fasting blood lipids and endocrine testing. Specific tests have been described in Chapter 5.

Assessment of support systems. A personal support system should include specially trained professionals and family involvement. Many times a partner is also obese and may be in even more danger and at higher risk than you are. His obesity is also dangerous to the family unit.

Dietary assessment. Often a seven-day calendar in which all food is recorded without an attempt to diet may serve to identify specific patterns that may not be self-evident, and may be easily changed. Assess not only what you eat, but also how you eat. In addition, attention should be paid to previous dieting experiences, interventions that have worked and why they failed.

Activity assessment. How much exercise do you get? How much can you exercise given your schedule? What do you like to do? What don't you like to do?

Step 2: Design a program

Each plan must be individualized. There is no standard diet. Personal preferences must be considered. Nutritional planning should take into account types of foods, meal size, meal frequency and meal timing. Just because we all have a long experience with eating does not mean that we know how to properly eat. Work with a skilled nutritionist, usually a registered dietician. This individual can be your teacher and coach. When lab results indicate need, consider drug therapy to help initiate the loss and correct metabolic disturbances such as hyperinsulinemia and hyperlipidemia.

Set measures of success. Be realistic. Set goals of what you think you can obtain, not what you want to obtain. Set yourself up for success, not failure.

Step 3: Intervene

Normalize food intake. Change eating behavior. Eat healthy. Continue to learn about food and how *your* body responds.

Increase activity. Start low; go slow.

Improve self/body image. Seldom is this done alone. It's a strange thing—we call it self-image, but it is really what we perceive others think about us. Working with a skilled mental health professional can provide that outside person looking in to help you along the way. Few like the idea of seeing a psychologist, however much it might help. Sometimes a physician can fill this role, other times a nutritionist or exercise specialist. (See Chapter 10).

Step 4: Evaluate progress

Markers must be established to evaluate success. In our PCOS patients on metformin we utilize a wide range subjective and objective criteria of success: establishment of regular menstruation, weight loss, feelings, medication tolerance and feelings of well-being, and an improvement in metabolic parameters such as lipids and insulin. It is uncommon to not make progress in some areas.

Keep a journal. Journals are great learning tools and can help in the process. Record not only the foods you eat, but also your hunger and satiety levels, your mood, thoughts and feelings. No one can ever know you as you can know yourself.

Step 5: Look to the future

Once you understand how better to get along with yourself, continue positive behavior. An identification of success in two years, and especially five years, is whether weight loss has been maintained rather than lost weight regained. If you don't achieve your goals, circle around and try again.

Too Sweet for
Our Own Good.
The Insulin Connection

At least 20% and possibly as many as 70% of individuals with PCOS also have a disorder of insulin secretion or glucose metabolism. Although only recently in the forefront of research, the relationship between PCOS and diabetes is not new. In 1921 a reference was made in a French medical article by Achard and Thiers to "diabete des femmes a barbe," or "bearded lady diabetic." Despite an increasing understanding of the important actions of insulin on the ovary, a clinical connection between PCOS and insulin resistance was not made until relatively recently. In the early 1980s, two distinguished researchers in reproductive endocrinology, Drs. Jeffrey Chang and James Givens, published reports linking PCOS with elevated insulin levels. The real coming of age and the solidification of the PCOS-insulin connection was with the sophisticated clinical studies of Dr. Andrea Dunaif in 1989. By the late 1990s, major strides had been made toward unraveling the role of insulin and insulin resistance in PCOS. Still, we are not much past the foundation level.

Fuel for the new understanding of the basic mechanisms of insulin resistance, as well as innovative therapies, have not come as much from the scientific community as from the pharmaceutical industry. Several new agents for the treatment of type 2 diabetes serendipitously were shown to alter weight, menstrual cycle function and/or fertility. For the first time we may have therapy aimed at the real root of the problem in at least some cases of PCOS. In making the PCOS-insulin connection, a new era dawned for scientists, clinicians, industry, and patients alike. Insulin altering drugs may provide heavy ammunition not only to win the battle of PCOS, menstrual function, and fertility, but also the long war against development of diabetes and heart disease. (See Chapter 15).

What is insulin? What does it do?

Insulin is a protein composed of a long string of amino acids produced by specialized cells in the pancreas called beta (ß) cells. The gene that codes for insulin production is located on chromosome 11. Like other hormones, insulin is released into the bloodstream to be carried to "target cells" throughout the body. Insulin specifically directs how the body regulates its energy supplies (metabolism). Proper insulin secretion is critical to ensure a constant and adequate supply of glucose, the basic fuel of the human engine. In turn, glucose, a sugar or simple carbohydrate, is the major controlling mechanism of insulin secretion.

The secretion of insulin is precisely controlled to maintain the blood glucose level to within a range of 60-150 mg/dl. If the glucose in the bloodstream falls below this level, the condition is called *hypoglycemia*. When glucose levels drop to very low levels, unconsciousness and even death can result. This is why diabetics are so careful with the use of insulin. If the glucose level rises and stays above 200 (*hyperglycemia*), the body compensates by increasing insulin, and if the action of insulin is not sufficient to hold the tide, excess glucose is cleared from the system by the kidneys. High levels of glucose cause *diuresis*, the process by which the glucose serves as a diuretic, resulting in excessive fluid loss through urination. This process is the cause of the frequent urination and thirst, which are the symptoms of hyperglycemia and diabetes.

In times of excess food (in the form of energy-producing glucose), insulin promotes storage of glucose. First, glucose is stored in the liver and muscle as glycogen, the most readily available storehouse of glucose. When this container is filled, glucose is then stored as fat, a more long-term energy resource. Insulin not only promotes the storage of fat and glycogen, but also retards the breakdown of fat (a process called *lipolysis*) and glycogen (*gluconeogenesis*). In summary, insulin acts to conserve energy. Given this purpose, it is natural that insulin excess should cause weight gain.

However, insulin is much more than just a glucose regulator. Its action is much broader and indispensable in the regulation of numerous body functions. The major targets of insulin action are the liver, muscles, blood vessels, pituitary gland, and brain, where it can alter expression and regulation of genes (DNA), protein synthesis, and steroid hormone metabolism. It is not only insulin's effects on glucose and fat metabolism, but also these other complex actions that are currently under investigation in PCOS patients.

Figure 9-1 Insulin Action

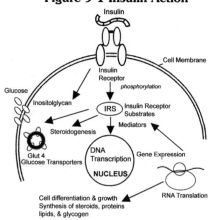

What is insulin resistance?

Defective insulin secretion, or a defect in the capacity to respond to insulin by the various target tissues, results in increased insulin secretion in the body's attempt to overcome this block. Insulin resistance is an impaired biological response to insulin, regardless of whether the insulin is derived from the body's own resources or is given by injection. In 1939, Himsworth and Kerr reported the possibility that defects exist in the sensitivity of different tissues to insulin, but it was not until recently that assays have been readily available to measure insulin levels. A clarifying analogy I frequently use is that of the speaker-audience. Think of the target tissue as being like an audience that is

Figure 9-2 Glucose - Insulin Curve

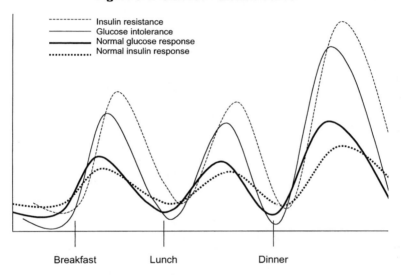

hearing impaired and the pancreas like a speaker trying to be heard. In this analogy the speaker (the pancreas) continues to increase the volume (produce insulin) until it can be heard. Increasingly greater concentrations of insulin become necessary to maintain a normal glucose response. When insulin can no longer control glucose elevations, hyperglycemia and diabetes result. The abnormally high levels of insulin produced in attempt to control glucose could adversely affect the many other functions of insulin. For example, hyperinsulinemia resulting in hyperandrogenemia.

Hyperinsulinemia has been linked to a number of seemingly unrelated abnormalities. Some of the disorders that have been suggested to have common roots in hyperinsulinism and insulin resistance include chronic fatigue syndrome, defects in the immune system, eating disorders, hypoglycemia, gastrointestinal disorders, depression and anxiety. These relationships are still very much unproven, but their similarities and suspected connections call for the attention of the medical profession and make it appropriate for those suffering from any of them to become more informed of the others and to make special note of their appearance in genetic family members.

Are there symptoms of insulin resistance?

It should be remembered that insulin resistance is a metabolic alteration, not a disease. As such, insulin resistance does not necessarily have signs or symptoms. However, most of us are enough in tune with our bodies so that the marked fluctuation in glucose can be recognized, even though the cause may not have been known. There are probably individuals who wake up energetic, tackle the tasks of the day with vigor and have no slumps, but they (you) must be a rare breed. All of us get a charge from a dose of sugar, but with insulin resistance these swings can be very pronounced and enough to alter productivity and interaction with others. With insulin resistance, there can be high peaks and deep troughs. It's amazing how many insulin resistant or glucose intolerant women have a unified group of symptoms, that, however vague, are universal. It is not uncommon for PCOS patients to answer yes to every one of the symptoms listed below.

- Early day irritability followed by late day drowsiness.
- Desire for an additional sweet after a large meal even with a dessert.
- Desire to eat again after a recent meal and eating to fullness
- Eating to over-fullness.
- Excessive irritability just before meals or intense need for food.
- Craving for bread, pasta or potatoes.
- Pronounced drops in strength or stamina at particular times of the day.
- A constant desire to graze on high carbohydrate or high fat foods.
- Night eating.
- Poor sleep habits.
- Constant hunger and cravings on a low calorie diet.
- Pronounced inability to lose weight despite caloric restriction.
- Believing, "There are so many people who eat more than I do."

How does insulin resistance develop?

The response of the body to a meal (intake of glucose) is to release insulin from the pancreas. Insulin stimulates uptake of glucose by the major customers in the energy market, including the liver and skeletal muscle. Skeletal muscle, the muscle that moves our bones, is the body's greatest consumer of glucose. About 30% of all calories go to muscle. Insulin resistance appears to be a defect in the manner in which individual cells process glucose. Reduced sensitivity of skeletal muscle to insulin appears to be the first manifestation of insulin resistance. A problem with skeletal muscle is a big problem and is magnified throughout the body. Defects in utilization of glucose mean that more glucose remains in circulation and more insulin is produced in an attempt to push it through the muscle cell's resistance. The beta cells of the pancreas attempt to compensate for the disordered action in muscle by making more insulin. Later the pancreas itself may become over stressed and have problems meeting the demands for insulin production.

It gets even more complex, in that as insulin is released from the pancreas, the pancreas makes more insulin. In the early stages of insulin resistance, the immediate release of insulin may also be impaired, but insulin production remains normal. As insulin resistance worsens, an abnormality in insulin production arises as well. The pancreas overcompensates by making more insulin than required; then, over time, it may exhaust itself because of its hard work.

As glucose levels rise there is an attempt to compensate by shunting glucose to the liver and converting glucose to fat. There may be an additional problem of abnormalities in glycogen synthesis by the liver. The ovary may be a small time investor in the energy market, but still get caught up in the trading frenzy with adverse consequences.

To understand insulin action one must understand the lock and key principle of hormone and receptor action that has been discussed Chapter 2. Hormones bind to hormone receptors in order that a particular activity of the cell will take place just as keys are inserted into locks to open doors. The gene that codes for the insulin receptor is located on chromosome 19. To have an effect, insulin must bind to insulin receptors on the membrane of an individual insulin sensitive cell. The binding of insulin to its receptor sets into motion a cascade of interrelated events including: 1) alteration of protein messengers (phosphorylation) that involves several intermediaries including insulin receptors substrates, which will ultimately send signals to the nucleus for DNA synthesis, 2) mobilization of glucose transporter proteins, specifically GLUT4, in muscle, that regulates how the cell manages glucose, and 3) regulation of inositolglycan generation which may have a role in steroid hormone (androgen) production. (See Figure 9-1) In insulin resistance, it seems as though the key fits, in that there are no problems with the receptor or its action, but the door has a safety latch that prevents it from fully opening. Insulin resistance may arise in a number of points along this scheme and many more mechanisms and genetic alterations than is feasible to present here have been proposed.

There is a strong familial tendency to develop insulin resistance, suggesting a genetic basis. Tracing the family tree of insulin resistance is complicated by the fact that insulin resistance is controlled by more than one gene. Several forms of insulin resistance have been linked to an alteration of a single gene. You either have it or you don't; it's either black or white. These conditions are uniformly rare. Multiple genes and their multiple interactions give rise to infinite shades of gray, depending on the particular genetic make-up of the individual. The genetic expression is even further complicated by environmental factors such as obesity.

What does obesity have to do with insulin resistance?

Fat itself, how fat is distributed around the body, and muscle mass all have independent effects on insulin sensitivity. Excess body weight is present in 80-90% of cases of type 2 diabetes and in 50-80% of cases of PCOS. The environment in which insulin resistance is most likely to arise is one of increased levels of glucose and fats circulating in the blood. Long-term hyperglycemia has been called *glucotoxicity*. Glucotoxicity, like obesity, is a curse of our present dietary habits and sedentary lifestyle. The body compensates for increased loads of glucose by increasing insulin production.

A central purpose of fat is to store energy for times of need. During times of reduced energy stores (starvation), free fatty acids are mobilized from fat cells called adipocytes, by insulin. Free fatty acids can be used by muscle as an energy source sparing precious glucose for use by the brain. In obesity, there are elevated free fatty acids in the face of high levels of glucose. Free fatty acids inhibit glucose metabolism and are stored in the fat of muscle giving it a typical "marbled" appearance. With obesity there is a reduction of the *GLUT4* insulin transporter molecules that further increases glucose and decreases the effect of insulin action; insulin resistance develops. Insulin is also stimulated. Obesity is an ironic condition in which the body believes itself to be starving despite high levels of glucose. In 1936, a model of adrenal function called the *general adaptation syndrome* was proposed by Selye to describe adrenal function. The system described an initial *alarm reaction* brought on by stress. If the stress persisted, *resistance* developed and under a chronic condition there was *exhaustion*. An analogy can be made with insulin. Untreated diabetics develop a severe wasting syndrome despite high levels of glucose and insulin.

Obesity is not the total problem; in fact, in some cases obesity may be only a symptom of insulin resistance. In studying the origin of PCOS in teenagers, some have stated that insulin resistance develops only after and as a result of obesity. This clearly does not seem to be the case. Many, if not most, will begin to have menstrual cycle irregularity before there is a weight gain. About 10% of obese women who ovulate have glucose intolerance, compared to 30% of obese women of the same age who have PCOS.

Obese women with PCOS have been shown to have a defect in the pancreatic ß-cell function, as well as action of insulin in the fat cells. While insulin resistance may improve with weight loss, the abnormal beta cell function remains. There are also a number of *thin* PCOS patients with quite severe insulin resistance. That there are women of entirely normal weight suggests that there is more to the insulin resistance of PCOS than obesity.

Is the insulin resistance of PCOS different?

This is a hard question and some researchers are convinced there is a completely different form of insulin resistance in at least some PCOS patients. However, due to the high frequency of the more "garden variety" of insulin resistance and its association with diabetes, it seems incorrect to state unequivocally that insulin resistance of PCOS is different. Certainly, PCOS is associated with insulin resistance. However, insulin resistance is not usually present in women with only polycystic ovaries on ultrasound, or in women who ovulate and have elevated androgens.

The question becomes, "Is there something special about insulin resistance in PCOS and the PCOS ovary?" One theory is that the PCOS ovary remains normally sensitive to insulin so that when insulin levels rise in response to insulin resistance, the ovary is placed in overdrive due to the excessive stimulation. In this variety, weight loss and treatment of hyperinsulinemia decrease insulin resistance. Insulin resistance is not altered by weight loss in some cases of PCOS.

A second theory is that there is a specific defect of the insulin signaling pathway related to the PCOS ovary. This theory is championed by Dr. Dunaif, who along with her co-workers, has found that there is a specific defect in insulin action which exists in cells isolated from women with PCOS. By removing a small piece of tissue from the body and placing the tissue in an *in vitro* culture system, the genetic programming of cells independent from the hormonal imbalances of PCOS can be studied. Using this technique, it was found that the insulin resistance there is most likely a defect in the body's ability to handle insulin, while in PCOS the defect seems more likely to be in insulin signaling. Granted, this is a very subtle distinction, but one which scientists are presently pursuing.

A third hybrid possibility is that there is a hormonal defect of the ovary that is made worse when insulin levels rise. Insulin may play a permissive or additive role. Dr. Nestler has pointed out that the ovaries of women with PCOS may be "uniquely susceptible" to the action of insulin. There may be a specific genetically programmed susceptibility present with PCOS. It seems logical that PCOS and insulin resistance are separate problems, in that some individuals have PCOS without insulin resistance and others have insulin resistance without PCOS. When you get both PCOS and insulin resistance, you get double trouble.

None of these theories exclude the other two, and it's entirely possible that a combination of more than one cause may be present in the same individual. We will be unable to know which theory or theories are correct until one mechanism has been fully worked out. (Also see Chapter 2 on biology and Chapter 3 on genetics for more detailed explanations of the origins of insulin resistance).

How does insulin affect the ovary?

The relationship between insulin and ovarian function is intertwined at many levels. A recent review by Poretsky proposes that insulin acts in the following ways that have been substantiated to varying degrees:

- Directly stimulates and alters steroidogenesis (increases androgen production).
- Interacts with gonadotropin (LH and FSH) (increases LH receptors).
- Affects the growth of the ovary and cyst formation.
- Decreases production of sex hormone binding globulin (SHBG).
- Alters insulin-like growth factors (IGF), their binding proteins and receptors.
- Interacts with leptin, and it effects on the hypothalamic-pituitary-ovary axis.
- Disrupts ovulation and luteal function.

Drs. Barbieri and Ryan at Harvard showed a relationship between insulin and androgen production in the human ovary as early as 1984. There is no doubt that there is a direct relationship between insulin and testosterone production by the ovary. It seems clear that insulin causes androgens (male hormones) to rise, but that the reverse is not true—androgens do not cause insulin to rise. The fact that men seem to be slightly more insulin resistant than women, and the fact that oral contraceptives containing androgenic synthetic steroids have a negative effect on glucose tolerance are given as supporting evidence for the theory that androgens cause insulin to rise. It is also possible that hyperandrogenism may worsen insulin resistance. However, it seems from several lines of evidence that high insulin levels resulting in hyperandrogenism is the most common situation. Women in whom the ovaries have been removed or androgens completely suppressed with GnRH analogs (Lupron) are still hyperinsulinemic and may have the risk factors that go along with this. They may be **hypoandrogenic**, which can have its own set of problems such as decreased libido. A second debate and looming question still to be answered is whether insulin acts alone to cause PCOS, or whether it has to work through a defective mechanism of the ovary. It seems that hyperinsulinemia itself is not important outside a permissive defect in the PCOS ovary. There needs to be a permissive defect to make the ovary responsive to LH. Hyperinsulinemia in a normal woman's insulin does not appear to have a serious effect on androgen production.

There are two hormones that primarily regulate androgen production from the ovary: luteinizing hormone (LH) and insulin. For all practical purposes, they are identical in their action, and insulin can be considered a gonadotropin. Perhaps the best way to understand the role of insulin in PCOS to is to refer back to Chapter 2 and the role of luteinizing hormone in the development of PCOS. Both insulin and LH seem to be interchangeable in their capacity to cause hyperandrogenism. Although the effects of insulin and LH appear similar, LH does not affect insulin levels. If GnRH analogs are used to block LH secretions, there is no change in insulin secretion in insulin resistant patients. High levels of LH may coexist with insulin resistance, or one may be high without the other. The more profound cases of PCOS are seen when both LH and insulin levels are elevated.

Insulin may directly interfere with normal follicle development by indirectly increasing ovarian androgens or by disturbing gonadotropin release from the pituitary gland. Androgens are known to arrest normal development of ovarian follicles and cause their degeneration (*atresia*). LH is known to stimulate the proliferation of androgen producing cells in the theca layer of the ovary. *Any action that can increase androgens or LH can cause PCOS.* Insulin may do both.

How does insulin affect the adrenal gland?

This is a tough one. DHEAS is a weak androgen that is almost exclusively produced in the adrenal gland. As such it is commonly used as a marker to determine an adrenal component of PCOS. It is possible that it is not the most appropriate marker, but it is what we have. Depending on the particular patient population, 20-50% of those with PCOS have elevated DHEAS. There is a very curious second group of about 10% that have low PCOS and abnormally low DHEAS levels. In men, insulin administration and insulin resistance both lowers DHEAS levels. One study has reported that metformin reduces DHEAS levels, but this would seem to be at odds with studies in men. We know that ovarian steroids and gonadotropins affect adrenal androgen production, but we don't know how. We will have to leave insulin action on the adrenal gland with the same vagueness.

How is insulin resistance measured in the laboratory?

There are several techniques for measuring insulin resistance in the laboratory. They include:

The euglycemic insulin clamp: With this technique, an IV is started and insulin is infused at a rate to maintain a constant blood insulin level. A second infusion of glucose is given at different rates determined by measurements of glucose every five minutes to maintain the plasma level of glucose at a constant level. The total amount of glucose given over the complete test time of one to three hours is calculated. The insulin resistant patient requires much more insulin or much less glucose to maintain the same baseline level. A number of insulin clamp studies have confirmed that PCOS patients are insulin resistant. There are problems with the test related to time, cost and complexity, and it is usually reserved for research purposes.

Minimal model: This method was developed as an attempt to provide an easier measurement than the clamp technique. With the minimal model, glucose and insulin are frequently sampled from an IV line during an intravenous, rather than oral, glucose tolerance test. Results are entered into a computer model to determine insulin sensitivity. This test is still too complicated to be used in the physician's office for routine testing and is relegated to research.

Fasting insulin: This is the easiest of all techniques and involves taking a single sample of morning blood after fasting since midnight the day before. There can be considerable variability between the various assays and there has been no central standardization. That means a level of 20 uIU/ml in one lab may correspond to 10, or 30, in another. The tests are equally good, but different. There is also considerable discrepancy about what constitutes abnormally high insulin. The original validation of assays included individuals with insulin resistance that skewed the entire population toward higher normal levels. Using the same assay, some labs report a level of 14 uU/ml as the upper limits of normal while others use twice that. Thin, "normal" women have an average level of about 10; while in obese women the level has increased to 15. It depends on how discriminating one wants to be with the test. Probably levels much under 15 are clearly normal and much over 25 clearly elevated.

Fasting glucose:insulin ratio: A ratio of less than 4.5 is suggestive of insulin resistance. While there is considerable overlap between normal and abnormal values, the test is easy and reasonably reliable.

Insulin after glucose challenge More information can be gathered by also measuring insulin after a glucose tolerance test. After one glucose load, the one-hour glucose tolerance should show a level up to 50 uU/ml in thinner patients and 60 in obese patients. However, the stimulated insulin levels do not always match the results obtained by more aggressive techniques. A more sophisticated evaluation can be obtained mathematically by plotting the values from the test and then studying the area under the curve (AUC) for this same test. This gives a better approximation of the total amount of insulin released, but again, this test can be cumbersome for regular clinical use.

What is the relationship between insulin resistance and diabetes?

The terminology of diabetes is constantly in a flux. Presently, the major categories of diabetes are type 1, type 2, gestational and other. The other categories are so small that they can be eliminated from our discussion. For all practical purposes, gestational diabetes is type 2 diabetes manifested in pregnancy (see Chapter 12). Type 1 diabetics are insulin deficient and must have insulin replacement. This form is not inherited, it begins in childhood, and it usually is due to an immunologic destruction of pancreatic B cells. Many, probably most, type 1 diabetics will develop insulin resistance over time. Some will exhibit classic polycystic ovaries on ultrasound scan, an acquired variety of PCOS. Type 2 diabetes usually has its onset in adulthood, is genetically programmed, and is universally insulin resistant. About 10% of type 2 diabetics are not insulin resistant. Severe type 2 diabetics will often develop insulin deficiency over time.

It is believed that insulin resistance is a pre-diabetic state and the direct cause of type 2 diabetes. Insulin resistance is inherited in most cases and its greatest predictor is other family members with type 2 diabetes. If there is a parent with type 2 diabetes there is about a 50% chance that you will be insulin resistant. If there is one grandparent there is at least a 25% chance. Still, all with insulin resistance will not become diabetics. Obesity significantly increases the risk that the insulin resistant individual will become diabetic. Some with insulin resistance are thin, young and have completely normal glucose levels. There is significant room for increasing or decreasing risks of diabetes by altering environmental factors such as diet and exercise. Insulin resistance can easily be present for many years before the body's compensation mechanisms are overpowered. As many as 40% of women with PCOS develop either impaired glucose tolerance or type 2 diabetes by age 40. PCOS should be considered a readily identifiable risk factor for diabetes. Diabetes itself has a number of adverse health consequences. (See Chapter 15).

| GENETICS DIET OBESITY | → | INSULIN RESISTANCE | → | GLUCOSE INTOLERANCE | → | TYPE 2 DIABETES |

When is it diabetes?

There is a gradual evolution from normal blood glucose levels (*euglycemia*) to hyperglycemia. Diabetes is presented further in Chapter 15. Diabetes is diagnosed when

- Blood glucose level is over 200 at any time.
- Fasting blood glucose level exceed 126 mg/dl.
- Blood glucose level above 200 mg/dl two hours after drinking a solution containing 75 g of glucose.

What can be done about insulin resistance?

The first step for most people is a lifestyle change (sorry, but there's no way to avoid this). Clearly, insulin resistance is a hazardous warning signal for the need of lifestyle change. The initial recommendation to improve insulin resistance is alteration in diet and exercise. While they may not "cure" insulin resistance, positive changes in diet and exercise have been shown very beneficial in reducing its effects. Even modest changes in lifestyle may improve fertility for those interested in conceiving a child, as well as postpone the progression of IR to diabetes. Insulin resistance may be reduced even before weight is lost when using a reduced calorie diet. (See Chapter 8). In addition to limiting foods that result in more pronounced elevations in glucose and insulin, a diet lower in fat is also recommended. Such a diet plan can have significant beneficial effects on the cardiovascular system and reduce the risk of heart attack, vascular disease and stroke. (See Chapter 15). Exercise can reduce insulin resistance in the absence of weight loss. A study in the *Journal of Clinical Endocrinology and Metabolism*, April, 1999, showed that gradual lifestyle changes alone, even without rapid weight loss, improved insulin sensitivity and restored ovulation. There is no doubt that suggested changes in diet and exercise are easier said than done, and soon both physicians and patients look toward pharmacological intervention.

There are now a number of drugs that in early trials show great promise in reversing many of the metabolic derangements of PCOS. These drugs may represent the first therapies that have an impact on a central causative mechanism of PCOS. Before use of insulin-altering drugs, beginning with metformin in 1995, there was no drug therapy that improved insulin resistance and the only oral medications for type 2 diabetes were the sulfonylureas, which increase insulin production and cause weight gain, both counter productive for the insulin resistance of PCOS. Insulin-altering drugs are listed below with additional general information in Chapter 16 and use in infertility in Chapter 11.

It should be noted that, as this book is going to press in the summer of 2000, *no medication has received FDA approval for treatment of PCOS, or even for treatment of insulin resistance*, although it is clear that the drug companies are very interested in these issues.

Metformin—good for what ails you?

Metformin (Glucophage™) was introduced in the United Sates in 1995 for the treatment of type 2 diabetes. It had established a long, successful record of accomplishment in Europe in diabetes therapy, but the association with successful PCOS therapy had not been made. In part, a delay in its use in the U.S. may have been due to an earlier similar drug, phenformin, with questionable safety and a high rate of side effects. In the last several years, metformin has reached cult status for the treatment of PCOS largely due to the dissemination of information over the Internet. Like most Internet phenomena, it fails to live up to all its claims. Regardless, it is increasingly prescribed by a wide range of physicians for "off-label indications" such as obesity, infertility and PCOS. It is neither a poison nor panacea, but can be a very useful therapy in PCOS. There are presently two wrongs in the dispensing of metformin. Some physicians are giving the drug indiscriminately without knowledge of its actions, indications, or time needed for effectiveness. The other problem is that there are PCOS patients that would benefit from the drug, but can't find a physician experienced in its use. Both of these will likely change.

Metformin does not appear to alter insulin secretion, but it may enhance tissue sensitivity to insulin. Its effectiveness rests in its capacity to suppress glucose production by the liver (gluconeogenesis) and to a lesser extent, decrease insulin resistance, primarily in muscle. Metformin alters how cells transport glucose. In the diabetic, glucose levels are lowered by making the body more efficient in the use of glucose. Therefore, it is virtually impossible that glucose levels are lowered below normal. (See Chapter 5).

As metformin was becoming available in the U.S., Charles Glueck at the Jewish Hospital of Cincinnati began a study to evaluate the effects of metformin on the insulin resistance seen in PCOS patients. They were met with a startling finding: seven of the first twelve women who had markedly abnormal periods became pregnant after use of metformin for IR. Dr. Nestler at Virginia Commonwealth University has been a leader in the study of metformin therapy. His group has shown reduced fasting and glucose stimulated insulin, but also a decrease in the P450c17a enzyme that has a primary responsibility for androgen production by the ovary and LH. It is now well substantiated that metformin improves fertility and its success may rival clomiphene. Dr. Nestler has also shown that infertility patients who were previously unresponsive to clomiphene ovulate when clomiphene and metformin are used together. Although the results have not been confirmed, concurrent metformin therapy seems to improve success with injectable gonadotropin therapy and in vitro fertilization. There now have been a substantial number of studies on metformin that have shown significant improvement in hormonal measurements and restoration of menstruation. Universally, insulin levels have been reduced.

Metformin also seems to have the advantage of causing weight loss, but how this works and whether weight loss can be maintained over the long term is not known. It has been argued that the effect of metformin is merely that of weight loss. Clearly, loss of as little as 5-10% of body mass improves menstrual function and glucose tolerance. Crave and colleagues reported no additive effect of metformin to alter hormonal levels outside that of weight loss.

It is quite possible that some degree of insulin resistance will always remain despite weight loss. Controversy still abounds. However, the results with metformin therapy are just too good to suggest weight loss alone is responsible.

In the appendix you will find a table summarizing many current studies concerning Metformin.

What are "glitazones"?

Commonly referred to as "glitazones," thiazolidinediones act on a different pathway than metformin and directly decrease insulin resistance. Initially there was a single drug marketed in the thiazolidinedione "glitazone" class of medications, troglitazone (Rezulin™). Now there are three, with more on the way. Troglitazone™, which was introduced in 1997 for treatment of type 2 diabetes, has a unique property of containing vitamin E as part of its structure. This may provide the additional benefit of an antioxidant, acting to decrease risk of the microvascular damage described above. Recently two other glitazones have received FDA approval, rosiglitazone (Avandia™) and pioglitazone (Actos™). The mechanism of action of these drugs is probably similar, but there may be subtle differences in such issues as cardioprotective effects and the possibility of liver damage. In part fueled by the success of metformin, troglitazone was immediately evaluated for its capacity to reduce androgen levels and improve insulin sensitivity in PCOS patients. Success was good. A study by Dr. Ehrmann and colleagues showed reduction in ovarian and adrenal androgen levels as well as improved insulin sensitivity. Dr. Dunaif has shown the effectiveness of troglitazone in both obese and thin PCOS patients with insulin resistance. They showed that improving insulin sensitivity independent of weight loss reduces the hyperandrogenism of PCOS.

There was not the weight loss of metformin, but neither were there the gastrointestinal side effects, and the drug was exceptionally well tolerated. Rezulin™ appeared to be a silver bullet aimed at the target of insulin resistance. Then came the bad news. Troglitazone appears to be linked with the possibility of liver damage leading to possible need for a liver transplant or even to death. It clearly seems that the press exaggerated claims. One possibility of the liver dysfunction of troglitazone stems from its incorporation of vitamin E as a part of its structure. It's possible that the vitamin E portion, known to have effects on the liver, and not the "glitazone" molecule itself which may be responsible for the liver problems. Troglitazone still remains an exceedingly important medication in the treatment of type 2 diabetes, but has moved to second line therapy in conjunction with other drugs such as metformin or sulfonylureas. It is interesting that they have received a FDA classification in pregnancy as C, whereas troglitazone remains category B. This probably reflects an uncertainty rather than true risk. Since "glitazones" are so effective in lowering insulin, they should not be excluded in the treatment of PCOS in association with hyperinsulinemia. Trials on the newer glitazones in the treatment of PCOS are underway and it is suspected that rosiglitazone and pioglitazone will be equally as effective as troglitazone. A responsible way to determine which to use is probably price. Routine liver function testing is mandatory with use of any glitazone.

What happened to Rezulin?

When Rezullin™ was introduced to the U.S. market in 1997 it was completely unrelated to other anti-diabetic agents available for general use. The safety profile appeared excellent and much lower than any anti-diabetic agent except metformin. Its action directly improved the insulin resistance of type 2 diabetes and the drug was quickly adopted into widespread use. Troglitazone was removed from the market in March 2000 due to its potential liver toxicity. Troglitazone was unique in its chemical structure due to an attachment of vitamin E molecule. This may have contributed to its beneficial effect on the heart, but also its potential for liver damage. Troglitazone relied on activation of the 3A4 pathway for its metabolism in the liver, which further increases its capacity for interaction with other drugs.

In over 2 million users, there were around 50 reported cases of deaths or liver transplants. About 1/3 of these patients either were alcoholic or began the drug before liver function was monitored. In most ways the removal of this drug was a shame. The FDA made this stand not because troglitazone was such a bad drug; it was that in their view, the other glitazones were superior because of the lack of reported liver toxicity. Unfortunately, it became a liability to the pharmaceutical firm to market the drug. The tragedy of troglitazone should not be taken as a negative comment about other glitazones. Presently two are in active use, pioglitazone (Actos™) and rosiglitazone (Avandia™) which was FDA approved June 1999.

Are the glitazones different?

In comparison of rosiglitazone and pioglitazone, each drug has favorable effects on insulin, both are well tolerated, and both seem to have an excellent safety profile. There are many more similarities than differences.

Much has been made about the difference in drug interaction between the 3 agents. Both troglitazone and pioglitazone induce a metabolic pathway called the cytochrome P450 3A4. This is the pathway through which many other drugs are metabolized creating the possibility of altered, higher or lower, concentrations depending on the circumstance. Rosiglitazone is metabolized by a different mechanism, CYP 2C8, which has less potential for drug interaction. Pioglitazone utilizes a combination of both pathways,only about 17% by the possibly less advantageous 3A4 pathway. Drug interactions can be serious and the lack of demonstrated interaction is important. While there has been no "head to head" comparisons, it is possible that pioglitazone has a more favorable effect on blood lipid levels which may give it a therapeutic advantage. You should also compare costs.

How do the glitazones stack up to metformin?

Although glitazones and metformin are both used to improve insulin sensitivity and hyperglycemia, they are very different classes of drugs.

Experience: Both have been used in the United Sates for a relatively short time, but metformin has had a twenty-year record of use in Europe. There has been much more experience with metformin than glitazones and much of that experience was with troglitazone.

Action: Glitazones may be better at improving the action of insulin (insulin sensitizer), while metformin may be better at lowering glucose production from the liver (gluconeogenesis). The obese glucose intolerant patients may do better on metformin; the thinner insulin resistant patients may do better on glitazones. In my experience, glitazones are superior in lowering insulin levels. Troglitazone decreases androgen production, while the effects of metformin are less clear and may be related to weight reduction.

Safety: Both drugs appear safe and their benefits of use almost always outweigh their risks. Metformin has been very rarely associated with a serious and perhaps fatal condition called lactic acidosis. It is unclear whether the PCOS patient is at risk. The experience with glitazones is still accumulating. It does not appear that they have liver toxicity.

Side effects: Metformin clearly has more gastrointestinal side effects than glitazones. Most patients put up with metformin, while they seldom know they're taking glitazones. With glitazones there may be slight fluid retention.

Weight: Some weight loss almost always accompanies metformin use in PCOS patients. It is still unclear whether this is long lasting. We have now had patients on metformin for over 2 years with good weight maintenance. Most do not have a weight loss on glitazones and usually gain 2-10 pounds. Weight loss sometimes occurs in the PCOS population. In my experience weight is often lost where glitazones are used as a part of an overall approach to better health, but not as much weight is lost as with metformin.

Lipid profile: Weight loss has been a significant reason to use metformin and has been shown to have a better effect of improvement in lipid profiles overall. Both drug classes reduce triglycerides about 10-15%. Glitazones raise or do not lower LDL cholesterol while metformin lowers LDL.

Dosing: Glitazones are often used once daily, sometimes twice. Metformin is often used twice daily, sometimes three times.

Precautions: Baseline kidney function testing (BUN and creatinine) is needed before starting metformin. Discontinue therapy with radiographic procedures using iodine, surgery, acute illness, heavy prolonged physical activity, and dehydration. With glitazones, pretreatment and periodic liver function testing are recommended.

Expense: The cost of 4 mg of Avandia™ is approximately equal to that of Glucophage™ or about $60 per month. A generic metformin is on the horizon. Avandia™ is maybe less expensive than Actos™.

Pregnancy: Each drug appears equally safe, but information is too sketchy to draw conclusions. Metformin is given a category B rating for pregnancy while glitazones are C. The safety profile in pregnancy may be better for metformin, but the information is still preliminary.

What are other drugs that might help with insulin resistance?

Glucosidase inhibitors: Members of this group include Glyset™ and acarabose (Percose™). Both slow the absorption of carbohydrates from the intestine and partially block the rise in glucose after meals. They have been used alone or in combination with sulfonylureas for treatment of type 2 diabetes. In theory, they should have the important effect of buffering the surge of glucose after meals, especially seen in individuals with impaired glucose tolerance. Glyset™ did not alter fasting glucose or insulin levels. In some ways these drugs do for sugar what orlistat (see below) does for fat. There are often significant gastrointestinal side effects of use. There may be fewer with the newer Glyse™t. There was a tendency toward weight loss with Glyset™. Glyset™ use in PCOS has not been substantiated although the FDA has rated Glyset™ Category B.

Lipase inhibitors: Orlistat (Xenical™), while classified as an antibody agent, produces weight loss which improves lipid profile and insulin sensitivity. How it would fare when compared to metformin would be a very interesting question. If weight loss is the, or at least a major, cause of the effectiveness of metformin, then orlistat should be equally good. It can have nuisance side effects of gastrointestinal upset, but the safety profile is very good. Since it is not absorbed into the system it should be safe in use in infertility patients, but should be stopped in pregnancy.

D-chiro-inositol: Molecules that contain D-*chiro*-inositol are known to be mediators of insulin action and glucose metabolism. A deficiency of D-*chiro*-inositol has been linked to insulin resistance. Inositolglycans modify the insulin action and may have direct effects on androgen production by theca cells. Dr. Nestler recently reported on a study in twenty-two PCOS patients who were given 1200 mg of D-*chiro*–inositol daily for six to eight weeks. The response of insulin to glucose decreased, suggesting an improvement in insulin sensitivity. Testosterone levels, blood triglycerides and blood pressure all decreased and six of twenty-two women had elevation in progesterone levels, suggesting ovulation. This is an exciting possibility for treatment, but remains an unsubstantiated treatment and is still under review and several trials are underway. D-*chiro*-inositol is a natural component of some foods. Do not confuse it with *myo*-inositol which is widely available and has NO effect on insulin sensitivity. and may not need to be branded a drug.

Other candidates: Growth hormone (GH) alters the production of insulin-like growth factors (IGFs) and may improve follicular recruitment for ovarian stimulation in previously under responsive patients. GH offers just enough hope to be tried, but reviews are generally unfavorable and the cost of the drug excludes its routine use. IGFs are known to alter insulin levels and affect ovarian function, but may be as much a culprit as insulin itself in hyperandrogenism. An interesting dark horse is vanadium which alters the insulin receptor and reduces insulin and glucose. There have been no trials in PCOS.

When should insulin-altering drugs be stopped?

If a pregnancy occurs, insulin-altering drugs are most often stopped, but this may change when more is known. An evaluation is carried out after a six-month trial. The decision to continue is based on tolerance, improvement in overall status, long term goals, and other options available. Suffice it to say, it is much easier to know when to start than to stop.

Should insulin resistance be treated?

The primary treatment for insulin resistance—and one that clearly works—is weight reduction and increase in physical exercise. Regular vigorous exercise improves insulin resistance, but it must be continued. Insulin resistance will return when exercise is stopped. The effect of exercise on insulin resistance is almost immediate when calories are reduced and even before weight is lost. Total calories seem to be more important than how the calories are distributed between fats, carbohydrates and proteins. Reduction of saturated fat may reduce the risk of heart disease. It is likely that weight loss followed by a rapid gain does little good and may worsen health. The best policy is to prevent weight gain.

Since we know that some of the medications described above can have a positive effect on treating insulin resistance, shouldn't we use them? At present, the American Diabetes Association, a very strong advocate of diabetes prevention, has not recommended medical therapy alone for insulin resistance or prevention of diabetes. This seems to be one of those scientific facts that very likely will change over time as more is discovered about the role of insulin. At present, however, it is not clear that treatment of insulin resistance will make people live longer, or even better. Still, it makes good sense to take insulin resistance very seriously. It appears that the problematic medical conditions related to diabetes are more a result of hyperglycemia (glucotoxity) than insulin resistance.

A specific trial, the Diabetes Prevention Program, has been designed to answer the question of whether insulin resistance should be treated as a preventative. In a National Institutes of Health (NIH) supervised study, 4000 men and women volunteers will be enrolled in studies in twenty-five centers across the United States. Participants must have fasting glucose levels between 100-139 mg/dl, and will participate in various lifestyle and drug interventions to determine if the development of diabetes can be delayed or prevented.

While not necessarily for general health concerns, it may be important to treat insulin resistance solely because of its effect of hyperinsulinism on the ovary in PCOS. Although the insulin resistance of PCOS may not be curable, there is increasing evidence that regular menstrual cycles with ovulation and subsequent pregnancy may be achieved with strategies to alter glucose and insulin metabolism.

So what's my formula for use of insulin-altering drugs?

Most patients do not respond to being told to go home, lose weight, and start to exercise more. Clearly, programs with focuses on life style improvement work, but I find a regimen that incorporates an insulin-altering drug often attacks the problems on more fronts.

Blood testing (including a comprehensive biochemical panel, lipids, fasting insulin and 2 hr glucose tolerance test with stimulated insulin levels) is used to assess presence and degree of insulin resistance. (See also Chapter 5 for further explanation of testing for PCOS). Tests are performed after a progestin withdrawal or in the first 5 days of natural cycles. If there is no evidence of insulin resistance, I am reluctant to start insulin-altering drug therapy. On the other hand, I have tried with reasonable success in individuals in which all other roads seemed blocked.

After the test results are evaluated, medication is started. For fertility patients, there may be an additional trial of clomiphene to ensure clomiphene resistance or for the quick fix since insulin-altering theory can be more protracted. In patients who desire fertility, clomiphene is usually used at least once as a diagnostic test as well as a therapeutic intervention. When insulin-altering drugs are selected, I prefer to start with metformin, especially in heavier patients. With thinner patients who also have higher insulin levels, a glitazone may be first line therapy. Many have indicated that they prefer to take metformin at night so that is when it is usually started. Usually 850 mg once a day is used for 1-2 weeks then the dose in increased to 850 mg twice daily. The maximum doses not exceed 2550 mg daily. Some stay on 850 mg or even 500-mg once daily.

Two parameters are used as benchmarks of success: weight loss and establishment of regular periods. Usually cycle regulation agents such as progestins or oral contraceptives, are not given for fear of inadvertent use in pregnancy or blockage of ovulation. Most patients are seen back at monthly intervals for a meeting with the nutritionist. A repeat of at least some of the lab tests is performed after an induced or natural menses at 3 months to evaluate endocrine response. If the insulin levels remain significantly elevated on metformin, a low dose of glitazone is added for two to three months and levels resettled. If insulin levels are elevated, and metformin cannot be tolerated, a switch is made to glitazones. In some cases a repeat clomiphene challenge is performed.

Learning to Love the One You're With. PCOS and Body Image

by Melissa J. Himelein, Ph.D[1]

"She was a beautiful woman, but proud and haughty... She had a wonderful looking-glass, and when she stood in front of it and looked at herself in it, and said, 'Looking-glass, looking-glass, on the wall, Who in this land is the fairest of all?' The looking-glass answered, 'Thou, o queen, art the fairest of all.'"
—from Snow White

The evil queen of *Snow White* may have looked approvingly at her reflection, but vain women are hard to find in modern society. Surveys of U.S. women reveal that most are quite unhappy with their bodies. They express dissatisfaction with the size or shape of countless body parts, and regardless of their actual size, they perceive themselves as too large. The "beauty industries"—from cosmetics to weight loss to plastic surgery—are thriving. Despite emptying their purses to these industries, women go right on glowering into the mirror.

Notions of beauty are narrow in Western culture. The women featured in fashion magazines are uniformly tall, a minimum of 5' 9", and slender, a maximum of size six. By height and weight criteria alone, these standards fit less than 2% of women. The weight difficulties of women with PCOS make conforming to this extreme level of thinness especially unlikely. Add to this the

---

[1] *Melissa J. Himelein, Ph.D., an associate professor of psychology at the University of North Carolina at Asheville (UNCA) and a licensed clinical psychologist, was the author of this chapter. She provides counseling to women and couples dealing with the emotional impact of PCOS, infertility, or other issues at the Center for Applied Reproductive Science in Asheville. Dr. Himelein also conducts research focused on topics of special importance to women, publishing her work in a wide variety of academic journals and books.*

characteristic skin problems and hair growth which accompany PCOS, "undesirable" characteristics that are routinely airbrushed away when models have them, and PCOS can be a recipe for a poor body image.

The first symptoms of PCOS emerge in adolescence, at a time when body preoccupation is especially strong. Girls who develop symptoms of PCOS, whether aware they have the disorder or not, are likely to feel strikingly dissimilar from their peers. As one teen girl diagnosed with PCOS screamed out in an Internet chat, "All I want is clear skin like my friends! I hate being different!" To be different during adolescence, especially in the physical arena, can be devastating.

To be chronically unhappy with your body is a heavy burden, one that likely spills over into many areas of your life. This chapter overviews the causes and consequences of body dissatisfaction in women with PCOS. I hope to convince you of the importance of trying to change a negative body image, and to provide you with some concrete suggestions for doing so.

Sources of Body Dissatisfaction

Body dissatisfaction is not unique to women with PCOS, but it is relatively unique to women. Psychologists Alan Feingold and Ronald Mazzella recently reviewed over 200 research studies focused on gender differences in body image. Women not only expressed far more body dissatisfaction than men, they also rated themselves as less physically attractive than men rated themselves–despite the fact that neutral judges rated the women as more attractive than the men! Even when men are not altogether satisfied with their bodies, their displeasure is rarely obsessive, or even excessive, in the way that it so often is for women. What accounts for this striking difference between the genders?

Women in our society are trained to care about their looks from an early age. For many women, attending to their appearance is simply part of being female. When they are unhappy with the final product, they feel somehow less female: "To me, PCOS...takes away your femininity. On the outside it makes me look like a freak. Or at least that is how I see it.... Just once I would like to know what it feels like to be a normal woman."

Cultural training about the importance of physical attractiveness in girls begins early. Even before birth, the most frequent question expectant parents are asked is the gender of their upcoming baby. Once gender is established, shower shopping is easy: Girls get the pink frilly dresses with matching headbands and boys get the rugged blue overalls. Parents quickly pick up on the focus on girls' appearance. A study by Katherine Karraker and associates showed that within two days of birth they describe newborn daughters as finer featured and more delicate than newborn sons. Likewise, infant sons are seen as stronger and hardier than infant daughters. From conception onward, we appear to concern ourselves most with girls' physical features but with boys' physical functioning.

Parents continue "beauty brainwashing" by decorating their daughters' hair, polishing their nails, and even piercing their ears, all within the first years of life. Walk down the aisles of your local toy store and note the make-up kits and vanities for girls. (Is it during girls' long beauty training sessions that their male peers are getting a jump on math?) The success of fairy tale heroines is largely dependent on their beauty. Sleeping Beauty was "so beautiful that [the prince] could not turn his eyes away," and Rapunzel, "the most beautiful child under the sun," was only rescued because of her magnificent long, golden hair. (Male heroes, in contrast, tend to be valued for their bravery, wisdom, strength, or wealth.) In her book, *Beauty Bound*, Rita Freedman notes that by elementary school, girls are receiving more compliments about their appearance than on any other characteristic. They are especially noticed and admired when wearing dresses. Not surprisingly, they want their Barbies™ to have as stylish and elaborate a wardrobe as possible.

And then there's adolescence. According to psychologists Linda Smolak and Michael Levine, girls not only start to perceive attractiveness as the ticket to success, good looks may well offer real advantages in both academic and social areas. Middle school girls tend to focus especially on their body size, believing that there is nothing more important than thinness. Yet, puberty dictates sudden and significant weight gain, moving them farther and farther from their thin "ideal." They respond by devoting increasing time and energy to their appearance. Because they believe (erroneously) that weight is the one area they can control, many adolescent girls begin dieting. Nearly half of all high school girls are currently on a weight loss program of some type.

Girls with PCOS symptoms may well find the beauty obsession aspect of adolescence traumatizing. Their dieting efforts are particularly likely to fail, and since most have no idea why, they are prone to feel shame or guilt over their supposed lack of will. The typical adolescent girl obsesses over one or two pimples, while the girl with PCOS is likely to have much more significant acne. Spending long hours in front of the mirror, girls are acutely aware of every facial hair. Smolak and Levine reviewed the results of several studies on the relationship between the onset of puberty and body image, and concluded that girls who begin menstruating either earlier or later than their peers tend to be more body-dissatisfied. Consequently, it is possible that the menstrual irregularities of PCOS also contribute to body dissatisfaction.

How important is body image? Among adolescent girls, body image is an important contributor to overall self-esteem. Girls who like their bodies, like themselves, but girls who are unhappy with their bodies are probably globally unhappy. According to research reported by psychologist Lydia Kwa, although physical appearance is the most important source of self-worth in girls, it is athletic ability that drives self-worth in adolescent boys. In our culture, girls are trained to feel good about themselves if their bodies look first-rate; boys are trained to feel good about themselves if their bodies function first-rate.

Does beauty really matter?

Unfortunately, there is just enough truth to the notion that looks matter to make preoccupation with appearance almost logical. In personal ads, men's ads tend to include mention of their desire for attractive female partners, and often thin ones; women's ads for male partners rarely contain this focus. Countless surveys indicate that men place a higher priority on looks than do women in choosing a mate. Overweight women may be at a particular disadvantage, subject to prejudice and even outright discrimination in Western society. In her doctoral dissertation, Kristen Davis demonstrated negative stereotyping toward large women among a sample of psychologists, a professional group we would hope to be especially empathic. In fact, psychologists viewed hypothetical female clients who were overweight more pessimistically than those of normal weight, expecting the heavier clients to expend less effort and to improve less in the course of therapy.

Women who are physically attractive do appear to benefit from their looks to some degree. Although research has been inconsistent, some studies have found that females rated as more attractive are more likely to marry, and more likely to marry men with high incomes. They also may make more money than less attractive women. The idea that beauty could be an advantage in the workplace is probably no surprise. As Naomi Wolfe reported in her popular book, *The Beauty Myth*, women earn more than men in only two professions, both of which value bodies, not minds: modeling and prostitution.

On the other hand, the beauty obsession is only "almost" logical because women tend to overemphasize the importance to which appearance, and especially specific aspects of appearance (usually those areas they perceive as "defects") are important. They are also notoriously poor evaluators of their own physical appearance. Women tend to judge their attractiveness by comparing themselves to others, and usually, to extraordinarily attractive others to whom they can't possibly measure up. Consequently, there may be little relation between objectively rated attractiveness and attractiveness that is self-rated.

The truth is that the rewards of beauty are not nearly so great as the fairy tales lead us to believe. Most of us, attractive or not, are merely victims of what social psychologists call the "physical-attractiveness stereotype": the belief that beautiful people have many desirable characteristics, or that "what is beautiful is good." But this effect is strongest in our initial impressions of people, when we know little else about them. Over time, the effect is weakened, because we are not so blind as to be permanently distracted by beauty. Perhaps highly attractive people are even judged more harshly in the end, when they fail to live up to the impossible standards we set for them. At least those of us of "average" attractiveness do not have to worry whether our friends, partners, or spouses value us merely for our looks. As the prince sang while agonizing over his feelings for Rodgers and Hammerstein's *Cinderella*, "Do I love you because you're beautiful?"

It is also important to remember that standards of attractiveness vary across time and culture, and most importantly, across individuals. There is not just one version of beauty. The current desirability for thinness is a huge deviation from the era of Botticelli's Venus, when heavier, curvier women were idealized and romanticized. Marilyn Monroe, considered perfect in her day, is often described as a size twelve or fourteen. Research conducted by Sheila Parker and her associates found that African-American females were much more flexible in their notions of beauty than European-American females, emphasizing thinness less and liking their bodies more. Outside of the U.S. and Europe, a wider variety of body types is also embraced. Even in the U.S., it may surprise you to learn that a study conducted by Paul Rozin and April Fallon demonstrated that men are not interested in women becoming as slim as women think they believe that they should be.

Media Influences

The mass media—magazines, television, and movies—are an important and unfortunate source of our ideas about what constitutes beauty. They are important because of the sheer magnitude of media we absorb on a daily basis, for example, seven hours of television per day, but unfortunate because of the truly restrictive range of body types displayed. Again and again, the same body confronts us: tall, thin, narrow-hipped, broad-shouldered, white, and youthful. Women come to believe that this image is the ideal, and worse, they imagine that it is attainable.

As psychologist Jean Kilbourne points out in her thoughtful and entertaining video, *Slim Hopes: Advertising and the obsession with thinness*, this body is very likely not even real. It is often artificially enhanced (large breasts do not come naturally with extreme thinness), and then carefully edited via high-tech photography techniques or computer enhancement. Frequently, advertising photographs are composites of several different bodies—the legs of one model, the waist of another, and the face of a third. I find that when I discuss these processes in classes or workshops, women are surprised—and then comforted. (The fact that even Julia Roberts was forced to use a body double in *Pretty Woman* is especially well received!) It is interesting that photographs of male models are rarely touched-up as are those of females; the industry apparently believes men's stubble, scars, and wrinkles to be appealing in their realism.

Teen girls' magazines feature these models almost exclusively, but messages about beauty are much more direct than this. Approximately half of the articles published in magazines such as *Sassy* and *Seventeen* focus on appearance and how to improve it. If the average reader isn't already worried about her body, she certainly will be after reading all about its likely imperfections. According to a review of the literature on media effects undertaken by Michael Levine and Linda Smolak, most girls who read these magazines (and most do) say that they are an important source of beauty and fitness information. Yikes! This market's bent on beauty is about as reputable as *National Enquirer* headlines.

Popular women's magazines continue the same trend. Beauty, and especially weight-loss, articles predominate, a focus that is comparatively rare in popular men's magazines. Consider that women's magazines also devote enormous space to food ads and articles, and the quandary is clear. Flipping through a magazine at the grocery store checkout counter produces an internal tug of war: "Have a candy bar!" beckons the ultra-thin model. "Lose 10 pounds in 2 weeks!" scream the headlines across the adjacent page. "Learn to make a strudel!" "Take a weight-loss supplement!"

The women of television and movies are no more realistic-looking than are those in print. Female characters in the sit-coms tend to have models' bodies; only a very small percentage of these actresses have larger body types. On the other hand, male characters are more frequently overweight, indicating that a different set of standards operates for males and females. Overweight men are attractive enough to be featured on television, but overweight women must be hidden.

We like to think we are immune to these images, but research suggests otherwise. When the typical woman is bombarded with the supposedly ideal body images of advertising, a comparison process is unleashed. "She has such thin legs; why aren't mine like that?" In a recent compilation of studies on the impact of media on body image, psychologists J. Kevin Thompson and Leslie Heinberg document numerous adverse effects. For example, just three minutes of viewing photographs of thin models in women's magazines resulted in increased psychological symptoms and body dissatisfaction in a sample of college women. These reactions did not occur when women viewed photographs of average-sized models. In another study, ten minutes of videotaped television commercials featuring bikini-clad women and diet ads produced depression, anger, anxiety, and body dissatisfaction in a female audience. If ten minutes can send self-esteem into a tailspin, what is the impact of the average 35,000 TV commercials the typical adult watches in one year? As you might expect, the more television young girls watch per week, the worse they tend to feel about their bodies.

And by the Way, Super Models Are Not Role Models

Based on modeling agency criteria, the average high fashion model is likely to be 5' 10" and 120 pounds. In comparison to the average U.S. woman of 5' 4" and 138 pounds, models are not only abnormal, but also unhealthy. To meet the diagnostic criteria of anorexia nervosa, a life-threatening eating disorder, women must be 15% below normal body weight, a level at which most models would be deemed too *heavy* to work. This is the extreme illustrated by Barbie™, who is rumored to be not only too thin to menstruate, but so off-kilter because of her measurements that she must walk on all fours.

In her light-hearted and thoughtful guide to beauty traps, *Real*

Gorgeous author Kaz Cooke describes the unhappy lifestyles of prominent models. They pay a heavy (pun intended) price for their bodies. To maintain their impossibly low weights, they may resort to extreme diets, starvation, purging, intense exercise, and/or laxative use. They are also prone to smoking and drug use (especially heroin) in the effort to maintain thinness.

These are clearly not women to emulate. And yet, the number one wish of females from adolescence to middle age is to lose weight. For women with PCOS, attempts to lose weight are likely to be especially frustrating. Most women with PCOS were not aware of their diagnosis through what may have been several years of unsuccessful dieting. Because of our societal myth that weight is controllable, women with PCOS likely blamed themselves for their inability to shed pounds. Here is the story of one such woman, now in her 30s:

> "By this stage I had been on a diet for more or less as long as I could remember, never succeeding in keeping the weight off.... No one emphasized to me enough that my metabolism would be so reluctant or that I would be fighting a constant battle against my own body, which I began to perceive as my enemy. I was left on my own to find the right diet. For years I starved myself with little or no success, and last year I joined Weight Watchers™. For the first time, I felt I had found the perfect lifetime diet. I was successful for a while, yet I found it much harder than many of the other women at my group. It was very discouraging to see other women shed the pounds like nothing, whereas I had to be far stricter to lose only a fraction of the weight they were losing. Then it got worse. I stopped losing weight altogether, while I was still at least ten pounds away from my target weight. And then it got even worse: I started putting on weight, which really frightened me, as I was doing 'all the right things'."

Consequences of Body Dissatisfaction

It's sad enough that modern generations of women dislike—even hate–their bodies. But body dissatisfaction doesn't end there. It often leads to other, more serious consequences. Viewing one's body negatively tends to spill over into more generalized despair. The link between dislike of one's physical self and one's whole self is clear in this woman's description of her PCOS:

> "No one ever asked how it affected my womanhood. My sexuality. Me. I was always so DEPRESSED. I plucked my face everyday from the age of thirteen. It makes/made me so sad. I never wanted to go out in the sun; I didn't want people to notice the hair on my face and still don't. I was afraid to have boyfriends. I didn't want many girl friends. I felt and still feel inferior to other 'normal' women. I've

always felt I've been dealt a double whammy since I have also been overweight most of my life and ridiculed for it. (Now I know it's related to the PCOS). My self esteem was crushed from early on."

In many countries in the world, including the United States, women are two to three times as likely as men to experience a serious, clinical depression. There is increasing evidence that body dissatisfaction contributes to depression and helps to explain this gender difference. Prior to adolescence, the rate of depression is approximately equal in girls and boys; however, after puberty, girls are at greater risk of depression than are boys, the same time period in which their body satisfaction sharply declines. Although other theories have been proposed for the gender difference in depression, psychologist Kathryn Grant concluded on the basis of research she conducted that "Poor body image alone largely accounted for gender differences in depression among adolescent and young adult females." Depression is not uncommon among women with PCOS. Perhaps the source of such feelings is not PCOS per se, as is sometimes assumed, but the associated body dissatisfaction.

It is probably no surprise that body dissatisfaction is strongly linked to the development of eating disorders (anorexia and bulimia). Girls who are most unhappy with their weight in early adolescence are more likely to exhibit symptoms of eating disorders as they age. Even when girls do not develop a bona fide eating disorder, there is a strong likelihood that their pursuit of thinness will lead to chronic dieting behavior, which in turn leads to a lifetime of disturbed eating.

Many of the desperate methods women employ to attain the "thinness ideal" are hazardous to their health. Nutritionist Frances Berg, editor and founder of the *Healthy Weight Journal*, notes that one of the driving forces in young girls' cigarette smoking is their belief that smoking will help them lose weight. Despite decades of anti-smoking education and ad campaigns, for the first time in history girls—and especially white girls—are more likely to smoke than boys.

In fact, the list of harmful beauty efforts is unending. The quest for a tan can lead to skin cancer. Cosmetic surgery is not performed without risk. Depending on whether you believe the surgeons or the malpractice companies, liposuction killed between five and two hundred people during the late 1990s. Breast implants have, to say the least, questionable safety. Fen-phen, a formerly FDA-approved, and widely prescribed diet drug, is now the subject of a lawsuit. Studies have revealed it to be linked to heart-valve defects and hypertension.

One of the saddest aspects of body dissatisfaction is the idea that because it is so widespread among women, it's okay to feel that way. We laugh at Cathy, the cartoon character who always harps on her appearance obsession, because she reinforces the idea that body despair is universal. It's as if hating one's body is as much part of being a woman as is the XX chromosome.

Likewise, for some women with PCOS, it seems there is a perception that because "everyone"–or at least, *every woman*–has body dissatisfaction, it isn't worth talking about. But women with PCOS are likely to have body
dissatisfaction to a far greater degree than other women, and therefore, it is
definitely worth talking about. Recently, I was working with a female client in
her late 30s who came to see me primarily because she was experiencing a
significant depression. I learned in the course of therapy that she has PCOS,
and that although she never struggled with weight as a young girl, she had
experienced significant weight fluctuations in the past few years. After talking
with her about a number of difficulties that she was experiencing, I eventually
found a way to ask her about her body image. "Oh, sure, that's there," she
shrugged, understanding my question immediately. "I feel terribly uncomfortable with my body." With encouragement, she then proceeded to spend a good
bit of time discussing the very deep pain she felt over appearance issues - so
much that she had lost confidence in social situations and had started avoiding
leaving her house altogether. But until I asked her about body satisfaction, she
hadn't planned on bringing it up; she assumed these feelings to be largely irrel-
evant and perhaps a byproduct of depression. I, on the other hand, wonder to
what extent her body image problem was the *source* of her depression. The
danger of normalizing body dissatisfaction is that we make no effort to change
it, and then by default, we accept its negative consequences.

Overcoming Body-hating

I hope I've convinced you that there are good reasons to give up a
body-hating attitude. The most important first step is the resolution—and the
determination—to do so. But understand that because most women have been
feeling badly about their bodies for many years, learning to "love the one
you're with" is not likely to happen overnight. So make it a goal, but give yourself some time to achieve it. How do you do it? Here are ten practical, concrete tips for achieving this goal:

1. Stop cosmetic dieting! Instead, practice healthful eating.
Let's be absolutely clear about this: The vast majority of time-limited diets
designed to produce weight loss fail. Even if a dieter manages to shed weight
short-term, few will maintain the loss beyond one year. This is true regardless
of the amount of weight an individual loses or the type of diet selected for
weight loss. Results of dieting research have been so discouraging that a panel
convened by the National Institutes of Health in 1993 concluded that
attaining and maintaining a reduced body weight is simply a goal out of reach
for most overweight Americans. And this pronouncement was not directed
at women with PCOS, where biological issues make losing weight even
more difficult.

This may not be the news you hoped to hear. If you are unhappy with
your current body shape, it is not easy to give up dreams of completely over-
hauling it. Perhaps you are a victim of the cultural mythology that bodies can
be shaped and molded at our command. Isn't it of some relief to give up this
fantasy? I'm betting that if you take careful stock of your history, considering
all the unsuccessful diets you have attempted in your lifetime, you will conclude

that your weight has *not* been under your control. There are few pursuits in life at which we are so willing to repeatedly fail. If I invested in a mutual fund that had the success rate of dieting, I hope I would withdraw my money, and fast!

Giving up dieting is not all bad: Consider its negative impact on mental health, well documented in a report by Traci McFarlane and associates. Women on diets experience lower self-esteem than non-dieting women. Very low-calorie or long-term diets are associated with a variety of serious psychological symptoms such as anxiety, irritability, anger, and depression. Chronic dieting tends to lead to increasingly dysfunctional eating behavior, such as bingeing followed by starvation followed by bingeing. It is all too often a precursor for eating disorders. The deprivation that goes along with dieting also leads to internal torment; dieters experience greater food preoccupation, intrusive thoughts about food, food-related impulses, and feelings of being out of control. Dieting is even associated with cognitive impairment, for example, distractibility, slower reaction time, and poorer recall.

So what is the alternative? Increasing numbers of researchers recommend a strategy of *healthful eating.* Such programs may result in some weight loss, but they are not "diets." Psychologists Janet Polivy and C. Peter Herman designed a program that promotes "natural eating," defined as eating when hungry (as opposed to eating for emotional, social, or other reasons) and eating what one desires. Conducted in a group format, participants are encouraged to examine the negative consequences of dieting in their lives and to set goals for the future without reference to weight loss. Research indicates that this approach has resulted in increased self-esteem, decreased depression, and decreased bingeing for participants. The key feature of programs such as this one is encouraging women to give up dieting—forever. Participants are not encouraged to lose weight, but rather, their preoccupation with doing so.

What about dieting for medical reasons? Many women with PCOS are advised to lose weight for reasons related to fertility, pregnancy, or overall health. Obviously, this is a decision you must make in collaboration with your physician, taking into account your own unique circumstances. Keep in mind, however, that some researchers believe that the medical risks of obesity have been overstated. For example, scientists Paul Ernsberger and Richard Koletsky recently wrote a comprehensive review of the literature on this issue and concluded that the health hazards of obesity are not so great as to justify the hazards of dieting, dieting failure, and weight cycling. Their advice, consistent with experts in many fields, is to pursue a healthy, rather than a thin, lifestyle. Whatever your conclusion, dieting is never a decision to make lightly (pun intended).

For more on the issue of PCOS and healthy eating patterns, see Chapter 8.

2. Exercise, but not exclusively for weight loss! (Go ahead, sneak a peek at all ten of my suggestions: You won't find any weight loss recommendations here!) Exercising for the express purpose of losing weight is probably the quickest way to turn exercise into a chore, and chores—like diets—tend to be quickly forgotten.

I'm recommending exercise—or "prescribing it," as I often tell clients— for its psychological benefits. Most relevant to the issue of body image is the finding that exercise can improve women's satisfaction with their bodies. Physical activity can change a woman's focus, with her body suddenly viewed in terms of its function as opposed to being a mere object of attraction. (I'd rather have the muscular thighs of speed skater Bonnie Blair or soccer player Mia Hamm were I lost in the woods than the sticks of a super-model). I have observed large women, in particular, delight in the discovery that their size may translate into strength in the weight room.

Psychologists Gregg Tkachuk and Garry Martin recently reviewed research on exercise "therapy" and concluded that regular aerobic exercise is as effective as individual and group psychotherapy in the treatment of mild to moderate depression. Improvements in mood were obtained with as little as twenty to sixty minutes of supervised sessions of walking or running conducted three times per week. Regular exercise also appears to be helpful in alleviating pain in patients with chronic pain and anxiety in patients with panic disorder. Given the prevalence of depressive symptoms among PCOS patients, regular exercise may provide a special benefit.

Some tips: Choose something you really enjoy (or can learn to enjoy), and choose something to which you have easy access (e.g., if it requires a gym, do the gym hours fit your schedule?). Walking tends to be the simplest activity to incorporate into a crowded schedule, and it doesn't require a gym, a partner, or special equipment. (If you do opt for a health club, be careful not to join one of the meat market variety. All-women's gyms are nice, and the members tend to wear less neon and actually sweat.)

Even though the minimum level of exercise recommended for cardiovascular benefit is thirty minutes, three to four times per week, I favor five or more times per week because I think it is more likely to become part of your everyday routine that way. Perhaps start with ten to fifteen minutes at a time and gradually work toward the full thirty minutes.

Some basic tips for beginning exercise, and more importantly, incorporating it into your regular routine:

- Find an exercise partner or partners. Why not make this a social occasion? You'll find yourself looking forward to the activity, less bored with it, and afraid to disappoint a friend with a no-show.
- Schedule exercise, writing it in your calendar as you would any other appointment. Morning exercisers tend to have more success at maintaining their routine long-term.
- Set realistic goals, starting very modestly and keeping expectations low. Keep records of your activity in an exercise journal so you can see your progress.
- Remember that you might not always feel good during exercise, but you surely will afterward. Take note of those feelings so that you can use them to motivate yourself to get out of the house on a rainy day.
- For women who have not previously been physically active, consider investing in one or two sessions with a fitness trainer in order to learn proper techniques. In addition, be sure to start very slowly and gradually.

3. Read a self-help book. This chapter can only be considered an introduction to the problem of body dissatisfaction. If you are among the many women with PCOS who see body image as a "core" issue, that is, one from which many other psychological problems stem, consider dedicating yourself to a deeper study of the topic. You can continue your education by reading a popular book on body image; many of these contain exercises and activities to help you on your journey. Jane Hirschmann and Carol Munter's *When Women Stop Hating Their Bodies* is a solid approach to overcoming weight obsession; Joni Johnston's *Appearance Obsession* is more broadly based on cultural beauty. For girls and women of all ages, Kaz Cooke's *Real Gorgeous* is a humorous, highly readable, and practical guide to "the truth about body and beauty." (See the Resource List at the end of this book for complete references.)

4. Emphasize the positive. Here's an exercise that is presented in various forms in different self-help books: Examine yourself in the mirror and make a list of all your positive attributes. Everyone can find some aspect that is satisfying. Consider not only body parts (e.g., eyes, nose, hair) but also body functions (stamina, coordination, reflexes, energy level). If you get stuck on a body feature with which you aren't happy, consider its genetic basis. Are those Mom's thighs? (You might also ask yourself what positive contributions Mom provided; you may dislike Mom's thighs but love the mind you inherited from her. Remind yourself you don't get one without the other).

Remember that your level of contentment with your body is potentially more important to the outside world than any objective assessment of your body is. When people feel good about themselves, they tend to exhibit more social self-confidence and interpersonal skill, and this leads to more acceptance and liking from others. The next time you find yourself in the midst of a new group of people, focus on your long, thick hair or winning smile rather than the hips you imagine are too large. The boost you get from this positive focus will likely create a favorable impression on others. And don't forget another truism from social psychology: The more we like someone, the more attractive that someone becomes in our eyes. The prince in *Cinderella* apparently knew this fact, too, when he asked, "Or are you beautiful because I love you?"

Another approach to accentuating the positive is to consider expending dollars previously squandered in the $30 billion per year diet industry on body "feel-good" activities. Treat yourself to a sauna or a massage, and pay attention to the positive body feelings these produce. Some women find that yoga classes have the same effect.

5. Regulate your media intake. Here's a diet I can recommend: trimming the magazines and television viewing. The obvious solution to the unrealistic and unrepresentative images of the media is to shut them out. Pay attention to how you feel when you flip through a fashion magazine. Are you someone who feels worse about your body afterward? Likewise, do you find yourself attending to the bodies of the women you see on television? (No wonder we hit the refrigerator during commercials!)

Now ask yourself: Do you really need the fashion magazines? Do you want to support the industry that creates them? Perhaps you could substitute a different style of magazine, or better yet, one that features a wide variety of body types. *Radiance*, which now has an Internet version, is an upbeat, optimistic magazine that describes itself as "the magazine for large women." Other excellent alternatives to traditional women's magazines include *Mode*, a fashion magazine featuring models who must be a minimum size 12 (the on-line version is called *ModeStyle*), *Bella Online Magazine*, designed as a forum for large women to voice concerns related to body image and self esteem, and *Maxi* (also Web-based), described as a "friendly environment in which to empower and inspire" women.

As for television, consider leaving the room during commercials. The mute button is not enough, because it is the visual imagery, not the sound, which is so harmful to esteem. Teach yourself to practice media literacy when you can't escape ads, analyzing and then attacking the negative messages they convey.

6. Become an activist. Spread your media literacy to others. Start by visiting the Web page of *About-Face* (http://www.about-face.org), a San-Francisco-based, non-profit media literacy organization focused on the presentation of female images in the media. Frustrated with "starvation imagery," the group not only educates about the negative impact of media messages on body image and esteem, but also presents creative strategies to prevent their spread. Some features of the Web site: a gallery of offensive images, along with names and addresses of the persons or companies responsible for each ad; for a dose of optimism, a positive image collection; and an extensive library of factual information, references, and resources. Best of all, you can purchase postcards, bumper stickers, posters, and tee-shirts with slogans such as "Bodies are not fashion accessories," "Quit playing Barbie™," and "Stop Starvation Imagery." You might find yourself walking twice your usual route if you are wearing a tee-shirt that reads, "Goddesses Have Hips."

If you are involved in a PCOS support group (see Chapter 18), consider devoting group time to media literacy discussions and activism. Media activism is not merely an academic exercise; it can be highly effective in bringing about change while simultaneously educating consumers. In the early 1990s, Hershey's advertised a chocolate bar with the slogan, "You can never be too rich or too thin." The company elected to remove this advertisement after it became the target of a letter-writing campaign and was also challenged publicly by a public interest group.

Beyond PCOS support groups, you might consider channeling activist tendencies into starting another type of support group in your area, one focused on the promotion and acceptance of diverse body types. Such groups can be tremendously rewarding and energizing for women, providing both emotional support and a shared sense of purpose. They tend to bring together a diverse group of women, because so many women can relate to the problem of body dissatisfaction. A similar focus of some such support groups is on the prevention of eating disorders. Dina Zeckhausen, a clinical psychologist in private practice in Atlanta, began such a group in Atlanta in 1995: "I started the Atlanta Anti-Eating Disorders League after hearing about a similar group in Vancouver, made up of women recovering from eating disorders who realized as they got healthier that their eating disorders were merely an outgrowth of a food- and weight-obsessed culture. They were ready to stop focusing so much on themselves and start trying to do something to change the culture around them. Their first act of defiance was in downtown Vancouver at the opening of a new GAP™ store, where a large poster in the window displayed an anorexically-thin woman in a sleek top with the caption, 'Just the Right Shape.' They stood outside of the store and handed out brochures to passersby that described the indirect message of the poster, the general impact of media images on self-esteem and body image, the address of GAP™'s executives, and a sample boycott letter to send them. They also handed out brownies!" Dr. Zeckhausen believes that women benefit from involvement in support groups by "feeling that they are part of the solution. They meet women who are farther along in the process of 'recovery,' who are channeling all of the energy that their weight obsession previously occupied into amazingly creative, life-changing activities, and they are encouraged and inspired to find their own creative outlet."

7. Resolve to give up social comparison. Social psychologists tell us that it is human nature to evaluate ourselves in relation to other people. It is probably unrealistic, therefore, to imagine we can stop altogether comparing our bodies to those of other women. Perhaps a better goal would be to add some questions to the internal dialogue-taking place in your head when scrutinizing the women around you.

"Was this woman's look artificially produced/enhanced?"

"How many women in the world really look like this?"

"I wonder how much time and expense were put forth in achieving the look this woman has?"

A friend of mine gave me another suggestion. Consider adding "age groups" to your social comparison, as is done in competitive athletics, where "master's" runners and swimmers aren't forced to compete against younger athletes. If you can't stop social comparison altogether, you might at least consider choosing age-appropriate models!

8. Be an activist at home, too. It is important to be public about a commitment to accept a wide variety of body shapes. That means taking a careful look at your own critical eye and editing or censoring your appearance-obsessed commentary. Examples:

Old comment: "You look great; have you lost weight?"

Underlying message: You didn't look great when you were heavier.

New comment: "How are you today?"

Old comment: "Wow, look at the gorgeous model in this magazine. I'd kill to have legs like that."

Underlying message: Isn't thinness great?

New comment: "Wow, look at this stick figure model. She looks so unhealthy to me. Wonder if she's addicted to drugs? I don't care how much they pay those women; nothing is worth anorexia."

Old Comment: "Can you believe that woman has the nerve to wear a bikini? Look at how her stomach hangs out of that thing! Bikinis are made to be worn by size twos only."
Underlying message: People who are overweight should hide this fact as best as they can. Only thin body types are allowed to show off their bodies.
New comment (if you must make one at all): "Isn't that woman inspiring? I'm trying hard to get comfortable with my body, and she looks content with hers."

Old comment: "Wonder how many fat grams this dessert has? I really shouldn't be doing this. I feel so guilty."
Underlying message: It is sinful to eat dessert, and I better let everyone else know that I'm sinning so they don't think I do this regularly.
New comment: "I really enjoy a good dessert every now and then."

9. Join a therapy program. Psychologist Thomas Cash developed an intervention program for body-dissatisfied women known as body image cognitive behavioral therapy. The therapy approach has been shown to be effective in either a group therapy approach or via a self-directed format. Cash recently published a workbook that boils the program down to eight steps; the workbook has also been demonstrated to produce significant improvement in body image and adjustment, regardless of weight or weight changes. Another session for a PCOS support group might be devoted to working through an exercise in the workbook together.

The cognitive behavioral treatment approach was recently pitted against other interventions in a doctoral dissertation authored by Anner Bates Eliot. Participants in an approach that combined cognitive-behavioral therapy with exercise made the greatest gains in body satisfaction.

Individual therapists can help with these issues as well. Based on the fact that some psychologists continue to show prejudice toward women who are overweight, you should interview prospective therapists carefully about their training and experience with regard to weight and body image issues. Specific workshops or psychoeducational classes on body image are increasingly available as well.

10. Help prevent beauty brainwashing in the next generation. I'll be honest; this suggestion benefits you only indirectly. But helping others is often a way to help ourselves. And if you are able to discourage just one adolescent girl from adopting a beauty-obsessed, self-hating attitude, you have earned your ticket to heaven.

- Stop discussing weight or eating habits (and definitively not diets!), your own or others', around young girls. Parental comments, especially by mothers, can be very powerful contributors to weight and body concerns.

- Encourage and support school-based prevention programs. The Eating Disorders Awareness and Prevention website provides information about body image curricula for girls in middle and high school (http://www.edap.org). For example, the Go Girls! (Giving Our Girls Inspiration and Resources for Lasting Self-esteem) project has culminated in a 12-week curriculum that focuses on body image, media awareness, and the power of speaking out in teenaged girls.
- You can also teach youth the messages of these curricula–through youth groups you have contact with or, if you're a parent, to your own children. Read magazines or watch television with adolescents so that you can be on hand to criticize the harmful beauty messages.
- Buy a teen girl you know a subscription to an alternative girls' magazine, one that doesn't focus primarily on beauty and improving appearance. You can find a list of girls' magazines on the About-Face website.
- An excellent contribution from psychologist Joni Johnston: Fight weight or appearance criteria in school systems, e.g., weighing of cheerleaders or dance team members or cross-country runners.
- Take a firm stand against teasing about physical appearance, however "light" the humor.
- Remember that modeling is a powerful source of learning (note: that's modeling of behavior, not of clothes!) For example, refrain from voicing your own appearance concerns. Demonstrate an enjoyment of physical activity. And above all, do not evaluate others in terms of physical appearance.

Yes, I Want a Baby! Infertility

"I just want to know if I will ever get to be a mother."

If PCOS is present, a primary causative factor for infertility has already been identified. It is a major mistake, however, to assume that PCOS is the only problem. Any single diagnosis does not exclude other causes of infertility, such as tubal obstruction, endometriosis, aging, or male factors. Combined male and female factor infertility is present in about a third of couples seeking infertility treatment. Fewer than 10% of couples who seek treatment cannot be diagnosed with a specific problem (and so are referred to as having *unexplained infertility*). Even then, pregnancy rates with treatment are good. It is likely that subtle alterations in hormones, perhaps a milder form of PCOS, may be the underlying cause of much unexplained infertility. A healthy approach for the individual with PCOS is to enter a fertility investigation with a partner who has expectations for taking equal responsibility in the quest to become pregnant. There is much hope and considerable help for PCOS patients to establish a pregnancy. Therapy may be as much as 90% effective for fertility problems related to PCOS.

This chapter will present an approach to the full spectrum of infertility evaluation and therapy for both partners, with emphasis on PCOS-specific concerns. Don't get bogged down. This is a long chapter, but deservedly so. The chapter is divided into three parts:

- DIAGNOSIS
- THERAPY
- OPTIONS

Am I the only one? Is it in my head?

As if dealing with the stress of PCOS were not enough, infertility further magnifies the threat to female identity. A fertility patient *never* wants to hear from her family and friends, "Isn't it about time you had a baby?" The curse of all infertility patients is the friendly statement, "Just relax; it will happen." When infertile, it seems that everyone in the world is pregnant and no one else has your problem. As an exercise in reality, the next time you are in the mall do not look at every baby or even pregnant women, but instead consider every woman of reproductive age who does not have a child in tow to have an infertility problem. Actually, many of these women do have a problem, and many of those with a child have had a problem.

One of every six couples in the United States will experience infertility. It is not a sign proudly displayed. There can be intense isolation and an over-riding feeling of loss of control. Up until this point, most major life decisions, such as whether or not to attend college, whom to marry, when to marry, choice of career, etc. have been self-determined. That doesn't mean that life has been easy, only that with perseverance and hard work, obstacles have been overcome. Infertility is different. This may be the first major barrier that hasn't been under self-control. Now, no matter what is done in the name of childbearing, it just doesn't seem to work. True, determination is necessary, but success can't be achieved by worrying more and pushing harder. In truth, for many with PCOS, outside help will be needed for that baby, so let's talk about how to find and use that help!

Infertility and PCOS—Twelve Basic Truths

- PCOS is the most common cause of infertility in women who don't ovulate. In some infertility treatment centers, PCOS may be the most frequent cause of infertility.
- If you have PCOS, think you might have PCOS, or have irregular periods, don't wait a year to have the diagnosis of infertility. Seek help early.
- Individuals with PCOS should undergo preconception counseling to identify special medical risks, such as insulin resistance and hypertension, before attempting a pregnancy. Allowing a six-month period before conception in order to make health changes is a good rule.
- Do not delay after birth control pills are stopped to attempt getting pregnant. Try the first month off the pill.
- The healthier, and if overweight, the thinner you are at the onset of pregnancy, the easier and healthier the pregnancy will be. It may be worthwhile to invest in lifestyle changes. Smoking is out.
- If menstrual cycles are over 35 days apart, forget about using standard methods of ovulation detection. Either you don't ovulate or ovulation is so delayed that the quality of the eggs is likely affected and the risk of miscarriage is higher. Move on to a therapy that will facilitate ovulation.
- Clomiphene therapy is seldom effective after six cycles. Use of gonadotropin therapy should be questioned after three cycles. Age alone is a major cause of infertility.
- The risk of early miscarriage is higher in a PCOS patient, both with and without fertility therapy. If a miscarriage occurs, it is not your fault and ninety nine out of one hundred times, nothing could have prevented it.

- Don't forget to check a semen sample. Never lose sight that it takes
two, and there may be problems other than PCOS. Infertility is a
serious life event that affects both partners.
- It is important to understand the multiplication principle. If you are 60% fertile, perhaps due to irregular ovulation, and your male partner is 60% fertile due to lower, but still normal sperm parameters, it does not mean that as a couple you are 60% fertile; rather, you are 36% fertile. With each additional factor, the percentage lessens. If you take away another 10% for frequency or timing of intercourse, a couple may be infertile without one clear cause.
- Have hope and resolve. The road may be rough; it may be rocky, but probably about 90% of women with PCOS will become pregnant, unless there are other, even more stubborn factors.
- It is relatively commonplace for additional pregnancies to occur without intervention in women with PCOS, despite the need for aggressive therapy to achieve the first pregnancy.

Why preconception counseling?

The general advice often given to couples considering a pregnancy is, "Try, and if you are not pregnant in twelve months, then you are infertile and we will see what needs to be done." With PCOS, this is bad advice for several reasons. The first is that the chance of infertility is very high if the menstrual cycles are irregular and to delay therapy is to waste time. Perhaps more importantly are the metabolic associations of PCOS, or the appearance of PCOS, which can have very adverse effects on maternal and fetal health and may compromise the well-being of both. A thorough medical evaluation including weight, blood pressure, assessment of diabetes risk and lipid status should be added to the preconception visit with PCOS patients. It's a sad reflection, but another all too common physician response is "Go home and lose 50 pounds." Not that this is an unreasonable approach, but any physician who suggests it should also be prepared to be a partner in its accomplishment. Although weight loss is exceedingly difficult, weight reduction in itself may result in a pregnancy. If weight reduction does result in ovulation, it may create a better hormonal environment, resulting in better success with medical therapy. (See Chapter 8). After alteration in lifestyle, some women with PCOS can avoid ever being seen in a fertility clinic. See Preconception Pointers in Chapter 12.

Was it the pill that caused my fertility problem?

If you didn't or don't want to become pregnant, the pill is the optimal choice of contraception for patients with PCOS. There seems to be no problem with its long-term use, even very long-term use. Often the pill takes the blame for menstrual cycle problems that occur after it is stopped. The regular pattern of bleeding while using OCs gives a false impression of normalcy and masks underlying PCOS problems. Pill users may have a decreased risk for uterine fibroids, endometriosis, or pelvic inflammatory disease, and ovarian function may be better preserved.

If oral contraceptives (OCs) are being used decide when you want to be pregnant, stop taking the pill, and attempt a pregnancy in the first month. The so-called "wash-out" period may be a time of greatest fertility. Previously, it was believed that the pill caused birth defects. This was based on scanty evidence and no longer is thought to be true.

If you have PCOS, you might be even more likely to ovulate on, than off, the pill, especially a low dose pill. In fact, if it were not for the pill, some women with PCOS that have been pregnant would never have been so. Immediately after the pill is stopped, there can be a rebound effect resulting in a window in which ovulation occurs. The miscarriage rate may be slightly higher in conceptions established during the first month off the pill, but an attempt at pregnancy may be a calculated risk worth taking. Often after the pill is stopped, cycles may remain normal for several months before the system returns to its old ways.

DIAGNOSIS

What does it take to make a baby?

Perhaps it's my obsessive-compulsive personality, but I have always been a list maker. In initial infertility consultations I make two lists. The first is the essential requirements for pregnancy, or what it takes to make a baby. The second list is the types of therapy available to achieve this goal. The concepts are very simple. If it isn't this, then it must be that. If you have tried this, then that's what is left. Most often, the list is the same regardless of the cause of infertility. In practice, the hard part is weaving through the complexities of a diagnosis and modeling therapy to fit each individual couple.

The overall goal of fertility should be to move from infertility to a successful pregnancy as quickly, safely, and cost-effectively as possible. Tests and therapies that do not advance this goal, regardless of how widespread their use may be, are identified as such.

There are four basic requirements for reproduction, and therefore four areas for investigation as to the cause of infertility.

- A **sperm** capable of fertilizing an egg
- An **egg** capable of being fertilized
- Open passages to allow the **egg and sperm to meet**
- A **uterus** to nurture the developing pregnancy

A Sperm

Unlike PCOS, male infertility may have no outward signs. The first step, indeed the single most important test in any fertility evaluation, is a *semen analysis* (SA). Even if a child has been fathered or a previous semen analysis has been reported as normal, this is still necessary.

Several years ago, an IVF laboratory director in a reasonably well-known program complained that a couple was having in vitro fertilization because the woman had blocked tubes. At the time the eggs were obtained,

there were no sperm in the husband's semen sample. No semen sample had
ever been obtained before. Their doctor was quoted as saying he "had not wanted to stress the male partner." What about the stress of a $7500 bill for an IVF procedure and nothing to show for it? There have been too many instances where female partners have undergone surgery or aggressive medical therapy when a semen sample had never been examined. Luckily, these cases are becoming increasingly scarce.

The Male Infertility Inventory (The Ten "I"s)
- Infection
- Illness
- Incision (surgical injury)
- Injury
- Impotence (erectile dysfunction)
- Environment* (toxins and stress)
- Intoxicants (smoking, alcohol, illicit drugs)
- Ingestants (medications, diet)
- Inheritance
- Idiopathic (unknown cases)

*Ok, so I fudged! But this *e* sounds like an *i*!

Who evaluates male infertility?

Most individuals with PCOS readily identify with difficulty in obtaining comprehensive quality care. If the semen sample is abnormal, referral to a urologist is common. Urologists, while very capable of a thorough exam, unfortunately often are not interested or trained in complete evaluation and treatment of the infertile couple. Probably the best route is a relatively quick referral to a fertility center. The reproductive endocrinologist (RE) receives training in both male and female infertility and may be the best individual to explain options and coordinate efforts. A question you should ask when selecting a facility is whether the team includes an andrologist and reproductive urologist. The andrologist may be either a scientist or a clinician specifically skilled in male reproductive biology and infertility. The reproductive urologist has an interest in andrology, as well as surgical treatment of male infertility, and is a valuable member of the comprehensive care team. Unfortunately there are too few of these professionals around.

Looking at and understanding the numbers

Sperm *count, motility,* and *morphology* are the big three in analysis of semen. The chances of pregnancy fall as the number of problematic factors in a semen sample increase from one to two and from two to three. Often there are abnormalities in all three categories (*oligoasthenoteratospermia*).

Standard recommendation is that semen samples should be analyzed after three to four days of abstinence in order to have the maximum chance of a satisfactory evaluation. In reality, it may be more appropriate to produce a sample at your natural intercourse interval. Regardless, it is most important that the days of abstinence be recorded. If there is a good sample after twelve hours of abstinence—that's real good. Semen quality among men of proven fertility can vary considerably between samples. Do not be alarmed with a single bad report. It may be a one-time occurrence. Sometimes the semen analysis can be performed as a part of a natural or clomiphene cycle, adding therapy to diagnosis.

Withdrawal sex should not be used for producing a sample for analysis. The best sperm may be lost in the first several drops of semen. Artificial lubricants may lower motility and viability. If successful masturbation is not possible, many fertility clinics have condoms especially designed for this purpose.

General Guidelines for Interpretation of Semen Samples

Measurement	Normal	Low
Volume	2-5 ml.(cc)	
Concentration (count)	>20 million per ml. (cc)	oligospermia
Motility (movement)	>60%	asthenospermia
Morphology (appearance)	>30% WHO criteria >14% strict criteria	teratospermia

The normal volume of semen is 2-5 milliliter (ml) (1 ml = 1 cc, these units are used interchangeably). Less semen may be seen when there was recent intercourse. Lack of seminal fluid is a sign of obstruction or retrograde ejaculation. Low volume could indicate partial obstruction or infection.

Concentration is expressed as the number of sperm in each ml of ejaculate. Often a SA is read as abnormal because only total sperm count is considered rather than the count per ml. If there are no sperm, the condition is called *azoospermia*. Causes of azoospermia can be genetic factors, an obstruction, and/or hormonal problems. To exclude *retrograde ejaculation* (passage of the sperm into the bladder instead of out the urethra) a second semen analysis with evaluation of urine sample after ejaculation should be performed. Endocrine testing should also be performed. Unless the cause is immediately obvious, genetic studies may be needed.

If the count is under 20 million per ml, the individual is said to have oligospermia. It is not really a diagnosis, but a finding, and virtually every source of male infertility has the finding of oligospermia. It shows the likelihood of pregnancy, not what is wrong.

Motility (movement of the sperm) is very seldom above about 80%. Samples under 10% should be scrutinized for lab or collection errors. Labs differ in what they consider normal motility. Normal ranges are probably about 40-70%. Be aware of the sample that looks too good on paper. Problems with motility are referred to as *asthenospermia*.

Morphology refers to the shape of the sperm. There are two different classification systems in use. According to the traditional World Health

Organization classification, normal forms (shape) should be over 30%. Using a more refined classification including the "strict" criteria developed by Kruger, fertilization after IVF was 37-47% when there were fewer than 14% normal forms and 85-88% when there were over 14% of normal shape.

Be aware of the laboratory that is performing the semen analysis. Hospital labs are notorious for letting the sample sit too long before analysis, and too often technicians interpret semen samples with little formal training in semenology. The quality of the semen may be much better than reported. Often when white blood cells (WBC's) are reported, these are actually immature sperm cells. The distinction between WBC's and immature sperm can save unnecessary treatment with antibiotics. The results of the semen analysis may also overestimate sperm quality, but generally a sample reported as too good is much less worrisome for everyone.

If one semen analysis is abnormal, it should be repeated. If two semen analyses are normal, male factor cannot be excluded but becomes much less likely.

What is too low?

The most useful parameter in evaluation of a semen sample is total motile sperm. Too often a sample is judged good or poor by looking at only one of the above parameters. The correct formula for use to judge a sample is *Total motile = (Volume of sample) X (Concentration of sperm) X (motility).*

When there are more than 20 million total motile sperm, the chances of fertility are good. When in vitro fertilization (IVF) is used, there is little difference in fertilization rates with samples above five million. Every fertility specialist has been surprised with a pregnancy that occurred with counts so low as to border on sterility.

In the past, the prognosis for men with very low sperm counts was very poor and often donor sperm became the most viable option for achieving pregnancy in the female partner. We are now in a new era of male infertility therapy. We can not absolutely predict the limits of male fertility and it truly may take only one good sperm. It may mean assisted reproduction, but virtually all-male factor infertility is now treatable with relatively good success. Direct injection of sperm into the egg, *intracytoplasmic sperm injection* (ICSI) has dramatically changed the boundaries of male fertility. The confines of male infertility have been pushed even farther back with the technique of removal of sperm directly from the testicles.

Are there other fertility tests for him?

If a repeat semen analysis is also low, the next step is hormone testing. The basic evaluation includes blood tests for luteinizing hormone (LH), follicle stimulating hormone (FSH), and testosterone. If FSH levels are high, there is reduction in sperm production, while low FSH and LH indicates a "stress" pattern or communication problem within the endocrine system. Normal levels may be seen with obstruction of the sperm ducts. This is only a basic guide and there is considerable variation. The advisability of more extensive testing of sperm and sperm function, such as sperm penetration assays, antibody testing, and sperm viability studies should be highly questioned on a cost benefit basis. These tests may be valuable experimental tools, but truly offer very little to alter course of therapy and are best performed and read only by highly specialized clinics.

What can he do to improve his fertility?

One major area in which change for the better can occur is in lifestyle. Individuals with PCOS often share many lifestyle evils with their partner. There is no better way than to work on the problems together. There is a clear relationship between male obesity and decreased testosterone and decreased libido. Smoking has been clearly linked with decrease in sperm function. This relationship is very clear and very real. Additionally, smoking frequently leads to difficulty in establishing an erection in men over 40. Caffeine has the effect of temporarily exciting sperm, but then they don't live as long. It is unclear if the occasional alcoholic beverage affects sperm counts or function, but chronic and heavy use is clearly dangerous. A survey of any medications used is important. For example, calcium channel blockers, which are excellent drugs for hypertension, have also been shown to block fertilization. Too much of a good thing can also have negative consequences. For example, running over twenty miles a week reduces fertility.

In many cases of couples with both PCOS and male factor infertility, if one were more fertile than the other was, that one might not be seen in a fertility clinic. Sometimes if we can improve the female fertility by increasing the number or quality of eggs, this alone will overcome the male factor.

Boxers or briefs?

There is probably no male undergoing a fertility investigation in the United States today who is still wearing briefs. While based on the sound theory that increased heat reduces sperm count, there is clearly no evidence that the type of underwear worn makes a difference. The famous lover Casanova was said to have used long hot baths as a contraceptive, but this story, as well as a recommendation, is suspect. Fertility seems to go down in the summer months, and men in certain occupations subject to long periods of high heat are possibly affected, but the risks have been exaggerated

Should a varicocele be repaired?

A varicocele is a varicose vein of the scrotum. It has been theorized that this dilation of the veins increases scrotal temperature and reduces semen quality. There are some very positive scientific reports on improvement in sperm after the veins have been closed (ligated, occluded) or removed. Sperm counts may rise somewhat after surgery, but the hard evidence is completely lacking in relation to varicocele repair having any positive effect on fertility. If a surgeon finds a varicocele, there is a good a chance the opportunity to "have it fixed" will be offered. There would seem more effective alternatives than surgery, especially if there is the combined problem of PCOS.

Do men feel differently about infertility?

There is always considerable performance anxiety before the first semen sample is produced and great pride when it is discovered to be normal. For a man to be told of an abnormal semen analysis is equivalent to a woman being told that she cannot carry a child. Men equate sperm counts with potency, potency with virility and virility with manliness. Men may not wake up each morning and go to bed at night thinking about infertility, but they certainly carry the burden with them. Infertility attacks the male self image as strongly as the female.

A "Good" Egg

The second essential component of establishing a pregnancy is an egg. This translates into both the necessity for a "good egg" and the capacity for it to be ovulated. PCOS patients may have difficulties with either or both. What constitutes a good egg is an elusive concept. The only definite distinction that can be made is that a good egg is one capable of being fertilized, of normal development, and of establishing a normal pregnancy. I worked with an embryologist who was constantly asked by patients about egg quality after eggs had been aspirated from the ovary for IVF. His reply was often, "Good." When asked what this meant, his reply would be " 'Good' is good."

Certainly we know from several vantage points that eggs from women with PCOS are not always "good." A recent study found that eggs extracted from the small cysts of PCOS ovaries have much less capacity to undergo development than do eggs from follicles of similar size women without PCOS.

In the past there have been no specific treatments to directly improve egg quality. We had to rely on drugs to ensure that ovulation would occur, often therapies that resulted in several ovulations in hopes of safety in numbers. This may be changing with drugs that specifically address the ovarian environment in which the egg and its follicle grow.

How can I tell if I am ovulating?

The only sure test of ovulation is a pregnancy. There are a number of indirect testing methods that provide a probability that ovulation will occur, or has already occurred. The more of these indicators that are used and that are positive, the more likely the individual is ovulatory. Methods for ovulation detection should only be used in PCOS if cycle lengths vary between 26 and 32 days either naturally, or with some form of fertility promoting agents.

Methods of ovulation detection and cycle monitoring

- Cycles 26-32 days
- Mid-cycle mucus changes
- Pain at mid-cycle (mittleschmerz)
- Basal body temperature (BBT) tracking
- Ovulation predictor kit (OPK)

- Day 21 progesterone level
- Ultrasound
- Endometrial biopsy
  (to be avoided)

Figure 11-1 Ovulation Detection

OVULATION DETECTION

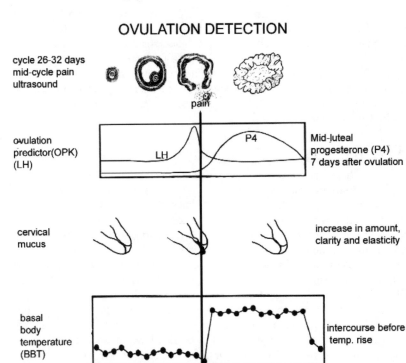

cycle 26-32 days
mid-cycle pain
ultrasound

pain

ovulation
predictor(OPK)
(LH)

P4

LH

Mid-luteal
progesterone (P4)
7 days after ovulation

cervical
mucus

increase in amount,
clarity and elasticity

basal
body
temperature
(BBT)

intercourse before
temp. rise

Day | 1 | 2 | 3 | 4 | 5 | 6 | 7 | 8 | 9 | 10 | 11 | 12 | 13 | 14 | 15 | 16 | 17 | 18 | 19 | 20 | 21 | 22 | 23 | 24 | 25 | 26 | 27 | 28

The best approach to ovulation detection and luteal phase responsiveness is to use the largest number of the most accessible, least invasive, and inexpensive tests. This combination might vary depending on the patient's distance from the clinic, activity schedules, and preference.

Physical signs

As a follicle grows toward ovulation, estrogen levels rise and the cervical mucus starts to increase in quantity, clarity and elasticity and a discharge becomes more obvious. Mucus production is associated with estrogen production and not necessarily ovulation. Mucus production is enhanced by gonadotropin stimulation for ovulation induction and inhibited by clomiphene therapy. *Mittleschmerz,* the mid cycle pain associated with ovulation, is felt in some, but certainly not all ovulatory women. It is unclear whether this pain represents the rupture of the follicle, or is a response from irritation caused by the fluid released from the follicle. The pain may alternate between the right side and left side since each ovary ovulates with about the same frequency. Most often pain occurs two days before the BBT elevation. If there are subjective signs that a period is nearing, such as fluid retention and breast tenderness, then there is a somewhat better chance ovulation has occurred.

Charting the basal body temperature using a special thermometer, which is used before getting out of bed, is a nuisance, but is also easy, cheap,

Figure 11-2 BBT

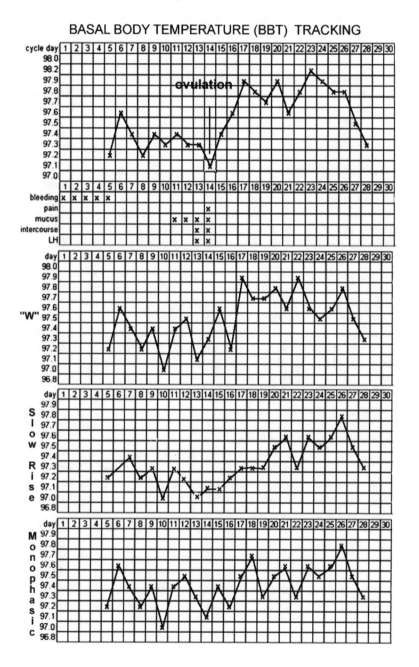

BASAL BODY TEMPERATURE (BBT) TRACKING

and relatively reliable. BBT tracking also provides a calendar on which other information about the cycle and therapy can be recorded. Unfortunately, it is one more daily reminder of infertility. Ovulation generally occurs one to two days after the lowest temperature point. A temperature elevation of about 0.4-1.0° F is evidence of progesterone production, which is presumptive but not conclusive evidence of ovulation. When there is a clear rise in temperature, this is called the *shift* and the chart is said to be *biphasic*. In a 28-day cycle, the shift should occur on cycle day 13-14. In longer or shorter cycles, the shift should occur ten to fourteen days before the next menses. The temperature should remain elevated until just before menses. If the temperature elevation occurs in fewer than ten days, or if there is a drop after a rise, this is evidence of ovarian dysfunction and possibly lack of ovulation. If the shift does not occur, the chart is said to be *monophasic*. A pronounced "W" pattern to the chart, a shift after day 16, or a slow rise in temperature may indicate disordered ovulation.

Ovulation predictor kits (OPK)

A valuable method to help determine if ovulation is occurring and when best to time intercourse or insemination is the home test kit that changes color when a certain level of luteinizing hormone (LH) is present in the urine. Ovulation usually occurs within forty hours of this color change, but there is individual variation ranging from twelve to sixty hours. The ovulation predictor kits are very sensitive and reliably measure LH. While there cannot be ovulation without LH, it may be elevated when ovulation has not occurred (false positive). Constantly, I hear the comment "I've tried those !?"&%@ kits and they don't work." Truth be known, the kits work just fine, it's the "!?*?!" ovary that's not working correctly. A relatively common observation in PCOS is that the test kit is always positive. This is also a diagnosis, but not the one desired. Another possibility for a falsely positive test is in patients using clomiphene, which elevates LH. Usually this is not a problem if testing is started at least three days after the last clomiphene tablet. Finally, although there can be a timely secretion and adequate LH to cause a color change, there may be insufficient LH to stimulate the ovary to ovulate.

Mid-luteal progesterone level

Use of progesterone measurements to check for ovulation can be a little tricky. The production of progesterone is limited to ten to fourteen days after ovulation unless a pregnancy intervenes. In a 28-day cycle, the height of progesterone production occurs on day 21 or seven days after ovulation and this is when the test should be performed. However, if ovulation occurs on day 20, the progesterone level would not be at maximum elevation until cycle day 27, still seven days after ovulation.

This is further complicated because progesterone is released in pulses. Although ovulation has occurred, progesterone levels may be abnormally low when caught at the trough of one of the pulses. Progesterone levels may be falsely high at a pulse peak although ovulation failed. High levels suggest that ovulation has occurred, low levels suggest that it hasn't. There is a broad gray area in the middle range. Remember that timing of this test is everything.

Endometrial biopsy

During an endometrial biopsy, a small sample of the uterine lining is taken as close to a period as possible (days 24-26 of a 28 day cycle). A pathologist then "dates" the endometrium according to established standards for that day of the menstrual cycle. If the histologic dating of the sample lags the menstrual dating by two or more days, there is said to be a *luteal phase defect* (LPD). The single most common cause for a LPD is lack of ovulation. Generally called the "gold standard," the endometrial biopsy has little utility at present. It is imprecise, expensive, painful when performed, and probably does not alter therapy. Biopsy can be valuable in some cases of abnormal bleeding when there is difficulty in evaluating the endometrium by ultrasound, or if cancer must be excluded (see Chapter 13), but I strongly believe it has no role in fertility evaluation. We have moved beyond that point.

My suggestion for ovulation detection

One scenario that I use to optimize data collection is as follows: BBT tracking is started on cycle day 7; ovulation detection kit monitoring on day 9 to 12, based on previous cycle length and continued at least five days, or until clear evidence of a color change; a progesterone determination seven to nine days after a shift/surge. In a subsequent cycle, the above is repeated and modified depending on findings. If there is clear lack of ovulation by two or three of the parameters, clomiphene citrate therapy is started (see below).

What if I am over age 35?

Advances in medical care systems and changes in demographics have changed our concept of "old" and "young." Some women have delayed childbearing while other life goals are being met; others are in new relationships at

Figure 11-3 IVF Success at Various Ages

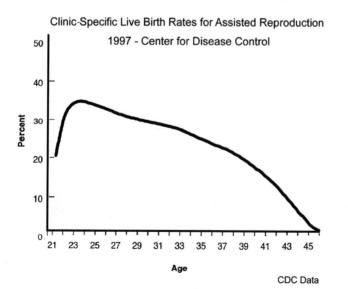

Clinic-Specific Live Birth Rates for Assisted Reproduction

1997 - Center for Disease Control

CDC Data

later ages, while others may be at the end of a very long path of unsuccessful fertility therapy. It seems everyone has a family member or friend of a friend who had a pregnancy after age 45, but pregnancy after age 42 becomes increasingly rare. Numerous studies show that the average age that the last child is born is age 41. Perhaps a little good news is that there is no evidence that PCOS causes faster aging. Unfortunately, there is virtually no information about PCOS and childbearing at later stages of the reproductive years.

Regardless, the biologic clock continues to tick as the supply of eggs is continually depleted from the ovary. There has been a steady decline of eggs since before birth, a decline which becomes more pronounced after age 30 and rapidly accelerates as age 40 nears. Any factor that results in the destruction of oocytes such as surgery, radiation, pelvic disease or genetic disorders serves to hasten the loss. There is theoretical concern that ovarian wedge resection or ovarian cautery (see Chapter 17) while temporarily beneficial, may reduce oocytes store, but this has not been confirmed.

A reliable marker to evaluate the remaining egg stores of the ovaries is a blood test for follicle stimulating hormone performed on day 2 or 3 of the cycle. Pregnancies are seldom achieved in women with FSH levels over 20 IU/L. Levels above 10 are very worrisome. FSH levels are determined in conjunction with a blood level of estradiol that adds to the integrity of the test. Estradiol levels should be below 50 PG/ML for the FSH test to be valid. Use of a clomiphene challenge test to stimulate FSH has been reported to further increase the sensitivity. In the future, special signals like *inhibin*, which is produced from the follicle, may give an even more accurate assessment of ovarian reserve.

It seems that the two consequences of reproductive aging are infertility and an increased risk of chromosomal abnormalities, especially Down syndrome. It is recommended that women over age 35 receive counseling and diagnostic testing. If a pregnancy exists, it seems there is an excellent chance that the mother and baby will do about as well as younger women. Again, specific studies on PCOS, pregnancy and advanced reproductive age have not been performed. The single largest issue appears to be infertility. As figure 11-1 clearly shows, there is a significant decline with even the most aggressive of therapies over age 40.

Sperm and Egg Must Meet

The third requirement for reproduction is that the egg and sperm must meet. This requires properly timed intercourse and a clear path.

How should we time intercourse?

This is a simple question, but it is amazing how much misinformation there is about timing intercourse. Ovulation occurs toward the end of a five to seven day time-span called the *fertile period*. In the idealized 28-day cycle, ovulation occurs on days 13 to 15. If the cycles vary within the acceptable 26 to 32 day range, the fertile period is from days 11 to 16. If you have intercourse three times during the fertile period there is probably adequate exposure. It doesn't matter if there are two or three days in a row, or even several days without intercourse. Chances are that over several months the timing will be perfect. Don't believe the sit-coms where the male partner is called home from the office or golf course because ovulation is occurring at that exact minute. No one ever knows her ovulation that precisely. More importantly, remember that sperm require up to six hours in the female reproductive tract before they develop the capacity to fertilize an egg, so plan ahead. Intercourse every day will drive down the sperm count, while intervals of over three days may not ensure the highest concentration of sperm, or may even miss ovulation.

The goal is to have healthy sperm at the site of fertilization awaiting ovulation. Once released from the ovary, the life span of an egg is short, probably twelve to twenty-four hours. However, sperm remain capable of fertilization for at least two days. I recently saw a pregnant couple where there had been a well documented six days between intercourse and ovulation. Rare, but it illustrates the point. Much too much emphasis has been placed on timing. Obviously, you have to have sex, but don't disrupt your bedroom.

Semen seems to drip out after sex, is this normal?

Yes. This is probably the single most common question couples ask, although usually with a slightly reddened face. The first and best part of the ejaculate is naturally placed in the deepest portion of the vagina and is least likely to be lost. Usually the discharge is from the natural process called liquefaction, when there is change in the consistency of semen. You should not douche after sex, but there are no other restrictions.

Is there a better position?

No. Change position for recreation, not procreation. There are many different sexual positions and many different positions of male and female anatomy. There may be one best for you, but not one best for everyone.

Could my body be killing sperm?

Sperm are deposited in the area of the vagina that surrounds the cervix called the *fornix*. The vaginal environment is very acidic and quite hostile to sperm. Semen, along with the cervical mucus, has relatively high pH and can protect sperm until they have a chance to enter the favorable environment of the cervical canal. It is only around the time of ovulation that there is sufficient mucus to entrap and protect the sperm. There are remedies that have been used to alter the pH of the vagina, such as baking soda and other special douches. It also has been suggested that the quality of cervical mucus is improved by use of the active ingredient of some cough mixtures, Guafinesin™. Neither of the two approaches is validated by scientific trials and is usually not advocated by fertility specialists. On the other hand, these approches probably do no harm.

Could I have a sperm allergy?

Most antibodies to sperm are produced in the cervix. Antibodies are real. Antibodies can bind and inactivate sperm. This barrier can be by-passed by either intrauterine insemination (IUI) or in severe cases, IVF. There has been no therapy shown effective in reversing the problem.

What does an abnormal post coital test mean?

The *post coital test* (PCT) is an evaluation of cervical mucus performed just before ovulation and immediately after intercourse. The test assesses the quality of cervical mucus and the presence and viability of sperm. PCT has much to be said for it. It's simple, painless, cheap and safe. It has only one serious disadvantage. Two different studies have now substantiated that PCT does not predict fertility or infertility. The poor PCT most likely arises from poor test timing. A second cause is lack of ovulation. Seldom does the PCT indicate cervical factor infertility. If a cervical factor does exist, it is mostly a moot point, because it is usually by-passed by intrauterine insemination that is a part of standard procedure in fertility therapy.

Do vaginal infections alter fertility?

Typical "run of the mill" vaginal infections are not serious, but could produce an abnormal vaginal and cervical environment. They can usually be evaluated by the presence of discharge on speculum examination and PAP smears. Cultures are not necessarily needed if there is a very low risk of sexually transmitted diseases. It is often easy to forget to keep PAP smears current during an infertility evaluation.

Can the cervix be too tight?

Probably not. There have been the rare cases when the cervical opening seems to be very small. It seems possible that if this was associated with abnormal semen parameters that there could be a problem, but one that should be easily correctable by IUI. An abnormally tight or closed cervix (*cervical stenosis*) sufficient to prevent sperm transport can result from surgery.

Surgery on the cervix?

Some have had cone biopsies for the evaluation and treatment of *cervical dysplasia*. During the procedure, a portion of cervical canal and its *endocervical glands* are removed or destroyed. These glands serve both to produce mucus and act as a reservoir for sperm, slowly releasing them over several hours to several days. The likelihood of a problem is related to the extensiveness of the surgery. Minor cryosurgery (the cervix frozen) usually causes no harm. Repeat PAP smears are essential when there has been a previous diagnosis of cervical abnormalities.

Could I have blocked tubes?

I often tell patients that if there is ovulation and there are sperm, what remains is an anatomic problem. For the PCOS patients, I still always consider PCOS to be the cause, but I change the statement into a question. When there is a diagnosis of PCOS, the question becomes, is there anything else, is there more than one problem? That "something else" can be a problem with pelvic anatomy. It might not matter if medical therapy is successful if the egg and sperm can't meet. There are three major ways to evaluate pelvic anatomy: ultrasound scan, hysterosalpingogram, and laparoscopy/hysteroscopy.

The *hysterosalpingogram* (HSG) is a screening test performed in a hospital x-ray department in order to evaluate the contour of the uterine cavity and to determine if the tubes are *patent* (open). During an HSG, liquid dye is passed through an instrument placed in the cervix. Passage of the dye and outline of the uterus and tubes can easily be visualized by a special x-ray technique called *fluoroscopy*. Some women conceive after an HSG without additional therapy. This is thought to be due to a "flushing out" effect on the tubes and the removal of small bits of scar tissue. HSG is an excellent method to evaluate the possibility of some congenital abnormalities of the uterus, but its overall usefulness may be limited.

About one in three cases will give a false HSG reading. Either there will not appear to be a problem when there actually is, or the test will be read as abnormal when no abnormality exists. If the HSG is abnormal, a laparoscopy or hysteroscopy is needed for confirmation and treatment. If the test is negative and nothing has been found, the results can't be trusted and a laparoscopy or hysteroscopy may be necessary to exclude a problem. It is also common for the tube to have a muscle spasm during the procedure and appear blocked. The ability of the tubes to be freely mobile is very important. The tubes may be open, but scarring (adhesions) may prevent the tubes from capturing the egg at ovulation. *Open tubes do not equal normal tubes.* Perhaps, finding the tubes open may be sufficient to progress to a more aggressive ovulation induction. A personal opinion is that as a screening test, HSG is too painful, too costly, and just isn't good enough.

Should I have a laparoscopy?

Although sometimes performed under sedation and local anesthesia only, laparoscopy is usually done under general anesthesia in an operating room of an outpatient facility. General anesthesia allows a more complete examination and more importantly, a more thorough therapy.

A small incision is made in or just below the navel (*umbilicus*). A small amount of carbon dioxide gas is placed into the abdomen to allow better visualization and a comfort zone from injury. A slender telescope-like instrument, the laparoscope, with a video camera attached is inserted through the umbilical incision and the internal organs are viewed on a television monitor. One to three more small (about 1/4") incisions are made just below the pubic hairline to allow operating instruments to be used as needed.

Direct evaluation can be made of the uterus, tubes and ovaries, as well as other pelvic and abdominal organs. Under direct observation, blue dye is passed through the cervix, uterus and out the tubes, *chromotubation*. The is similar to the procedure for HSG, but you are asleep and colored dye is used instead of x-ray contrast to see if the tubes are free and clear.

A videotape is often made and can be used to discuss surgical findings, as well as a precise important record for the future. Sometimes photos of important findings are made instead of a video. One of these two methods should always be used. It is recommended that a *hysteroscopy* be performed at the same time. It is very useful to put a check mark in the column signifying that the uterus is normal. This is good insurance for the future.

Some experts regard laparoscopy with or without hysteroscopy to be the most valuable single procedure in evaluating female fertility. Others, who are in the minority, suggest avoiding laparoscopy with concentration on medical therapy and assisted reproduction. The decision for laparoscopy is even more difficult in the PCOS patient where one diagnosis is already known. The decision to proceed should take into account age, suspicion of pelvic disease and whether ovarian cautery procedure to treat PCOS is planned. Laparoscopic therapy for PCOS is discussed in Chapter 17.

The Three Values/Purposes of Laparoscopy
- Diagnosis – What's wrong
- Therapy – A chance to correct the problem
- Prognosis – What the future holds

When should a laparoscopy be considered?

Your doctor may suggest a laparoscopy when any of the following conditions exist:

- Pelvic pain (to exclude adhesions and endometriosis).
- Obvious abnormalities on ultrasound scan.
- Suspected previous pelvic infection or pelvic.
  inflammatory disease (PID).
- Previous pelvic or abdominal surgery.
- No other cause has been found—normal semen.
  and ovulatory parameters.
- Before proceeding to injectable fertility drugs, or IVF.

What might be found?

Laparoscopy offers an opportunity to visualize and thus confirm diagnosis of several conditions for which there are no lab tests, including

- Endometriosis
- Tubal blockage, damage, or impairment of movement
- Adhesions (pelvic scarring)
- Congenital abnormalities (birth defects)
- Uterine fibroids
- Ovarian cysts
- PCOS

A benefit of laparoscopy is that practically any fertility problem that can be seen by laparoscopy can also be treated by laparoscopy. A surgeon who has experience in correction of the problems related to infertility should be chosen. There is no use to look but not correct a problem. However, it is better to look and discuss rather than incompletely or incorrectly treat.

What's it like to have a laparoscopy?

In the preoperative visit, a full discussion of the possible diagnoses, planned treatments, potential benefits and risks are presented in detail. This is your time to make sure all your questions are answered and you and your surgeon are in agreement. An ultrasound evaluation of the uterus and ovaries to identify potential problems is useful at some point before the surgery.

Laparoscopy is often performed after menstruation stops, but before ovulation. This prevents an interruption of an unknown pregnancy. There are also reports that the healing process is better during this time. The ovary is also quiet and cyst formation is less likely.

Although sometimes performed under sedation and local anesthesia only, laparoscopy is usually done under general anesthesia in an operating room of an outpatient facility. General anesthesia allows a more complete examination and more importantly, a more thorough therapy. That night and the next day it is common to have shoulder pain due to a small amount of gas remaining in the abdomen. Your body will tell you what to do or not do. Many times it is suggested that you try for a pregnancy in the same month as surgery. Recovery is usually complete in a week or less.

A Place to Grow (The Uterus)
What are the possible abnormalities of the uterus?

Problems of the uterus are less common than anovulation, male factors, tubal disease or endometriosis, but still must be considered and their diagnoses excluded. A good prognosis is a previous pregnancy and normal delivery. Any lesion that distorts the endometrial lining either directly, such as a polyp, or indirectly from pressure in an underlying structure, usually a fibroid, (see Chapter 13) can alter the capacity to conceive and increase the risk of pregnancy complication.

Problems may exist with the uterine lining due to past infection, a too aggressive dilation and curettage, or incompletely removed pregnancy. In these conditions, the regenerative cells are removed from the lower endometrial lining and since the lining cannot renew the cells, it scars. Sometimes a similar condition is selectively induced to stop irregular bleeding. Regardless the uterine lining can not be primed to accept or keep a pregnancy.

The uterus is formed from the fusion of two embryonic tubes called the *Müllerian, or paramesonephric ducts*. They remain separate in the upper portion as the fallopian tubes, but are joined to form the uterus with cervix and upper vagina. Embryology of this area follows Murphy's Law that "if it can happen, it will." Variations range from a complete double system of two separate and equal uteri and vaginae (*uterus didelphys*) which is easily diagnosed, to a diagnosis of intermediate difficulty, a "y"-shaped *bicornuate* uterus, to a uterus with only a small thin vaginal septum which might be diagnosed only by hysteroscopy. The defect may be symmetric, with equal portions, or asymmetric, with unequal portions or perhaps even a segment that is isolated and blocked (*non-communicating*). Endometriosis, as well as abnormalities of the urinary system, for instance a double ureter, are more common and a test to evaluate the status of the kidney and collecting system (intravenous pyelogram -IVP) is often used for evaluation. There has become more of a tendency not to surgically correct embryologic disorders unless there is recurrent loss, or all other causes of infertility have been completely excluded.

Conditions that may affect the uterus
- Uterine fibroid(s) (myoma or leiomyoma)
- Endometrial polyps
- Intrauterine adhesions (Asherman's Syndrome)
- Congenital anomalies

How is the uterus evaluated?

Ultrasound is the first diagnostic tool for evaluation of the uterine lining (endometrium) and the wall of the uterus (myometrium). Most fibroids and many polyps are seen during an ultrasound scan. The endometrial cavity can be further evaluated by sonoHSG.

Sonohysterography (*sonoHSG*) involves passage of a small plastic tube through the cervix into the uterus through which to pass water or other substances while watching with ultrasound. This is performed as an office procedure and avoids the higher cost of a conventional HSG and radiation. It is superior for evaluation of the uterus for abnormalities such as polyps or fibroids. Its drawback is that it is not a good technique for evaluation of whether the tubes are patent. Sometimes water can be seen passing through the tubes and accumulating in the pelvis, which is an indication that at least one tube is open. Like an x-ray, sonoHSG is a screening test and if a problem is found, it will need to be evaluated by hysteroscopy.

Hysteroscopy is the definitive test for evaluating the architecture of the inside of the uterus. With hysteroscopy, a slender telescope is placed in the cervix and the uterus is filled with a solution or a gas allowing direct observation of its inside. Abnormalities of the uterus including scar tissue, polyps, and some fibroids can be identified and often treated at the same time.

Is there an immunologic basis of infertility?

In no topic of reproductive medicine are the lines so well drawn and the sides entrenched as in the debate over the value of immunologic testing and therapy. I am clearly against it. It is not because immunologic processes do not have a critical part of many reproductive functions. On the contrary, ovulation and implantation clearly share many similarities to an inflammatory response. I am against it because, thus far, tests have failed to accurately discriminate disease. There have been a number of scientific reports that indicate women with and without antibodies achieve pregnancy equally. More importantly, if a problem is found, there is no proven effective therapy. While testing may involve only a blood test, some of the therapies that have been proposed are potentially dangerous. It is unclear why there is so much discrepancy. This fact alone is worrisome.

It has been said that there is no important disease for which an immunologic cause has not been proposed. Both PCOS and infertility are prime candidates for an immunologic diagnosis. Individuals with these problems are often desperately in search of solutions that have not been forthcoming. It is unclear why there is so much discrepancy. We all must wait for greater scientific clarity. In the meantime, make sure evaluation and therapy stays on course with the highest degree of efficiency.

THERAPY

Regardless of the cause of infertility, there are only three broad areas of therapy. PCOS may be amendable with treatment by any or all of these major methods. All work, but none work in all individuals, none is guaranteed, and none is without risks and possible side effects. The therapies are

- Ovulation induction (fertility drugs)
- Laparoscopy and hysteroscopy (surgery)
- Assisted reproduction (IVF)

What are fertility drugs?

If ovulation is not occurring or not occurring regularly (a simple fact in most cases of PCOS), there are two different types of drugs approved by the FDA and traditionally used for ovulation induction—oral clomiphene citrate and injectable gonadotropins.

Each month there is a group (*cohort*) of one to twenty follicles, that are "recruited" from the resting pool (remember the follicle is the small cyst that contains an egg; one follicle = one egg). From this group, usually *several* are "*selected*" to continue their growth, while the others degenerate (become *atretic*). From this small group, one follicle achieves "*dominance*" over the others and will progress to ovulation. The symphony is conducted by pulses of gonadotropin releasing hormone (GnRH) secreted in short *pulses* from the hypothalamus resulting in release of gonadotropins (LH and FSH) from the pituitary gland. (presented in detail in Chapter 2).

Fertility drugs stimulate the ovary by increasing the concentration of gonadotropins. A higher level of gonadotropins means less atresia and translates into more follicles available for ovulation. The drug clomiphene citrate works by a pharmacological trick that promotes the release of the pituitary gland's own storage of gonadotropins and thus, indirectly stimulates the ovaries. Injectable gonadotropins stimulate the ovaries directly. An important point is that neither of these medications depletes the ovary of follicles or eggs. Therapy only reduces the normal falling by the wayside of follicles during their development.

One of the drawbacks of all fertility drugs is that they tend to work in only one cycle (month), having usually little impact on the next cycle. The developing follicle may take as long as three months (cycles) to go through the entire process of growth and maturation. The importance of this for PCOS is that the follicle and its egg have progressed through 80-85% of their growth and development in an abnormal hormonal environment. This may contribute to poorer egg quality despite aggressive stimulation and explain why many more women can be caused to ovulate than get pregnant.

Clomiphene Citrate

Clomiphene citrate (CC) (brand names—Clomid™, Serophene™) is usually the first-line of therapy in PCOS patients who want to become pregnant. Experience and research seem to show that different brands of CC are equally effective. In comparison to the injectable medications, CC is quite safe, inexpensive, easy to use, and offers a chance of pregnancy in the initial month of use. CC is not a hormone, but a synthetic *anti-estrogen*. As such, it "fools" the body's regulatory mechanisms into perceiving that more estrogen is needed. This challenge is met by increased gonadotropin release from the pituitary gland as well as by a breakdown in the barriers to successful follicle growth and ovulation. However, this anti-estrogenic action is a double-edged sword also extending its anti-estrogenic effects to other 'target' organs such as the lining of the uterus (*endometrium*) and cervix. CC retards endometrial development and may decrease the possibility of implantation of the embryo. CC also markedly decreases the amount and quality of cervical mucus, which may impede sperm transport. Some investigators have proposed a detrimental effect of CC on the follicle, egg, or embryo, but this is much less well substantiated. It is clear that ovulation rate on CC exceeds the pregnancy rate. CC is certainly far from perfect. (See further explanation in Chapter 17)

Gonadotropin injections

The injectable gonadotropin drugs are natural hormones, the fuel on which the ovaries run. They directly stimulate the ovaries in the same manner as the naturally secreted hormones do, just more. Success results from either improving the *quality* of all individual follicles therefore eggs, and can be likened to improving aim, or from increasing the number of eggs, thus enlarging the target.

There are three disadvantages of gonadotropin injection:
- **Route of administration.** Gonadotropins are given by injection and most people do not like shots. Fortunately, the procedure of the injections is safe, easy and less painful than most injections. In the past these were given in the hip (*intramuscular*); now some varieties are given with a small needle under the skin (*subcutaneous*) in the thigh; much like insulin or allergy shots.
- **Cost**. Gonadotropin injections are expensive. The cost of the medication alone runs from several hundred to several thousand dollars per cycle. Insurance companies vary in their willingness to cover the charges, which are usually from $500 to $2500 for the medications alone, with an additional $500-$1500 for labs and monitoring. The

average cost of a traditional cycle should be about $2000, all inclusive.
- **Hyperstimulation**. It is difficult to determine in advance whether an individual will over- or under-stimulate with gonadotropin injections. The threshold level between too much and too little can sometimes be very narrow. PCOS is one of the definite risk factors for ovarian hyperstimulation syndrome (OHSS) and multiple pregnancy. You must be fully informed about the considerable dangers and the emotional risks and problems in a multi-fetal pregnancy. Most infertility patients initially think of the possibility of twins or triplets as exciting. This is just not an issue of having one's hands full and one's pocketbook emptying after the babies are born! Multi-fetal pregnancies carry high physical risks for both mothers and babies. The mothers of recently publicized septuplets and octuplets were given these drugs. With careful and proper monitoring and close attention to detail, the medications are safe and effective. (See further explanation Chapter 17).

What about the other drugs?

There are many other drugs, old and new, that may improve ovarian function and have fertility promoting effects. The listing included below is supplemented by a more detailed explanation in Chapter 17.

Prolactin-inhibiting agents. It is still speculative whether there is a direct association between elevated prolactin levels and PCOS. Hyperprolactinemia is relatively common, so they are necessarily sometimes seen in association. Prolactin levels should be determined in all with irregular cycles. Therapy should be considered in all individuals with even a minimally increased level when still present on repeat testing. If the level is over marginally elevated, a MRI scan of the pituitary gland should be performed. There has been an occasional suggestion for the use of prolactin inhibiting agents in PCOS in the absence of prolactin elevation. Their effectiveness has not been substantiated and their use cannot be recommended. Cabergoline (Dostinex™) and bromocriptine (Parlodel™) are the agents most commonly used to reduce prolactin levels.

Thyroid replacement. Thyroid disease, especially hypothyroidism is especially common in women. A thyroid stimulating hormone (TSH) level should be obtained in all patients with any evidence of ovarian abnormality or family history of thyroid disease. If the TSH is elevated, replacement therapy should be started and dosage changed to ensure that the TSH levels are kept in the mid-normal range. Unless an abnormality has been identified, thyroid hormone should not be used in an attempt to lose weight or increase fertility. Over replacement can have serious medical consequences.

Corticosteroids. Low doses of prednisone or dexamethasone are sometimes used when there is an excess of adrenal androgen production. One marker of this is an elevated dehydroepiandrosterone sulfate (DHEAS) level. Long term therapy with these drugs is often poorly tolerated and the success questionable. I have had some success and may use a short course of low dose steroids for ten to twelve days in addition to clomiphene.

GnRH analogs. GnRH analogs, commonly Lupron™, are used for a variety of fertility promoting reasons. They can be used over the long term to reduce endometriosis. In the short term, they are used for cycle synchronization, to reduce LH levels and possibly improve egg quality and to prevent an unwanted mid-cycle surge of LH before adequate follicle development has been achieved using gonadotropins. Recently, a new type of GnRH analog, a GnRH antagonist, has been introduced into clinical practice, one that can be used for immediate and short term suppression of LH and does not cause the "flair" of gonadotropin release seen with the previously used agonists.

Insulin altering agents. Around 50% of PCOS patients have a component of insulin resistance (see Chapter 9) and use of insulin altering agents has become widespread despite their lack of FDA approval for this purpose. There are three very different drug classes that work on different steps in the pathway of the insulin/glucose utilization. Two groups are presently available, biguanide (metformin) and thiazolidinedione ("glitazones") while a third agent, D-*chiro*-inositol, has shown promise in research trials, but has not been released for general use. Although the information about effectiveness of these agents is still preliminary, there appears to be additive effects when used with clomiphene, gonadotropins, and IVF. Success in their use alone may rival success with clomiphene alone, but more information is needed.

Surgery

Laparoscopy and hysteroscopy are described in the above section on diagnosis and continued in Chapter 17 on therapy. The leading diagnoses to exclude at time of laparoscopy are endometriosis and tubal disease. Hysteroscopy evaluates the internal architecture of the uterus. Laparoscopy is not a part of the diagnosis of PCOS, but enlarged polycystic ovaries can be confirmed during the procedure. In some cases, ovarian "drilling," presented in Chapter 17, may be performed for the treatment of PCOS and improvement in fertility.

Assisted reproduction (ART)

The definition of ART is somewhat vague. Does "T" stand for technology, technique or therapy? It really doesn't matter. A reasonably accepted definition of the ARTs is that they are a group of therapies that employ manipulation of the egg and/or sperm and/or early conceptus in order to establish a pregnancy. Assisted reproduction, especially in vitro fertilization, has revolutionized the treatment of infertility. It is a final common pathway on which all forms of fertility problems may converge for a single treatment.

Intrauterine insemination (IUI)

IUI is the removal of sperm from the semen during a sperm prep and placement of the "washed" sperm into the uterus. IUI is about the simplest form of ART available. Although artificial insemination (AI) has been performed for a very, very long time, it was not until the techniques of sperm preparation were refined from IVF technology that IUI became widely used. It has now replaced other types of insemination procedures such as intracervical and vaginal.

IUI is used in cases of male factor infertility to improve the number of sperm reaching the site of fertilization. IUI may by-pass the cervix, which is the main site of sperm antibody production. It may also be used in conjunction with fertility promoting agents in order to increase their effectiveness. Also, IUI may be used for semen testing. Rather than discarding the semen sample after it has been analyzed, why not do an insemination to add therapy with diagnosis?

To begin the process of IUI, the sperm have to be removed from the seminal fluid and concentrated. The process of sperm preparation is called washing. The semen is then mixed with a nutrient medium and placed in a centrifuge. The fluid is taken from the top and discarded, and the pellet of sperm remaining is again mixed with the medium for a second centrifugation. The sperm pellet is suspended in a drop of medium and the insemination is performed by passing a small plastic catheter (a tube about the size of a ball-point pin refill) through the cervix and into the uterine cavity. An ultrasound scan may be used before the insemination to check for follicle and endometrial development. At the time of the insemination the amount and quality of cervical mucus is recorded.

During the sperm washing, the sperm are activated so that capacity to fertilize is immediate. Unfortunately, it also means that their life span is limited, so timing is critical. The natural reservoir of sperm in the cervix has been bypassed so the sperm don't have the same lasting power. Often insemination and ovulation are synchronized either by the LH surge as determined by an ovulation predictor kit (see above), or by giving an injection of the hormone hCG (see Chapter 17). Instructions may be given to have intercourse the night before and/or after the insemination to increase the amount of sperm available, but some clinics rely solely on IUI.

Semen cannot be placed directly into the uterus without the risk of severe contractions. This is due to the high levels of prostaglandins present and is a reason why the sperm must be washed prior to IUI. There is usually no, or minimal cramping with IUI. Severe pain and especially fever should be reported.

Here are some facts you should know about IUI.

- There is no advantage to remaining lying down or limiting activity after the procedure. Unlike conventional insemination, it is unlikely the sperm will escape.
- IUI does not increase risk of multiple pregnancies, but fertility drugs do.
- IUI is of questionable benefit after about three unsuccessful attempts unless the ovulation induction drugs have changed. In any case, more than four to six attempts are not recommended.
- The procedure costs $100-$500, and another $200-$1500 with fertility drugs.

In vitro fertilization (IVF) and embryo transfer (ET)

In vitro, literally meaning "in glass," refers to a natural process that is performed outside the body. It is from this literal translation that the term "test tube baby" arises. IVF-ET represents the flagship of assisted reproduction. It is from IVF-ET that other technologies draw their impetus and scientific foundation. The American Society for Reproductive Medicine states, "in vitro fertilization for infertility, not solvable by other means, is considered ethical." For some, assisted reproduction may represent the last hope at the end of a long path of infertility therapy. For others, it may be the best place to start, depending on age and cause of infertility. IVF is being used increasingly for treatment of PCOS. The major factor limiting its greater use is its high cost.

IVF offers several distinct advantages that make it more cost-effective than it might seem initially. Perhaps the largest benefit, a desire shared by both clinician and patient, is to evaluate the capacity of the oocyte to be fertilized. As expected, the chance of fertilization failure is higher in PCOS patients than in those with anatomic abnormalities. Lack of fertilization in one cycle does not necessarily prove that by altering the stimulating regimen or timing that fertilization will fail in subsequent cycles. It may be more the environment in which the oocyte develops than the oocyte itself. An additional advantage is that a more aggressive approach can be taken toward ovarian stimulation. With PCOS, hyperstimulation is somewhat less of an issue because the preovulatory size follicles are aspirated and a limited number of embryos are replaced. Not only does this decrease the chance of multiple pregnancies, it reduces the risk of more pronounced cystic change. Many PCOS patients either over or under stimulate with gonadotropin therapy. The use of GnRH analogs and gonadotropins in conjunction with IVF may maximize control and ensure the greatest chance of pregnancy in any one cycle.

What are the chances of pregnancy with IVF and PCOS?

Theoretically, this would be a hard question to answer. Since the egg quality is a major issue, IVF success should not be different from ovulation induction in individuals with open tubes and no male factor. It seems to be significantly better than ovulation induction. This may be due to different stimulation protocols, or that all the follicles are aspirated including some that probably would not have ovulated. Overall, the success with IVF is dependent on the individual center and it is usually at, not above or below, their average reported success. In most cases, no more than 3 cycles of gonadotropin stimulation should be used before IVF is given strong consideration. If there are other possible causes, such as age or male factor, IVF may move up considerably in priority.

Can the risk of hyperstimulation in PCOS be lessened?

It is common to have an exaggerated response to ovarian stimulation with PCOS. More follicles lead to more eggs. Often there are more eggs than good eggs, causing the fertilization in PCOS patients to be decreased. The IVF program at Cornell University uses a regimen of two cycles of oral contraceptives, followed by higher doses of Lupron™ (1mg) and often lower gonadotropin doses (2 amps). With this regimen, their success rate matches their Center rate compared to a much poorer success rate with a conventional stimulation regimen.

Why IVF?
- Diagnostic and prognostic procedure for egg assessment
- Less chance of multiple pregnancy than with gonadotropin injection
- Ensure egg collection by-pass needed for ovulation
- Treatment of male and tubal factors
- Superior success rates over all other methods

Why not IVF?
- High financial, time, and emotional cost
- Pain of the aspiration procedure
- Ethics about freezing embryos
- Success is not guaranteed

In theory, the IVF-ET procedure is simple. An egg is taken from the ovary and healthy sperm are selected from a sample produced by the male. Egg and sperm are then mixed together in a culture dish, which is where fertilization takes place. The resulting embryo is transferred into the uterus in about the time it would take to arrive there in a natural conception. Does it sound easy? It isn't!

In practice, IVF-ET demands a high level of attention to detail and requires a precisely coordinated effort among all involved. IVF-ET is a very emotional and encompassing experience. It seems to focus all hopes and fears about fertility and pregnancy into a "procedure."

What is necessary for IVF?
The Five stages of the IVF-ET Process
- Controlled ovarian stimulation
- Follicle aspiration
- In vitro fertilization and culture
- Embryo transfer
- Luteal implantation and support

Step 1: Controlled Ovarian Stimulation
Each month a woman usually releases a single egg from the ovary. For IVF, we know that the more eggs there are (to a point), the more embryos there are, and the better the chance of a pregnancy. To obtain more than one oocyte, fertility drugs are given to stimulate the ovary so that more than one "preovulatory" follicle develops. Usually these are the injectable drugs, but some centers use clomiphene for selected patients.

There is some degree of disorder in the normal follicular development of every woman's ovary. Several different medication regimens, including birth control pills and progestins, may be used to synchronize the ovary in hopes of obtaining the best quality eggs. Most IVF programs use Lupron™, one of the analogs (see Chapter 17), to suppress, regulate and better synchronize the development of follicles. These GnRH analogs not only lower the high LH levels of PCOS, but also block the natural LH surge, both of which can reduce success. If used for an extended time, these medications would create a reversible medical menopause. It is used only for a short time, several days to

Figure 11-4 IVF Schedule

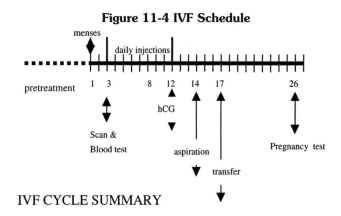

IVF CYCLE SUMMARY

several weeks, and generally has few, if any side effects. An alternative is to use a GnRH antagonist (Antagon™) after gonadotropin stimulation has been underway for several days. It is unclear whether Antagon™ will be as successful as pretreatment with Lupron™ for patients with PCOS.

When the next menses occurs, a *baseline scan* and estradiol level is drawn to make sure the ovary is suppressed, no cysts have formed, and the uterine lining is thin.

Gonadotropin therapy is started in order to stimulate multiple follicles to develop. This step is no different than when these drugs are used for ovulation induction. Individuals with PCOS may require a lower starting dose and then a quick step down in doses to prevent over stimulation of the ovaries. Ultrasound scan and estradiol levels are used to monitor follicle growth and response to stimulation. When a sufficient number of follicles are judged to be mature, both by size (16-22 mm) and estradiol level (above 200 pg/ml for each large follicle), an injection of human chorionic gonadotropin (hCG) is given to allow the follicles to complete their last stages of maturation.

The follicle aspiration (the procedure where the eggs are removed from the ovary) is scheduled about thirty-six hours after the hCG. By that time, the egg is floating in the follicle.

Step 2: Follicle Aspiration

In the past, aspiration of follicles required laparoscopy. Now virtually all centers use a transvaginal ultrasound guided approach that is often performed as an office procedure. In the procedure of follicle aspiration, a needle is passed through the upper vaginal wall, and, with the use of vaginal ultrasound, fluid is removed from the follicles by a gentle suction. The procedure is not painless, but it is generally well tolerated. The procedure may last from

five to about fifteen minutes with few exceptions. Centers vary in their sedation; anything from a pain pill to general anesthesia is used.

Immediately after aspiration of a follicle, the oocyte is isolated from the follicular fluid and placed in a culture dish that contains nutrient media. It is then transferred to the incubator.

Shortly before or after the aspiration procedure, the sperm are isolated from the semen that was obtained earlier. During this procedure, the most active sperm are selected and transferred to a culture dish for completion of the changes necessary for fertilization.

Step 3: In Vitro Fertilization

Oocytes and sperm are placed together in a culture dish, which is placed inside an incubator, thus providing a controlled environment. There, they are left undisturbed until the next day, at which time they are examined for fertilization. Over the next day, the 1 cell embryo will divide (cleave) into a 2-cell embryo, 2 cells into 4, 4 cells into 8 and so on.

Step 4: Transfer of Embryos

Traditionally, on the second or third day following follicular aspiration when the embryos have reached the four to ten cell stage, the embryo(s) is transferred into the uterus. With the development of new types of media, embryos can be cultured for longer periods of time in the laboratory. The term *blastocyst* refers to the stage of embryo development just prior to implantation and is reached after about five days in culture. By extending the culture period, *blastocyst stage culture*, the best embryos can be selected and, theoretically, pregnancy rates improved. This technique may be of greater importance in PCOS patients who produce more embryos, rather than good quality embryos. Fewer embryos transferred translates into a reduced risk of multiple pregnancy and the serious consequences that can result.

Blastocyst culture is an important scientific advance, but the practical advance in terms of IVF success is much less clear. Unfortunately, the technique has been the subject of some major hype. In some cases the uterus may still be a better incubator than the laboratory. Extending the culture period and delaying transfer may lose some pregnancies. There will be fewer embryos for cryopreservation because of the need to keep more embryos in culture to see which will continue to best develop. An additional attempt at success using frozen and thawed embryos may be lost. Also, an extended culture can mean an extended cost.

Cryopreservation, freezing of surplus embryos is routinely performed. This allows the possibility of an additional attempt at pregnancy without the necessity of the fertility injections or aspiration procedure. It is not known for how long embryos can remain frozen, but successful pregnancies have occurred ten years after the initial transfer of embryos. As few as 50% of the embryos survive the thaw process, but there is no evidence that cryopreservation is harmful to children born from the technique.

The transfer takes only a few minutes and involves placing a small plastic tube through the cervix into the uterine cavity. No anesthesia is required and usually only minimal or no discomfort is felt.

Step 5: Implantation Support and Monitoring

It is unknown when implantation takes place or what can be done to ensure the best chance of implantation. Because of the extreme manipulation of the ovaries that has taken place, additional supplements of hCG and/or progesterone are given to help ensure the optimum environment for implantation.

Does aspirin improve success?

Low dose aspirin, one baby aspirin or a half tablet daily, has been suggested to improve pregnancy rate and success with IVF. Aspirin belongs to a group of drugs called nonsteroidal anti-inflammatory drugs that block prostaglandin production. Large doses could potentially block ovulation and implantation, which are both prostaglandin-related events. Small doses are thought to improve blood supply to the ovary or uterus and improve pregnancy rates. Many large successful centers do not use aspirin therapy. The beneficial effects of aspirin await substantiation.

What about Viagra?

Viagra™ has been used in infertility programs to improve male performance with good success. A report in March 2000 showed an improvement in IVF success when Viagra™ was given to women with previous IVF failure. It is hypothesized that Viagra™ can increase blood flow to the uterus and improve implantation rates. Only four patients were included in the first report and validation of findings is needed.

Should blocked tubes be removed?

In-vitro fertilization was initially developed as a means of allowing women with blocked or absent fallopian tubes to conceive. Women with fallopian tubes damaged by prior infection or scarring from surgery or endometriosis were considered perfect candidates for in vitro fertilization. Unfortunately, many of these high prognosis young women had a very difficult time conceiving through IVF. Only recently has it been recognized that success is markedly reduced when one tube (hydrosalpinx) or both tubes (hydrosalpinges) are blocked and filled with fluid. It is theorized that this fluid flows back into the uterus from the tubes and either washes away, poisons, or in some other way hinders the implantation or growth of the embryos. While some experts look for and remove the tubes aggressively, others wait until the first failed cycles. It is possible that tube removal could damage the blood supply to the ovary. Sometimes the hydrosalpinx can be drained and the tube repaired, but more often the damage is permanent and failure to remove or close off the tube increases the risk that the hydrosalpinx will reform. There is also the risk of ectopic pregnancy when the tube is repaired rather than removed.

Why not GIFT, ZIFT?

Gamete intra-fallopian transfer (GIFT) is a technique where follicle aspiration is performed through the laparoscope and the eggs obtained are immediately mixed with sperm and placed into the fallopian tubes. The theory was that the fallopian tube allowed a superior environment for fertilization and development. That this is more natural can be called into question, but it initially allowed centers with poorer laboratories to have success rates that were thought to be superior. Laboratories are universally better today than they were ten years ago. Now when groups of equivalent patients are examined, there is no advantage in success rates. GIFT does permit a laparoscopy for diagnostic purposes, but corrective surgery is ill advised because of the possible reduction in success rate. The major downside of GIFT is that it requires a laparoscopy, which has a substantially higher cost than an office procedure. GIFT is questioned in the PCOS patient because of the relatively low fertilization rate that is sometimes seen. It is better to evaluate fertilization and pick the best embryos before transfer.

Zygote intrafallopian transfer (ZIFT) and tubal embryo transfer (TET) combine the potential advantages of IVF and GIFT. The eggs are removed by laparoscopy, fertilized in the laboratory and the conceptus replaced into the tubes at laparoscopy in either the zygote (fertilized egg to two cell stage), or later as a cleaving embryo. Very high success rates were reported by some centers, but two surgical procedures are required and the cost is largely prohibitive.

With the recent increase in success rates and relative ease of the IVF-ET procedure, GIFT and ZIFT are probably on the way out.

Does ICSI have a role in treating PCOS?

Intracytoplasmic sperm injection (ICSI) was introduced in 1992, and it is possibly the most important advance in the treatment of infertility since IVF-ET. ICSI, when coupled with sperm aspiration directly from the testis, can correct a majority of male infertility, regardless of cause. ICSI is a technique whereby a single sperm is directly injected into an egg. ICSI bypasses the outer coverings of the egg and thus, some of the barriers to fertilization. Since a very small number of sperm are needed for this procedure, it has a very important advantage for men with extremely low sperm counts or sperm motility. ICSI is generally unsuccessful when used to treat fertilization failures that are primarily due to poor egg quality, a common problem of PCOS. However, when there has been fertilization failure with conventional IVF, ICSI may be tried as a method of bypassing a possible male factor and exhausting all means available.

What is assisted hatching?

The *zona pellucida* (ZP) is a protein halo surrounding the egg and later the embryo. The ZP prevents attachment of the embryo to the wall of the tube as it travels down to the uterus. Once in the uterus, the ZP dissolves and the embryo "hatches." There are several studies suggesting the ZP abnormally thickens or "hardens," thereby causing a reduced success with IVF. Theoretically, older women and those with PCOS are at a higher risk for this hardening. In assisted hatching, the ZP is thinned mechanically by physically puncturing it, or chemically by using an acid solution to partially dissolve it. Some excellent centers swear by the technique. Others with equally good success rates condemn the procedure as unnecessary. While the procedure may improve the chances for pregnancy, it is more costly and could destroy the embryo.

What are some of the experimental techniques?

At any given time since the early 1980s, several experimental techniques were being used at various centers around the world. Within a short time some proved to be so effective that they become standard procedure, while others were shown to be of little merit. In the first decade of the 21st Century current areas of experimentation are these:

IVF with immature oocytes.

Aspiration of immature oocytes from small ovarian follicles and their development in vitro has been proposed as therapy for three of the plagues of resistance to ART: age, poor response and fertilization failure. With this technique, minimum, if any, stimulation is used and eggs are aspirated from much smaller follicles than with conventional IVF. The eggs are matured in a special media that could theoretically by-pass some of the problems of PCOS.

Despite early enthusiasm, the procedure has not met its expectations or been adequately successful to presently count it as a viable therapeutic option. This technique may become very important in the future as a way to harvest large quantities of eggs from donor ovaries or to harvest eggs to be stored for later use, for example with cancer patients. One trial of the procedure with PCOS was met with dismal success, while a second seemed to be more rewarding.

Donor cytoplasm

Some women with repeated failure of IVF may have specific and correctable abnormalities of the egg cytoplasm and not the egg nucleus. There has been a case report of one such patient having success with this procedure after about 5% of cytoplasm was removed from a donor egg and placed into a recipient egg at the time of IVF. This stirred controversy and excitement, with an over-reaction about the potential success of this technique. The technique has not shown to be the magic bullet searched for, although the theory remains intriguing. In PCOS, there could easily be cytoplasmic alterations that result in poor oocyte development and fertilization failure. A patient with PCOS would seem to be an ideal candidate for this procedure. Although it is new science and new hope, it is unclear whether this will become a viable therapy.

Success rates, an editorial

The bottom line in worldwide experience with IVF-ET provides a realistic expectation of 25-50% for delivering a baby from any one IVF-ET cycle in women under age 40. This equals or exceeds the natural pregnancy rate in fertile couples having unprotected intercourse (though, admittedly, at considerably more trouble and considerably higher expense than it takes to conceive naturally). One fact that makes reproductive medicine unique is a specific well-defined quantifiable end point, a healthy baby. Obviously, the purpose of assisted reproduction is to facilitate a pregnancy. Each infertile couple and each assisted reproduction technology (ART) program is vitally interested in success rates. Truly, success breeds success. A well-placed report of superior success rates can ensure survival of that center in a competitive market and can be translated into substantial financial rewards and acclaim. The stakes are high—so high as to restrict entry into the program, alter therapy, and at least open the possibility of misleading the reporting of statistics. There is always some degree of desperation in every ART patient and perhaps in every ART program, as well.

There seems to be something unprofessional about discussion of cost. Cost is an absolute barrier to therapy for many couples. In other cases, couples with a good prognosis for pregnancy must stop short of realization of their goal for financial reasons. It is common for lifestyle to be altered and discretionary income to be entirely allotted to ART. In some cases, houses are mortgaged, vehicles sold, and retirement accounts depleted in order to pay for a single ART cycle. This monetary factor is never officially reported, but in fact, if an IVF cycle costs 50% less at one center with the same success rates as another center, and if money is the limiting resource, the center with lower costs is in principle twice as successful as the more expensive center.

It is very difficult for a center, or for that matter the infertile couple, not to choose the option that gives the highest chance of pregnancy, even if the increased risk of multiple pregnancy is known. Many couples clearly profess their preference of twins and naively underestimate the risk of pregnancy-induced hypertension, gestational diabetes, premature labor and birth, and c-section. Still, most would consider multiple pregnancy as a sign of success even though the reverse, in terms of medical and financial costs, is true. In terms of the total health cost for ART, more is spent on the care of resultant multiple pregnancies from a few than the total cost of IVF for all. Several countries have mandated the limits of embryo replacement to two embryos.

The universal declaration of human rights proclaims the right of a couple to form a family. Unfortunately, insurance companies have not adopted this principle. What a better condition we would be in if the maximum number of embryos transferred was two and family building was covered by health insurance.

When do we stop?

Although many of the pregnancies established are in the first cycle, chances of pregnancy appear to be equal with each try through the first four attempts. The average couple will undergo two to three IVF attempts before either achieving a successful pregnancy or abandoning therapy. Once established, a pregnancy after IVF-ET is no different from pregnancy established without fertility therapy and is not considered high risk.

OTHER OPTIONS

To this point we have talked about options in treatment which offer couples the hope that they will give birth to a healthy child genetically related to both of his parents. This is, of course, what all couples—fertile and infertile—initially expect when they decide that they want to be parents and stop using birth control. But despite amazing treatment advances, it remains the case that just under half of couples who are faced with male factor, female factor or combined factor fertility impairment (not just those dealing with PCOS) will not be able to give birth to a baby genetically related to both of them. There are, however, other options that will provide the infertile couple with the opportunity to become parents.

Just as PCOS is not a one issue medical problem, infertility is not just about not giving birth. Infertility involves multiple potential losses, including control over many parts of life, loss of genetic continuity, loss of the expectation of blending our genes with those of a much loved partner to make a new life from the best of us both, loss of the impregnating and pregnancy experiences and the loss of the taken-for-granted opportunity to parent. While a single section of a single chapter in this book about PCOS can't provide all of the answers, it can provide you with some of the questions you will need to ask yourselves and some information about where to begin finding answers should you feel interested in exploring one of these options more seriously.

Donor Gametes

It is possible that some PCOS patients will eventually want to consider *oocyte donation*, that is, using an egg from another woman mixed with your partner's sperm and then implanted using an IVF technique into your uterus. The first oocyte donations were performed in 1982-1983, about three years after the birth of the first IVF baby. Initially oocyte donation was considered a heroic attempt to allow young women with premature ovarian failure a chance to reproduce. In these individuals, the ovaries had "run out of eggs." Otherwise, the uterus was normal and capable of carrying a pregnancy. Soon it was shown that the uterus could be "programmed" by use of oral, transdermal, or injectable hormones to accept and carry a pregnancy normally. It became strikingly obvious that pregnancy rates for recipients was as good as, and often even exceeded, that of conventional IVF-ET. While the option of donor eggs is not as common as using donor sperm, oocyte donation is considered a vital part of many, if not most, of the larger IVF-ET programs.

The need for ovarian stimulation using injectable medications and the procedure for harvesting eggs from the ovary require considerable commitment from the donor. This limits the availability of oocytes from donors in the general population, though they are available.

An alternative is a "known donor," using the eggs of a family member such as a sister or a cousin. While this option does preserve the genetic connection to the mother that is important to some women, it carries a substantial social and emotional risk and should be considered very carefully. The IVF-ET procedure is very taxing. It may be much easier for a family member to offer to be a donor than for the recipient to accept the offer. Many centers

require that both donor and recipient undergo evaluation and counseling by a
psychologist before starting the procedures.

With oocyte donation, the male partner of the recipient fertilizes the donor oocyte. This means that the male partner will be the genetic (natural) father of the child. If oocytes from a family member are used, the mother will be genetically related to the child. The embryos are transferred into the recipient, whose uterus has been primed with hormones (estrogen and progesterone) to support the pregnancy. Therefore, the recipient will be able to carry and deliver the pregnancy. The recipient is the birth and legal mother, although not the genetic mother. Oocyte donation allows the male partner a natural child and the mother a chance to nurture her child. Oocyte donation involves all of the expenses of an IVF cycle, in addition to the not insignificant expense of purchasing the egg by covering the induction and other medical expenses of the "donor" and often paying her a fee.

A corresponding (though less invasive, significantly less expensive and less medically complex) procedure available to couples with combined factor infertility where the PCOS problem has been overcome but the male factor has not is *donor insemination*. Insemination with the sperm of a donor (most often unknown) has been used to establish pregnancies in ovulating women since the 1800s. This technically simple procedure can involve using technology as simple as a turkey baster to deposit a semen sample from a donor into the uterus of a woman who hopes to become pregnant. Used in conjunction with a viable egg, donor sperm carries a very high rate of success in establishing a pregnancy.

Most often today (and especially among women who have already been involved in infertility treatment) the procedure is done as an IUI (see above). Much more often than not sperm is obtained (usually frozen) through a commercial sperm bank which has carefully screened donors and provided significant non-identifying information about genetics, intelligence, social interests, talents, etc. to help recipient couples select a donor. Sometimes couples choose to use a related donor—the father, brother, or cousin of the infertile male partner—in order to preserve the paternal genetic connection. This choice, however, like using donor eggs from a relative, carries significant social and emotional risk and so should be considered carefully.

Embryo adoption

Embryo adoption is a third way for couples unable to conceive together to experience a pregnancy. Technically, this involves the IVF implantation of an already fertilized egg into the uterus of an infertile woman who, through therapy with many of the hormones we have discussed here, has prepared her uterus to receive and implant a blastocyst. Though a few practices around the country are actually able to "commission" the production of an embryo for this purpose using the sperm and egg of donors unknown to the couple and unknown to one another, this practice is fraught with so many ethical questions, that it is not widely available.

Considered to have fewer ethical problems, is the use of "left over" embryos created during the IVF process for other couples. These "extra embryos," however, are not readily available. Though many embryos are created and stored for future disposition by couples using ART procedures, and while many of these couples go into the IVF process expecting that they will eventually want to donate their unused embryos to other infertile couples who need them, it has been the case throughout the world that these couples do not ultimately make the decision to donate. Their options are to donate the eggs to another couple, to donate them for research, or to have them destroyed. Having completed their families through successful treatment or simply having decided that enough unsuccessful cycles is enough, most couples asked by their clinics to make a decision about what to do with excess embryos in storage have a difficult time with their decision. Psychologists working in these clinics report that for many of these couples the thought of having their genetic children "out there somewhere" being parented by someone unknown to them is simply too difficult to consider. These couples opt to have their embryos destroyed when they cannot opt for unlimited storage time.

Adoption

People who, after examining their feelings about the multiple losses that accompany unsuccessful infertility treatment, discover that the greatest loss for them is the loss of the opportunity to parent, are perfect candidates for adoption. Adoption today is fraught with myth and misunderstanding caused primarily by media misrepresentation and exaggeration. Adoption is a viable option, and throughout the world millions of children are in need of parents. Despite myth, many of these children are babies, many are healthy, and one neither has to be married nor be rich to adopt.

Adoption is, however, complex, involving a variety of decisions to be made. Do you want to adopt a baby or an older child? The answer may not be as simple as it seems. Do you want to adopt from the U.S. or will you consider adopting from Asia, Eastern Europe, South or Central America, the South Pacific or the Indian Subcontinent? Do you wish to use an agency, or does going on your own adoption quest in an independent adoption appeal to you? What does "healthy" mean to you? Many children with so-called "special needs" may have issues that you are perfectly suited to assist. There are financial options. Most children who have been adopted grow up to be healthy, productive adults with close bonds to their parents and siblings by adoption. Indeed, a large federally funded recent study (done by the Search Institute of Minnesota) of adolescent adoptees who had joined their families in infancy and toddlerhood were compared to a "general population" of adolescents who had not been adopted and were found to be just as stable, just as confident, just as emotionally healthy, just as racially identified and just as connected to their parents as their non-adopted peers.

The bottom line is that investing finances and energy in adoption is more of a "sure thing" for the overwhelming majority of couples and singles than is any form of medical treatment. If you manage your personal finances—however high or low—effectively, can provide a safe and healthy environment for a child to live in, and are a stable individual or couple with reasonable expectations for longevity, you can adopt if you are willing to put energy into the process of making it happen.

Living childfree

Though more and more adults are choosing not to give birth to or adopt children but instead to live childfree, this remains a lifestyle choice misunderstood by the population at large. Those who have decided that they want to become parents and <u>then</u> found themselves faced with fertility impairment have a particularly difficult time looking at this option objectively. There are now some support groups for childfree adults and many infertility support groups have groups for those considering or already living childfree.

The truth is that some who examine the losses of infertility find that what they wanted most when they decided to become parents was a genetic connection to their child or to their partner that the alternatives beyond treatment cannot provide for them. Others discover that their loss of control is so powerful that the adoption process is unappealing. When they open their hearts and minds to it, many such people indeed find the idea of reinventing themselves and directing their lives in a child*free* rather than child*less* direction holds a lot of appeal.

Getting more information

To explore further the alternative options discussed above, we can recommend four books from the publisher of this book, Perspectives Press: The Infertility and Adoption Publisher. They are

Taking Charge of Infertility by Patricia Irwin Johnston (Perspectives Press, 1994) This book is not a technical guide to infertility, but an emotional and social guide to enhancing communication between partners, making more effective and synergistic decisions, and becoming one's own best advocate in making treatment decisions and choosing lifestyle options.

Choosing Assisted Reproduction by Susan Cooper and Ellen Glazer (Perspectives Press 1998), which is a guide to the emotional, social and ethical considerations that couples need to take into account when considering any of the ARTs, using donor gametes, and talking to their children about their high-tech conceptions.

Adopting after Infertility by Patricia Irwin Johnston (Perspectives Press, 1992) is a guide to deciding whether or not adoption can be a positive and satisfying path to parenthood and exploring and choosing adoption's many options, from domestic to international, infant to older child, open or confidential, through an agency or privately, etc.

Sweet Grapes: How to Stop Being Infertile and Start Living Again by Michael and Jean Carter (Perspectives Press, revised and expanded 1998) offers an infertile couple's (he a college professor, she an ob-gyn) personal explorations and tools for enthusiastically embracing a childfree lifestyle after ending infertility treatment.

Each of these will lead you to other books and to websites and resources, as well as to education and support and advocacy organizations that can help you to achieve your new goals.

Now I'm Pregnant. Is the Pregnancy at Greater Risk?

"I have had two miscarriages and I am worried about a third. My friends tell me they have also lost a pregnancy before they were successful and that I should relax. My doctor doesn't seem concerned and tells me it's nature's way of protecting itself from unhealthy babies. That doesn't help very much. I'm scared! I have just read a magazine article that talks about PCOS. My cycles are irregular and I am a little overweight. Could PCOS be a factor in my pregnancy loss? Can I do anything to prevent another miscarriage?"

"I failed to get pregnant on clomiphene, but got pregnant in my second month on metformin. My insulin levels are high and although I tried to lose weight before my pregnancy, I still weigh 220 pounds. Is my pregnancy high risk?"

By the National Institutes of Health's 1990 consensus definition of PCOS as hyperandrogenic chronic anovulation, it might be logical to assume that PCOS no longer exists when a pregnancy is established. After all, the patient must have ovulated to become pregnant and she may not even be hyperandrogenic during pregnancy. Often, an infertility specialist has treated the PCOS patient and once a pregnancy has been achieved the patient is considered "cured."

In my opinion, this is a very narrow view of PCOS. It would seem overly naïve to say that because a woman has achieved a pregnancy she no longer has PCOS. Since PCOS is often associated with significant metabolic alterations, it logically follows that these could adversely affect a pregnancy.

Human pregnancy is unique in the animal world in its close association between the mother and her fetus. Most of these complex interactions remain a mystery. For instance, we do not know for sure what causes labor to begin (*initiation of parturition*). It could be reasoned that the fetus exceeds capacity of the mother to support its continued growth. Nutrition is the central dogma of both pregnancy and PCOS.

As has been the reccurring theme throughout this book, we really know very little about PCOS and we especially do not know very much about its effect on pregnancy or pregnancy's effect on PCOS. Only the very basic generalizations can be made and theories presented. In the following chapter, normal pregnancy is presented and superimposed with how PCOS, as we now understand it, may alter it. In order to accomplish these goals, this chapter has been divided into the following sections:

- PRECONCEPTION
- ESTABLISHMENT AND MAINTENANCE OF PREGNANCY
- MEDICAL COMPLICATIONS OF PREGNANCY
- MISCARRIAGE
- BREASTFEEDING
- ADDITIONAL PREGNANCIES

PRECONCEPTION

How can I best prepare for a pregnancy?

Consider preparing for pregnancy as if you were training for a great race. This is a race of endurance, not speed; a race in which a teammate must be carried; and a race that must be finished without being short of breath. This race both figuratively and literally requires great cardiovascular conditioning.

Outcome has everything to do with the state of your body (and mind) at the start of a pregnancy. Many unprepared women have had pregnancy thrust upon them; fortunately, youth and good health will overcome most obstacles. The truth remains that those nine months of development in the womb can affect the health of a child for a lifetime. So plan. The greatest chance for a good pregnancy outcome occurs when the body is at maximum harmony—metabolic balance.

Before Becoming Pregnant
- Use folic acid supplementation (minimum 400 mcg daily)
- Achieve maximum nutritional status possible
- Stop smoking
- Consume alcohol and caffeine in modest amounts
- Reduce your stress level
- Get a rubella vaccination, if not already immune
- Get a hepatitis B vaccination, if at social or occupational risk
- Discuss any chronic medical conditions or prescription drug use
- Live well, live happy

Am I pregnant?

Implantation of the embryo occurs about five days after ovulation. Very shortly after implantation, small amounts of *human chorionic gonadotropin* (hCG) must be produced to prevent the demise of the corpus luteum, which is the power house of progesterone. Even before a missed period, the early hormonal changes are often translated into fatigue, breast tenderness, and frequent urination. These feelings may be especially prominent if fertility drugs have been used and cysts remain on the ovary. Many report flu-like symptoms, which in part may be due to the immunologic reaction to implantation. Most, but certainly not all, women have a "second sense" that they are pregnant. With all the hormonal instability of PCOS, there can be false symptoms of pregnancy.

All *pregnancy tests*, whether the one bought in the local pharmacy or the blood test in a physician's office, detect hCG. HCG is made by the primitive placenta (*trophoblast*) as it embeds into the uterine wall. Except under very unusual conditions, hCG is present only during pregnancy. The qualitative tests give a yes or no answer by a color change. Using sensitive assays, it is possible to give a numerical result (quantitative hCG). A positive test indicates a pregnancy has occurred even if subsequent tests are negative. Any positive test is an important finding, in that it signifies that a number of important steps have had to take place. If you are past your period date, do the test before calling your physician because "Did you do a pregnancy test?" is often the first question asked.

Figure 12-1 Establishment of Pregnancy

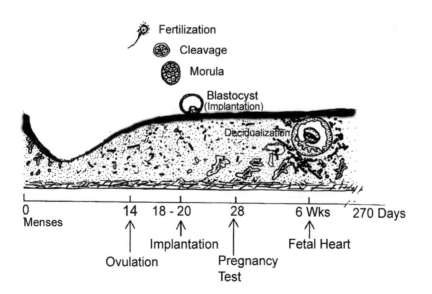

Are home pregnancy tests reliable?

Yes. If the test turns positive you are pregnant. False positive tests are very unlikely. If a test is negative, it means that it may be too early for the measurement. Home pregnancy tests (HPT) are based on hCG in urine causing a chemical reaction resulting in a color change of a specifically designed dye indicator. There needs to be 25-50 IU of hCG in the urine for the test to change colors (become positive). *Home pregnancy tests turn positive about the time of the first missed menstrual period*, or twelve to fourteen days after ovulation. Delayed ovulation may occur in PCOS patients and will delay a positive pregnancy test. Tests are rarely negative at any time two weeks after ovulation. A false negative test rarely occurs outside of timing errors.

How quickly does the hCG level increase?

Two weeks after ovulation, the hCG level should be 15-200 IU/L. After this, the level approximately doubles *every* forty-eight hours over the next two weeks. A multiple pregnancy has a faster rise in hCG level. In cycles where supplemental hCG was used for ovulation induction, as many as eight days from the hCG injection may be required before it has cleared the system and the pregnancy test is valid. Slower hCG rises may be a sign of an ectopic pregnancy or impending pregnancy loss. A falling level is an ominous sign for the health of the pregnancy.

Is there a value of measuring progesterone?

Progesterone levels may be evaluated at the same time as hCG and can help in the differentiation between healthy and problematic pregnancies. Ectopic (tubal) pregnancies often are associated with low progesterone levels, but the progesterone level alone will not distinguish between an ectopic and intrauterine pregnancy. Because progesterone is secreted episodically, levels may vary between samples and minor ups and downs of several points are of little importance. Unlike hCG, which should steadily rise, progesterone levels remain relatively constant in early pregnancy. Progesterone levels can be considered as reassuring (usually above 20 pg/ml), probably indicating a compromise in the pregnancy (less than 10 pg/ml), or equivocal (10-20 pg/ml).

Should supplemental progesterone be used?

Most pregnancy losses are due to genetic abnormalities present from the point of conception. Progesterone may prolong such a pregnancy, but it will not prevent the destined loss. There is no evidence that progesterone supplementation has a detrimental effect on the embryo/fetus other than a postponement of the inevitable miscarriage.

At the same time, there may be some theoretical value in progesterone supplementation in that it may relax the uterus' smooth muscle and prevent contractions. Theoretically, progesterone may also help the body accept the pregnancy by suppressing the immune response. In many ways a pregnancy is like an organ graft from a different person.

Traditionally, progesterone has been used in an attempt to overcome inadequate progesterone production from the ovary (the so-called *luteal phase defect*). I also use supplemental progesterone if there is good evidence of timely ovulation and low mid-luteal phase progesterone levels, but this is an uncommon finding. Actually, the problem usually arises in the follicular phase and therapy should be aimed at correcting the problems with follicle growth and ovulation rather than covering up the trail. I use progesterone supplementation in the luteal phase more for cycle regulation than luteal support. It may better prepare the next cycle and most often will not delay menses.

As soon as a home test turns positive, I usually measure hCG and progesterone and will start supplementation with borderline or low progesterone levels. Supplementation is continued until levels normalize and the viability of the pregnancy can be ascertained by ultrasound.

After nine weeks, the placenta is capable of making all necessary progesterone and the ovaries could be removed without detrimental effect on the pregnancy. Conclusive benefit for use of progesterone is lacking in any clinical situation other than with IVF and GnRH analog use.

Overall, the usefulness of supplemental progesterone is thought to be limited and has not passed scientific scrutiny.

How pregnant am I?

Pregnancies are dated by weeks since the last menstrual period (*LMP*). The typical pregnancy lasts 280 days or 40 weeks from the last menstrual period. A due date can be calculated by the formula of adding twelve months minus three months plus one week to the LMP to predict the estimated delivery (due) date (*EDD*). A *term* pregnancy is one that has gone on for between 37 and 42 weeks before the baby is delivered. If over 42 weeks, the pregnancy is said to be *post-dates* and under 37 weeks, *preterm*.

Historically, conception was thought to occur during menstruation and pregnancy was dated from the onset of the last period. The tradition remains, but it is subject to several flaws. First it is common for patients with PCOS to have ovulated later in the cycle. The number of days ovulation occurred past day 14 must be added onto the due date. The second problem occurs because there may be a slight amount of bleeding during either ovulation or during the implantation process so the pregnancy may be off by two to four weeks.

Pregnancy is divided into three *trimesters* of three months each. The first trimester is one of rapid change and adaptation to pregnancy. Virtually every single body part has some degree of change. The second trimester is a time when all generally seems 'right with the world' and complications are uncommon. In the last trimester, pregnancies become very tiring as the delivery day approaches and I have never heard anyone say, "if this could only go on for a little longer."

Is a PCOS pregnancy a high-risk pregnancy?

Risk is a relative term. Given what can go wrong, every pregnancy ever achieved has risks, some may even say high risks, whether you have PCOS or not. Do you need to see a specialist in perinatal medicine if you have PCOS? Probably not. There can be medical complications that might arise more commonly in a PCOS pregnancy and referral to, or consultation with, a subspecialist in perinatal medicine may be in order when those complications do occur.

Certainly it appears that the risk of miscarriage is increased in mothers with PCOS, as are the risks of gestational diabetes and pregnancy-induced hypertension (PIH, toxemia, preeclampsia), unusually small (growth restricted) and large (macrosomia) babies, and c-section rates. All of these are more common in first pregnancies and after many pregnancies. Some risks may be independently related to increased pre-pregnancy weight, others to insulin resistance regardless of weight. Smaller growth may be specific to hormonal alterations of the PCOS ovary itself.

What is most important is that an obstetric practice is found that provides education, answers to your questions, a systematic process allowing early identification of potential problems, and care for you and your partner as individuals. Believe it or not, there are a lot of practices out there that meet these requirements.

Should I have an ultrasound scan?

I am a believer in early ultrasound scan to precisely date a pregnancy and serve as a bench mark to better understand the cause of pregnancy loss, if it were to occur. The best reason for an early scan is to give a great sense of relief that all is well. If there is a problem, why not find out as quickly as possible? I'm not sure that all physicians and insurance companies share this view.

Ultrasound scan will show a pregnancy in the uterus when the hCG level reaches about 1500 IU, or about five weeks after the last menses. An hCG level over 2500 IU without evidence of an intrauterine pregnancy should raise the suspicion of an ectopic pregnancy. Fetal heart activity is usually seen at about six weeks after last menses (four weeks after conception). At eight weeks the embryo measures about 1 cm and movement can sometimes be seen. If all parameters are normal to this point, the risk of miscarriage has markedly dropped and there is an excellent chance the pregnancy will progress to term. At ten weeks gestational age (eight weeks after conception), the embryo measures about 23 mm (one inch), all the foundation has been laid for the various organ systems and the embryo becomes a fetus. At twelve to fourteen weeks a detailed analysis of the body systems can be performed by ultrasound and most anatomic abnormalities excluded.

I am not advocating that an ultrasound machine be kept at the bedside for daily measurements, but an early scan to determine viability and dating and a second for an anatomic survey would seem to be reasonable.

Are there restrictions when a woman with PCOS becomes pregnant?

Pregnancy is not a disease; it is a normal physiologic process (condition). Even though pregnant women can be a little difficult to get along with at times, they are sturdy creatures. There is no evidence that work, exercise, stress, or travel have adverse effects on pregnancy. Stress is always a danger—in pregnancy, in medicine, and in life. This is one that you will have to handle yourself.

The cardinal rules of should I/can I?

If you have a question about any activity, ask yourself two questions. First, does this seem like the wrong thing to do and second, if something were to happen would I blame myself? If the answer to either is yes, don't do it. Do not be faced with the comment "I knew I shouldn't have, but...." It is amazing how many questions can be answered by this exercise; it's really common sense after all. If in doubt—ask. Follow these guidelines:

Stop short—-don't push. This may mean getting off work early, working less, or giving up a commitment. No one is as dependent on you as your baby. Give yourself a margin of safety.

Listen to your body. It will tell you what's going on in there. If you are tired, rest. If you are hungry, eat. If you are sleepy, sleep. If you think there's a problem, have it evaluated.

Nutrition in pregnancy

In general, obstetricians have become much more lenient about what is considered "normal" weight gain in pregnancy and have focused more on good nutrition. If the expectant mother is eating right, weight gain is thought to be less important. The average weight gain in pregnancy is about 12.5 kg (28 lbs.), but this still leaves a margin of at least five pounds or so. If over thirty pounds are gained, it becomes much more difficult for a mother to return to pre-pregnancy weight. Weight gain in the first trimester is variable and there can be considerable increase due to fluids in fertility drugs which have been used. In the second and third trimesters, about one pound per week is appropriate.

Dieting in pregnancy specifically to lose weight is definitely out. Still, it is common for obese patients not to gain, or possibly to lose weight, in the early stages of pregnancy. The very obese may gain little weight throughout the entire pregnancy.

Average caloric intake for women of normal weight and height should be 2100-2500 cal with somewhat less in the first trimester. Diets under 1800 cal are not recommended. The pregnancy itself will require about 300 additional calories a day over your standard dietary needs. Even more calories will be needed while breastfeeding. The entire calorie cost of the pregnancy is about 80,000. It has been suggested that intake of simple type carbohydrates (sweets) increases maternal weight gain and fetal growth more than with complex carbohydrates (starches). The U.S. governmental guidelines suggest 20%

of the diet should come from protein, 40% from carbohydrate, and 40% come from lipids.

I tell all of my newly pregnant PCOS patients to consider themselves to have gestational diabetes (GDM) right from the start. Women with PCOS should ask their obstetricians for diet information and nutritional counseling. *It really doesn't matter how many do not develop gestational diabetes, only how many do.* Why wait until thirty weeks and think about what might have been done? Every pregnancy is a premium pregnancy. Besides, the pregnant diabetic diet is complete and offers good nutrition.

There is evidence that exercise during pregnancy can reduce the incidence of GDM. Pregnancy is not the time to start aerobic training, but gentle, steady exercise will prepare you for the rigors of parenthood. There are specific exercise programs for pregnancy. Yoga gets high marks.

Develop a mental image of a small engine inside you that is always running. It runs best when there is a constant and even supply of fuel. Too much and the engine gets flooded, too little and the tank starts to run a little dry. For the mother, this means rather than three big meals a day, think six small meals. Think grazing, not gorging. You will still consume the same amount of calories; they will just be spread out. You will feel better and so will your baby.

Can nutrition in pregnancy change risk?

A 1999 article in Lancet (Napopi et al). suggested that elevated cholesterol levels in mothers induced changes in the fetal aorta that would predispose the offspring to fatty streak formation and atherosclerosis. Although it could be argued that these children inherited this risk for atherosclerosis, the authors favored it was more acquired during pregnancy. It is thought that some signal transverses the placental circulation and alters the early development of fetal arteries.

Can there be bleeding in a normal pregnancy?

There will be bleeding, or at least spotting, in about one in three pregnancies. About 50% of these pregnancies eventually will be lost. While there is no such thing as "normal bleeding," bleeding does not necessarily indicate a serious problem. With pregnancy, the cervix softens and the surface may easily bleed with even minimal trauma, such as an exam or intercourse. During implantation, which occurs at about the first missed menstrual period, a small amount of bleeding or spotting may be seen. Bleeding may also occur during the process of placenta formation (placentation) when the intimate relationship between the fetal and maternal blood circulation is established. A general rule is the greater amount of bleeding and the more cramping, the greater the chance of pregnancy loss. I have been amazed at the how much bleeding can occur and the pregnancy still continues normally. So first of all, **DON'T PANIC. CALL YOUR PHYSICIAN. REST**. Although there is a great tendency to want immediate reassurance, it may be more diagnostic to wait eighteen to thirty-six hours at home. Too quick an assessment can be falsely reas-

MEDICAL COMPLICATIONS OF PREGNANCY
Big babies, little babies

Generally, the average birthweight of babies born to PCOS mothers is reported not to differ from the general population. The key word here is average. Consider that if there were an equal number of high and low birthweight babies, then the average would not be altered. It is probable that many with PCOS deliver infants with normal birth weights (3000 to 3600 g or 6 1/2 to 8 pounds). But, equally likely is a relationship between PCOS and the extremes of birth weight, both high and low. When interviewing new PCOS patients, I also ask about their own birth weight and there seems to be a disproportionate number of patients who have started their lives heavier or lighter than the average baby.

Infants born before 37 weeks are said to be *premature* and do not have the same risks as babies that are *small for gestational age* (SGA) or *growth restricted* (less than 2500g or about 5 pounds). Growth restriction is usually a result of *utero-placental insufficiency*, a decreased blood supply to the placenta, and is associated with substantial perinatal problems. There can be many causes of growth restriction, but of most importance to PCOS patients are vascular problems arising from long-standing diabetes and chronic hypertension. Detection of growth restriction is based on poor maternal weight gain, a smaller uterus on exam, and ultrasound confirmation. When growth restriction is suspected, much more intensive monitoring is indicated.

Babies *large for gestational age* (LGA or *macrosomia*) probably outnumber growth restricted and SGA babies in mothers with PCOS. The major risks for macrosomia are related to gestational diabetes, obesity, and postdates. The incidence of macrosomia at delivery in the general population is about 1% for babies 4500 g (about 10 pounds) and 5% for over 4000 g (about 8 1/2 pounds). When the risk factors of gestation of 40 weeks, obesity, and gestational diabetes (GDM) are added, the incidence is 10-15%. One or more risk factors are found in about 40% of macrosomia. Sometimes the parents are large people and sometimes the baby is just big. It is still possible that in pregnancies where no risk factors can be identified that an underlying and undiagnosed cause of macrosomia is hyperinsulinemia. Maybe we just haven't looked hard enough. All pregnancies with excessive fetal growth should be monitored closely for GDM and hypertension. There is a significant increase in c-section rate and risk for shoulder injury due to obstructed labor (dystocia) during delivery. All larger babies should be watched closely after delivery for evidence of hypoglycemia.

Does growth restriction lead to future insulin resistance?

There is a confirmed relationship between low birth weight and development of insulin resistance, impaired glucose tolerance, and type two diabetes. As many as one-third of young adults born with growth restriction later become insulin resistant. The mechanism is not completely known, but is thought to involve the altered development of adipose (fat) tissue so important in glucose homeostasis.

A second finding has been that low birth weight predisposes to precocious adrenal (pubertal) development and this then to PCOS.

A third, and at first seemingly unrelated, mechanism is that prenatal exposure to corticosteroids was later associated with development of PCOS. Individuals at risk for preterm delivery are commonly treated with large doses of corticosteroids. While these treatments were controversial for many years, it is now considered the standard of care to accelerate the fetal lung development and decrease the risk of respiratory distress syndrome (RDS). The value of steroid use is clearly established, but the long-term risks of this therapy, specifically the possibility of PCOS, may be underestimated.

As a group, these observations can be interpreted in several ways. One possibility is that prenatal stress, either from growth restriction, prematurity, or adrenal steroid administration leads to a greater probability of the development of PCOS. It is possible that early adrenal programming is responsible for later PCOS in some cases.

This is especially interesting in that it would represent a different pathway for development of PCOS that had little or nothing to do with genetics. Looking up and down the family tree would be an interesting exercise in this group.

Does macrosomia cause PCOS?

Do big babies make big babies? It is back to the question of nature or nurture, of genetics and environment. Clearly, insulin resistance and type 2 diabetes are in part inherited. Women who will develop type 2 diabetes are more likely to have gestational diabetes and were probably abnormally insulin resistant during their pregnancy. Gestational diabetes is uniformly associated with larger babies. Since PCOS and diabetes are related, it is reasonable to project that the PCOS patient will have bigger babies and that PCOS patients will have a greater risk of GDM. Now, could it be that macrosomia alone alters the fetal metabolism to such an extent to predispose to later development of PCOS in the absence of genetic factors? Could a glucose rich environment, in itself, cause later PCOS or insulin resistance? This we do not know. Complex, isn't it?

Does PCOS increase the risk of diabetes in pregnancy?

Yes. True, there have been no studies large enough to make a statement of the number of patients with PCOS who will develop gestational diabetes mellitus (GDM), or the number of gestational diabetic patients who have

PCOS. It is very difficult to sort out the effects of obesity alone versus the effects of insulin resistance alone. Both are components of PCOS, but not all of PCOS. But, the association is clearly there and the research would not seem all that difficult; it just hasn't been done. Several small studies suggest 41-45% of the women with GDM have ultrasound appearance of PCOS.

Gestational diabetes is defined as any degree of glucose intolerance with first onset, or recognition during pregnancy. GDM complicates 2-4% of pregnancies, about 135,000 cases per year, and is the second most common medical complication of pregnancy. Complications of GDM include macrosomia, increased risk of cesarean section and hypertension. It is logical that those with PCOS and insulin resistance would be at higher risk of GDM. We don't know how many with PCOS develop GDM.

Making the diagnosis of gestational diabetes

In the past, whom to screen for GDM was the subject of extensive lists; now it becomes common practice to screen virtually all patients. It is known that the risks of GDM increase slightly with maternal age, but some who develop GDM have no risk factors identified. It is amazing how many PCOS patients we screen for insulin resistance and glucose intolerance would be classified as GDM even before pregnancy. One can only suppose that pregnancy will worsen their insulin resistance.

The time-honored method of screening for GDM is to perform a one-hour glucose tolerance test (GTT). This is accomplished by a blood test in the morning after nothing to eat or drink after midnight the night before. The test is more reliable if there have been several days of heavier carbohydrate intake. Do not diet for the test. A bottle of some really horrible glucose rich liquid is drunk and a second blood test is measured after one hour. This is considered positive if the initial fasting level is over 90-95 mg/dl., and after drinking 50 grams of glucose and waiting one hour, the level is over 140. If this screen is positive, then a three hour test is performed using a 100 g glucose drink with blood samples at one, two and three hours. If two of the three levels are abnormal, a diagnosis of GDM is made and diet restrictions enforced. Monitoring is usually by blood testing two hours after a big meal (postprandial).

Far be it from me to go against the establishment. I think the GTT is a good tool to equally evaluate patients, but I have a different idea, at least for those with PCOS. As above, you have already been given the diagnosis of PCOS and are known to be at risk, so skip this test and throughout the remainder of the pregnancy, with variable frequency based on performance and risk factors, have routine two hour blood samples performed after a wholesome breakfast or lunch. When you are no longer remaining in the normal glucose range, you have GDM.

It has been reported that 40-66% of GDM could be diagnosed on the first prenatal visit, but there have been conflicting views as to whether the testing should be performed. The diagnosis GDM by GTT is associated with a much greater chance of pregnancy induced hypertension. An early identification of risk may alter how the remainder of the pregnancy is approached and intensify vigilance.

This risk for GDM may be thought of as a gradient, listed in terms of increasing risk of GDM—non-obese, non-PCOS, obese non-PCOS, non-obese insulin resistant, obese insulin resistant PCOS.

Why is there insulin resistance during pregnancy?

Pregnancy creates a significant nutritional drain on the mother. Insulin resistance is a normal and necessary part of normal pregnancy. During pregnancy, fat storage is promoted, especially in the areas of gynoid fat distribution in the thighs and hips. This fat is relatively resistant to mobilization. Relative insulin resistance allows a more constant state of availability of glucose. There must be sufficient food stores created to maintain not only the pregnancy, but also provide for the breast feeding that follows. The initial stages of pregnancy are characterized by an increase in insulin sensitivity, that is more nutrients going into fat stores. In the later stages of pregnancy nutritional stores are maintained for the growing baby's higher nutritional needs by insulin resistance.

Insulin resistance in pregnancy may arise from the same mechanisms as insulin resistance at other times, namely alteration in the glucose transport proteins (GLUT 4) and actions resulting after the binding of insulin to the insulin receptor (post receptor defects) (discussed in insulin chapter). In GDM glucose transport is decreased and GLUT 4 levels are reduced. As an aside, increasing GLUT 4 may be the principle action of metformin and at least the mechanism by which metformin reduces pregnancy loss. If the individual is insulin resistant when she should be insulin sensitive, there may not be enough nutrient supply, the embryo may be starved, and miscarriage result.

The placenta secretes human pregnancy lactogen (hPL) which is very similar to human growth hormone. Human growth hormone is intimately related to insulin and insulin-like growth factors after birth and in the adult; hPL is a diabetogenic force in pregnancy. HPL increases in the second half of pregnancy and may be responsible for the IR seen as pregnancy progresses. HPL works to insure the constant supply of glucose and amino acids demanded by the fetus. As glucose decreases between meals, hPL rises, stimulating breakdown of maternal fat stores. When there is an abundance of energy substrates, the fetus, like all of us, grows. Still, there are problems with the interpretation of this mechanism, because there have been normal pregnancies despite absence of hPL. HPL may be one of the adaptive mechanisms, a reserve fuel tank switch, which has been held over from our earlier days when food supplies were not nearly so plentiful.

How is gestational diabetes treated?

The first step is a modest increase in activity and reduction in calories. The goal is to have a fasting glucose under 100 mg/dl and a glucose level two hours after meals no higher than 140 mg/dl. Most with GDM will respond to this intervention, some will not. At present, insulin is the only treatment of GDM not responsive to diet therapy. Typical oral agents (sulfonylureas) should not be used because they pass through the placenta circulation and may cause fetal hypoglycemia. We are probably not far away from routine use of insulin-altering drugs, but at present it is still experimental.

A high definition genetic ultrasound to look for potential birth defects is reasonable to perform at eighteen to twenty weeks and/or as soon as the diagnosis of GDM is made. Know where you are starting. More vigilant ultrasound studies to check fetal growth might be indicated as well as frequent office visits for sugar checks. Like it or not, you will probably be a frequent visitor to your physician's office. During the third trimester when there is an increase in unexplained fetal death, vigilance should be increased. In part, this may be performed by self-testing of fetal movement by a "kick" chart. You may also have biophysical profiles that use ultrasound and a number of parameters to evaluate fetal well-being. A portion of the ultrasound evaluation will be to check for the amount of amniotic fluid. The patient with GDM is at increased risk for polyhydramnios (excessive accumulation of amniotic fluid).

Pregnancies with GDM are not usually allowed to progress much past term. C-section is much more common. When there has been maternal hyperglycemia, there is a greater chance of neonatal hypoglycemia and close vigilance is required with babies born to a mother with GDM.

What does GDM mean for the future?

GDM may be a risk factor for the future development of metabolic syndrome (dyslipidemia, hypertension and insulin resistance) in mothers. It is thought that women with GDM have a 50% chance of developing type 2 diabetes within twenty years of delivery. Considering these risks, women who develop GDM should be rescreened with a glucose tolerance test several months after delivery.

What if there is diabetes before pregnancy?

Pregnancies in diabetics are risky business, but they are also successful. Planning is everything. Hypertension, prematurity, and unexplained fetal death are common complications of diabetic pregnancies. A pre-pregnancy evaluation should also be performed to check for cardiovascular fitness and kidney function.

Maternal hyperglycemia results in fetal hyperglycemia, which results in fetal insulin resistance, just as in adults. Increased glucose levels also increase oxygen demand for the metabolism of these substances, and in the absence of the ability to do this, blood and oxygen may be compromised. There may already be a problem with the vasculature of the placenta due to hyperglycemia, but added to that is the frequent association of diabetes and hypertension. Around 30% of diabetic women will develop hypertension in the third trimester of pregnancy. Most preterm delivery is associated with worsening hypertension. Premature delivery may be of even greater risk because elevated insulin and testosterone have been reported to delay lung maturation and can place the fetus at risk if delivered prematurely. Close evaluation of the fetus with care to observe evidence of vascular compromise should begin at about thirty-two weeks for women with preexisting diabetes. It is generally thought that diabetic pregnancies should not be carried past forty weeks.

How the pregnancy is finished is in many ways dependent on how the pregnancy is started. By all we know, the most harmful effects on the fetus are due to elevated glucose levels. There should be absolute normalization of glucose levels and hemoglobin A1c (glycosulated hemoglobin, a marker of long term glucose control), before a pregnancy is attempted. Whether this requires an insulin pump and/or insulin-sensitizing agents, just do it. Diabetics on insulin synthesizing agents and in good control should continue them in pregnancy. Even without approval, this may be a case where the real benefit may exceed a theoretical risk.

Diabetes and birth defects

Women with established diabetes before pregnancy have a four-fold increase in major birth defects. Evidence of birth defects is directly correlated with hemoglobin A1c. This rate can be markedly reduced with good glucose control. Almost 50% of deaths of children born to diabetic mothers are related to congenital malformation (birth defects). Animal and human studies indicate that these effects arise very early in the pregnancy, by eight weeks. Hyperglycemia appears to be a major contributor, but is complicated by vascular alterations. Over one third of the major defects are heart-related. Skeletal defects occur in 15% of patients, central nervous system in 10%, and multiple defects in16%.

Should insulin-altering drugs be used during pregnancy?

Two unplanned human experiments, DES and thalidomide, have molded the entire pharmaceutical industry's thought about use of medication during pregnancy. At the time, use of thalidomide for morning sickness seemed to be safe, but the offspring were born with limb abnormalities. In the case of DES, physicians thought they were helping to prevent miscarriage by giving estrogen, but the daughters exposed to DES while in the uterus were born with abnormalities of the uterus. No one wants to be the first to try new drugs, and physicians are generally cautious about almost any drug use in pregnancy. It is virtually impossible to have any drug approved for a pregnancy indication.

Having said this, one should revert to that FDA admonishment of "the potential benefit should exceed the potential risk." Use of insulin-altering drugs in pregnancy may have very significant benefits of reducing pregnancy loss. The risks, although generally unknown, would appear to be very small. Diabetics who are using the drugs for glucose management would seem the best candidates to continue their use. Older, uncontrolled research has studied metformin's use in diabetic women throughout pregnancy, and no measurable increases in miscarriage or congenital anomalies were identified compared to expected norms. Then, possibly the drug should be extended to those with recurrent pregnancy loss and those at high risk for developing gestational diabetes. These drugs should not be considered risk free, but neither should PCOS in pregnancy or gestational diabetes.

Pregnancy-induced hypertension

Hypertension is defined as a systolic pressure (top number) above 140mm over a diastolic (bottom number) pressure over 90mm. Blood pressure may vary greatly with temporary stress and, in the obstetric patient, position can affect the blood pressure greatly. It is best to take the blood pressure while the patient is lying down after a few minutes rest. The early stages of pregnancy are associated with a drop of blood pressure.

Maternal hypertension (increased blood pressure) is the most common medical complication of pregnancy (6-8% of pregnancies). It is responsible for 15% of all maternal deaths and ranks second to thromboembolism (blood clots) as the major cause of maternal mortality. While chronic hypertension is a risk factor in developing *pregnancy-induced hypertension* (PIH), they are very different problems. PIH is not just blood pressure elevation; it can be a wild fire, involving multiple organs and systems. Patients are usually said to be *preeclamptic* when blood pressure exceeds 140/90 and there is protein found in the urine (*proteinuria*). *Eclampsia,* which luckily is uncommon, is secondary to PIH. A serious sequel of PIH is *HEELP syndrome* consisting of hypertension, elevation of liver (hepatic) enzymes often with abdominal pain, blood clotting abnormalities, edema and proteinuria.

PIH usually does not develop until after twenty weeks gestation. If blood pressure is high before that time, it may have been a chronic problem. *Antiphospholipid antibody (APL) syndrome* often presents with early second trimester hypertension. With APL there are multiple small infarctions of the placenta microcirculation due to abnormalities in the blood coagulation system. APL should be tested in all cases of second trimester loss associated with hypertension.

PIH results in constriction of the vessels (vascular bed) of the placenta with diminishing blood flow. This can restrict fetal growth and prematurely age the placenta. There are few ways to prevent PIH. It is a fact of life for some pregnant women. Because the first pregnancy has been affected by PIH does not mean the second pregnancy will always be affected.

Can PIH be predicted?

The following is a list of the risk factors for PIH, in increasing order of risk. The more risk factors that are positive, the greater likelihood that PIH will occur.

- Family history of PIH
- Chronic hypertension
- Twin gestation
- First pregnancy
- Age over 40
- Diabetes

How is PIH treated?

Spending more time lying on the left side, which takes pressure off the major vessels and allows maximum blood flow to the uterus, and bedrest can sometimes slow progression of hypertension. Reducing salt intake can also help, as can preventing an excessive weight gain in pregnancy. In reality, the only definitive treatment is delivery.

Does obesity make the pregnancy high risk?

Obviously many obese women (BMI>27) become pregnant and many deliver healthy babies without problems. Still, obesity clearly increases risks to the woman and her fetus. It is very difficult to separate simple obesity from that associated with PCOS. Those with PCOS may be at higher risk for the complications of pregnancy when compared to the obese without PCOS. Women with a waist hip ratio over 0.8 are at further increased risk.

Chronic hypertension is an indication of a *high-risk* pregnancy and must be carefully monitored. ß-Blockers have been shown to have adverse effects on early embryonic development and may cause fetal heart problems in later pregnancy. ACE inhibitors have been shown to cause fetal death in the last two trimesters, however, early pregnancy use may be safe. The long-standing drug of choice for treatment of chronic hypertension in pregnancy is Methyldopa (Aldomet™), which is a vasodilator.

Incidence of severe PIH may be as much as tripled in the obese woman. Gestational diabetes complicates about 10-20% of pregnancies when weight is 150% of the ideal. Specific congenital anomalies include neural tube defects (spina bifida) in which the risk is doubled. There is a greater likelihood of heart defects as well. In one study, when BMI was over 39, the c-section rate was nearly doubled over that of women whose BMIs were less than 29.

> **Risks of Obesity for Pregnancy**
>
> - Chronic hypertension
> - Pregnancy-induced hypertension
> - Gestational diabetes
> - Macrosomia
> - Operative delivery (c-section and forceps)
> - Obstructed delivery (shoulder dystocia)
> - Birth defects
> - Blood clots (phlebitis and pulmonary embolism)
> - Hemorrhage and anemia
> - Extended hospital stay
> - Infection
> - More neonatal intensive care unit admissions
> - Increase risk of perinatal death in the first week

Who's the boss—mother, baby, or placenta?

Its gross bloody appearance at birth would never suggest it, but the placenta is a fascinating organ, an unsung champion of pregnancy, and an organ to which much homage is due. The placenta forms the interface between the mother and the fetus and the site where the complications of pregnancy can occur that theoretically are associated with PCOS. Both hypertension and diabetes have the microvasulature of the placenta as their target.

While commonly called the "after birth," this does not honor its contribution to the pregnancy. Perhaps it would more properly be referred to as the "before birth." The placenta is an organ that is born, lives a full life, ages, and dies within a span of forty weeks. It also serves many bodily functions, including acting as circulatory, digestive, excretory (renal), immune, and endocrine systems. It has diseases and pathology just as any organism. Professor Sam Yen, a patriarch of reproductive endocrinology, has referred to the placenta as the "third brain". It may be the placenta that decides when its job is finished and initiates labor. Surely we know that it forms a major interface and communication network between the mother and her fetus. The placenta regulates the nutrient supply from the mother to the fetus by accessing each of their needs and supplies. Through signals to the placenta, the fetus controls the way the mother handles the food she takes to maintain an uninterrupted supply of nutrients. (See human placental lactogen above). Whether there is a boss or a committee is not known, but the thankless job of the placenta is under appreciated.

MISCARRIAGE

What is a miscarriage?

A *miscarriage* is loss of pregnancy before twenty weeks gestation. In the medical community this is more widely called a spontaneous abortion. After twenty weeks a pregnancy loss is called a *stillbirth*. There have been pleas to use the more widely understood term *miscarriage* to designate the undesired, or spontaneous loss of pregnancy, but the term *abortion* is still used by most physicians to describe all losses regardless of cause.

The time surrounding a miscarriage is a time of intense feeling of failure and despair. An emotional scar will almost always remain regardless of future pregnancy success.

What is the chance of miscarriage?

A couple in their mid-twenties having intercourse regularly will usually take about three months to become pregnant. It is possible that most women who are regularly ovulatory and not using contraception achieve a pregnancy in most months, but the pregnancy is lost soon after conception and goes unnoticed. One in four couples will have a recognized miscarriage. The chance of a miscarriage after a positive pregnancy test is 8-15% for all pregnancies in all age groups. This rate increases to about 15-25% in women over age thirty-five and those who have irregular menstrual cycles. Overall, about 80% of couples with two miscarriages, and 50-60% of couples after four losses still will have a successful pregnancy. As the pregnancy progresses, the risk of miscarriage decreases. Over 90% of miscarriages occur during the first twelve weeks.

What are the causes of miscarriage?

The circumstances around the miscarriage are extremely important in determining the cause of the pregnancy loss. A detailed history, clinical and ultrasound findings should be carefully recorded. Perhaps most important is the number of weeks gestational age at which the loss occurs. This may be difficult to determine in some cases because accurate dating has not been made. The number of weeks between loss of viability of the pregnancy and its clinical diagnoses is unknown and the length of the pregnancy often is over estimated. Early first trimester losses are most often due to genetic and hormonal causes. Later first trimester losses, after eight weeks, may be a result of uterine anomalies. Second trimester losses are often due to disorders of the placental-maternal unit and sometimes due to chronic diseases. While genetic problems are less common, they are still possible. Losses during the third trimester are often maternal in origin and may be related to various diseases of pregnancy including diabetes and hypertension.

When Can Tell Us Why
When a pregnancy is lost often determines the cause of the loss.
The following are general guidelines.
- First trimester: EMBRYO—hormonal and/or genetic in origin
- Second trimester: UTERUS—less often genetic and more often anatomic
- Third trimester: MATERNAL—immunologic, medical complications

How are miscarriages characterized?

Various terms are used to describe the circumstances surrounding the pregnancy loss, each term taking into account when the loss occurred, clinical findings, ultrasound findings, cause, and whether the loss is recurrent. This has resulted in confusing and overlapping terminology. Listed below are several clinical distinctions used to characterize pregnancy loss.

- Blighted ovum
- Missed abortion
- Threatened abortion
- Incomplete abortion
- Complete (spontaneous) abortion

The first evidence of a pregnancy on ultrasound is the *gestational sac* containing a smaller *yolk sac* as definitive evidence of an intrauterine gestation (pregnancy). Occasionally an irregular structure appearing to be a gestational sac, a "pseudo sac," can be seen with an ectopic pregnancy.

A pregnancy that has implanted, but has failed to grow to the stage where an embryo can be identified on ultrasound scan is called a *blighted ovum*. Evidence of a pregnancy is seen by ultrasound by the presence of a yolk sac, but because it lacks evidence of an embryo, it is often called an *"empty sac."* These pregnancies are uniformly believed to have a genetic or endocrine reason for their poor outcome. Although gestational sacs vary somewhat in size, smaller sacs are worrisome. A larger or smaller yolk sac can be an early indication of an endangered pregnancy. In the early stages of pregnancies that will subsequently be lost, progesterone levels may be normal or decreased. HCG titers may increase normally or more slowly. The cause of a blighted ovum is virtually always a problem with the conceptus itself, rather than the uterus or maternal factors. While male factors may contribute, the blighted ovum is more commonly of oocyte origin—the reason for the designation of a blighted ovum. Most are a result of genetic abnormalities in eggs that are satisfactory to be fertilized and go through the early stages of development, but not sufficiently normal for further development. Usually, there is insufficient tissue for genetic testing on these pregnancy losses.

Sometimes, the pregnancy will spontaneously resorb and no intervention is necessary. In other cases, there may be persistence of the pregnancy requiring either a D&C and/or hysteroscopy to identify and remove the pregnancy. Since the pregnancy is small, care has to be taken with the dilation and curettage procedure to avoid missing the pregnancy. In some cases, it is wise to do the procedure under direct ultrasound guidance. The D&C is performed in an outpatient capacity, but usually in a same day surgery facility.

A *missed abortion* is diagnosed when viability of the pregnancy has been lost, but there has been no expulsion of the pregnancy. The blighted ovum is an early type of missed abortion in which fetal heart activity was not identified. Fetal heart activity may have also been seen, but then lost. In some cases, a short time in wait for spontaneous loss may be given before intervention. This may be especially important as a time to accept that the pregnancy will not continue.

Like the blighted ovum, most cases of missed abortion in the first trimester are due to problems in the conceptus. In some cases, there is a much greater chance that this has been a sporadic and non-reccurring problem related to egg quality rather than an inherited genetic problem. The blighted ovum and missed abortion are the most common types of pregnancy loss in PCOS and a hormonal etiology should be suspected in all cases.

In cases of a *threatened abortion* there is bleeding but the cervix is closed. When the cervical canal opens, miscarriage is usually *inevitable*. If only a portion of the pregnancy has been lost, the miscarriage is said to be *incomplete* and intervention is warranted in all cases. Often there will be a *complete* and total expulsion of the pregnancy. If ultrasound scan shows that there are no retained products of conception, bleeding is slowing and the cervical opening is closed, no operative intervention is needed.

Recurrent pregnancy loss

After three, some authorities say two, consecutive pregnancy losses, diagnosis of *recurrent* or *habitual pregnancy loss* is made. Every pregnancy loss is associated with despair, but there are few that grieve more deeply and fear more intensely than those who have had repeated pregnancy losses. It is a common feeling that an additional loss could not be withstood. About 1% of couples trying to conceive will have three or more losses. The best news is that even after three successive losses, the chance of a successful pregnancy is generally greater than 70% and after four losses, still 60%. Usually after successive losses, a medical evaluation should be initiated. In the early stages, this may consist of nothing more than tracking temperatures, using ovulation detection kits, and possibly using luteal progesterone levels.

What causes recurrent pregnancy loss?

When evaluating pregnancy, most physicians go through the process of a mental listing then an exclusion of the possibilities based on individual characteristics. In the final analysis, if it isn't one cause, it must be another.

Causes of Recurrent Pregnancy Loss:
- Endocrine/genetic
- Anatomic
- Inherited
- Infectious
- Chronic disease
- Immunologic
- Unexplained

Endocrine/genetic

Previously, it was thought that over 50% of recurrent pregnancy losses were unexplained. We now know that many of these cases are due to subtle hormonal abnormalities. Unless another reason can clearly be identified, such as a strong family history of pregnancy loss or clearly evident uterine abnormality, it may be reasonable to treat with clomiphene or possibly progesterone before extensive testing is performed. After three losses, a karyotype can be considered, if no other cause is evident. Even if the genetic studies are abnormal, that does not mean a normal pregnancy is impossible.

Anatomic

Pregnancy losses that occur after a normal pregnancy has been established and all appears to be progressing well followed by cramping and loss of the pregnancy are more likely due to congenital anatomic abnormalities in the uterus. These can be identified by either *hysterosalpingogram* (HSG) or *hysteroscopy*. There are approximately 15% false positive and negative rates with the HSG and it may fail to identify the more subtle anomalies such as a uterine septum. It is unclear whether congenital anomalies of the uterus cause infertility, but it is clear that it is associated with a greater risk of recurrent pregnancy loss and preterm labor. Milder forms are easily corrected by hysteroscopic surgery. It is important to note that there is a high incidence of associated abnormalities of the urinary tract and an intravenous pyelogram is indicated when a uterine anomaly is identified. The more severe uterine anomalies may be easily seen on ultrasound scan. MRI has been suggested for a definitive diagnosis; however, this is very costly and the information can be gained by other sources.

Inherited

The chance of an inherited genetic condition that is passed from either the mother or father as the cause of recurrent pregnancy loss is about 3-5% of cases. These can be identified by karyotype performed on a blood sample. These can be very valuable, but are also extremely costly. Karyotype should probably not be performed in individuals with fewer than three pregnancy losses. Even if a genetic defect has been identified, it may not prevent a normal pregnancy but it may indicate that the chance of a recurrent pregnancy loss is greater.

Infectious

Both *mycoplasma* and *ureaplasma* have been identified with a greater risk of pregnancy loss. While there are tests to detect their presence, testing can be inconclusive and it is often easier to treat with a two-week course of antibiotics than identify the specific organism. The chances of recurrent pregnancy loss due to infection are probably very slim, but the treatment is easy and sometimes rewarding.

Chronic disease

Patients with virtually any type of chronic disease may be at increased risk for recurrent pregnancy loss. Chronic diseases such as high blood pressure and diabetes create a much higher risk for recurrent loss. An under-appreciated chronic disease may be obesity. Chronic disease probably primarily affects establishment of the maternal fetal circulation. The best treatment in these cases is preconceptional counseling and making sure that the disease is under the best control possible before a pregnancy is attempted.

Immunologic

Clearly, many of the immunologic diseases have multiple organ system involvement and have a higher rate of pregnancy loss. An uncommon but particularly dangerous type of recurrent pregnancy loss is the antiphospholipid antibody syndrome characterized by hypertension, poor fetal, and placental development. There are a number of small infarctions that occur in the placenta due to a disorder in the blood clotting mechanisms. Pregnancies are most often lost in the mid-second to early third trimester. A variety of therapies including aspirin, heparin, corticosteroids, and immunoglobulin injections have been tried with marginal success.

This is different from the otherwise healthy individual without overt immunologic disease, in whom I believe immunologic causes of recurrent pregnancy loss to be rare. Granted, immune mechanisms are intrically related to implantation and there is considerable area from which problems might arise, I just don't think it happens very often. Our greatest problem is that there is no extensive testing without clinical associations and no proven efficacious therapy exists. There still could be very important developments in this field.

Unexplained

Philosophically, I refuse to accept the diagnosis of unexplained pregnancy loss. Probably most cases are either undiagnosed or misdiagnosed problems in one of the above categories. Most cases of recurrent loss are probably related to egg quality and therefore related to the environment in which the egg develops.

Is miscarriage more likely with PCOS?

Probably. This is a real tough question and I personally believe the answer is yes. Initially, it appeared as if everyone agreed, but as the studies have been repeated, the results are less clear. One fact stands out. Women with recurrent pregnancy loss much more often have polycystic ovaries on ultrasound. The most comprehensive study to date by a group lead by Lesley Regan reporting on 2199 women attending a recurrent pregnancy loss clinic in London found that 40.7% of women had polycystic ovaries; that's about twice the normal reported incidence. In this study, women who had three or more losses had a pregnancy rate of about 60% regardless of whether they had polycystic ovaries or, not. On the surface their results may appear as if PCOS did not cause pregnancy loss, but that would assume that the group of other women with recurrent loss were "normal," which we just don't know. This just means that women with polycystic ovaries have no less chance of success.

An area of more debate is the role of LH and androgens in pregnancy loss. Several studies have shown that pregnancy rates and outcome are improved when GnRH analogs (Lupron™, etc.), which reduce LH secretion, are used in conjunction with gonadotropin stimulation. Others have a found that pretreatment with oral contraceptives before ovarian stimulation, also known to reduce LH secretion is associated with improved success. The authors of these studies tend to place the blame on LH as the main culprit of poor success. I personally believe that there is significantly higher first and repeat loss rate in PCOS compared to the general population. The cause of the altered egg quality is yet to be determined.

Can insulin-altering drugs reduce miscarriage rate?

There is a very close correlation between the effect of LH on ovarian function and that of insulin. Both cause androgen hypersecretion from the ovary and this may be but one of many alterations that the two share. If LH results in an increase in pregnancy loss, so should increased levels of insulin. If pretreatment of PCOS patients with GnRH analogs reduces LH and pregnancy loss, then insulin-altering drugs should do the same for the hyperinsulinemic patient.

Preliminary evidence suggests this fact may be the case. Dr. Glueck in Cincinnati reported at the Annual Meeting for Experimental Biology 2000, (CJ Glueck et al, J *Invest Med* 2000) his experience with fifty-nine women with PCOS who established a pregnancy while on metformin. Of these, twenty-three continued metformin when a pregnancy resulted while the other thirty-six discontinued therapy. The miscarriage rate was 45% without metformin and 9% with metformin. This must be taken as a very preliminary finding, but it is clear there will be a proliferation of reports and I suspect encouraging results in spontaneously achieved pregnancies and those established after fertility therapy. Several studies are underway to evaluate metformin use as adjunctive therapy in IVF. The safety of insulin-altering drugs is discussed below.

Can a miscarriage be prevented?

Probably not. Generally, all patients with impending loss are placed on bed rest. Unfortunately, there is no scientific proof that indicates this is of benefit. It doesn't hurt and it may help to ease anxiety and avoid guilt associated with activity. Sexual intercourse should be avoided. Sex can cause uterine contractions. Generally, once a pregnancy is established, very little can be done to alter its course. This becomes less true in the second and third trimester. Stress may have an adverse effect on pregnancy. Don't be your own worst enemy. Remember, that nothing you did caused the pregnancy loss. Reassurance by ultrasound can be helpful. It is always great to see the fetal heart beating.

After a miscarriage what are the chances of a healthy baby?

In cases where no cause is discovered and no treatment prescribed, the chance of achieving a healthy pregnancy despite having had three miscarriages is still better than 60%. Generally, the risk of a second loss is only slightly higher after a single loss. Of course, the first loss rate is probably higher than the non-PCOS population. The American College of Obstetrics and Gynecologists (ACOG) now recommends testing after a second loss-especially for women over the age of thirty-five. A recent study has shown that a high percentage of patients that conceive and miscarry during fertility therapy will subsequently have a healthy baby.

When can we try again?

The answer to this is dependent on the size of gestational sac, dates and the circumstances around the loss. There are several studies that suggest that if there is not a waiting period of six months, then there is a greater chance of a subsequent low birth weight pregnancy. These studies were mostly performed in indigent patients with borderline nutrition. There is also the concept of a grieving period and a chance to get over the loss. I believe this is a worn approach on two counts. It's not the concept of "jump back on the horse after being thrown off." It's a matter of reaching a peace and moving on. There must be all the processes of grieving that accompany the death of a family member. A scar is left that will heal but will never go away no matter what success there is in the future. A pregnancy can be attempted as soon as you can accept the possibility of another loss. It is common to hear "I can't go through that again." The only answer is, "then don't try." There is never a guarantee of pregnancy success and virtually never a guarantee of its failure.

Medically, it is probably prudent to wait through at least one normal menstrual cycle after an early first trimester loss, possibly two cycles, if the pregnancy was in the later stages of the first trimester. Second trimester losses may require three months. HCG blood titre should be followed to zero.

It is surprising how many couples will quickly and even spontaneously establish a pregnancy after a recent loss. A pregnancy loss can have a positive effect on PCOS making the next pregnancy both easier to achieve and more likely to be successful.

Why do doctors seem not to care about pregnancy loss?

After losing a pregnancy, or with an impending loss, couples have tremendous amounts of anxiety and despair. In actuality, the chances of having been pregnant and delivering a healthy child are probably much greater than their counterparts seeking fertility therapy.

Physicians view miscarriage as common, natural and a situation that offers little opportunity to treat (prevent). As obstetricians, we know that miscarriage is going to occur in a certain percentage of our patients regardless. Unfortunately, physicians can be very matter-of-fact about pregnancy loss. This doesn't excuse our behavior, just explains it (partly).

So when can I stop worrying?

You can't, you won't. I was having dinner with one of the medical students one evening when he turned to me in all sincerity and said, "You know my mom didn't consider me a viable pregnancy until I was selected to Yale Medical School." There will always be the next horizon, whether it will be the first positive pregnancy test, the first evidence of fetal heart activity on ultrasound, a healthy baby at birth, the first step, the first day from home, or their 21st birthday. You will always worry. Stick to worrying about the things you can change.

BREASTFEEDING

Breast is best when it comes to nutrition for babies. There's virtually no arguing that fact anymore. Additionally, breastfeeding can be a great way to lose the weight gained with pregnancy and maybe a little pre-pregnant weight too.

There are two mostly independent processes required for breast feeding (*lactation*)–milk production and milk letdown. Milk production is a multifaceted hormonal process involving *prolactin*, other pituitary hormones, steroids, and a variety of growth factors. Milk let down is under control of oxytocin produced from the posterior lobe of the pituitary gland. *Oxytocin* is the same hormone that was given to some to stimulate uterine contractions. It's a good system; suckling stimulates oxytocin release and at the same time causes the uterus to contract. Initially, this controls bleeding; later it helps return the uterus to its once pear-size form through a process called *involution*. Over the first two days, only a small and variable amount of fluid called *colostrum* is released. Colostrum is rich in fat and protein, but poor in lactose, a major nutrient of breast milk. Colostrum is also rich in antibodies providing partial immunologic protection to the newborn.

Does PCOS impair the ability to breast-feed?

This question of PCOS and breastfeeding keeps arising and there seem to be two entrenched camps. Some report little problem and others, despite the best intention and preparation, are not successful. Many with PCOS, after surviving the ordeal of becoming pregnant, are extremely desirous of the breastfeeding experience as well. When they cannot do so successfully they are once again disappointed by a failure of their body to perform on expectation.

Initially my thoughts were that breastfeeding with PCOS was no different than it was for anyone else, but experience with many patients has led me to wonder. Truly, many women have only marginal success with breastfeeding; but is there something special about PCOS? Although some failure of lactation is due to anatomic "nipple" factors, it would seem that there should be no difference in PCOS there. Since lactation is such a complex hormonal process, this could be the source of the problem. Androgens, diabetes, hypertension, hyperprolactinemia have all been implicated in decreased milk production. As much as I hate to bring it up, we know for sure that stress will negatively impact the pituitary gland and milk production. It is possible that some incidences of lactation failure may be due to just working too hard at it. Local LaLeche League support groups can provide assistance in such cases, but don't be surprised if they seem uniformed about PCOS.

ADDITIONAL/SUBSEQUENT PREGNANCIES
Will my next pregnancy be at increased risk?

Not necessarily. Each pregnancy is unique. The greatest determinant may be the time factor between pregnancies and the maternal age at which the next pregnancy is attempted. There can be planned, or unplanned, long gaps between pregnancies. Health status may improve or deteriorate during this period. Disorders such as hypertension and diabetes have a definite age related increase in risk, but then PIH is also more common in the first pregnancy, so the risk may be lessened. Obstetricians once operated under the adage "once a cesarean section, always a cesarean section." We now know that larger babies can be successfully delivered vaginally after a previous c-section performed because it was judged the baby was too large (cephalopelvic disproportion-CPD). These deliveries are called vaginal birth after c-section (VBAC). Much will have to do with maintaining good health, then a bit of luck.

What does a pregnancy mean for my future?

Often good news. Pregnancy has a positive health benefit on breast and reproductive cancer. I am constantly surprised by how an additional pregnancy may follow so effortlessly after a pregnancy achieved after a long wait or very aggressive fertility therapy. One should never fall victim to the belief that once fertility impaired, one will always be fertility impaired. If an additional pregnancy is not immediately desired, contraception should be used.

The Estrogen Link:
Endometriosis, Fibroids,
and Cancer

Ann, 35, was an infertility patient with very obvious PCOS on physical examination, laboratory testing and ultrasound. After the third month of metformin therapy her cycles became regular, but exceedingly painful. In the past her periods had not hurt, but again, she only had two or three a year. Despite apparent ovulatory cycles she still failed to achieve a pregnancy. A laparoscopy showed severe endometriosis and very limited tubal function. She could have ovulated for the next twenty years and not established a pregnancy.

Jane was a 44-year-old woman who had had two pregnancies and normal deliveries despite cycles that were often 35 to 50 days apart. There wasn't any evidence of abnormal hair growth or skin problems. Her periods became increasing heavy and she thought it was probably the "change" starting. An ultrasound scan showed a softball-size fibroid tumor of the uterus. Although a hysterectomy was necessary, she now feels that a lead weight has been lifted from her pelvis and now is able to travel between rest areas without having to stop for relief.

Mary was 52 and had never been told that she had PCOS, but on review of past history, the diagnosis seemed obvious. She was initially seen for postmenopausal bleeding. An endometrial biopsy confirmed a low-grade cancer of the uterine lining. She is now five years past her surgery and for all practical purposes she is cured.

As my wife is fond of telling me, "Age does not come alone." Many of the disorders of the female reproductive system are estrogen dependent. Estrogen specifically causes the proliferation of cells that are sensitive to its action, that is those that have an estrogen receptor. While estrogen is a great hormone in some respects, it does have its dark side. While unique, each of the disorders included in this chapter has a common bond: abnormal cell growth that is influenced by hormones.

Patients commonly ask whether there is a relationship between endometriosis and PCOS. And of course, the greatest dread of most women is the "C" word—cancer. Since fibroids are tumors, it is common for women to wonder about their relationship to cancer as well. Please do not assume, though, that all cases of cancer are caused by hormonal problems or that endometriosis or fibroids even increase the risk of cancer. There may (or may not) be a link between endometriosis, fibroids, cancer, and PCOS. The exploration of these common problems and how they may be connected to PCOS is the subject of this chapter.

Setting the Stage

To prepare, let's challenge your thinking about the female menstrual cycle. You may think that having regular menstrual cycles is "normal." It is not. In fact, menstruation represents a system failure.

Because the underlying drive of the reproductive system is the preservation of the species, through much of human evolution a woman's reproductive life looked something like this: Intercourse probably started in the early to mid-teenage years, although regular ovulation might not have been established for several additional years. There could easily have been one or more intervening early miscarriages as cycles started to normalize. Soon after regular ovulation was established, a pregnancy followed. A pregnancy lasts 40 weeks from the last menstrual period and there is no evidence that this has changed during the course of human evolution. Until very recent history, by necessity, breastfeeding was essential and its failure was almost as serious as lack of ovulation. Breastfeeding usually continued for about one year. Prolactin, the pituitary hormone essential for milk production, prevents release of luteinizing hormone, therefore preventing ovulation. If the rigors of childbirth were survived, the pattern of pregnancy and breastfeeding usually produced about an eighteen-month interval between pregnancies. Some miscarriages occurred, but on average four to six children may have been born to a sexually active female and of that, half survived to adulthood. A female's life expectancy at that time was only twenty-five to thirty years. Truly, through much of human history before the twentieth century, the average woman spent much of her time barefoot and pregnant.

A lot has changed. By the last quarter of the twentieth century, life expectancy had increased by 2.5 times and it had become increasingly common to electively postpone childbearing into the twenties and possibly the thirties. "Today's woman" may have years of ovulation without an intervening pregnancy. In women with PCOS, there can be years of lack of ovulation. In either case, that's a lot of estrogen coursing through a woman's body unopposed by the pregnancy hormone progesterone!

UTERINE FIBROIDS

Fibroids are the most common tumors in the female reproductive system. They increase with age and as many as 50% of women at age 50 have one or more fibroids. They are the most common cause for hysterectomy. While fibroids are common in all races, studies have shown that they are more common in African-Americans.

What are fibroids?

Uterine fibroids, also called myomas or leiomyomas, are a benign tumor of the muscle of the uterus. Fibroids may range from the size of a pea to that of a basketball. They may be single or multiple.

Fibroids are usually described by the position they occupy in the uterus. Some fibroids may be connected to the uterus only by a thin stalk. These are called *pedunculated fibroids* and are the least symptomatic of all types of fibroids. If the fibroid is on the outside of the uterus, it is called *subserosal*. Subserosal fibroids usually cause fewer problems than those located deeper in the uterine wall, which are called *intramural*. The last type of fibroid, and perhaps the most significant for abnormal bleeding and fertility, are the *submucosal fibroids*. These fibroids lie just under the endometrium and have an "iceberg" effect—there is actually more there than is exposed at the surface. (See Figure 13-1).

What makes them form and grow?

A fibroid forms from a single muscle cell that begins to multiply. The exact stimulus that causes this growth, or the stimulus that limits fibroid growth, is not known. While the cells of the fibroid multiply and the fibroid grows, it is very different from a cancer in that the fibroid does not invade surrounding tissues; it just pushes on them. Luckily, fibroids are universally benign, although malignant transformation is not impossible.

It is clear that fibroids are under the control of estrogen and progesterone. After menopause, when the estrogen levels fall, fibroids decrease in size. During pregnancy, fibroids often increase in size. Some fibroids grow very quickly and undergo death (degeneration) of the middle portions, thus causing pain. Degeneration of fibroids is more common during pregnancy.

How do I know I have them?

Patients with fibroids most often are seen in their gynecologist's office with abnormal pain, abnormal uterine bleeding and enlargement of the uterus. Back pain, frequent urination, and alteration in bowel function are common symptoms. Often the fibroids are suspected by pelvic examination and can be readily confirmed by ultrasound scans. Sometimes they are discovered during an infertility evaluation.

Usually an ultrasound scan is all that is necessary to make the diagnosis. Most often fibroids have a characteristic finding by ultrasound of what is called the homogeneous echo of the "ball of muscle cells" surrounded by a capsule. While most fibroids have a uniform appearance, some older fibroids will have bright ultrasound shadows, suggesting calcification. This is a normal and benign finding. A problem looks similar to a fibroid on ultrasound is an *adenomyoma*, which is an area of endometriosis within the muscle of the uterus. If the fibroid is near the uterine lining (submucosal) it may be difficult to distinguish from an endometrial polyp, but is treated the same.

How big is big? When to remove?

"Big" is always a relative term colored by the degree of discomfort caused and fears of both the patient and physician. When it is agreed that a fibroid is large and it has become unmanageable in other ways, it's time for surgery. If pregnancy is not desired this may mean a hysterectomy. Most who have had hysterectomies because of fibroids are much improved. Bleeding is gone and other symptoms at least improved. The decision for hysterectomy is based on the size of the fibroid, how fast it is growing, the amount of problems it is causing and the desire for future pregnancy.

Unfortunately, there have been only a few studies that have specifically addressed the role of fibroids in fertility. Most believe that the fibroid must be above 3 cm in size to have a deleterious effect on fertility. Obviously, the position of the fibroid may be more important than its size. If it is found by evaluation using hysteroscopy, hysterosalpingography, or sono-hystersalpingography that the fibroid is not impinging on the uterine cavity, therapy may not be necessary. Large fibroids, however, can further enlarge and cause pain in early pregnancy, possibly altering the implantation site and causing early or obstructed labor. There is probably adequate justification for removing all fibroids greater than 6 cm regardless of their position.

How are fibroids removed?

Submucosal fibroids are usually removed by hysteroscopy. Intramural and subserosal fibroids are removed by a procedure called myomectomy, which can be performed either through an abdominal incision (laparotomy) or by "band aid surgery" (laparoscopy). Some surgeons believe that any fibroid which is sufficiently easy to remove at laparoscopy may be insignificant in its capacity to affect fertility. Certainly, the laparoscopic procedure has a much shorter recovery time, but the decision for laparoscopic removal should be carefully considered. There are recent studies advocating a destruction of the fibroid by an electric current without actually removing the fibroid. This procedure is questionable when a pregnancy is desired. It is not known whether this technique will abnormally weaken the wall of the uterus.

Once the fibroid is removed, the surrounding muscle is usually closed with sutures. Inside the body, the area where the fibroid has been removed forms a scar. This scar may not expand as well as the muscle during pregnancy and can result in a uterine rupture. Every patient who has had a fibroid removed should also be informed as to whether cesarean section should be performed to deliver subsequently conceived babies. Certainly, the obstetrician should be made aware of a previous myomectomy.

Are there therapies other than surgery?

Since fibroids are under the control of ovarian hormones, agents that suppress ovarian functions such as the GnRH analogs will also cause suppression of fibroids. Unfortunately, even though the suppression may reduce the fibroid size by 50%, the fibroid will quickly return when the suppressive therapy has been stopped. Sometimes pretreatment with GnRH analogs will control bleeding and will allow surgery to be carried out with less blood loss and in some cases this will allow an easier procedure. Pretreatment with GnRH analogs is especially important with hysteroscopic removal of larger fibroids. Unfortunately, suppressive therapy that lessens bleeding also increases scarring around the fibroid, thus making the removal more difficult. The effect of oral contraceptives and progestins such as Provera™ on fibroid growth is unclear. Overall, it is believed that women who use birth control pills have a lower incidence of fibroid changes. The horizon may include pirenidone, an anit-fibrotic agent and/or tibolone, a unique anti-estrogen.

A procedure for treating fibroids that is gaining acceptance is uterine artery embolism. In this procedure, under X-ray guidance the main blood supply to the fibroid is disrupted, causing it to shrink. It is unclear whether this technique can be safely used for those desiring a future pregnancy. It may weaken the uterine wall, or more importantly, it may alter the necessary blood supply to the uterus that is needed for normal placental function. At the same time this procedure avoids a surgical scar in the uterus, and thus lessens the chance of uterine rupture.

Are fibroids more common in women with PCOS?

Partially because PCOS is under-diagnosed and partially because fibroids are so common the answer to this question is unknown. There is no doubt that fibroids are related to estrogen. It is probable that fibroid development is affected first by inherited tendency, then by hormones. Whether estrogen unopposed by progesterone, as seen with anovulation and prolonged cycles of those with PCOS, is more likely to cause a fibroid to form and grow is unknown. Some with PCOS are relatively hypoestrogenic. Are low levels of estrogen protective? This is also unknown.

What about polyps?

Polyps are small, universally benign growths that may be found attached to the surface of the uterine or cervical lining. They seldom cause pain but are frequently associated with abnormal bleeding. Endometrial polyps can sometimes be seen by ultrasound and often by a sonoHSG, but the definitive test is by hysteroscopy. Polyps are easily removed. Cervical polyps are often removed in an office procedure. (See Figure 13-1). Polyps of less than 1 cm are not thought to interfere with pregnancy.

Figure 13-1 Uterine Pathology

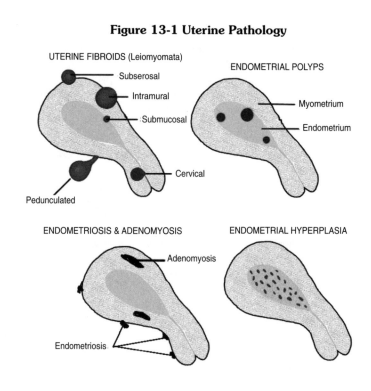

UTERINE FIBROIDS (Leiomyomata)

Subserosal

Intramural

Submucosal

Pedunculated

Cervical

ENDOMETRIAL POLYPS

Myometrium

Endometrium

ENDOMETRIOSIS & ADENOMYOSIS

Adenomyosis

Endometriosis

ENDOMETRIAL HYPERPLASIA

ENDOMETRIOSIS

Whether or not an association exists between PCOS and endometriosis, sufferers of each share a common bond. Both problems are chronic; both alter lifestyle; both lack a known cause or cure; and both are subject to delay in diagnosis.

What is endometriosis?

The endometrium is the inner lining of the uterus that is shed each month at menstruation. When the cells that have the same appearance under the microscope as the endometrium are found outside the uterus, the condition is known as endometriosis. Just as endometrium is under hormonal control, so is endometriosis. It progresses through the typical cycle changes of the endometrium under the influence of estrogen and progesterone.

How common is endometriosis?

It is difficult to know the true incidence of endometriosis in the general population. It is commonly stated that approximately 30% of infertile women will have endometriosis to some degree. In the general population, estimates of 5-10% have been reported. The statistical co-incidence with PCOS is unknown.

What causes endometriosis?

There have been over 5,000 scientific publications about endometriosis, yet the disease remains poorly explained. There seem to be numerous factors that collectively alter an individual's predisposition to develop endometriosis. While endometriosis is not directly inherited, it is more common in some families. A specific endocrine, immunologic or even lifestyle may be a predisposition to endometriosis.

There are two well-entrenched theories about how an individual develops endometriosis. The first and longest standing theory is that of retrograde menstruation. According to this theory, endometriosis comes as a result of a back flow of blood from the uterus through the tubes and out into the pelvis. The problem with this theory is that most, if not all, women have some degree of menstrual fluid back flow. Maybe it's an issue of quantity, but then maybe there is an additional factor.

A second theory of origin of endometriosis is that the cells lining the pelvis and ovaries are transformed into endometrial cells by some internal or external stimulus. Perhaps blood and all the growth factors it contains are good candidates for being this stimulus. This makes good theoretical sense. The lining of the pelvic cavity, including the surface of the ovary, has the same embryologic origin as the endometrium. Whether by genetic predisposition, alteration of immunology, stimulation by hormones, or chronic irritation from menstrual reflux, the peritoneal cells are transformed into endometrium.

These theories are not mutually exclusive and it is quite possible that they act in concert in the development of endometriosis. An experiment supporting this combination of two theories has been carried out in nature in women with a congenital anomaly that naturally blocks the normal blood flow through the cervix at menstruation. Endometriosis is a very common finding in these individuals. Several studies have linked the diameter of the cervix with the propensity to develop endometriosis. The tighter cervix, the smaller the cervical diameter, the greater the chance of menstrual back flow and the development of endometriosis. It is possible that endometriosis is slightly more common in individuals with a retroverted or tipped uterus.

The most common sites of endometriosis formation are the areas that are most easily bathed in menstrual blood. These common sites include the ovaries, with their close approximation to the tube in order for egg pick up at ovulation. Other sites are the uterine sacral ligaments that stretch from the cervix to the sacrum in shelf-like folds of peritoneum. These are very common sites of menstrual fluid accumulation. Adjacent to the uterine sacral ligaments are a rich supply of nerves supplying the cervix and uterus. Endometriotic implants along these ligaments are commonly associated with painful intercourse and dyspareunia. Occasionally, nodules can be felt by pelvic examination, or in severe cases, the uterus may be felt to be fixed and not movable. The third most common site is along the anterior folds of peritoneum above the bladder. Endometriosis along the surface of the intestine is relatively common and can explain the high association with altered bowel function. Endometriosis of the appendix sometimes occurs.

Who gets endometriosis?

In the past, endometriosis was thought to be most commonly seen in the thin, "type A," professional woman who had regular menses and postponed childbearing. This is obviously not the case, and we now recognize that endometriosis transcends all ages and races. While less common, severe endometriosis is occasionally found in teenagers. Even in this young group, pain should not be dismissed or attributed to "just a normal part of growing up." Additionally, just because a diagnosis of anovulation and PCOS has been made in an infertility diagnosis, it doesn't mean that there cannot also be endometriosis. There should especially be concern about the possibility of co-existence of endometriosis in PCOS patients when it seems that ovulation induction therapy is working but a pregnancy is still not forthcoming.

The chance of endometriosis increases as the number of these factors increases. The two central risk factors for endometriosis include pain and infertility.

> **Risk Factors
> for Endometriosis**
>
> • Short time between periods (less than 26 days)
> • Long periods (over 5 days)
> • Heavy bleeding
> • Congenital uterine abnormalities
> • Cervical stenosis
> • Postponed childbearing
> • Lack of oral contraceptives
> • Infertility
> • Pain
> • PCOS

Can endometriosis be inherited?

Endometriosis is not inherited as such, but it is more common in some families. It is best to consider that the *propensity* for endometriosis is inherited rather than that the disease itself is inherited. The development of endometriosis can be related to certain modifiers, such as the tendency not to ovulate, to have heavier periods, to have the uterus tilted such that back-flow of blood is more likely or an immunologic incompetence, each of which itself may be inherited. Clearly, however, inheritance of endometriosis is not direct and predictable. One family member who decides to postpone childbearing may develop endometriosis, while a second with the same genetic tendencies and two children may remain endometriosis-free.

Does PCOS increase or decrease the chance of endometriosis?

Since endometriosis has been reported in about 30% of infertile women and since PCOS is a leading cause of female infertility, it would seem statistically likely that many women would have both PCOS and endometriosis. Many women have endometriosis and not PCOS, and a fair number of women with PCOS do not have endometriosis. When two disorders are this common, it is difficult to determine a clear and convincing association. Both of these disorders appear to have a genetic predisposition and both are interrelated with the body's hormonal environment. In my experience some of the worst cases of endometriosis have been in PCOS patients.　　　　　　　Estrogen

251

Classically, endometriosis was thought to occur in women with regular menstrual function. Regular menses will certainly subject the body to the constant waxing and waning of hormones and subject the pelvic organs to the periodic back flow of blood in the pelvic cavity. Heavy frequent periods clearly place one at risk of endometriosis, and considering the above theories about how endometriosis forms, it is easy to see why. But what if periods are lighter and less frequent? Does this reduce the risk of endometriosis?

Endometriosis is estrogen dependent. Endometriosis can be thought of as a fire. The fuel for the fire is estrogen. When there is estrogen unopposed by progesterone, the endometrium, whether in the lining of the uterus or in small implants scattered throughout the pelvis, is in a constant state of proliferation. It would seem logical that endometriosis would be more common in women with PCOS, but this will have to wait until both the diagnosis of endometriosis and PCOS is more uniformly made and reported.

In the final analysis, it is still unclear why all women who menstruate do not have endometriosis and all women with PCOS do not have uterine hyperplasia. There must still be an overriding issue of sensitivity.

Pelvic PAIN!?

Abnormal pain associated with menstruation or ovulation is endometriosis until proven otherwise. The triad of painful menstruation (*dysmenorrhea*), painful intercourse (*dyspareunia*), and painful bowel movements (*dyskezia*) are the most common reported pain abnormalities. Often, patients have been misdiagnosed with irritable bowel syndrome when diarrhea and constipation, along with intestinal pain, are related to menses. Certainly if there is a bleeding sore on the rectum, the bowel would be irritable. During intercourse, the upper portion of the vagina is adjacent to the most likely areas of endometrial involvement. The relationship between PCOS and other bowel disturbances such as Crohn's disease and ulcerative colitis have not been reported. These diseases would seem to have a hormonal relationship in that they can be made better and worse by pregnancy.

Pelvic pain is much more likely in the times of marked hormonal change, such as ovulation and menstruation. Individuals with endometriosis are known to produce much more prostaglandin and that is clearly related to the amount of pain. Anti-inflammatory agents such as ibuprofen, naprosyn, and aspirin are effective in relief of menstrual pain in some individuals.

How is endometriosis diagnosed?

While ultrasound scan cannot detect the scarring or implants of endometriosis, it may yield a high suspicion for the disease by highlighting the characteristic cystic changes of the ovary. Endometriosis, which is a surface lesion, incorporates into the ovary and eventually forms a walled-off cyst, an *endometrioma*. It is possible that endometriomas are more likely to form from a raw area of the ovary at the time of ovulation and the formation of the corpus luteum. An endometrioma is a particularly ominous finding that will almost always indicate some degree of ovarian compromise. It is often called a *choco-late cyst* because of the enclosed endometrial fluid, which is a combination of old blood and endometriotic tissue, and has the consistency of chocolate syrup.

While history and pelvic exam may suspect the diagnosis of endometriosis, direct viewing at surgery can only make the definitive diagnosis.

What are the types of treatment available?

Endometriosis can be thought of as having two different components. There is an active component that represents the cyclic changes seen with waxing and waning of the endometrium. This form may be amenable to either medical or surgical therapy. The second portion of endometriosis, a fixed variety, is represented by the residual scarring from the endometriosis and is only corrected by surgery.

Surgery

Since endometriosis is a surgical diagnosis, and surgery is invasive and thus always carries an inherent risk, virtually all physicians recommend that endometriosis be treated at the time it is found rather than be treated in a second, subsequent operation. Endometriosis has been classified due to the findings at surgery as either minimal (stage 1), mild (stage 2), moderate (stage 3), or severe (stage 4). There is little correlation between the stage of endometriosis and the amount of pain. However, the more severe the endometriosis, the more likely it is that the patient will be infertile. Minimal and mild endometriosis is associated with infertility, but it is unclear if the early stages "cause endometriosis."

Endometriosis may have a variety of presentations at surgery. They correspond to the progression of the disease from inflammation of the peritoneum to dense scarring as the lesion heals. Endometriosis may be seen as clear blobs or reddened blister-like lesions with abnormalities of the associated small blood vessels. In the past, many lesions thought to be the earlier stages of endometriosis were overlooked. The typical lesion of endometriosis has been described as a "powder burn" lesion connoting that there has been bleeding at the site of the endometriosis and deposition of black pigment as the area of bleeding heals.

The small areas of endometriosis can be compared to a small open sore that is constantly being irritated. There is associated inflammation and finally a slow healing process by scar formation. The end results of endometriosis are dense whitened areas of scarring and adhesions (abnormal attachments). Sometimes, adhesions produce no symptoms while in other cases there can be severe pain. Adhesions can limit the mobility of the pelvic organs and cause infertility.

Surgical techniques fall into two categories—excision and destruction. Many experts believe that an excision is preferable, but this may be more difficult around the vital organs and large areas of dissection may increase the amount of post surgical adhesion formation. Certainly, all areas of endometrio-

sis should be treated and this may involve surgery around vital structures such
as the ureters, bladder, major blood vessels, and intestines. A variety of techniques including a laser, electro-cautery, and a new device called a harmonic scalpel, which uses ultrasound waves to destroy tissue, may be used. The latter differs slightly in its method, but none have been shown to be more superior to the others. Treatment probably relies on the skill of the surgeon rather than the equipment.

Medical therapy

There are a variety of medical treatments for endometriosis. Two gold standard treatments are Danazol (Danocrine™) and GnRH analogs. Danazol is an androgen-like drug shown to suppress ovulation and cause the regression of endometriosis. Its side effects include weight gain in virtually all users. Occasional side effects of the androgen include acne, abnormal hair growth, and mood changes. Danazol should not be used in PCOS patients (who are already hyperandrogenic) for the above obvious reasons.

The primary therapy for endometriosis is the gonadotropin releasing hormone (GnRH) analogs that shut down the stimulation of the ovary and in doing so, create a reversible menopause. The side effects of the GnRH analogs relate to induction of a menopausal state with vasomotor instability, vaginal dryness, insomnia, and bone loss. GnRH analogs may potentially improve PCOS and is probably the treatment of choice. (See Chapter 16). Usually the GnRH analogs are limited to a six-month treatment. In an attempt to reduce side effects and to prolong therapy, "add back" regimens involving giving low doses of hormonal replacement in addition to the GnRH analogs are used. It is unsure how long this therapy could be maintained, but it should have a positive effect on PCOS and has been recommended but is expensive therapy.

Other medical therapies include continuous use of oral contraceptives. Using the pill in the usual cyclic fashion with "dummy" pills and regular withdrawal bleeding may retard the development of endometriosis, but it is often not sufficient to treat the disease. Progestins such as Depo-Provera™ have also been used, but the effectiveness is less reliable. Unfortunately, all medical therapy is probably temporary, and endometriosis may continue to progress.

Can endometriosis be cured?

There is no cure for endometriosis. The objectives remain to move from infertility to a successful pregnancy and from intolerable pain to tolerable discomfort.

CANCER AND PCOS

What is cancer?

Cancer results when cells escape their normal mechanisms that control growth and replication. When these escaped cells start to invade surrounding tissues they are called *malignant*.

What causes cancer?

There's the hang up. It is probably no one single event that causes cancer, although as with PCOS research, scientists are still looking for the first defect from which all others arise. It is most widely believed that cancer involves a slow process of change. The process probably begins with a specific genetic predisposition. That does not mean that a specific cancer runs in families, although some do. The predisposition may alter the response to the environment. Cervical cancer is a cancer for which there seems to be no inherited basis. Ovarian and breast cancers seem to have a genetic basis in about 10% of cases. There then seems to be a long-term chronic promoter. For lung cancer the promoter may be smoking, for uterine cancer that promoter may be estrogen. The reason that a cell is induced to become cancerous is still a much-sought secret.

How are cancers described?

In many cases cancer is thought to march through specific stages. This may start with *hyperplasia*, a simple overgrowth of cells. If left untreated, hyperplasia may progress to a very localized cancer, *carcinoma in situ*, followed by local invasion and then distant *metastasis*. How far a cancer has spread is referred to as its stage, with stage 1 representing minimal invasion to stage 4 when there is involvement of distant organs. Cancers that tend to remain very similar to the cell they arise from are called "well differentiated," and those that have lost their identity are called "poorly differentiated." The greater the stage and the less differentiation, the poorer the prognosis is thought to be. Each type of cancer behaves somewhat differently, and perhaps each cancer in each individual behaves differently.

Why are some types of cancer more common?

Some cancers are more common because of the extent of the offending agent. For example, skin cancer is directly related to the number of hours under the sun. Many cancers arise from the surface of an organ. Since this is both the protective shield and the area that is most subject to wear and tear of life, it is logical that this would be the area first to be affected. In both males and females, some of most serious cancers arise from glandular cells. These cells are constantly active. Under the best of circumstances they take a lot of abuse. A large part of this abuse in the reproductive cancers (uterine, ovarian, and breast in the female and prostate in the male) comes from hormonal bombardment.

Does PCOS cause uterine or endometrial cancer?

YES. Under the influence of estrogen, the cells of the uterine lining multiply (proliferate). If this proliferation is left unopposed by progesterone, periodic loss of endometrium at menstruation is prevented and a build-up of the endometrium occurs. The earliest signs of abnormal endometrial development may be erratic and heavy bleeding. Left unchecked, this may result in an overgrowth of the endometrium called hyperplasia. While certainly not cancer, hyperplasia is moving in that direction and certainly should be considered a warning sign.

The Centers for Disease Control in their Cancer and Steroid Hormone study reported that women who specifically reported a history of PCOS had a five-fold increase in endometrial cancer. The good news is that the literature regarding endometrial cancer in those with PCOS has a very favorable diagnosis. The cure rate is very high.

The association is so strong that most would conclude that PCOS does cause endometrial cancer.

Risks factors for endometrial cancer:
- Post-menopausal
- Obesity
- Nulliparity (having had no children)
- Lack of oral contraceptive use
- Family history

This constellation of predictors sounds like we are describing PCOS, doesn't it?

So where does the estrogen come from?

The primary estrogen of the reproductive age woman is estradiol. Most estradiol is formed from the developing preovulatory follicle. A second estrogen, estrone, while weaker than estradiol, is more widespread. Estrogen can be produced in a number of so-called peripheral tissues including the liver, fat and muscle. Fat cells have the capacity to convert precursor hormones in the blood to estrogens. Estrone is also the most abundant estrogen after menopause. Because estrone is a weaker estrogen it acts as an anti-estrogen and blocks the full action of estradiol. These estrogens may further inhibit ovulation or may act on the uterus directly to promote hyperplasia.

How is the uterus evaluated for hyperplasia or cancer?

The time-honored way to make the diagnosis of hyperplasia is an endometrial biopsy. Ultrasound can be very helpful, but is less sensitive after age 40. In some cases of uncontrolled bleeding, a dilation and curettage (D&C) may be needed both for diagnostic as well as therapeutic reasons. Hysteroscopy can also be used to aid in maximum evaluation of the uterine lining. Most often in the premenopausal patient, ultrasound is all that is needed for the evaluation of the uterus and abnormal bleeding. The first treatment strategy in premenopausal women is to treat medically with progestins to mature the endometrium and cause a more complete sloughing. Many cases of hyperplasia can be treated with progestins alone.

So what's the good news about endometrial cancer?

If you have to have a cancer, this is one of the least bad. Almost all endometrial cancers are found early in their development because of their association with abnormal vaginal bleeding. Any unexplained bleeding after menopause should be considered an early warning sign. Since this cancer is found early in most cases, the cancer is potentially totally curable by hysterectomy. Numerous studies about PCOS and endometrial cancer seem to concur that the prognosis is quite favorable.

Uterine cancer before age 35 is exceedingly rare. Several reports have stated that most, if not all, cases of endometrial cancer involve women with PCOS.

What about ovarian cancer?

Is ovarian cancer increased in PCOS? Maybe, maybe not. Certainly the risk factors for ovarian cancer are the same as those listed above for uterine cancer, but the relationship is not nearly so obvious. A big problem in answering this question has been the under-recognition of PCOS and the complexity of its association with obesity, fertility and altered hormonal environment. Perhaps one of the only studies to date, by Schildkraut and others, suggests a modest increased risk, while pointing out at the same time the problems of the complexities of PCOS and the small number of PCOS patients included in this study. It is possible that the ovarian cancer risks in obese PCOS patients may be different from those in thin patients. Those with insulin resistance may be completely different from others with PCOS. The jury remains out on the question of relationship here.

Is there a cause of ovarian cancer?

A decrease in the incidence of ovarian cancer is seen in women who: 1) have been pregnant, 2) have used oral contraception 3) have an early menopause. Ovarian cancer rates go down with an increased number of childbirths and the years of oral contraceptive pill use. Later age at first childbirth may also be protective. The role of incomplete pregnancy and cancer risk is unsettled. Each of these groups has had a protective time off from ovulation. The theory of "incessant ovulation" has been proposed to emphasize the monthly distortion of the ovarian surface. Equally likely is the avoidance of the high levels of estradiol that are seen in the preovulatory period. A possible connection has been the release of relatively large amounts of follicular fluid over the surface and into the pelvis. This fluid might contain growth-promoting factors that could influence later development of cancer. It seems that if the ovulations predicted the risk of cancer, then an early puberty and late menopause would place an individual at increased risk. This seems to be only a weak predictor when all studies are examined together.

Among my colleagues who study ovarian cancer, there is not universal agreement that estrogen is the major offender. It has been hypothesized that androgens or even progesterone may also be involved. This could be bad news for PCOS sufferers, or on the other hand, elevated androgens may prevent normal follicle development and ovulation, reducing the risk of ovarian cancer. A study by Helzlsouer in 1995 reported that ovarian cancer was increased in those with low gonadotropin levels, but high androgen levels. This characterizes the insulin resistant patient and is an area that needs additional investigation.

A different theory is that since ovarian cancer is most commonly seen after age 60, it is the high levels of gonadotropins appearing with menopause that induces the cancerous changes of the ovarian surface. This theory would seem to implicate PCOS as an increased risk due to the associated chronic levels of gonadotropin.

Other theories include exposure to environmental carcinogens or a back-flow of contaminants through the tubes much like the theory of endometriosis. A theory has been advanced (but with little support) that pregnancy has a tumor-clearing effect based on the immunologic alterations in pregnancy. To date, no theory has received confirmation of universal support. There may be multiple paths that lead toward ovarian cancer and equally as many that lead away. Which path the PCOS patient is treading is not yet clear.

Do fertility drugs cause ovarian cancer?

Let's start with a couple of truths. First, individuals who are infertile use fertility drugs, and second, individuals who are infertile have an increased risk of ovarian cancer. It is a classic illogical conclusion then that infertility drugs cause ovarian cancer. It is the individual to whom the drugs are given, rather than the fertility drugs themselves, that creates the risk. The risk of cancer seems highest in those who do not ovulate or have unexplained infertility, whether fertility drugs have been used or not.

If we accept the incessant ovulation theory (all that estrogen running unopposed through the body) and extend it to the multiple ovulations caused by fertility drugs, as is the source of the increased risk of ovarian cancer, then there is a problem. Over the reproductive life span of the regularly ovulatory woman, there are 200 to 400 ovulations. It would seem that even with the most aggressive stimulation, there would be only a modest increase in the total number of lifetime ovulations. The total may not even approach the usual quota, if it is considered that ovulation is not regularly occurring in women who have PCOS.

Unfortunately, one well placed sensationalistic story on a night time news magazine linking fertility drugs with ovarian cancer can do more harm than all the scientific proof can undo. Clearly some women who develop ovarian cancer will have used fertility drugs (remember, one of six couples is infertile). When a cancer develops forty years later, that news story and those three cycles of clomiphene use will undoubtedly be remembered. We always look for a reason. There will be the thought "if only..." and the blame placed on the clomiphene, the doctor, and the patient rather than on the real culprit, chance.

There have been two well-publicized studies on ovarian cancer and fertility drugs. One involved the relationship of ovarian cancer and clomiphene. In this study, results show that there needed to have been twelve cycles of clomiphene use before a significant risk for cancer was reached. This is twice the recommended length of therapy and also signifies a relatively seri-ous problem with ovarian function. Chemically, clomiphene is very similar to tamoxifen, which is used in the treatment of breast cancer and its capacity to induce cancerous change is low. Ovulation is often single and the hormonal changes are often not far exceeding those of a normal cycle. It just doesn't seem to add up.

The second and even more often quoted study by Whittemore and her colleagues surveyed and compared twelve U.S. studies (a study on studies) about the use of fertility drugs after a diagnosis o.f cancer. This relied on par-ticipant recall and the drug could have been anything from a shot of proges-terone to multiple cycles of gonadotropin injections. It was reported that a rel-ative risk of cancer in infertile users of fertility drugs was 2.8 times that of fer-tile patients. The risk of cancer markedly increased in infertile patients who stayed infertile while pregnancy seemed to remove the risk, but the significance of this finding was removed when patients had never been pregnant. The study has been criticized on a number of grounds and has not been substantiated in other trials before or since. It could be concluded that if an individual is infer-tile, then fertility promoting therapy *should* be used to establish a pregnancy for its protective effects.

Reproductive endocrinologists and the American Society for Reproductive Medicine as a group believe that fertility drugs *do not* cause cancer. Future studies may prove us wrong. The value of this controversy is that it has made the scientific and clinical community ever vigilant about this issue. It may be reasonable for PCOS patients to use oral contraceptives, which are known to lower risk of ovarian malignancy, when not pursuing fertility therapy.

What makes ovarian cancer so scary?

Ovarian cancer is the sixth most common cancer in females and is a leading cause of death from gynecological cancer in the U.S. At birth a woman will have about a 1 in 70 chance of developing ovarian cancer during her life-time. Most ovarian cancer occurs in the postmenopausal years, but there are exceptions. It is very rare that we unexpectedly find an ovarian cancer during an infertility investigation or at a routine laparoscopy. Luckily, the incidence of ovarian cancer is not rising, but it is too bad that it is not falling either. A major problem comes from the usually silent progression and its discovery at late stages. The symptoms of ovarian cancer include abdominal fullness, alteration in bowel function, and fatigue, but all are very vague. Many women have vis-ited multiple physicians before a diagnosis is suspected. The diagnosis is usu-ally easily made by ultrasound scan and this is a simple and important tool that can usually be used to exclude the diagnosis.

Are there screening tests for ovarian cancer?

A good screening test should be sensitive enough not to miss the dis-eases in question (low numbers of false negatives) and specific enough to iden-tify only the disease (low number of false positives). For the test to be widely used, it also must be relatively easy and inexpensive. No such test for ovarian cancer yet devised meets all of these criteria. Ultrasound is easy and may be used as a screening tool, but its endorsement is lacking for widespread use as a screening test only. The CA125 blood test has been used to follow response of ovarian cancer to therapy and some have suggested that it be used for screening, but this has not been approved for general use. CA125 may be falsely elevated with gall bladder disease, endometriosis, benign/malignant breast disease and other conditions of chronic abdominal or pelvic inflammation.

The vast majority of ovarian cancer is sporadic, but from 5-10% of breast and ovarian cancers can be attributed to an inherited mutation in the BRCA1 tumor suppressor gene. Women who inherit a BRCA1 mutated gene have a greater than 80% lifetime risk of breast cancer and a 45% chance of ovarian cancer by age 70. About 1/800 women carry this gene and DNA testing has been recommended only for women judged to be at high risk.

Is the risk of breast cancer increased in PCOS patients?

The breast is dependent on hormone stimulation for its development and function; as such, it becomes an integral part of the reproductive system. Although breast cancer is a relatively common malignancy and this is a question for which we should know the answer, no clear decision has been reached about its association with PCOS. A small number of studies suggest either an increased or decreased risk. Genetics and family history are clearly important. Routine mammography and self-examination are essential. For now we need to assume that the risk for breast cancer is increased for women with PCOS.

Does It Ever End?
Menopause—Before
and Beyond

"I'm 55 and have recently been reading and hearing about PCOS. I'm sure that I have (had) it. The diagnosis of PCOS was never made, but I had all the symptoms and still have some. I was pregnant once, but miscarried. I had a hysterectomy in my early forties, because of heavy bleeding. There is a scattered history of heart disease and diabetes in my family. I'm in reasonably good health, but I'm worried."

You are not alone!

Female life expectancy first exceeded age 50 around the 1900s. Currently, life expectancy for women exceeds eighty years. This means a third of a woman's life will be lived after menopause. The over-50 group is a rapidly expanding segment of our society with 35 million postmenopausal women in the United Sates today. After 2000, the only age group likely to have significant growth is the one consisting of adults over age 55. This increase is partly due to more people and a surge from the baby boomers; however, the greatest source is the reduction of the causes of early death.

Is menopause a more troubled time than are other life passages? I don't know. It would be easy to offend someone no matter what my stance on such a question. It's too euphemistic to equate menopause with a "new dawn," "new freedom," or a "lift of the curse," as some have proposed. The fact is that there is no stage in life that is completely easy, so it is probably unreasonable to expect that menopause will be any different. There may be a number of trade-offs to be made during menopause, but there is also the capacity for great accomplishment and happiness. Certainly at age 50 you should be getting a reasonable idea of who you are. Still, health issues are becoming even more at the front of our thoughts as we become increasingly aware of our lack of immortality. Physicians are trained to evaluate pathology. We are much more interested in the exclusion of disease than evaluation of health. In menopause we must serve a dual role of diagnostician of diseases and counselor of health.

The reality is that we know shamefully little about how women age. It should be of no surprise that we know almost nothing about how those with PCOS compare to women without PCOS. With more research, there may be some surprises. Women with PCOS might fare quite well in comparison. On the horizon is the Women's Health Initiative, a multi-center study conducted by the NIH of the postmenopause in the general population. The SWAN study, another multi-center NIH funded project, is compiling information on the perimenopausal woman. Although these studies do not have a mechanism to address PCOS specifically, they are forward looking and will be an advance as to how medical risks materialize.

At least we can hope.

Hey, maybe it's your turn!

Menopause happens to all women. The woman with PCOS may be better adapted to handle this change. At least let's try this concept on to see if it fits. We'll start with body image. Women with PCOS have been facing an altered body image and working on self-esteem since puberty. For those women who have not dealt with PCOS and whose esteem has been vested in their appearance, coping with that first wrinkle, gray hair, or an extra ten pounds may be difficult. These women may be equally disturbed by the development of erratic bleeding, and alternating heavy and light periods, which have been a way of life for many with PCOS.

There have been only a handful of studies on the long-term evaluation of PCOS and disease risks. Most of these studies have used only women who have had ovarian wedge resections. These long-term studies suggest that while there is an increased risk of cardiovascular diseases among women with PCOS, the actual incidence is less than expected. Osteoporosis is a leading cause of death and disability in postmenopausal women. With PCOS there is a significant reduction in its risk.

While there should be a push for more long-term studies of PCOS, and we should continue to make the case by expounding on the potential risks, there may possibly be a little glimmer that the risks might be over-stated. We will have to wait and see. For now, we must extrapolate from general studies on menopause and mold them around what makes PCOS different.

How is menopause defined?

Menopause is defined as the last menstrual bleeding. It is a diagnosis that cannot be made until after a year of no bleeding. Like the menarche, or first period, menopause is a point in time and while an important marker, it is not nearly so important as the surrounding events. Previously, the years around menopause were called the *climacteric,* but this term seems to have been largely discarded for a more properly descriptive term, the *perimenopause.* The perimenopause, with variable menopausal symptoms, precedes the menopause by four to five years, and a loss of fertility precedes menopause by as much as ten years. The average age of menopause is 50 to 52, and there is little evidence that the age of menopause has changed over the last 2000 years.

What causes menopause?

The mechanism of menopause is much easier to explain than that of puberty. Females are born with all of the eggs/follicles they will ever have. Each month a few are lost until at menopause when a critical level of follicles is reached and ovulation and normal menstrual function cannot be supported. Menopause is simply an exhaustion of the egg/follicle store of the ovary. This does not mean that the ovary is completely devoid of eggs, but there are just too few. As the follicle number diminishes, so does the capacity of the ovary to produce estrogen. When the estrogen secretion is erratic, periods are erratic. At menopause the estrogen production of the ovary is insufficient to stimulate the development of the uterine lining and so, bleeding stops.

Are there factors that hasten or delay menopause?

There seems to be little correlation between the onset of menses (menarche) and menopause. Women who smoke experience menopause an average of one and a half years earlier than non-smokers. Very early menopause and premature ovarian failure (menopause before age 40) tend to run in some families. On a larger scale, there tends not to be a consistent relationship in the time of menopause between mothers and daughters, but this is subject to considerable variation from other life events, such as ovarian surgery. Menopause may occur sooner after hysterectomy or the removal of one ovary. Any factor that might destroy a part of the follicle pool, such as endometriosis, severe infection, or ovarian surgery, could hasten menopause. There is a small amount of evidence that long-term use of oral contraceptives (OC) may have a minimal protective effect on ovarian egg stores and perhaps slightly extend reproductive life. This effect could be from the reduction in reproductive system problems with OC use. There is no information as to whether women with PCOS go through menopause earlier or later than others.

What hormonal changes occur with aging?

Generally, there is a decrease in all steroid hormones with aging; adrenal and ovarian, estrogen and androgen. Of course, the big one is estrogen. Most of the principle estrogen, estradiol, produced from puberty to menopause, is from developing follicles and principally the preovulatory follicle. Until ovulation ceases, the mid-cycle estrogen may change very little. However, during the time around menses there are fewer and fewer developing follicles, hence less estrogen. This is the cause of the increase in hot flushes and other signs of hypoestrogenism experienced at that time.

As the follicle store nears depletion (menopause) androgen production does not increase, but because estrogen is lower, the relative concentration of androgen to estrogen rises. This may be the cause of the slight increase in hair growth reported by some (both women with and without PCOS) during perimenopause.

The ovaries produce only small amounts of estrogen after menopause, but the androgen production, which is also relatively small, persists much longer. Much of the estrogen in women who do not ovulate is generated from the conversion of androgens to estrogen by fat, the so-called *peripheral conversion*. Most of this estrogen is not estradiol, but a weaker estrogen called estrone. Peripheral conversion is why overweight women have higher estrogen levels than their thinner counterparts. While this may increase some risks, such as endometrial hyperplasia, other risks are decreased, such as osteoporosis and possibly cardiovascular disease. It stands to reason that PCOS may make the menopausal transition easier.

With aging, there is a slow constant decline in DHEAS, the principle androgen of the adrenal gland. If one listens to the glowing testimonial from "health food" suppliers, every one should take DHEAS to live longer and better. It stands to reason that if with PCOS the levels are higher to start with, then the decline may be slower or take longer. You already have too much of what they are trying to give others some of. Of course this is purely conjecture but why not put a positive spin on it? Once again, studies are sorely lacking.

Are there tests to determine if menopause is nearing?

There are several markers for evaluation of the aging ovary. Medium size growing ovarian follicles produce relatively large amounts of a substance called *inhibin*. As the follicle develops, inhibin is produced as a signal to the brain and pituitary gland to decrease or "inhibit" follicle stimulating hormone (FSH) production. As the follicle store is depleted, inhibin levels fall and FSH rises in an attempt to compensate. The hormonal network does everything possible to maintain normal estrogen production and follicle development.

Cycle day 3 FSH and estradiol levels are usually used when there is a question of fertility reserve. A level over 10mIU/ml suggests that there may be a reduction in follicle store, enough to threaten fertility. If FSH levels on day 3 are above 20 mIU/ml, the use of fertility drugs is associated with very poor response. Levels of FSH can vary from cycle to cycle, and although we usually use the highest levels of FSH as a marker for fertility, individuals with very elevated levels of FSH occasionally and spontaneously establish a normal pregnancy.

A random FSH over 40 mIU/ml is suggestive of menopause. Some have advocated measurements of inhibin levels, but both really show the same thing. Often there is no need to measure estrogen levels, or for that matter even FSH levels, because the symptoms and age speak for themselves. FSH levels are of no value in monitoring hormone replacement.

Does PCOS exist after menopause?

This is probably the most asked question by women over age 40 with PCOS and one that becomes almost philosophical in its answer. In many ways it is similar to the question, "Does removal of the ovaries cure PCOS?" The answer to which is, "No!"

women now have a diagnosis for a variety of medical and physical problems
that had been previously unexplained and had plagued their lives. Sometimes
the diagnosis emerges during their daughter's infertility evaluation. Although
there had been the classic signs of irregular periods, obesity, and abnormal hair
growth present forever, little attention was given to the symptoms by health
professionals and the diagnosis just wasn't made. Now these women learn they
are insulin resistant and have abnormal blood lipid levels. Certainly, infertility
and regular menses are no longer issues, but there are major concerns about
general health.

In some cases PCOS may be exchanged for a new syndrome—*metabolic syndrome* (also called *Syndrome X*)—with its associated hypertension,
type 2 diabetes and abnormal blood lipid levels. PCOS patients who are
insulin resistant are at an estimated five-times greater risk for type 2 diabetes.
Risk for heart disease may be more complex. It may be difficult to sort out
PCOS from obesity when it comes to abnormal lipid levels.

Women with PCOS and obesity may have higher estrogen levels after
menopause. This may have protective effects on bone, as well as other positive benefits. However, it can also have the negative effect of unopposed estrogen on the uterus and possibly on the breast, resulting in an increased risk of
uterine hyperplasia and breast cancer. (See Chapter 13).

So, does PCOS exist after menopause? The short answer is yes. Just
because you are 50 (plus), and even if your ovaries have been removed, your
genetics have not changed. Since PCOS is a multi-system disorder, a *panendocrinopathy*, it stands to reason that it will be baggage that is carried for an
entire lifetime.

OK, then, can PCOS improve with age?

A study completed earlier this year by Etling evaluated 205 women
with PCOS seen an average of twelve years before the study. Analysis of a
questionnaire showed clear association of age and the possibility of normalization of menstrual bleeding. Those who started having regular cycles tended
to weigh less, but changes in smoking, excessive hair growth, fertility drug use,
or pregnancy did not seem to be significant. It seems likely that PCOS
improved as the follicle store reduced. The authors of the study likened aging
to the reduction of follicles that occurs after ovarian surgery (wedge resection).
Certainly, more studies of this kind are desperately needed.

When can I stop contraception? Can I get pregnant?

Those with years of infertility may find it amusing to discuss contraception along with menopause, but it's important that we do. As FSH levels
start to rise, there is possibly an increased chance of pregnancy. The average
age at which the last baby is born is 41 to 42 years in previously regular cycling
women not using contraception. Everyone knows someone who knows someone who delivered a baby at age 44 to 45, but this is *exceedingly* rare. It is
possible that this was an effect of slight increases in FSH that may have had

the same result as being placed on low doses of injectable fertility drugs. Some women may start hormone replacement therapy with a resulting favorable effect on ovulation.

One of my colleagues was evaluating a patient in her mid-40s who clearly had menopausal symptoms and an elevated FSH level. She had many years of infertility and never thought a pregnancy likely, although he did warn her that it could happen. In her second month of therapy, she became pregnant. She was furious and not only left his practice, but also threatened to sue him. Pregnancy happens and sometimes at the least expected or desired time. The risk of miscarriage after age 42 is above 30%.

Sometimes a good transition into hormone replacement therapy is accomplished by using the new lowest dose contraceptives. They may offer good bleeding control during this time. The bottom line is that pregnancy is very unlikely after age forty-five, or after the FSH levels are above 40.

Is perimenopause different for women with PCOS?

Normally an early sign of the menopausal transition is an altered bleeding pattern, but those with PCOS may have been experiencing this since puberty. This makes it more difficult to assess when those with PCOS are nearing menopause. Some will have an abrupt cessation of bleeding, or they will alternate between frequent bleeding and very infrequent bleeding. Initially cycles tend to shorten. In women who have had regular periods, higher FSH levels at the start of a cycle result in an extra push for follicle growth. Since the follicle has an accelerated development, cycles tend to shorten. Often cycles that were 27 to 29 days become 26 to 27 days. By all we know, menopause and its associated symptoms are not different in women with PCOS.

Does menopause cause excessive hair growth and weight gain?

There is a bit of good news for women with PCOS here. In most women, maximum body weight is achieved around menopause and then weight tends to slowly decrease. Of course we do not know about PCOS, but in the general population there is usually a weight gain of only several pounds. It could be argued either way for hair growth. Normally, many women have a slight increase in unwanted hair growth because of the changing androgen/estrogen ratio around menopause. This could be the same for the woman with PCOS. However, for some with PCOS and hirsutism as a constant problem, androgen levels may fall more than estrogen levels and unwanted hair decrease, especially if estrogen replacement therapy is used.

How should bleeding after menopause be evaluated?

Bleeding irregularities are common during the menopausal transition. To distinguish normal from abnormal can be problematic even for the best clinician and these problems can be magnified in those with PCOS. The only advice is to ask your physician. Pap smears, ultrasound, and possibly endometrial biopsy are all tools that may be used in the assessment. Negative tests are always reassuring to both patient and physician. There are no real rules for the evaluation other than honest communication and concern.

All postmenopausal bleeding should be evaluated. The bleeding may be easily explained and is usually is not serious, but it must be evaluated. Individuals with PCOS are at a higher risk for endometrial hyperplasia and even endometrial cancer. (See Chapter 13). Early diagnosis is the key. If diagnosis is not immediately forthcoming hysteroscopy and/or dilation and curettage (D&C) may be necessary.

Does PCOS increase the need for hysterectomy?

The most common reason for hysterectomy is abnormal pain and bleeding, (a very non-specific diagnosis) often related to uterine fibroids or endometriosis. (See Chapter 13). Sometimes a hysterectomy is the result of both the patient and physician running out of, or perhaps not looking for options. Many women with PCOS will have a hysterectomy; whether more attention to the disorder or more aggressive therapy could have prevented it is unknown.

A very good question is "Do I have to have a hysterectomy?" The answer to this is most often "no," at least in the short-term. Certainly, if there is abnormal bleeding that cannot be controlled by medications, or large growing fibroids, hysterectomy may be the only answer. Despite widespread and true stories about the quickness and questionable diagnosis for which hysterectomies are performed, this represents a relatively small percentage. If it does not seem to be a logical decision based on a complete explanation, a second opinion is probably warranted. Most women do not regret their decision; especially if it is a decision well thought out and prepared for.

The support is lacking.

All pelvic tissues are under the influence of estrogen. As estrogen levels wane, there can be a decreased integrity of the supporting *connective tissues* and muscles of the pelvis resulting in a common condition called uterine *prolapse*. With even minor descent of the uterus and cervix into the vagina, there can be an intense feeling of pressure, back pain, and bowel or bladder symptoms. Prolapse is most common near or after menopause and directly related to the number of vaginal deliveries. Some have postulated that prolapse is more common after difficult labors and in fact, difficult deliveries can damage the supportive structures. However, it is more likely that prolapse occurs after relatively quick and easy deliveries, indicating a larger pelvic capacity. The more rounded gynecoid, or female, pelvis is inherently more unstable than the heart-shaped male, or android, pelvis. Although I know of no study that can either substantiate or refute the possibility, it may be that the pelvic architecture of PCOS may be more male-like and inherently stronger. This may result in less tendency for prolapse. Estrogen therapy can sometimes improve the integrity of the supportive structures and should be the first line of therapy for patients with prolapse.

Other associated conditions include bulging of the rectum the posterior vaginal wall (rectocele) and/or descent of the urethra and bladder (urethrocele and cystocele). These likewise may respond to estrogen, but surgery may be needed in the final analysis.

Is there a greater frequency of urinary tract problems?

With removal of estrogen, there is thinning of the lining of the urethra that can result in painful urination (*dysuria*). Like the prolapse described above, there is a loss of the supportive structure and prolapse of the bladder and alteration of the urethra can occur, making loss of urine with coughing, laughing, or exertion—*stress urinary incontinence*—more likely.

Kegel exercise helps to strengthen the perineal muscles surrounding the urethra, vagina, and anus and maintain their tone and may improve continence. This exercise is done by tightening the pelvic floor muscles, as if trying to stop a flow of urine, and holding them tense for ten seconds. This is repeated ten to twenty times in a row at least three times each day. These exercises help improve the ability to hold urine.

The risk factor and the above explanation for uterine prolapse should be applied, as well as the suggestion of estrogen therapy. Like prolapse, the relative risk on PCOS is not known.

Do I have a vaginal infection?

Probably not. It is true that with decreased estrogen stimulation the vaginal environment may change and vaginal health suffers. Yeast infections are reasonably common, but many more nonprescription yeast preparations are sold for non-infection than infection. Frequent yeast infections could be a sign of a more serious disease process such as diabetes and warrant medical evaluation. Adding yogurt and lactobacillus to the diet may help but vaginal application is discouraged. Copious amounts of discharge or discharge with a bad odor should also be evaluated.

The most common cause of irritation is estrogen deficiency. The vaginal lining thins and normal moisture decreases in a perimenopausal women (*vaginal atrophy*). *Atrophic vaginitis* results when the vaginal wall becomes inflamed. The treatment is to replace estrogen. Although it should not matter whether estrogen is used orally or as a vaginal cream, response may be quicker and dosages smaller when estrogen is directly applied. In some cases a small amount of cortisone cream may help, but this should be used very sparingly since it can thin tissues even more. In resistant cases a very small application of testosterone cream may be needed to restore integrity.

Regular sexual activity has been shown to help maintain vaginal health, but nature needs a little help. Lubricants and moisturizers do not restore or promote vaginal health, but may relieve symptoms. Water-based products, such as K-Y Jelly™, Lubrin™, and Astroglide™ are lubricants and short acting, while Replens™ and K-Y Long-Lasting™ act directly on the tissue to increase moisture and also have the advantage of lowering the vaginal pH and possibly making the vagina less inviting for infection. Oil-based prod-

ucts should be avoided. Douches can often worsen the problem.
Antihistamines can worsen dryness.

I can't remember the question.

It has been difficult to sort out the association between the alteration in memory, sleep disturbance and other dynamics of this stage of life. Women who may have never had a problem with remembering minute details in their daily life are often surprised to find themselves suddenly unable to call to mind common ordinary information such as an address, telephone number, or even someone's name. They are dismayed to find themselves unable to concentrate or focus on a simple task that previously was performed effortlessly.

Clearly there is a decrease in short-term memory function at menopause. Most studies would suggest an improvement in cognitive function (clear thinking) among women who use HRT.

I can't SLEEP!

Virtually every perimenopausal woman has a sleep disorder although sometimes the association with menopause is not made. The 3 AM awakening is common place. The source is unclear, but the effects are not. Poor sleep leads to daytime fatigue, lethargy, poor concentration and irritability. HRT usually improves sleep pattern, somewhat. In PCOS there may be an additional problem of sleep apnea resulting in the same symptoms. Clearly, sleep apnea is related to obesity, but it may also be related to insulin resistance.

Am I depressed?

Menopause for most is a time of introspection and review. Many women report that they feel discouraged, irritable, tired, out of control, "numb" or just "blue" during the perimenopausal/menopausal years. Sometimes things are OK and other times, not so good. They wonder if they are depressed. Scientific proof that menopause causes *clinical* depression is completely lacking. Many studies and opinions have been formed by surveys of women presenting to their physician with a problem. These women are then used to study other issues about menopause. From the start these studies are extremely biased toward disease and illness adaptation of patients. It is safe to say that we know very little about the issue of the general make-up of women around menopause. What your mother told you may be as reliable as many medical books. That's not a comment on how good the information is, but how bad!

This does not mean that hormonal rhythms are not markedly distorted and menopause does not cause alteration in mood and mental functioning. Many women who begin hormone replacement therapy for relief of symptoms such as hot flushes or insomnia often report improvement in mood as well.

Often, feelings of anxiety and depression are the result of life changes other than menopause. The timing of these events just happens to coincide with menopause. There is often a death or extended illness of a parent. The last child has sought independence, emptying the nest. Sadness over the pregnancy that was lost, never was, or never can be may resurface. The upper limits of one's career are in sight. A husband is having a mid-life crisis or possibly even a heart attack. A wife may find herself divorced or widowed. If these are not enough, add waking in the middle of the night with hot flashes, and then overlay a poor sleep pattern at night with forgetfulness during the day. In this environment, it is hard to consider menopause as liberation. It is hard not to question sanity. Stress, fatigue, insomnia, and feelings of sadness often blamed solely on menopause are often the result of the *time* of life rather than the *change* of life.

Depression is tough to define. It can be a mood (one that many know well), a symptom, or an illness. Depression may be "situational" and entirely related to a normal adjustment reaction. In this case, symptoms should not last over six months. Health care providers should tune in enough to diagnose depression. Sometimes we are not well enough in tune, and we need a suggestion. Medications ("nerve pills") don't solve problems and, while very useful for treatment of illness, they are less successful for mood. Prolonged feelings of sadness, irritability, loss of interest in the activities that once gave pleasure, and feelings of worthlessness or hopelessness should be discussed with a mental health professional.

Is the PCOS perimenopausal patient more likely to be depressed? I will venture to guess that her likelihood is less; don't prove me wrong.

What about sex?

For the modestly overweight woman with PCOS, there is perhaps some more good news. Her slightly higher androgen levels may preserve libido. This is another edge over her thinner counterparts.

Humans are sexual beings from before birth until death. There is the need for human companionship, love, and intimacy, but also for sex. Sexual feelings can be repressed for a number of reasons. Often in later ages it is because of a lack of an outlet due to the death or illness of a partner. Over 50% of women and 70% of men are sexually active after age 65. Most often decreases in function are due to a repression when there is no socially acceptable outlet. A source of the problem is more likely to be of male origin than female origin. As men age, sexual interest often declines along with a capacity to achieve and maintain an erection. Use of Viagra™ may help. The use of Viagra™ in women is also being evaluated. Many women say the arousal phase of sexual excitement is slower. Blood pressure medications, antidepressants, tobacco, and alcohol can each have a negative effect on sexual functioning.

As estrogen levels drop, there is a tendency for there to be increased vaginal dryness and decreased lubrication during sexual intercourse. The vaginal lining thins and there may be burning and spotting during intercourse. There is also a loss of the elasticity of the tissue surrounding the vagina. There may be a feeling of tightness and also burning. A vicious circle is established with painful intercourse decreasing the pleasure for the female resulting in even less lubrication and increased pain that causes a combined feeling of guilt and performance anxiety in the male. Intercourse becomes easier to avoid and the decreased frequency worsens the problems, all around.

Water-based lubricants can help with these problems. Estrogen replacement helps, but usually does not completely resolve these issues. Sexually active women note fewer problems than the rarely active woman does. It is quite possible that regular sexual activity improves the blood supply to the reproductive organs. Especially in the absence of a sexual partner masturbation can be considered a healthy expression of sexuality. There may be some truth to the phrase, "use it or lose it."

At our center, Judy McCook is writing her Ph.D. thesis on PCOS, sexuality, body image, and family relationships. It is her hypothesis that PCOS patients, because of the testosterone, have healthy libidinal function. It is common to find that the thinner perimenopausal patients have decreased levels of androgens. This is also the case in the very obese, whether male or female. Many obese men have decreased sex drive.

Always remember that the most important sex organ lies between our ears. Many perimenopausal and postmenopausal women are reluctant to discuss sex with their physicians. The physician may be young enough to be her son or daughter and outdated cultural training takes over. Physicians may also feel somewhat embarrassed for the same reasons. Make the first step if your physician doesn't.

Those aren't hot flashes; they're power surges!

You don't "think" you are having hot flashes; you know. The hot "flash" or "flush," which first begins around the time of menses, is usually more common at night. There is a feeling of intense heat that spreads over the entire body and is occasionally associated with perspiration. Although there is an increased reddening of the face, neck, and chest, it is more easily felt than seen. These 'personal summers' may be more frequent during times of stress. Virtually all women have flushes and they can be of variable intensity and duration. Most often hot flashes start to decrease about two years after they begin, and there is much less frequency and intensity after five years. Some PCOS patients complain of intermittent hot flushes throughout their lives. The flushes coincide with a surge in LH, but it is not solely due to LH release. Hot flashes cause no health risk other than the

Triggers for Hot Flashes

• Stress
• Hot foods
• Hot drinks
• Alcohol
• Caffeine
• Warm rooms

unneeded embarrassment that results when a woman believes that every one in the room can tell that she is having a hot flash. Estrogen replacement dramatically reduces hot flushes. Progestins also may have a limited effect. There is a suggestion that 400 IU of vitamin E might help. It also has been suggested that an increase in soy-based products can lessen hot flashes. (See *phytoestrogens* below). If no other therapy is working, some women are helped by the prescription medication clonidine (Catapres™).

What is osteoporosis?

Bone is in a constant state of remodeling; it is being laid down and absorbed continually. Bone cells called *osteoblasts* lay down bone, at the same time cells called *osteoclasts* remove bone. This ensures the body a steady state of calcium that is critical for many of its cellular activities. When the resorption is greater than deposition, osteoporosis results. Bone loss is as sure as aging itself for both men and women. Bone deposition occurs throughout childhood and in to the teenage years. Bone loss starts in the twenties. If there are fewer deposits, the account cannot withstand as many withdrawals.

Osteoporosis is a disease of the skeleton in which the amount of calcium present in the bones slowly decreases to the point that bones become brittle and prone to fracture. Often referred to as the "silent crippler," this devastating disease currently affects nine million American women, while another sixteen million are at high risk for fractures because of low bone density. There are no warning signs for this crippling and sometimes deadly disease. Often the first indication that there is a weakening of the bones is a fracture that occurs from a minor fall or even a typical movement. Hip fractures and their complications result in the deaths of more women than deaths from cervical, ovarian and uterine cancer combined.

Most women tend to believe that osteoporosis is a disease that afflicts them only during menopause and that they need not be concerned until age 50 or later. Even then, many women believe that they obtain enough calcium in their diet and do not consider bone loss to be a major health risk. Unfortunately, while osteoporosis is largely a disease of older women, it can affect women of all ages. Any woman who is estrogen deficient as a result of infertility or early menopause (due to surgery or naturally occurring) is at risk for developing osteoporosis. Moreover, decreasing levels of estrogen hasten bone loss, so that 30-50-% of women over age 50 will have a fracture caused by osteoporosis.

We should not rely on therapy, but aim at prevention. Fortunately, there are preventive measures that can be taken, beginning in the teenage years and continuing for a lifetime. Encourage good nutrition and exercise in adolescence; continue good nutrition as an adult.

What are the risk factors?

Risk increases with age as bone begins to lose density after the mid-thirties. Individuals who are thin, with a small-boned frame are at a greater risk because they have less bone mass originally. Caucasian and Asian women are at a greater risk than women from other ethnic backgrounds, and women are at greater risk than are men for developing osteoporosis. Genetics also plays a large role in determining risk. In fact, 80% of bone density is genetically determined. Fortunately, the remaining 20% involves diet and exercise; factors that are within one's control and factors that can make the difference between healthy bones and osteopenital bones. Women whose female relatives have been diagnosed with *osteoporosis*, especially on their maternal side, are at an increased risk.

Because of the decline in estrogen, one-third of all women develop osteoporosis after menopause. Early menopause, either naturally occurring or due to the surgical removal of the ovaries, increases the chance of developing weak bones. The use of certain medications for lengthy periods of time may also increase the risk of developing osteoporosis. Among these are corticosteroids (hormones used as anti-inflammatory medications to treat asthma, arthritis and certain cancers), thyroid hormones, and some anti-seizure medications. Osteoporosis may also be a complication of various medical conditions, such as overactive thyroid. If an individual is on thyroid medication, too much supplementation can hasten bone loss. TSH levels need to be checked at least annually. Lifestyle choices that include smoking, excessive alcohol consumption, being sedentary and a diet low in calcium, fruits and vegetables can also increase the risk.

Can osteoporosis be prevented?

We cannot overemphasize that osteoporosis in not just a concern of old age. Women especially should begin taking preventive measures early in life in order to build bone mass. This healthy lifestyle should then continue throughout a lifetime to prevent bone loss. By learning what happens at the different stages in life, a woman can assess her risk factors and know what steps to take toward maintaining the healthiest bones possible.

During early childhood and the teen years, bones lengthen and mature. In fact, 45% of the adult skeletal volume is formed during this time, and the bones store calcium at a faster rate then at any other time in life. Teenagers who diet, eat mostly junk food, become anorexic/bulimic, or start smoking are putting themselves at risk. This age group needs to participate in regular weight-bearing exercise and eat a calcium-rich diet, which includes 800 mg of calcium daily for children under 12 and 1000 mg daily for those 12 and older. Fruits and vegetables may also play a role in building strong bones. Too much protein, salt, and phosphorous (an ingredient in carbonated soft drinks) drain calcium from bones.

Bones gradually begin to thin during the mid-30's. Because smoking has a toxic effect on bone-building cells and can accelerate menopause by up to five years, women in this age group are at an extreme risk. Additionally, persons who have had a hysterectomy, dieters, and those with a family history of osteoporosis are at an increased risk. If one is in this age range and at a high risk, it is time to discuss a bone scan with the doctor. Additionally, a calcium rich diet and weight-bearing exercise continue to be of importance.

Bone loss continues to be gradual in the 40's, except in the case of early menopause. Women who have early menopause or a family history of osteoporosis are at an increased risk. In the case of early menopause, one should consider hormone replacement therapy. A calcium-rich diet with 1500 mg of calcium daily is important in this age group. Weight-bearing exercise and a diet containing soya-rich products are also helpful.

Bone loss increases from 1% per year to 5%-6% and continues at that rate for up to seven years after menopause. Those at the greatest risk for developing osteoporosis are women with any of the above-mentioned risk factors and women not taking hormone replacement therapy. After menopause, it is strongly encouraged that women take estrogen. A proper diet as well as vitamins and calcium supplements are important in reducing the risk of fractures. Weight-bearing exercise continues to increase bone density.

Calcium absorption from the intestine slows after menopause. Supplemental calcium is important, but calcium therapy alone is not enough to turn the tide of osteoporosis. Calcium supplementation should be considered to help slow loss. A daily calcium intake of 1500 mg a day is recommended. Is one type better than the rest? Probably not. Antacids, oyster shells and various other preparations are more similar than different.

Exercise is an important part of a preventative regimen for osteoporosis. It need not be vigorous, but it should be weight bearing, such as walking and calisthenics. There needs to be about 30 minutes of exercise at least three times weekly for it to have a strong beneficial effect.

How is osteoporosis detected?

A dual energy X-ray absorptiometry (DXA) scan is the most effective way of assessing bone strength. This painless diagnostic tool uses a very low-dose radiation to produce accurate images of spine and hip bones. A significantly lower than average bone density indicates osteoporosis. Scores between normal and lower range indicate low bone density and an increased risk for developing osteoporosis. Often osteoporosis is diagnosed because a fracture occurs. Regardless of how the disease is detected, once it is discovered, it is time to begin therapy.

What treatments are available?

Therapy usually includes increased calcium intake; exercise and medications, in addition to regular monitoring of bone density. Presently there are only a few medications approved by the Food and Drug Administration (FDA) for the treatment of osteoporosis. These are hormone replacement therapy (HRT), raloxifene (Evista™), calcitonin (Miacalcin™) and alendronate (Fosamax™).

Medications are important for some patients experiencing rapid bone loss. Bisphosphonates (alendronate, Fosamax™) are absorbed by bone and block its resorption. Simplistically, the bisphosphonates are taken up into bone, give it a "bad taste" and ruin the appetite of the osteoclasts that have been devouring bone. The largest problem with the bisphosphonates has been their gastrointestinal side effects, especially gastric and esophageal irritation. New, improved formulations and proper administration have decreased frequency of gastrointestinal side effects. Pills should be taken with only plain water at least thirty minutes before the first food. Standing for at least thirty minutes after taking the medication reduces chance of irritation of the esophagus. Raloxifene (Evista™) is an estrogen receptor modulator (see SERM below) that is FDA approved for prevention of osteoporosis. It does not improve the other symptoms of menopause and is considered third line therapy. *Calcitonin* is a hormone produced by the thyroid gland that is involved

with calcium and bone metabolism. It is approved for treatment of osteoporo-
tered as a nasal spray and has minimal side effects, but is expensive. It has no
effects on other menopausal symptoms. (See Chapter 15 and Chapter 17).

While no cure exists for osteoporosis, we empahsize again that preventive measures begun early in life can make the difference between fragile
bones and healthy bones in later life. The best precautions one can take are
building maximum bone density early in life and reducing loss as much as possible as one matures. Accomplishing this is not difficult. It requires eating a
well-balanced, calcium-rich diet and performing regular weight-bearing exercises. Additionally one should guard against risk factors in order to take extra
steps to prevent future fractures.

Does PCOS increase the risk for osteoporosis?

No, just the opposite is true! It seems that PCOS has a protective
effect on bone density. This may be due to the increased weight; thin patients
have a higher risk than heavier patients do. In a study by Professor Jacobs in
London, 610 new PCOS patients had bone densitometry performed as a part
of their evaluation. Both patients with amenorrhea and those with regular
cycles were scanned. PCOS patients diagnosed on ultrasound scan had higher bone density than their non-PCOS counterparts.

What about increased risk of cardiovascular disease after menopause?

Cardiovascular disease is the largest killer of both men and women
after age fifty. While there are volumes of research, risk factors for cardiovascular disease include smoking, obesity, type 2 diabetes, and family history (see
Chapter 17). The risk in men is significantly greater than that of women. This
may be due to the atherogenic potential of androgens, which are, of course,
higher in women with PCOS, but it has also been hypothesized that it may be
due to the male lifestyle. These topics are more fully presented in Chapter 9.
The best advice that can be given here is that all women must do the best they
can at removing, reducing or treating the risk factors for cardiovascular disease
and other factors that put women with PCOS at risk for cardiovascular disease
and health problems.

Must I use HRT? Is it for everyone?

Most animal species do not survive long enough to spend time past
their reproductive years. As has been earlier stated, at the time of Christ, the
average life expectancy was less than twenty-five years. Not too long ago, surviving to menopause for the human female was a plight restricted to few and
it was not until around 1900 that the average female life expectancy reached
50 years. Most women who reach age 65 will also reach age 85 or more. The
average life span of women is now eighty years. One third of a woman's life
span will be spent after menopause and unless corrected, these years will be
spent in an estrogen deficient state.

Since estrogen is related to all things female, why would it not be replaced? Generally, the benefits of hormone replacement therapy (HRT) far exceed the risks. HRT is not for all and its use should remain an individual decision, but when this is an informed decision based on our present scientific information available, it is difficult not to choose HRT. Still it is amazing that only about 50% of postmenopausal women have ever used HRT and most will discontinue use after only about five years.

Menopause creates a hormone deficiency that should be corrected. Generally I am in favor of HRT for all women. I believe the quality of life is increased and overall disease risks are lessened. In the following, I am going to reiterate the "company" policy of what I believe is the present standard of care in our profession for menopause and HRT in general. It (I) may be accused of having a shortsighted, lack of a "natural" approach, but the stand is completely defensible based on our present scientific understanding.

HRT can improve longevity and quality of life, but the side effects and medical risks can preclude its use. HRT is not for everyone.

Benefits of HRT
- Alzheimer's/cognition: Debated, but suggested decrease in Alzheimer's or improved memory and mental functioning.
- Cardiovascular: probably cardioprotective due in part to improved lipid status.
- Dental/mouth: less tooth loss, less gingival inflammation, less oral pain.
- Hot flashes: clearly decreased.
- Osteoarthritis: protection.
- Sexual function: preserved or improved.
- Sleep: improved.
- Skin: reduction of collagen breakdown and improved collagen quality.
- Stroke risk: no change or reduced, especially in severity.
- Urinary incontinence/pelvic support: less incontinence, improved support.
- Vaginal dryness/thinning (atrophy): lessened.
- Vasomotor instability: decreased hot flushes.
- Vision: improved visual acuity, less dry eyes, protection against lens opacities.

Estrogen and Alzheimer's?

The possibility that estrogen therapy decreases the relative risk of developing Alzheimer's, premature senile dementia, is presently a controversial study. More data supports a beneficial effect of estrogen rather than refutes it. There is also evidence that estrogen may improve the mental function of individuals already afflicted with Alzheimer's. It's a fascinating topic to consider whether the PCOS patient may have an increased or decreased risk of the devastating disease for patients and their families.

Does HRT cause weight gain?

Despite the thoughts to the contrary, women on HRT gain less weight than those not using the therapy.

Does HRT decrease the risk of heart disease?

Estrogens clearly improve the HDL levels and lessen the LDL level. Abnormal lipids, especially triglycerides and LDL, are thought to be a major risk factor for cardiovascular disease. Whether estrogens actually protect against heart attack is presently actively debated. The result of the large HERS study suggested that estrogens may not be as cardioprotective as once thought. The first results of The Women's Health Initiative have returned with a suggestion that in the first two years of HRT use there was a slight and inconclusive trend toward a higher incidence of heart attacks and strokes. The risk was no greater after two years. In the final analysis it is unlikely that HRT causes cardiovascular disease, but it also may not be as protective as once thought. Most still believe and there is ample evidence to support that estrogens have beneficial effects on the cardiovascular system. (Also see Chapter 17). We need to know.

Can HRT be used with hypertension?

HRT may cause a mild elevation in blood pressure thought to be due to fluid retention. High blood pressure does not prevent use of HRT. A mild diuretic may be added, if needed.

Estrogen and migraines?

Estrogen withdrawal can initiate migraine syndrome. Headaches are usually more a result of change in hormone status than hormone use. In some cases, migraine will be improved by HRT and in others, worsened. (See further explanation in Chapter 15).

Do estrogens improve insulin resistance?

Estrogens certainly do not worsen glucose tolerance and insulin sensitivity. It has been generally suggested that there is an improvement in insulin sensitivity, reduction in the likelihood of type 2 diabetes, and improved blood glucose control. This is probably due to the positive effects of estrogen on the liver. A recent study by Dunbar failed to show an improvement with transdermal estrogen alone, or when norethindrone was added. This study could be criticized because it used the patch, which bypasses the "first pass" effects in the liver and may be less likely to show positive effects. Oral medications absorbed through the intestine are first taken to the liver where they are metabolized. It is here that the beneficial effect on lipid metabolism occurs and at least some effects of insulin resistance are found. This is another critical area of research.

What are the major risks of HRT?

Liver: Individuals with impaired liver function may have a worsening of the condition. Close monitoring and guidance is necessary.

Hypertriglyceridemia: Individuals with markedly elevated triglyceride levels, above 300, are at risk of worsening their problems and even acute pancreatitis. A non-oral route is suggested. A level above 750 is an absolute reason not to use estrogen replacement. There might be a slight increase on gall stone formation and gallbladder disease in estrogen users.

Gall bladder disease: There is increased risk.

Thromboembolism: It is generally considered that combination HRT increases the risk of blood clots (thromboembolism) in individuals at risk. Most of the risk comes in the first year of use. The risk factors include previous deep vein clots, marked obesity, and importantly, family history. If there is a strong family history, specific tests for clotting tendency may be considered. The overall incidence of thromboembolism is low, about 1/10,000 in each year. The risk with HRT may be increased to about 3 times that amount. HRT does not appear to cause elevated blood pressure.

Other: There is fragmentary evidence that HRT may worsen asthma but these individuals who have used corticosteroids may be at higher risk of osteoporosis. HRT may worsen lupus and is best not to be used in active disease. Again, there may be cardiac protection and reduction of risk of osteoporosis after steroid use.

Does HRT cause cancer?

Answers vary with type of cancer.
- *Breast*: This is very hotly debated issue. If the risk of breast cancer is increased and it could very well be slightly, it still may not outweigh the benefits of HRT. Some studies have shown a decreased risk. If all studies are taken together (meta-analysis,) it appears that the relative risk is increased less than 5%. A study by the American Cancer Society reported a 16% reduction in the risk of "fatal" breast cancer in estrogen users. It cannot be said that the progestin component of HRT is protective and itself may stimulate breast proliferation. Under close guidance and after informed consent, some breast cancer survivors are using HRT.
- *Cervical:* probably no change.
- *Colon:* probably decreases in the HRT user.
- *Melanoma:* inconsistent data, probably no change.
- *Ovarian:* inconsistent data, probably no change.
- *Uterine:* clearly yes, if unopposed with progestin therapy. Rate of uterine cancer is lower than for those who do not use HRT, if a progestin is added. (See Chapter 13).

Can HRT be used if there is endometriosis?

A hysterectomy does not cure endometriosis. The removal of the ovaries only removes the hormonal signals and the stimulation of endometrial

tissue to grow. Clearly estrogen stimulates proliferation of the endometrium
and with estrogen replacement; it can worsen or activate endometriosis.
Usually the lower doses are not sufficient to have a significant effect. After a
hysterectomy for endometriosis, it still may be advisable to use a continuous
regimen that incorporates a progestin to block the unopposed effect of estrogen. Whether this should be continued long-term is unclear. There is always
the option of temporarily stopping HRT and allowing the endometriosis to
regress, if pain returns.

When to start HRT, when to stop?

When to stop is an easy question to answer. Stop when hip fracture,
urinary continence, and mental functioning are no longer important. When to
start is a slightly more difficult question to answer. Most women start HRT
because of the symptoms of the perimenopause, which serve as a good bio-
marker of estrogen deficiency. Usually HRT is started by age 50 or soon thereafter. Benefits still can be gained even when HRT is started in later years.

What's different about HRT with PCOS?

Outside the well-documented common risk of endometrial hyperplasia (see Chapter 13) both with PCOS and HRT, there has been little specific
information on which to base our decisions to use HRT in PCOS. In the total
absence of any specific guidelines, common sense should prevail with an
increased awareness, and good medical practice as our guide. Don't ignore
warning signs. Don't assume anything. Be aware that every physician will be
a product of his/her training, experience and interest, that there may be a
variety of opinions and levels of concern.

If there is a segment of the population that may need HRT less, based
in hypoestrogenism alone, it may be those with PCOS. Bone density is higher when menopause is entered, as well as androgen and estrogen levels.
However, this will confer only temporary protection and while the decline may
be slower, it will occur. Even then the potentially beneficial effects on the heart
may be reason enough to use HRT. We just don't know enough and the decision about HRT should be individualized.

While total androgen levels may drop after menopause, ovarian
testosterone may slightly increase under the influence of elevated
gonadotropins in all women. It is possible that this rise will be greater in
PCOS. The ovary has more stroma and androgen producing tissue with which
to work. This should also increase estrogen production, but the higher androgen levels could also move to a more atherogenic lipid profile, one more likely
to cause atherosclerosis (hardening of the arteries). Increased androgens may
also worsen insulin resistance. A recommendation has been made that women
with type 2 diabetes should consider HRT due to its cardioprotective effects.
Estrogen has been shown to improve glucose metabolism and insulin resistance. Long term studies are desperately needed.

Which estrogen?

First there was Premarin™, which is still one of the most widely pre-scribed of all drugs in the United States. Premarin is derived from the urine of pregnant mares noted for high levels of estrogen production. Estrone is the major estrogen of Premarin™, but it also contains other less active estrogens such as equilin, so named because of its association with horses. Other estrogens are derived from the Mexican yam and are largely estrone. It is interesting that the Mexican yam also contains traces of equilin. Contrast this to estradiol-17ß, which is the exact estrogen produced by the developing follicle, but it is synthetically produced. Still, estradiol is rapidly converted in the liver to estrone. All in all, there is no evidence that one estrogen is therapeutically better than another.

Is there a substitute for estrogen?

No. All are less effective alternatives. If all alternative therapies are taken together, they cannot match the protective effect of estrogen on bone, reduction of hot flushes, and other symptoms of estrogen deficiency.

What are phytoestrogens—do they help?

Many plants contain estrogenic compounds. Farmers attempt to keep the cows away from certain clovers because of their adverse effects on the estrus cycles. The legumes are the plant group richest in phytoestrogens. The majority of studies have evaluated soybean products. Clearly they have an estrogenic effect of reducing hot flashes. In areas of the world where soy intake is highest, women have a lower incidence of breast and endometrial cancer. Soy consumption reduces the amount of circulating estradiol. Phytoestrogens bind to estrogen receptors, but it is unclear whether they should be considered estrogen or anti-estrogen. There are isolated reports that phytoestrogens may inhibit growth of breast cancer cells in culture. Studies have been inconclusive as to a positive benefit of phytoestrogens on reduction of FSH levels, improvement of the vaginal lining or prevention of osteoporosis.

The recommended intake has been about 50 mg, but there is great variability in absorption and bioavailability. The amount of soy protein necessary to equal the lowest dose of estrogen therapy, 0.5 mg of estradiol, is 165 mg. While arguably more natural than other HRT combinations, soy is not without its detractions, specifically GI side effects.

Soy supplementation has caught the eye of both scientists and pharmaceutical firms. We will know much more soon. I will have to draw a bye on this one as opposed to herbal preparations that I am uniformly concerned about (see Chapter 17). Soy supplementation is not a substitute for HRT; it could turn out to be a useful additive therapy.

Is one hormone preparation more natural than another?

Patients often ask for the most natural method of HRT. It is a term we have grown fond of and this has not escaped the notice of pharmaceutical firms. In many ways all estrogens are natural in that they are either derived from plant or animal sources or, if man-made in the lab, are identical to the hormones produced by the ovary.

There is more variation in progestins. Some like medroxyprogesterone acetate (MPA), norethindrone and levonorgestrel are synthetic and distinct from the naturally occurring progesterone. The term progestin is variously used to describe only synthetic progestins or both the synthetics and progesterone. It is common to precede progesterone with "natural" as if there could be an unnatural. Progesterone equals progesterone and estradiol equals estradiol. There is no difference in whether they are derived or made in the laboratory.

What are SERMs?

Selective estrogen receptor modulators, or SERMs, alter the estrogen receptor and in some ways mimic estrogen action, but not exactly. Raloxifene (Evista™) is an example of this new class of drugs that have clearly been shown to reduce bone loss. There is a reduction of LDL (bad cholesterol) in users of SERMs, but not the improvement of HDL as seen with estrogen therapy. SERMs do not improve the symptoms of hypoestrogenism such as hot flashes. They should have at least a neutral, if not protective, effect on breast cancer. The major raloxifene trial can be accessed on the Web at www.asco.org.

Why is a progestin added when I need estrogen?

All women who have not had a hysterectomy must use a progestin or progesterone to lessen the chance of endometrial hyperplasia. Endometrial hyperplasia occurs in about 25% of women using (unopposed) estrogen alone and is probably more common with PCOS. The progestins of HRT are the same as those used by many with PCOS for menstrual cycle regulation, namely medroxyprogesterone acetate (Provera™, Cycrin™, Amen™), norethindrone acetate (Aygestin™) or progesterone (Prometrium™, Crinone™).

Progesterone or progestin?

The typical dose of MPA is 5-10 mg for twelve to fourteen days or 2.5 mg daily. After several large studies over the last few years, there has been a tendency to extend the progestin therapy from ten to fourteen days and decrease MPA from 10 to 5 mg. The most common side effect of these progestins is breast tenderness, which is much more common in sequential therapy.

There is much less information on use of progesterone for HRT than progestins. It would seem that progesterone would be superior, but problems of less absorption from the intestine may make blood levels more erratic. If oral progesterone is used, the dose is usually 200 mg for sequential and 100 mg for continuous. Because peanut oil is used as a base in Prometrium™, individuals with peanut allergies should not use this preparation. Crinone™ is progesterone that has been suspended in a special gel that is used vaginally. It offers very good absorption and perhaps direct uptake by the uterus without having to go through the circulation. Its disadvantage is that it is messy and expensive. Vaginal gel available as Crinone™ can also be used. Various capsules, creams, and vaginal suppositories are sometimes compounded by individual pharmacies. These may vary in their absorption and bioavailability.

There is evidence that women who cannot take estrogens receive some relief from vasomotor instability and endometrial protection from progestins alone. This should be considered a less advantageous alternative. Some seem to tolerate norethindrone acetate (Aygestin™) better than MPA (Provera™).

Should testosterone be added?

Giving testosterone to those with PCOS may be like taking coal to Newcastle. Hyerandrogenism is what PCOS is about. Logically, it would seem that if the ovary has more testosterone-producing tissue before menopause, it would have more <u>at</u> menopause and probably in the following few years. Of course, this is another one of these things we've not yet proven.

Most often the reason to add testosterone to HRT regimens is to improve libido and a sense of well-being. I have a few patients that swear by the addition of small amounts of testosterone, but more are dissatisfied that it either has not helped or the side effect of fluid retention has increased. In addition, testosterone can worsen skin problems and adversely alter the lipid profile, which already may be in need of help in PCOS.

The goal in all HRT is to replace what is lacking. Just as in diabetes where the goal is to keep sugar levels normal (euglycemia), the goal should be the same for the reproductive hormones. The overall feeling of wellness may be the best assay for adequate replacement.

What's the standard HRT regimen?

There are many options, but those below are the most commonly used regimens.

Estrogen (every day)
1 mg of estradiol
or 0.625 mg of conjugated estrogens
or 1.25 mg of estropipate

Continuous progestin (every day)
5 mg of medroxyprogesterone acetate (MPA)
or 200 mg of oral progesterone
or 1 mg of norethindrone acetate
or 4% vaginal gel twice weekly

Sequential progestin (14 days each month)
5 mg of medroxyprogesterone acetate (MPA)
or 200 mg of oral progesterone
or 1 mg of norethindrone acetate
or 4% vaginal gel daily

Continuous or sequential therapy?

The continuous regimen involves daily use of both estrogen and progestin, while the sequential therapy combines estrogen alone for fourteen to sixteen days followed by estrogen plus progestin for twelve to fourteen days. Within about six months most women on the continuos regimens completely stop bleeding. Early in the transition, there may be spits and spurts of hormone production that lead to erratic bleeding. The continuous regimen may control this less effectively than the sequential.

Which is right for PCOS? It could be argued that a constant level effect may be best, but it is possible that there may be less stability and therefore a greater tendency for bleeding. The majority of women using the sequential method will continue to have periods, while over the long term most on the continuous will completely stop bleeding. The cyclic side effects of bloating, breast tenderness, and mood changes are usually less on the continuous therapy. Patients with PCOS who are already at risk of endometrial hyperplasia should be watched more closely.

There is no need for a pill-free period in either the continuous or sequential regimens.

Does it matter when the pills are taken?

There is so much individual variation that a specific regimen cannot be suggested. The regimen that offers the best chance to be remembered and followed is probably best. Compounds called flavanoids present in fruits and vegetables can inhibit the breakdown of estrogen and therefore increase the circulating concentration. It is possibly better to take pills at bedtime.

Patch or Pill?

There are two delivery systems in general use for HRT, transdermal (patches) and oral (pills). Much less commonly used are long acting injections or creams/gels. Gel absorption is variable. Implanted estrogen would seem easy in their twice-yearly injection. However, the implants are hard to remove if needed and in some cases estrogen from an implant may persist for up to two years after removal. Estrogen is sometimes prescribed as a vaginal cream, especially when there is the specific problem of atrophic vaginitis. Absorption is direct and even low doses can be beneficial. A small supplement of vaginal cream in the initial stages of therapy is often appreciated.

The newer patches are smaller and skin irritation is less common than with the older models. There are differences in transdermal and oral systems. With the transdermal method, the estrogen is absorbed differently and the "first pass" through the liver is avoided. Initially this was a selling point. It now appears that this may be a disadvantage because the metabolism in the liver is associated with reduced LDL (bad) cholesterol and increased HDL (good) cholesterol.

Patches are changed once or twice weekly, avoiding the need for a daily pill. In the past, patch users who had not had a hysterectomy had to also take oral progestin. There is now a patch (Combipatch) that provides both estrogen and progestin.

When is bleeding abnormal?

It is reasonable to perform an endometrial biopsy and/or an ultrasound scan before initiation of HRT in those with PCOS. There is no hard and fast rule. Since there is an increased risk of endometrial hyperplasia, it may be reasonable to know the baseline starting point. Pre-treatment evaluation could save worry and numerous return visits.

On the sequential therapy, there should be a timely withdrawal bleeding as the progestin is finished. On the continuous regimen, spotting can be expected for the first six months, even after a year of use. After a year, about one out of every six women will continue to have irregular bleeding. Initial evaluation of abnormal bleeding is usually by ultrasound. Sometimes the bleeding is not hormonal, but due to uterine fibroids or polyps. Fibroids may or may not grow under the influence of estrogen. Lower doses are associated with less likelihood of growth. A very thick lining indicates a need for an endometrial biopsy; a thin lining does not completely exclude cellular abnormalities and an endometrial biopsy may be necessary. Polyps can often be identified by an office ultrasound procedure called a sonoHSG during which a small amount of water is instilled through the cervix into the uterine cavity for a better view. In some cases, hysteroscopy and/or D&C may be needed for an evaluation to be completely thorough.

If bleeding persists, the options are to change to a sequential regimen, discontinue therapy and reevaluate after several months, or proceed to surgery. If hysteroscopy fails to identify a cause and hysteroscopic directed biopsy is unrevealing, the options may remain to either perform an endometrial ablation where only the lining of the uterus is destroyed, or at last resort, a hysterectomy.

Can adequacy of hormone replacement be tested?

Although the FSH levels may be a good indication as to when to start therapy, it is poor for monitoring. Usually no monitoring is necessary and the standard doses (0.625 of conjugated estrogen or 1 mg of estradiol) will provide proper bone and heart protection. Estradiol levels are usually 50-150 pg/ml on this regimen. Reported estradiol levels will very much depend on the individual laboratory and to some degree on the type of estrogen used. Despite no estradiol in conjugated estrogen, there is interconversion in the body and measurement of estradiol is still valid. Levels above 200 pg/ml should be considered excessive and avoided.

So how do you want to spend the next 30 years?

You are not a kid anymore, but 50 is hardly old. The life expectancy tables would suggest another thirty years or so to your life. Like it or not, health problems, both real and imagined, will start to take precedence. It is not too late to make significant changes that can not only extend life, but improve how the years are spent. First an assessment needs to be made.

Step 1—Self-assessment

An important part of the midlife health assessment you already know. It is of no use for a physician to tell you to lose weight and stop smoking until you are ready to do it. If you are smoking, you know that you must stop. If you are overweight, weight has to be lost. If you are completely sedentary, you've got to move. Overall, the key is *optimum metabolic balance.*

Step 2—Evaluate specific disease risks

For this, additional help is required. This involves a complete medical and family history and then checking for different specific diseases. This may be heresy, but very little is found on a general physical examination. It is time to bring up specific concerns and general worries. It can also be a vehicle into the medical system, which is infinitely more important than listening to your chest or pressing on your abdomen. Not only should risks such as heart disease, diabetes, and cancer be of concern, but also issues such as urinary incontinence, thyroid disease, osteoporosis, and sexuality are included.

Step 3—Make plans

It does not have to be an ambitious plan, nor does it necessarily have to include medications. Set goals that can be accomplished. See if it is within your own power to make a difference before medications are used.

Step 4—Take action

The following is a general medical screen recommended at age 50.

- Pap smear (after a long history of normal smears, this can be less frequent.
- Mammogram (yearly after age 50).
- Bone densitometry (first at 40 to 45, every 2 years after 50).
- Comprehensive biochemical profile.
- Complete blood count (CBC).
- Lipid panel.
- Thyroid stimulating hormone (TSH) to exclude thyroid disease.
- Pelvic ultrasound. There is an increased use of ultrasound as a part of routine examination. There is a much better view of the pelvis through ultrasound than biannual examination can provide. Ultrasound can be particularly useful in overweight individuals in whom adequate examination is more difficult. Availability of equipment, skill requirements, cost and lack of third party reimbursement all contribute to a lack of more universal acceptance of this screening. Routine ultrasound use should be easily available and inexpensive. Separate hospital visits and an expensive extensive scanning still should be reserved for evaluation of suspected pathology.
- Colonoscopy (screening at age 50 has been recommended).

A Coat of Many Colors.
PCOS' Relationship with
Other Medical Problems

*"I've passed the time when reproduction is an issue.
I'm concerned about what PCOS means for my future
health. Heart disease runs in my family."*

*"I don't get periods very often, but when I do it's a
'dilly.'"*

"I get terrible migraines."

"Could I be depressed?"

The roots of any endocrine or metabolic disorder run deep. There are
a number of medical problems that have hormonal relationships, although not
all are necessarily related to PCOS. We will start with metabolic syndrome,
which may have PCOS as its origin, and move into other disease processes
that may not be so clearly related.

METABOLIC SYNDROME
What is metabolic syndrome?

There is much more difference in opinion as to what to call this group
of interrelated metabolic disturbances than there is concerning its serious consequences. Metabolic syndrome has been variously referred to as syndrome X,
dysmetabolic syndrome, insulin resistance syndrome, plurimetabolic syndrome,
chaos syndrome or the deadly quartet. Whatever its name, there is a "cluster-
ing" of diseases and risk factors revolving around insulin action (*insulin resistance*) and altered health of blood vessels and blood pressure (*hypertension*),
with an interweaving abnormality of blood lipid levels (*dyslipidemia*). Together
these factors blend to form a "metabolic soup," where the sum is greater than
the total of the parts. Some researchers include obesity (especially android,
centripetal, or visceral obesity) in this grouping to make a quartet, while oth-

ers leave it out of the definition. Regardless, obesity seems to be strategically posed in the middle of it all and few have the other components of metabolic syndrome and are not obese. Taken as a whole, this derangement accounts for most cases of cardiovascular disease, the number one cause of death in adult women and men.

Many women mistakenly believe (fear) that cancer, especially breast cancer, is their leading cause of death. However, the risk of dying from a complication of cardiovascular disease (CVD) is twice that of all types of cancer and more than equals all other causes of death combined. CVD accounts for over 50% of all deaths of women age 35 years and older. More and more research is showing that this risk can be changed by lifestyle modification assisted by medications. The PCOS patient seems to embody metabolic syndrome. She often has all the risk factors for CVD except the Y chromosome (she is not male); however, there are exciting new findings that suggest that PCOS may *not* have the risks previously expected.

METABOLIC SYNDROME		CARDIOVASCULAR DISEASE
	nitric oxide	
	vascular muscle	
INSULIN RESISTANCE	vascular bed	MYOCARDIAL INFARCTION
	endothelial injury	
	inflammation	PERIPHERAL VASCULAR D
OBESITY	plaque formation	
	fibrin deposition	THROMBOEMBOLISM
DYSLIPIDEMIA	clot formation	
	vasoconstriction	STROKE
HYPERTENSION	prostaglandins	
	angiotensin	
	fluid retention	

Figure 15-1 Metabolic Syndrome

The dyslipidemia factor
What are lipids?

Lipids (biologic fats) are used by both plants and animals as food and building sources. Some lipids must come from our diet (essential fatty acids), while others are constructed by our bodies from non-essential fatty acids, which in turn have come from carbohydrates. Many of the carbohydrates we eat are converted and stored as fat before they are released back into the circulation to meet the daily energy requirements. Fat is an excellent way to store energy. It has twice the caloric value of sugars and is associated with very little water. Since fats are insoluble in water and blood, special transport mechanisms exist for transport of fat through the bloodstream. Lipids are hooked-up with protein to form lipoproteins. As more fat is attached to a protein carrier, the density decreases and they become lighter. Their density classifies different circulating lipoproteins.

Cholesterol Despite its bad press, cholesterol is an essential nutrient necessary for repairing cell membranes, manufacturing vitamin D on the skin's surface, and creating hormones such as estrogen and testosterone. The body obtains some cholesterol through diet, but about two-thirds is produced in the liver. A diet rich in unsaturated fats stimulates cholesterol formation. More information is emerging that cholesterol itself is neither good nor bad. It has to do with the company it keeps, the lipoproteins.

Lipoproteins Cholesterol and other lipids, including triglycerides, are carried in the bloodstream packed into lipoproteins. Lipoproteins are categorized by size into five major types:

chylomicrons (largest in size and lowest in density). After a fat rich meal, the serum can be cream colored with the chylomicrons carrying fat globules floating to the top.

very low density lipoproteins (VLDL)

intermediate density lipoproteins (IDL)

low density lipoproteins (LDL). LDL is generally referred to as bad cholesterol, but there is a further division into the small dense LDL, which is the biggest offender in cardiovascular disease. LDL comprises the majority (60% to 70%) of cholesterol in the blood.

high density lipoproteins (HDL). HDL is the smallest and most dense, accounting for 20% to 30% of total cholesterol. It is a scavenger for LDLs and mitigates the adverse consequences of LDL. HDL concentration is raised by estrogen and reduced by androgens. HDL, on the other hand, removes excess cholesterol from peripheral tissues, reducing risk. Studies indicate that the higher the HDL the lower the cardiovascular risk.

Triglycerides: Triglycerides have a backbone of glycerol with fatty acids attached. Free fatty acids are the basic currency of the fats and have profound effects on insulin release. Triglycerides are the wrappers that hold these coins together, serving both as transporters and as a storage depot in adipocytes (fat cells). High triglyceride levels are often associated with other lipid abnormalities, such as low HDL and elevated LDL. High triglyceride levels, which are associated with insulin resistance and obesity, can be an independent predictor of CVD risk in women and a more important predictor in women than in men.

What are the normal levels?

The National Cholesterol Education Program (NCEP) classifies total cholesterol levels by assigning a category that describes the potential for risk associated with the value. A high-risk classification (total cholesterol ≥240 mg/dl) means that a person with this cholesterol value has a high likelihood of developing some form of atherosclerotic disease in the near future. A total cholesterol level of 200-239 mg/dl is borderline/high and <200 mg/dl is considered desirable. Using these cutoffs, approximately 20% of the American adult population can be classified as having high cholesterol. Using low-density lipoprotein cholesterol values and risk factor assessment, approximately 30% of the U.S. adult population qualifies for dietary intervention. Risk factors include elevated LDL cholesterol, men ≥45 years, women ≥55 years or premature menopause without estrogen replacement therapy, family history of premature CVD, cigarette smoking, hypertension or use of antihypertensive medications, diabetes mellitus, and low HDL cholesterol (<35 mg/dl).

In healthy people LDL cholesterol levels should be 160 mg/dl or below and in people with coronary artery disease LDL needs to be below 100 mg/dl. The lower the better. HDL levels should be well above 35 mg/dl. (An HDL level above 60 may offer enough protection to cancel out a risk factor). Triglyceride levels should be under 200 mg/dl, although some experts recommend that they be under 100. Twenty percent of adult women have dyslipidemia and 40% to 50% have at least borderline high risk or undesirable lipid levels.

Cholesterol, Lipoproteins, and Triglycerides			
Type	Target Normal	Increased Risk Lifestyle change	High Risk Medical intervention
Total Cholesterol	< 200 mg/dl	200-239 mg/dl	240+ mg/dl
HDL Cholesterol	> 35 mg/dl		
LDL Cholesterol	< 160 mg/dl	>160 mg/dl	
Triglycerides	< 200 mg/dl	200-400 mg/dl	400-1000 mg/dl

What are apoproteins?

When lipoproteins are made in the liver and intestinal wall, various apoproteins are attached. Apoproteins are genetically determined and influence the structures, receptor binding and metabolism of lipoproteins. Four classes have been identified, A, B, C, and E. Apoprotein A-1 and B are also thought to be important indicators of heart disease risk. Apoprotein B may actually turn out to be a very accurate indicator of heart disease risk in women.

Who's at risk?

Genetics plays a major role in determining a person's blood cholesterol levels. Children from families with a history of premature heart disease should be tested for cholesterol levels after age two. Genes may influence whether one has low HDL levels, high LDL levels, or high levels of other lipoproteins.

In women, dyslipidemia is most common in late middle age and beyond. Young and middle-age women generally have higher levels of HDL, which is protective against CVD. Mean lipid levels in women increase with age, catching up with those in men by age 45 to 54 and exceeding those in men at age 70 and beyond. One view is that cardiovascular risk is inversely related to the capacity of the ovary to make estrogen. As ovarian estrogen production diminishes, risk of cardiovascular disease increases.

Risk factors for dyslipidemia include age ≥55 years, premature menopause without hormone replacement, family history of early heart attacks, hypertension, and diabetes. Obviously major targets for intervention are smoking, obesity and physical inactivity.

Diabetes is one of the most frequently missed secondary causes of high LDL. Another frequently missed cause of high LDL is hypothyroidism. Hypothyroidism is easily treated with replacement and "we didn't look for elevated TSH levels" is never an excuse. Other secondary causes of high LDL include some kidney and liver diseases, obstructive liver disease, multiple myeloma, and various drugs, such as anabolic steroids, corticosteroids, and some antihypertensives.

Women with polycystic ovary syndrome are at increased risk for high triglyceride and low HDL levels. Whether due to inherited alterations in the way the body handles lipids, the increased risk of lipid disorder due to elevated androgens, insulin resistance, or obesity itself, those with PCOS frequently have dyslipidemia. Those with PCOS universally have high LDL levels. So much so, that the LDL levels could serve as a secondary marker for the disorder. This risk may be due to higher levels of testosterone in these women.

Everyone with PCOS should have a lipid profile performed early and then repeated annually.

What is saturated fat?

Dietary fats are either saturated or unsaturated. Fat saturation has to do with how the carbon molecules that make up the fat molecule are hooked together. The number of "double bonds" between carbon atoms determines the degree of saturation. If there are no double bonds the fat is said to be saturated; one double bond, monounsaturated; and multiple double bonds, polyunsaturated. The longer the carbon chain, the more double bonds, the higher the degree of unsaturation, the less association with CVD. Animal fats contain more saturated fats, while vegetable oil more unsaturated. Calorie per calorie, polyunsaturated fats may be no different for carbohydrates in CVD risk, but they are very energy dense.

Why lower cholesterol?

Diets high in saturated fat and cholesterol are associated with raised blood cholesterol levels. The benefits that can be gained by lowering these levels have been recognized through the results of epidemiological trials, including the landmark Framingham Heart Study, the Lipid Research Clinics Coronary Primary Prevention Trials, and the Multiple Risk Factor Intervention Trial. The National Cholesterol Education Program (NCEP) was launched in 1985 under the direction of the National Heart, Lung, and Blood Institute of the National Institutes of Health with the goal of reducing the prevalence of high blood cholesterol in the United States and thus, reducing related morbidity and mortality. The NCEP has established recommendations for detection, evaluation, and management of high cholesterol to be used by health professionals, for persons with elevated cholesterol, and for the American public as a whole.

There are no warning signs for high LDL cholesterol levels. When symptoms finally occur, they usually take the form of angina or heart attack in response to the buildup of atherosclerotic plaque in the patient's arteries. This is definitely an affliction where it pays to invest in preventive medicine before dangerous complications occur.

What makes bad cholesterol bad?

The main source of problems with cholesterol is not cholesterol itself but low-density lipoprotein (LDL), especially the *small dense LDL*. LDL transports about 75% of the blood's cholesterol to the body's cells, and is ordinarily harmless. However, LDL penetrates the walls of the artery where it can interact with unstable molecules called oxygen *free-radicals*. Free-radicals are released naturally during the body's maintenance processes and increase during stress, such as exposure to products of tobacco smoke, or exposure to environmental toxins. Free radicals are essential in the body's defense, but in excess, like all components of the immune system, can cause more harm than good. Free radicals are hungry for a missing electron that would restore the oxygen molecule to a more stable form. LDL is a juicy source of electrons, just ripe for the picking.

When LDL collects on arterial walls it is attached by free radicals released from the membranes of the cells lining the vessel wall, the *endothelium*. The resulting oxidized form of LDL triggers immunologic response with white blood cells gathering at the site causing inflammation. As a part of this process fat is eaten by inflammatory cells called macrophages and they accumulate their deposits in the vessel wall as a *fatty streak*. Trauma and inflammation continue, causing proliferation of the muscle of the vessel wall with more fat accumulation to form an atheroma, or *plaque*. In addition, the body attempts to repair the endotheial damage by patching the damaged area initially with a protein glue called fibrin, then with a blood clot and finally, with calcium to wall off the area. Pieces of the brittle calcified plaques can be sheared off as blood flows through the artery forming an embolus that may block an artery at some distant site. If this were an artery of the brain, the result would be a cerebrovascular accident (CVA or stroke).

As the plaque continues to build, the arterial walls slowly constrict reducing blood flow. Imagine a water pipe slowly rusting. The rust gathers more rust, but it also is a great place for other mineral deposits. If you have ever seen a water pipe of an old house, you have a very good understanding of plaque formation, *atherosclerosis*.

No artery is immune from atherosclerosis, but a particularly dangerous situation occurs when the arteries of the heart are affected, coronary heart (artery) disease. The heart muscle, which must function continuously with a high level of efficiency, demands large quantities of blood-borne oxygen. If blockage occurs, the result is a heart attack, myocardial infarction (MI). Alteration of the vessels of the arms and legs, called peripheral vascular disease, can cause pain and loss of function due to the muscle starved for blood and oxygen supply.

Is there protection against oxidative stress?

The best defense is a good offense. Reduce fats, stop smoking, and ensure good cardiac function by exercise. With PCOS, we already know that this will be a real uphill battle because of the strong genetic component of dyslipidemia and insulin resistance. It just means you have to work harder and sometimes enlist the help of medications.

Some advocate supplemental vitamin E, which is a *free-radical scavenger* thought to reduce oxidative stress. Use of small doses of aspirin (1/2 adult or 1 "baby") daily does not alter free-radicals, but its use prevents small clots from forming on the damaged vessel walls (microvascular disease). Alteration in dietary lipids also is clearly shown to help.

Why is good cholesterol good?

Our body has its own protection system against levels of LDL that are too high. High levels of high density lipoprotein serve to remove cholesterol from the walls of the arteries and return it to the liver. High HDL levels (above 45 mg/dl) appear to protect arteries from dangerous narrowing and thus help prevent heart attacks. HDL formation is promoted by estrogen and exercise.

How can my diet be improved?

First and foremost is a reduction in calorie intake. (See Chapter 8). However, it is not only how much, but what you eat that's also important. Polyunsaturated fat has been linked to improved lipid profiles when substituted for saturated fat. The omega-6-type polyunsaturated fatty acid linoleic acid reduces LDL and HDL levels. Vegetables and the vegetable oils olive, soybean, safflower, and sunflower are rich in this fatty acid. The omega-3-type polyunsaturated fatty acid alpha-linolenic acid and its breakdown products have been linked with lower rates of heart disease, an effect that may be independent of their effects on lipid profiles. Omega-3 fatty acids, especially a type found in fish, lower triglycerides but may have little effect on other serum lipids.

Increase fiber. Dietary (soluble) fiber binds cholesterol and increases intestinal transit time, so there is less chance for fat absorption. Foods rich in soluble fiber are beans and oat bran. Insoluble fiber found in wheat and vegetables have less effect on lipids.

What drugs help?

Use of lipid-lowering drugs is reserved for patients who do not achieve target lipid levels after an adequate trial (six months) of dietary intervention. Even after drug therapy is initiated, dietary therapy should continue to ensure maximal lipid lowering. LDL levels and the number of risk factors help determine when drug therapy should be added to dietary therapy. Drug therapy should be considered when LDL remains at 190 mg/dl or higher, despite dietary intervention in low risk cases and 160 mg/dl in high-risk cases.

Like the metformin and glitazone story, this is a case where the pharmaceutical industry has been a leader in innovation. Previously, many of the lipid-lowering agents were associated with a list of undesirable side effects. The "statin" class of drugs is making progress on several fronts and has the potential of significantly reducing the deaths from cardiovascular disease. While there are advantages to others agents, the "statins" have become the preferred treatment for hyperlipidemia in association with insulin resistance.

I once prescribed Metformin to a patient I thought would be an excellent candidate for its use. I expected a weight loss to occur. When she came back after the holidays, she said, "This holiday was the best ever. I ate and ate and gained not a pound." I was happy for her, even envious, but that was not the point. Use of a lipid-lowering agent is not a free ticket to eat fatty foods. It is that extra boost that can overcome the naturally adverse conditions under which the body has been operating. Still, work toward reducing the calories, saturated fats and cholesterol in the diet and increasing exercise.

There are four major categories of lipid lowering agents. Each category works at a different step in the production and metabolism of lipids. There also may be slight differences between the individual drugs of each of the categories. The reason for use is clear. Less lipid, less cardiovascular disease; less cardiovascular disease, a longer and better life.

Bile acid sequestrants: Cholestyramine (Questran™) and Colestipol (Colestid™). These agents bind bile acids in the intestines. This complex combination cannot be absorbed and is then eliminated in the feces. Since circulating bile acids are decreased, cholesterol in the liver is converted into bile acids that are further eliminated.

The use of the bile acid sequestrants must be carefully timed in patients taking other medications. These agents will also bind many other drugs and dietary vitamins A, D, K, and E. Patients must take other drugs one-hour before cholestyramine or colestipol or wait four hours before taking the other drugs. A vitamin supplement is generally recommended, with carefully timed administration, in patients on these agents.

Niacin/nicotinic acid Niacin inhibits the breakdown of fat in tissues. Niacin can cause flushing of skin and a sense of warmth, especially of face and upper body. This effect is seen more commonly at higher doses and when first started. Dizziness may occur, especially with sudden changes in posture. While niacin is generally considered the first choice of agents when HDL is also low, it may increase insulin resistance, so it is not a good choice for the PCOS patient.

Fibric Acid Derivatives Clofibrate (Atromid-S™) and Gemfibrozil (Lopid™). These agents lower triglycerides & VLDL by altering the breakdown of VLDL to LDL and decreasing the liver synthesis of VLDL. These agents may be most useful with elevated triglyceride levels. An increase in the risk of gall stone formation and muscle disease may occur. Commonly the taste of food is altered and annoying gastrointestinal side effects may occur.

HMG-CoA Reductase Inhibitor ("statins")

Cerivastatin-Baycol™	Pravastatin-Pravachol™
Lovastatin-Mevacor™	Fluvastatin-Lescol™
Simvastatin-Zocor™	Atorvastatin-Lipitor™

The HMG-CoA Reductase Inhibitors frequently referred to as
"statins," lower elevated total and LDL cholesterol by inhibiting the enzyme that promotes cholesterol formation.

It is now thought that pravastatin is also effective in reducing the "stickiness" of the vessel walls and likelihood of fat deposition on the vessel walls. While pravastatin is the first drug to get an FDA approval indication for this benefit, it is likely that the other statins will be found to provide the same benefit. Because the CYP3A4 pathway of the liver metabolizes them, drug interactions may occur with all of the statins, except pravastatin and fluvastatin. Muscle wasting may occur, especially in patients with liver disease or those who consume moderate or greater amounts of alcoholic beverages. Baseline liver function testing with regular monitoring of liver enzymes is recommended. Muscle pain, tenderness or weakness should be reported.

Can lipid-lowering agents be used while pregnant?

The short answer is no. Most who use these agents are past childbearing age, but with increasing awareness, more young individuals will become candidates for therapy. While usually withheld in both those pregnant and those trying to be pregnant, no studies have confirmed either risk or safety (FDA pregnancy category C) in the agents other than the "statins." Bile acid sequestrants are not absorbed systemically, niacin is a naturally occurring substance which should be acceptable in lower doses, and while clofibrate crosses the placenta, it is unlikely that the fetal metabolism is mature enough to be altered. However, statins (category X) cause skeletal deformities in animals and pose a definite risk in humans. For now it is probably better to be safe and not use these agents during pregnancy.

The hypertension component

Hypertension, high blood pressure, is a measurement of how hard the heart must work to circulate blood through (perfuse) the vascular bed. Hypertension is another one of the body's adaptation mechanisms. As the vessels become stiffer or narrow, blood pressure must increase to keep the flow going. Hypertension and elevated pulse rate place more strain on the heart, which itself may be having its own problems with blood supply.

Classification of Hypertension
- optimal 120/80
- mild 140-160/90-99
- moderate 160-179/100-109
- severe 180-209/110-119
- critical >210/120

For proper measurement, blood pressure should be taken using the appropriate size cuff; larger arms require larger cuff size and smaller arms a smaller cuff. If the examiner is struggling with the cuff, it may not be the appropriate size. If there is any deviation in normal, the pressure should be taken in both arms. The most accurate reading is after lying in a resting position for 20 minutes. There really is a "white coat" effect where some are hypertensive only in the physician's office. Hypertension which is sometimes up and at other times not is called *labile hypertension*.

What causes hypertension?

Every cell in the body needs energy, and in order to properly utilize that energy, it needs oxygen. The source of both energy and oxygen is the blood stream. Without adequate perfusion and the transfer of oxygen, tissues begin to die. Red blood cells are small dump trucks that load up with oxygen in the lungs and dump it out in the miles of capillaries scattered throughout the body. Foodstuffs are carried in the plasma, the non-cellular portion of the blood.

As the pipes start to clog with plaques, clots, etc., two mechanisms try to compensate for this increased resistance—increased blood pressure and increased pulse rate. The systolic pressure indicates how hard the push might be, while the diastolic tells of the resting pressure that must be present to keep up a "head of steam."

It is slightly more complicated than just increased resistance due to atherosclerosis. In fact, if atherosclerosis were all that there was to it, lower blood pressure would be detrimental. In fact in older patients, this may be the case because a higher blood pressure is needed for adequate perfusion. Blood vessels are under the control of the *autonomic nervous system*. Specifically the *sympathetic nerves* control the tone of the small muscles that encircle all arteries. This allows for *shunting* of blood to where it is most needed. When stress is perceived, muscles tighten and blood pressure rises. A good system when we are running from a wooly mammoth, not so good when we are listening to our boss. With stress our pulse rate and

The Central Role of Nitric Oxide
• *Decreases* smooth muscle proliferation
• *Inhibits* plasminogen activator (PA-1)
• *Reduces* platelet adhesion and clot formation
• *Decreases* lipid peroxidation, interaction with free-radical formation
• *Facilitates* muscle relaxation and vessel dilation

blood pressure increase. The same sympathetic alterations are seen with nicotine and to a lesser extent caffeine. Smoking has extremely serious consequences for cardiovascular health. As a consequence of atherosclerosis, there has been an increase in hypertrophy of the muscle, further increasing vessel tone and requiring higher perfusion pressure.

Hypertension is interrelated with insulin resistance. As many as 50% of hypertensive individuals are also insulin resistant and hypertension is associated with most cases of type 2 diabetes. Hyperinsulinemia increases muscle tone of the arterial wall. Hyperinsulinemia also results in sodium retention and therefore, fluid retention. With more fluid, the heart has a tougher pumping job. Insulin levels have a direct impact on increasing triglycerides and LDL cholesterol in the blood creating an atherogenic environment.

An active area of recent research has centered on nitric oxide (NO) as a major player in endothelial function. Insulin resistance has been suggested to be associated with a defect in nitric oxide production, although researchers have not fully worked out the mechanism.

As presented in Chapter 9, hyperinsulinemia predisposes one to accumulation of visceral fat, which then contributes to hyperinsulinemia. Stress has been shown to increase visceral fat in men . Obesity alone has a direct effect on hypertension by adding a large bed of blood vessels that must be kept supplied with blood.

Who's at risk?

After natural menopause, a woman's risk of heart disease gradually rises over a 10-year period. Before the age of 60, only one in 17 women will have a coronary event, whereas after age 60, one in four women will die of cardiovascular disease.

The good news is that many of the risk factors for cardiovascular disease are modifiable. For example, smoking represents a significant risk factor for myocardial infarction in women, even among those who are pre-menopausal. Smoking alone is thought to account for one-fifth of cardiovascular disease deaths. Smoking as few as one to four cigarettes a day doubles a woman's risk and smoking twenty or more cigarettes may double or quadruple it. Additionally, a woman who uses oral contraceptives and smokes heavily increases her risk of coronary artery disease up to 39 times. However, smoking cessation results in a rapid decline in risks within three to five years.

> **Cardiovascular Risk Factors**
> - Can't change
>   - Sex
>   - Race
>   - Age
>   - Genetic parents
> - Can change
>   - Stress and coping
>   - Nicotine
>   - Sedentary lifestyle
>   - Nutrition

Women who are overweight and those who have excess abdominal and upper body fat are at greater risk for developing CVD than slim women and those with excess weight on the hips and thighs. A desirable waist-to-hip ratio for middle-age women is <0.8. A desirable body mass index is <25. Research has shown that woman with a BMI of >29 had triple the risk of CVD when compared to women with a BMI of <21. Moderately overweight women (BMI of 25-28.9) had almost double the risk of CVD.

More than two alcoholic drinks per day increase the risk of death from CVD and other causes. The excessive alcohol consumption can also elevate blood pressure and increase the risk of breast cancer. But, there is evidence to suggest that low-to-moderate alcohol intake may reduce the risk of CVD.

Lab tests for CVD?

Obviously since CVD is such an important health risk, researches are trying to find markers that can predict the amount of vessel wall damage and extent of the disease, especially in asymptomatic individuals. Unfortunately, warning signs may be absent and the first sign of a problem is sometimes a heart attack. As described above, the inflammatory response mediates plaque formation and so inflammation should be a logical choice for a marker. The leading candidate has been high sensitivity C reactive protein (hs-CRP). hs-CRP appears to be closely related to endothelial cell damage. It has been suggested that hs-CRP added to total cholesterol-HDL ratio enables the most effective marker for risk of future MI. Others argue the test is no better than standard risk assessment: hs-CRP has a high correlation with obesity.

Other less successful candidates have included lipoprotein α, homocysteine, fibrinogen, and plasminogen activator antigen.

Pass the salt?

Salt (sodium chloride—NaCl) makes food taste good. To reduce the amount of salt in your diet is the same as using a diuretic. A reduction of sodium (Na) to 2.6 mg (100 mmol) reduces blood pressure an average of 6.3/2.2 mm Hg.

Dietary alterations should be considered before supplementation. Insuring that your diet contains adequate amounts of other salts may help control blood pressure. At least 90 mmol of potassium (K) is recommended. In part, this can be obtained through vegetables, but you might consider using the salt substitute that contains potassium instead of sodium when possible. Adequate calcium improves blood pressure control as well as reducing osteoporosis. If the guidelines for osteoporosis prevention are followed (see Chapter 14), calcium intake should be appropriate for control of hypertension. Supplementation of magnesium beyond dietary requirements is not recommended.

What are the treatment options?

The treatment and prevention of hypertension begins with, once again, lifestyle changes and the same ones previously promoted. Not to harp, but stop smoking, improve nutrition and increase activity. Once again, drug therapy isn't usually considered until at least a six month trial of adequate dietary therapy and increased physical activity has been attempted.

When drug therapy is needed, a bewildering array of antihypertensive agents is available; yet none are perfect. There's a catch. Drug studies have mostly been on men and older women. Significant gender differences may exist, both in drug action and side effect profile of antihypertensive agents. It is possible that after age 60 the effects may be similar, but under age 50, who knows?

The goals of hypertensive agents are either to reduce fluid, dilate vessels and decrease vascular resistance, or slow the heart; all with the same objective of reducing cardiac work load. The following represent the major classes of antihypertensives, each with a different action and a potential for side effects. Only a representative sample of drugs commonly used is given. Specialist referral should be considered if good results are not forthcoming.

- *Diuretics.* Diuretics cause the body to excrete water and salt. The most common diuretic is hydrochlorothiazide (HCTZ). Caution must be observed in diuretic usage because of possibility of electrolyte (salt) imbalance. Diuretics are inexpensive and usually considered first line therapy, but often are not potent enough to achieve the desired effects. Sometimes diuretics are combined with a second drug for their synergistic effects. Higher doses possibly worsen lipid profiles. These drugs may aid in treatment of osteoporosis. Adequate potassium intake is essential. Spironolactone (Aldactone™) may be a good option for a diuretic in PCOS. It is an anti-androgen and is used in the treatment of hirsutism.

- *beta ß-blockers.* ß-blockers block the effects of adrenaline and widening blood vessels, slowing pulse, and easing the heart's pumping action. In general, ß-blockers are often the first line of therapy for uncomplicated hypertension. Older agents like propanolol had more side effects than the newer more "selective" ß-blockers {atenolol (Tenormin™), bisoprolol (Zebeta™) metoprolol (Lopressor™)} One possible side effect may be lowering of libido and increased feelings of fatigue. More importantly, ß-blockers may worsen glucose tolerance and lipid profiles. There is an additive benefit of possible reduction in migraine occurrence. It's possible they might not be the best choice in PCOS, but this is still unknown.

A Note on Hypertension and Pregnancy

There is virtually no human data to suggest which antihypertensive agent is superior or even risky while a pregnancy is being attempted. My preference is not to use ß-blockers or calcium channel blockers. ß-Blockers has been shown to have adverse effects on early embryonic development and may cause fetal heart problems in later pregnancy. ACE inhibitors have been shown to cause fetal death in the last two trimesters, however, early pregnancy use may be safe? The long-standing drug of choice in pregnancy is Methyldopa (Aldomet™) which is a vasodilator. Chronic hypertension is an indication of a *high- risk* pregnancy

- *Angiotensin converting enzyme (ACE) inhibitors.* {captopril, benazepril (Lotensin™), quinapril (Acurpil™); fosinopril (Monopril™); linisopril (Zestril™). ACE inhibitors reduce the production of angiotensin, a chemical that causes arteries to constrict. The side effect of cough is possible and more common in women than men. They are clearly the drug of choice for those with type 2 diabetes and probably are a good choice for PCOS.
- *alpha α-Blockers* {doxazosin (Cardura™), prazosin (Minipress™) a-Blockers are vasodilators, that is they work by dilating blood vessels and decreasing peripheral resistance. The side effect can be postural hypotension, a feeling of faintness when moving from a sitting to standing position. They should be neutral to positive effects in glu-

cose and lipid metabolism and although usually not considered first line therapy, they are another good choice for PCOS.

- *Calcium channel blockers* (CCBs){diltiazem (Cardizem™ and others), verapamil (Calan™ and others), amlodipine (Norvasc™), nifedipine (Procardia™, Adalat™)} CCBs help decrease the contractions of the heart and widen blood vessels. In men, CCBs are associated with decreased sperm function. The effects of female fertility have not been studied in detail, but there are a number of calcium dependent events in reproduction, ovulation for one. Some of the possible side effects include ankle swelling, flushing, gum swelling and headache.

- *Others* There are a variety of older agents and combination agents that may be successful, but clear benefit should be shown over the above drugs.

Is hormone replacement therapy cardioprotective?

Here is another controversy (addressed as well in Chapter 14). Pick up most medical books and the value of HRT and the positive (cardioprotective) benefits of HRT on cardiovascular disease are stated unequivocally. Numerous observational studies have suggested that women using HRT may have much reduced risk of CVD. For instance, the Nurses Health study of 59,000 women found that the risk of major coronary artery disease was as much as 50% reduced in present estrogen alone (ERT) users and 40% in combination estrogen and progestin (HRT) users. The wind may be changing.

The Heart and Estrogen/Progestin Replacement (HERS) study looked at the risk of serious cardiovascular event in 2900 women with known CVD. Women who received HRT were more likely to have a coronary artery event in the first year of use (52% increase) over women receiving a placebo. However after 3 years, there were fewer events in the HRT groups than in the placebo group. The results of this study show that HRT should not be used to protect against heart attacks in women with known CVD. Additional data from their trial indicates those with elevated lipoprotein A had decreased risks on HRT while those with normal lipoprotein A have an increased risk. The protective effect of healthy women was not addressed. Studies from the recently completed Estrogen Replacement and Atherosclerosis (ERA) trial showed neither an improvement nor worsening of plaque build-up in postmenopausal women with preexisting coronary artery disease.

The Joslin Diabetes Center study of a small number of patients with diabetes showed that estrogen actually improved vascular function and that HRT should be considered in this group.

The most controversial findings to date have been the first reports out of the 27,000 participant Women's Health Initiative (WHI). During the first two years of HRT use women had more cardiovascular complications, heart attacks, strokes and blood clots than those using no medication. The incidence was still less than 1%. Caution was issued that it was too early to make recommendations. The longer life span of women results in more women dying of cardiovascular disease than men. Women also have poorer prognoses than men after a heart attack. As women pass menopause their risk for CVD increases and approaches that of men by age 70. That pre-menopausal women have such a lower risk of heart attacks has been taken as evidence of the cardioprotective effects of estrogen.

The cardioprotective effects of estrogen has been attributed to many factors including raising the ratio of the vascular dilator (prostacyclin) to the constrictor (thromboxane), lowering fibrinogen levels and the risk of clotting, endothelial function and nitric oxide production, improvement in insulin sensitivity, and alteration of lipid profile.

The lipid-lowering effects of ERT/HRT vary, not only among preparations but also among patients. Women whose LDL consists predominantly of large, buoyant particles may not experience as much beneficial effect on their lipid profiles with ERT/HRT as women whose LDL consists mainly of small, dense particles. Women with the latter pattern, however, are more likely to have worse lipid profiles and insulin resistance. ERT reduces LDL levels by about 15% and increases HDL by 15%. ERT/HRT may raise triglycerides as much as 25%. A woman who has triglycerides above 250 mg/dl or whose triglycerides rise to that level after starting ERT/HRT should be switched to transdermal hormone replacement, which does not elevate triglycerides as much. The progestins in HRT regimens may offset some of the beneficial effects of estrogen, especially elevation of HDL. The effect is less pronounced with hydroxyprogesterone derivatives than with the more androgenic progestins (norethindrone and levonorgestril). Micronized progesterone may at least offset estrogen's benefits.

So where does this leave the PCOS patient considering HRT? There are very many positive benefits to HRT, some neutral effects, and a few negative ones. Therapy must be individual and based on specific therapy goals. It can no longer be recommended that HRT be used for cardiac protection, but again, it seems that the PCOS patient may need it less than we originally thought.

How is insulin resistance related to metabolic syndrome?

Insulin resistance is more fully presented in Chapter 9. There is still much to learn about how insulin resistance develops and its consequences: however, in short, insulin resistance arises because insulin is simply not doing its job. It is probably not the fault of insulin itself, but the way the cells handle insulin and the signals that are sent out. Although insulin resistance is not considered a discrete disease it seems to have its tentacles attached to all components of the metabolic syndrome.

Skeletal muscle is a big user of energy and a prime target for insulin action. It's possible that the primary defect in insulin resistance is due to an isolated defect in insulin sensitivity and action in skeletal muscle. Increasing levels of insulin are produced to overcome this block. Other tissues, whether the ovary, blood vessels, or fat deposits, don't have the same problem as muscle. Nothing is wrong with their insulin metabolism, they are simply subjected to too much of a good thing. Insulin does more than regulate glucose homeostasis; it has profound effects on cell growth and function. After constant stimulation from high levels of insulin, each target tissue shows its wear in a different way and the effects of insulin resistance are multiplied.

There are at least two insulin-related factors at work in metabolic syndrome, insulin resistance and altered glucose regulation leading to hyperglycemia. Outright, it is known that hyperglycemia is associated with widespread organ damage. Kidneys, eyes, and peripheral circulation are a few of the targets. Insulin resistance also has a number of metabolic consequences outside glucose homeostasis. As described above, insulin has a direct action on the walls of blood vessels and may promote vascular disease. Insulin resistance alters fat metabolism and increases free fatty acid production in the face of already high lipid levels. Insulin also promotes formation of visceral fat, which worsens insulin resistance and stimulates even more fat accumulation.

Let's round it out with obesity.

Fat (adipose tissue) is an endocrine organ. Fat cells (adipocytes) have hormone receptors for response and make hormones, especially estrogen. "Metabolic fat" is largely stored in visceral tissue in and around the abdomen. Visceral fat is so closely related to metabolic syndrome that it becomes a cause rather than an effect of the metabolic changes. Visceral fat is more androgen-related, leading to the more typical "apple-shaped" habitus as opposed to the "pear-shaped" gynoid form. Reduction of fat stores (weight) by 10% can result in significant improvement in overall metabolic and endocrine parameters. It is not a matter of looking better, feeling better, or even overcoming infertility; it is a matter of self-preservation and extension of life expectancy.

Putting metabolic syndrome back together for PCOS.

What you see may not be what you get. Presently we are faced with a paradox in PCOS research. By all we hold to be true, the PCOS patient with increased visceral fat, dyslipidemia, elevated androgens, and insulin resistance should be metabolic syndrome personified. There should be increased incidence of hypertension and cardiovascular events. While the results are still preliminary, the risk of CVD appears to be much less than expected.

It is truly incredible that we know so little about the non-reproductive health risks of PCOS. Our knowledge is limited to speculation, several small research reports, and a couple of observational studies. There have been two major studies that lave looked at long-term follow up of women with PCOS. The first study by Dahlgren et al. surveyed the records of women in Goteborg, Sweden, who had ovarian wedge resections, or an ovary removed for PCOS 25-30 years before. Thirty-three of the 49 cases of PCOS agreed to answer a questionnaire. Twenty-one percent of the women subsequently had a hysterectomy compared to 7% in the control population. They found over 1/3 of the PCOS group had been treated for hypertension (39 versus 11%) and 15 versus 2.3% had been treated for diabetes. 85% of the respondents reported that at least one parent had diabetes, cardiovascular disease, or both. They estimated that myocardial infarction would be seven times more common than PCOS. This study has been referred to by virtually every author on PCOS since it was published in 1992. While an important contribution, it is very easy to see many flaws. First there were a very small number of women studied. All had PCOS severe enough to warrant ovarian surgery. Today, for better or worse, many patients would not have had surgery. After their surgery most had resumption of normal menses and many achieved a pregnancy. How does this compare to today's PCOS patient?

A large and well designed study of this issue was reported by Pierpoint et al. in 1998 where 786 British women diagnosed with PCOS between 1930 and 1979 were traced from hospital records of ovarian wedge resection and followed for 30 years. From a literature review of PCOS and its risk factors, they derived a theoretical risk of coronary artery heart disease of three times normal. There were 59 deaths from all causes; thirteen deaths were from breast cancer compared to an expected eight, indicating an increased risk. There were fifteen deaths from circulatory disease, 13 were from heart attacks, and only one from stroke. The rate of observed to expected deaths from circulatory disease was lowest in the 40-59 age group. It was expected that 1.7 women would die from diabetes, but on analysis six had diabetes listed as cause of death on their death certificates. Their conclusion states that "despite unfavorable risk factors... the risk of dying before age 75 is no higher than normal." The study suggested that the long periods of unopposed estrogen due to anovulatory cycles may have had a protective effect. It could also explain the increased risk of breast cancer. This study has received most of its criticism on the use of death certificates, which are notoriously unreliable. This group too had all had ovarian wedge resection, which could alter androgen levels, but it is not thought to change insulin resistance. Dr. Sarah Wild of this group has continued their research and still reports no increase in risk of death from cardiovascular disease. The update reports a two-fold increase in diabetes and a 3.4 fold increase in non-fatal stroke. Another bit of good news is that they have failed to confirm an increase in risk of breast cancer.

A preliminary report by Dr. Caren Solomon at the late 1999 American Heart Association meeting using the over one million strong Nurses' Health Study database reported that 4.3% of the women who reported irregular menses between ages 20 and 35 had a fatal or non fatal coronary disease event, a 50% increase over those with normal menses. This is the first study of this kind.

Mounting evidence is generally positive. Elevated androgens in PCOS do not appear to be related to thickness of the carotid wall and there appears to be normal endothelial function despite insulin resistance in healthy women with PCOS. There have been several reports of increased levels of plasminogen activator system, which is correlated with increasing risk of blood clots. Contrary to this, it appears that women with PCOS have higher levels of vascular endothelial growth factor (VEGF) which is associated with improved vascular perfusion and endothelial cell health. Increased levels of VEGF have been proposed as the protective mechanism in PCOS against cardiovascular disease. It may be ironic that the same factor that caused the increased risk of ovarian hyperstimulation syndrome with fertility drugs will be cardioprotective. The most important work is still to come. It will be the study of many of you who are reading the book. With our new awareness and sensitivity about the many facets of PCOS, I wonder what the future holds. Hopefully, some good news.

Because a reprieve has been granted this does not mean to relax. CVD is still the number one cause of death in both women and men. Because your risk may not be as high as expected, this does not mean that it is low; nobody's is. We still don't know about PCOS.

GALLBLADDER DISEASE

Who's at risk and how much?

Between 10 and 20 percent of all adults over age 40 have gallstones. Women are at an increased risk because estrogen stimulates the liver to remove more cholesterol from blood and divert it into bile. Increased risk of gallstone formation has been observed in women who take oral contraceptives and in those taking estrogen replacement therapy and during pregnancy. In medical school we learn the five "F's"as risk factors for gallbladder disease—female, fat, forty, fair and fertile. Although the incidence of gallbladder disease in PCOS is unknown, I expect it is quite high. It seems that about one in five women with PCOS that I see have had their gallbladder removed. Most of these are women under age 35—some are under age 25. It would seem the greatest risk factor is obesity.

Research suggests that gallstones are more likely to develop in those who are obese and who consume a diet high in saturated fats and refined sugars. "YO YO" dieting increases the risk for gallstones. Gallstone formation does not correlate with overall cholesterol levels, but persons with low HDL cholesterol levels or high triglyceride levels are at increased risk. Gallbladder disease may progress more rapidly in patients with diabetes.

How is GB disease diagnosed and treated?

Diagnosing gallstones often presents a challenge because it may be difficult to determine if the abdominal pain is caused by stones or some other condition. Gallbladder pain is most common after a fat-filled or spicy meal. Ultrasound or other imaging techniques easily find gallstones. However, because gallstones are common and most cause no symptoms, finding stones does not necessarily explain pain.

Most surgeons remove the gallbladder if there is pain and stones. Gallbladder removal (cholecystectomy) is increasingly performed laparoscopically as outpatient surgery. The recovery time is short, but there can be the lasting effects of fat intolerance.

To reduce the risk of gallstones, one should maintain a normal weight and avoid fasting. Exercising regularly and vigorously may reduce the risk of gallstones and gall bladder disease. Some researchers believe that in addition to controlling weight, exercise helps normalize blood sugar levels and insulin levels, which, if abnormal, may contribute to gallstones.

DEPRESSION

Who's depressed?

If it didn't rain we would not appreciate sunshine. None escape the "blues." The periodic lowness that we all feel is a necessary time of recharging our emotional batteries. The word depression is unfortunate because it can imply anything from a momentary disappointment to a disease state that warrants immediate medical intervention. The seriousness of depression depends on its recurrence, time course, severity and alteration in capacity to go about everyday activities. True clinical depression is usually an easy diagnosis to make and immediate medical intervention is warranted. There is a large gray zone that encompasses situation depression, depression as a personality trait that is difficult for all involved to know how to proceed.

Depression is commonly associated with any chronic medical problem, and unfortunately, with many of the medications we use to treat chronic illness. Thyroid and adrenal disease can cause depression. In fact, these diseases may even be misdiagnosed as depression and go undetected. A number of studies have associated low cholesterol and high triglyceride levels with depression, although it is not clear whether these factors or accompanying health problems reduce spirits. One study reported that nearly half of people with chronic tension headaches met criteria for either anxiety or depression; it wasn't clear whether the psychological disorder preceded or followed the onset of headaches. Some experts believe that a syndrome of migraine headaches, anxiety, and depression, which occurs in some people, is caused by a single genetic defect that regulates dopamine – a chemical messenger in the brain.

Medications linked to depression include at least some of the drugs used for pain relief, cholesterol lowering, hypertension and heart problems, and bronchodilators. It is essential that a thorough medical history is taken with special attention to medications used.

Is being female a risk factor for depression?

Most studies indicate that depressive disorders are at least twice as likely to affect women as men. Although largely unsubstantiated, it has been suggested that girls with early puberty are more prone to experience depression during adolescence. Married women with children have a higher risk for depression than do married childless women, single women, or single or married men. Isolation at home or a job that fails to provide social support creates an environment favorable to depression.

It is unclear as to the reason for the sexual difference in depression. All sorts of theories abound. Some believe depression is due to a greater role overload and role conflict, higher rates of victimization, childhood socialization patterns that support their internalization of stress, and a greater tendency toward negative self-evaluation. Others contend that there is a neurobiologic and hormonal basis for the difference.

While I would not fully dismiss the former, I believe that hormones and the cyclic changes, daily, monthly and throughout the reproductive life cycle, have a major affect on mood. Those with a tendency toward depression are particularly vulnerable during these times. Major hormonal shifts occur after delivering a baby and after miscarriage.

What about PMS?

I once saw a cartoon of a woman sitting on the exam table holding a smoking gun. The caption read "my gynecologist didn't believe I had PMS, so I shot him." First of all, there is no argument from me, PMS (*premenstrual syndrome*) is real. A diagnosis of PMS requires that the symptoms start 5 to14 days before a period and—most importantly for the diagnosis—that they resolve within a couple of days after menses. The most common symptoms include depression, anxiety, emotional liability, tension, irritability, anger, and sleep and appetite disturbances. The emotional symptoms are often coupled with physical symptoms of headache and fluid retention. We know it's hormonal, but we don't know what causes PMS or how to treat it. There is a long list of therapies for PMS including progesterone, oral contraceptive, GnRH analogs, diuretics, calcium supplements, exercise, massage, and herbal preparations. None seem to work for all, while all seem to work for some.

A common complaint is "I have PCOS, infrequent periods, and horrible PMS." This is quite possible. Many with PCOS report almost a constant PMS. Most likely this is an interrelated combination of hormones and fluid retention. It is one of several reasons that regular menses are important.

Depression as an illness

It is not a question but it is a fact: depression is an illness. There should be no stigma, just understanding and treatment. Severity, duration, and the presence of other symptoms are the factors that distinguish normal sadness from a depressive disorder. Depressive disorders can begin at any age, but they most commonly begin in the 20s and 30s.

In major depression, at least five of the symptoms listed below must occur for a period of at least two weeks, and they must represent a change from previous behavior or mood. Depressed mood or loss of interest must be present. Alcohol and drug use must be excluded.

- Depressed mood on most days for most of each day.
- Total or very noticeable loss of pleasure most of the time.
- Significant increase or decrease in appetite, weight, or both.
- Sleep disorders – insomnia or excessive sleepiness most days.
- Feelings of agitation or a sense of intense slowness.
- Loss of energy and a daily sense of tiredness.
- Sense of guilt and worthlessness nearly all the time.
- Inability to concentrate occurring nearly every day.
- Recurrent thoughts of death or suicide.

How is depression treated?

It's very hard not to give a mixed message here. I do not believe the treatment for what most patients call depression comes in a brown pill bottle; on the other hand, in severe depression, this pill bottle is exactly what is needed. Major depressive illness should be treated by or at least after consultation with a psychiatrist.

Situational depression should be self-limiting, resolving in several weeks to several months. If there has been a death, whether a grandparent or an embryo, it is normal and necessary to grieve. During the recovery period a supportive environment that may include professional counseling can sometimes ease and speed the recovery.

In the absence of the signs of serious depression listed earlier, I will venture another suggestion. Many individuals are both private and like to feel in control. A personal reassessment may be in order and action to include a change in environment, diet and activity taken. Some have suggested that exercise can be as good as psychotherapy. Alteration in eating patterns and foods can also have a significant effect on the sense of well-being. If this plan is not working, ask for help; this is also a sign that you are in control.

Between major clinical depression and situation depression, there still remains a considerable middle ground. Unfortunately, some of the tendency for depression is genetic and cannot be cured, but it can be successfully managed. I have the fortunate association with a talented psychologist whom I rely on to help both my patients and me. Sometimes intervention might involve prescription medications and sometimes not. Individuals who feel that they need antidepressant medications will not have to look far for a physician willing to prescribe them. They are relatively safe and sometimes they work exceedingly well and sometimes they don't. They work better when given under continued supervision of a mental health professional. The objective of treatment is not improvement of symptoms, but full remission. This can be an easily accomplished mission for some and a life-long battle for others.

SO, is depression more common in PCOS?

Given the concerns listed in this book to this point, all PCOS patients have a right to be depressed. Is this so? Of course not. Is there a greater chance of depression or other psychiatric problems among those with PCOS? This is not known, but an increase is clearly not obvious in my long-term dealings with PCOS .

A questionnaire to be used by health care providers that has been-specifically designed to address quality of life for women with PCOS has been designed by Cronin et al.

MIGRAINE HEADACHE

For some a headache is almost a daily occurrence; for others it's a rare event, but few of us truly escape this misery. There are basically three types of headaches: tension, sinus, and migraine. If you want to add a fourth it could be a combination of any, or all. The tension headache, also called a frontal-occipital headache, is of muscular origin. The pain is usually constant. Tension headaches usually respond to a couple of aspirin or Tylenol™, possibly a neck rub, and getting out of the environment that is causing it. Sinus headaches are characterized by the feeling of fullness and association with other signs of allergies. Treatment is by decongestants and antihistamines. The migraine headache stands above all others and is important here because of its close association with hormonal status.

What is a migraine?

Migraines are the most common type of vascular headache. They are generally described as severe pain on one or both sides of the head, an upset stomach, and occasionally problems with vision. The two most common types of migraine caused headache are classic and common. The primary distinction between the two types is the appearance of neurological symptoms 10 to 30 minutes before a classic migraine attack. The person may see flashing lights or zigzag lines, or may temporarily lose vision. Other classic symptoms include speech difficulty, weakness of an arm or leg, tingling of the face or hands, and confusion.

The pain of a classic migraine headache, which can last from one to two days, is intense. Most sufferers describe the pain as a throbbing or pounding that is felt in the forehead, temple, ear, jaw, or around the eye. A classic migraine begins on one side of the head but may eventually spread to the other side. Contrastly, during the headache phase of a common migraine, a person may have diarrhea and increased urination, as well as nausea and vomiting. Common migraine pain can last three or four days.

What triggers a migraine headache?

Many factors can trigger migraines, and identifying them is an important component of patient assessment. These factors may be environmental, behavioral, dietary, pharmacologic, or physiologic. Additionally, people who suffer from migraines may have an inherited susceptibility to headaches. Headache diaries can be used to identify migraine triggers, a potential relationship with the menstrual cycle, and assist in diagnosis and management. The headache diary should contain the following information:

- Date and time of migraine.
- Date of onset and duration of menses.
- Dietary intake.
- All medications, including oral contraceptives, herbal preparations, and vitamins.
- Lifestyle factors (stress, exercise, amount of sleep).

It is useful to keep the diary for at least three months so that patterns and initiating factors can be identified. You may find, for example, that you are among those who experience migraines triggered by certain foods. Some common triggers for some (but not all) migraine sufferers include chocolate, coffee, caffeine containing soda, spinach, onions, beans, cabbage, tomatoes, citrus fruits, licorice, avocados, alcohol, cheddar cheese, eggs, red meats, fatty fried foods, seafood, home-bade bread, pastry or pasta (what's in the flour?), sodium nitrate in cold cuts, foods with monosodium glutamate(MSG), Others may find that certain activities (exercise, constrictive clothing) or environmental issues (noise, weather) trigger migraines, while still others may find causes related to physical changes in their skeleton or muscles, etc.

How are hormones related to migraines?

Although both sexes are affected by migraines, the condition is much more prevalent in adult women. In fact, about three times as many women as men have migraines, and this holds true throughout the world and in every culture. Most migraines in women develop during the hormonally active years between menarche and menopause. It is often not the hormone itself, but fluctuations of estrogen and progesterone that seem to trigger the headache. About half of women with migraines report headaches associated with their menstrual cycle, although true menstrual migraines may be less common. The relationship between female hormones and migraine is still unclear.

Migraines that regularly and predictably occur in close proximity to the onset of menstruation are termed menstrual migraines. Menstrual migraines can be subclassified as true menstrual migraines or menstruation-associated migraines. A true menstrual migraine is usually defined as migraine (without aura) that always occurs in the perimenstrual period and at no other time. True menstrual migraines occur most frequently on the first day of menses, unlike PMS headaches, which generally resolve with the onset of menses. Like true menstrual migraines, menstruation-associated migraines occur perimenstrually. Women suffering from menstruation-associated migraines also experience migraines at other times of the month. However, the menstruation-associated migraine usually lasts longer, is more difficult to treat, and is more debilitating than a migraine unrelated to the onset of menses.

Late luteal fall in estrogen levels is the primary trigger for migraine associated with menstruation. There is no evidence to indicate, however, that migraine associated with menstruation is due to abnormal or aberrant hormone levels. Rather, the problem is the response of the central nervous system to normal fluctuations in hormone levels.

Many PCOS patients report migraine syndrome, but I know of no studies that have looked at the relationship directly.

How are migraines treated?

Migraines have probably been around for a long time and our treatment strategies have improved. During the Stone Age, pieces of a headache sufferer's skull were cut away with flint instruments to relieve pain. Native Americans used to drive cow horns into the skulls to let out the evil spirits. Many suffers have probably thought about self-administering one of these therapies during an attack.

Today drug therapy, biofeedback training, stress reduction, and elimination of certain foods from the diet are the most common methods of preventing and controlling migraine and other vascular headaches. It is also believed that regular exercise can lessen the severity and recurrence of migraines.

There are two options when making a decision of how to treat migraines using drug therapy. A patient can use drugs intended to prevent the headaches, or drugs to relieve the pain. It is important to remember that treatment of menstrual migraines can be very difficult and standard migraine medications may be inadequate to control them.

Ergotamine tartrate is an older drug and has been commonly used. It is a vasoconstrictor that helps counteract the painful dilation stage of the headache. It's interesting that this is the same drug that has been used in the past to treat hot flashes of the peri-menopause. For optimal benefit, the drug is taken during the early stages of an attack. If a migraine has been in progress for about an hour and has passed into the final throbbing stage, ergotamine tartrate will probably not help.

Monamine oxidase inhibitors (MAOI) may help prevent migraines. These drugs block the enzyme called monoamine oxidase which normally helps nerve cells absorb the artery-constricting brain chemical serotonin. Several drugs for the prevention of migraine have been developed in recent years, including drugs that mimic the action of a key brain chemical called serotonin, serotonin agonists. Prompt administration of these drugs is important. MAOIs have a long list of drug interactions and you should inform your physician and pharmacist about MAOI use with each new prescription.

"Triptans" act on serotonin receptors in the brain. Sumatriptan was the first drug specifically developed for use against migraine. More recent oral triptans include zolmitriptan, naratriptan, rizatriptan, eletriptan, avitriptan, frovatriptan, and almotriptan. Triptans are structurally related to serotonin and cause blood vessels to narrow. These drugs have become the mainstay of current therapy and are the ones you will most likely see advertised.

A small percentage of migraine sufferers will benefit from a treatment program focused solely on eliminating headache-provoking foods and beverages. Other migraine patients may be helped by a diet to prevent low blood sugar. Low blood sugar, or hypoglycemia, can cause dilation of the blood vessels in the head. This condition can occur after a period without food.

OTHER POSSIBILITIES

PCOS and epilepsy?

Epilepsy has been associated with menstrual cycle disturbance in several studies, as has obesity. Whether these individuals have enough of the clinical findings to make the diagnosis of PCOS is unclear. Drugs used in treatment of epilepsy can alter prolactin levels and this may be one source of the menstrual cycle disturbance.

Does valproic acid cause PCOS?

This is a debated issue. More studies support valproic acid (Depakote™—a drug commonly used to control seizures) as a causative factor of PCOS than refute it. While valproic acid is a useful drug, individuals using valproic acid should be aware of its association with menstrual cycle disturbance. If symptoms of PCOS develop, or worsen, an alternative medication may be in order.

Autoimmune disease

PCOS is clearly a disorder of the endocrine and probably nervous system. It would be a short leap to associate PCOS with alterations in the third of the body's communication systems, the immune system. Certainly steroid hormones have an effect on the immune system, but this is highly variable among individuals. Research studies have reported very mixed results. Certainly, any stressor like PCOS *could* have an impact on immune function. Conditions known to have an immunological basis include, Crohn's disease/ulcerative colitis, rheumatoid arthritis, lupus, most thyroid disease, and others. Scattered reports show an improvement of arthritis with hormonal supplementation and a possible deterioration of lupus. Glucocorticoid use to treat autoimmune conditions can clearly worsen osteoporosis. Bone densitometry is suggested on all women who have repeated long-term use.

Despite a very rare attempt, the issue of PCOS and altered immune response has not been addressed and is needed. I wouldn't even hazard a guess on what the results of a study would be. It would be easy to offer a sound scientific basis whatever the outcome.

Asthma

The effects of hormones on asthma are unclear. It is possible that estrogen can worsen asthma.

Liver and kidney disease

It is unlikely that disorders of the liver and kidneys are directly related to PCOS. Since the liver and kidney are the primary organs that clear drugs from the body, their preexisting disease and alteration of function is important.

Chronic fatigue syndrome and fibromyalgia

I believe that both of these disorders are very real, but their etiology remains illusive. It is possible that they could be more common in women with PCOS, but proof is lacking.

The bottom line

No body system or disease process is immune from the effects of hormones, and therefore could be a target for PCOS. Studies on the effects of hormones fall into two categories, those that separate males from females and those that involve various hormonal supplementations, such as oral contraceptives or hormone replacement. A part of the role of a medical care provider is as a medical detective. Because there is as yet so little known with absolute certainty and so much to learn about PCOS, physicians should keep their eyes open to various disease associations.

From Surviving to Thriving! Becoming Your Own Advocate

With Luann Johnson[1]

Lisa, one of our patients, is a woman who is not only surviving PCOS but is thriving! Her story begins like many others. At puberty, Lisa and her mother realized something was amiss with her periods, and the long journey from doctor to doctor—including prescriptions for birth control pills—began at age 13. Lisa acquired symptoms of weight gain, hair growth, and hot flushes along the way. By the time she was 21, after many tests, Lisa's collection of symptoms was finally given a name—Stein Leventhal syndrome. But naming the symptoms did nothing to relieve them. Lisa read what little she could find and after awhile began to accept that this condition was a part of who she was (and is).

But Lisa knows something that it takes many PCOS patients a long time to learn: while PCOS is a part of her life, it is not all of her life. PCOS is not who Lisa is as a person, but it has helped to shape her as a person. Living with PCOS has taught Lisa many things that she is graciously sharing with you through this book....

Lisa is devoutly religious and her faith and trust in

[1] Luann Johnson, B.S., is the Patient Advocate at the Center for Applied Reproductive Science in Johnson City, Tennessee. Before joining the Center, she worked as a microbiologist in research and industry. She has been an infertility patient and has many years of experience as a volunteer infertility support group leader. She now serves in a professional capacity to help maximize the Center's responsiveness to individual patient's needs. She serves as a liaison between the patient and the clinical staff, supplementing education and emotional support as well as smoothing out any "rough spots" patients may encounter along the way. She also represents patient interests on advocacy issues at the local, state, and national levels.

God is the basis for all aspects of her life, including PCOS. Lisa believes that God has never made a mistake and certainly He did not err in allowing her to have this condition known as PCOS. She strongly believes in prayer, and her prayer about her PCOS has led her to help others to find a place for PCOS and leave it in its place. With an approach like this, Lisa finds that the more she concentrates on other aspects of her life and especially in helping others, PCOS finds the proper place to occupy.

Lisa has been luckier than some PCOS patients because her parents, husband, family, and friends have been extremely encouraging. Not everyone is fortunate to have such support. Very often PCOS patients have to create their own support. Lisa knows that knowledge is the key here. Lisa has come to believe that it was up to her to help others understand just as she was trying to understand and to share what she knew with those she was closest to. Lisa had to ask questions of others as well as let them question her. She came to understand that remarks that hurt or offended her came from ignorance. She decided that she would do her part to correct this ignorance with knowledge.

After finding a doctor who would work with her and take her condition seriously, Lisa knew it was up to her to take the steps necessary to assure good health and quality of life. Her doctor could recommend, but it was up to Lisa herself to do it. She takes her medication, keeps all of her follow up appointments for monitoring, exercises, and has adopted a healthy eating plan. She knows that these steps will help her to enjoy a long, full life, regardless of achieving a pregnancy, regardless of developing diabetes, regardless of PCOS. Lisa knows that she has only one chance at this life!

Looking at her own experience, Lisa observes, "Yes, PCOS is a condition that is a part of your life but it is not your entire life. Concentrate on all that life has to offer you and all that you have to offer others. Life is to live to the fullest, so don't just survive—THRIVE!"

For now, we cannot cure PCOS, but with proper evaluation, therapy, education and support many may move from infertility to a successful pregnancy, from a situation of poor metabolism and increased risks of serious disease to one of better quality of life and longevity. That's what this chapter is all about.

How can I feel more "in control" of my PCOS?

Symptoms of PCOS may appear to control a woman, but it should be the other way around! Some women with PCOS say they feel their bodies and indeed their lives are controlled by their hormonal imbalance. If they are successful in getting one area in line, it seems that another area soon falls out. Women with PCOS need to find ways to feel more "in charge" of their bodies, and they can.

It's true that symptoms of PCOS can have a negative effect on feminine identity. It's hard to hide obesity, in a culture obsessed with thinness. It's not socially acceptable for women to have facial hair, so women may do everything they can to hide the condition, even from a supportive spouse. Blemishes or acne are considered an adolescent problem, and some women with this condition are made to feel "dirty." Even dermatologists and skin care experts do not fully understand the hormonal connection and that costly treatment for hair and skin problems can be in vain without addressing the root of the problem—high androgen levels.

In order to "take charge," women must first understand that, despite the tendency to isolate oneself with "embarrassing" visible symptoms such as hair, skin, or weight problems, these are very common among PCOS patients. You are not alone in your frustration. Secondly, women must educate themselves about treatment options available before making decisions about which path to take. Gain knowledge by visiting related Web sites, reading books, magazine and medical journal articles about symptoms, asking your doctor, or participating in a support group for women with PCOS. Third, understand that treatments available for the most visible symptoms of PCOS are not permanent, but are ongoing, and the need to repeat them may depend on your commitment to following instructions and guidelines. Finally, since some treatments for non-life threatening symptoms of PCOS are not covered by insurance, consider the expense and effectiveness of each treatment before investing in that option. In the meantime, or until treatments are effective for you, there is no reason to be ashamed. Use the tips which follow in this chapter to do the best you can to maintain control over the condition and take the time to accentuate your best features. Remember that you are probably more aware of and sensitive to the cosmetic symptoms of your PCOS than others around you are. Insulin resistance is another matter entirely. This side effect of PCOS is a serious condition. Once it appears, it will probably be a lifelong struggle. Gaining control of this condition involves adhering to a carefully managed food plan (a diet focused on enhancing health rather than weight reduction), exercise, and possibly medication. Lifestyle changes are never easy, especially if one has established unhealthy behaviors over long years. Poor dietary habits and avoidance of exercise are common in our society. These tendencies can be dangerous for a woman with PCOS.

While it is tempting to try to ignore insulin resistance, this is not a good option. Many women just think their bodies are betraying them or that they are just in poor health. However, ignoring or leaving PCOS untreated can result in more serious conditions such as endometrial cancer, diabetes, obesity, heart disease or infertility. Sadly, because information about PCOS was so scarce, until very recently many women ignored their condition because they did not know they should be paying attention to the symptoms which appeared to be unrelated. Having read this book, perhaps you are now aware for the first time of the very scary consequences that can accompany unmanaged, uncontrolled PCOS. Ignoring the symptoms of PCOS is just a plain bad idea. The physical costs of PCOS are high, and only through the earliest possible awareness can they be decreased. Women with PCOS must seek treatment before the costs become too high. Taking charge of this aspect of your life can be the key to the success of your treatment for other conditions, including infertility. So listen to your doctor and follow treatment guidelines to make the changes necessary. Improving your diet and beginning an exercise program can be one of the best things you can do for yourself—you will feel better physically and mentally within days! The feeling of being "out of control" is one of the most frustrating parts of dealing with any chronic medical condition and PCOS *is* a chronic health problem. Establishing a plan with your doctor (Chapter 6) is one of the most important ways that patients (and their partners) can feel more in control of their bodies and their lives. Plans can be periodically examined and adjusted if necessary. This plan should include an open and frank discussion about your personal resources—the time, the money, the physical resources, and the emotional energy that you bring to the treatment of your PCOS.

Budgeting the "Real" Costs in a Plan

More and more people are coming to recognize that making any long range plan involving personal lives—for family, housing dreams, a vacation, retirement—demands budgeting resources. PCOS, infertility, or any other long-term health issue requires this kind of multi-resource budgeting, too. Budgeting resources determines the type, the number, and the length of treatment options that are available to you. The "real" costs of dealing with PCOS involves building such a budget: evaluating and allocating our limited reserves of money, time, physical capacity and emotional energy.

What Are Your Resources?
• Money
• Time
• Physical capacity
• Emotional energy

Budgeting Money

Treatment for PCOS can become very expensive. It's important that you determine for yourself what treatments are imperative and what are elective. While treatment for insulin resistance would not be considered elective, treatment for hair, skin and obesity-related symptoms might be. Treatment may not be covered by insurance. In those cases, women must make individual decisions about spending money out of pocket for therapy. Women experiencing strongly negative self image issues with their symptoms may consider finding funding for these treatment high on their list of priorities, while others may feel that they can "live with" these symptoms. For some women having a child genetically related to themselves and their partner is of such importance that

they are willing to go into serious debt attempting to conceive, while for other
women becoming a parent is the goal and they prefer to forego more expensive infertility treatments and invest their limited monetary resources in adopting a child. Once you have set your own priorities concerning treatment, you
can begin to explore where the money for those treatments will come from.
To what extent are the treatments you are considering time-limited expenses
and what will be long-term, ongoing expenses? Part of your plan must involve
trying to predict, from the outset, what the financial impact of your treatment
will be and what options you have to assist you with these expenses. How
much coverage, if any, is available through health insurance? How much
money will need to come from savings or from loans? Do you anticipate that
most expenses will be in the area of diagnostic procedures or from medication? What about lab charges to cover drug monitoring? It is entirely proper to
ask any care provider quite directly about the costs of his services. Will your
doctor require you to pay as you go if your insurance does not cover? Are there
sliding fee scales or payment plans available?

Budgeting Time

Treatment for chronic medical issues involves a tremendous investment of time: time off from work or school for appointments, time undergoing treatment, or time waiting for results. In short, you should understand that
time spent on treatment is time spent NOT doing something else. How will
this affect the time demands from the other areas of your life? How might the
stress and pressure of spending this time away from other needed or desired
activities affect you emotionally and impact your important relationships with
others? It is important to factor in this "opportunity cost." Patients pursuing
treatment for PCOS should have a time frame for that treatment which may
be symptom specific. For example, patients being evaluated for hirsutism may
have treatments in block visits for hair removal. Periodic touch up visits may
be required. Insulin resistant patients on metformin therapy may have visits
every four to six weeks for laboratory blood work to measure fasting insulin,
glucose tolerance, or other hormone levels. Patients undergoing weight loss
therapy will need follow up appointments at regular intervals for diet and nutritional assessment. Infertility therapy will follow a particular regimen for a limited number of menstrual cycles before reevaluating its likely success and looking at other treatment or family planning options. Consult with your doctor
about the number of months of treatment you will undergo before moving on,
either to another protocol, another drug regimen, or stopping entirely. Once
you establish what you are willing and able to do, it is easier to make decisions.
As you progress through treatment, reevaluate your plan as necessary. It is
important that you not feel pushed or rushed into any treatment timetable.
Take time to make decisions. Take time to educate yourself about new medications or protocols. Take time off from doing anything if you need to
regroup.

Assessing Physical Capacity

Many women go to their physicians expecting a "cure all" pill for
PCOS. Clearly this is unrealistic. Since PCOS is a group of related conditions

and affects many parts of the body, treatment will probably involve several "layers" of lifestyle changes. Of all the things you can do for yourself, healthy eating and exercise are probably the most important for gaining control of PCOS. Establish eating and exercise plans that are realistic and can result in lifelong changes. Do not have unrealistic expectations of yourself. You may never attain your ideal weight, but you can become healthier and decrease the negative effects of PCOS on your body. There's just so far that our bodies can go in "changing" or in responding to various treatments. PCOS takes a physical toll, one that is too often unacknowledged by physicians eager to "fix" the problem. Yet, a woman's investment of time, money and emotional energy are sometimes limited primarily by her physical capacity. Although PCOS can deplete physical energy, you have the ability to build up your physical resources. This can be accomplished through both physical and psychological means. The "wellness" perspective incorporates both the mind and the body in attempting to build a healthier self. All women, and especially women with PCOS, can benefit from establishing an ongoing, personalized wellness plan. Healthful eating and a consistent exercise program, described in chapters 8 and 10, are important components of wellness. Freedom from addictions, such as smoking, alcohol, and even caffeine, is another critical goal. Making time for regular, meaningful contact with friends and family—something psychologists term "enhancing social support"—has also been shown to produce physical benefit. Support groups, for example, have been demonstrated to lengthen the lives of terminally-ill patients. Daily relaxation rituals have numerous health benefits, including enhancing sleep quality, improving cardiovascular functioning, building up the immune system, and decreasing chronic pain. Many different types of relaxation strategies can be effective, including progressive muscle relaxation, deep breathing, meditation, or imagery. Finally, a strong spiritual commitment, described later in this chapter, has been linked to fewer medical problems.

The Emotional Budget

Your greatest investment may not be in time, money, or physical capacity, but in emotional commitment. The body image issues, the ups and downs of treatment successes and failures, the impact on relationships, and the sometimes overwhelming nature of being "a patient" take a toll on emotional reserves. Examine your source of emotional support and comfort. Will your support come from a partner? A close friend or relative? If neither of these sources of support is available to you, now may be a good time to explore whether there is a support group available in your area or to join one of the growing number of Internet discussion groups for women with PCOS and women with infertility. Expect feelings during treatment to range from the ultimate highs to the deepest lows. There may be tremendous relief and happiness over finally having a name for your condition and a plan to deal with it. At the same time, there are often feelings of sorrow in identifying oneself as having a chronic condition, fear and loss about not being able to conceive a child, disbelief at the many physical changes occurring in your body, or anger over a body that is out of control and not doing what it is "supposed" to do. Finally it's tough to acknowledge that there is, at present, no cure for PCOS, so dealing with the manifestation of symptoms will be a lifelong battle. Do not expect too much of yourself! How will you validate these feelings? If your treatment is unsuccessful or if you decide to discontinue treatment, who will be disappointed? How will you deal with any regrets that may arise? What is the most difficult part about your struggle? Is it body image or self-esteem (Chapter 10)? Do you feel somehow defective or abnormal? Acknowledging the way you feel will help you to navigate any rough waters you encounter in your treatment. Finding, nurturing, and using sources of support will be discussed at greater length in sections to follow, but in considering emotions as a budgetable item, it's important to realize that emotional energy is one of the few resources with the potential to be renewable when effective support is available. Support sources already in place may include family members, close friends, a spouse or partner. There are additional sources of emotional support for those who are willing to reach out to face-to-face support groups, Internet support boards and listservs, a religious community, a mental health professional, or some combination of these. (See Chapter 18). Those dealing with chronic medical conditions such as PCOS are at higher risk for depression than the average woman. Finding and using appropriate emotional reservoirs can go far toward preventing this difficult "side effect."

What can I do to help myself?

Be an informed and aware consumer of PCOS medical care! Until recently, there has been little information available to the public on PCOS. The book you are holding now, if not the very first, is one of the first handful of books ever written for consumers on the subject of polycystic ovarian syndrome. Increasingly, media outlets such as women's magazines or news programs are offering articles or segments on the disease. Women will often read the article or see the program and express relief saying, "That's me! That's what I have!" These women are thrilled that there is a name for the disorder that has wreaked havoc on their lives for years. Often a woman will bring an article in and ask her doctor if he/she has seen it. Because the medical community has become more knowledgeable of the ramifications of PCOS, chances are that her primary care physician may have at least a nodding acquaintance with new thinking about PCOS through professional journals, meetings, etc.

Should I "just relax?"

Certainly well meaning but uninformed family and friends often recommend relaxing as a "treatment" for various medical problems! While relaxing isn't enough, there is some evidence among researchers that relieving stress can go a long way toward alleviating some symptoms associated with PCOS. We are learning more and more about the role that stress can play in complicating various medical conditions. For example, Dr. Alice Domar, the director of the Mind/Body Center for Women's Health at the Mind/Body Medical Institute at Harvard Medical School has done extensive research with the role of stress reduction and relaxation techniques on the success rates of women undergoing infertility treatment. The results are striking. In her two books—*Healing Mind, Healthy Body* and *Self-Nurture: Learning to Care for Yourself as Effectively as You Care for Everyone Else*, Dr. Domar provides practical strategies for reducing stress through exercise and increased physical activity, prayer, meditation (including using tapes, Yoga, Qi Gong and T'ai Chi), self affirmation, restructuring destructive thought, guided imagery, managing one's diet, time management, and receiving adequate amounts of sleep each night. However, even with increased awareness, better diagnosis and treatment options, living with PCOS can still be an ordeal. There have been very few scientific evaluations done in this area. However, one study by Dr. Lisa Cronin et al. published in *The Journal of Clinical Endocrinology and Metabolism* (83: 1976, 1998) measured the quality of life of PCOS patients ages eighteen to forty-five. Domains of weight, menstrual problems, body hair, infertility, and mood swings were studied. The respondents were concerned about being overweight and expressed difficulty with remaining at the ideal weight. They noted frustration at not being able to lose weight. Many reported increased appetite that interfered with weight loss attempts. These women also reported that they did not feel sexy because of their weight. Irregular menstrual periods ranging from six weeks to six months were also commonly reported. Associated headache, abdominal bloating and menstrual cramping were also described. Very heavy bleeding, often associated with clots, was a complaint as well. With regard to body hair, visible growth anywhere on the face, including upper lip or chin caused feelings of embarrassment. The women reported that they felt different from other women and tried to avoid talking about the problem. Many women reported that they did not feel sexy because of excessive hair growth, especially on the abdomen. A variety of negative feelings related to infertility were reported. Conditions caused by PCOS can be profound and have a perceived threat to feminine identity regardless of age, marital status, education level, or ethnic origin. Doing whatever one can to reduce this stress can have a dramatic impact on quality of life!

Life Cycle Issues—PCOS is forever

The plain facts are that there is no cure for PCOS; therefore, living with this disorder will be a constant throughout a woman's life. PCOS will be there at adolescence, during the reproductive years, and at menopause... even after a hysterectomy with removal of the ovaries, PCOS is there. Stress varies as symptoms are manifested during each cycle of life. It is important not to blame yourself for your PCOS and its symptoms. You didn't "do" this to yourself, and while you have some control over it, that control is limited.

From the appearance of acne, unwanted hair or weight management issues as early as the pre-teen years, to the infertility that may interrupt the reproductive years, to the insulin resistance that often accompanies menopause, PCOS is forever. Anyone dealing with a chronic health problem—

PCOS through the Life Cycle

- Puberty/Teens
- Dating
- Marriage
- Family building
- Menopause

and PCOS must be counted as a chronic health problem—can attest to the extent that their health issues affect their personal relationships and the way they interact with the world. For example, certain health problems require medications or treatment to be taken on a strict timetable. Failure to do so compromises the ability of the drug or procedure to control a specific symptom or event. If treatments for some conditions are to work, social schedules must conform to the clock or the calendar. Decisions such as whether or not to schedule a weekend getaway or an evening on the town may be dependent on treatment. The quality of a prospective employer's health insurance plan can influence whether or not to accept a position! The availability of appropriate medical care may be the deciding factor in whether or not to accept a transfer. Medications and procedures often impact the way the patient feels both physically and mentally. The amount of physical strength and mental stamina available then affects relationships with partners, coworkers, family and friends. Whether or not to discuss health problem with others, and if so, how much to reveal, is a source of concern because there is often fear or uncertainty surrounding the responses of others. In addition, living with a chronic medical condition such as PCOS also produces grief reactions. For example, an initial response might be surprise or denial that a problem really exists. "There's nothing wrong with me. All the women on mom's side of the family are heavy." or "I've had irregular periods all my life. That's just normal for me." Eventually when the problems persist or worsen, bargaining may set in. "If I can just lose twenty pounds everything will be O.K." If weight continues to rise, if insulin resistance develops into diabetes, if hair growth worsens, the woman often feels different from everyone else around her, causing isolation. She may also feel anger which may be directed either at her own body for being "different" because it is not working normally or at women around her who do not struggle with PCOS as she does. Because the medical professional is still relatively uninformed about the breadth of the spectrum that defines PCOS, depression or despair may result from going to doctor after doctor with no firm diagnosis. Girls and women of any age may go through these grieving steps in a different sequence, but most will encounter each step in the grief and loss process to one degree or another and for some, grief may be re-encountered in subsequent stages of life.

What can I do for my daughter?—
a special word to parents

Parents of daughters with PCOS need to be aware of the consequences of their reactions to the physical changes that are taking place in their child. Fathers, in particular, can influence how a girl begins to view herself as a female because he is the first male she learns to relate to. If an adolescent female is rejected by her father physically, it can form the basis for self-esteem issues throughout her life. Negative comments about weight or skin problems can be particularly damaging. Any comment about these conditions should be carefully considered, made in a private setting and in a helpful, not hurtful manner. Daughters will face enough negativity about this condition outside of the family circle. For now, guidance counselors and health educators in public schools are not usually well aware of PCOS. However, as a parent of a child with PCOS, one of the best things you can do for your daughter and others with PCOS is to make those professionals aware. If you feel inadequately prepared or informed to do this, send information or ask your daughter's physician to speak with these professionals. Once your daughter is diagnosed, it is imperative that she not ignore the condition. Most teens to try to downplay or to ignore the existence of PCOS in their life. Monitor your daughter's condition with her and keep an open dialogue. Remind her that ignoring the problem will only result in a worsening of the symptoms. Don't harp. Encourage a healthy lifestyle and set a good example for her to follow. It will do no good to insist that she diet or exercise regularly if you the parents are not good role models. Since PCOS carries a strong genetic component, the whole family may benefit in the end from the changes that are necessary to treat PCOS. Parents always want things better for their children than they had for themselves. If you have a family history of PCOS, to make things better for your daughter, there must be a plan from birth involving eating and exercise. Good eating and exercise habits can only result in better health for everyone. Parents should assist their daughter in a plan of education. PCOS is a lifelong condition but it does not have to control one's life. The earlier you can help your daughter to see this, the better her chances for successful treatment and healthy self esteem. It is also important that moms, nurses, lab techs, and doctors involved in caring for your daughter be gentle in their approach to her. Telling her that she has a lifelong condition is likely to be upsetting. She is at an awkward stage. She may already feel that her body is ugly. Now she must be told that her body isn't working exactly like it is supposed to. She may have to take medication to control this condition for the rest of her life and she may be at higher risk for serious diseases later on in her life. The diagnosis of PCOS may be scary. It also may mean that she is different from everyone else she knows. No girl is happy about hearing any of this. The adults in her life need to be sensitive to this fact.

Who's the right doctor for my daughter?

Diagnosing and treating PCOS during these "in between" years is often frustrating for doctors, parents, and the girls themselves. Pediatricians may have limited information on PCOS because it is not an area that they are accustomed to seeing frequently in their practices. Some pediatric offices only see girls up to age 14-16 before referring them to a family medicine practice. It may be difficult for many pediatricians to deal with fourteen to sixteen year old young women. Other pediatric groups see patients up to age eighteen to twenty, even doing college entrance physicals if necessary. Some practices have a female partner who will do physicals on adolescent girls if they are uncomfortable seeing a male physician during these years. If a problem is detected, the girls are usually referred to a gynecologist. It may be difficult to find a gynecologist or reproductive endocrinologist who will treat a girl under the age of fifteen, so some girls may "fall through the cracks" when trying to find care. There are pediatric gynecologists and endocrinologists who specifically treat adolescent/teenage females. Ideally, a mutual decision as to when to

visit a specialist can be reached by doctor, parents, and patient. Ask what is
involved in the first visit. A physical exam may not be needed but an ultrasound
scan might be. One of the definitive ways of diagnosing PCOS is via ultrasound
scan of the ovaries. This ultrasound is done by means of a slender vaginal
probe. Although this procedure is not painful, many young girls who are not
sexually active or have not yet had a Pap test are fearful of the ultrasound
scan—and their mothers are fearful for them. Physical symptoms and blood
testing can also make the diagnosis of PCOS, so it is possible that a vaginal
scan may not be a mandatory part of a diagnostic visit. This practice varies
from clinic to clinic. A relaxed attitude about this can help it to be a positive
experience for all concerned. The bottom line remains that the sooner a girl is
diagnosed, and begins treatment for PCOS, the better. Be sure to read Chapter
5 for a thorough discussion of how PCOS is recognized, diagnosed and treated during puberty. If you are not satisfied with the care your daughter is receiving or if some of her symptoms are not being adequately treated, it may be necessary to seek more specialized treatment elsewhere. It is better to be proactive early than sorry later.

PCOS in puberty and the teen years

Physical issues of PCOS are uncommon before the age of eight and
are most often seen at puberty. The first symptom may be a hair or weight
issue. Pediatricians may notice weight gain (though they are unlikely to connect
this to PCOS) and may encourage parents to monitor the eating habits of the
child. While poor eating habits and sedentary lifestyle do contribute to overweight children, PCOS should also be considered as a possibility. If you suspect that your daughter has PCOS or if she has already been diagnosed, discuss this with your pediatrician or primary care provider. Give him or her the
opportunity to be a part of the treatment team for your daughter.

Most often symptoms of PCOS begin to manifest in the teenage
years. Comparing experiences with their friends at slumber parties or on the
telephone, a teenager may suspect something may be different when her periods do not come like clockwork every month. Open communication with
adults, especially parents, often declines during adolescence, so a girl may not
discuss her developing symptoms with anyone. Not having to deal with a period may be seen as a positive thing to a girl active in athletics or marching
band. If a girl does talk to her mother or even a school nurse, she may be told
that irregular or absent periods are the young body's way of adjusting to the
hormonal changes it is undergoing. However, irregular bleeding can be a negative, in that when a period does come, it can be especially heavy and painful.
Participation in school or social events is affected by fear of soaking through
pads and having embarrassing accidents.

Painful, irregular periods may send the teen with undiagnosed PCOS
to a gynecologist at an earlier age than most of her peers. A prescription for
oral contraceptives is most often given which does help some young women.
(See Chapter 4). However, some are not able to take birth control pills due to
side effects. Also, many parents are reluctant to see their teens on birth control pills and some girls are reluctant to let it be known they are taking birth

control pills because it may be wrongly assumed they are sexually active when they are not.

Weight gain, acne, or hirsutism often occur with rapid onset during the teen years. Parents, unaware of the underlying cause of such problems, may caution their daughter to "cut out all that pizza and Coke™!" In fact, the PCOS teen may be eating a very healthy diet and be physically active. She may try every skin and makeup product sold at the mall in an attempt to cover up blemishes or excess hair, all to no avail. Poring over the latest teen magazine for tips on fashion and guys, most young women start to view their bodies negatively; for young women with PCOS, body image may be an especially unsettling issue (see Chapter 10). While few women ever look like the models on those pages, the PCOS teen with weight ballooning, facial acne, and hair on her lip or chin feels different from females she sees—whether in the magazine or in her class at school. At an age where being one of the crowd is coveted, being different in any way is definitely out.

Sadly, some classmates may tease or ostracize a teen whom they perceive as different because of appearance. The stress of this, coupled with the stress of the symptoms themselves may cause the teen to withdraw academically and/or socially. Stress can cause the symptoms to worsen and the cycle continues. Parents, teachers, or guidance counselors are often at a loss to explain or understand the reason for such withdrawal. The suggestions for overcoming body dissatisfaction presented in Chapter 10 can be applied to teen girls, too. Parents of teen daughters with PCOS might pay special attention to the tips about preventing beauty brainwashing in the next generation provided there. In addition, parents should carefully examine their own attitudes about the importance of physical attractiveness; is it possible that beauty, and especially weight, have been overemphasized? Parents must be careful role models in this regard, demonstrating through their own behavior the importance of respecting people of all body types and looks, eating healthfully and normally, exercising for enjoyment, and accepting their own bodies. Above all, parents should discourage, if not forbid, dieting, educating daughters about the impossibility of losing weight through dieting and the hazards of attempting to do so.

Parents can also educate daughters with PCOS about the media as well. Watch television with your daughter, commenting critically about the ultra-thin female characters on her favorite show: "Oh, dear, I probably shouldn't say this, but don't you think poor Allie looks half-starved? I can't imagine how she makes it through a show; she's obviously so unhealthy! I certainly hope she's not addicted to drugs or eating-disordered, but I hear that's not uncommon for models and actresses." It wouldn't hurt to casually mention a few statistics when you have a chance, such as the height and weight of average U.S. women (5'4" and 138 pounds) versus those of models. Girls are notoriously ignorant about what's real and what's ideal. Actively discourage purchase of teen girls' fashion magazines and try substituting with the new girls' sports magazines or alternative, feminist teen magazines. Likewise, replace women's magazines in your home with magazines that feature larger models.

Kaz Cooke's *Real Gorgeous*, already recommended in Chapter 10,
is the popular book on body image most appropriate for teens. Cooke, both a writer and cartoonist, has a casual and inviting style that will appeal to younger readers. She addresses the myths of adolescent beauty magazines directly, for example, refuting the efficacy of anti-cellulite creams, calling attention to the dangers of cosmetic surgery, and poking fun of "pricey sniffs" (expensive perfume). Girls will especially appreciate her advice on handling the "body police"— family members or friends who insist upon commenting on a teenager's changing body. How to respond to "You're getting a bit fat"? There's the tame "No, I'm not, I'm just growing"; the more assertive "Yes, thank you, I have put on weight and I feel great"; the sassy "You're right. I guess I should become anorexic immediately. Would that be all right?"; and the more aggressive "You are quite right. I do not have the body of a 12-year old boy. Do you have one you're not using?"

It is not uncommon for teenagers riding the emotional hormonal roller coaster to feel that the biggest problem they have in their life is that no one understands what they are going through. In PCOS, it is quite true that this is the case! Teenage girls may develop depression as a result of their symptoms and there may be an abrupt change in behavior. The girl may previously have been happy and carefree, successful in school, excelling in extracurricular activities and suddenly become anxious, tense and withdrawn. Parents, teachers, and guidance counselors may be at a loss to explain this change in behavior. It is important that these adults become involved as much as possible, researching symptoms, networking with other professionals and just being there in all possible ways for the girl whose body is changing so rapidly as a result of PCOS.

Coping strategies for Teens

PCOS is enjoying increased publicity at present and many women are taking advantage of this opportunity to support other women known to have PCOS or who suspect they may have it. An example of this is the BigCyster/PCOTeen program of the Polycystic Ovarian Syndrome Association. In this program a young woman is paired with an older "cyster" to help her deal with symptoms as they manifest. The young woman is given suggestions about what works, what doesn't, and in general what to expect with PCOS. This will help make life a little bit easier to deal with. The Big Cyster is not a physician but she is someone who is farther along in living with PCOS and willing to share what she has learned to help others.

Any activity that develops a healthy self-esteem should be encouraged. Effective coping skills can be developed to make living with PCOS easier. The earlier in a woman's life that she acquires these skills, the brighter her future. Need and type of coping methods vary. Many keep a journal for recording thoughts and feelings before, during, and after various treatments. Looking back over the journal reminds them of where they were and how far they have come. Others find that taking a class in theater, photography, cooking, or another area that has always interested them helps them to focus less on themselves and have a sense of personal accomplishment. For still others, even caring for a pet who returns their affection and does not care about their physical appearance is rewarding. Regular physical activity is a great stress reducer. Running, bicycling, swimming, horseback riding, or softball are among the most common types of exercise women report enjoying. Less strenuous forms might include walking or golf. These activities can be continued for many years. Physical activity not only improves the body, it also calms the mind.

PCOS and the Dating Game

How does having PCOS affect a woman's choice of a partner or a partner's choosing her? It would be nice to think that your intelligence and winning personality would take precedence over physical appearance when it came to being noticed by and attractive to someone else. However, the sad fact is that physical appearance is one of the first things a person notices about someone else. Very often one person's response to another's physical appearance determines whether or not to take a next step of engaging in conversation to get to know the other person better. A woman struggling with facial hair or extreme weight may not get the chance to reveal her personality. It is a sad commentary on our society that some people discriminate against these women, dismissing them as being "lazy" or lacking self discipline.

What can also be true is that this can become a self-fulfilling prophecy! Women who are not comfortable with their own appearance or who fear rejection sometimes create that same rejection in a variety of ways they can change. Be especially attentive to self care (see later section "How can I be good to myself?") Work to overcome any innate shyness or self consciousness. Develop your sense of humor.

Most men don't get married for reasons of attractiveness. Some may date for it, but unless it is a whirlwind courtship, they don't marry so much for it. If they do marry for it, they may also divorce for it. There really are people who do not dwell on physical appearance at all. They focus on what is inside that makes you special. For that matter, there are also men who find women of size extremely attractive. Finding such matches can lead to meaningful relationships that are long term.

A woman does not need to worry about an in-depth discussion about PCOS with every person she dates. If the relationship progresses to serious dating or engagement, then it becomes more important to educate the partner about PCOS and reveal the potential impact it has on fertility in addition to its other long term health consequences and possible worsening "cosmetic" symptoms. The bottom line is that early on in the dating game it is important to remember that attractiveness is less important after that first date and that it is more important that a woman *feel* attractive than *be* attractive. Women tend to perceive themselves as less attractive or more overweight than men think they are.

PCOS and Marriage—My Partner and Me

Like any chronic health problem, PCOS can have an impact on a marriage or long term partnership. As discussed above, the treatment plan and symptom management themselves can be timing consuming and costly. This is one of the most important reasons for making your partner a part of your treatment and management planning and decision making.

The impact of PCOS on sexuality is one of those proverbial "elephants in the living room" that is often "there" but not discussed, as everybody wants to pretend that it isn't there. We wouldn't be honest if we didn't acknowledge that, since in many women the outwardly visible symptoms of PCOS may not appear in young adulthood or may worsen with age. PCOS symptoms such as hair problems and obesity may not even have entered the picture when you and your spouse were dating. If your PCOS symptoms do not begin to appear until after you have been with your partner for awhile or if they worsen later, it may be difficult for both of you to deal with these changes. Your partner may struggle with symptoms of hair growth, hair loss, or obesity as much as you do. The truth is that in some relationships, in addition to feeling turned off sexually by their partner's appearance, men may also feel enormous guilt at their own response. They may wish that they felt differently but they have trouble getting past the fact that the woman they are with now bears little resemblance to the woman they met originally. Your partner may make comments to you about your weight, your skin or hair, or some other aspect of your appearance in hopes that you will "fix it." He may believe that you are somehow not the same person that he met and liked initially. He may have difficulty feeling sexually attracted to you. He may not speak these feelings to you initially, but he may think them, and he may feel enormous guilt for even entertaining these thoughts.

Having hair on the abdomen or face may make you feel less sexy as a woman. If you do not like your body and the way it is "behaving," it may be difficult for you to believe that your partner finds it attractive either. In order to deal with these sexual insecurities, it is important for you to develop a healthy body image and good communication using the skills in Chapter 10.

It's common to fear that difficulties like these will automatically lead to rejection and divorce. This does not have to happen. Your relationship with your partner may need a little extra nurturing even as you nurture yourself while living with PCOS. Communication is of vital importance here. Don't assume that you know what your partner may be thinking. Your partner needs to be able to say out loud that this is a problem. He needs to be educated about weight, in case he, like lots of Americans, assumes that the body can be shaped or molded if one just *tries* hard enough. He may think that you are using PCOS as an "excuse for not dealing with" the weight. Include your partner in treatment planning and listen to his concerns as part of decision making. Encourage your partner to exercise with you. You will feel better about your body, tightening up your larger frame, and he can see that you are making an effort to be healthy and conscientious about managing PCOS. Take the time to look your best, of course, but try not to get hung up on physical appearance. You are more than your dress size or waistline. Helping your partner to understand that there are reasons for the undesirable changes which are taking place in your body is always a good idea.

Remember that the emotional and intellectual characteristics that drew you and your partner together initially are still valid. There is much more to you than your body, and there is much more to your body than your poly-cystic ovaries! Nurture your relationship with mutual kindness such as mas-sages, long walks, long talks, or whatever activities keep communication open. If problems continue and you feel the need, do not hesitate to seek the advice of a marriage or relationship counselor. Sometimes a mediator can make all the difference in the world.

Most of all take care of you. Remember that you have done nothing to cause your PCOS and you are doing everything you can to manage it. Do not allow someone else's perception of you to negatively affect your self-esteem.

Family Building—PCOS and Infertility

At some point in their life together, most couples see children as a part of their life's plan. Many women who struggle with PCOS also face infer-tility, and this has been discussed from a medical perspective in Chapter 11. For one in six couples today, getting pregnant is difficult. One of two events can happen: either a pregnancy will not be achieved or an achieved pregnan-cy will not be carried to term. Either of these outcomes results in tremendous stress and frustration for a couple because each represents a blocked desire of the heart in an area of life over which the couple has no control—while at the same time most of their peers among this second generation after the advent of reliable birth control take family planning very much for granted.

Most couples assume that they are fertile and that whenever they are ready to conceive, they will. Because of these assumptions, they may have a difficult time admitting that there may be a problem. Women who have been seeking medical care for other factors of PCOS—such as weight management or hair or skin problems may have no idea that these symptoms are a part of a syndrome that can include impaired fertility as well. They are often shocked or dismayed when they cannot produce a child. Emotions might also include anger that life is not going as planned, denial that a problem may exist, guilt at a body that won't produce a child, blame from a spouse, fear that a spouse may leave for a fertile partner, regret over past lifestyle choices, or jealousy of other people with children.

The inability to conceive a child is often one of the first events in a person's life that he or she is unable to control. Up until this time, most of life's major decisions, such as choice of schooling or profession, whom to marry, or where to live, have been carried out with few problems. Personal goals and professional achievements have been acquired with skill, hard work, and per-severance. Producing a child is often the first goal that a person is unable to achieve by effort alone. For most women, this inability to make a baby is espe-cially upsetting. Most women were taught from the earliest days when they played with dolls that they would have a baby someday. They have no difficulty seeing themselves in a motherhood role. A woman believes that if she just takes good care of her body with proper diet, rest, and exercise, or if she does-n't abuse drugs or alcohol, then her body won't let her down when it comes time to conceive a baby. Sadly, this is not always true. Some women, no mat-ter what they do, will be unable to make their body achieve or maintain a preg-nancy. This results in feelings of sadness, emptiness, and low self-esteem.

Many women dealing with infertility, no matter what its cause, fear that they are infertile as a consequence of past behavior or decisions that they have made. Perhaps an elective abortion resulting in scar tissue or a sexually transmitted disease leaving adhesions is the reason for their infertility. Many women feel tremendous guilt that they are somehow to blame for their infertility or they see it as a punishment from God. While it is important to remember that all choices have consequences, most of the causes of infertility involving sperm quality, heredity, anatomy and hormonal functions are beyond the patient's control. This is especially true for a woman with PCOS. Her hormonal disturbance is definitely not a result of anything she has done.

Infertility patients are well aware that their treatment can overshadow everything they do as a couple. Everything from the social calendars to entertaining new job offers to buying a new car to choosing a style of underwear can appear to be dominated by infertility. Couples may not feel comfortable in gatherings that include young children because their family seems incomplete. Holidays are particularly difficult because they mark the passage of still more time gone by without children. The problems with Mother's Day and Father's Day are obvious. Seemingly simple activities such as shopping in the mall or grocery store are potentially difficult because seeing pregnant women or mothers pushing strollers is painful. Attending baby showers for coworkers or christenings at church are impossible for some.

When hopes are dashed month after month, couples may finally seek medical help. Many infertility treatments are painful, invasive, and financially demanding. They may destroy a couple's privacy, distract the couple from their occupations, and generally consume their lives. This results in many emotional issues, which must be addressed. In dealing with these aspects, many couples ask, "Why us? What did we do to deserve this?" They may feel shame or embarrassment over a body that is not functioning "normally." A couple may feel isolated from family or friends because they do not yet have children. Often there is frustration directed at each other or toward self. They may feel intense jealousy toward those who have children or who are pregnant. They feel out of control in the situation. The PCOS patient in particular must feel confident that her doctor is up to date on rapid advances in endocrinology that have shown that "standard" ovulation induction treatments may be a waste of time for the PCOS patient. Additionally, her physician must be one of those who works with both members of the couple to insure that the subfertility of one is masked, to the extent possible, by the enhancement of the fertility of the other.

For those living in metropolitan areas, sources of emotional support for those dealing with infertility have been available since the late 1970s through the chapters of RESOLVE around the country, the Infertility Awareness Association of Canada and various independent groups. Five years ago the Internet added to the sources of support through INCIID (International Council on Infertility Information Dissemination) and several other on-line support systems. Only in the last three years, however, has there been specific support for PCOS-related infertility. PCOSA, the national support and advocacy organization, offers seminars, meetings, and many quite narrowly focused Internet support groups. The American Infertility Association offers both face-to-face seminars and meetings, and an Internet support board on PCOS.

PCOS and Menopause

Menopause. Change of life. End of fertility. To some women, these words sound ominous and evoke feelings of dread. To others they indicate still another season of life. Seasons provide the change that permit growth for all living things and the season of menopause allows you to continue the personal growth you have begun to this point in your life.

As has been earlier discussed in Chapter 14, menopause is confirmed when a woman has not had a period in twelve consecutive months. The period of time leading up to menopause—perimenopause—is marked by hot flashes, night sweats, insomnia, mood swings, and menstrual irregularities. All women should work with their doctors to establish an individual treatment regimen for dealing with these characteristics that result from decreased hormone production by aging ovaries.

Women who have PCOS often have had a lifetime of managing hormonal side effects, so for many, the symptoms of menopause are just added to the list. For such a woman, this change in her life may not really be much of a change in her life. However, some women who are presently in perimenopause or who have already experienced that passage never heard the words "polycystic ovaries" until recently. In fact, for many women a name was never attached to their specific symptoms, nor might their symptoms have been recognized as related as they struggled with PCOS over the years. For women who came of age in the mid-sixties through the seventies, the feminist movement brought about vast changes in reproductive health issues of birth control, abortion rights and childbirth options but little recognition, let alone advancement, for PCOS.

Because most PCOS patients have had a lifetime of managing PCOS symptoms associated with skin, hair, weight, menstrual problems and more, they may be at a significant advantage when it comes to living with menopause. For example, many menopausal women who have never suffered with PCOS look in the mirror and decide they are no longer happy with the way they look. They may spend vast amounts of time and money on make up and hair products to cover up wrinkles, age spots, or gray hairs. The PCOS patient is already a pro at "plucking and powdering" to mask hair and skin imperfections. The PCOS patient already knows what products and procedures work well to let her look her best. This is nothing new for her.

Other women fear gaining weight as they get older. As midlife approaches, it is normal for a woman's breasts to thicken, her waist to enlarge, and fat deposits to increase as lean muscle is replaced by fat. These are unwelcome changes for many women. They often avoid healthful foods, skip meals, diet, or exercise to extreme to remain thin. If a PCOS patient has battled weight issues all her life, then she has probably come to accept her size and shape and will not waste time and energy disliking her body. She already knows the importance of proper nutrition. She should already have an eating plan and an exercise program as part of her lifestyle for living with PCOS. There is nothing new here either.

Likewise, menstrual irregularities are another area in which the woman with PCOS has the edge of experience over her non-PCO sister. One sign of menopause is change in the menstrual pattern. Changes may begin in the late thirties or forties and result from dropping hormone levels. The flow may become lighter and thinner or heavier and gushing. Cycles may shorten or lengthen, finally ceasing altogether. Absent or irregular bleeding may have been a fact of the PCOS patient's life since her periods began. Here again, there is nothing new about this.

One aspect of menopause with which those with PCOS may struggle more keenly than their non-PCO sisters is the fact that menopause does signal the end of the reproductive years. Fertile women sometimes grieve during this stage of their life but they have had the experience of pregnancy to help them cope. If a woman battled infertility along with PCOS and was unsuccessful in ever achieving a pregnancy, she may have renewed grieving, sadness, and loss during this transition. For both fertile and infertile women, adoption or third party reproduction may continue to offer family building options during menopause if desired.

A menopausal PCOS patient will want to continue under the care of the doctor who knows her and her disease best. Whether this doctor is a general practitioner, gynecologist, or reproductive endocrinologist, she will need to continue to receive regular gynecologic care as well as advice on areas such as hormone replacement therapy, osteoporosis prevention, and continued insulin/diabetes monitoring. It remains important that she continue healthy habits of diet and nutrition, as well as continuing to exercise for her cardiovascular health.

Menopause can be a bittersweet time for all women, seen as both loss and relief. It is important that menopause is seen as just the end of reproduction, not the end of life. Many women may experience increased vigor during this time. This season of life is just that—another season with opportunities for new growth, new adventures, and new opportunities in all areas of life.

What if my friends think I'm "crazy"? Am I losing my mind?

Many women experience vast mood swings and feelings of sadness or irritability during the perimenopausal/menopausal years. They may ride a roller coaster of emotions in a very short time frame. They often report feeling calm and serene one minute but totally out of control the next. Innocent questions or comments form a spouse or co-worker may be met by a flood of tears or a verbal rampage. Some women may have prided themselves on the fact that their mind was razor sharp. In the past, they were able to work at multifunctional tasks and remember a myriad of details. These same women are now dismayed to discover that they are often easily confused, no longer able to focus on specific tasks or remember the simplest of details. Now they walk into a room and forget why they came in. Their minds come up blank when they try to recall names or telephone numbers that they have known for years. They will be speaking and lose the word they mean to say in mid-sentence. Our office has coined a phrase to describe this characteristic: estrogen-deficient mush brain syndrome—EMB for short. If only it had a diagnosis code that the insurance companies would recognize!

These changes in mental stability and mood are still more symptoms caused by fluctuating hormonal levels. Women who begin hormone replacement therapy (HRT) for other menopausal symptoms such as insomnia, night sweats, etc. sometimes report relief from the cognitive symptoms as well. They report that the estrogen gives them more energy, relieves the hot flashes, and in general makes them just "feel better." This in turn leads to a more positive outlook on life. Others however, report that the progestin aspect of HRT only aggravates the more negative symptoms. They report feeling "blue," fatigued, crampy, irritable, sad and depressed.

There is a strong possibility that not all of a woman's emotional and cognitive issues at this time in her life are tied to the physical issues of menopause and/or PCOS. Not only is her body undergoing physical changes, but her environment is likely undergoing changes as well. She may be at or near the peak of her career with a multitude of job responsibilities. She may be newly divorced or widowed. If she is married, she may be adjusting to a spouse facing life changes of his own. If she has children, they may have left the nest. If there are children still in the home, she may find herself in the sandwich generation, having to provide both childcare as well as eldercare for parents, in-laws or others. Any or all of these life "passages" at this time in her life can represent loss or areas for concern or worry. They can create stress, leading to fatigue, interrupted sleep, sadness, or other mental characteristics often associated only with menopause.

Women have always helped each other through such times but they have not always openly discussed "the change." In our grandmothers' day, there were church circles and quilting bees where women came together often to commiserate among themselves. Multigenerational families living under one roof gave young women role models for dealing with events and circumstances as they occurred but more often than not, values were "caught, not taught" because the change of life was not openly discussed. Women were expected to suffer in silence. The most they could hope for from their doctor was a prescription for Premarin™ as they prepared to "ride it out." Today it may be difficult to find a quilting bee but with organized support groups and the Internet only a mouse click away, women continue to provide information and support for each other, not only through the discomforts of menopause but for the other experiences they will face in midlife as well. There is NO reluctance to share information on treatment choices or experiences.

So, the answer to the question posed at the beginning of this section is NO. You are not crazy and you are not losing your mind. You are normal and you can take comfort in the fact that you are not alone. Some days will be better or worse for you than others. If you are having a "down day" and don't feel like being around a lot of people, know that it is ok if you aren't. Friends and relatives will understand if you explain to them. You've begun educating them on PCOS; you might as well continue educating them. Try to work from home or arrange your workday so that contact with others is minimized. If you are feeling irritable, take a block of time from your schedule and do something just for yourself such as taking a walk, reading a book, shopping, or going to a movie. If memory lapses are a concern, make lists. The list will remember for you. Try slowing down and doing only one task at a time and completing it before moving on to the next thing. Group like tasks on your list together so that you don't have duplication of effort and your brain will feel less likely to "short circuit."

Two things your mother probably told you were "Keep your wits about you," and "This too shall pass." Both are true statements regarding your menopause and PCOS symptoms. Your mind hasn't left you but you may think it has gone into hibernation for awhile. It is also important to remember that this is just one more season in your life. For a woman today, nearly half of her adult life will be lived as post menopausal. These can be some of her most productive years professionally, emotionally, and personally.

Facing the World

Dealing with a chronic medical condition creates complications in both our internal and external worlds. In this section we hope to offer you not just acknowledgement of what some of the most common of those issues are, but practical tools for beginning to address them.

Spiritual Issues

We all struggle with issues of religion and faith. While the church can certainly be a source of solace and support, it can also be a source of stress as well. Infertility patients can be told at the beginning that the reason they are not pregnant is because they do not have enough faith, they are not praying diligently enough, or it is not God's will that they have children. Many patients fixate on certain scriptures about children being blessings and they wonder why they don't "qualify" or if they are somehow not spiritual enough. Many infertility patients are reluctant to use procedures such as donor inseminations or IVF using donor eggs because their church says that it is technical adultery or that it violates the "one flesh" marital relationship.

The Catholic Church's view inseminations, in-vitro fertilization, the use of donor gametes, donor embryos or surrogates as inappropriate because these procedures separate human procreation from intercourse. Procreation cannot be performed by a physician but physicians can assist a couple in conceiving by using corrective techniques such as medications for ovulation induction that do not directly involve procreation. Any procedure such as GIFT, which allows fertilization to occur "naturally" in the fallopian tube, is allowed.

The Jewish religion believes that the centrality of family is critical. Procreation is an obligation and responsibility. Practitioners in orthodox and conservative Jewish hospitals are limited in procedures they can perform as well. Hebrew law suggests that couples be treated as a single unit. IUI, IVF, and corrective surgeries are acceptable methods for treating infertility. Gamete donation is considered inappropriate because of issues related to adultery, inheritance, and the legitimacy of the child since there is no genetic link. Orthodox Jewish women may be particularly concerned with any test procedure that may result in bleeding because they must refrain from intercourse for eight days and undergo purification rites.

Practitioners of Islam also consider procreation a duty in marriage. Treatment for infertility is encouraged as long as procedures do not involve gamete donations. The use of donor sperm, eggs, or embryos is viewed as adulterous or against legal inheritance. Islamic women stigmatized by poor body image and/or infertility associated with PCOS, may face additional problems depending on their culture. In many homes, even if a woman is fortunate enough to receive an early diagnosis, she is often discouraged from talking about it, especially by her mother who often believes that she will not receive any proposals of marriage if there is a chance she will not be fertile. Other women believe that their condition should be openly discussed with any prospective suitors so they will be courted by men only interested in them as a person and not in the condition of their ovaries.

For devout individuals, the organized church may create obstacles to treatment plans by prohibiting certain procedures, limiting treatment options, or otherwise creating conflict for those who choose to engage in treatments of which their faith does not approve. Regardless of the particular faith of an individual, this statement by Chicago's Cardinal Joseph L Bernardin sums up the situation well:

> "I have heard the pain of loving couples, Catholic and non-Catholic, who desperately want the gift of a child. My heart reaches out to them. Theirs is a difficult burden, and I share their pain. We must offer them love, support, and understanding. And in the end, after careful and conscientious reflection on this teaching, they must make their own decision."

For the PCOS patient, there is an extra societal and personal burden. Issues of faith and religion may surface in additional ways. For example, body image is important to any woman. Many faiths teach that man and woman were made in God's image. A PCOS patient may look at her overweight, hairy body and have trouble reconciling the image she sees in the mirror with an image of God's perfection. God may have known what he was doing when He created Adam and Eve, but what did He have in mind with the body He gave her?

Many religions teach that gluttony is a sin. A woman with PCOS may eat normally but her weight status may label her as "glutton" to everyone else. A woman may be taught that her body is God's temple and that she is to glorify God with her body. A woman unhappy with her body is often not able to glorify God when she is unhappy with the size and shape of her "temple."

A positive effect the organized church has had in recent years is the development of an interest in diet and nutrition to help people take better care of their bodies. There are weight loss programs such as Weigh Down, First Place, and others that meet in church fellowship halls across the country. Sections in religious bookstores contain books on diet, recipes, and meal planning such as *Eating By The Book* by nutritionist David Meinz. These programs and books explore what the Bible says about food, fat, fitness, and faith. They discuss what foods God said were good to eat and how to prepare them for best nutrition value.

Self-control is a virtue encouraged by many religious denominations. A woman with PCOS may believe that she could lose weight by diligently following a diet. She may have tried countless diets with little or no success. She may believe she is missing self-control and because she lacks this particular trait, perhaps her degree of faith is somehow in question, She may believe she is not spiritual enough and is unable to lose weight on her own strength. For many devout women, this would induce major guilt.

A woman struggling with these issues should remember that she is of no less value and is no less loved by God because of her body. Her responsibility is to be a good steward of all that God has given her, including her body. This includes finding good medical care and educating herself as much as possible about PCOS.

Regardless of denomination or faith, living with PCOS can represent a spiritual crisis. It impacts a woman's concept of God as a fair and just provider, enabler, and healer. Some women experience a deep crisis of faith when they feel that the spiritual power in which they believe has somehow let them down. They may find it difficult to pray or be a part of any organized spiritual group. It is important to somehow find the inner strength to connect or reconnect to the faith or belief system that has sustained you in the past.

How can I educate the public?

PCOS does not have a famous spokesperson (though some of us may wonder if certain of those high-profile celebrity large ladies might be candidates for such a job!), nor is it a "high profile" disease. PCOS is no less difficult to live with and in fact, it may put a woman at increased risk for cardiovascular disease, endometrial cancer, and infertility. Because symptoms are varied and often misunderstood, they have sometimes not been acknowledged. As connections to insulin resistance, genetic links, and new drug developments are made through research, public awareness and sensitivity will increase. Until that happens on a large scale, it is often up to the individual PCOS patient to do her part to increase awareness in the people that she encounters. Now you know that you have PCOS. Become an advocate. **Tell people!!**

Insensitive Comments

Hurtful remarks are difficult to deal with no matter how much practice one has had in receiving them. Unless someone has experienced PCOS symptoms firsthand, it is unlikely they will completely understand. You might receive "lip service" from others and they may be sympathetic to some degree, but not empathetic. A person may mean well and think they are being supportive in their concern but the comments they make often strike the PCOS woman as cruel. No doubt you have heard the following:

- "You have such a pretty face!" (Unspoken, but clearly implied, is that the rest of you is not so pretty and you ought to do something about it).
- "You would be so much more attractive if you would just lose that weight." (The assumption being both that there is little else appealing

about you and that you could manage that weight if you wanted to).
- "What is that thing on your face?" (It could be a pimple. It could be an ingrown hair. It could be a skin tag. Bottom line, though, is that the question is insensitive and intrusive).
- "You're doing _____for treatment?? I read/heard somewhere that causes cancer." (The unspoken judgment being...Are you sure your doctor knows what he is doing? Shouldn't you be seen by Dr. Great?)

It is normal to feel upset over such observations. It is important to have an abundant supply of self-control so as not to snap back at the person making such a comment. As you encounter comments surrounding PCOS, your response may reflect your particular coping style in one of the following ways.

- **Repression** You may choose to ignore the remark or deny that it was directed at you. You may try not to think about it or you may think that it is not really a problem at all.
- **Humor** You may automatically react with jokes or funny stories to reduce stress and ease tension. Laughing at yourself may indicate that you don't take yourself or your troubles too seriously. Laughter may also hide intense emotional pain. Be sure that you do not laugh with others, then cry when you are alone.
- **Altruism** is another way that you may respond, putting the day-to-day needs of family, friends, and coworkers ahead of yourself to avoid dealing with your own needs.
- **Activism** A few women may decide to adopt PCOS as their *cause celebre* and unselfishly devote their time to helping others understand the disease by doing such things as coordinating a support group or developing a Web site.

OK, so the comments are a fact of life—a reality of living with PCOS. Do you just accept them? Is acknowledging your own natural coping style the only answer? We don't think so. Knowing how to respond when nearly everyone says the wrong thing can help you feel less isolated and more empowered! If you want to thrive with PCOS instead of just surviving, you need to take charge! So here are some suggestions we have for dealing with comments ...

If the person who made the comment is someone close to you, talk with the person privately and explain why such a comment, however well intentioned, is hurtful or not factual. If the person is merely an acquaintance or a stranger, how you respond will depend on whether you have the energy to correct or educate. How you choose to respond becomes a matter of balancing your need for understanding and emotional support with the general need to educate people about PCOS. Taking this approach, you might respond to the four comments above with...

- "Thanks. I have a great hair stylist/makeup regimen." (This ignores the unspoken criticism and deals with the comment at face value. You DO have a pretty face).
- "Almost everybody battles weight. I have an endocrine imbalance that

causes it. I'm working with a physician/nutritionist/exercise program but as you know, there is no easy way to lose weight. Would you care to walk/work out/ diet with me?" or, "I have a medical condition that makes that extraordinarily unlikely. Please be more sensitive to others when you don't have full information about their private medical history."

- "I have PCOS—a hormone imbalance which causes acne/extra hair growth."
- "It took a long time for me to find a doctor who knew about my disease. I am confident that he/she knows what treatment will work best in my case. I'm glad you are interested in my care. Would you like to read some articles my doctor researched?" or "Thank you for your concern, but you can rest assured that I've investigated my options carefully before choosing my medical practitioners and my treatment."

Another way to look at such comments is to keep in mind that in polite society we do feel it appropriate to set privacy boundaries. When rude comments or intrusive questions come from a stranger, rather than from someone in your "inner circle" it is entirely appropriate to ignore the question, to deflect the question, or to take yourself OFF the defensive and put the rude querier ON the defensive with responses like these:

- No comment at all
- Blank stare
- "I beg your pardon! Perhaps I misunderstood your very rude comment."

Tips for dealing with friends and family

It is a fortunate woman who struggles with PCOS who also has a supportive friend. As she struggles with her physical symptoms, treatment options, medications, and side effects, it is helpful to have someone who will be there to listen if and when she needs to talk. Perhaps you, the reader of this section, are not a woman who struggles with PCOS, but perhaps you know someone who does. In that case, there are some important Do's and Dont's that can qualify good friends as good listeners and effective supporters. These include:

- Don't patronize.
- Don't offer unsolicited advice, especially if you are not positive that your advice is factual. Chances are that your friend has already seen the latest magazine article on her condition, and she most likely has a good doctor to whom she is paying good money for advice.
- Do not assume that you have the answers or that you know exactly what she needs.
- Don't second-guess your friend's choice of physician or treatment. Getting in as a patient under the care of a good physician has probably been an uphill battle. Don't raise your personal objections to a decision she has made regarding her care.

- Do be realistic and flexible. Don't deny that a problem exists for your friend in an attempt to sound encouraging. Sometimes your friend may want to socialize; at other times she may prefer her own company.
- Do acknowledge that it may be difficult for your friend to be around you if you are a size 6 and she is not or if you are pregnant and she is not. Let her know that you are sensitive to the issue and that you want to understand about this.
- If you don't know what to say, it is perfectly fine to say nothing at all. Very often this is the best medicine!
- Do be sensitive and patient. PCOS can involve issues of an intimate nature. If you have not experienced it personally, chances are good that you don't know exactly what your friend is thinking/feeling. Wait for her to tell you.
- Become an advocate for PCOS yourself! The fact that you are not dealing with the implications of this condition allows you to be less sensitive. Correct inaccuracies and insensitivities you hear from others about your friend's condition or symptoms! Volunteer for the support and advocacy group your friend depends on.

Workplace Issues

Many women try not to discuss their disease in the workplace but often find it necessary to be away from work for various periods of time for medical treatment. Taking extended time off from work can sometimes cause problems with a boss or with coworkers who have to cover for you in your absence. This is true for fellow office workers who need to be away for child care issues as well as those needing time for medical concerns. Whether or not to disclose the medical reasons for extensive absences is a personal decision. However, as a general rule, it is best to disclose only that you are undergoing medical treatment for a non life-threatening condition. This would apply to any infertility treatment, as well as treatment for PCOS. Disclosing eliminates speculation that you have a terminal illness. Many employers have mandatory attendance policies allowing only a specified number of absences. Once this number is exceeded for ANY reason, the employee is terminated. This is often the policy in manufacturing industries where production and shipping quotas must be met around the clock. Other businesses and industries will excuse an absence for doctor visits if there is a letter from the physician stating the necessity for the visit. If a written excuse will not suffice, very often the physician, or his designee, can discuss the situation with an employer within the limits of confidentiality. The Family and Medical Leave Act requires employers to allow employees unpaid leave for pregnancy and related matters without losing their jobs. Many employees are applying FMLA to treatment for infertility and PCOS with varying degrees of success. Certain smaller employers are not bound by FMLA so this provision may not be of benefit in every situation. It can be problematic for both you and your employer for you to be away from work and your career track can suffer as well.

Getting emotional support

Internet sites

There are several Internet sites that have chat rooms and bulletin boards where computer savvy patients can share their experiences with others. These are listed in Chapter 18. When obtaining information from a chat room or bulletin board on the internet, it is important to remember that what you read there is tempered by the experience of the person writing the message. Every treatment one person swears by, another person will swear at. You cannot always accurately compare your situation and your physician's treatment plan with someone else's. Every patient is different and every response is different. Do not second-guess your doctor based on someone's Internet diagnosis. Your doctor knows your situation best. This does not mean however, that you should refrain from bringing up with your doctor and his staff intriguing information and questions that have arisen from your Internet research and chatting. Doing so and getting the "take" of the professionals you trust is part of being a good self-advocate!

Support groups

Support groups may not be for everyone, but we want to encourage you to give them a try. Support groups can be a wonderful way to obtain education and emotional support. Connecting with other people going through similar circumstances has tremendous benefits for you as a patient. You can learn new methods of coping, talk to people who understand what you are going through, navigate medical options, and even decide when "enough is enough." Support groups for PCOS are available in a variety of "styles."

Face-to-face small groups led by a mental health professional may be available through your physician's office or through a local hospital. These are most often limited to eight to ten sessions, though often ongoing one-on-one support grows from friendships made in such groups.

Chapter 18 will also lead you to organized support, education and advocacy groups through PCOSA, RESOLVE, or the American Infertility Association. Such groups are available on the local, state, and national levels. They offer an opportunity for you to learn from the experiences of others. PCOS and its effects on the body are of an intimate nature. This makes it difficult to discuss with people who do not know first hand what you are going through. The women in a support group are just like you. You can learn more about your specific condition and associated coping skills as well as share medical information and personal concerns such as how your disease affects other aspects of your life.

Despite these advantages, many women are reluctant to go to an organized support group because they feel that it would be like undergoing therapy. They don't see themselves as "desperate enough" to need therapy. In fact, a support group is not supposed to be therapy. Therapy is individually focused and is led by a mental health professional. Support groups are of course "therapeutic" in the general sense of that word in that they give a woman an outlet to identify her feelings and acknowledge losses, but they are far less formal than professional therapy. Talking with others lets you know it is ok to cry when you feel like it and accept that grief is a normal response to an often abnormal situation. A woman is not required to "bare her soul" in a support group. She decides how much she wants to relate to the other members. Another misconception is that a support group will go on for a long period of time. Most organized groups only last for ten sessions or even less. Many women find that the friendships that begin in a support group often last long after the support group fulfills its role. Social support goes a long way toward combating feelings of isolation and loneliness that women often experience.

Should I see a professional counselor?

Whether or not a woman chooses to avail herself of the benefits of a support group, it is important that she identify her feelings and acknowledge them. According to mental health professionals, it is time to seek professional counseling when any of the following occur:

- a change in eating or sleeping habits
- feelings of isolation, loneliness, or hopelessness
- difficulty on the job
- inability to focus on or complete specific tasks
- loss of interest in activities that previously provided enjoyment
- suicidal thoughts
- increased use of alcohol or drugs

If you find yourself identifying with the above list, be sure to speak with your physician or a member of his staff so that they can help you find more help.

Who Should I See?

A qualified professional may be a psychiatrist, psychologist, social worker, marriage/family counselor, or clergy. If you decide to seek professional counseling, mental health experts agree that it is important to look for one with experience in dealing with the specific issues you need to address. For women coping with PCOS, this may be easier said than done. Because PCOS is only now being extensively studied and publicized, there is not a great deal of information available to counselors on PCOS specifically. As more information becomes available this will change. It is important not to reject a counselor solely on his or her lack of experience with PCOS. Many issues surrounding PCOS such as self-esteem, body image, or infertility, are commonly treated by mental health professionals. Your medical doctor may refer you to an appropriate mental health provider. If not, groups such as the American Society for Reproductive Medicine, National Association of Social Workers, or the American Psychological Association has lists of qualified professionals that you may choose from.

According to RESOLVE's 1999 book *Resolving Infertility*, the following questions should be answered satisfactorily before selecting a counselor:

- Schooling: What school was attended? Is it accredited? What degree was earned? How long was the clinical training and in what area of concentration?
- Practice: When was the practice established? What percentage of the practice deals with infertility/PCOS? What treatment approaches are used? Are medications prescribed? If so, are they compatible with other medications used to treat infertility/PCOS? How many sessions would be needed? What is the cost? What is the phone call policy? How are appointments scheduled?
- After a counselor is selected and you have had the first session, you need to assess your feelings about him/her. Do you feel comfortable? Do you feel that your issues are understood? Are questions answered directly and honestly? Are you given a sense of hope? If not, or if you begin to feel you are not progressing after several sessions, you may want to consider changing to another counselor. (See Chapter 6).

How can I be good to myself?

Living day to day with symptoms of PCOS forces women be creative in finding ways to look and feel their best. When you look good on the outside you feel good on the inside.

Skin

Mild cases of acne are usually treated with over-the-counter preparations. For moderate to severe cases, a doctor may prescribe stronger medication such as Azelex™ (azelaic acid), which is sometimes given to teenagers with acne problems. It is important to use hypoallergenic makeup products such as Almay™ or Clinique™ if a woman has sensitive skin. If the problem is oily skin, no matter what brand of makeup is used, it is important that the product be powder based or oil free so as not to exacerbate the problem.

Hair

Chapter 7 offered information on professional care for hair problems. Here are some practical suggesions from women with PCOS...

Many women with excess facial hair bleach the hair. The bleaching process changes the pigment of existing hair but some women's skin tone is not right for bleaching so that bleaching can actually make the hair more obvious. Other women use waxing or depilatories to remove hair because these methods leave no stubble. The advantages of these first two options are that they are less expensive than laser hair removal or electrolysis. They can also be done either at a salon or at home in private and do not require medical assistance. The disadvantages are that none of these methods are permanent and they may irritate sensitive skin types.

A few women must actually shave every morning to keep hair growth at bay. These women often eventually decide to undergo electrolysis or laser hair removal. These procedures are longer lasting but more expensive. They may also be painful and cause inflammation. Very often insurance will not cover these treatments because they are considered cosmetic rather than as treatment for a medical condition.

For women with thinning scalp hair, there are products such as TIGI™ Thickening Shampoo and Cream, which add body and thickness to thinning and fine hair. There are also shampoos such as Nioxin™ to boost the process of regrowth. As with any product, if you decide to use it, read the label first to see if it is the right product for you. For many women who have darker hair, thinning hair makes the scalp more visible. They find that lightening their hair color or adding highlights to selected area helps to minimize the problem.

Weight/Clothes

While you are following the eating plan tips in Chapter 8 you should pay particular attention to clothing styles that look flattering on you. Some manufacturers skimp on fabric allotment while others are more generous in size, cut, and seam allowance. Try on outfits from different designers and manufacturers to note the difference in fit. Many clothing manufacturers such as Liz Claiborne, Donna Kaaren, and Hanes have plus sizes in styles or designs equivalent to their regular sizes. Bigger retail clothing stores have departments catering to larger sized women. There are also specialty-clothing boutiques.

Web site and catalog shopping can offer privacy to those women who are self conscious about shopping for larger sizes. Most such resources make returns easy, so shoppers can afford to experiment some until they find the right brands and sizes for their bodies.

Catalogs/websites offering wide selections of stylish larger sized, well fitting clothes for office, casual living, dressy occasions and lingerie and intimates include Bloomingdales, Nordstrom, Lane Bryant, Silhouettes, Roamans, J.Jill, Coldwater Creek, Drapers & Damons and QVC among others.

Getting on with it!

Resolution is the emotional goal when living with PCOS or any chronic medical condition or health crisis. Resolving means coming to accept the presence of this condition in your life and incorporating it into your sense of yourself as a worthwhile human being. Resolution involves making decisions about treatment options in positive, productive ways. It is an ongoing process, accomplished in degrees over time with gains as well as losses along the way. It is important as you are living with PCOS that you be patient and good to yourself in as many ways possible. You can be in control, but your control does have limits. You can't remake your basic self, so you will need to work at appreciating the changes you can effect. As eager as you may be to see results quickly, changes are usually more lasting if they are made slowly. You cannot remake yourself in a matter of a few days, weeks or months. It took awhile for you to get to this place in your life and it will take awhile for you to get to a better place.

Women often struggle with putting the needs of others before their own. In the interest of being good to yourself, take time to reconnect with yourself and indulge in things that you enjoy. This might include reading a book, going shopping, taking a long walk, calling up an old friend, or renting a good movie. You are your own best friend and best advocate so treat yourself with kindness.

How do women with PCOS become more like Lisa, whose story
began this chapter? How can you move from just surviving to thriving?

- Become an educated, informed consumer.
- Devise a personal management plan for your PCOS.
- Bring your family and friends onto your personal "team."
- Get additional support as needed.
- Accept what you can't change and work with gusto to change what you can!
- Celebrate the gift of life and really **live it**!

No Cure Yet, So Let's Manage. Therapy Options

I just delivered my son conceived on metformin. I don't want to be pregnant right away, but can I please be started back on the drug. I felt so good....

I would rather stick needles into my eyes than use one more day of metformin. I can't stand the diarrhea, I feel horrible....

Shall we start with the cliches? *There is no silver bullet. One size does not fit all.*

These are ways of emphasizing from the start of this very complex chapter that no therapy for PCOS is right for everyone, nor does any single therapy deal with all of PCOS' symptoms and consequences. Therapeutic options are almost as varied as are the individuals with PCOS and *treatment for PCOS must be individualized..*

For now, we cannot cure PCOS, but with proper evaluation and therapy many may move from infertility to a successful pregnancy, from a situation of poor metabolism and increased risks of serious disease to one of better quality of life and longevity. It is my belief that the role of support and lifestyle changes in treatment should be considered as important as are surgical or medical treatments. These have not been included in the following, but are suggestions that have been scattered generously throughout the previous chapters.

The following may not be an exhaustive discussion of treatments available for PCOS, but it is as thorough as we could make it at the time we went to press. It certainly is not a "how to" manual, and we want to be clear that the information here should not be construed as an endorsement of any particular therapy. It is also important that readers understand that few interventions for PCOS are without risk.

Furthermore, we are well aware that this chapter would be a "tough read" for most. Few, if any, who use this book are likely to read this chapter straight through, and that's fine! We've designed it as a handbook of reference material. We are attempting here to provide you with education and information, hoping that this chapter can serve as a practical database of many of the current therapies available. Its most important function should be to help you understand the questions you need to ask in managing your own treatment since we cannot provide individualized answers.

That said, let's look at the therapeutic approaches to treating PCOS. There are three:

- SURGICAL
- MEDICAL
- COMPLEMENTARY

SURGICAL THERAPY

Ovarian Wedge Resection

Ovarian wedge resection is now a rarely performed procedure, but it has been a foundation of therapy in the past and still provides important clues about the nature of PCOS. During this surgery one half to three-quarters of the ovary is removed in a wedge and the ovary is then sewn back together. The original description of PCOS by Drs. Stein and Leventhal in 1935 followed this surgical procedure performed on seven women who had amenorrhea and markedly enlarged ovaries. The wedge resection had been a previously described therapy for ovarian cysts, and these operations were performed more for diagnosis than as therapy. The only consistent finding in the removed slices of ovary was a large number of small follicle cysts. Surprisingly, soon after surgery all of the women in Stein and Leventhal's study regained normal menses, and two of the seven patients treated became pregnant. A finding that was also unsuspected was that wedge resection appeared curative and long-term establishment of regular menstruation was noted. This report of restoration of menses after wedge resection did much to popularize the technique. It was correctly concluded that polycystic ovaries were a consequence of a hormonal disturbance, but incorrectly assumed that lack of ovulation was due to the mechanical factor of overcrowding.

Over the next 50 years ovarian wedge resection became the major treatment option for PCOS. Multiple studies of about 1500 cases have shown a restoration of menses in an average of about 80% (range 6-95%) of cases and pregnancy in 65-70% (range 10-90%). Why there is so much variation between studies is not known. Even the earliest investigators warned of the substantial risk of pelvic scarring after the procedure and, while uncommon, complete destruction of the ovary has been reported. With the traditional approach to wedge resection it has been reported that about 30% of patients will have scar tissue formation around the ovary, with the result that this procedure used to promote fertility can in itself cause infertility.

Laparoscopic Ovarian Drilling

Virtually every surgical procedure performed on the pelvic organs through a large abdominal incision (laparotomy) is now possible by laparoscopy. (A description of laparoscopy is provided in Chapter 12). The same can be said for the wedge resection. The drilling procedure is most often performed for infertility and promotion of ovulation. This does not mean that it might not be used for other indications, but it probably is far down on the list of treatment options. Androgens are reduced, but there is little change in insulin resistance.

Since the early 1980s there have been various reports of laparoscopic methods used to partially disrupt or destroy a portion of the ovary. The objectives are the same as with traditional wedge resection, but major surgery is avoided and the potential scar tissue formation is probably lessened. Techniques have included multiple needle punctures (four to twenty in one or both ovaries) to disrupt the cysts, as well as lasers or electric current to selectively destroy a portion of the ovary. When electric current is used it may be called *ovarian diathermy* or *microcautery*. It seems simplistic, but by reducing the amount of hormone producing tissue, the endocrine environment is improved. It has been shown that both wedge resection and ovarian drilling substantially reduce levels of luteinizing hormone and testosterone.

Figure 17-1 Ovarian Drilling

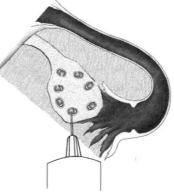

There is debate over whether laser or electric cautery forms less scar tissue. Theoretically, cautery using a small thin needle inserted into the ovary would create less chance for scar tissue to form around the ovarian surface, or when it occurs, it is likely to be less severe. The chance of scar tissue (adhesion) formation is reported to be less when one of the surgical barriers, such as Intercede™, is used to wrap the ovary at the completion of the procedure. There is a constant search for ways to prevent adhesion formation and in the future this too-frequent complication may become less of a problem. At this time, it seems that the success of the procedure and the chance of scar tissue may be more related to the surgeon than to the specific technique, so it would be very important to determine the experience of the surgeon when considering this procedure.

As with wedge resection, the reported pregnancy rates for drilling have varied. The pregnancy rates in some studies are similar to the best reported with traditional wedge resection. Over a dozen studies have been published with success rates for ovulation between 50% and 95% and pregnancy rates between 30% and 85%. Obviously, the higher success rates cannot be guaranteed, and few investigators are prone to report their lack of success. There would be much less need for this book if we had a technique that was permanent and universally 85% successful. I must say that my success rates with these procedures have not been this good.

There are limited long-term observations after ovarian drilling. While there is a chance of permanent restoration of regular menstrual cycles, there is also a small risk of permanent ovarian damage. The greater the chance of cure, the greater the chance of injury.

Studies seem to show that success rates may be better when patients are closer to their ideal weight. Whether this identifies a special population of PCOS patients is not known. Even if the procedure is not fully successful in restoring normal ovarian function, ovulation, and pregnancy, it may improve the responsiveness to clomiphene stimulation.

A benefit of ovarian drilling is that by avoiding fertility drugs the risk of multiple gestations is very much reduced. By altering the abnormal ovarian hormonal environment, there could be the chance of improved egg quality. One study has reported a significant reduction in miscarriage rates as compared to pregnancy achieved after gonadotropin injections.

It also may be considered an appropriate option for those who are unwilling to use gonadotropins, or in cases where a laparoscopy is being performed for other reasons. If IVF represents the next option, it may be reasonable to try ovarian cautery to avoid the high cost and inherent risks of this technology. A clear indication for the procedure could be in cases where there is such a hyper-responsiveness to gonadotropin injections that this becomes an unduly risky therapy, even when used for IVF.

There has been at least one report of the procedure being performed using transvaginal ultrasound guidance. While avoiding the need for surgery altogether, this approach is still considered too risky by most for fear of injury to the nearby intestines.

Removal of the Ovaries and Hysterectomy

Hysterectomy and PCOS is a curious topic on which there is little written. This is an area where new endocrine theory and standard gynecologic practice collide and there are few answers. In general, I consider a hysterectomy as a failure of our capacity to adequately treat the various problems of the female reproductive system. Hysterectomy may be a good option for therapy in some instances, but it should be considered the last resort, not the first. Many women do fantastically well after hysterectomy, while to others, a hysterectomy is a curse on their existence. Most women, however, do not regret the decision and many say that they wish the procedure had been performed years before.

Hysterectomy is most often performed either for bleeding problems that cannot be controlled medically or specific abnormalities such as fibroids or uterine prolapse. It is surprising how many PCOS patients tell of family members who "needed" a complete hysterectomy. (Note: when surgeons use the term *complete hysterectomy*, they mean removal of the entire uterus, including the cervix. *Total hysterectomy with bilateral salpingo-oophorectomy* is the correct surgical terminology for removal of the uterus, both tubes, and both ovaries. Maybe "complete" is still a better term). Often hysterec-

tomies are performed for reasons, that if examined more closely, would be
seen to be consequences of PCOS.

Therapy
349

Does removal of the ovaries cure PCOS?

Previously it was stated that after wedge resection many women had
normal menstrual cycles. Sometimes removal of <u>one</u> ovary will have the same
result. Presently, we do not know the specific cause of PCOS, so it cannot be
said with certainty that removal of the ovary will cure PCOS.

PCOS, as has been emphasized over and over throughout this book,
is much bigger than the ovary. If it were only the ovary, PCOS should be
"cured" by menopause, which it isn't. PCOS of the reproductive years
becomes the Metabolic Syndrome (type 2 diabetes, heart disease, abnormal
blood lipid levels) of the post-reproductive years. This is true whether by age,
or by removal of the ovaries. If removal of the ovaries cured PCOS, women
should lose weight after oophorectomy, which is generally not the case.

What oophorectomy does do is result in a significant reduction in
androgens, and therefore PCOS-related skin problems often improve, especially after estrogen replacement is started. Removal of the uterus certainly
cures the problem of irregular bleeding regardless of whether the ovaries are
absent or present. Removal of the uterus and ovaries might be considered a
treatment for the *symptoms* of PCOS, rather than as a treatment for the complex disorder itself. Simply to remove the ovaries as treatment of PCOS is not
justified in our present standards of practice. Perhaps it should be. If hysterectomy is to be performed for reasons other than PCOS, it may be justified to
remove the ovaries of the PCOS patient as well. It is possible that in the future
removal of the ovaries may become more common, or we might find on the
balance of positives and negatives that ovaries are more beneficial than detrimental and should not be removed.

MEDICAL THERAPY

There are no medications that have been approved for the specific
purpose of treatment of PCOS. However the manifestations of PCOS offer a
number of targets at which to aim medical/pharmacological therapy.
Throughout the previous chapters, information about drug therapy has been
interspersed with theory and clinical practice. This section is designed as a reference listing of the various drug therapies that may be employed in the management of PCOS. It includes the most common medications, but to include
all would be outside the scope of this book. To make information gathering
quicker and easier, the following format is used in discussing each medication:

- Description
- Rationale/Indications for Use
- Potential Benefits
- Disadvantages
- Risk of use during pregnancy
- Administration

A risk factor rating (A, B, C, D, X) has been assigned by the Food and Drug Administration (Federal Register 1980; 44:37434-67) based on the level of risk the drug poses to the fetus. They tend to oversimplify issues and the system falls short on many counts, but it is the best presently available. The table which follows describes these categories, which will be referred to in the "Risk of Use during Pregnancy" section on each medication.

FDA Risk Factor Categories

- **Category A:** Controlled studies in women fail to demonstrate a risk to the fetus in the first trimester (and there is no evidence of a risk in later trimesters), and the possibility of fetal harm appears remote. Very few drugs fall into this category.
- **Category B:** Either animal-reproduction studies have not demonstrated a fetal risk but there are no controlled studies in pregnant women or animal-reproduction studies have shown an adverse effect (other than a decrease in fertility) that was not confirmed in controlled studies in women in the first trimester (and there is no evidence of a risk in later trimesters).
- **Category C:** Either studies in animals have revealed adverse effects on the fetus (teratogenic or embryocidal or other) and there are no controlled studies in woman or studies in women and animals are not available. Drugs should be given only if the potential benefit justifies the potential risk to the fetus.
- **Category D:** There is positive evidence of human fetal risk, but the benefits from use in pregnant women may be acceptable despite the risk (e.g., if the drug is needed in a life-threatening situation or for a serious disease for which safer drugs cannot be used or are ineffective).
- **Category X:** Studies in animals or human beings have demonstrated fetal abnormalities or there is evidence of fetal risk based on human experience or both, and the risk of the use of the drug in pregnant women clearly outweighs any possible benefit. The drug is contraindicated in women who are or may become pregnant.

Medication Groups

Steroid hormones	Anti-androgens	Anti-obesity	Insulin altering	Fertility agents	Others
oral contraceptives	estrogen	flutamide	others	clomiphene citrate	GnRH
progestins	corticosteroids	finasteride orlistat	metformin	gonadotropins	GnRH analogs
progesterone	spironolactone	sibutramine	"glitazones"	hCG	prolactin inhibition

STEROID HORMONES

Oral Contraceptives (OCs)

Description

OCs employ synthetic steroid hormones to block ovulation and render the uterine environment hostile to implantation. There are subtle differences between various OC formulations and this may translate into an individual woman's better tolerance for a particular type of formulation. However, there are many more similarities between OCs than differences. There are often several brands of OCs that contain the same ingredients. I have seen a patient who was placed on three different name brands in an unsuccessful attempt to prevent spotting, but all brands tried had been the same formulation of medication! The intentions of the physician in this case were unclear, but most of the possible explanations are unsatisfactory.

OCs are usually described by the following terminology:

Composition
combination	combined estrogen and progestin
progestin only	progestin alone without estrogen

Pattern of administration
monophasic	same dose every day
multiphasic	various doses throughout cycle

Progestin type
1st generation	norethindrone
2nd generation	norgestrel / levonorgestrel
3rd generation	norgestimate, desogestrel,

Amount of ethinyl estradiol
"High" dose	over 35 micrograms (mcg)
"Low" dose	30-35 mcg
"Mini" dose	less than 30 mcg

Most OCs are a combination of an estrogen and progestin. There are a few progestin-only pills, but progestin-only OCs are now thought to be of limited usefulness. Naturally occurring steroid hormones such as progesterone and estradiol are not easily absorbed in the stomach and intestine, so the hormones have been modified in the laboratory to improve solubility in water and absorption by the body. For all practical purposes, all combination OCs contain ethinyl estradiol (EE). The "strength" of an oral contraceptive is generally measured by how much estrogen is present. The pill introduced in the sixties had three times the dose we now consider a high dose of estrogen (50 mcg). It is no wonder that the present side effect and risk profile differ so from those of early versions of the pill.

Various regimens of increasing and decreasing the amounts and ratios of estrogen to progestin have been tried in PCOS patients, more to prevent abnormal bleeding than to mimic a natural cycle. Multiphasic OCs tend to lower the overall steroid used, but may not be useful in PCOS patients, where a flat-line ovarian and uterine suppression is desired. The variation in formulation is the source of a billion-dollar industry with each firm trying to make the better-tolerated product.

Presently, the most distinguishing characteristic between OCs is the type of progestin each contains. The first generation progestin, *norethindrone,* is the standard by which other agents are measured. The second generation progestin, *levonorgestrel,* is the most potent progestin and is the most androgenic. Theoretically, the more androgenic a progestin is, the greater its capacity to suppress LH as well as control bleeding. However, the more androgenic, the more potential for negative effects on lipids levels, glucose tolerance, and adverse effects on the skin. PCOS patients should, in general, avoid the more androgenic OCs. The third generation progestational agents, such as *desogestrel* and *norgestimate,* are the least androgenic and most estrogenic of the progestational agents. In one study, even the most androgenic progestin, levonorgestrel, was insufficient to increase androgens if used in the newer lower dose formulations. The risks/benefits between progestins in very low doses may be inconsequential, but may be enough to alter tolerance. There is still a concern that even low doses of levonorgestrel may adversely alter glucose tolerance and increase insulin resistance. For this reason some have avoided use of levonorgestrel.

In late 1995, a controversy arose about whether third generation progestin, *desogestrel*, increased the risk of thromboembolism (blood clots). This remains an unsettled issue. The problem is that this medication is excellent for controlling the skin problems of PCOS and may have the least adverse effect on glucose tolerance and insulin resistance. Another third generation progestin, *norgestimate*, should have similar benefits and disadvantages but was not included in the analysis. It was thought that the pills were prescribed not only to women at the greatest risk, but also to those who would have the greatest value of their use. The risks are still considered low and are probably offset by the benefits.

Overall, it is very difficult to decide which OC is best for the PCOS patient. There is too little research to draw a conclusion.

Rationale for Use

Oral contraceptives (OCs) are a mainstay of treatment of PCOS in women who do not want to become pregnant. On the balance OCs have many more positive than negative points. Obviously they are a method of birth control, about 99% effective, but they have a number of non-contraceptive uses as well. OC's most valuable asset is their capacity to regulate menstrual bleeding, but are also effective in treatment of hyperandrogenism.

OCs directly reduce the amount of LH released from the pituitary gland and therefore testosterone production from the ovary. The estrogen component of OCs increases sex steroid binding globulin (SHBG) which binds testosterone circulating in the bloodstream, thus preventing its action on targets like the hair follicles of skin. A decrease in production and a removal of active hormone from circulation translates into less androgen effect on the skin.

The largest problem that faces OC designers is not how to make a contraceptive, but how to best control the uterine lining (endometrium) to prevent unwanted bleeding. Too much estrogen has the side effect of headache, while too little estrogen increases the risks of untimely breakthrough bleeding. The combination of EE and a progestin is much like having ones foot on the accelerator and brake at the same time.

Since both an estrogen and progestin are present at the same time, the hormonal environment has been compared to that of pregnancy. The goal is to put the reproductive system in a state a suspended animation. OCs do a relatively good job of this. There is even scant, but positive evidence that OCs may preserve the store of eggs and marginally delay menopause. By reducing problems such as endometriosis, fibroids, and pelvic inflammatory disease, an individuals fertility may be better preserved.

A recent study at a major university health service showed that women of all ages had a poor understanding of the risks and benefits of oral contraceptive use. Many believe that the Pill causes cancer, when in fact, it lowers the risk of breast and ovarian cancer and has no promoting effects on others. Much of our early information about OCs is no longer valid. With the newer "low" and "minidose" pills, even the few risks formerly attributed to the pill have largely disappeared.

Potential Benefits:

Decreased
- Androgen levels
- Acne and hirsutism
- Endometrial hyperplasia and uterine cancer
- Menstrual bleeding and risk of anemia
- Menstrual pain and PMS
- Endometriosis
- Ovarian cancer
- Growth of uterine fibroids
- Ectopic pregnancy
- Pelvic inflammatory disease
- Fibrocystic breast disease
- Rheumatoid arthritis

Increased
- Menstrual cycle regulation
- Bone density
- Contraception
- Fertility

Disadvantages
- Weight gain (usually less than 10 lbs).
- Headache, nausea, breast tenderness
- Light erratic bleeding
- Risk of stroke in smokers over age 35
- Worsening of glucose tolerance
- Increased insulin resistance
- Worsens gall bladder disease

Weight gain Although weight gain is often attributed to pill use, scientific data is lacking and experts feel that this is a problem of perception. I am not so sure. Weight gain remains the most frequent reason after wanting to become pregnant that women stop OC use. Unfortunately, no one seems to loose this weight, reportedly gained because of OC use. If weight gain occurs as a result of OC use alone, it is minimal. There are some women who lose weight on OCs.

Headache, nausea, breast tenderness Frequent migraine headaches that are made worse by OCs may be a good reason to stop OC use. It is unclear whether the actual frequency of headaches is increased, but it remains a frequent complaint and the reason some women stop OC use. Nausea and breast tenderness are caused by the estrogen component of the OC and while relatively common, are usually mild and decline over several months of use.

Abnormal bleeding pattern Some women will not have periods. This is not a bad side effect. We know that there is sufficient hormone to offer proper hormone replacement, as well as uterine and bone protection. There may just be too little stimulation to cause withdrawal bleeding when the pill is stopped. Perhaps the greatest problem with loss of periods while on OCs is the anxiety caused about not being "normal" and the fear that there has been an establishment of pregnancy.

The most frequent reason an OC is stopped is due to breakthrough bleeding (BTB). The estrogenic portion of the OC is necessary for the support of the uterine lining. If there is too little estrogen, the integrity of the uterine lining may be compromised and spotting occurs. While a nuisance, it is of little medical significance and often will resolve after several months of pill use. The brands Demulen™ and Lo-Estrin™ have been frequent offenders and there may be better alternatives now.

Hypertension The older pills seem to increase blood pressure in about 5% of users. A small increase in blood pressure is seen with the 30 mcg pill with all progestins. This increase is not seen with the multiphasic preparations. Women who have developed hypertension while on the pill are more likely to have pregnancy-induced hypertension. OCs also may be used in cases of mild hypertension controlled by medications. While of no clinical significance in the population of pill users at large, I am prepared to keep an open mind about the effects on PCOS.

Lipid levels Low-dose OCs have limited effects on lipid profiles and except with very high levels, do not present a reason not to use OCs. It is important that those at risk have a lipid profile determined before OCs are started and if abnormalities are found, that routine testing be performed. The more estrogenic contraceptive agents are more likely to increase HDL, the good cholesterol, but it is not known whether this increase is significant. Adverse effects in lipid profile seem limited to the monophasic preparation of levonorgestrel at a strength that exceeds that of multiphasic preparations.

Once again, there have been no studies of birth control pills in which PCOS was appropriately targeted for impact on hypertension, insulin resistance or abnormal lipid levels.

To use or not to use?

Internists and medical endocrinologists are often at odds with reproductive endocrinologists and gynecologists about the relative benefits of OCs.

I am not sure why this is, but I am quite sure we REs are right. With the older higher dose medications many women had an impaired glucose tolerance test, an increased level of insulin and greater insulin resistance. This insulin resistance may be of enough to increase cardiovascular disease risks. OCs can be used in diabetics who are under age 35 and do not smoke. There has been no reported increase in diabetes or cardiovascular disease in patients that took even the older, more potent OCs.

Absolute reasons NOT to use OCs
- History of blood clots
- Known coronary artery disease
- Heavy smokers or smoking over age 35
- Breast cancer
- Markedly impaired liver function
- Undiagnosed vaginal bleeding

Thromboembolism The risk of deep vein thrombosis or pulmonary embolus increases 4-fold, but this is from 1 case per 10,000 use years to 4 per 10,000. The risk of stroke and serious blood clots has been eliminated with 20 mcg pills. If there is a family history of unexplained blood clot formation or pulmonary embolus, or if a blood clot has developed while on oral contraceptives, a search for an abnormality that could be inherited is warranted through special coagulation tests.

Heart attack (MI) The risk of myocardial infarction in a non-smoker may actually be less in OC users than in nonusers. The studies that identified most of the cardiovascular disease risks were with oral OCs no longer used. Smoking does not cause blood clots; however, it does increase the risk of MI.

Smoking OCs should not be used in smokers over age 35. If more than one pack a day is smoked, there is a relative contraindication at any age. Someone who has been an ex-smoker for more than one year can be considered a non-smoker. Don't smoke.

Risks of Use during Pregnancy
OCs were previously listed as Category X (though this has now been withdrawn. There are several studies that suggest women take somewhat longer to become pregnant when they have used OCs. There is no evidence that there is a greater risk of infertility after OC use, nor is there increased incidence of miscarriage. In fact, former pill users have a very slight reduction in miscarriage rates, and some IVF protocols use OCs to regulate cycles. There may be a slight increase in fraternal twinning after the pill is stopped. *OCs do not increase the possibility of birth defects.*

Administration
OCs are usually supplied in punch packs with some mechanism for identifying days of cycle. The 28-day packs contain twenty-one hormone pills and seven "dummy" or sugar pills that contain no medication. The 28 days represent the 28-day normal cycle. The purpose of the bleeding is to convey

a feeling of normalcy and ensure that a pregnancy has not occurred. It could have been that the pill pack contained eighteen or thirty-five active pills. In fact, in treatment of endometriosis, OCs are given continuously without a break to achieve maximum suppression of bleeding and endometriosis. The pills are usually started and stopped on Sunday, with bleeding occurring after 1-3 days of the dummy pills. The Sunday start is used to avoid bleeding on the weekend.

Progestins (progestagens)

- Medroxyprogesterone acetate (MPA) (Provera™, Cycrin™, Curretab™, Amen™)
- Norethindrone Acetate (Aygestin)

Description

A *progestin* is a medication that mimics the action of progesterone. The primary reason to use progestins is to regulate menses or to prevent an abnormal build-up of the endometrial lining. It is not the progestin itself that results in a period, but the progestin "matures" the uterine lining and its withdrawal causes menstruation.

Rationale for use

Progestins are most commonly used in PCOS to 'bring on a period' and to regulate menstrual cycles. They are also a necessary part of hormone replacement protocols in menopausal women who have not had a hysterectomy.

The small follicles (cysts) of PCOS produce enough estrogen to stimulate the proliferation of the uterine lining. In the absence of ovulation, the uterus is subject to unopposed estrogen stimulation. Left unchecked, this can lead to an overgrowth of the lining of the uterus (endometrial hyperplasia) and over the long-term (probably years), even uterine cancer. While uterine cancer is rare under age 40, most cases occur in association with PCOS.

The most common use for progestins is in combination with estrogen for hormone replacement therapy after menopause or ovarian failure in women who have not had a hysterectomy. The risk of uterine cancer is too high to use estrogen alone. In some PCOS patients the estrogen levels are not sufficient for the progestin to have an effect. For a progestin to work, the uterus must first be "primed" with estrogen.

In some cases of PCOS, a progestin alone will not induce bleeding. A regimen first using estrogen to cause endometrial proliferation and then progestin to mature the lining may be tried to more adequately reproduce the normal endometrial maturation process. The risk of endometrial hyperplasia is probably much less in these individuals.

In select cases progestins may be used to partially suppress the ovary and regulate bleeding in preparation for use of fertility drugs. There are also those who use progestins in treatment of endometriosis.

- The principle benefit of progestin is its capacity to regulate uterine bleeding. The medical benefit is improved uterine health. There is decreased fluid retention and reduction in the feeling of pelvic fullness that can occur with infrequent menses. MPA may be less detrimental to glucose metabolism that norethindrone, but since it is used for such a relatively short time, these differences may not matter. Some patients report better tolerance of norethindrone than MPA.

Disadvantages

- While progestins may regulate the menstrual cycle and blood levels of LH may be reduced with their use, they appear to be of little value in reduction of hair growth or metabolic derangements of PCOS. Acne and hair growth may even be increased with progestin use. Some patients report depression or PMS-like symptoms with the synthetic progestins, which may be lessened with the progesterone. There is spotty evidence that progestins can increase the growth of uterine fibroids. Progestins may increase the risks of serious blood clots in susceptible, or at risk individuals.

Risks of Use during Pregnancy

FDA has removed rating and substituted a caution that progestins should not be used in pregnancy. As one might expect, progestins are relatively frequently, but unintentionally, used in early pregnancy. There is no evidence that pregnancies are adversely effected, or that use leads to birth defects. Still it is advised that use of progestins in early pregnancy is avoided and it is a good idea to check at least a home pregnancy test before starting therapy. Progesterone is sometimes used for early pregnancy support, but not progestins. The risk of a male baby being born with the urethral opening on the underside of the penis, rather than at the tip (hypospadias) has been reported to be double the natural occurrence of about five per thousand births. Rarely, female fetuses may be born with a slightly enlarged clitoris if exposed to these medications. This is probably less common than reported and is based on the use of progestins in the past as opposed to during pregnancy. The drugs would have to be used in the critical time of genital development, three to six weeks after a missed period. Progestins still carry pregnancy category X warning, but this was clearly over-stated.

Administration

A regimen of MPA 5 to 10 mg for ten to fourteen days monthly is used for normalization of cyclic bleeding. Norethindrone can be used at 5 mg daily in a similar regimen. Some prefer therapy every three months. It is possible that less frequent use is also less effective in reducing the risk of hyperplasia.

MPA 2.5 mg daily is often used in conjunction with estrogen and is often used in a regimen of daily hormonal replacement after menopause or ovarian failure.

There is a long-acting form of MPA (Depo-Provera™) that may have some usefulness as a contraceptive. Use in teens has become relatively common because of poor compliance with OCs. The long-term effect on reproduction is unknown in this age group, but an increased risk of osteoporosis has been reported. Depo-Provera™ is occasionally used as second line treatment of endometriosis. Outside of contraception, its usefulness is uncertain and in an occasional case may result in long term disruption of ovulation and menstrual function even after discontinuation. Although Depo-Provera™ may prevent endometrial hyperplasia, there have been limited reports of its specific usefulness in PCOS. I have a personal bias against this medication and have seen more problems than solutions with its use.

Progesterone

- Crinone™ (vaginal)
- Prometrium™ (oral)

Description

Progesterone (P_4) (*pro* = for, *gest* = pregnancy) is the hormone produced by the corpus luteum following ovulation. Progesterone is available for use in oral, vaginal, injectable and cream forms.

Rationale for Use

Progesterone is a naturally occurring hormone that reaches high levels after ovulation in the normal cycles. Use of progesterone in PCOS is in attempt to mimic the luteal phase of the cycles and add integrity to the uterine lining. Like the progestins listed above, supplemental progesterone can be used to mature the uterine lining that has been estrogen primed. When discontinued, a period will result. In this role it is used to regulate menstrual bleeding.

Progesterone is also used to supplement luteal function after IVF, especially when Lupron™, or another GnRH analog, has been used along with stimulation. GnRH analogs have the advantage of blocking an unwanted LH surge and ovulation, but also suppress the production of progesterone by LH in the luteal phase. Using a combination of supplemental estradiol and progesterone, the uterus can be precisely programmed to exactly mimic a normal natural ovulatory cycle. As such, progesterone is often used in managed cycles for oocyte donation and replacement of previously frozen embryos resulting from IVF.

Progesterone has also been used in the treatment of PMS, but with equivocal results.

Progesterone changes the uterine lining that has proliferated under the influence of estrogen into a lush environment of uterine secretion that is receptive to pregnancy. Progesterone is sometimes used as an aid in supporting the uterine environment for an early pregnancy. By about eight to nine weeks after the last period, the placenta has taken up the role of hormone production and the ovary ceases to be important. In fact, at nine weeks, we know the ovary can even be removed without detriment to the pregnancy.

Supplemental progesterone use for prevention of pregnancy loss is questionable, but virtually all gynecologists and reproductive endocrinologists use progesterone for this reason. Progesterone use is based on the premise that there is inadequate progesterone being produced by the ovary and that this is the reason for miscarriage. The amounts of progesterone actually needed to sustain a pregnancy are really very low. I have seen successful pregnancies resulting from progesterone levels as low as 4 pg / ml. However, progesterone is a reasonable marker of the health of a pregnancy and lower progesterone levels can signify a problem. Can the problem be fixed with progesterone supplementation? Probably not. This is usually a problem of egg quality that was determined either before ovulation, or at the time of fertilization. By giving progesterone we are treating an effect, not the cause of the problem. There is evidence that progesterone relaxes the uterus and also may assist in implantation by helping block the natural immunity the body has to the embryo, an invading foreigner. Therapy would be better addressed at improving egg quality.

Potential Benefits
- Menstrual cycle regulation
- More physiologic ("natural") than progestins
- Support of luteal function
- Hormone replacement

Disadvantages
- Overall, minor side effects are common. Serious side effects are very rare. Remember this is a supplement of a natural hormone given in amounts to approximate what the body should be making during a normal menstrual cycle. In this context, it should not be considered a drug. Progesterone may share some of the potential for blood clots as progestins, but incidence should be less.
- With injections of progesterone there may be pain or irritation at the site of the injection. With vaginal applications there may irritation and/or discharge, which is commonly mistaken for a yeast infection. Crinone™ uses a superior vehicle for delivery of progesterone and is generally better tolerated than other vaginal preparations. Oral progesterone is much less effective in increasing blood and therefore uterine levels of progesterone and larger doses are needed to achieve the same effects as other routes of administration.
- Progesterone should not be used in cases of persistent vaginal bleeding or liver disease. If there is a significant change in health while on the medications, your physician should consulted.

> ### Side-effects of Progesterone Use
>
> - Lethargy/drowsiness/insomnia
> - Depression/mood swings
> - Breast soreness/enlargement
> - Nausea/constipation/diarrhea
> - Headache
> - Muscle pain/joint pain
> - Increased urination

• The progesterone of Prometrium™ is mixed with peanut oil and should not be used by individuals with an allergy to peanuts

Risks of Use during Pregnancy

Previous Category X (now withdrawn), the FDA has now approved the administration of progesterone (Crinone™) in conjunction with assisted reproduction when a progesterone deficiency may be possible. Progesterone is progesterone regardless of the route of administration. Also understand that progesterone is the hormone that the ovary normally makes.

Will the use of progesterone harm the pregnancy? Probably not. The greatest fear is that it may delay an early miscarriage of an abnormal embryo. This loss is still inevitable, but the miscarriage is postponed. Progesterone appears safe and it may be a useful addition to give a pregnancy the best chance. After good levels of progesterone are determined, therapy can often be tapered and stopped. If there is poor growth of the pregnancy on ultrasound, then it may be in the best interest to stop progesterone and allow a miscarriage to occur.

We know that individuals who have undergone ovulation induction have progesterone levels that may be as much as ten times that of a normal pregnancy and these pregnancies do just fine. It is quite possible that pregnancies in individuals who receive progesterone are at higher risk of miscarriage from the beginning. The incidence of birth defects seems not to be significantly increased. In fact, the idea that progesterone is harmful is a relic of bygone days and is unsubstantiated.

Administration

While progesterone therapy is not new, it has required compounding by a pharmacist and so was relatively difficult to obtain. Preparations varied between different pharmacies and probably in their capacity for progesterone absorption into the blood stream. No pharmaceutical company wanted to bother with a drug that could not be patented. Many health food stores sell progesterone in lanolin or other emollients. While this is probably of no harm, it is several times less potent and several times more expensive than prescription progesterone, but still the same medication. Now there are brand name prescription compounds available for vaginal (Crinone™) and oral (Prometrium™) use.

Crinone™ is emulsified in a hypoallergenic gel that allows even absorption. It should be noted that since there is a direct absorption into the uterus, blood levels of progesterone are much lower and do not adequately reflect the true concentration of the medication reaching the uterus. Usually the 8% strength is used, but it is also available in a 4% application. Unfortunately, Crinone™ is too expensive to be used outside assisted reproduction and in the short term.

Prometrium™ is dispensed in 100 or 200 mg capsules (100 mg is approximately equal to 2.5 mg of MPA). The medication may be better tolerated than the progestins mentioned above. Absorption of progesterone is much less effective and erratic in an oral form.

For injection, progesterone is pre-mixed, usually with sesame oil. The
injections are usually given in the hip. The dose is usually 25-50 mg.

Therapy
361

Generally, it doesn't matter what time of the day medication is taken.
If drowsiness occurs, it is best used in the evening.

Estrogens

Description

The are three major estrogens produced in the human female: estradiol, estrone, and estriol. Estriol (E_3) is made from the placenta and is important only in pregnancy. Estrone (E_1) is the major metabolite of estradiol and
the major estrogen produced outside the ovary. Estrone is also the most common estrogen produced after menopause and is used in some hormone
replacement preparations. Estradiol (E_2) is the most potent of the three estrogens and principally comes from the developing ovarian follicles. The are a
number of synthetic, plant and animal derived estrogens that are used for supplements and hormone replacement and more are arriving monthly. If there is
a difference in effectiveness of oral preparations it is not clear, but tolerance
may vary. See Chapter 14 for more information on hormone replacement
therapy (HRT).

Rationale for Use

All estrogens have the capacity to induce endometrial development.
Some physicians use estrogen supplementation to enhance development of
the uterine lining, possibly increase the implantation rate and reduce the
chance of miscarriage. Other physicians recommend using estrogen in the follicular phase in addition to clomiphene to counteract the anti-estrogen effects
of clomiphene. There is a new study using estrogen supplementation with
clomiphene showing increased pregnancy rates. This may rekindle an enthusiasm for this regimen that is not thought effective by most.

Estrogens are most commonly used in hormone replacement therapy
(HRT). HRT has a number of positive benefits in reducing the large number of
signs and symptoms of estrogen deficiency. Estrogen is essential for bone
health. There is increasing awareness that there may be positive metabolic consequence of estrogen use. These benefits must be weighed against the potential increase risk of breast cancer.

Potential Benefits

- Promotion of endometrial development
- Relief of menopausal symptoms
- Retard osteoporosis
- Possibly decrease risk of coronary artery disease
- Possibly decrease risk of senile dementia (Alzheimer's)
- Add integrity to the tissues of the pelvis

Disadvantages

- Unwanted endometrial proliferation
- Breast tenderness
- Mild fluid retention and hypertension

- Increased risk of breast cancer (?)
- Stimulates growth of endometriosis
- Increased risk of blood clots

Risks of Use during Pregnancy

Category X. The FDA classification is an older and more general warning and does not apply. Estrogen is used at relatively high levels in artificially programmed cycles for frozen –thawed embryo replacement or fresh embryos after oocyte donation. There does not seem to be any adverse consequence of this therapy in hundreds of pregnancies. The package inserts still contain strong warnings about the use of estrogen in pregnancy, but are probably unfounded.

Administration

Estradiol can be dispensed in either an oral or transdermal route. Synthetic estradiol comes in 0.5, 1 and 2 mg tablets representing the dose given for hormone replacement. This is equivalent to 0.375, 0.625 and 1.25 mg of conjugated estrogens. In comparison, 1.0 mg of estradiol is roughly equivalent to 0.1 mg of transdermal estrogen. If used for hormonal replacement and the uterus has not been removed, a progestin must be added to prevent endometrial hyperplasia.

Corticosteroids

- hydrocortisone, dexamethasone, prednisone

Description

Corticosteroids (glucocorticoids) are hormones that have their origin in the cortex of the adrenal gland, or mimic the actions of these hormones. Corticosteroids, whether synthetic or natural, have the capacity to reduce inflammation and the body's immune response.

Rationale for Use

Steroid therapy is most often used in PCOS for the suppression of excessive amounts of adrenal hormone production. Some have hypothesized that as many as 50% of PCOS patients have some degree of hyper-secretion of adrenal androgens. Although all hormones of the adrenal cortex are controlled by the same pituitary adrenocorticotropic hormones (ACTH), the other major adrenal hormones, cortisol and aldosterone are seldom elevated in PCOS. Adrenal steroids can be reduced when small amounts of high potency adrenal steroids are given. This principle is used for therapy in select patients with PCOS. Some have reported reasonably good success with adrenal steroid therapy while others have had no improvement with the discontinuation rate quite high due to side effects. Dehydroepiandrosterone sulfate (DHEAS) is almost entirely of adrenal origin and has been used as the principle marker of adrenal hyperandrogenism. The individuals most likely to benefit from corticosteroids are those with elevated levels of dehydroepiandrosterone sulfate (DHEAS) found on blood testing.

Cortisol (cortisone) represents the standard by which other drugs are measured, but due to its mineralocorticoid action and salt retention, cortisone has been largely abandoned if favor of the synthetic preparations, prednisone and dexamethasone. In comparison, 25 mg of hydrocortisone is equivalent to 5 mg of prednisone or 0.5 mg of dexamethasone. The longer half-life of dexamethasone may work in favor of desired adrenal suppression, but also it may be more likely to over suppress.

Complete replacement of cortisol requires about 50-75 mg of cortisol daily. The desired objective for adjunctive glucocorticoid use in ovulation induction has been to normalize without suppressing adrenal steroid production. Therefore, less than replacement levels are used. Typical dosages are dexamethasone 0.25-0.5 mg, or 5-10 mg of prednisone. Lower dosages potentially have fewer side effects and unwanted adrenal suppression, but may also achieve less desired suppression.

There are two different philosophies and regimens on duration of therapy. Some have started therapy with onset of clomiphene and stopped when ovulation has been confirmed. Others give the medication continuously. Since the ovarian follicle may take up to100 days to undergo its complete development, it would seem that a continuous regimen offers the best protection against hyperandrogenism, but also the highest incidence of adverse effects. In general medical use, an every other day dosing regimen is used to minimize unwanted suppression and side effects, but this regimen has not been reported in ovulation induction.

Potential Benefits

- Steroids have the ability to suppress adrenal androgen production and may be useful in treatment of PCOS with an adrenal component. Overall, their use is better in theory than practice and use is often discontinued because of unwanted side effects. The effectiveness of corticosteroids in control of hirsutism is questioned and they should probably be considered third-line therapy. Some have reported an additive effect with clomiphene and patients with elevated DHEAS may be candidates for a trial of therapy. Doses as low as 0.25 mg. of dexamethasone can be used chronically with little fear of overly suppressing adrenal function. Because of the higher cortisol levels at night, suppression therapy is probably better given at bedtime.

Disadvantages

- Major complications from use are extremely rare. Patients on glucocorticoid therapy are at risk for adrenal suppression and inability to properly respond to stressful stimuli such as major surgery, or accidents. It is generally believed that doses equivalent to 5 mg of prednisone daily (0.5 mg of dexamethasone), or use for less than 3 weeks does not cause undesired suppression and can be abruptly stopped at any time.
- Weight gain is very common and in my experience, this is the most frequent complaint and the most common reason to stop therapy. One study reported that over 3/4 of patients using corticosteroids gained at least 10 pounds after 6 months of therapy.

Potential Side Effects
- Weight gain
- Worsening of glucose tolerance
- Osteoporosis
- Skin changes
- Gastric hypersecretion
- Hypertension
- Lipid abnormalities
- Insomnia and psychological changes

Risks of Use During Pregnancy

Category C. Corticosteroids have been used extensively in pregnancy for treatment of asthma and to help mature the fetal lungs when preterm birth is suspected. There has been a single report that suggests that PCOS may result from prenatal exposure to large amounts of corticosteroids used for prematurity.

Administration

I prescribe one of two regimens of corticosteroids. The first is to use 5 mg of prednisone nightly from cycle day 2-3 for the next 10 –14 days in conjunction with clomiphene 100-150 mg taken days 5-9. The success seems better and the steroid exposure shorter than the alternative regimen. Here I prescribe 0.25 mg of dexamethasone every night for up to six months. At one and three months of therapy, DHEAS and total testosterone are measured to evaluate success in the improvement of androgen levels. Monitoring of stimulation cycles is not altered. Therapy is stopped when a pregnancy test returns positive.

ANTI-ANDROGENS

Rationale for Use

All anti-androgens have a single reason for their use in PCOS, to reduce the adverse effects of androgens on the skin and thus lessen excessive hair growth. Each has a related, but slightly different method of action. Each is available in the U.S. and is used primarily for reasons other than hirsutism. None are specifically approved by the FDA for hirsutism. Each has been shown effective to some degree, but no one is effective in all cases and one is not better than another. Each has distinct advantages and disadvantages. (Also see Chapter 7).

Risks of Use during Pregnancy

Category X. No anti-androgen should be used when attempting a pregnancy, or without adequate contraception. Although there has been inadequate human study to draw a conclusion, at least a theoretical risk exists in males exposed during pregnancy to anti-androgens of alteration in the external male sex organs and their appearance. There are scattered reports of spironolactone used in fertility therapy, but this cannot be advised.

Spironolactone (Aldactone™)

Description

Spironolactone is a diuretic used to treat hypertension. It has an idiosyncratic action as an anti-androgen and can reduce excessive hair growth by blocking the effects of androgen. It is the most widely prescribed anti-androgen in the United States.

At high doses spironolactone blocks the metabolic pathway called the cytochrome P-450 system that affects the capacity of the ovary and adrenal gland to make androgens. It also alters the conversion of testosterone to dihydrotestosterone (DHT) by 5 alpha-reductase enzyme.

Potential Benefits

- Spironolactone is the least expensive of the alternatives listed below. Since it is a diuretic, it can be especially useful in hypertensive patients.

Disadvantages

- Irregular bleeding occurs in about 30% of patients unless used with an oral contraceptive
- Some patients report the side effects of nausea, indigestion, or fatigue

Administration

The usual starting dose is 50 mg. once or twice daily and may be increased to 100 mg. twice daily. It is prudent to have initial blood testing and to be reassessed after several weeks of therapy. Although an adverse effect of spironolactone use may be hyperkalemia (high levels of potassium in the blood), it is rarely seen in young healthy women. Because spironolactone is metabolized in the liver, baseline liver function testing should performed.

Cyproterone acetate

Description

Cyproterone acetate (CA) is a potent anti-androgen and weak progestin. CA is used specifically for control of excessive hair growth. In Britain and Canada it is also combined in the oral contraceptive Diane.

Potential Benefits

- Its effectiveness in treatment of hirsutism is well substantiated. Most patients will report decreased hair growth and some patients become amenorrheic.

Disadvantages

- While CA is usually well tolerated, its glucocorticoid activity may cause weight gain. Drug induced hepatitis has been reported and it is prudent to monitor liver function.

Administration
The usual dose is 50 mg.

Flutamide (Eulexin™)

Description
Flutamide is a non-steroidal anti-androgen indicated for treatment of prostatic cancer. Its action is similar to spironolactone and cyproterone acetate in that androgen action is reversibly blocked at the androgen receptor.

Potential Benefits
- Flutamide is theoretically superior to cyproterone due to its absence of prednisone (steroid) like activity and to spironolactone because of its lack of alteration in kidney function.

Disadvantages
- A majority of patients report the side effect of dry skin. Less common side effects are hot flushes, increased appetite, headache, fatigue, and nausea. It is metabolized by the liver and fatal liver toxicity has been reported. Its similar efficacy, but higher cost and potential liver toxicity make flutamide a second line therapy. Many feel the drug is safe, especially in lower doses in healthy individuals. I have heard of one serious complication possible related to flutamide. I suggest flutamide be limited to physicians experienced with its use.

Administration
The usual dose is 125-250 mg. once or twice daily.

Finasteride (Propecia™, Proscar™)

Description
Finasteride is not a true anti-androgen, but inhibits the enzyme 5 alpha-reductase, which is responsible for the production of the active skin androgen, dihydrotestosterone. Finasteride is indicated for use in the management of benign prostatic hypertrophy and more recently male pattern baldness.

Potential Benefits
- Good safety and tolerance profile

Disadvantages
- High cost

Administration
The dose of 5 mg. daily is usually prescribed.

ANTI-OBESITY AGENTS

It is known that weight loss alone can restore menstrual cyclicity and fertility, as well as improving general health parameters. Medications may be useful in helping the individuals begin a weight loss program. These agents do not work alone. Eating habits must be changed, moving toward smaller portions of well-rounded meals. With weight loss there is often an improvement in the endocrine abnormalities of PCOS. Weight loss however is a huge challenge.

Orlistat (Xenical™)

Description

Orlistat is a lipase inhibitor released in the United States in 1999. Orlistat's site of action is in the intestines, where it blocks absorption of approximately 30% of the fat that is eaten from being absorbed. The unabsorbed fat is then eliminated in the feces.

Rationale for use

Weight loss. Blocks absorption of fat.

Potential Benefits

- Orlistat would appear to be the best "diet pill" for the obese PCOS patient. Its effectiveness in weight loss has been clearly shown. There is also evidence that patients who have used orlistat maintain their weight loss over a two-year study period, compared to a placebo control group. In addition to facilitating weight loss, orlistat reduces fat intake, thereby lowering cholesterol and triglycerides. Orlistat appears to lower insulin levels and possibly improve insulin resistance. Most other weight reduction medications are contraindicated in pregnancy.

Disadvantages

- While a safe drug, orlistat is not necessarily an easy drug to take. The risk of gastrointestinal side effects may be as high as 30%. Side effects are most pronounced after fat filled meal. Some are using orlistat as an agent for purging. Fat laden meals are consumed then Xenical™ is used to induce diarrhea. This may help with weight control, but is ill-adaptive behavior.

  #### Side effects
  - Diarrhea or frequent loose stools
  - Malodorous stools
  - Fecal urgency
  - Fecal incontinence
  - Fecal staining

Risks of Use during Pregnancy
Pregnancy category B. Since the drug is not systemically absorbed its risk to a pregnancy that might be conceived while using the medication would appear very small.

Administration
Taken with fat-containing meals up to three times daily. Vitamin supplementation is required because of increase loss and decreased absorption in the intestines.

Sibutramine (Meridia™)

Description
Sibutramine (Meridia™) is thought to work by increasing the activity of norepinephrine, serotonin and dopamine in the brain. This decreases appetite and creates a full feeling.

Rationale for Use
Weight loss. Alters the hunger and satiety centers of the brain.

Potential Benefits
- Tolerance is less likely to occur with sibutramine, making possible extended use (beyond 12 weeks). Sibutramine does not directly stimulate adrenergic nerve fibers so stimulation is less. Long term studies have been encouraging.

Disadvantages
- Blood pressure usually increases by 1-3 mm hg and pulse by 4-5 beats per minute. Sibutramine has the potential of interacting with a number of other classes of drugs including all central nervous system stimulants and depressants. It may increase the sedative effect of alcohol.

   Possible drug interaction:
   - Antidepressants
   - Other weight loss medication
   - Cold preparation containing PPA
   - Migraine headache medication such as Imitrex™
   - Tryptophan supplementation
   - St John's wort
   - Narcotic agonists (Talwin™)

   Individuals with the following conditions should not use sibutramine:
   - History of seizure or epilepsy
   - Heart attack , cardiac arrhythmia or irregular heartbeat,
   - Glaucoma

Risks of Use during Pregnancy
Pregnancy Category C. Contraception is recommended. Sibutramine should not be used in pregnancy or nursing mothers.

The usual starting dose is 10 mg once daily. Blood pressure must be
monitored. Pills are available as 5, 10 and 15 mg.

Other Agents

Below is a summary of medications that have been reported to cause
weight loss and still may be available. They cannot be recommended either
because of safety issues or inability to produce sustained weight loss.

Adrenergic (Amphetamine–like) agents:

- Phenteramine (Adipex™, Fastin™, Oby-trim™, Ionamin™)
- Diethylpropion (Tenuate™, Dospan™),
- Phendimetrazine (Bontril™, Plegine™, Prelu-2™, X-Troxine™)
- Mazindoil (Sanorex™, Mazanor™),
- Phenylpropanolamine (Acutrim™, Dexatrim™),
- Ephedra

The amphetamines belong to a class of drugs known as adrenergics
or sympathomimetics. All, more or less, have the adrenalin effects of stimulation of the central nervous system and suppression of the appetite center in
the hypothalamus. The newest drugs have had modification in their chemical
structure where there is less CNS stimulation and less potential for abuse.
None of these agents are recommended for other than short-term use. With
all these drugs their effectiveness decreases over time as the body grows accustomed to the effects (tachyphylaxis). Blood pressure monitoring is important.

Common side effects of all of these agents include nervousness and
agitation, palpitations, dry mouth, insomnia, constipation, tremor, difficulty
with urination, and headache. All can increase blood pressure, pulse rate and
may worsen glucose tolerance. They can be particularly dangerous in individuals with hypertension, hyperthyroidism, and glaucoma.

Phentermine is a sympathomimetic appetite suppressant.
Previously it was combined with fenfluramine in the now infamous (phen-fen)
combination. Fenfluramine was shown to increase the risk of valvular heart disease; lawsuits are still pending. Phentermine appears to have a reasonable
safety profile. Phentermine acts on the appetite center of the hypothalamus to
reduce the desire to eat. The greatest disadvantage of phentermine is the stimulation it causes. Many people feel nervous or have trouble sleeping. Side
effects include hypertension, euphoria, nervousness and insomnia. As the
effect of the drug decreases over time, there may be episodes of decreased
alertness. Phentermine is taken before breakfast and 10 to 14 hours before
sleep. Its benefit diminishes within a few weeks and should be continued only
if the patient continues to lose weight. Long term weight reduction is questionable and many regain any weight lost while using the medication within
one year.

Phenylpropanolamine (PPA) is the agent most commonly used
in non-prescription formulations. It is more commonly added to cold prepara-

tion as a decongestant. It is somewhat less stimulating and probably less effective than prescription, but it should not be considered an unconditionally safe drug. If PPA is taken with bromocriptine, used for prolactin suppression or another groups of drugs, MAO inhibitors, a serious hypertensive crisis can result.

Ephedra is used in traditional Chinese medicine for its bronchodilation and drying action similar to pseudoephedrine in the U.S. There have been claims, subsequently disproved, that the herb can cause weight loss. If it were so, it would be temporary. At the most the preparations are similar to PPA, but it has the potential for considerable toxicity, especially hypertension.

Serotonergic Agents

Theoretically these agents can reduce the desire to eat or over eat. Fenfluramine previously given weight phentermine was one such agent. Selective serotonin re-uptake inhibitors (SSRIs) which prolong the action of serotonin by inhibiting its uptake at nerve endings are widely used in the treatment of depression.

Fluoxetine (Prozac™) is a SSRI touted to promote loss. Follow-up studies reported that weight lost was temporary and regained within one year. These drugs are no longer indicated for treatment of obesity alone.

5-hydroxytryptophan (5-HP). Although several studies have shown a positive effect on weight loss, the loss was short term and quickly regained. It is not presently recommended for weight loss.

INSULIN-ALTERING DRUGS

The use of insulin-altering drugs has done more to bring the entity of PCOS to the surface than any single advancement since the disorder was first described. Undoubtedly, this is the portal through which a good deal of our future understanding and potential for making a change in quality of life of those with the disorder will flow. Surely, soon after this book is published, there will become new agents available and some of the present agents may fall into disfavor. The concept of insulin resistance is presented in Chapter 9 and use of some of these medications in infertility in Chapter 11.

Disclaimer

The insurgence of interest in PCOS has been firmly associated with insulin-altering drugs, but it must be remembered that they are not "miracle" drugs. They do not work for everyone, and there are risks of use. It should be remembered that the FDA has not approved insulin-altering agents for treatment of either insulin resistance or PCOS. Use of these medications for PCOS is considered "*off label*", although they are commonly prescribed. There should be a close patient-physician working relationship that includes discussion of risks and benefits of its use. Some have suggested that the major effect of metformin is to induce a temporary weight loss and this reduction is responsible for the improvement seen in metabolic parameters. The effectiveness of metformin has been questioned in severely obese individuals (over 300 pounds).

Metformin (Glucophage™)

Description

Metformin is an oral insulin sensitizer that was FDA approved in 1994 to lower glucose when sugar levels cannot be controlled by diet alone. Metformin is now used in over ninety countries and by three million in the United States alone. Metformin enhances the body's sensitivity to insulin and inhibits glucose production from the liver without the risk of hypoglycemia.

Rationale for use

Glucophage has been shown to improve the endocrine imbalances associated with PCOS. It decreases insulin resistance, which has a very positive effect on ovarian function. There are repeated studies that show spontaneous ovulation in previously anovulatory patients using glucophage.

There seems to be a great reluctance by some physicians to trying metformin. Doctors are a conservative lot and we must respect the physician who says that he or she is reluctant to give the drug without FDA approval or because they are not familiar with its use. A much worse scenario is the physician who, taunted by a patient with a drug and dosage written down from an Internet excerpt, prescribes the medicine without full knowledge of the drug, the patient, or the indication for use. Several recent cases illustrate the point. One was a physician who had heard about the improvement of clomiphene responsiveness with metformin, so prescribed metformin for five days each month along with clomiphene. When it didn't work he considered both metformin and clomiphene to be failures. In another case, a patient used metformin for the first two weeks each month and stopped it at mid-cycle to avoid exposure during an early pregnancy. The patient had two weeks of severe GI distress in each of three months. Each time she would start to feel better and believe the drug was actually helping, she stopped use, only to repeat the problem the following month. This went on for three months, until the patient decided she couldn't stand it any longer. She is now using metformin continuously (the appropriate method), feeling great, and having regular menses.

Why not give it a try? This is how we approached our first metformin patients in 1997. We were failing miserably in our treatment with PCOS. They couldn't get pregnant even with the most aggressive therapy; they would over or under stimulate on fertility drugs; they needed to lose weight and couldn't; or they just wanted to try another approach. After fully considering the benefits, suggested but not clearly known at that time, and the risks, thought to be very low, we concluded why not give this treatment a try? Our patients did and they continue to undergo a basic endocrine evaluation as outlined in Chapter 5. We are still attempting to determine whether specific types of patients with PCOS are better candidates for metformin than are others. The point here is that there does not have to be a lock-tight indication for use of metformin, but there should be.

I often see patients with PCOS on the Internet posting complaints that a physician will not prescribe metformin. There is a time-honored tradition in medicine to "first do no harm" and this may be the crux of the matter. The risks of metformin appear quite low and it is hard to make someone more infertile than they are already are, so why argue? We might learn something. Certainly we are far from knowing how successful metformin can be in fertility therapy, or for that matter, general health maintenance.

I find it much harder to answer the question of when to stop metformin therapy rather than when to start. If there is a long-term health benefit, can we postpone development of type 2 diabetes with ongoing use of metformin? Do all women that have taken and lost weight keep the weight off? We don't know. We generally consider a six-month course of metformin as a trial. We will stop it sooner or continue it longer based on the individual's own personal assessment. Is it helping? Do you feel better? Do you want to continue?

This is difficult in that the greatest reason for use is that a good alternative has not been found.

Potential Benefits*
- Improvement of glucose tolerance and insulin sensitivity
- Does not lower glucose outside the normal range
- Favorable effect on blood lipid levels
- Stabilization or possible loss of weight
- Improved fat distribution
- Reduction in blood pressure independent of weight loss
- Reduction of circulating androgens
- Restoration of regular menstrual cycles
- Increased fertility
- Induction of ovulation with clomiphene after previous treatment failure
- Improved success with in vitro fertilization
- Postponement or prevention of diabetes
- Improvement in well-being and energy level
* Some findings suggested but not yet substantiated through large trial research

Possible Disadvantages
- Metformin appears to have an excellent safety profile. After having treated a large number of otherwise healthy PCOS patients with metformin, there seem to be specific patterns that develop in terms of side effects. The list below is a combination that must be included due to medical concerns and many are from accounts of patients' personal experiences. How well the drug is tolerated and how the individual responds must be factored into the equation to determine of how long the drug should be used.

Gastrointestinal disturbance Gastrointestinal (GI) upset and a tendency toward looser stools or more frequent bowel movements are reported in at least 1/3 of users. These problems are much more common in the initial month of use and can be decreased by starting at lower doses and taking the medications less frequently. GI problems are most often experienced after a meal rich in fats or sugars. If there is recurrent vomiting or persistent diarrhea, a physician should be consulted.

In warning patients about the side effects of metformin, there are several analogies I use that are more or less correct. The first is that metformin is similar to Antabuse™ which is given to alcoholics in that it causes a quite severe reaction when alcohol is used. The same will often occur while on metformin if a "Big Mac attack" is launched. If the thought of a piece of chocolate cake, or an order of French fries becomes a little repulsive due to resulting intestinal problems, one is less likely to partake of the evil. The early stages of metformin use afford a reasonable chance for behavior modification.

An additional analogy of metformin action is that it regulates the body's need for glucose. If more is taken in than needed, the excess will be "dumped". That dumping can be the source of the GI side effects. And the third analogy used is that metformin adjusts the carburetor on the body's engine. It is running on too rich a fuel and by "leaning out" the mixture, performance is increased. None of these examples may be scientifically correct, but taken together I believe they accurately portray an assessment of the actions of metformin and the reason for the GI side effects. It may be less than kind. I am not opposed to responding to complaints of GI side effects after initiation of therapy by the comment – "Good. It's working". Certainly the side effects can be so severe that the medication must be discontinued and a physician should be immediately informed if a problem is perceived. Clearly, metformin is not a "one size fits all" drug.

Those who continue to have persistent GI symptoms after the first month of use should reexamine their diet.

Generalized feeling of unwellness It seems that about 30-40% of patients on metformin really feel better. They may have mild GI effects; overall the energy level is increased and their appetite is decreased. They appear to almost be addicted to the drug. Another 30-40% is more in the "take it or leave it" category. They see or feel advancement in some areas, maybe a little decline in others, and often no real change one way or the other. A third group of 10-20% feel that metformin is the work of the devil. They feel unwell and have a number of varied complaints. Common sense would dictate that the medication be stopped in this group. The question is whether physical response and tolerance of the drug can be related to its effectiveness and alteration in laboratory findings.

Precautions: before starting therapy

Metformin is cleared from the body by the kidneys. One half the drug has been removed in 6 hours and another 50% in the next 6 hours. If there is a reduction in kidney function, the clearance of metformin is slowed and can build up in the body. Renal (kidney functions) is tested by measurement of blood urea nitrogen (BUN) and creatinine levels in the blood and repeated yearly. A complete blood count (CBC) and comprehensive biochemistry panel that will include tests for liver and kidney function should be performed at onset of therapy and at least yearly.

Warnings

Lactic acidosis is a potentially fatal disorder that has been reported to complicate a small number of cases of metformin use. The reported incidence of lactic acidosis is 3/100,000 using the drug for one year. Some have argued that there is no risk in healthy individuals and that the problem only occurs in those already compromised by other illnesses and/or medication use. For now we should be vigilant. The symptoms of lactic acidosis are hyperventilation, slow and erratic pulse, weakness, muscle pain, sleepiness, and feeling of extreme unwellness. It will not just happen; there will be warning signs. There is some fear that if we no longer consider it a possibility and fail to inform our patients, then the one case might occur that could be prevented.

X-ray dye Glucophage should be stopped at the time of, or just prior to a procedure using X- ray dye containing iodine. The kidneys clear X-ray dye and rare cases of diminished kidney function have occurred because of the dye. Since the kidney clears metformin, it could cause a build-up of metformin and potentially increase the risk of lactic acidosis. The procedures that use iodinated dye include the hysterosalpingogram (HSG) in evaluation of infertility, intravenous pyleogram (VIP) often to exclude a kidney stone or evaluate the urinary tract for recurrent infection and abnormalities, evaluation for gall bladder disease (cholangiogram), and tests to evaluate for blood clots, coronary artery function (angiogram), and CT/MRI scans. Metformin can be safely started in 48 hours if there have been no problems with the procedures.

Surgery The same rationale for withholding metformin before procedures using X-ray dye, can be said for surgery. This is a very stressful time on the body and metformin should be discontinued until a regular diet and fluid intake has resumed.

Alcohol use A social drink or two should pose no problems, but since alcohol may worsen lactic acid metabolism, excessive intake should be avoided.

Liver disease Again it's the lactic acid problem. Metformin is not metabolized by the liver but individuals with markedly altered liver (hepatic) function may be at increased risk of lactic acidosis.

Exercise and dehydration Prolonged aggressive exercise may cause build-up of lactic acid. Aggressive exercise routines should be discussed. Kidney function can also be altered by dehydration. Metformin should be withheld if there is not adequate fluid intake.

Vitamin absorption Use of metformin may alter the body's capacity to absorb vitamins from the digestive system, specifically vitamin B-12. A daily multivitamin and perhaps increased calcium supplementation may be a good idea.

Drug Interaction Use with other drugs. This list is too long to list all the possible interactions. Your physician should be kept informed of all medications used It may be possible to have different medication from different doctors, make sure they know.

Risks of Use during Pregnancy

Pregnancy category B. Safety has not been established, but no study has shown an adverse effect. Studies are underway and at least one preliminary study by Dr. Glueck in Cincinnati has found that the risk of early miscarriage is decreased when metformin is continued in early pregnancy (See Chapter 12). It is known that diabetics have a very high early pregnancy loss, but it has been thought mostly due to high glucose levels. It is also known that the pregnancy loss is higher in PCOS, this may be due to an inherent egg quality that may not be correctable Pregnancy in all individuals is a natural state of insulin resistance. In the more extreme cases gestational diabetes may result. Still the use of metformin is a calculated risk. Although it has yet to be considered safe, the risks appear quite low. Use of metformin in pregnancy must involve a close working relationship with one obstetrician. Metformin is excreted in milk and use during nursing is highly questionable.

Administration

Metformin is available in 500, 850 and 1000 mg tablets. The initial PCOS studies were performed using 500 mg of metformin three times daily. Because the midday dose is the hardest to remember, most now recommend twice daily dosing at either 850 or 1000 mg for PCOS. Treatment of type 2 diabetes is often at 1000 mg twice daily. The maximum dose under all circumstance is 2550 mg (850 mg three times a day). Most often a once a day dose is used for about a week then increased at weekly intervals to minimize GI side effects. Personal preference dictates whether to first start with a morning or evening dose in PCOS.

Glitazones

Description

- Troglitazone (Rezulin™) no longer available
- Rosiglitazone (Avandia™)
- Pioglitazone (Actos™)

The above three drugs are thiazolidinedione class of agents and are often commonly referred to a "glitazones". These drugs have been approved by the FDA for treatment of type 2 diabetes unresponsive to diet. They may be used alone (monotherapy) or combined with metformin or other anti-diabetic therapy (combined therapy). The concept of insulin resistance and mechanism of action is presented in Chapter 9.

Rationale for use

Insulin resistance is a characteristic of about 50% of PCOS. Glitazones improve insulin sensitivity. Like metformin and different form the other anti-diabetic drugs, the glitazones do not cause hypoglycemia. Glitazones bind to the PPAR- gamma (peroxisome proliferator-activated) receptors in the nucleus of target tissues of insulin action such as fat, muscle and the liver where it alters genes that promote insulin action, or decrease insulin resistance. When a glitazone binds to the PPAR receptor they alter the genes that control glucose production, transport and utilization and improve sensitivity to insulin. It appears that rosiglitazone is more potent in binding to the insulin receptor than either troglitazone or pioglitazone, but this should not be taken that rosiglitazone is stronger than pioglitazone.

Potential Benefits

- There has been no substantiated evidence of liver toxicity with rosiglitazone and pioglitazone. The typical anti-diabetic drugs can cause fatal hypoglycemia, which does not occur with troglitazone alone. The deaths from hypoglycemic episodes with other drugs were and are, much higher than with glitazones. Triglyceride levels are often decreased by 10-20% while HDL (good cholesterol) levels are increased by about 10%.

Disadvantages

- Glitazones increase the number of fat cells (adipocytes) in the body. This may, in part, account for the minor weight gain seen in some individuals
- While increasing HDL levels, there is also an increase in LDL levels.
- A potential complication that has not been addressed in the reproductive medicine literature is that rosiglitazone is a calcium channel-blocker at higher doses. While this is potentially a positive effect for blood pressure control, it has been reported that calcium channel blockers can prevent fertilization in IVF cycles. Calcium channel blockers could have implications for female fertility as well. On the other side, the relaxation of smooth muscle that occurs is an effect similar to progesterone and could improve implantation, Probably the effects of glitazone are insufficient to make a difference either way, but this is yet to be proven.
- At doses 20-200 times the recommended human dose there were lowered levels of progesterone and estradiol in rats. In monkey's doses of 3-15 times the normal human dose the normal rise in estradiol during the follicular phase diminished and the LH surge is blunted. No effects were noted in a typical human dose. It was hypothesized that this may be due to a direct inhibition of steroid hormone production. This could be interpreted as both a positive and negative effect for the PCOS patient.
- Since all glitazones are metabolized in the liver, the drug will be cleared more slowly in patients with liver disease. This doesn't mean the drug cannot be used; however, more aggressive monitoring is needed.
- The side effects are few and mild with the most common that of fluid retention. At least in diabetes, there is a weight gain of 2-10 pounds. This is thought to be evidence of improved metabolism.

Pregnancy category C. Treatment during mid-late gestation was associated with fetal death and growth retardation in rats and rabbits when over 4 times the usual human dose was given. There was no increase in birth defects even at very high doses. There is insufficient information to determine positive or negative effects in human pregnancy. Certainly in diabetics who achieve pregnancy while taking glitazones it may be better to continue the medications. High glucose levels are associated with a higher incidence of birth defects, fetal and neonatal death. The consequences of poorly controlled glucose levels are clearly shown to influence pregnancy health and these may outweigh the risks, which are largely unknown. The manufacturers say that the glitazones should not be given to nursing mothers.

Administration

Rosiglitazone comes in 2, 4 and 8 mg tablets (maximum dose 8 mg) and is taken orally once or twice a day. For diabetic management the recommended does is 4 mg daily. For pioglitazone 15 mg once daily increasing to a maximum dose of 45 mg daily. For PCOS, lower doses may be tried, especially if metformin is already being used. Although the incidence of liver toxicity is low, it is advised that ALT (alanine aminotransaminase- a liver enzyme) levels be performed before starting therapy and every other month for the first year of use.

FERTILITY AGENTS

Clomiphene Citrate (CC) (Clomid™, Serophene™)

Description

CC is not a hormone but a synthetic estrogen-like substance that binds and partially "deactivates" estrogen receptors. In effect, CC is a pharmacologic trick for increasing gonadotropin release for the pituitary gland to promote ovulation. Unfortunately, CC's action as an *anti-estrogen* extends to other tissues, such as the uterine lining and cervix where clomiphene has the negative effect of blocking the physiologic response to estrogen and may hamper fertility. (Also see infertility chapter)

Rationale for Use

CC is usually the first line therapy for induction of ovulation in PCOS. In binding to estrogen receptors of the hypothalamus and pituitary gland, it is perceived that the body is estrogen deficient. The natural response to estrogen deficiency from any cause is to compensate by the release of gonadotropins, LH and FSH. An increase in gonadotropins stimulates further follicle development. It is hoped that this increase is sufficient to break the barrier of PCOS that prevents the final stages of follicle development and thus, promote ovulation and normal function of the corpus luteum. For a description of normal follicle development see Chapter 2.

Potential Benefits

- While not a great drug, CC is a reasonably good drug. It is easy to use, safe, and relatively inexpensive. It is a useful first step in treatment of disorders of ovulation. Over 70% of pregnancies are achieved during the first 3 months of use. In the first 3 cycles an expectation of 5-25% is not unreasonable. There is generally reported to be a cumulative pregnancy rate of about 30% after six cycles

Disadvantages

- CC retards endometrial development and may decrease the possibility of implantation of the embryo. CC also markedly decreases the amount and quality of cervical mucus that may impede sperm transport. There has been a hypothesized direct negative action on egg quality, but this has not been substantiated in humans. Each of these negative actions has been proposed as the reason why the ovulation rate with CC is much higher than the pregnancy rate.

Side effects of clomiphene use
- Headache
- Blurred vision / double vision
- Hot flashes
- Pelvic pain
- Mood alteration

Since the drug is used for a brief time, side effects are generally considered more of a nuisance than serious and resolve quickly. One study reports that there is an increase in ovarian cancer in patients that have used twelve or more cycles of CC. Still, this may be more related to the woman who has difficult infertility and ovarian dysfunction than to the drug itself. Ovarian hyperstimulation is very uncommon and may be more related to stimulation of residual cysts from the previous cycle rather than multiple cystic development in a current cycle.

Risks of Use during Pregnancy

Clomiphene increases the number of preovulatory follicles, ovulations, and therefore the chance of multiple pregnancy. The risk of twins is 5-10%. Since the twins resulted from fertilization of two different eggs, the twins will be fraternal. Triplets and greater are very uncommon (less than 1 percent) when the drug is used as prescribed. Inadvertent use in pregnancy would appear to cause no harm. There is no evidence that there is an increase in birth defects after CC. The risk of miscarriage is probably slightly greater, but probably not related to the drug itself.

Administration

How much? The lowest dose of CC that results in ovulation should be used. The usual starting dose is 50 mg (1 tablet) which can be taken morning or evening, during or between meals. The dose is usually increased by one pill (50 mg). until ovulation is achieved. Success is usually limited at doses over

150 mg (three tablets per day). There is some evidence that a ten-day trial at 50 or 100 mg. may be effective in some PCOS patients who are otherwise unresponsive. Some respond on 25 mg (1/2 tablet).

The 'more is better' rule does not apply to CC because higher doses increase the anti-estrogenic effects and prevent rather than promote pregnancy. The dose may need to be adjusted according to body weight with obese individuals requiring more. It also takes longer for CC to clear the system in obese individuals and may prolong the negative effects of CC. After several cycles, a "wash-out" period may be useful. CC will accumulate over time in fat cells with a potential of increasing its negative effects.

When to start? CC may be started on cycle day 2, 3, 4, or 5 and usually is given for five days. Each physician will have a preference and there is no conclusive evidence that one regimen is superior to the others. I usually count the first day of any bleeding or spotting as day 1 and then start CC on day 5. Others may wait to the first full day of bleeding and start the next day. The question of when to start is complicated by not knowing which day of the cycle is truly day 1.

How long to use? Except under very specific circumstances, CC therapy should not be used more than six months.

Clomiphene "plus":

- *HCG:* The most common additive therapy is an injection of human chorionic gonadotropin (hCG) to facilitate ovulation. A shot of HCG, which is perceived by the follicle as the LH surge, substitutes for or boosts the natural LH surge and promotes ovulation and helps ensure normal luteal function. While routinely used, its effectiveness is unsubstantiated. If the hCG injection is given too early, it may prevent ovulation. The follicle size should be over 20 mm to properly respond to hCG.

- *Gonadotropins:* CC may also be used with medications such as Gonal- F™, Follistim™, or Repronex™. This extends and possibly heightens the response to CC while reducing the risk of multiple pregnancy. Use of CC may help prevent an unwanted LH surge common when gonadotropins alone are used, but the anti-estrogenic effect on the uterus remains.

- *Estradiol:* In an attempt to get around the anti-estrogenic effects of CC, either natural estrogens, for example Estrace™ (1-4mg) or the synthetic estrogens, ethinyl estradiol (0.05 - 0.1 mg) for 5-10 days have been added to the CC regimens. It in uncertain why the additive of more estrogen in the presence of already high estradiol levels from the developing follicles would improve the uterine lining and cervix, but there have been several positive reports. It may be worth a try if there has been very poor endometrial development in the presence of good follicle development.

- *Corticosteroids:* In cases of increased adrenal androgens, dexamethasone (0.25 or 0.05 mg) or prednisone (5 mg) may be added.

- *Metformin:* It is becoming increasingly common practice to either start with metformin and then add CC if the metformin is not effective alone, or add CC after several months of metformin when CC alone has been ineffective alone. There are several studies that support the effectiveness, as does my personal experience.

- *IUI:* intrauterine insemination (IUI) may by-pass the unfavorable cervical environment caused by CC, but must be properly timed to be effective.

Monitoring: In some cases, CC can cause the ovulation detection kit to be falsely positive on the first day of use. Some women with PCOS have repeatedly shown positive ovulation detection kits because of their elevated LH. If the first measurement is negative, other tests should be reliable. It is probably good advice to have a baseline ultrasound scan performed before the first CC cycle. This will usually exclude ovarian cysts and some other pelvic abnormality that may complicate therapy or make it less effective. Some form of exam, ultrasound or less preferably a bimanual (pelvic) exam should be performed each time CC is used, although this may be modified depending on the particular circumstances.

Some physicians aggressively monitor CC cycles while others do not. The advantage of close supervision is that, if the drug is not effective, therapy can be modified. Monitoring can also offer the patient and clinician a better understanding of the dynamics of ovarian function. The disadvantages are cost and inconvenience.

Gonadotropin Injections

Human menopausal gonadotropin
- HMG—Pergonal™, Humegon™, Repronex™

FSH enriched urinary gonadotropins
- Metrodin™, Fertinex™

Recombinant gonadotropin
- FSH - Follistim™, Gonal-F™
- LH - (in development)

Description

Post-menopausal women produce large amounts of FSH and LH that are cleared from the body in urine. FSH and LH are isolated from the urine of postmenopausal women, processed, and packaged for use for controlled ovarian stimulation to promote fertility. The first well-known human menopausal gonadotropin (HMG) preparation was *Pergonal™* produced by Serono and first used in the mid-1960's. More recently others have marketed HMG, *Humegon™* by Organon and *Repronex™* by Ferring. All HMG preparations consist of equal quantities of FSH and LH and should be identical in action. The choice of which to use can be made on relative cost.

Since high levels of LH appear detrimental to oocyte quality, a search was on for a better product. A purified HMG product from which most of the LH had been removed was introduced in the mid-1980's, *Metrodin-*
Corticosteroids: In cases of increased adrenal androgens, dexamethasone (0.025 or 0.05 mg) or prednisone (5 mg) may be added.

Later a further purification of urinary FSH of Metrodin led to *Fertinex™ (Metrodin HP™)* in the mid- 1990's. The greatest advantage of

Fertinex™ was that it could be self-administered by a small skin (subcutaneous) injection. In the near future, Ferring, the producers of Repronex™ are expected to release a product similar to Fertinex™.

A major change in the way gonadotropins were obtained was made possible by genetic engineering and recombinant DNA technology. Here, specific cells that produce massive amounts of absolutely pure hormone are cultured in the laboratory. This type of production has obvious advantages, but at present, the disadvantage is a higher cost. Presently, the recombinant FSH (recFSH) preparations available in the U.S. are *Gonal-F™* (Serono) and *Follistim™* (Organon).

Rationale for Use

Gonadotropins are required for follicular development and ovulation. Use of gonadotropin injections can override most of the various blocks to ovulation. (The normal process of follicular development is discussed in chapter 2).

Both FSH and LH are needed for follicle development, but how much LH is unknown and debated. High as well as extremely low amounts of LH are thought to be detrimental to egg quality. This has led to a variety of stimulation regimens ranging form recFSH to HMG, with regimens that use a mixture of the two preparations. Serono has a recombinant LH preparation, *Ladi™* in clinical trials that will allow precise formulation of LH/FSH combinations.

Although there are many claims, to date, no specific formulation or product has emerged as superior for controlled ovarian stimulation. Some patients respond equally well to all preparations and some better to a specific type of preparation. Since PCOS is associated with higher levels of LH, it would seem that preparations without LH would be superior. This is not the case universally and it has been impossible to predict in advance which regimen is best.

Potential Benefits

- These drugs work! Few will not have follicle growth using these agents. The problem is that for many, especially with PCOS, there is a narrow therapeutic window between too much and too little. (See below) Like all fertility therapy, success declines with age. In the early twenties to mid-30's the chance for initiation of pregnancy is 15-30% per cycle of use. Nothing short of IVF is this effective. There seems to be a 3-5% added benefit of combining gonadotropin injection with IUI.

Disadvantages

Gonadotropin injections have four major disadvantages:
- They are injections and inconvenient.
- They cost from $40 to $100 per ampule (5 to 50 amps per cycle).
- They carry a significant risk of ovarian hyperstimulation and cyst formation.
- Sometimes they work too well (multiple pregnancy)!

Ovarian Hyperstimulation Syndrome (OHSS):

Ovarian Hyperstimulation Syndrome (OHSS) should be differentiated from the hyperstimulation that occurs as a result of induction of the growth of multiple ovarian follicles. Most pregnancies are associated with mild hyperstimulation. Multiple pregnancies increase the risk. It is unknown whether this is due to enlargement of follicles that do not ovulate or further growth of follicles too small to ovulate with the HCG injection, but which continue to grow.

While the cause of OHSS is unknown it seems to be a discrete disease process associated with altered permeability and leakage of protein-rich fluid from the small vessels of the ovary into the pelvic, abdominal and possibly pleural cavities. A link has been found between higher levels of vascular endothelial growth factor (VEGF), which increases capillary permeability and fluid leakage, and OHSS. PCOS is associated with higher levels of VEGF.

OHSS is said to be mild when there is abdominal swelling, ovarian enlargement with cysts up to 5 cm and discomfort. Mild OHSS is relatively common and is often seen with PCOS where it may be indistinguishable from the natural effects of the ovaries to gonadotropin injections.

In severe OHSS there is marked fluid accumulation in the pelvic and abdominal cavities. Occasionally this extends to spaces around the lungs (pleural cavity). Pleurocentesis, drainage of fluid from the pleural cavity, or paracentesis, drainage of fluid form the abdominal cavity may be necessary to relieve the pain. The greatest concern is that there is so much loss of fluid from the blood vessels that there is a concentration of blood cells and the possibility of blood clot formation. In some cases hospitalization and intravenous fluid is needed. Deaths have been reported from severe OHSS. A major objective during controlled ovarian stimulation should be the avoidance of severe OHSS.

Consideration should be made to cycle cancellation when the estradiol level is over 2000 pg/l or there is a markedly exaggerated ovarian response on ultrasound. Some have attempted to avoid multiple pregnancies and OHSS by withholding therapy for several days allowing the smaller follicles to regress (*coasting*) before hCG is given. If OHSS appears likely, the hCG injection should be withheld. In cases of IVF, it is sometimes reasonable to proceed with aspiration, but freeze all embryos for later transfer rather than transfer in the stimulation cycle.

Daily weight should be taken. Your physician should be contacted if there is over 5 pound weight gain, difficulty breathing, severe abdominal pain, vomiting, fever, or reduced output of urine. Strenuous exercise and sexual intercourse should be avoided. There should be adequate intake of fluids containing salt (electrolytes). Juices are better than water or soft drinks.

Advance management approaches for OHSS
(not in order of preference)

- *Low-slow protocol* where low doses of gonadotropin are given over along period of time. Lower pregnancy rate, but much safer.
- When GnRH agonists have not been used, a shot Lupron™ may be given in lieu of hCG to induce ovulation. There has been reported less chance of hyperstimulation with t

- GnRH analogs, such as Lupron™, lower the response of the ovary to gonadotropin stimulation ovarian suppression and lessen OHSS risk, but are not used specifically for this purpose.
- IVF. Less hyperstimulation after follicles are aspirated. If you are traveling a long distance consider going this next step. Pick a successful program.
- Ovarian drilling. Laparoscopic cautery lessens the chance of hyper•stimulation. Besides it may be therapeutic in itself.
- Insulin lowering agents. May work when injections did not. May possibly improve pattern of stimulation

Risks of Use during Pregnancy

There is no evidence that a pregnancy achieved after gonadotropin therapy has any greater risk of birth defects. Miscarriage rate is higher, but is more related to altered egg quality and unrelated to gonadotropin therapy itself.

The greatest threat to a successful pregnancy is a multiple gestation. The risk of twins with gonadotropin injections is about 20% and the risk of triplets about 5%. These rates can be much higher in IUI than in IVF cycles depending on the number of embryos replaced. The tendency to produce more follicles coupled with the reduced egg quality is a tough dilemma for deciding when to cancel an ovulation cycle or how many embryos to replace after IVF. There is a great desire to push toward that goal of a pregnancy and sort out the number later. Wrong! It is impossible to estimate the health care and emotional costs of multiple gestation. There are resounding success stories that receive much recognition. Tragically, there are also many failures. Each clinic has it own standard as to when to cancel an ovulation induction cycle due to excessive risk for multiple gestation. An alternative is to change to a "rescue" IVF cycle. After IVF, I advocate that never more than 3 embryos are transferred under any circumstances and if the embryo quality is good, no more than 2 embryos are transferred. Extended culture of embryos to *blastocyst stage transfer* may help make the decision as to the best embryos.

Administration

Route**:** Gonadotropins must be given by injection. HMG (Pergonal™, Humegon™, and Repronex™) are given by intramuscular (IM) injection (deep into the muscle) in the upper leg or hip either once or twice daily. Repronex™ has been approved for subcutaneous (sub-q or S.C). injection, but it is associated with increased pain and irritation. RecFSH and purified FSH can be administered subcutaneously. The injection is much like an insulin injection. The needle is very small and the injections are often self–administered.

It is most common for the partner to be the "shot-giver." Keep him involved. Believe it or not, you will be impressed as to how good of a job he does. Do not rely on neighbors and friends, they might not be there when you need them. Although the injection process can be intimidating, complications of the injections are very rare, except for slight bruising and soreness. There are really few things that can go wrong. Often an instruction video is available at the physician office. Expect full-instructions on administration techniques.

Time of day: By convention injections are usually given in the early evening. This is because most office appointments are in the morning, its takes several hours to have the blood test results returned and it is the most convenient time for the designated shot-giver and receiver to get together. Studies suggest that a once-daily injection is equally as effective as are spit dosages given in twice-daily injections. However, twice-daily injections may still be advantageous, especially when particularly large doses of gonadotropins have been prescribed.

Dose: Gonadotropin for injections comes in ampules or vials. The dose varies from 1-6 ampules nightly. Low doses are usually tried initially with PCOS in attempt to avoid excessive stimulation. The dry medication must be mixed with its accompanying vial of solution shortly before its use to retain its maximum potency. With each ampule of gonadotropin powder, there is usually a vial of solution for mixing. Up to 4 ampules of gonadotropin powder can be dissolved in one vial of diluent. In the near future it is likely that there will be available a new multi-dose vial which will lessen preparation.

"Goldilocks phenomenon:" It is sometimes hard to get it just right. Too little and there is inadequate response; too much can lead to potentially serious hyperstimulation. This is where you require the skill of your physician—not so much to know what drug to use (there aren't that many or different), but how and how long to use it.

The amount of gonadotropin to be given is determined by expected and previous response. The amount of drug needed may be difficult to predict in advance. Low dose stimulation is considered 1 amps daily, high dose 4-6 amps daily. Most ovulation induction is performed with 2-3 amps. The lower dose has a greater chance of cycle cancellation due to poor response. The larger doses a greater chance of hyperstimulation. Some REs employ a "step-up" method where you start low and increase as needed to stimulate follicle growth. Often this is more prolonged and may not change the overall number of preovulatory follicles. Other REs use a "step-down" approach where number of amps used each night is decreased once a good response has been established. The step-down approach may better match the physiology of how the system normally operates. Lowering the dose may reduce the risk of hyperstimulation, but starting with a higher dose may also increase the risk of hyperstimulation. Still other REs start and stay at the same dose for a complete cycle and go up in the next cycle if the response has not been satisfactory. Gonadotropin therapy is used for a total of 5-12 days, usually 6-9 total.

Success rates of 10-15% per cycle have been reported with a low-slow protocol where a single ampule of injection is used over a prolonged time. This can take several weeks. I find the extended period of injections, the inconvenience and expense of repeated monitoring and prolonged anticipation to be difficult.

Monitoring: Usually you will be seen for injection instructions, ultrasound and possibly blood work on either day 1, 2, or 3. You will take four to six nights of injections depending on your history and the amount of medications used. From then until the follicles are mature you may be seen daily or every other day for vaginal ultrasound and estradiol levels. The ultrasounds tell the number and size of the follicles. The estradiol level tells about their

activity and indirectly, their health. Sometimes an LH level will be added to the
blood test or you will be asked to do a home ovulation predictor kit to test for the presence of an early LH surge. As the cycle progresses, the endometrium grows; the uterine lining on ultrasound is called the endometrial "stripe." When ovulation nears, the stripe is usually over 8 mm and has a halo appearance suggesting appropriate development. When follicles reach the 16-20 mm range, you are ready for an hCG injection.

Consider that there should be direct communication between you and your physician or his staff after each time an ultrasound or blood testing is performed. Do not assume anything during gonadotropin therapy.

Human Chorionic Gonadotropin (hCG) (Profasi™, Pregnyl™)

Description
Human chorionic gonadotropin (hCG) is a gonadotropin made not by the pituitary gland, but by the trophoblast, specialized cells present in great abundance in the placenta. Biologically, hCG is identical to LH. It binds to the same receptors as LH and causes the same responses. This is logical because hCG takes over responsibility for maintenance of the corpus luteum after ovulation.

Rationale for Use
Since hCG is relatively easily acquired in large quantities, it is cheaper to manufacture and use than is urinary extract of LH. hCG can be equally substituted for LH in any therapy. Some HMG preparations use hCG to balance out the LH: FSH ratio so they are equivalent. Most commonly hCG injection are used to mimic the LH surge in ovarian stimulation regimens. In clomiphene cycles it is very optional, but hCG is required in gonadotropin cycles because of an erratic, often low and possibly untimely release of LH. HCG is also used as in the luteal phase to enhance or ensure progesterone release from the corpus luteum.

Potential Benefits
• Relatively inexpensive. Effective when used as indicated.

Disadvantages
• It's an injection. If the injection is given too early, ovulation can be blocked instead of promoted. Increases risk of hyperstimulation and cyst formation. May cause false positive pregnancy test. Usually 7-9 days is required for an hCG injection to clear the body.

Risks of Use during Pregnancy
No known risk of use as directed.

Administration
Usually this is an intramuscular (IM) injection, but some prefer a subcutaneous route. Often the injection is precisely timed and you should inquire about specific scheduling. Follicle aspiration for IVF is usually is scheduled for 35-37 hours after the hCG. Insemination timing may range from 12-40 hours

after injection. Sometimes a second smaller booster of hCG may be given. If there is any hCG remaining from the first injections, put it in the refrigerator for safe keeping

Errors in administration occur and if hCG is not given, a condition known as empty follicle syndrome can occur resulting in no oocytes recovered from normal-appearing follicles at follicle aspiration for IVF.

Gonadotropin releasing hormone (GnRH) (Lutrepulse™)

Description

Gonadotropin releasing hormone (GnRH) is secreted from the hypo-thalamus and promotes production and release of the gonadotropins (LH and FSH) from the pituitary gland.

Rationale for use

Pulsatile GnRH administration is capable of over-riding the distur-bance in the release of GnRH from the hypothalamus and normalizes gonadotropin secretion, follicle growth and ovulation.

The hypothalamus is the pacemaker (pulse generator) of the endocrine system. It receives signals from throughout the brain and body trans-lating them into short bursts (pulses) of releasing hormone. The pulses may vary in frequency and amplitude throughout the menstrual period. PCOS is associated with altered pulse hypothalamic pulses. GnRH therapy is most use-ful when there is a low output of hormones as seen in the hypogonadotropic patients (low LH and FSH). It is less useful in hypergonadotropic (high LH) conditions, such as PCOS.

Potential Benefits
- GnRH may be successful when clomiphene and gonadotropin injec-tions have failed. GnRH is the most "natural" of all fertility therapies, usually leading to the development of a single preovulatory follicle. Hyperstimulation or multiple pregnancies are uncommon when used in the prescribed manner.

Disadvantages
- Therapy is very costly, at least $2000 per month. There is often irri-tation around the needle site that has to be changed routinely. In some cases, infection at the needle site can occur

Risks of Use during Pregnancy

Since GnRH restores normal ovarian function and ovulation, there should be no risk to the pregnancy. It is possible that if ovulation is delayed, the rate of miscarriage may be higher.

Administration

For GnRH to be effective, it must be administered in brief pulses, thus mimicking the natural secretion of GnRH and the normal cycle. The user wears a small pump attached to her belt, much like the insulin pump diabetics wear. Every 90 minutes a small amount of GnRH is released either through a small needle placed under the skin (subcutaneous) or by a catheter placed in a vein.

OTHER AGENTS

GnRH Analogs (GnRHa)
- Agonists—luprolide acetate (Lupron™), nafarelin (Synarel™), gosereliv (Zoladex™)
- Antagonists—ganirelix acetate (Antagon™)

Description
GnRH has a relatively simple chemical structure of 10 amino acids linked together. A pulsatile secretion required for normal ovarian function, but if GnRH is administered continuously, gonadotropin (LH and FSH) production is shut down. Soon after the chemical structure of GnRH was discovered, scientists started producing analogs by substituting one amino acid for another. Some of these new substances shared many of the same properties of the native GnRH, but had extended time of action. This mimics a continuous GnRH secretion with reduced gonadotropin secretion, reduced ovarian follicle growth and reduced estrogen and androgen production. In effect, GnRH analogs induce a reversible medical menopause.

There are two types of analogs: agonists and antagonists. Agonists first stimulate the release of LH and FSH ("flare"), then block their production and release. There are three agonists used in the United States: Lupron™, Zoladex™ and Synarel™. Their action is identical, but they differ in route of administration; monthly to tri-monthly injections, implant, or daily nasal spray. Antagonists directly block the action of GnRH. Presently a single agent, Antagon™, has been FDA approved There are more on the way. Antagonists differ from the agonists in that there is no sudden burst of LH/FSH release and suppression is immediate.

Rationale for Use
There are a number of situations where there is a desire to place the ovary at rest. They include

- Puberty before age 9
- Endometriosis
- Reduction of LH , prevention of premature LH surge, cycle management with injectable fertility agents
- Cycle management to receive donor or frozen embryos
- Hirsutism due to ovarian hyperandrogenism unresponsive to more conservative therapy
- Reduction of fibroid size before surgery
- Recalcitrant PMS
- Unresponsive chronic pelvic pain
- Other disorders thought to benefit from medical menopause

In the mid 1980s it was discovered that there were two different conditions of abnormal or unwanted LH secretion that hampered success with ovulation induction with injectable fertility drugs and IVF. The first was chronic elevation of LH and the second was a premature surge of LH and ovulation. Both were associated with a decreased number of "good" eggs, and both could be successfully treated with GnRH analogs.

Now virtually all IVF programs use GnRHa in conjunction with gonadotropin injections. A disadvantage of GnRH analogs is in some ways the same as the advantage: ovarian suppression. This leads to more days of injections and a higher number of gonadotropin ampules needed for stimulation. In some cases, the suppression may be so strong as to block development of follicles. In about 5% of cases the LH surge is not suppressed, but this is considerably better than the premature surge that previously occurred in 30% of patients with a 50% reduction in success rate.

In the case of IVF, GnRHa is used from several days to several weeks and generally has few side effects. If used for an extended time, all the problems of menopause begin to show their ugly heads. For example, GnRHa is commonly used in a 3-6 month regimen for the treatment of endometriosis. The side effects of extended use can be reduced when estrogen and progestins, either separately or in combination as an oral contraceptive are given in addition to GnRHa. This "add back" therapy offers the advantages of increasing SHBG and reducing the risk of osteoporosis, and symptoms of menopause. We still can't get around the cost of $300-600 per month price tag.

Theoretically, GnRHa should be a very good group of drugs for long term treatment of PCOS, but high cost and undesirable side effects limit therapy. In using GnRH analogs for PCOS, there is a reduction in ovarian and to a lesser degree adrenal androgens, but no change in insulin resistance

Disadvantages

High cost. Often an injection. Longer therapy almost always associated with significant side effects. Can overly suppress the ovary when used in conjunction with injectable drugs. The initial response of the agonist is to case a "flare" in gonadotropin release. In endometriosis this can increase pain. In ovulation induction this can increase the risk of cyst formation.

Risks of Use during Pregnancy

Inadvertent use of GnRH analogs in early pregnancy is relatively common and has not been reported to be associated with increased pregnancy loss or birth defects. The "flare" of LH release that occurs with initiation of therapy can cause ovulation if there is a follicle in the appropriate stage of development. The official line is that contraception should be used in the cycle in which GnRH analog therapy is started. It is not known how many follow this guideline. The reason why we don't tend to worry is that hCG from the early pregnancy directly stimulates the ovarian production of estrogen and progesterone and takes the previous suppression out of the picture. It is customary to check an estradiol level if menses has not started after 10-12 days of suppression. If the estrogen level is elevated and the endometrium is thickened on ultrasound scan, a pregnancy test should be performed.

Administration

Lupron™ is given by a daily (usually morning) subcutaneous shot. It is usually administered in the thigh and most patients usually choose to give themselves the injection. Long term therapy is given by long acting injections, either 3.75 or 7.5mg Lupron Depot™ doses, that are repeated every 25-28 days. Daily injection are 0.25 - 1.0 mg (0.05 - 0.2 cc or if an insulin syringe is used 5-20 µ) In cases of very poor ovarian response even similar doses have been tried, but must be specially mixed.

Different analog regimens are used in attempt to control follicle development and improve egg quality for IVF. The traditional approach with agonist therapy is to start on day 21 of the cycle *before* gonadotropin injections are give. When gonadotropin injections start the dose is often reduced by 50%. The next most popular regimen of agonist use is a "flare" where GnRH and gonadotropin injections are started almost simultaneously with the agonist. With the "flare" there can be an added boost of gonadotropin release assisting in follicular development, but also the suppression of the "long protocol" is avoided. This "*flare protocol*" is usually reserved for previous or expected "low" or "poor responders."

The "new kids on the block" are the antagonists, presently Antagon™. These drugs cause immediate suppression of gonadotropin release for the pituitary gland. There is no waiting for the flare to resolve and down regulation is immediate. Antagon™ is started *after* gonadotropin injections, usually around cycle day 8, or after five nights of injections and continued for several days until the follicles are ready for hCG.

Prolactin Inhibiting Agents

- bromocriptine (Parlodel™)
- pergolide (Permax™)
- cabergoline (Dostinex™)

Description

Prolactin is produced by the pituitary and has a role in breast development and milk production. Prolactin secretion is unusual in that inhibition, rather than stimulation, regulates its release. Any condition that removes the inhibition can cause the prolactin level to rise. The substance that prevents prolactin release, prolactin inhibitory hormone, is dopamine, a neurotransmitter of the central nervous system. All the above agents are similar to dopamine (dopamine agonists).

Rationale for use

There is an association of PCOS and hyperprolactinemia, but the cause and effect is not clear. There have been isolated reports of empiric or unsubstantiated use of prolactin lowering agents in PCOS. The present recommendation is that these medicines not be used without documented elevated prolactin levels. Excess prolactin alters LH release, reduces estrogen levels, and inhibits ovulation. Prolactin has been suggested to inhibit progesterone and alter the luteal phase. Some patients have no period (amenorrhea) and are severely estrogen deficient. Like PCOS, hyperprolatinemic patients are at more risk of hyperstimulation with fertility drugs.

Hyperprolactinemia can be one of the easiest and most rewarding diagnoses to make and disorders to treat. All individuals with irregular cycles or milk secretion from the breast (galactorrhea) should have a prolactin level checked, regardless of whether the diagnosis of PCOS has been made. At the same time a thyroid stimulating hormone (TSH) level should also be measured. Individuals with an underactive thyroid (hypothyroidism) have elevated TSH levels and this is related to an increase in prolactin. If the prolactin level is slightly elevated, a MRI of the pituitary gland to exclude a small benign prolactin secreting tumor, prolactinomas should be performed.

Potential Benefits
- Treatment is considered safe, even if therapy extends for several years. Studies show that about 80 percent of women with galactorrhea and amenorrhea will start to have normal menses when a pituitary tumor is absent. Success is somewhat less good when a pituitary tumor is present. Almost all prolactin secreting pituitary tumors (adenomas) will regress with drug therapy. As many as 65 percent of uncomplicated patients conceive.

Disadvantages
- The side effects of these medications include nausea, nasal stuffiness, dizziness, drowsiness, and headaches. These agents can cause a lowering of blood pressure and a feeling of faintness is common, especially when therapy is started. Rarely, mental problems including hallucinations have occurred. It was common place to use Parlodel™ for post partum milk secretion in those that did not want to breast-feed. There were several cases of stroke reported in these patients and this indication has been removed. The first few days of treatment can be very uncomfortable, but the side effects usually mostly, if not completely, resolve.
- Usually, over time, prolactin levels naturally fall. There is controversy over whether the small pituitary tumors ever totally resolve. There is a risk of recurrence in many patients when their prolactin levels normalize and regular menstruation returns only to become amenorrheic any time the medication is stopped. If there is intolerance to the medications and a pituitary tumor has been identified, surgery may be indicated.

Risks of Use during Pregnancy
In the United States, medications are usually stopped as soon as a pregnancy is confirmed. In Britain the medication is often continued for risk of worsening hyperprolactinemia caused by the high estrogen levels of pregnancy. There have been no studies that suggest the drugs are harmful. Severe headaches and vision changes should be reported. Some advise routine visual field testing.

Administration
 Usually starting at a low dose and gradually increasing help to control side effects. Treatment can be started with 1/2 a 2.5 mg tablet of bromocriptine nightly. Generally no more than 2.5 mg daily should be used. Pergolide, which is longer acting, and has fewer side effects in some, is given as a single daily dose of 50-150 micrograms. Cabergoline is usually best tolerated and the advantage of one or twice weekly dose of 0.25 mg. Neither cabergoline nor pergolide is FDA approved for treatment of hyperprolactinemia, but most see no reason not to substitute for bromocriptine.

COMPLEMENTARY THERAPY

 I am not quite sure what this term means. With that, I obviously confess a personal bias. Like most physicians of my era, until recently I usually have only considered *good medicine* and *bad medicine*. Somewhat better is the term *complementary medicine*, in that the use of the term may recognize that other approaches can add to and not subtract from a more traditional western medical approach.

 Physicians have a long history of respect within a community but are also equally subject to ridicule. As a group we are egocentric, self-righteous, often pompous, and dogmatic. Whether we are born this way or have it thrust upon us is unclear. We are much more versed in pathology than physiology. If we can predict the future by studying the past, the medicine we are practicing today will be considered wrong in fifty years or at least so primitive as to be tragically amusing. Then again, perhaps we will look back and see the origins of our understanding. What is all of this leading up to? The simple fact is that there are many things we do not understand and many more that our particular path of training as physicians will cause us to ignore.

 Since the field of complementary medicine is largely one of experience and anecdote, allow me to illustrate my point by using several anecdotes.

 I recently received an e-mail from a patient stating that after years of seeing a variety of physicians in multiple specialties without answers to her problems, a chiropractor had found a malalignment of the cervical spine. After the first several treatments her hair stopped falling out, her menses became normal, and she says she feels better than she has in years. How does that work?

 A nurse with whom I worked told me an amazing story of how after years of suffering from endometriosis, during a particularly painful episode she visited a Chinese naturalist physician. He spoke little English, but muttered that her liver was much too hot. "I fix, I make baby," were his words. Although she had experienced many years of infertility and kept trying to persuade the naturalist that this was not why she was there, and in fact fertility was the last thing she wanted, he kept repeating "I will fix, I will fix." The next month she was pregnant.

 I confess I do not know very much about the various non-medical treatment modalities, but I do know the field of reproductive physiology reasonably well. When I read various articles and books on "naturalistic" and "alternative" remedies I am struck by the lack of understanding of basic hormonal and physiologic mechanisms of health and disease that I find there.

They might purport that agent X is effective in Y, but it worries me that they don't understand disease Y. Could it be that they do not understand X as well?

Throughout this book the concept of *metabolic balance* has been stressed. Several levels up, there is a balance, or harmony, of mind, body, and environment. Sometimes a proper metabolic balance may be the first step to this higher level of living. Sometimes self-realization will permit metabolic *im*balance to be corrected. A physician's capacity to "heal" is in part vested in the trust and confidence of the patient that she can be healed. Any form of activity that permits a greater realization of the mind-body-environment connection and at the same time not have a detrimental effect is worth a try. Complementary approaches might include yoga, Weight Watchers™, Zen philosophy, a church revival, acupuncture, aromatherapy, a vacation, or a day in the woods. Who couldn't stand daily message therapy? I am sure I don't have most of the answers here and so I'll have to stick to what I know, as rudimentary as it is, and attempt to be governed by a fundamental foundation, *primum non nocere*—first, do no harm.

Supplements

I cannot recommend using supplements. True, they may not harm anything, but you will have to show me that they can help. The safety testing is just not there. There is a significant risk that adding one supplement may result in one positive action, but may lead to a cascade of events that may distort the overall balance of the body in a negative way. There is also serious concern about the effect of supplement on the interaction of drugs that may be used. *Be sure to discuss supplement use with your pharmacist and physician.* As discussed in the chapter (fat) there is no substitute for a properly balanced diet.

Listed below are several of the most commonly used supplements and their reported use and benefit. This should *not* be taken as a recommendation from me for their use.

5-hydroxytryptophan (5-HP): 5-HP is a naturally occurring amino acid. 5-HP is a precursor of serotonin production has been suggested for treatment of depression, migraine, insomnia, and obesity. Several studies have shown a positive effect on weight loss and energy balance with 5-HP use. In clinical trials the doses have varied from 150 to 900 mg daily. GI upset has been reported. 5-HP can potentiate the action of antidepressants and antihypertensives and use should be cleared by the physician prescribing the drugs.

Gamma linolenic acid (GLA): GLA is a polyunsaturated fatty acid of the omega 6 series. It is derived form linolenic acid and is the precursor of arachidonic acid, the backbone of prostaglandins. GLA is commercially available as oil of evening primrose, borage extracts and black currant seed oil. Positive health interventions have been attributed to its use, including reduction of inflammation in arthritis, prevention of nerve damage in diabetes, suppression of tumor growth, reduction of osteoporosis and improvement in PMS and menstrual dysfunction. The side effect profile appears very good and the theoretical basis is sound; the scientific proof that substantiates its effectiveness is just lacking. Successful treatment may be dependent on each individual as described for vitamins below.

Brewer's Yeast: More appropriately called nutritional yeast. It is a rich source of B vitamins and chromium. Using nutritional yeast may cause an overgrowth of another yeast, Candida. Since nutritional yeast is rich in phosphorus, which binds calcium, possibly it should be avoided or additional calcium supplementation used.

DHEAS: *Dehydroepiandrosterone sulfate* is an adrenal hormone that decreases with age. It has been put forward as a rejuvenator. Its proven usefulness as a supplement is completely lacking and many with PCOS would come closer to selling the product than buying it. For the rest of us, a recent survey found that about half of the supplements tested had no active ingredient in the sample. It is common to check for DHEAS in PCOS and some individuals have low levels. A trial may be in order in this group.

Flaxseed oil: *Alpha-linolenic acid* (ALA) is an omega-3 fatty acid and is found in relatively large quantities in flaxseed oil. ALA is an essential fatty acid that is it is not made by the body. It is also a precursor of prostaglandins, but has other action than the gamma-linolenic acid described below. ALA may have beneficial response on the immune system and inhibit autoimmune reaction. ALA may lower blood pressure. Flaxseed oil is an alternative to fish oil and each has their individual benefits and disadvantages. Flaxseed oil may be a safer alternative to fish oil, which may worsen lipids and blood glucose control. Flaxseed oil can add calories/fat and compensation must be made. It is also very sensitive to storage conditions. Use can neither be encouraged or discouraged.

Glutamine: Glutamine is an amino acid important in the syntheses of DNA. It is also important in muscle metabolism and is widely used by body builders. It is possible that glutamine reduces sugar cravings. Many foods such as milk, meats, and raw dark green vegetables contain glutamine and a deficiency would be rare.

Melatonin: About the only function of the pineal gland at the back and base of the brain is the secretion of melatonin. Little is known about the pineal or melatonin. It may not be a black box, but it is a dark box. Melatonin is altered in sleep-wake periods, night-day cycles, travel, and aging. Melatonin has a complex relationship with virtually every reproductive and adrenal hormone. We know that it is important, but when and how to use supplementation still awaits study.

Selected vitamins and minerals

Vitamins and minerals promote and permit most steps in cell function and metabolism. They are critical for energy production and expenditure. The government has issued a minimum daily allowance (MDA) and a recommended daily allowance (RDA). While this is a guideline of proven safety, it may not be optimal for all. There are no specific vitamin or mineral deficiencies that have been linked directly with PCOS.

One thought is that the body will rid itself of any surplus that is not needed. On the other side, it has been stated that we get all the vitamins in our daily diet, but do we, or could be benefit from more? Will more benefit some and hurt others? Multi-vitamins are so packed full of various compounds that it is possible that the may block out each other's effects. With minerals, the problem is getting the balance right. By altering one mineral, the relatively fine balance may be altered to a more negative than positive balance. All the minerals compete to one degree or another for absorption in the intestines.

The same advice holds for vitamins as for supplements above. A truly healthy diet is the most sensible mechanism for providing adequate amounts of all the body requires. Women on average are calcium and iron deficient. An effort should be made to ensure adequate concentration of these elements. It would seem foolish to be using a bark of a tropical plant of no proven efficacy, while bone is dwindling due to obvious calcium deficiency.

Some drugs including, metformin and orlistat, alter intestinal absorption of vitamins. A multipurpose vitamin supplement is suggested. *Be aware that various drugs can increase or reduce vitamin and mineral needs.*

Calcium: About 2% of our body in calcium. Our calcium supply is always in a state of flux. It is a reasonably sturdy building substance as well. The movement of calcium in and out of bone is under the control of vitamin D and parathyroid hormone. Most American women do not have adequate calcium intake. This deficiency results in calcium being taken from the bone and resulting in bone loss. Over time this leads to osteoporosis, which is accelerated when the protective effects of estrogen are lost in the perimenopause. Like magnesium, calcium has been proposed as a treatment for PMS and a trial of calcium supplementation should be tried by all with PMS. Excessive calcium consumption can cause constipation and kidney stones. Commercial preparations vary, Calcium citrate is the most easily dissolved, digested, and absorbed. Calcium carbonate (Tums™, Rolaids™) containing supplements are less expensive and less well absorbed. Also available are calcium gluconate and calcium lactate. Women need 1000 -1500 mg of calcium daily. Daily diet supplies about 500 mg of calcium.

Chromium is a trace element that must be taken in the diet. Some studies have shown that modern diets may be deficient in chromium, but the amount needed is so small that true deficiency is probably rare. Chromium plays a vital role in insulin action, improves glycemic control, and has lipid-lowering effects. Its action is related to its role in increasing insulin receptor receptivity and glucose transport. Deficiency has been associated with, but is an unproven cause of infertility, decreased sperm counts, and cardiovascular diseases. It is possible that chromium decreases urinary excretion of calcium and may help preserve bone in menopausal women, but proof is lacking again. A suggestion for chromium supplementation varies among physicians treating diabetes. The ADA advises against its routine use. Excessive intake can worsen insulin resistance. Chromium is found in brewer's yeast, meat, cheese and whole grains. Use of chromium for weight loss requires potentially toxic amounts and is of marginal if any benefit. Smaller doses may cause weight gain. Multivitamin supplements contain chromium. It is also available as a single supplement, chromium picolinate. Doses over 200 mcg should be avoided.

Magnesium: Magnesium and calcium metabolism goes hand in hand. They are cofactors in a number of cellular mechanisms from a muscle contraction to fertilization. It appears that the calcium/magnesium ratio may be altered in PCOS. Alteration of magnesium has also been suggested in accelerated atherosclerosis and diabetes. Low magnesium levels have been related to PMS and restless leg syndrome at night. Getting magnesium supplementation right is more difficult than calcium supplementation. Increases in magnesium can inhibit actions of calcium. Supplemental use, except under the care of a physician is discouraged. Total magnesium intake should not exceed 400 mg daily and no more than 200 mg from supplementation.

Iron: Iron is an essential mineral that has varied functions in general cell metabolism, but it is most remembered for its role as an integral component of hemoglobin. Red blood cells are designed to carry hemoglobin and hemoglobin carries oxygen to cells throughout the body. Now this is a case were there is some work to be done on supplementation. Many women are iron deficient because of poor dietary intake and menstrual bleeding. The more bleeding, the greater the chance of iron deficient anemia (IDA). PCOS may protect from, or cause, IDA. IDA is particularly prevalent in the teen years and during pregnancy when the blood volume substantially increases. Heme iron that comes from meat is absorbed 3 times more readily than non-heme iron from plants and supplementation. Iron supplements are universally difficult to take with gastrointestinal side effects common. If taken with other vitamins, the absorption may be compromised. Vitamin C enhances iron absorption while those agents taken for relief of indigestion inhibits absorption. Symptoms of iron deficiency are fatigue and exercise intolerance. Dried beans, dried and fresh fruits, whole grains, molasses and dark colored vegetables are good sources of iron. Iron delivered as ferrous sulfate is the most harsh on the intestines; other compounds may be easier and different sources and splitting doses should be tried if there is a problem with one preparation. The RDA for iron in reproductive age women is 15 mg and 30 mg when pregnant.

Folic acid: Folic acid (FAA) and its inactivated form folate are one of the B complex of vitamin (B9). It functions with vitamin B12 in many genetic, metabolic and nervous system functions. About 15% of individuals have a minor mutation that causes as defect in protein metabolism with resultant increase in levels of homocysteine. Folate reduces homocysteine levels. Folic acid supplementation has clearly been shown to reduce heart disease in women (*JAMA* 279; 359,1998). Homocysteine can interfere with collagen g cross-linking in bone and may reduce the risk of osteoporosis. Oral contraceptives increase folate requirement and supplementation is suggested. Supplementation is universally recommended in women of childbearing age. Individuals of Scottish, English and Irish ancestry are at risk for neural tube (spine) defects and folic acid supplementation has been clearly shown to reduce risks. All women who can become pregnant can and should take folic acid to reduce the incidence of this disorder. A minimum additional supplementation of 400 mcg is required and this is contained in most multivitamins. Often I prescribe 1000 mcg especially in PCOS. Even a higher amount, 4 mg daily begining 1 month before pregnancy through the first trimester, is indicated when there is family history of neural tube defects (spina bifida). Supplementation may reduce the risk of occurrence by 70%. Grains, beans, greens, orange juice, peanuts and whole-grain products are rich in folate but cooking lessens folic acid. In pregnancy, 800 mg is needed.

Vitamin A: Vitamin A like vitamin D is a fat soluble vitamin indicating the potential for a buildup and toxicity if more excessive amounts are used. Vitamin A has a role in skin, eyes, growth and immunity. Vitamin A is only found in foods of animal origin. Milk has been fortified with vitamin A and is an excellent source. Vitamin A can be derived from beta-carotene found in dark vegetables. Women should not take more vitamin A than is found in an all-purpose multivitamin (5000 IU). Skin preparations of vitamin are used in acne and are not absorbed into circulation to an appreciable degree. High levels of vitamin A have been associated with birth defects.

Vitamin C: Ascorbic acid is an antioxidant that is used as a food preservative. There is controversial evidence dating from the Nobel laureate Linus Pauling about the overall effectiveness of supplementation. The role of vitamin C is much clearer than whether supplementation is necessary or beneficial. Vitamin C is an antioxidant; it is critical in collagen formation and is clearly associated with insulin action and glucose metabolism. It appears safe and excess is excreted in the urine.

Vitamin D: The only vitamin that is a hormone. Its role is to balance serum calcium and phosphorus levels. Low levels lead to osteoporosis and have been implicated in diabetes. Vitamin D can be generated in the skin by sunlight. Vitamin D is fat-soluble and overdose is possible. Dosages above that in a multivitamin should not be used. Care should be exercised by those with liver, kidney, or heart disease.

Vitamin E: Vitamin E is a key antioxidant and most studies show a positive role of supplementation in prevention of heart disease. Vitamin E may also improve insulin action. Vitamin E can interfere with the vitamin K and clotting. Liver toxicity is possible at high doses. Generally considered safe at the recommended doses for disease prevention is 400-800 IU daily. This may be a reasonable vitamin to supplement.

Zinc: Next to iron, zinc is the most abundant trace element in the body. It is involved in the function of several hundred enzymes. It has an important role working with superoxide dismutase and protecting cells from the damage caused by scavenging free radicals (anti-oxidation). Zinc also increases immunological competence. Situations that may increase the need for zinc include oral contraceptive use, diabetes, pregnancy, lactation, male infertility, and acne. Red meats and shellfish are the foods richest in zinc. It is present in beans and soy products but may be less absorbable. The RDA for zinc in women is 15 mg; a therapeutic dose is about twice that amount.

Herbal remedies

And now for my experience with herbs. I am very concerned about the use of herbs in an unscientific or unproven method. It is my respect for the potency and unwanted side effects of herbs and the knowledge that they are not subject to review by the FDA as medication rather than my doubts about effectiveness that are the basis of my concern. I am simply afraid. That said, let's talk about the use of herbs.

One of my biology classes required a collection identification of local plants. While on the side of the river I discovered a May apple. The name was pleasant enough sounding and there was a small bulbous fruit at the base of the leaves. Being cautious by nature, I took only a small taste and immediately spat it out. A blister quickly was raised on my lip. I now know that the scientific name for this plant is podophyllum. As a gynecology resident I learned to use podophyllum as a topical agent to burn off venereal warts.

I used to be fond of comfrey root tea. I really thought it caused me to mellow. But then every time I drank it, I was sitting on my friend's back porch in the country. Was it the atmosphere, or the tea? The root has now been taken from the market because of its relationship with liver disease. Maybe I should have tried a beer?

And one more. Recently I was browsing through reviews for new garden books. I was amused about a new herb book whose reviewer states that it is divided into three parts—gifts to make with herbs, recipes for cooking with herbs, and healing with herbs. No offense, but this seems incongruous. It reminds me of the shop I pass on my way home each night that sells guns and vacuum cleaners. How did that happen? Something for everybody I guess!

I am fascinated by herbs and herbal medicine. I have a garden filled with as many herbs with as rich a history as I can cram into it. For centuries plants have been the mainstay of our medicine chest and clearly there is much more work to be done. Most of our present drugs have their roots, so to speak, in plants. Only several years ago extracts from the common yew, taxus, was shown to have important chemotherapeutic effects in treatment of ovarian cancer (Taxol™). Ginseng has been used for thousands of years. A recent study of ginseng showed reduced fasting blood sugar, weight and improved sense of well-being. (*Diabetes Care* 18:1373, 1995), but the study has not been substantiated. Extracts of the saw palmetto bind to androgen receptors of the prostate gland and act as an androgen similar to the drug finasteride (*Prostate* 29:231-240, 1996). It is possible it may have a role in treatment of hyperandrogenism. Still, our lack of controlled scientific knowledge about this makes me cautious about recommending their use.

Our information on herbs and on herbal medicine is growing and being refined thanks to initiatives like the World Health Organization, the European Scientific Cooperative on Phytotherapy (ESCOP) and the Commission E of the German Institute for Drugs and Medical Products. They are applying principles of the scientific method in randomized control trials with factual information emerging. Perhaps the United States should follow the lead. A reasonable source of information in the U.S. is the American Botanical Council (www.herbalgram.org). Included in the bibliography are several, I believe sound, references to sources of herbal information.

Herbal preparations are big business. So big, that the pharmaceutical firms are realizing the profit potential and moving very quickly to buy smaller companies. Herbs occupy an unusual position in the US in that they must carry a warning that they are not indicated for treatment or prevention of any ailment, illness or medical condition. As such they are not subject to review by the FDA as medication. In 1998 over $150 million dollars was spent in the US on ginkgo alone. A real cash crop and possibly deservedly so (see below). The total revenue from herb sales increased 50% from 1997 to 1998 to more than $700 million. Does anyone think that the pills are bought because of their pretty colors? It's not that the physicians and pharmaceutical magnates are immune to the profit motive. The buyer should be an informed consumer in both instances.

Will a cup of raspberry tea have an adverse effect? No. But the same cannot be said for an herb such as St. Johns Wort, which can have a toxic interaction with a number of prescription medications. Most herbal remedies are taken in such small quantities that the risk of damage is not great. It very much depends on the margin of safety between useful effect and toxicity. A pharmacist who reviewed this section noted that every week he receives more and more bulletins containing warnings about dangerous interactions between the prescription medicines he dispenses and widely available and unrestricted herbal remedies and supplements.

Any agent that has no disadvantages probably has no advantages either. It can cost 10–100 million dollars for a drug to be shown safe and marketed with a specific indication for its use. Will this ever happen for valerian root? Probably not. Take the recent issue of Rezulin, really a very useful drug, but taken from the market because one in 40,000 users develop a seriously or fatal liver disease. Will any herb ever come under this degree of scrutiny? Another issue is that the plant grown in your back yard may have completely different potency of its active ingredients than one grown in mine. If herbal preparations are used, they should have a guaranteed analysis and list the percentage of the active ingredient. A third concern is that herbal products have been shown to contain appreciable amounts of heavy metals. In addition, most herbal products are not recommended for long term use or should be used a limited number of times each year, so if there is an effect, it will be temporary.

Let me leave it as this. It isn't that I disbelieve; it is just that herbs as drugs have not met the scrutiny of the scientific method. I just don't know.

The following discussion includes information about several agents that have been proposed to have actions in PCOS or gynecologic concerns. It has been derived from the Natural Medicines Comprehensive Database (www.NaturalDatabase.com) or Commission E monographs.

Black Cohosh (cimicifuga racemosa): Beautiful native woodland plant that grows well once established. Black Cohosh is used as a treatment of menopausal estrogen deficiency, PMS symptoms, and dysmenorrhea. Its action is that of a weak estrogen which binds to estrogen receptors. General favorable reports about lessening menopausal symptoms include reduction in hot flashes, vaginal wall thinning and anxiety. (*J Women's Health* 5:525,1998) A laboratory study showed lack of stimulation of estrogen dependent breast cancer cells and an additive effect on tamoxifen in preventing cancer recurrence. May inhibit LH with little effect on FSH and theoretically could block ovulation. Clearly more information is needed and the plant may have potential. Should not be considered a substitute for standard hormone replacement therapy. Stimulates uterine contractions and is unsafe in pregnancy and lactation.

Chasteberry (vitex agnus castus): An ornamental shrub or small tree of the mid-south with a colorful past and potential for future use. Chasteberries are thought to have anti-androgenic properties, but at the same time may contain testosterone. Monks were thought to chew chasteberry

leaves to maintain their celibacy. A testimony to the chastity of a Greek sol-
dier's wife was a bed strewn with chasteberries on his return. Traditional
herbalists used chasteberry extracts to bring on menses and relieve uterine
cramps. Other reports show induction of uterine contraction and regulation of
menstrual flow. There are reports of improvement in breast pain and PMS.
Reported active ingredients bind to dopamine receptors and reduce prolactin
secretion. Also, the extract possibly decreases FSH and increases LH, which
is *opposite* the effect desired as PCOS therapy. A report in a reputable British
women's magazine had a testimonial of complete reversal of the symptoms of
PCOS with use of vitex. It is commonly used among naturalist physicians.
Vitex seems worthy of more study. In the final analysis, use of this herb may
or may not alter prolactin, may or may not contain estrogen, and may or may
not be an anti-androgen. There exists the possibility of interference with other
types of hormonal therapy. Considered unsafe in pregnancy and lactation.

Don Quai (Angelica sinesis): Taken for menstrual cramps and
irregularities, and for menopausal symptoms. Several components are similar
to Coumadin™ (warfarin, rat poison) and have potentially dangerous blood
thinning activity. Possibly causes cancer and birth defects. Unsafe in pregnancy and lactation.

Echinacea (echinacea pupurea) (coneflower): The perennial
flower of the year several years back. There exists a special Tennessee variety
that is on the endangered species list. Echinacea is vigorously promoted as a
stimulant to the immune system. It was about the only alternative for treatment
of infections before modern antibiotics. It appears to lessen the common cold.
Use in diabetics has been associated with worsening metabolic conditions.
Oral use has been questioned in Germany with rigorous herbal testing. The
herb should not be used during pregnancy.

Evening Primrose (Oenthera biennis): A beautiful plant, but
the flower is seen only every other year. The plant is very rich in the essential
fatty acids, especially gamma linolenic acid. Fatty acids are involved with
prostaglandin synthesis and prostaglandins are intimately involved in inflammation. It may be individual specific with success of therapy dependant on relative deficiency of essential fatty acids. Myriad uses have been suggested, but
widely known in gynecologic circles as therapy for PMS, endometriosis, and
breast pain. Scientific studies are still inconclusive, but most have supported
minimal or no effect. Safety profile appears good and for those conditions
where other agents have failed, it may be worth a try. Safety in pregnancy is
unknown.

Garlic (Alium sativum): Shown effective in reducing blood pressure and lipid profile. In larger quantities can induce bleeding and uterine contraction. May increase insulin and lower blood sugar. May cause bleeding in
pregnancy but also has been shown effective in reducing blood pressure and
lipids. Large quantities not considered safe in pregnancy.

Ginkgo (Ginkgo biloba): Ginkgo is a most ancient tree originat-
ing over 200 million years ago, but destroyed in North America as an indige-
nous tree by the Ice Age. In the case of the ginkgo, an infertile tree is wel-
comed because of the lingering rancid smell of its seedpods, as those who have

experienced the fertile bloom can attest. There have been over 400 studies of more or less value written over the last thirty years. The extract of leaves is used for improvement in cognitive function. Ginkgo has shown a therapeutic potential in early stages of Alzheimer's disease (*JAMA 278:1327,1997*). There is some evidence that ginkgo improves peripheral circulation and even that it may improve sexual functioning No study has been flawless nor totally convincing, but there appears to be a very good safety profile and low level of toxicity. No restrictions in pregnancy have been stated.

Ginseng: (Chinese - Panex ginseng. American - quinque-folium, Siberian - Eleutherococcus senticosus). A tradition of the Southern Appalachians is "sanging", or collecting ginseng. Even Daniel Boone was a "sanger". In 1773, 55 tons of the roots were exported to China. The minimum of five years of growth is taken to develop the medicinal properties and its massive over harvesting has virtually depleted ginseng from natural ranges in the U.S. and China. Most is now farm-grown in the Orient. Pan (all) Akos (cure) compare panacea is of Greek origin, while gin (man) and (man) seng (essence) is from the Chinese ideogram for crystallization of the earth's essence in the form of a man. The roots of ginseng often have a human like form and are traditionally thought to be more potent. In Asian medicine, gin-seng is used to replenish vital energy (*qi*) and to build resistance and promote health. Present use does not differ from it use for thousands of years as a restorative. American, Asian and Siberian varieties have not been proven to be different. Although a traditional use of ginseng has been to promote fertility, safety in pregnancy has neither been established nor rejected. It should not be used by individuals with hypertension.

Goldenseal (Hydrastis canadenesis) Early settlers to the Southern Appalachians learned about goldenseal form the Cherokees. At different times, both have been threatened. Most Goldenseal is now farmed. Used also as a yellow dye, goldenseal is thought by herbalists to potentiate the effects of insulin and help heal gastric, intestinal, and reproductive tract inflammations. Goldenseal is used by some to alter results of urine testing for control drugs. It has been recommended that The National Toxicology Program evaluate goldenseal as a possible cause of developmental problems and reproductive tract cancers. May cause abortion and is considered unsafe in pregnancy and lactation.

Grapefruit Usually considered safe but has the potential to increase the bioavailability of numerous drugs through its activity on the CYP3A4 system in the liver involved with drug metabolism. It may potentially increase the absorption of estrogens, lipid lowering agents and pioglitazone.

Kava kava (piper methysticum) Root of the plant comes from the south pacific where it is used ritualistically with Valium™-like effects. It seems to be effective in reducing anxiety and has been used in the perimenopause. It seems to me to be much like a glass of wine, since its proponents say promotes sociability not hostility. I wonder if anyone has ever seen a mean kava user. Long term use is questioned. Use may potentiate the effects of sedatives and alcohol. It is not recommended for use in pregnancy or lactation.

Licorice (glycyrrhiza glabra): Real licorice is a rare commodity that is now too expensive to use for its usual flavor. Its action, similar to the adrenal gland hormone aldosterone, can cause fluid retention, and electrolyte imbalance. The possibility of serious toxicity exists and its use in PCOS should be questioned. Licorice flavoring has no toxic effects.

Sage (salvia officinalis): Used for galactorrhea and dysmenorrhea. Thought to lower blood sugar. Safe if used in seasoning amounts. May cause uterine contraction and induce abortion. Unsafe in pregnancy and lactation.

St John's wort (hypericum perforatum): SJW is a great garden plant for dry ground where not much else will grow. It has been used since the glory days of Greek civilization and no less authority than Hippocrates, of medical oath fame, reported its value in mood disorders. It appears to be an effective antidepressant and seems useful in the perimenopause. The National Institute of Mental health does not presently recommend its use for depression. More randomized control trials are needed. The mechanism of action is unclear. It has been thought to be a monoamine oxidase inhibitor (MAOI), but recent studies indicate that this might not be the case. It has the potential for interaction with numerous other drugs including steroids, antihypertensives and antidepressants. Its potency should not be underestimated. It may elevate blood pressure, cause skin sensitivity, and has gastrointestinal side effects in some. It should be considered unsafe in pregnancy and lactation.

Saw palmetto (Serenoa repens): The saw palmetto grows throughout the Deep South and was used as a staple food of the native Floridians. Presently, is widely used for its capacity to reduce or prevent the progression of benign prostatic hyperplasia (BPH) for which it has been shown to be reasonably safe and effective. It has received the euphemistic title of "old man's friend." Extracts of the active ingredients are anti-androgens with weak estrogenic activity that bind to receptors in the prostate. Conversion of testosterone to dihydrotestosterone is blocked by inhibition of the 5-alpha reductase enzyme in an action similar to finasteride. It is possible that it could lessen unwanted hair growth. Although it has been said to increase the flow of milk, because of its other possible hormonal actions, it should not be used in pregnancy or lactation. I wonder if the PCOS patients that have had difficulty breastfeeding would benefit?

Shepherd's Purse (Capsella bursa pastoris): Shepherd's purse is found worldwide and even in the stomachs of ancient corpses. I have fond memories of the plant from walks with my grandfather who called it pepper grass and was constantly chewing on a few seeds. It has been used by traditional herbalists to reduce menstrual flow and in menstrual disorders although the mechanism of action is unknown and studies substantiating its use are lacking. It should not be used in pregnancy or lactation.

Stinging nettle (urtica dioica): A relatively common pest in the garden whose nettles (hairy spines) contain histamine and formic acid the agent responsible for ant stings. Ironically, nettle sap relieves the sting. Extracts of the plants contain a wide variety of active agents. Traditionally the plant has been used to stimulate milk production and treat uterine bleeding after childbirth with properties similar to oxytocin. It has also been touted to reduce glucose. Nettle root extracts interfere with testosterone synthesis, possibly by alteration of aromatase enzyme, but only unsuitably high doses. Like saw palmetto, it seems to be effective in benign prostatic hypertrophy. Nettle has been used to induce abortion and should not be used in pregnancy and probably lactation.

Valerian (valeriana officinalis): There are many varieties of this common garden plant. In early texts the plant was named "phu" due to its offensive odor. Since the time of Hippocrates, the root of the plant is widely recognized for mildly sedating and sleep enhancing qualities. In one trial valerian-hop combination has been considered as effective as Valium™ without withdrawal symptoms. Rarely it may have the opposite effect. It is being evaluated as a non-prescription sleep-aid, but again, randomized controlled trials are lacking. Valerian has been suggested to reduce menstrual pain, but without scientific justification. Cultured cells undergo cytotoxic and mutagenic changes when exposed to valerian extracts, but specific human risks are unclear. Valerian may interfere with other drugs used for the same purposes. Valerian has been approved as a food additive/dietary supplement in the U.S. It is generally considered safe (GRAS). Safety in pregnancy and lactation has not been established.

Herbs to be Avoided During Pregnancy & Lactation		
Pregnancy		**Lactation**
Angelica root	Licorice root	Angelica root
Black Cohosh root	Motherwort herb	Black Cohosh root
Blessed Thistle herb	Myrrh	Blessed Thistle herb
Buckthorn bark	Orange peel, bitter	Buckthorn bark
Cascara Sagrada bark	Parsley herb and root	Cascara Sagrada bark
Chaste Tree fruit	Rosemary leaf	Cinnamon bark
Cinnamon bark	Sage leaf	Chinese
Cinnamon bark, Chinese	Senna leaf	Ephedra
Echinacea Purpurea herb	Senna pod	Echinacea Purpurea root
Ginger root	Shepherd's Purse	Ginger root
Ephedra	Thyme	Horehound herb
Fennel oil	Turmeric root	Horseradish
Fennel seed	Uva Ursi leaf	Juniper berry
Fenugreek seed	Watercress	Kava Kavarhizome (root)
Ginseng root	Yarrow	Orange peel, bitter
Horehound herb		Sage leaf
Horseradish		Senna leaf
Juniper berry		Senna pod
Kava Kava rhizome		Uva Ursi leaf

Where Can I Find More Information? PCOS Resources

By Paula Puffer [1]

Before I was diagnosed, I knew I had a problem with my hormones. I didn't have a name for what was happening with my body, but I knew that the hairiness on my neck, the lack of menstruation, and my thinning hair had to be related. Then, in 1998, I found (in a magazine) a name for what I had—Polycystic Ovarian Syndrome (PCOS). I was overjoyed that I had this name and could do some research on PCOS, but overwhelmed when I started to read all of the information about PCOS. Everyone's story was similar but somewhat different from my own.

Where do you go to get help? Who in your area treats PCOS? Where do you find information about PCOS? How do you decide that a resource is an excellent resource for PCOS? Until this book, the main patient resources for PCOS information were found on the Internet. The Internet is an important place to get needed information and a way to get up-to-date information quickly. It is not, of course, the only source of support and information, and we have included here some important resources such professional societies, consumer organizations with both a Web presence and significant off-line presence, contact information for face-to-face support groups, and a long, but by no means comprehensive list of specializing physicians.

Collecting and assessing information about PCOS (or any medical condition) and its treatments can be scary, especially if you are just starting on your journey toward healing. However, the benefits of being able to better com-

[1] *Paula Puffer, B.A., B.S. lives with PCOS on a daily basis. She is a technical writing consultant and Web Design instructor in Houston, TX. She volunteers her time as the Director on Online Services for the PolyCystic Ovarian Syndrome Association. When she isn't doing any of the above activities, she is finishing her thesis about the PCOSupport Web site for her Masters in Technical and Expository Writing and spends time with her boyfriend, Pat.*

municate with your healthcare professionals about PCOS, its associated symptoms and its treatments, will make your research worth it.

The information in this chapter is meant to be a guide for you to use in getting the help and support you need to treat your PCOS symptoms. There are four main areas in this chapter.

PCOS Support Groups and Infertility Groups which are not-for-profit consumer education and support organizations. These can lead you to good information and help you to find nearby medical care. The organizations in this section have face-to-face local presences and/or are accessible on the Internet in the form of e-mail lists, discussion boards, and newsgroups to which you can subscribe.

Internet Resources about PCOS.

Professional Societies and Organizations consist of associations for professionals working in allied fields. These are resources from throughout the English-speaking world that present solid information about PCOS and its side effects. These organizations can also help you to find healthcare professionals and other professional services in your area to treat your PCOS and its symptoms.

Health Care Professionals by region. Many of these doctors are professional members of the support organizations listed in the section above. This listing is not exhaustive, of course, especially since true expertise in this growing field is unusual (but increasing every month). Subsequent editions of this book may well carry much longer lists. It might even be possible that as PCOS becomes more and more well known and understood among the medical community the need for such a list could become unnecessary. That is not the case now, however, and this list should serve to help you (and perhaps your local primary care physician) to find help within your geographic area if not within your own city.

Using the Internet for Research

Many of the resources we are recommending can be accessed via the Internet. Searching the Internet can be time-consuming. You put in a term and you get thousands of entries back.. Then you start following the links generated by your search and you find that you have some unexpected results—some of the sites are no longer active or do not contain the kind of information you expected. You give up—frustrated because you didn't find the information you needed to take to your physician.

Unfortunately, because there is no one way of cataloging the information on the Internet, searching is not going to get any easier. However, there are some ways that you can speed up your search so that you find the information you need and want.

Focusing your Internet Research

The key to getting the information you need is to do a focused search. Even with with well-defined searches, you can get a huge number of results. Pick the key terms for which you want to search. Be careful when choosing the terms you use. It can make a significant difference in the number and type of results generated.

For example, when using the term *PCOS* to search, you get 7010

If you specify *Polycystic Ovarian Syndrome*, the results drop to 4000 entries.
If you specify *Polycystic Ovarian Syndrome Hirsutism* in the search box,
about 40 entries are returned. Forty entries are much more manageable than
4000 entries.

Once you have your search narrowed to a manageable number of
Web sites, you can start looking at the information available to you.

Evaluating the Available Information

PCOS information on the Web basically comes from three sources—
the media, the women who have PCOS, and the healthcare community.

The first PCOS information source women often find are stories in
the media. Women read an article about PCOS by accident, like I did, or they
happen to see a piece on a news program. Media stories often combine the
other two types of resources—professionals who treat and work with PCOS
patients and the women who have PCOS—and are written at a level that the
general public can understand. These articles are often reprints or transcripts
of traditional media stories and will point women to Internet Web sites related
to PCOS in an effort to give women the information they need.

A well-rounded media piece will cite information from healthcare professionals (along with the professional's credentials and affiliations) and then
give examples of how particular aspects of PCOS have affected the women
being interviewed. By the time you have finished the article, you should have
a sense of what kind of impact PCOS might have in your life and have an idea
where you can go for additional help.

Another primary source of information is personal, or anecdotal, stories about PCOS. Some women who write about PCOS have formal medical
training, but most do not. These women write about their personal experiences so that others don't go through what they did when trying to get a
PCOS diagnosis. Their experiences may provide insight on how to handle a
particular aspect of PCOS (such as insulin resistance). Many Web sites by
women will have links to other sites by women, the media and medical professionals, or support organizations. But the most important function these
anecdotal sites serve is to validate the fact that women with PCOS are not
alone and there are other women out there that know what you are experiencing.

If you have read many of the anecdotal and media sites, the next logical place is healthcare-related sites, such as doctor Web sites or support associations and sites for journal or research articles. The list of questions that follows will help to determine how valuable an article may be for your purposes:

- Does the healthcare professional cite numerous outside sources?
- Is he or she someone who's name you have run across in your
  research about PCOS?
- Is he or she a professional member of any related support associa-
  tions?
- Is the information reviewed by a board of peers, or in the case of

associations, are articles reviewed by a medical or editorial advisory board?
- Does the site follow the HON code or Medindex Code of Ethics? Both of these codes require that that information be reviewed for medical accuracy, cite the resources being used to write a particular article, and have a disclaimer on the site telling people that the information provided is for information purposes only and that for diagnosis and treatment, the user should see professional healthcare providers.

Consumer Education, Advocacy and Support Organizations

Polycystic Ovarian Support Association
P.O. Box 7007
Rosemont, IL 60018-7007
(877) 775-PCOS (7267)
http://www.pcosupport.org

PCOSA is the oldest support association for PCOS and focuses on all health issues related to PCOS. Established in 1997 with an immediate Internet presence, the PCOSupport Web site provides a host of support options for women of all ages. The site hosts online chats, discussion forums, and a number of e-mail lists, has contact information for worldwide local support groups as well as a Professional Members Directory, and provides information about national and regional PCOSupport Symposia.

General membership dues are $40 a year and are tax deductible. Membership benefits include the quarterly newsletter *The PCOS Bulletin*, membership in your local chapter, and discounts on PCOSA-sponsored symposia and other events.

Professional membership dues are $150. Professional members are listed in the PCOSupport Professional Directory, receive *The PCOS Bulletin*, patient referrals, discounts to symposia and conferences, and patient/client information materials as needed.

To become either a general or professional member, visit the membership section at the PCOSupport Web site (http://www.pcosuppport.org/Membership/) and follow the links to the secure server where you can submit your information using your credit card.

PCOTeen
P.O. Box 7007
Rosemont, IL 60018-7007
(877) 775-PCOS (7267)
http://www.pcoteen.org

PCOTeen, a division of PCOSupport, focuses on PCOS issues related to young women. In addition to the PCOTeen e-mail list, there is a quarterly newsletter, a weekly chat and the Big Cysters program which

teams young women with older cysters who have PCOS.
General membership dues are $40 a year and are tax deductible.
Membership benefits include the quarterly newletter *The PCOS Bulletin*, membership in your local chapter, and discounts on PCOSA sponsored symposia and other events.

To become either a general member, visit the membership section at the PCOSupport Web site (http://www.pcosuppport.org/Membership/) and follow the links to the secure server, where you can submit your information using your credit card. Be sure to indicate if you are a PCOTeen member on the application.

Polycystic Ovarian Syndrome Association of Australia
PO Box E140
Emerton NSW 2770
http://www.possa.surak.com.au

The Polycystic Ovarian Syndrome Association of Australia is a sister organization to PCOSA. This site provides information for women in Australia and its states. In addition to PCOS resources it also has links to Australian infertility groups.

Verity
52-54 Featherstone Street
London England EC1Y 8RT
http://www.verity-pcos.org.uk

Verity is the PCOS support organization for women in the United Kingdom. Its website has a variety of links and resources for women in the UK.

American Diabetes Association
1701 North Beauregard Street
Alexandria, VA 22311
http://www.diabetes.org

The American Diabetes Association has a lot of great information about dealing with diabetes and insulin resistance. You will also find a few articles about PCOS on their Web site.

American Infertility Association
666 Fifth Avenue, Suite 278
New York, NY 10103
(718) 621-5083
http://www.americaninfertility.org

The American Infertility Association is a not-for-profit organization that focuses on the infertility issues. In their PCOS area, AIA has online chats, a message board, some articles on PCOS, and information about their various support groups.

**The International Council on Infertility Information
Dissemination (INCIID)**
P.O. Box 6836
Arlington, Virginia 22206
(703) 379-9178
http://www.inciid.org

INCIID is a five-year-old non-profit organization devoted to helping men and women find online information about the latest infertility techniques. The largest and most inclusive general infertility site on the web, INCIID offers dozens of specially focused support boards as well as medical information forums staffed by specializing physicians. Primarily an Internet resource, INCIID sponsors occasional symposia.

RESOLVE
1310 Broadway
Somerville, MA 02144
(617) 623-0744
http://www.resolve.org

Started in 1974, RESOLVE is one of the most extensive networks for infertility and adoption resources in the United States. Nationally the organization offers telephone support to members and a quarterly newsletter. The RESOLVE chapter system includes 54 meetings sites throughout the country, each of which sponsors face-to-face informational meetings on a monthly basis, support groups, a local newsletter, symposia, and more. Information covered on their not particularly expansive Web site includes, chapter contact information, infertility information, advocacy information, physician referrals, and several fact sheets.

Premature Ovarian Failure Support (POFSupport) Group
P.O. Box 23643
Alexandria, VA 22304
(703) 913-4787
http://www.pofsupport.org/

Premature Ovarian Failure Support is an organization devoted to women who are menopausal due to ovarian failure.

PCOS Support Groups
Local PCOSupport Groups
The following is a list of local face-to-face PCOSupport groups arranged alphabetically. The listing includes the group name, an e-mail contact, and phone number where applicable. Please note that this information was current at the time of printing. However, for the most accurate listings, please visit the PCOSupport Web Site at
http://www.pcosupport.org/Chapters/index.html.

PCOSupport Group Name	Contact	E-mail
Alabama	Victoria Valdes	sflorida@pcosupport.org
Alaska	Jodi Synder	jodi@alaska.net
Arizona	Heather Nottingham	WSWCDC@aol.com
Arkansas	Angie Coleman	ACOLE@PCOS.itgo.com
Asheville and Whittier, North Carolina	Lesa Childers	WNCPCO@aol.com
Australia	Kerri Cottell	kcottell@pnc.com.au.
Brantford, Ontario	Lori Peeling-Hill	lapeelinghill@yahoo.com
British Columbia	Claudia Whitworth	Claudia@pcos.net
Calgary, Alberta	Ann Smith	Lazuli_blue@hotmail.com
Cape Town, South Africa	Theresa de Villiers	PCOSACapeTown@yahoo.com
Caracas, Venezuela	Morella Hernández Rivero	shamresh@telcel.net.ve Central
Florida	Laura Perez	VPLP25@aol.com
Central New Jersey	Lisa Weinstein	wafin@pipeline.com
Central Pennsylvania	Sally Jo Bronner	Bronner@culturalpartnerships.org
Charlotte, North Carolina	Judith Hasak	PCOCharlotte@aol.com
Cinncinati, Ohio	Nancy Felson Brant	nfbrant@aol.com
Cleveland, Ohio	Judy Oschip	PCOCC@email.com
Colorado	Susan McEachern	ColoradoPCOS@yahoo.com
Connecticut	Lisa Weinstein	wafin@pipeline.com
Dallas, Texas	Shelby Fontaine	Sfont@airmail.net
Delaware	Melanie Crawford Or Anne Miller	Crawdoug@juno.com Paulmiller1@home.com
Denmark	Ulla Johannessen	johannessen@teliamail.dk
East San Francisco Bay Area		eastbaypcos@hotmail.com
Eastern Massachusetts	Amy Anderson	Amy4edu@mindspring.com
Edmonton, Alberta	Loralee Hutton	Lhutton@powersurfr.com
Georgia	Melissa Meyerhofer	PCOSupportGA@mindspring.com
Germany	Beate Rahmati	Rahmati.Synesis@telelev.net
Greenville, North Carolina	Leah Daughety	Lgdrn@hotmail.com
Haiti	Cara	Cara@can2.net
Hawaii	Victoria Valdes	sflorida@pcosupport.org
Houston, Texas	Paula Puffer	HoustonPCO@xoommail.com
Idaho	Kim Littlejohn	kim_littlejohn@yahoo.com
Illinois	Nicole Barbeau	Illinois@pcosupport.org
India	Dr. Aniruddha Malpani, MD	malpani@vsnl.com
Indiana	Beth Gould	Indiana@pcosupport.org
Iowa	Janine Lamb	IowaPCO@aol.com
Ireland	Clodagh Fitzpatrick	Clodagh.Fitzpatrick@medianet.ie

PCOSupport Group Name	Contact	E-mail
Israel	Bozmat Libovsky	Libv99@hotmail.com
Jamaica	Jessica McCurdy-Crooks	jessdel@hotmail.com
Johnson City, TN	Alisa Frazier	tnpcos@yahoo.com
Kansas	Kathy	kcregpcos@yahoo.com
Kansas City	Kathy	kcregpcos@yahoo.com
Kentucky	Patricia Barfield Hicks	PBHSCHUG@aol.com
Johannesberg, SouthAfrica	Nerishni Shunmugam	nerishni@mweb.co.za
Layetteville/Lurinburg, North Carolina	Carol Shulter	gshutler@carolina.net
Long Island	N/A	LIChapPCO@aol.com
Los Angeles Metro Area	Lisa Rowley	lametro@pcosupport.org
Louisiana	Nanette Wilson	NanStarrrr@aol.com
	Julie Rainwater	Rainwater@yahoo.com
Maine	Angi Ingalls	Angi@adoptasap.com
Maryland	Wende Peters	Pcos-md@xoommail.com
Minnesota	Joanne Binder	skydwellers@mindspring.com
Montana	Catherine L. McConnell	mcconnel@bigsky.net
Nashville, Tennessee	Alisa Frazier	Tnpcos@yahoo.com
Nebraska	Laurie Stallman	avicenna@ix.netcom.com
Netherlands	Raquel Ardon	ardongutierrez@hotmail.com
Nevada	Danielle Blomquist	DTBlomquist@aol.com
New Hampshire	Cindy Pelletier	cpelletier@mediaone.net
New Jersey	Lisa Weinstein	wafin@pipeline.com
New Mexico	Heather Nottingham	NMPCO@aol.com
New York	Lisa Weinstein	wafin@pipeline.com
New York City	Marjorie Anne Carroll	nycpcosa@msn.com
New Zealand	Nikki Hoare	Hoare.m@xtra.co.nz
North Dakota	Laurie Stallman	avicenna@ix.netcom.com
Nova Scotia	Brenda Bisbee	angeltpal@yahoo.com
Oklahoma	Tavia Armstrong	Pcosok@yahool.com
Orange County PCOSupport	Cindy Troyer	Cindytroyer1@hotmail.com
Oregon	Inga Black	Oregon@pcosupport.org
Ottawa, Ontario	Kathy Galleta	kgalleta@attcanada.net
Philadelphia	Maggie Freidenberg	Pac-pcosa@pcosupport.org
Phoenix	Amy Small	phoenixpcos@hotmail.com
Puerto Rico	Wendy Montañez	Wmontanez3206@prtc.net
Richmond,	Virgina Judith Tolenko	Tolenko@erols.com
Rhode Island	Lisa Weinstein	Wafin@pipeline.com
Rio Grande Valley, Texas	Jennifer Bradford	RGVPCO@aol.com
Rochester/Buffalo/ Syracuse New York	N/A	RochesterPCO@aol.com

PCOSupport Group Name	Contact	E-mail
Sacramento		
PCOSupport	Patty	Rockysfan@aol.com
San Antonio, Texas	Laurie Stallman	Alamopco@pcosupport.org
San Bernadino – Inland Empire Area	Kristin Lindberg	lindbergs@earthlink.net
San Diego		
PCOSupport	Julia Spencer	BandJSpencer@cs.com
Saskatchewan	Linda Henderson	Linda@massload.com
Southeast Michigan	Jennifer Lay	jalay@umich.edu
Southeast Nebraska	Renee Ybarra	ReneesPCO@aol.com
South Carolina	Sharon Lee	Sharon1227@aol.com
South Dakota	Laurie Stallman	avicenna@ix.netcom.com
South Florida	Victoria Valdes	sflorida@pcosupport.org
Southern Connecticut	N/A	northsuburbnypco@mindsping.com
Springfield, Missouri	Dani Abel	dani@positech.net
Tennessee	Dianne Ware-Furlow	Ware.furlow@gateway.net
Toronto, Canada	Ligaya Horhager	pcostoronto@medmail.com
Trinidad/Tobago	Ian Levia	ianlevia@hotmail.com
Ventura County	Alexis Schmidt	ebolahunter@aol.com
Waco, Texas	Elisa	Gospelstudy@interlinkcc.com
Westchester, Rockland, Western Massachusetts	Mary Ann Hanlon	RMKHanlon@compuserve.com
Western Michigan	Mary Mihovich	MJMSLS@aol.com
United Kingdom (Verity)	Catherine Williams	sewingcw@freeuk.com.
Utah	Chris Martinelli	Cmartin189@aol.com
Venezuela	Raquel Ardon	ardongutierrez@hotmail.com
Vermont	Lisa Weinstein	Wafin@pipeline.com
Virginia Beach Area,	Jennifer Midgette	VirginiaPCO@aol.com
Virginia-Northern Washington DC	Lahle Henninger	NOVAPCOChapter@aol.com
Washington State	Ashlyn Leahy	PCOSAWA@pcosupport.org
Washington DC	Lesa Childers	Wncpco@aol.com
West Virginia	Donna Hager	nonniejeen@yahoo.com
Wisconsin	N/A	wisconsin@pcosupport.org

Using the Internet for Support

Because the Internet is a rapidly growing and constantly changing resource, once helpful established sites disappear and new ones appear frequently. The specific sites, boards and e-mail addresses we have provided here were current as our book went to press in mid 2000, but are subject to change.

Discussion Boards

INCIID PCOS Cafe –
http://www.inciid.org
A PCOS bulletin board that offers support from other women. Doctors area also available to answer questions about PCOS. There are also links to various kinds of journals related to infertility and adoption.

OBGYN.net PCOS Discussion Forum—
http://forums.obgyn.net/pcos OBGYN.net's PCOS Discussion Forum
was created for women, physicians and medical providers to discuss
Polycystic Ovary Syndrome and share information.

OBGYN.net PCOS Medication Discussion Forum
http://forums.obgyn.net/pcos-medication
OBGYN.net's PCOS Medication Discussion Forum was created for
women, physicians and medical providers to discuss the medical treatments of Polycystic Ovary Syndrome and share information

Email Lists

E-mail lists are the main way that many women with PCOS get the
support they need. The following e-mail lists offer support for women who are
dealing with PCOS as this book goes to press in mid-2000. In each entry, a
description, the subscription information and the main mailing address are
included. You must be subscribed to a list to participate. The list names are
written as they appeared in 2000.

PCOSupport Lists.

PCOSupport hosts many lists including the PCOS, the PCOS-
Menopause, PCOTeen, and PCOLavender lists. The complete and
comprehensive list of PCOSupport Lists along with information about
how to subscribe to each lists can be found at http://www.pcolist.org.

AdvancedHope

This list is a friendly group targeted towards women who are in intermediate to advanced stages of TTC/Infertility (i.e. trying to conceive
for more than one year, dealing with infertility, Clomid™, injectibles,
IUI, IVF or PCOS) or who have suffered miscarriage/pregnancy loss.
Women seeking testing and treatment from a reproductive endocrinologist or other fertility specialist, who would like the support and information that a smaller group can provide are encouraged to join. This
group is active (lots of email) and flaming will not be tolerated.
Members must participate. To subscribe, send a blank e-mail to
AdvancedHope-subscribe@egroups.com. To send a message E-mail
AdvancedHope@egroups.com.

Aussie_cysters

A supportive mail list for women in Australia diagnosed with Poly
Cystic Ovaries (PCOS). This list is for women who would like some
support in their experience with PCOS and/or are trying to conceive
with PCOS. To subscribe, send a blank e-mail to aussie_cysters-sub-
scribe@egroups.com. To send a message E-mail aussie-
cysters@egroups.com.

Bearded_Lady

For many women, excess facial and body hair is a fact of life, not something that is funny. This list is for those dealing with the problem of unwanted hair. Hair removal techniques, tips, disasters, and support for each other are covered topics. To subscribe, send a blank e-mail to Bearded_Lady-subscribe@egroups.com. To send a message E-mail Bearded_Lady@egroups.com.

Christians-with-PCOS

This is a list for Christian women who are dealing with PCOS (polycistic ovarian syndrome). A women can join whether she has or has not been diagnosed. The list allows a woman to deal with her physical ailments, while keeping Christ at the center of her life and the Healer of her body and heart. To subscribe, send a blank e-mail to Christians-with-PCOS-subscribe@egroups.com. To send a message E-mail Christians-with-PCOS@egroups.com.

Cysterhood

This list is an announcement list that announces the update for the Cysterhood.com Web site. To subscribe, send a blank e-mail to Cysterhood-subscribe@egroups.com. Messages cannot be posted to this list.

DealingwithPCOS

This group is for women who are dealing with Polycystic Ovarian Syndrome and are experiencing Infertility. It is also for women who have conceived after a diagnosis of PCOS. Women with PCOS can share their feelings, vent their frustrations, and find the support they need. To subscribe, send a blank e-mail to DealingwithPCOS-subscribe@egroups.com. To send a message E-mail DealingwithPCOS@egroups.com.

emptyarms

This list is for all of those who are suffering from Polycystic Ovarian Syndrome (PCOS) in addition to primary infertility (no other children). If you suspect that you may have PCOS, but have not had a medical diagnosis, you are also encouraged to join. The goal of this list is to provide support and education to those dealing with all aspects of PCOS while trying to conceive their first child. To subscribe, send a blank e-mail to emptyarms-subscribe@egroups.com. To send a message E-mail emptyarms@egroups.com.

endobabies

This list is for women with such issues as endometriosis, PCOS, or any other illness that may cause fertility problems. This list is for venting, supporting and sharing ideas and knowledge. To subscribe, send a blank e-mail to endobabies-subscribe@egroups.com. To send a message E-mail endobabies@egroups.com

Just_Diagnosed_PCOS

Just_Diagnosed_PCOS is dedicated to those women who have recently been, or think they may be diagnosed with PCOS. This list was started in hopes of bringing women together who have recently been diagnosed with PCOS (Polycystic Ovarian Syndrome) and are still in the process of figuring it all out! So many questions...so few answers. The women on the list have been there and would like to help others who need that "beginners" PCOS support. To subscribe, send a blank e-mail to Just_Diagnosed_PCOS-subscribe@egroups.com. To send a message E-mail Just_Diagnosed_PCOS@egroups.com.

LDS-PCOSers

This email list is for Latter-day Saints (LDS) women to discuss PCOS and its effects on their lives. Women who have been diagnosed or think they may have it are welcome. It is also a place for fellowship of LDS women who are looking for a place that is non judgemental of each other, and is caring and supportive of each other. Discussions of about the LDS religion are a part of this list. The owner asks that all discussion be G or PG Rated. To subscribe, send a blank e-mail to LDS-PCOSers-subscribe@egroups.com. To send a message E-mail LDS-PCOSers@egroups.com.

MilitaryandPCO

This is a list is for all active duty military and military dependents who have PCOS. To subscribe, send a blank e-mail to MilitaryandPCO-subscribe@egroups.com. To send a message E-mail MilitaryandPCO@egroups.com.

NonIR-PCOS

This list is for women who have been diagnosed with PCOS but do not have the Insulin Resistance Component of the syndrome to share information. Women can share their experiences, treatments, and give tips on how to deal with PCOS in ways other than those used for IR PCOS women. It is open to all women with PCOS who are not IR or anyone interested in more information about PCOS/Non IR for a friend, family member, or support. To subscribe to this list, send a blank e-mail to NonIR-PCOS-subscribe@egroups.com. To send a message E-mail NonIR-PCOS@egroups.com.

PCOS-australia

This list is for women in Australia who have PCOS. To subscribe, send an e-mail message to pcos-australia-subscribe@egroups.com. To send a message E-mail PCOS-australia@egroups.com.

PCOS_CAN_Lose_Weight

This list is for PCOS women who want to lose weight. To subscribe to this list, send a blank e-mail to PCOS_CAN_Lose_Weight-subscribe@egroups.com. To send a message E-mail PCOS_Can_Lose-Weight-@egroups.com..

PCOS-Families

PCOS-Families is for the family and friends of women with PCOS can come and chat about PCOS affects their lives. It is hoped that husbands, family members, and friends can better understand what woman with PCOS mental and physical states are. women's body and mind. Women with PCOS are encouraged to subscribe to provide insight which helps others understand and become aware how PCOS affects them. This list has a Christian approach and discussions about faith do occur as an integral part of the list. To subscribe send a blank e-mail to PCOS-Families-subscribe@egroups.com. To send a message E-mail PCOS-families@egroups.com.

PCOS-Gals

This list is for women in their teens/late teens - 20's who are not concerned with trying to conceive, although they are concerned with the characteristics surrounding PCOS (weight gain, hair growth, acne, mood swings). To subscribe to this list, send a blank e-mail to PCOS-Gals-subscribe@egroups.com. To send a message E-mail PCOS-Gals@egroups.com.

PCOS_Pagans

This list is for women who are pagan and have been diagnosed with or think that they may have polycystic ovary syndrome. It is for the discussion of how we can take back our health in a natural way. All topics related to this are welcome. Mostly this is for support and to share success stories and disappointments. To subscribe, send a blank e-mail to PCOS_Pagans-subscribe@egroups.com. To send a message E-mail PCOS_Pagan@egroups.com.

PCOS-Low-Carb

This list is for all women suffering from PCOS, who would like to discuss low-carb dieting as an alternative way to alleviate symptoms, either in conjunction with, or in addition to, other medicinal treatments. All PCOS women, family members, and low-carb dieters welcome. To subscribe, send a blank e-mail to PCOS_low-carb@ egroups.com. To send a message E-mail aussie-cysters@egroups.com.

PCOS-PKD

This list is for women who have Polycystic Ovarian Syndrome and/or Polycystic Kidney Disease. To subscribe, send a blank e-mail to PCOS-PKD-subscribe@egroups.com. To send a message E-mail PCOS-PKD@egroups.com.

PCOS-UK

This list is for women in the United Kingdom who have PCOS. To subscribe, send an e-mail message to PCOS-UK-subscribe@ egroups.com. E-mail PCOS-UK@egroups.com to send a message.

PCOS_Weightloss

This list is for women with PCOS (polycystic ovarian syndrome) who is struggling with weight loss. This list is open to women wanting to lose any number of pounds and using their preferred diet may join. This list is a place where women who are struggling can come for advice, encouragement, and hints and tips from others who have been there, or are still struggling with their weight-related issues due to PCOS. To subscribe send an e-mail to PCOS_weightloss-subscribe@egroups.com. To send a message E-mail PCOS-weightloss@egroups.com.

PCOSAdoption

This list is designed to help women who are thinking about adopting or are in the process of adopting and the effects that PCOS plays in their lives. To subscribe, send a blank e-mail to PCOSAdoption-subscribe@egroups.com. To send a message E-mail PCOSAdoption@egroups.com.

PCOSandChildfree

This list is for women who are dealing with PCOS and are childfree by choice. It discusses the challenges of suffering from this disorder and trying to navigate the different treatment options and vent a little about being child free and suffering from a disease with such a strong fertility slant. Open to adult women who suffer from PCOS or suspected PCOS and who are childfree by choice. To subscribe, send a blank e-mail to PCOSandChildfree-subscribe@egroups.com. To send a message E-mail PCOSandChildfree@egroups.com.

PCOSJ

This list is for Jewish women who are diagnosed with Polycystic Ovary Syndrome and their family members. This should be a place to share feelings, treament, information, and support relating to PCOS issues including, but not exclusively, fertility and food. To subscribe, send a blank e-mail to PCOSJ-subscribe@egroups.com. To send a message E-mail PCOSJ@egroups.com.

PCONatural

This list discusses natural approaches to PCOS Treatment. To subscribe, send a blank e-mail to PCONatural-subscribe@egroups.com. To send a message E-mail PCONatural@egroups.com.

PCOSIreland

This list is a place where Irish sufferers of PCOS can discuss issues pertinent to their own country. To subscribe, send a blank e-mail to PCOSIreland-subscribe@egroups.com.
To send a message E-mail PCOSIrelance@egroups.com.

PCOSPreciousDreams

This list is for all women who have been diagnosed/undiagnosed with PCOS or Infertility. It is a warm and loving community of women to

discuss and give support in ALL areas of PCOS such as hirsutism
infertility, body image, depression, mood swings, insulin resistance and
the medications used to treat PCO. Support, advice and being informative are the BEST tools to make it through this frustrating medical
condition. To send a message Email emptyarms@egroups.com.

PCOSWeight
PCOSWeight unites women who suffer from PCOS with emphasis on
weight issues. The participants of this list share and empower each
other while dealing with life situations. To subscribe, send a blank e-
mail to PCOSWeight-subscribe@egroups.com. To send a message
E-mail PCOSWeight@egroups.com.

PCOSWomen
This list is for women who are not concerned with infertility but are
concerned about the other effects of Polycystic Ovarian Syndrome.
This is the place for support and "cystership" for women who were
blessed with children and now need a place to share information on
treatments for the other symptoms of PCOS. To subscribe send a
blank e-mail to PCOSWomen-subscribe@egroups.com. To send a
message E-mail PCOSWomen@egroups.com.

Sugarbusters_PCOS
This list is for females of all ages who have been diagnosed with
PCOS (Polycystic Ovarian Syndrome) and are trying to improve their
overall health with the SugarBusters™ nutrition plan. Discussion will
include list members' experiences with PCOS as it relates to their diet.
Weight loss will be the primary discussion. To subscribe, send a blank
e-mail to Sugarbusters_PCOS-subscribe@egroups.com. To send a
message E-mail Sugarbusters_PCOS@egroups.com.

ThinCysters
This group is for women with polycystic ovarian syndrome who do not
have the weight issues that affect the majority of women with PCOS.
Discussions cover every aspect of PCOS, including diet and insulin
resistance, infertility, hair loss and hirsutism. To subscribe, send a
blank e-mail to ThinCysters-subscribe@egroups.com. To send a
message E-mail ThinCysters@egroups.com.

ttcwithpcos
A group of individuals joining together to offer love and support during
the trials of trying to conceive while dealing with Polycystic Ovarian
Syndrome. This group are for those still trying to conceive or have
successfully conceived with PCOS. To subscribe, send a blank e-mail
to ttcwithpcos-subscribe@egroups.com. To send a message
E-mail tccwithpcos@egroups.com.

Cyster Sites

Beth Ager's PCOS page

http://www.win.bright.net/~mickbeth/pco.htm

Beth's PCOS Page shares her personal journey with PCOS as she has tried to conceive. She has several ancillary pages that talk about different things that worked for her. This page does mention miscarriages.

Callalil's Polycystic Ovarian Syndrome Pages

http://pcos.freeservers.com

An excellent site for women who are just beginning to find out about PCOS. Callalil's page is well written and includes citations at the end of each page when needed. The site hasn't been updated recently.

Dawn Overmyer's PCOS Page.

http://www2.dmci.net/users/candylady/pco/default.htm

Dawn's Site gives a good personal account of how PCOS affected one woman. Dawn talks about her experiences with traditional treatments and dietary changes. Some of the e-mail resource information is dated and should be sought through other sources in this appendix.

Isabel's Personal PCOS Victory

http://www.geocities.com/pcosvictory

Isabel's Web discusses what she did to have a successful pregnancy with PCOS. She gives a very good description what PCOS is and had links to several sites that talk about PCOS.

KJenn's PCOS Korner

http://www.geocities.com/BourbonStreet/3032/pcos.htm

A great resource for women who are just starting their journey with PCOS. KJenn has lots of links that deal with all aspects of PCOS. She also has some great laproscopic pictures of what a polycystic ovary looks like (this is not for the squeamish).

Shelby's PCOS Page

http://www.homestead.com/thelivingimage/WhatIsPCOS.html

Shelby's PCOS Page gives a brief overview of PCOS. It also discusses herbal remedies and the PCOSupport group for the Dallas-Fort Worth area.

Local PCOSupport Chapter Web Sites

The PCOSupport Chapters below have Web pages. The pages below have information about local PCOSupport meetings as well as links to various local and national resources.

PCOSupport Dallas-Fort Worth Chapter
http://dallas-pcos.dhs.org

PCOSupport Houston Chapter
http://members.xoom.com/HoustonPCO/index.html

PCOSupport Illinois Chapter
http://www.pcosupport.org/illinois/index.html

PCOSupport Kansas City Chapter http://sites.netscape.net/kly-bolt/kcpcosupport

PCOSupport Kentucky Chapter
http://pcos-ky.dreamhost.com

PCOSupport Maine Chapter
http://www.adoptasap.org/PCOS.html

PCOSupport New Mexico
http://www.geocities.com/nmpco

PCOSupport Oklahoma Chapter
http://www.geocities.com/pcos_oklahoma

PCOSupport Oregon Chapter
http://www.pcosupport.org/oregon

PCOSupport Philadelphia Chapter
http://www.pcosupport.org/philadelphia

PCOSupport Rio Grande Valley Chapter
http://hometown.aol.com/rgvpco/page/index.htm

PCOSupport San Antonio Chapter
http://www.pcosupport.org/sanantonio

PCOSupport South Florida Chapter
http://www.pcosupport.org/sflorida

PCOSupport Washington Chapter
http://www.pcosupport.org/pcosawa/index.html

PCOSupport Wisconsin Chapter
http://www.pcosupport.org/wisconsin/index.html

Media Sites

The Cysterhood. A Celebration of Women with PCOS.
http://www.cysterhood.com
The Cysterhood is a pictorial testament of women with PCOS and the things they have accomplished. It had links to a variety of Web sites and has recently added a teen section and a Cyster's Kids section so that women know that it is possible to conceive when they have PCOS.

OBGYN.net's PCOS Pavilion.
http://www.obgyn.net/pcos/pcos.asp
The PCOS Pavilion is a joint association between OBGYN.net and PCOSupport. This site has reviewed articles written by women and healthcare professionals related to PCOS. Recent topics covered include PCOS and Fertility, PCOS in Teens, and A Parent's Perspective on PCOS. All articles are archived and there are also links to other Web sites that are related to PCOS.

The PCOS Quilt
http://www.obgyn.net/scripts/cfml.exe?template=pcos.cfm
This virtual quilt demonstrates the global implications of Polycystic Ovary Syndrome and stands as a silent testament of the need for proper education to assist in a timely diagnosis of this life-altering syndrome. Women can read and share their stories about PCOS. The quilt also gives the total number of health years that women have been affected by PCOS.

Suite101 Polycystic Ovarian Syndrome
http://www.suite101.com/welcome.cfm/polycystic_ovarian_syndrome
This site has a number of article and links to other sites. Articles cover a broad variety of topics including various studies, how symptoms affect women, and the medications that are being used for treatment of PCOS symptoms.

Health Sites

Agency for Health Care Policy and Research
http://www.ahcpr.gov
This is a government site that covers all aspects of health research and policy.

American College of Obstetricians and Gynecologists (ACOG)
http://www.acog.org
This site provides information on all facets of women's health. It is an excellent reference site which provides book lists and e-mail addresses for numerous other resources.

American Dietetic Association (ADA) http://www.eatright.org
Professional and classified listings on nutrition.

American Heart Association (AHA)
http://www.americanheart.org
Includes a tremendous amount of information on women's health.
Additionally, there are search engines, links, professional referrals and
diets.

American Medical Association,
Women's Health Information center
http://www.ama-assn.org/women
The portion of the AMA's Web site that is dedicated to women's
health.

American Psychological Association (APA)
http://www.apa.org
This site contains search engines, lists of professional associations and
information on emotional problems.

Centers for Disease Control and Prevention (CDC)
http://www.cdc.gov
This government site is devoted to studies of disease causes and cures.

Clinical Trials: Polycystic Ovarian Syndrome
http://www.centerwatch.com/studies/cat313.htm
The Clinical Trials page shows current registered clinical trials going on
around the country related to PCOS. Gives a good idea about what
kind of research is being done in the United States related PCOS.
NOTE: Research studies are generally not open to women who are trying to conceive.

Dr. Legro's Web Site
http://www.collmed.psu.edu/obgyn/pcos.htm
Doctor Legro has a lot of plain-English information about PCOS and
its effects. Information includes general information about PCOS and
links to The Ask the Doctor column by Dr. Legro.

Dr. Orzeck's Web Site.
http://www.orzeck.com
Dr. Orzeck's Site is targeted at people with diabetes. It very good
information about management of diabetes and numerous articles that
Dr. Orzeck has published in various medical journals.

Female health links
http://www.femalehealthlinks.com
This site provides many links to magazines, journals, and conferences
on women's health.

Fertile Thoughts

http://www.fertilethoughts.net

A comprehensive site offering forums on infertility, and adoption issues as your seed to build your family.

Findings: The Woman's Healthcare Advocacy Service

http://www.findings.net

Links to many aspects of women's health care.

Food and Drug Administration

http://www.fda.gov/fdahomepage.html

This is another very large government site providing an incredible amount of information about food, drugs, cosmetics, and other related resources.

Go ask Alice!

http://www.goaskalice.columbia.edu

Columbia University's Health Education Department sponsors this site. There is information on sexual health, relationships, physical health, and sex-related questions from viewers.

Healthfinder

http://www.healthweb.org

Supported by the National Library of medicine, this site provides links to Internet resources chosen by librarians and information professionals at leading Midwest academic medical centers.

Hormone Foundation

http://hormone.org

Download a free booklet, "Managing menopause: A Change for the Better," cosponsored by the Endocrine Society.

International Food Information Council (IFIC)

http://www.ificinfo.health.org

Presents scientific information pertaining to food safety, nutrition, and health in a manner that is useful and understandable for consumers.

MEDLINEplus

http://medlineplus.nlm.nih.gov

Site provides access to MEDLINE, which finds articles in the literature on specified topics.

Medscape.

http://www.medscape.com

Medscape is one of the best medical sites for conducting research. Users have access to a large number of articles from a wide variety of journals. Users can also subscribe to a number of newsletters that they receive via e-mail that discuss Women's Health, Endocrinology and many other topics.

National Cancer Institute, National Institutes of Health

http://www.nci.nih.gov
Complete listing of information on the effects of hormones on
breast cancer and the use of anti-estrogens. Decision tree software
for determining relative risk for breast cancer within the next year
and by age 90.

National Center for Complementary and Alternative Medicine,

National Institutes of Health http://nccam.nih.gov
A federal agency that conducts and supports basic and applied
research and training and provides information on complementary and
alternative medicine.

National Women's Health Information

http://www.nlm.nih.gov
This site is sponsored by the US Department of Health and Human
services Office on Women's Health. Provides an extensive library of
frequently asked questions, news stories, links, and dictionaries and
glossaries of health terms.

OBGYN.net

http://www.obgyn.net
In addition to the PCOS Pavilion, users can find information about
endometriosis, infertility, and a host of other aspects about Obstetrics
and Gynecology. They also host a number of e-mail forums and two
quilts devoted to PCOS and Endometriosis. This site targets both the
patient and the healthcare professional.

Professional Societies

American Association of Clinical Endocrinologists

1000 Riverside Ave.; Suite 205
Jacksonville, FL 32204
(904) 353-7878
http://www.aace.com
The American Association of Clinical Endocrinologists is a professional
medical organization devoted to the field of clinical endocrinology. The
mission of the American Association of Clinical Endocrinologists is to
enhance the practice of clinical endocrinology.

American Society for Reproductive Medicine

1209 Montgomery Highway
Birmingham, Alabama 35216-2809
205) 978-5000
http://www.asrm.org
The ASRM is a professional organization including members who are
physicians, nurses, technicians, mental health professionals, etc. who
are devoted to advancing knowledge and expertise in reproductive
medicine and biology. Established in 1944 as the American Fertility

Society, the Society has since achieved national and international recognition as the foremost organization promoting the study of reproduction and reproductive disorders. The ASRM is a voluntary non-profit organization with several subspecialty societies, most of which publish journals and papers in addition to the ASRM's highly respected *Fertility and Sterility*. Members must demonstrate the high ethical principles of the medical profession, evince an interest in reproductive medicine and biology, and adhere to the objectives of the Society.

The Hormone Foundation

4350 East West Highway, Suite 500
Bethesda, MD 20814-4426
Phone: 1-800-HORMONE
Fax: 301-941-0259
The Hormone Foundation is the public education affiliate of The Endocrine Society. The Hormone Foundation is dedicated to improving the quality of life by promoting the prevention, diagnosis, and treatment of human disease in which hormones play a role.

Society for Endocrinology

17/18 The Courtyard,
Woodlands,
Bradley Stoke,
Bristol BS32 4NQ, UK.
+44 (0)1454 619036
http://www.endocrinology.org
The Society for Endocrinology was set up in 1946 to promote the advancement of endocrinology. The Society currently has about 1900 members and is increasing its size and range of activities rapidly. As well as being the major endocrine society outside North America, the Society is a founder member and organizer of the British Endocrine Societies, to which all the main British endocrine groups are affiliated.

The Endocrine Society

4350 East-West Highway
Suite 500
Bethesda, MD 20814
https://www.endo-society.org
The Endocrine Society is the primary professional organization for both clinical and basic science in endocrinology. They publish *The journal of Clinical Endocrinology and Metabolism,* and *Endocrine Reviews*, plus other journals.

Health Care Professionals

For ease of use, the Health Care Professionals section has been arranged alphabetically by the state in which the practice is located. Look for a specialist in an adjacent state if there is no one specializing in PCOS yet located in your state. Physicians with a special interest in PCOS are sometimes difficult to locate. Most medical, pediatric and reproductive endocrinology specialists have a general understanding of PCOS, but they may not have a special interest in the disorder. The following physicians were identified either by the research in PCOS or their identification with PCOSA. Their listing below is far from complete and is not an endorsement of competence. Many excellent clinicians are not included because there is presently no mechanism for recognition of this special interest or competence. You should urge any physician who has a specific interest in PCOS to *join PCOSA*, so that they may be identified.

Alabama

Ricardo Azziz, M.D., M.P.H.
The University of Alabama at
Birmingham
OB/GYN Dept.
618 South 20th Street
Old Hillman Building, Room 549
Birmingham, AL 35233-7333
(205) 934-5708
Specialty: Reproductive Endocrinology

California

R Jeffrey Chang, M.D.
Dept of Reproductive Medicien UCSD
9500 Gilman Dr., BSB 5040
San Diego, CA 92093
Specialty: Reproductive Endocrinology

Linda C. Giudice, M.D., Ph.D.
Dept Gynecology and Obstetrics
300 Pasteur Dr. Rm. HH333
Stanford University Medical Center
Stanford, CA 94305
Speciality: Reproductive Endocrinology

Robert A. Greene, M.D.
The North State Women's Center
1441 Liberty Street, Suite 306
Redding, CA 96001
(530) 244-1003
Specialty: Reproductive Endocrinology
Secondary specialty: Gynecology

Deborah A. Metzger, M.D.
Helena's Woman's Health
780 Welch Road Ste. 206
Palo Alto, CA 94304
(650) 833-7900
Specialty: Reproductive Endocrinology

Armand Newman, M.D.
9301 Wilshire Blvd. #301
Beverly Hills, CA 90210 USA
Phone: (310) 888-8877
Fax: (310) 273-5601
Specialty: Dermatology

Colorado

Gerald Poticha, M.D.
8120 S. Holly Street
Suite 110
Littleton, CO 80122 USA

Delaware

Ron Feinberg, M.D.
Reproductive Associates of Delaware
4600 New Linden Hill Road
Brownstone Plaza, Suite 102
Wilmington, DE 19808
(302) 633-9533
Specialty: Reproductive Endocrinology

Barbara McGuirk, M.D.
Reproductive Associates of Delaware
4600 New Linden Hill Road
Brownstone Plaza, Suite 102
Wilmington, DE 19808
(302) 633-9533

Florida

Kenneth Mark Gelman, M.D.
1150 N. 35th Avenue
Hollywood, FL 33021
(954) 963-7100
Primary Specialty: Reproductive
Endocrinology
Secondary: Medical Endocrinology

Neil F. Goodman, M.D.
9150 SW 87th Ave # 210
Miami, FL 33176
(305) 595-6855
Specialty: Reproductive Endocrinology

Georgia

Elbridge Bills II, M.D., F.A.C.O.G
Alliance OB/GYN P.C.
3400C Old Milton Pkwy, Suite 425
Alpharetta, GA 30005
(770) 777-4933

Mark Perloe, M.D.
Georgia Reproductive Specialists
285 Boulevard Northeast
Suite 320
Atlanta, GA 30312 USA
(404) 843-2229
Specialty: Reproductive Endocrinology

E. Scott Sills, M.D.
Georgia Reproductive Specialists
285 Boulevard Northeast
Suite 320
Atlanta, GA 30312 USA
(404) 843-2229
Specialty: Reproductive Endocrinology

John J.Vogel, D.O.
755 Mt. Vernon Highway #230
Atlanta, GA 30328
(404) 257-3002
Specialty: Women's Health

Illinois

David A. Ehrmann, M.D.
Dept. of Medicine/Endocrinology
University of Chicago
5841 S. Maryland Ave., MC1027
Chicago, IL 60637
(773) 702-9653
Primary Specialty: Medical
Endocrinology
Secondary Specialty: PCOS,
Reproductive Endocrinology

Mary Ghorbanian
M.G. Institute Ltd.
46 E. Oak Street
Suite 200
Chicago, IL 60611 USA
Specialty: Laser Hair Removal

Randy S. Morris, M.D.
2001 95th St., Suite 108
Naperville, IL 60540
(630) 357-6540
Or
680 N. Lake Shore Drive, Suite 1428
Chicago, IL 60611
(312) 573-3700
Specialty Reproductive Endocrinology

K. Nelson, M.D.
Advanced Reproductive Center
435 N. Mulford
Suite 9
Rockford, IL 61108-5100 USA

Maryland

Nathan G. Berger, M.D.
200 E. 33rd St. #487
Baltimore, MD 21218
(410) 554-2683

Rosella Smith, M.D.
110 West Road
Suite 102
Towson, MD 21204

Massachusetts

Andrea Dunaif, M.D.
Chief, Division of Women's Health
Associate Professor of Medicine,
Harvard Medical School
Brigham & Women's Hospital
75 Francis Street
Boston, MA 02115
(617) 732-8798
Primary specialty: Medical
Endocrinology
Secondary specialty: PCOS,
Reproductive Endocrinology

Janet Hall, M.D,
Reproductive Endocrine Associates
BHX - 5 Massachusetts General
Hospital
55 Fruit Street
Boston, MA 02114 USA
(617) 726-8433

Frances Hayes, M.D.
Reproductive Endocrine Unit
Massachusetts General Hospital
Bartlett Hall Exit 5
Boston, MA 02114 USA
(617) 726-8434

Kathryn A. Martin, M.D.
Reproductive Endocrine Associates
Reproductive Endocrine Unit, BHX-5
Massachusetts General Hospital
55 Fruit Street
Boston, MA 02114 USA
(617) 726-8433

Ann E. Taylor, M.D.
Reproductive Endocrine Unit
Massachusetts General Hospital
55 Fruit Street BHX-5
Boston, MA 02114
(617) 726-8433
Specialty: Reproductive Endocrinology

Corrine K. Welt
Reproductive Endocrine Associates
BHX 511
Massachusetts General Hospital
Boston, MA 02114 USA
(617) 726-8437

Minnesota

Daniel L. Dumesic, M.D.
Charlton 3A, Mayo Clinic
200 1st Street SW
Rochester, MN 55905
Specialty: Reproductive Endocrinology

New Jersey

Michael C. Darder, M.D.
IVF New Jersey/Fertility and
Gynecology PA
1527 Hwy 27 Suite 2100
Somerset, NJ 08873
(732) 220-9060
Or
193 Rt. 9 South
Manalapan, NJ 07726
Specialty: Reproductive Endocrinology

Annette Lee, M.D.
IVF New Jersey/Fertility and
Gynecology PA
1527 Hwy 27 Suite 2100
Somerset, NJ 08873
(732) 220-9060
Or
193 Rt. 9 South
Manalapan, NJ 07726
Specialty: Reproductive Endocrinology

Susan L. Treiser, M.D., Ph.D.
IVF New Jersey/Fertility and
Gynecology PA
1527 Hwy 27 Suite 2100
Somerset, NJ 08873
(732) 220-9060
or
193 Rt. 9 South
Manalapan, NJ 07726
Specialty: Reproductive Endocrinology

New York

Alan Barry Copperman, M.D.
Mount Sinai School of Medicine
Department of Obstetrics and
Gynecology
Box # 1170
One Gustave L. Levy Place
New York, New York 10029
(212) 241-5927

Walter Futterweit, M.D., F.A.C.P.,
F.A.C.E.
1172 Park Avenue
New York, NY 10128
212 876-6400
Specialty: Medical Endocrinology

Richard V. Grazi
Brooklyn IVF
1355 84th Street
Brooklyn, NY 11228

Kevin V. Kelly, M.D.
85 East End Ave. STE 1-G
New York, NY 10028
Phone (212) 249-2298
Specialty: Psychiatry

Rogerio Lobo, M.D.
Dept. Obstetrics and Gynecology
Columbia-Presbyterian Medical Center
622 W. 168th Street
16th Floor
New York NY 10032
Specialty: Reproductive Endocrinology

Martha McKittrick, RD, CN, CDE
436 E. 69th Street
Suite 5D
New York NY 10021
Specialty: Nutrionist for PCOS

Zev Rosenwaks, M.D.
Ctr for Reproductive Medicine &
Infertility
505 East 70th St
New York, NY 10021
Specialty: Reproductive Endocrinology

Irene N. Sills, M.D.
Pediatric Endocrinology
New Scotland Ave.
Albany, NY 12208 USA

Daniel Stein, M.D.
Division of Reproductive Endocrinology
St. Luke's-Roosevelt Hospital Center
425 West 59 Street (Suite 4G)
New York, New York 10019
(212) 523-8959

North Carolina

Stephen W. Sawin, M.D.
Samuel S. Thatcher, M.D., Ph.D.,
FACOG
Center for Applied Reproductive
Science
520 Biltmore, Suite A
Asheville NC 28801
(828) 285-8881
Specialty: Reproductive Endocrinology

Ohio

Charles Glueck, M.D.
The Cholesterol Center
ABC Building
3200 Burnet Ave.
Cincinnati, OH 45229 USA
(513) 585-7800
Specialty: Medical Endocrinology

Geoffrey Redmond, M.D.
Center for Health Studies
Five Commerce Park Square
23250 Chagrin Blvd
Cleveland, OH 44122
(216)292-5800
Specialty: Medical and Pediatric
Endocrinology

Oklahoma

Robert A. Wild, M.D.
Dept. Gynecology and Obstetrics
2410 Williams Pavilion
920 S. Stanton Young Blvd.
Oklahoma City, OK 73104
Specialty: Reproductive Endocrinology

Oregon

Kenneth Bury, M.D.
1750 SW Harbor Way, #100
Portland, Oregon 97201
(503) 418-3700
Specialty: Reproductive Endocrinology

Jan Gorril, M.D.
1750 SW Harbor Way, #100
Portland, Oregon 97201
(503) 418-3700
Specialty: Reproductive Endocrinology

Tori Hudson, M.D.
A Woman's Time
2067 NW Lovejoy St.
Portland OR 97209
(503) 222-2322

Philip Patton, M.D.
1750 SW Harbor Way, #100
Portland, Oregon 97201
(503) 418-3700
Specialty: Reproductive Endocrinology

Linda Price, M.D.
364 SE 8th Avenue, #205
Hillsboro, OR 97123
(503) 418-5525
Specialty: OB/GYN

Pennsylvania

Sarah Berga, M.D.
Dept. Obstetrics and Gynecology
University of Pittsburgh
McGee Women's Hospital
300 Halket St
Pittsburgh, PA 15213
Specialty: Reproductive Endocrinology

Michael D. Birnbaum, M.D.
8380 Old York Road, Suite 200
Elkins Park, PA 19027
(215) 886-9116
Specialty: Reproductive Endocrinology

Richard S. Legro, M.D.
Dept. of Ob/Gyn
Penn State University College of
Medicine
500 University Drive
Milton S. Hershey Medical Center
Hershey, PA 17033
(717) 531-8478
Specialty: Reproductive Endocrinology

Shahab S. Minassian, M.D.
MCP Hahnemann University Division
of Fertility and Reproductive
Endocrinology
Suite 100, Monroe Office Center
4000 Presidential Boulevard
Philadelphia, PA 19131
(215) 581-6200

Tennessee

Samuel S. Thatcher, M.D., Ph.D
Joseph L. Kennedy,III, M.D.
Center for Applied Reproductive
Science
408 N. State of Franklin Road
Suite 31
Johnson City, TN 37604
(423) 461-8880
Specialty: Reproductive Endocrinology

Texas

Amin Jamal, M.D.
8181 North Stadium Drive Suite #200
Houston, TX 77054
(713) 797-9922
Specialty: Medical Endocrinology

Eric Orzeck, M.D., F.A.C.E., F.A.C.P.
8181 North Stadium Drive, Suite
#200
Houston, TX 77054
(713) 797-9922
Specialty: Endocrinology
Specialty: Internal Medicine

Ivor Safro, M.D., P.A., F.A.C.O.G.,
F.A.C.S, F.R.C.O.G., F.R.C.S.,
F.C.O.G., S.A.
920 Frostwood, Suite 530
Houston TX 77024
(713) 465-9390
Specialty: Obstetrics and Gynecology

Vicki Schnell, M.D., F.A.O.G.
450 Medical Center Blvd
Suite #202
Webster, TX 77598
(281) 332-0073
Specialty: Reproductive Endocrinology

Utah
Eli Y. Adashi, M.D.
Health Science Center
1231 East Chandler Cir.
Salt Lake City, UT 84103
Specialty: Reproductive
Endocrinology

Virginia
John E. Nestler, M.D.
Professor and Chairman
Division of Endocrinology and
Metabolism
Medical College of Virginia
Virginia Commonwealth University
P.O. Box 980111
Richmond, VA 23298-0111
(804) 828-9695
Specialty: Medical Endocrinology

International
Marco Filicori, M.D.
Reproductive Endocrinology Center
University of Bologna
Via Massarenti 13
Bologna, 40138 Italy
Italian phone number: +39-051-342820
Italian Fax number: +39-051-397350

Kevin Gangar, FRCS, MRCOG
6 Kingsmead
Gower Road
Weybridge
Surrey, KT13 0HB United Kingdom

Ellen M. Greenblatt, M.D., F.A.B.O.G.
200 Elizabeth St. STE. EN6-242
Toronto, ON M5G2C4
Phone: (416) 340-4491
Specialty: Reproductive Endocrinology

What's Ahead?
Research Directions

"The theme... is not the advance of science as such; it is the advancement of science as it affects human beings." – foreword to Brave New World *by A. L. Huxley*

In 1935, Drs. Stein and Leventhal reported a series of seven women with irregular periods and enlarged ovaries who were operated on for diagnostic purposes. On microscopic examination, no tumor was found in these patients, but the ovary of each one was enlarged by an increased number of follicular cysts that appeared to be actively producing hormones. With removal of a portion of the ovary, these patients had restoration of menses and two became pregnant. It has been said of this original work "from a biopsy a syndrome was born." It's ironic that sixty years later a similar scenario was repeated when women with insulin resistance were treated not with a scalpel, but with insulin-altering drugs. The background of PCOS and its therapy have been inauspicious. Although several thousand research papers have been published on PCOS, they have not nearly generated the impact as has the recent insurgence of demand from information-hungry consumers.

There appears to be a coalescence of theory and practice of consumer and physician around PCOS. It is not yet a perfect fit. That there is, or should be, a single diagnosis of PCOS indicating that the various manifestations can be grouped into one disorder is disputed by some. With more information, the critical mass of what we now know as PCOS could break into multiple fragments and the disorder as we now view it will become of historical interest only. Whether PCOS is a unifying diagnosis or not is not nearly so important as the fact that it represents a flag to rally round, a flag that is bringing overdue attention to important issues of health and well-being of millions of women the world over.

The obvious gaps in our understanding of PCOS make it very difficult to predict what the future holds. Ten years ago this book might never have made it to bookshelves, much less be taken off the shelf and read. PCOS is a microcosm of what is happening in the evolution of medicine. Unfortunately, as in the study of biologic evolution, there is some blind stumbling until something is found that works. However, it seems clear that we are moving from disease treatment to disease prevention. We know that PCOS is related to some serious health threats such as diabetes and possibly cardiovascular disease. How strongly related, we don't know yet. Before we hang our heads too low in frustration and fear, we must also acknowledge that PCOS may also offer some health advantages. We know, for example, that the risk of osteoporosis, a major and increasing cause of female mortality, is reduced in women with PCOS.

Is the sky going to open and a miraculous cure for PCOS drop out anytime in the near future? I doubt it. When the basis of PCOS is finally worked out, it will be in the genetics and molecular biology labs investigating how the genes that affect ovarian function are altered and passed from one generation to another. Quite likely there will be many variations on the PCOS theme, sharing a common heritage of a small group of gene alterations. The words that are now being defined in the genetic dictionary, known as the Human Genome Project, will form a reference to study the language of PCOS.

A single fat gene, for example, may never be identified, but the causes of obesity will become much better understood. We are all hopeful that there will be a movement away from diets for weight loss and toward nutritional balance. In the future, safe therapies may be designed to alter metabolism and allow a much better utilization of food, but many other human frailties will be overcome before that of our eating habits.

While identifying the precise cause of PCOS may be many years away, effective therapy may not be. New insulin-altering agents will be increasingly used for infertility, diabetes in pregnancy, and to slow the progression of type 2 diabetes, possibly even its prevention. Development of drugs that affect the way in which we digest, absorb, and utilize our food have been identified as a priority by most pharmaceutical firms. It would seem a reasonably reachable objective that effective anti-androgens be developed for the treatment of skin problems.

To study the real issues presently confronting us doesn't take more than recording and comparing data about how women enter puberty, have children (or not), and grow old. It became a tedious exercise throughout this book to try to find new ways of stating what may have felt to the reader like the book's mantra—"This is an important topic on which we do not have enough information to draw a conclusion."

Why should it be so hard? Obviously, our major block to date has been the failure to make the diagnosis of PCOS. Scientific studies give us little glimpses, but often too few women were studied to offer a concrete foundation on which to build our understanding. Strides are being made. The two major federally funded multicenter NIH initiatives on perimenopause and post-menopauseal women's health are well under way. Although no provision is made in these studies for gathering information about PCOS, it may help us to define what is normal, so that future PCOS studies may have a benchmark for comparison. It is not that PCOS has been singled out and ignored; it is just that investigation of how it relates to all ages and aspects of life has not been studied. PCOS databases are now being started that can track the course of the disorder over the long term. It's reasonable to hope that a new NIH initiative will be a better characterization of PCOS.

It is a great boost to a physician's ego to make a diagnosis that has been missed in the past. To see the gratitude of a patient who has been evaluated and dismissed by a double handful of physicians and then finds out that there is a name behind and a cause for her multiple and seemingly unrelated problems strikes the cord that makes some of us remember why we practice medicine in the first place. Fortunately for our patients, the correct diagnosis of PCOS is being made with increasing regularity. Due both to physician and consumer education and advocacy, this "breakthrough diagnosis" phenomenon will become much less common.

A goal for the future is that an accurate description of what PCOS is and what it means can be uniformly given by health care providers. It is hoped that there will be easily available and identified centers for the evaluation and treatment of PCOS. Such centers will have an integrative group of health care providers including endocrinologists, nutritionists, exercise physiologists, psychologists, and dermatologists.

It is certain that the future study of PCOS will be a group effort. Women with PCOS and their partners and families are presently fighting too hard for the disorder not to be recognized and addressed. It is expected that PCOS advocacy will remain an identified and positive force. PCOS and its accompanying medical problems are an excellent target for new drug therapies and this has not passed unnoticed by the pharmaceutical firms that are increasingly becoming partners in health maintenance. PCOS is just too interesting not to be the subject of scientific research. Our new techniques of probing the origins of diseases and their transmission through our genetic makeup will take on more and more importance. At the center of this advancement will be the informed physician who can address the problems and design individualized intervention on a personal one to one basis.

As interest builds in studying PCOS and developing treatments to manage its various signs, symptoms and medical consequences, PCOS patients may be able to participate in studies and clinical trials. Check these two Web sites on a regular basis for information as it breaks:

Center Watch at http://www.centerwatch.com/studies/cat313.htm> or

PCOSupport at http://www.pcosupport.org/PCOSinfo/research.html>

I sincerely hope that the future holds a second edition of this book, if for no other reason than to reflect on where we were.

> *"The Future is a world limited by ourselves; in it we discover what concerns us, and sometimes, by chance, what interests those whom we love the most."*
> *—Maurice Maeterlinck, from Joyzelle*

Appendices

Laboratory Test Results Chart

Date	Test	Results	Normal Range	Comments

Medications Used Chart

Medication	Dose	Started	Stopped	Side-effects

NAME _____ age _____ date of birth _____

Have you had a physician give you the diagnosis of PCOS?   **No**   **Yes**
How was the diagnosis made:

DEVELOPMENTAL HISTORY
Were you born 1st   2nd   3rd 4th other?
How many siblings do you have? _____ brothers _____ sisters
Did your mother have problems getting pregnant?   **No**   **Yes**
Did she take any medications during her pregnancy with you?   **No**   **Yes**
Did she experience any complications during her pregnancy?   **No**   **Yes**
        Bleeding   Diabetes   High blood pressure   Other

Where you born on the expected due date?   **No**   **Yes**
        If not, how many weeks? _____
How much did you weigh at birth? _____ pounds   _____ ounces
At what age was your first pubic hair noticed?   _____ yrs.
At what age was your first breast development?   _____ yrs.
At what age was your first period?   _____ yrs.
At ages 14-17 were your periods? ($\sqrt{ }$)
        __regular __varied long and short   __usually over 40 days apart
        __never without medications
At what age did you first see a physician for weight, hair, period or
gynecologic problems? _____
              What was the treatrment?
Was there a time when things seemed to change?

MENSTRUAL HISTORY
What is the date of your last period? _____
How far apart are your cycles? (first day to first day)
        Under 26 days   26-32 days   32-40 days   over 40 days
        erratic   never
How many days do you usually bleed? _____
Do you consider your bleeding excessive?   **No**   **Yes**
Is your menstrual pain excessive?   **No**   **Yes**
Do you have mid-cycle pain (Mittelshermz)?   **No**   **Yes**
Do you have PMS?   **No**   **Yes**
What medications have you used to regulate your periods? ($\sqrt{ }$)
        _____ Medroxyprogesterone acetate (MPA) (Amen, Cycrin, Provera)
        _____ Norethindrone acetate (Aygestin)
        _____ Progesterone (Crinone, Prometrium)
        _____ Oral contraceptives (OC's)
        which brands   how long   problems

_____   _____   _____
_____   _____   _____
_____   _____   _____
        other medications:

Were you regular while on the pill?   **No**   **Yes**
After stopping, how many months before your periods became regular?

Has there been any change in your periods over the last year? (describe)

METABOLIC / ENDOCRINE HISTORY

Do you have acne ? **No** **Yes**
> Treatment(s):

Do you have excessive hair growth? **No** **Yes**
Location
> face _____ chest _____ abdomen _____ thighs _____
> (grade severe = 4, moderate = 3 mild = 2 , minimal = 1, none = 0)
> Treatment(s):

Other skin problems:

What is your present weight? _____ height? _____
Weight 1 year ago _____ 2 years ago _____ 5 years ago _____

Weight age 16_____ age 20_____ age 24_____ age 30_____ age 36 _____ 40_____
What do you consider YOUR ideal weight? _____

Do you avoid any types of foods or place restrictions on your diet?

What diet plans have you used?
> Name pounds lost over months to regain
> Name pounds lost over months to regain
> Name pounds lost over months to regain
> Name pounds lost over months to regain

Do you drink alcoholic beverages? **No** **Yes** rarely occasional social over 2 drinks /week
Do you drink caffeinated beverages? **No** **Yes**
Do you use vitamins or nutritional supplements? **No** **Yes** **list:**

DO YOU HAVE ANY OF THE FOLLOWING CONDITIONS?
( ) thyroid disorder or goiter ( ) diabetes ( ) breast secretion (galactorrhea)
( ) increased blood pressure ( ) hypoglycemia ( ) elevated triglycerides or cholesterol

DO YOU HAVE ANY OF THE FOLLOWING SYMPTOMS?
( ) excessive thirst/urination ( ) poor sense of smell ( ) visual disturbances
( ) hot flushes ( ) hot or cold intolerance ( ) frequent headaches
( ) excessive fatigue/weakness ( ) night sweats ( ) vaginal dryness
( ) pelvic pain ( ) painful intercourse

CONTRACEPTIVE HISTORY
Have you ever used any form of birth control?   **No**   **Yes**
List methods of birth control used:

OBSTETRIC HISTORY
total number of pregnancies _____full-term _____ premature _____ abortion
_____ miscarriage _____ectopic_____

ages of all living children _____   _____   _____   _____

year	months to conceive ?	current partner is father? (Y/N)	fertility therapy needed? (Y/N)	length of pregnancy?(wks)	vaginal or C-section delivery?	weight of newborn?
1st						
2nd						
3nd						

Were there any complications to your pregnancies?   **No**   **Yes**
( ) Bleeding   ( ) Diabetes of pregnancy (gestational)
( ) High blood pressure (toxemia, PIH)

Did you breast feed? **No**   **Yes**   Problems breastfeeding?   **No**   **Yes**

GYNECOLOGIC HISTORY
Have you ever had a genital or sexually transmitted infection?   **No**   **Yes**
when?   type?   treatment?
Do you have a history of vaginal infections (yeast, etc).?   **No**   **Yes**
Do you have a history of urinary tract infections (bladder, cystitis)?   **No**   **Yes**
Have you had, or been immunized, to Rubella (German Measles)?   **No**   **Yes**
Have you ever had an abnormal Pap smear?   **No**   **Yes**
when?   treatment?
Date of most recent PAP smear?

Is there a history of any of the following? (√)
( ) endometriosis   ( ) uterine fibroids
( ) ovarian cysts   ( ) breast lumps or fibrocystic breast disease

Which, if any, of the following have you had? (√)
( ) D&C   ( ) endometrial biopsy
( ) ultrasound scan?   ( ) hysterosalpingogram (HSG)
( ) laparoscopy?   ( ) hysteroscopy

If there is infertility
How long have you been attempting to get pregnant?   months
Which, if any, of the following have you had? (√)

( ) temperature charts	( ) urine LH kits	( ) blood monitoring
( ) clomiphene citrate (Clomid, Serophene) date:	number of months	maximum pills / day
( ) injectable fertility drugs date:	number of months	maximum amps / day
( ) semen analysis date:	results: normal abnormal borderline	
( ) intrauterine insemination date:		
( ) assisted reproduction (IVF) date:	attempts	

GENERAL MEDICAL HISTORY
Hospitalizations?

date   hospital   reason

_____

_____

_____

_____

Surgery?

date   hospital   operation

_____

_____

_____

_____

List medical problems you have been evaluated for in the last 5 years.

List any prescription or non-prescription medications used on a routine basis.

Have you had an allergic reaction to any medication? (List medication and type of reaction).

Do you have any environmental allergies? **No**   **Yes**

Have you ever had the following?

( ) anemia	( ) blood clots	( ) varicose veins
( ) hemorrhoids	( ) sickle cell	( ) heart murmur
( ) rheumatic fever	( ) pneumonia	( ) bronchitis
( ) asthma	( ) colitis	( ) gall bladder disease
( ) stomach ulcers	( ) diverticulosis	( ) appendicitis
( ) arthritis	( ) kidney disease	( ) back problems
( ) head injury /unconsciousness	( ) easy bleeding /bruising	
( ) emotional illness	( ) migraine	( ) seizures
( ) hepatitis	( ) heart disease	( ) hernia
( ) irritable bowel syndrome	( ) AIDS	

Have you ever been treated for cancer or any pre-cancerous condition? **No**   **Yes**

when?   for what?

Have you been exposed to ( ) toxic fumes   ( ) solvents/chemicals   ( ) radiation

SOCIAL/PERSONAL HISTORY

Marital status: single   engaged   separated married   divorced

What is your race or ethnic group?

What is your occupation?
        How many hours per week do you work?

What leisure time activities do you enjoy?

Do you participate in any form of strenuous exercise?
      type   hrs/week

Is there any abnormality in your sleep pattern?   No   Yes
       average N° hours of sleep each night

Do you smoke? **No Yes** — __less than 10 cigs. /day __10-20
                      __20-40   __over 40

Do you believe you or your partner has a problem with sexual function? **No**   **Yes**

FAMILY HISTORY

( ) PCOS   — who _____

( ) infertility   — who _____

( ) menstrual problems   — who _____

( ) hormone problems   — who _____

( ) diabetes   — who _____

( ) excessive hair growth   — who _____

( ) obesity   — who _____

( ) thyroid   — who _____

( ) miscarriage   — who _____

( ) heart disease   — who _____

( ) cancer   — who/type _____

( ) birth defects   — who/type _____

( ) male premature balding — who _____

BMI Calculation Chart

HEIGHT feet and inches

WEIGHT pounds	5'0"	5'1"	5'2"	5'3"	5'4"	5'5"	5'6"	5'7"	5'8"	5'9"	5'10"	5'11"	6'0"
100	20	19	18	18	17	17	16	16	15	15	14	14	14
105	21	20	19	19	18	17	17	16	16	16	15	15	14
110	21	21	20	19	19	18	18	17	17	16	16	15	15
115	22	22	21	20	20	19	19	18	17	17	17	16	16
120	23	23	22	21	21	20	19	19	18	18	17	17	16
125	24	24	23	22	21	21	20	20	19	18	18	17	17
130	25	25	24	23	22	22	21	20	20	19	19	18	18
135	26	26	25	24	23	22	22	21	21	20	19	19	18
140	27	26	26	24	24	23	23	22	21	21	20	20	19
145	28	27	27	26	25	24	23	23	22	21	21	20	20
150	29	28	27	27	26	25	24	23	23	22	22	21	20
155	30	29	28	27	27	26	25	24	24	23	22	22	21
160	31	30	29	28	27	27	26	25	24	24	23	22	22
165	32	31	30	29	28	27	27	26	25	24	24	23	22
170	33	32	31	30	29	28	27	27	26	25	24	24	23
175	34	33	32	31	30	29	28	27	27	26	25	24	24
180	35	34	33	32	31	30	29	28	27	27	26	25	24
185	36	35	34	33	32	31	30	29	28	27	27	26	25
190	37	36	35	34	33	32	31	30	29	28	27	26	26
195	38	37	36	35	33	32	31	31	30	29	28	27	26
200	39	38	37	35	34	33	32	31	30	30	29	28	27
205	40	39	37	36	35	34	33	32	31	30	29	29	28
210	41	40	38	37	36	35	34	33	32	31	30	29	28
215	42	41	39	38	37	36	35	34	33	32	31	30	29
220	43	42	40	39	38	37	36	34	33	32	32	31	30
225	44	43	41	40	39	37	36	35	34	33	32	31	31
230	45	43	42	41	39	38	37	36	35	34	33	32	31
235	46	44	43	42	40	39	38	37	36	35	34	33	32
240	47	45	44	43	41	40	39	38	36	35	34	33	33
245	48	46	45	43	42	41	40	38	37	36	35	34	33
250	49	47	46	44	43	42	40	39	38	37	36	35	34
255	50	48	47	45	44	42	41	40	39	38	37	36	35
260	51	49	48	46	45	43	42	41	40	38	37	36	35
265	52	50	48	47	45	44	43	42	40	39	38	37	36
270	53	51	49	48	46	45	44	42	41	40	39	38	37

	normal		normal		normal			normal

METRIC CONVERSION TABLE

		deci (d)	1 / 10	micro(μ or mcg)	1 / 100,000
Length	meters (m)				
Mass	grams (g)	kilo (k) x 1000	centi (c) 1 / 100	nano (n)	1 / 100,000,000
Volume	liters (l)	mega x 100,000	milli (m) 1 / 1000	pico (p)	1 / 100, 000, 000,000

Length

1 meter (m)	= 39.40 inches	1 yard(yd)	= 0.914 m = 91.4 cm
1 centimeter (cm)	= 0.394 inches	1 foot (ft)	= 0.305 m
1 millimeter (mm)	= 0.039 inches	1 inch (in.)	= 2.54 cm

Mass

1 kilogram (kg)	= 2.20 pounds	1 pound (lb)	= 0.454 kilogram
1 gram (g)	= 0.03 ounces	1 ounce (oz)	= 31.103 g

Volume

1 milliliter(ml)	= 0.034 ounces	1 ounce	= 29.573 milliliters
1 liter (l)	= 1.057 quarts	1 quart (qt)	= 0.946 liter

NOTE 1 cc = 1 ml

PCOS Family Tree

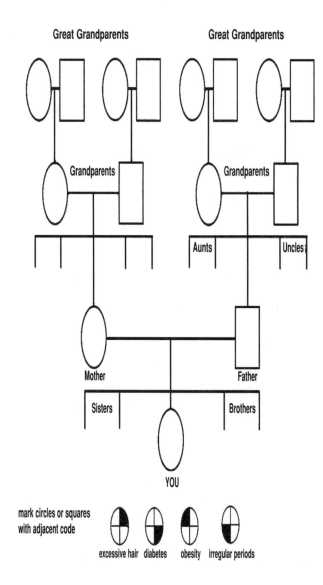

Great Grandparents   Great Grandparents

Grandparents   Grandparents

Aunts   Uncles

Mother   Father

Sisters   Brothers

YOU

mark circles or squares
with adjacent code

excessive hair   diabetes   obesity   irregular periods

Study	N°	Age (years)	Metformin dose / length	Fasting Insulin	SHBG	Free Testost	LH	FSH
Diamanti-Kandarakis *Eur J Endo1998*	16	18-31	850 mg TID 6 months	↓	↑	↓	ND	ND
Morin-Papunen *Fert Steril 1998*	20	20-40	500 mg TID 4-6 months	↓	↑	↓ (NS)	↓ (NS)	↑ (NS)
Nestler *N E J Med 1998*	59	28-29	500 mg TID +Clomiphene 50mg QDx5d	↓	↑	↓	ND	ND
Zarate *Ginec O Mex 1997*	15	16-20	400 mg BID 6 months	ND	NS	(NS)	ND	ND
Casimirri *Int J Obes 1997*	24	not given	500mg TID 6 months	↓	ND	ND	ND	ND
Ehrmann *J Clin Endo & Met 1997*	14	21-31	titrated to max dose 2550mg	no effect	ND	no effect	ND	ND
Nestler *J Clin Endo & Met 1997*	31	18-35	500mg TID 4-6 weeks Non-obese PCOS	↓	↑	↓	ND	ND
Velazquez *Metabolism 1997a*	16	18-33	500mg TID 8 weeks assess PAI-I, Lp(a) effect	↓	ND	↓	↓	↑(NS)
Velazquez *OB GYN 1997b*	22	mean 25	500mg TID 8 weeks	↓	ND	↓	↓	↑
Nestler *N E J Med 1996*	25	18-35	500mg TID 4-8 weeks	↓	↑	↓	↓	ND
Acbay *Fert Steril 1996*	16	mean 31	850mg BID 10 weeks	no change	ND	no change	no change	no change
Crave *J Clin Endo & Met 1995*	24	not given	850mg BID 4 months	no change	↑	no change	ND	ND
La Marca *Hum Rep 1999*	14	20-28	500mg TID x 30-32 days	NR	↑	↓	↓	↓
Glueck Diab Ed Faculty Conf	43	16-46	Titrated to max dose of 2550mg x 1.5 to 24 months	↓	↓	↓	↑	↓
Moghetti *J Clin Endo & Met 2000*	23 / 32	18-35 / 18-35	500mg TIDor placebo (up to 2 years)	↓	↑	↓	↑	↓
De Leo *Fert Steril 1999*	20	24-32	500mg TID 30-35 dys	D/C	D/C	↓	↓	↓
DeFronzo *J Clin Endo & Met 1991*	14	Mean 60±3	500mg BID 3-4 days max 2.5g daily	↓	D/C	D/C	D/C	D/C
Kolodziejczyk *Fert Steril*	35	18-37	500mg TID 12 weeks	↓	↑	↓	↑	↑
De Leo *J Clin Endo&Met 2000*	14	Mean 26	500mg TID 30-32 days	↓	↑	↓	NC	↑
Velazquez *Metab 1994*	29	18-33	500mg TID 8 weeks		↑	↓	↓	↑

Abbreviations

ADA- American Diabetes Association

AID -artificial insemination by donor

AIH - artificial insemination husband

ALT - alanine aminotransferase

AODM - adult onset diabetes, now called type 2

ASRM - American Society for Reproductive Medicine

ART - assisted reproductive technology

BMI - body mass index

BP - blood pressure

BUN - blood urea nitrogen

CAH - congenital adrenal hyperplasia

CAL - calorie = kcal

CBC - complete blood count

CC - cubic centimeters = milliliters (ML)

CC - clomiphene citrate

COH - controlled ovarian hyperstimulation

CVD - cardiovascular disease

CYP - cytochrome

D& C - dilation and curretage

DES - diethylstilbestrol

DHEAS - dehydroepiandrosterone sulfate

DHT- dihydrotestosterone

DI - donor insemination

DM - diabetes mellitus

DNA - deoxyribonucleic acid

E2 - estradiol

EDD - estimated date of delivery

ERT - estrogen replacement therapy

FAI - free androgen index

FBS - fasting blood sugar (glucose)

FDA-Food and Drug Administration

FSH - follicle stimulating hormone

GnRH - gonadotropin releasing hormone

GDM - gestational diabetes mellitus

GTT - glucose tolerance test

hCG - human chorionic gonadotropin

HMG - human menopausal gonadotropin

HDL- high density lipoprotein (good cholesterol)

HRT - hormone replacement therapy

HSG - hysterosalpingogram

ICSI - intracytoplasmic sperm injection

IDDM - insulin dependent diabetes mellitus

IGF- insulin-like growth factor

IGT - imparied glucose tolerance

IM - intramuscular

IR - insulin resistance

IU - international units

IUI - intrauterine insemination

IV - intravenous

IVF - in vitro fertilization

LDL - low density lipoprotein (bad cholesterol)

LMP - last menstrual period

LH - luteinizing hormone

MRI- magnetic resonance imaging

NIH - National Institute of Health

OC - oral contraceptive

OHSS - ovarian hyperstimulation syndrome

OMI - oocyte maturation inhibitor

P4 - progesterone

PP - precocious pubarche

PID - pelvic inflammatory disease

PIH - pregnancy induced hypertension

POF - premature ovarian failure

RCT – randomized control trial

RE - reproductive endocrinologist

RMR - resting metabolic rate

RNA - ribonucleic acid

SC - subcutaneous

SERM - selectivre estrogen receptor modulators

SHBG - sex hormone binding globulin

SSRI - selective serotonin reuptake inhibitor

T4 - thyroxine thyroid hormone

TSH - thyroid stimulating hormone

ZP - zona pellucida

Acanthosis nigricans: velvety, raised, pigmented skin changes, most often seen on the back of the neck, axillae and beneath the breasts. often seen in association with skin tags (acrochordons). Associated with insulin resistance, obesity, and very rarely some forms of cancer.

activin: A growth factor that enhances FSH action, increases FSH and LH receptors and prevents premature luteinization.

adenoma: An abnormal growth of glandular cells. More often benign, but can be malignant.

adhesion: Abnormal anatomic attachment of one structure to another.

adrenarche: Onset of "sexual" hair development (pubic, arm pits) as a consequence of adrenal gland production of androgens.

adrenal androgens: Male hormones produced by the adrenal gland which in excess may lead to excessive hair growth and infertility.

adrenocorticotrophic hormone (ACTH): The regulatory hormone of the adrenal gland produced by the pituitary gland. Its excess can lead to overproduction of adrenal hormone function, Cushing's disease.

allelle: Each cell has two copies (alleles) of a gene, one from the maternal side and one form the paternal side. Alleles are the complementary genes.

alpecia (androgenic): Balding.

amenorrhea: The absence of periods for over 3 months.

analog: A drug which is similar in action and sometimes structure to a natural substance.

androgen: A group of the sex hormones responsible for male sexual characteristics. All female hormones are made from male hormones and a certain amount are necessary in all women.

androstenedione: A weak androgenic steroid hormone produced in the ovary, testis and adrenal gland that is a precursor to many of the other steroid hormones.

anovulation: Absence of ovulation.

anti-estrogen: A synthetic or natural substance that mimics or blocks the action of estrogen.

antrum: The cavity inside the follicle that expands with fluid as the follicle grows.

aneuploidy: The gain or loss of chromosomes resultingin change from the normal number 46.

aromatase: Enzyme in the granulosa cells, fat, liver and other cells responsible for the conversion of androgens to estrogens.

asthenospermia: Abnormal sperm motility.

assisted reproductive technologies (ART): A group of procedures including intrauterine inseminations and in vitro fertilization that employ manipulation of egg and sperm to establish a pregnancy.

atherogenic: facilitating atherosclerosis. atherosclerosis: "Hardening" of the arteries due to deposits of lipids and plaque formation; associated with hypertension and increased risk of heart attack.

atresia: An orderly process of removal (death, degeneration) of ovarian follicles.

autocrine: Communication by chemical messengers from a cell that affects its own function.

autosome: A non-sex chromosome; in humans there are 44 autosomes and one pair of sex (X and Y) chromosomes.

azoospermia: A type of male factor infertility caused by having no sperm.

Basal body temperature (BBT): The temperature of the body at rest. Often charted through the menstrual cycle as a predictor of ovulation.

beta ß cell: Cells of the pancreas responsible for insulin production.

blastocyst: A stage of embryonic development that occurs just prior to implantation.

blighted ovum: A pregnancy that failed in its development before fetal structures or fetal heart activity could be identified by ultrasound scan; most often of genetic origin, with abnormality present from fertilization.

body mass index (BMI): A calculation of the weight divided (in kilograms) by height (in meters) and expressed in square meters.

Cardiovascular disease: Detrimental alteration of the blood vessels of the body making the individual more prone to peripheral vascular disorders (decreased muscle function and clot formation), myocardial infarction, and stroke.

chromosome: Structures in the cell nucleus that contain DNA.

chromotubation: Instillation of dye solution into the uterine cavity and fallopian tubes to evaluate tubal status.

climacteric: (see perimenopause) The transition from reproductive to non-reproductive life associated with decline in ovarian function and estrogen deficiency.
contraindication: A reason not to do, or use.

cortex: Outer portion.

cortisol: An adrenal steroid hormone involved in stress and inflammation. Too little results in Addison's disease, while too much causes Cushing's Syndrome.

Cortrosyn™ stiimulation: Diagnostic test where a small amount of ACTH is injected to evaluate adrenal gland function.

cryopreservation: Freezing and storage.

cumulus cells: A cloud-like layer of supportive cells around the egg.

Cushing's disease/syndrome: a hormonal disorder resulting from an over-production of cortisol from the adrenal gland. If the origin is from a pituitary tumor (small and benign) that produces adrenocorticotrophic hormone (ACTH) it is called Cushing's disease. If the hypercotisolism arises from another cause it is called Cushing's syndrome. Often vague symptoms including upper body obesity, severe fatigue and muscle weakness, hypertension, easy bruising and bluish-red marks (striae) on the abdomen. The skin is fragile and bruises easily, the cheeks are usually very red. Women often have irregular menses and hirsutism. Many patients have high blood sugar. Most cases occur in women between ages 20-50. Occasionally clinical presentation can be confused with PCOS.

cyst: A fluid filled structure consisting of a wall and a cavity. A *follicular* cyst results from a follicle that has grown but failed to ovulate A *luteal* cyst forms after ovulation and contains trapped blood. Both types of cysts are said to be *functional* cysts because they arise from normal functions of the ovary.

Deoxyribonucleic acid (DNA): The hereditary material contained in a chromosome that carries the specific blueprinting for each individual.

ehydroepiandrosterone sulfate (DHEAS): An androgen mostly produced by the adrenal gland used as a marker of adrenal involvement in PCOS.

examethasone suppression test: Dexamethasone (Decadron™), usually 1 mg, is given in the evening and a blood cortisol level obtained the next morning to evaluate the presence and cause of adrenal gland hyperactivity.

diabetes mellitus (DM): A disordered carbohydrate metabolism due to difficulty of the body to make or properly respond to insulin. Type 1 (insulin deficient), which is usually not inherited, occurs early in life and is associated with low insulin levels. Type 2 (insulin resistant) previous called adult onset, characterized by high insulin levels, but poor utilization.

dilation and currettage (D&C): mechanical opening of the cervix sufficient to pass a small metal instrument (currette) into the uterine cavity to remove a portion of the uterine lining , or pregnancy for evaluation; performed either for evaluation or treatment.

dihydrotestosterone (DHT): For testosterone to exert its effect on the skin, it is converted by the enzyme 5 alpha-reductase to dihydrotestosterone, the active skin androgen.

dysfunctional uterine bleeding: Abnormal bleeding from the womb (uterus) due to lack of ovulation or other hormonal problems. Bleeding caused by hormonal as opposed to anatomic (structural) problems.

dyslipidemia: an alteration, unusually excessive amounts of one or more metabolic fats (lipids, cholesterol and lipoproteins); generally related to an increased risk of cardiovascular disease.

dysmenorrhea: Painful periods.

dyspareunia: Painful intercourse.

Endocrinology: The study of the hormone producing organs, the hormones they produce, their action and interrelationships.

endometrial biopsy (EMB): A diagnostic procedure that samples tissue from the uterine lining to evaluate its development and receptivity, or for overgrowth (hyperplasia) and to exclude cancer.

endometrial hyperplasia: Excessive proliferation (overgrowth) of the cells lining the inside of the uterus (endometrium).

endometriosis: A condition where cells identical to the lining of the uterus (endometrium) are present and growing in a site other than in the uterine lining. Associated with chronic inflammation, adhesion formation, progressive pelvic pain, and infertility.

endothelium: Inner lining of cells in the wall of a blood vessel.

enzyme: A protein that facilitates (catalyzes) biochemical reactions.

estradiol (E2): An estrogen and principal hormone produced by the growing ovarian follicle.

estrone: A weak natural estrogen commonly produced in fat cells; also used in hormonal replacement therapy.

estrogen: The major female reproductive hormone.

ethinyl estradiol: A synthetic estrogen primarily used in oral contraceptives and hormone replacement.

Fasting: Nothing to eat or drink (usually after midnight the day before).

Ferriman and Gallwey score: A method of recording the amount of hair at eight different body sites on a scale of 1-4. A score greater than 8 denotes hirsutism.

fibroid: A benign fibrous tumor of the uterine muscle.

follicle: A small fluid filled sac in the ovary that contains an egg. The follicle ruptures and releases the egg at ovulation.

follicle stimulating hormone (FSH): A hormone produced by the pituitary gland that promotes the ovarian follicle development.

folliculogenesis: The growth and development of the ovarian follicles.

follistatin: A growth factor that opposes activin and regulates follicular growth.

free radical: An electron poor substance that can bind to lipids and other biological substances triggering an immune response, destruction or aging. Free radical scavengers are substances such as vitamin E which bind to free radicals and remove them from circulation.

Galactorrhea: Secretion (milk) from the breast, often indicating hyperprolactinemia.

gene: Basic unit of heredity; bits of DNA working together to achieve a single function.

genotype: The genetic makeup of an individual that determines the phenotype (physical action or appearance).

germinal epithelium: The surface covering of the ovary.

gestational diabetes: The development of diabetes (abnormal elevation of blood sugar) during pregnancy.

glucose tolerance testing (GTT): A test to exclude altered carbohydrate metabolism and diabetes. A blood test for glucose is performed, a sweetened drink with a known amount of glucose is given and a blood test for glucose repeated.

gonadotropins: Hormones (FSH, LH) produced by the pituitary gland to stimulate the ovaries to produce eggs and the testes to produce sperm. Also includes human chorionic gonadotropin (hCG) which is produced by the developing placenta stimulating the ovary to continue its production of progesterone.

gonadotropin releasing hormone (GnRH): The hypothalamic hormone controlling the production and release of gonadotropins (LH and FSH) from pituitary gland resulting in the stimulation of the gonads to make estrogen, progesterone, and androgens.

Graafian follicle: The preovulatory follicle.

granulosa cells: Supportive cells lining the ovarian the follicle that support egg development and convert androgens into estradiol.

growth factors: Substances that alter the growth and differentiation of the cell; the forerunners of hormones.

Heterozygous: Having two different versions (alleles) of a gene.

hidradenitis suppurtiva: Inflammatory condition of the modified sweat glands (apocrine glands) of the arm pits (axillae) and groin.

hirsutism: An increase in amount and/or coarseness of hair distributed in the male pattern in a female.

homeostasis: The body's internal balance; in equilibrium.

homozygous: Having the same version (allele) of a gene.

hormone: A substance made in small quantities by an (endocrine) organ which is secreted into the blood and has its effect(s) on distant and specific cells, tissues, or organs.

hormone replacement therapy (HRT): Medications used to replace estrogens, progestins, and androgens after the natural capacity to produce these hormones has been lost either naturally at menopause, or surgically.

hyperandrogenism: Increased amounts of male hormone in women and /or the associated clinical findings of such an increase.

hyperglycemia: Elevated blood sugar levels.

hyperplasia: Overgrowth of cells.

hyperprolactinemia: Excessive production of prolactin by the pituitary gland.

hypertension: Elevated blood pressure where the systolic (top number) is greater than and 140 and the diastolic (bottom number) is greater that 90.

hypoglycemia: A drop in the amount of sugar in the blood.

hypothalamic-pituitary-ovarian axis: The invisible wiring system that relates the ovary to the other components of the endocrine system and reproduction with the body's internal and external environment.

hypothalamus: Area in the brain just above the pituitary gland that integrates signals from the outside and inside environments and processes them into other signals that control body function including hormone release from the pituitary gland. The hypothalamus contains the "feeding" and "satiety" centers as well as "the pulse generator" producing short bursts of GnRH responsible for FSH and LH secretion form the pituitary.

hyperthecosis: A condition marked by few follicles and marked increase in steroid production in ovarian stroma cells.

hysterosalpingogram (HSG): An x-ray procedure whereby a special dye is passed through the uterus and tubes to test for structural abnormalities, such as blocked tubes and birth defects of the uterus.

hysteroscopy: A procedure whereby a small lighted telescope (hysteroscope) is passed through the cervix into the cavity of the uterus, which has been distended with either a gas or liquid, to evaluate the inside of the uterus for birth defects, polyps, fibroids, adhesions, or other factors that may compromise a pregnancy or cause abnormal bleeding.

Iatrogenic: Physician induced.

idiopathic: Unexplained, no known cause.

indication: Reason for therapy.

infertility: The inability to conceive after a year of unprotected intercourse or carry a pregnancy to term.

inhibin: A growth factor produced by the granulosa cells of the growing follicle that decreases FSH release from the pituitary gland.

insulin: A hormone produced by the pancreas that regulates the energy use of the body.

insulin clamp: A diagnostic test for insulin resistance where an IV is started amount of insulin needed to keep glucose at constant level;usually limited to research situations.

insulin resistance (IR): A condition where the body steadily becomes less responsive to the actions of insulin.

intracytoplasmic sperm injection: The mechanical insertion of a single sperm into an egg as a part of the in vitro fertilization process.

Karyotype: A picture of chromosomes arranged according to size and position.

Laparoscopy: A surgical procedure usually performed in a outpatient setting in which small telescope is inserted through an abdominal incision to examine the ovaries, uterus, and fallopian tubes. Conditions such as polycystic ovaries, endometriosis, or adhesions can be diagnosed and often treated.

leptin: Hormone-like regulatory protein produced by fat cells and involved in signaling of the body's energy requirements.

luteal phase defect: A condition characterized by insufficient progesterone production by the corpus luteum or the response to the uterus of that progesterone.

luteinizing hormone (LH): Hormone produced and released by the pituitary gland. In the female it is responsible for ovulation and the maintenance of the corpus luteum. In the male it stimulates testosterone production and is important in the production of sperm.

luteinization: The process under the influence of LH whereby the ovarian follicle is converted into the corpus luteum.

Macrosomia: An abnormally large fetus: birth weight greater than 4500g.

magnetic resonance imaging (MRI); A form of diagnostic imaging where the internal portions of the body are visualized using magnetic fields. Particularly useful in evaluation of the pituitary gland.

meiosis: The genetic basis of sexual reproduction where the normal complement of 46 chromosomes (diploid number) is reduced to 23(haploid number) so that when the egg and sperm unite the normal functioning constitution of 46 chromosome is restored.

menarche: The first period.

menorrhagia: Heavy periods.

menstruation: The periodic shedding of the uterine lining (endometrium) as a result of the failure to establish a pregnancy.

menses: A period.

meta-analysis: A statistical study combining a group of previous studies. It has the advantages of larger number of patients, but suffers from the constraints of the worst study added.

metabolic syndrome (dysmetabolic syndrome, syndrome X): Disorder characterized by insulin resistance, hypertension and dyslipidemia.

metrarrhagia: Bleeding between periods.

miscarriage: Loss of pregnancy before twenty weeks gestation.

Mittlesschmerz: Mid-cycle lower abdominal pain usually assumed to be associated with ovulation.

Missed abortion: Death of the fetus without expulsion from the uterus. Often associated with little bleeding and cervical opening.

myometrium: The dense muscle layer of the uterus whose contactions are responsible for menstrual cramps and delivery of the infant at birth.

Obesity: An excessive storage of body fat; a weight more than 20% above average.

oligomenorrhea: Menstrual periods greater than 35 days apart.

oligospermia: Decreased concentration (low number) of sperm.

osteopenia: Low bone density.

osteoporosis: The most common bone disease characterized by reduced bone mineral density and deterioration of the internal structural support within bones leading to increase bone fragility and fracture.

oxidative stress: Free radical biding (oxidizing) to lipids of the vessel wall resulting in inflammation and plaque formation (atherosclerosis).

ovarian cys: A fluid filled sac in the ovary. It may be found in conjunction with disordered ovulation (functional cysts), endometriosis (chocolate cysts) benign neoplasia (adenomas) and rarely cancer.

ovarian drilling: A surgical technique used in the treatment of polycystic ovary syndrome where a laser or high electrical current is used to destroy the small ovarian cysts which characterize the syndrome.

ovarian dysgenesis: A genetic abnormality where the ovary does not properly form with resulting signs of amenorrhea and estrogen deficiency.

ovaries: The female sex glands that produce eggs and secrete the female hormones estrogen and progesterone.

ovulation: The releasing of a mature egg from a follicle every month.

ovum: An egg.

Paracrine: Communication by chemical messages from a cell that affects neighboring cells.

perimenopause: Usually the 5 years prior and the first year after menopause in which there is declining ovarian estrogen production. Menstrual cycles tend to shorten as FSH levels rise in response to a declining store of follicles in the ovary. Symptoms of vasomotor instability (hot flushes/flashes/night sweats), poor sleep patterns, reduced memory, mood alteration, and alteration in the vaginal lubrication are often associated with this time.

phenotype: The outward appearance ofgene expression.

phlebotomy (venipuncture): Taking a blood sample.

pituitary gland: A less than dime size organ located at the base of the brain that is divided by origin into anterior and posterior lobes. The anterior lobe produces the "tropic" tropic hormones ACTH, FSH, LH, prolactin and TSH that control the action of the gonads, adrenal, breast and thyroid, and the posterior lobe that releases oxytocin responsible for milk "let -down" and vasopressin for fluid balance.

placebo: sugar pill, given in clinical trials to avoid bias about taking medications

polyp: A usually benign growth of glandular cells that is raised from the tissue of origin, for example the endometrium, by a stalk of tissue.

post coital test: An evaluation of cervical mucus and presence and viability of sperm performed just before ovulation and immediately after intercourse.

precocious puberty: The appearance of pubic and/or axillary hair before the age of eight.

pregnancy induced hypertension (pre-eclampsia, toxemia): hypertension with onset usually during the later stages of pregnancy associated with edema (swelling) and loss of protein in urine (proteinuria). In its severe form can cause blood coagulation problems and liver function abnormalities (HEELP syndrome).

progestin (progestogen): A synthetic agent that mimics the action of progesterone.

progesterone: A hormone produced by the corpus luteum of the ovary after ovulation has occurred that prepares the uterus for a pregnancy.

prolactin: A pituitary hormone which assists in milk production for breast-feeding; too much results in hyperprolactinemia and menstrual cycle disturbance.

Receptor: Usually a protein which may be attached to the cell membrane (wall) or free in the cell cytoplasm which recognizes and binds to other substance and permits a signal or event to be relayed or a particular action to take place.

recombinant: Technology whereby a specific gene is inserted into bacteria so that a specific protein is made in precise structure and in large quantities.

Sclerocystic: A term describing the appearance of the polycystic ovary; characterized by a tough, thick, white ovarian covering overlying numerous follicular cysts.

selective estrogen receptor modulator: A class of drugs that alter the estrogen receptor and mimic some, but not all, effects of estrogen; reduces bone loss, but has no effect on hot flashes.

sex hormone binding globulin (SHBG): A blood test used as a marker of PCOS. Low levels are a relatively good indicator of insulin resistance. Age, weight, diet, steroid and thyroid hormone levels, all affect the concentration of SHBG.

songram: see ultasound.

sperm washing (prep): Semen cannot be inserted into the uterine cavity without the risk of serious allergic reaction. For intrauterine insemination sperm must be isolated from the semen. Washing is performed by mixing the semen sample with nutrient media and placing the sperm in a centrifuge whereby the rapid spinning separates the sperm from the semen and media and then "resuspending" the sample in a small amount of media for insemination. The washing procedure may be performed once or twice before the sample is inseminated.

Stein-Leventhal syndrome: PCOS.

steroid: A biologic chemical similar to and having it origin form cholesterol. Depending on minor changes in structures, the steroid maybe classified as an estrogen, androgen or progestin. The major steroid producing organs are the ovary, testis, adrenal gland, fat and liver. Steroids are usually converted in the liver to inactive substances (metabolites) which are secreted in the urine and feces.

stroma: Connective tissue that fills the interstitial spaces of organs. In the ovary a source of hormone producing cells.

syndrome: A specific disorder characterized by a unified and identified group of signs and symptoms.

syndrome X: See metabolic syndrome.

Teratospermia: A type of male factor infertility caused by problems in the morphology of the sperm.

testosterone: The principal male sex hormone.

theca: a layer of vascularized steroid producing cells that arise from the ovarian stroma and surround the outer portion of the developing follicle.

thelarche: First breast development.

testosterone: Principle male hormone. Also produced in the ovary as the precursor of estradiol, the principle hormone of the ovary. About 50% of circulating testosterone in derived from conversion of other steroids by fat, liver and skin. The remainder comes equally from the adrenal gland and ovary.

thyroid gland: An endocrine gland in the front and base of the neck that secretes thyroxine and regulates general body metabolism.

threatened abortion: Bleeding during pregnancy with cervical dilation. May or may not indicate a problem with the pregnancy.

thrombus: Blood clot. A thromboembolism is a clot that moves from its site of origin to another area of the body.

thyroid gland: An endocrine gland in the neck that secretes thyroxin and regulates hormone balance in the body.

thyroid stimulating hormone: A pituitary hormone that stimulates the production of thyroxin in the thyroid gland.

thyroxine (T4): The hormone secreted by the thyroid gland, regulated by TSH produced in the pituitary gland.

tissue: Biologic combination of organized cells and supportive substances designed for a particular purpose.

trophoblast: The "extra"embryonic portion of the conception that initially attaches to the wall of the uterus and later differentiates into the placenta. HCG is produced from these cells.

Ultrasound: Imaging technique where sound waves are passed through a hand held transducer and the various densities of tissues examined . Fluid is said to be echolucent, it will appear black on the monitor while bone, the most echodense tissue appears bright white. The technquie is most often performed transvaginally (the transducer is placed in the vagina to enable the best visualization of the uterus and ovaries, but it can also be performed by placing the transducer on the abdomen (transabdominal), but the bladder must be very full to allow the best image.

uterus: A pear shaped reproductive organ of the female that nurtures the developing baby until birth. It is nulliparous if a woman has never given birth and multiparous after a delivery. It may be retroverted, tipped toward the backbone, or anteverted, tipped toward the front of the body.

Virilization: A condition where male sex characteristic (balding, voice change, enlargement of the clitoris, increase muscle mass, loss of breast contour) become prominent in a female.

Waist-hip ratio: Distance around the mid portion, greatest diameter of the hip divided by the waist measurement. defines type of obesity and specific disease risks.

wedge resection: see ovarian drilling.

withdrawal bleeding: Menses produced by giving medication to induce a period.

Zona pellucida: A protective coating around the oocyte which protects the oocyte and later, the developing embryo; sperm must penetrate this covering for fertilization to occur.

References

General Reviews

Adashi, E. Y., Rock, J. A., & Rosenwaks, Z. (eds). "Reproductive Endocrinology, Surgery, and Technology", 2 Volumes. (Philadelphia: Lipincott-Raven, 1996)

American College of Obstetricians and Gynecologists (2000). *2000 Compendium of Selected Publications.*

Azziz, R., Dewailly D., & Nestler, J.E. *Androgen Disorders in Women.* (Philadelphia, Lippincott-Raven, 1997)

American Diabetes Association: "Clinical Practice Recommendations" 2000. *Diabetes Care.* January 2000. Clark, Charles, editor-in-chief.

Ehrmann, D. A., Barnes, R. B., & Rosenfield, R. L.(1995) Polycystic ovary syndrome as a form of functional ovarian hyperandrogenism due to dysregulation of androgen secretion. *Endocrine Reviews, 16,* 322-353. Franks, S. (1995). Polycystic ovary syndrome. *New England Journal of Medicine, 333,* 853-861.

Kazer, R. R. (ed.). (1997). The polycystic ovary. *Seminars in Reproductive Endocrinology, 15,* 101-194.

Polycystic ovary syndrome: Metabolic challenges and new treatment options (1998). *American Journal of Obstetrics and Gynecology (supplement), 179,* S87-S116.

Redmond, G. P *Androgenic Disorders.* (New York: Raven Press, 1995).

Sperof, L., Glass, R. H., & Kase, N. G.. *Clinical Gynecologic Endocrinology and Infertility.* 7th edition. (Baltimore: Williams & Wilkins, 2000)

Stein, I. F., & Leventhal, M. L. (1935). "Amenorrhea associated with bilateral polycystic ovaries". *American Journal of Obstetrics and Gynecology, 29,* 181-191.

Yen, S., Jaffe, R. B., & Barbieri, R. L. *Reproductive Endocrinology: Physiology, Pathophysiology, and Clinical Management.* (Philadelphia, Pennsylvania: W. B. Saunders Company, 1999)

Biology (Chapter 2)

Barbieri, R. L., Makris, A., Randall, R. W., et al. (1986). Insulin stimulates androgen accumulation in incubations of ovarian stroma obtained from women with hyperandrogenism. *The Journal of Clinical Endocrinology & Metabolism, 62,* 904-910.

Beckers, N. G. M., Pieters, M. H. E. C., Ramos, L., Zeilmaker, G. H., Fauser, B. C. J. M., & Braat, D. D. M. (1999). Retrieval, maturation, and fertilization of immature oocytes obtained from unstimulated patients with polycystic ovary syndrome. *Journal of Assisted Reproduction and Genetics, 16,* 81-86.

Gougeon, A. (1986). Dynamics of follicular growth in the human: A model from preliminary results. *Human Reproduction, 1,* 81-87.

Hillier, S. G. Cellular basis of follicular endocrine function. In Hillier, S. G. (ed). *Ovarian Endocrinology.* (Oxford: Blackwell Scientific Publications, 25-72., 1991)

Magoffin, D. A., & Erickson, G. F. "Control systems of theca-interstitial cells." In Findlay, J. K. (ed). *Molecular Biology of the Female Reproductive System.* (London: Academic Press, 39-66, 1994)

McGee, E. A. & Hsueh, A. J. W. (2000). Initial and cyclic recruitment of ovarian follicles. *Endocrine Reviews, 21,* 200-214.

Genetics (Chapter 3)

Franks, S., Gharani, N., & Waterworth, D. (1997). The genetic basis of polycystic ovary syndrome. *Human Reproduction, 12,* 2641-2648.

Legro, R. S. (1999). Polycystic ovary syndrome: Phenotype to genotype. Endocrinology and Metabolism Clinics of North America, 28, 379-396.

McKeigue, P., & Wild, S. (1997). "Association of insulin gene VNTR polymorphism with polycystic ovary syndrome" (letter). *The Lancet, 349,* 1771-1772.

Puberty (Chapter 4)

Grumbach MM, Sizonenko PC, Aubert ML (eds). "Control of the onset of puberty". (Baltimore: Williams and Wilkins, 1990).

Herman-Giddens ME Slora EJ, Wasserman RC et al: (1997) "Secondary sexual characteristics and menses in young teens seen in office practice: a study from the Pediatric Research in Office Settings Network." *Pediatrics* 99: 505-512.

Legro, R. S., Lin, H. M., Demers, L. M., & Lloyd, T. (2000). "Rapid maturation of the reproductive axis during perimenarche independent of body composition." *The Journal of Clinical Endocrinology & Metabolism, 85,* 1021-1025.

Lucky AW, Biro FM, Simbartl LA et al. (1997) "Predictors of severity acne vulgaris in young adolescent teens: results if a 5 year longitudinal study." *Journal of Pediatrics* 130;30-39.

Mitamura, R., Yano, K., Suzuki, N., Ito, Y., Makita, Y., & Okuno, A. (2000). "Diurnal rhythms of luteinizing hormone, follicle-stimulating hormone, testosterone, and estradiol secretion before the onset of female puberty in short children." *The Journal of Clinical Endocrinology & Metabolism, 85,* 1074-1080.

Remschmidt H; (1994) "Psychosocial milestones in normal puberty and adolescence." *Hormone Research* 1 41; (suppl 2) 19-29

Roche AF, Wellens R, Attie KM, et al; (1995) "timing of sexual maturation in a group of US white youths." *Journal of Pediatric Endocrinology and Metabolism* 8;11-18.

van Hooff, M. H. A., Voorhorst, F. J., Kaptein, M. B. H., Hirasing, R. A., Koppenaal, C., & Schoemaker, J. (1999). "Endocrine features of polycystic ovary syndrome in a random population sample of 14-16 year old adolescents." *Human Reproduction, 14*, 2223-2229.

Diagnosis (Chapter 5)

Azziz, R. (1995). "21-Hydroxylase deficient non-classic adrenal hyperplasia". *The Endocrinologist, 5*, 297-303.

Allen, S. E., Potter, H. D., & Azziz, R. (1997). "Prevalence of hyperandro-genemia among nonhirsute oligo-ovulatory women." *Fertility and Sterility, 67*, 569-572.

Anttila, L., Ding, Y., Ruutiainen, K., Erkkola, R., Irjala, K., & Huhtaniemi, I. (1991). "Clinical features and circulating gonadotropin, insulin, and androgen interactions in women with polycystic ovarian disease." *Fertility and Sterility, 55*, 1057-1061.

Buckett, W. M., Bouzayen, R., Watkin, K. L., et al. (1999). "Ovarian stromal echogenicity in women with normal and polycystic ovaries." *Human Reproduction, 14*, 618-621.

Dale, P. O., Tanbo, T., Valler, St., & Abyholm, T. (1992). "Body weight, hyperinsulinemia, and gonadotropin levels in the polycystic ovarian syndrome: evidence of two distinct populations." *Fertility and sterility, 58*, 487-491.

Legro, R. S., Finegood, D. & Dunaif, A. (1998). "A fasting glucose-to-insulin ratio is a useful measure of insulin sensitivity in women with poly-cystic ovary syndrome." *The Journal of Clinical Endocrinology & Metabolism, 83*, 2694-2698.

Polson, D. W., Wadsworth, J., Adams, J., et al. (1988). "Polycystic ovaries: a common finding in normal women." *The Lancet, ii*, 870-873.

van Santbrink, E. J. P., Hop, W. C., Fauser, B. C. J. M. (1997). "Classification of normogonadotrophic infertility: polycystic ovaries diagnosed by ultrasound versus endocrine characteristics of polycys-tic ovary syndrome." *Fertility and Sterility, 67*, 452-458.

Hair and Skin (Chapter 7)

Azziz, R., Waggoner, W. T., Ochoa, T., et al. (1998). "Idiopathic hirsutism: an uncommon cause of hirsutism in Alabama." *Fertility and Sterility, 70*, 274-278.

Moghetti, P., Tosi, F., Tosti, A., et al. (2000). "Comparison of spironolac-tone, flutamide, and finasteride efficacy in the treatment of hir-sutism: A randomized, double blind, placebo controlled trial." *The Journal of Clinical Endocrinology & Metabolism, 85*, 89-94.

Olsen EA (editor). "Disorders of Hair Growth: Diagnosis and Treatment". New York, Mcgraw Hill 1994,

Obesity (Chapter 8)

AACE/ACE obesity Task Force (1998). "AACE/ACE Position Statement on the Prevention, Diagnosis, and Treatment of Obesity" (1998 Revision). *Endocrine Practice, 4,* 297-350.

American College of Sports medicine (1998). "The recommended quantity and quality of exercise for developing and maintaining cardiorespiratory and muscular fitness, and flexibility in healthy adults." *Medicine and Science in Sports and Exercise, 22,* 265-274.

American Dietetic Association (1997). "Position of the American Dietetic Association: Weight management." *Journal of the American Dietetic Association, 97,* 71-74.

Anderson, P., Selifeflot, I., Abdelnoor, M., et al. (1995). "Increased insulin sensitivity and fibrinolytic capacity after dietary intervention in obese women with polycystic ovary syndrome." *Metabolism, 44,* 611- 617.

Bray, G. A. (1996). "Obesity." *Endocrinology and Metabolism Clin North America, 25,* 781-1048.

Bray, G. A. (Ed). (1998). *Contemporary Diagnosis and the Management of Obesity. Handbooks in Health Care.* Newton, Pennsylvania.

Carek, P. J., & Dickerson, L. M. (1999). Current concepts in the pharmacological management of obesity. *Drugs, 56,* 883-904.

Guzick, D. S., Wing, R., Smith, D., Berga, S., & Winters, S. (1994). "Endocrine consequences of weight loss in obese, hyperandrogenic anovulatory women." *Fertility and Sterility, 61,* 598-604.

Miller, W. C. (1999). "Fitness and fatness in relation to health: Implications for a paradigm shift." *Journal of Social Issues, 55,* 207-219.

Kopelman, P. G., & Stock, M. J. *Clinical Obesity.* (Malden, Massachusetts: Blackwell Science Inc., 1998)

Report of a WHO Consultation on Obesity (1997*).* "Obesity: Preventing and Managing the Global Epidemic". Geneva: World Health Organization.

Shape Up America and American Obesity Association (1996). *Guidance for Treatment of Adult Obesity*

The National Heart, Lung, and Blood Institute (1998). "Clinical Guidelines on the identification, evaluation, and treatment of overweight and obesity in adults: executive summary." *American Journal of Clinical Nutrition, 68,* 899-917.

Vgontzas, A. N., Papanicolaou, D. A., Bixler, E. O., et al. (2000). "Sleep apnea and daytime sleepiness and fatigue: Relation to visceral obesity, insulin resistance, and hypercytokinemia." *The Journal of Clinical Endocrinology & Metabolism, 85,* 1151-1158.

Wadden, T. A., & Vanitallie, T. B. (1992). *Treatment of the Seriously Obese Patient.* (New York: The Guilford Press 1992).

Weyer, C., Pratley, R. E., Salbe, A. D., et al. (2000). "Energy expenditure, fat oxidation, and body weight regulation: A study of metabolic adaptation to long-term weight change." *The Journal of Clinical Endocrinology & Metabolism, 85,* 1087-1094.

American Diabetes Association (1997). "Consensus development conference on insulin resistance." *Diabetes Care, 21,* 310-316.

Dumesic, D. A., Nielsen, M. F., Abbott, D. H., Eisner, J. R., Nair, K. S., & Rizza, R. A. (1999). "Insulin action during variable hyperglycemic – hyperinsulinemic infusions in hyperandrogenic anovulatory patients and healthy women." *Fertility and Sterility, 72,* 458-466.

Dunaif, A., Scott, D., Finegood, D., Quintana, B., & Whitcomb, R. (1996). "The insulin-sensitizing agent troglitazone improves metabolic and reproductive abnormalities in the polycystic ovary syndrome." *The Journal of Clinical Endocrinology & Metabolism, 81,* 3299-3306.

Dunaif, A., Xia, J., Book, C. B., et al. (1995). "Excessive insulin receptor serine phosphorylation in cultured fibroblasts and in skeletal muscle. A potential mechanism for insulin resistance in the polycystic ovary syndrome." *Journal of Clinical Investigation, 96,* 801-810.

Ehrmann, D. A. (1997). "Relation of functional ovarian hyperandrogenism to non-insulin dependent diabetes mellitus." *Baillere's Clinical Obstetrics and Gynecology, 11,* 335-347.

Ehrmann, D. A., Schneider, D. J., Sobel, B. E., Cavaghan, M. K., Imperial, J., Rosenfield, R. L. & Polonsky, K. S. (1997). "Troglitazone improves defects in insulin action, insulin secretion, ovarian steroidogenesis, and fibrinolysis in women with polycystic ovary syndrome." *The Journal of Clinical Endocrinology & Metabolism, 82,* 2108-2116.

Elkind-Hirsche, K. E., Valdes, C. T., & Malinak, L. R. (1993). "Insulin resistance improves in hyperandrogenic women treated with Lupron." *Fertility and Sterility, 60,* 634-641.

Inzucchi, S. E., Maggs, D. G., Spollett, G. R., et al. (1998). "Efficacy and metabolic effects of metformin and troglitazone in type 2 diabetes mellitus." *New England Journal of Medicine, 338,* 867-872.

Moghetti, P., Tosi, F., Castello, R., et al. (1996). "The insulin resistance in women with hyperandrogenism is partially reversed by antiandrogen treatment: evidence that androgens impair insulin action in women." *The Journal of Clinical Endocrinology & Metabolism, 81,* 1952-1960.

Nestler, J. E., & Jakubowicz, D. J. (1996). "Decreases in ovarian cytochrome P450c17 a activity and serum free testosterone after reduction of insulin secretion in polycystic ovary syndrome." *New England Journal of Medicine, 335,* 617-623.

Nestler, J. E., Jakubowicz, D. J., Reamer, P., Gunn, R. D., & Allan, G. (1999). "Ovulatory and metabolic effects of D-chiro-inositol in the polycystic ovary syndrome." *The New England Journal of Medicine, 340,* 1314-1320.

Nestler, J. E., Jakubowicz, W. S., Evans, R., et al. (1997). "Metformin increases spontaneous and clomiphene-induced ovulation in the polycystic ovary syndrome." In: *Program of the 53r Annual Meeting of the American Society for Reproductive Medicine.* Cincinnati, p 51. Abstract 0-186.

Reaven, G. M. (1988). "Role of insulin resistance in human disease." *Diabetes, 37,* 1595-1607.

Robinson, S., Kiddy, D., Gelding, S. V., et al. (1993). "The relationship of insulin insensitivity to menstrual pattern in women with hyperandrogenism and polycystic ovaries." *Clinical Endocrinology, 39,* 351-355.

Velazquez, E. M., Acosta, A., & Mendoza, S. G. (1997). "Menstrual cyclicity after metformin therapy in polycystic ovary syndrome." *Obstetrics and Gynecology, 90,* 392-395.

Zhang, L. H., Rodriguez, H., Ohno, S. et al (1995). "Serine phosphorylation of human P450c17 increases 17,20-lyase activity: implications for adrenarche and the polycystic ovary syndrome." *Proc National Academy of Science USA, 92,* 10619-10623.

Body Image (Chapter 10)

About-Face (*http://www.about-face.org*).

Bella Online Magazine (web-based). http://www.bella-mag.com/

Berg, Frances. "Three major U.S. studies describe trends." *Healthy Weight Journal,* 11(4), 1997.

Cash, Thomas. "Cognitive-behavioral body-image therapy: Extended evidence of the efficacy of a self-directed program." *Journal of Rational Emotive and Cognitive Behavior Therapy,* 15(4), 1997.

Cash, Thomas. *The body image workbook: An 8-step program for learning to like your looks.* (Oakland, CA: New Harbinger, 1997).

Cooke, Kaz. *Real Grgeous.* (New York, NY: W.W. Norton, 1996).

Davis, Kristen. "Fat bias among psychologists: Impact of client weight on clinical judgments and treatment planning." *Dissertation Abstracts International: Section B: The Sciences and Engineering,* 58(7-B), 1998.

Eating Disorders Awareness and Prevention. (http://www.edap.org).

Eliot, Anne. "Enhancing women's body image: A comparison of treatment interventions." *Dissertation Abstracts International: Section B: the Sciences and Engineering,* 59(3-B), 1998.

Ernsberger, Paul, & Koletsky, Richard (1999). "Biomedical rationale for a wellness approach to obesity: An alternative to a focus on weight loss." *Journal of Social Issues,* 55(2), 221-260.

Feingold, Alan, & Mazzella, Ronald. "Gender differences in body image are increasing." *Psychological Science,* 9(3), 1998.

Freedman, Rita. *Beauty bound.* (Lexington, MA: Lexington Books, 1986).

Grant, Kathryn, et al. "Gender, body image, and depressive symptoms among low-income African American adolescents." *Journal of Social Issues*, 55(2), 1999.

Hirschmann, Jane, & Munter, Carol. *When women stop hating their bodies: Freeing yourself from food and weight obsession.* (New York, NY: Fawcett Columbine, 1995).

Johnston, Joni. *Appearance obsession: Learning to love the way you look.* (Deerfield Beach, FL: Health Communications, 1994).

Karraker, Katherine, Vogel, Dena, & Lake, Margaret. "Parents' gender-stereotyped perceptions of newborns: The eye of the beholder revisited." *Sex Roles*, 33(9/10), 1995.

Kilbourne, Jean. "Slim hopes: Advertising and the obsession with thinness." [Videorecording.] (Northampton, MA: Education Foundation, 1995).

Kwa, Lydia. "Adolescent females' perceptions of competence: What is defined as healthy and achieving." In Joanne Gallivan, Sharon Crozier, & Vivian Lalande (Eds)., *Women, girls, and achievement* (pp. 121-132). (North York, Ontario: Captus University Publications, 1994).

Levine, Michael, & Smolak, Linda. "Media as a context for the development of disordered eating." In Linda Smolak, Michael Levine, & Ruth Striegel-Moore (Eds)., *The developmental psychopathology of eating disorders: Implications for research, prevention, and treatment* (pp. 235-257). (Mahwah, NJ: Lawrence Erlbaum, 1996).

Maxi Magazine (web-based): http://www.maximag.com/.

McFarlane, Traci, Polivy, Janet, & McCabe, Randi. "Help, not harm: Psychological foundation for a nondieting approach toward health." *Journal of Social Issues*, 55(2), 1999.

Mode Magazine. On-line version (ModeStyle) at http://www.modestyle.com/.

National Institutes of Health Technology Assessment Conference Panel. "Methods for voluntary weight loss and control." *Annals of Internal Medicine*, 119, 1993.

Parker, Sheila, Nichter, Mimi, Nichter, Mark, Vuckovic, Nancy, Sims, C., & Ritenbaugh, C. "Body image and weight concerns among African-American and White adolescent females: Differences that make a difference." *Human Organization*, 54(2), 1995.

Polivy, Janet, & Herman, C. Peter. "Undieting: A program to help people stop dieting." *International Journal of Eating Disorders*, 11, 1992.

Radiance: The Magazine for Large Women. Information at *http://radiancemagazine.com/.*

Rozin, Paul, & Fallon, April. "Body image, attitudes to weight, and misperceptions of figure preferences of the opposite sex: A comparison of men and women in two generations." *Journal of Abnormal Psychology*, 97(3), 1988.

Smolak, Linda, & Levine, Michael. "Adolescent transitions and the development of eating problems." In Linda Smolak, Michael Levine, & Ruth Striegel-Moore (Eds)., *The developmental psychopathology of eating disorders: Implications for research, prevention, and treatment* (pp. 207-233). (Mahwah, NJ: Lawrence Erlbaum, 1996).

Thompson, J. Kevin, & Heinberg, Leslie. "The media's influence on body image disturbance and eating disorders: We've reviled them, now can we rehabilitate them?" *Journal of Social Issues*, 55(2), 1999.

Tkachuk, Gregg, & Martin, Garry. "Exercise therapy for patients with psychiatric disorders: Research and clinical implications." *Professional Psychology: Research and Practice*, 30(3), 1999.

Wolf, Naomi. *Beauty myth: How images of beauty are used against women.* (New York, NY: William Morrow, 1991).

Infertility (Chapter 11)

Balen, A. H., MacDougall, J., & Jacobs, "H. S. Polycystic ovaries and their relevance to assisted conception." In P. R. Brinsden (Ed)., *A Textbook of In Vitro Fertilization and Assisted Reproduction: The Bourn Hall Guide to Clinical and Laboratory Practice* (pp 109-129). (New York: The Parthenon Publishing Group Inc., 1999).

Cooper, Susan Lewis and Ellen Sarasohn. *Choosing Assisted Reproduction: Social, Emotional and Ethical Implications.* (Indianapolis: Perspectives Press, 1998).

Johnston, Patricia Irwin. *Taking Charge of Infertility.* (Indianapolis: Perspectives Press, 1994).

Family Building Alternatives

Carter, Michael and Jean Whitmore Carter, M.D. *Sweet Grapes: How to Stop Being Infertile and Start Living Again.* (Indianapolis: Perspectives Press, rev. 1998).

Johnston, Patricia Irwin. *Adopting after Infertility.* (Indianapolis: Perspectives Press, 1992).

Pregnancy (Chapter 12)

Bartha, J. L., Martinez-Del-Fresno, P., & Comino-Delgado, R. (2000). "Gestational diabetes mellitus diagnosed during early pregnancy." *American Journal of Obstetrics and Gynecology, 182*, 346-350.

Buchanan, T. A. & Kjos, S. L. (1999). "Gestational diabetes: Risk or myth?" *The Journal of Clinical Endocrinology & Metabolism, 84*, 1854-1857.

Cunningham, F. G., Clark, S. L., Grant, N. F., & Gilstrap, L. C., Hankins, G. D., Leveno, K.J., MacDonald, P. C. *Williams Obstetrics.* (Prentice Hall: Stanford, Connecticut., 1997).

Holte, J., Gennarelli, G., Wide, L., Lithell, H., & Berne, C. (1998). "High prevalence of polycystic ovaries and associated clinical, endocrine, and metabolic features in women with previous gestational diabetes mellitus." *The Journal of Clinical Endocrinology & Metabolism, 83*, 1143-1149.

Jaquet, D., Gaboriau, A., Czernichow, P., & Levy-Marchal, C. (2000). "Insulin resistance early in adulthood in subjects born with intrauterine growth retardation." *The Journal of Clinical Endocrinology & Metabolism, 85*, 1401-1406.

Napoli, C., Glass, C. K., Witztum, J. L., Deutsch, R., D'Armiento, F. P., & Palinski, W. (1999)." Influence of maternal hypercholesterolaemia during pregnancy on progression of early atherosclerotic lesions in childhood: Fate of early lesions in children (FELIC) study." *The Lancet, 354*, 1234-1241.

Radon, P. A., McMahon, M. J., & Meyer, W. R. (1999). "Impaired glucose tolerance in pregnant women with polycystic ovary syndrome." *Obstetrics and Gynecology, 94*, 194-197.

Rai, R., Backos, M., Rushworth, R., & Regan L. (2000). "Polycystic ovaries and recurrent miscarriage – a reappraisal." *Human Reproduction, 15*, 612-615.

Reece, E. A., & Hobbins, J. C. *Medicine of the Fetus and Mother.* (Philadelphia, Pennsylvania: Lippincott-Raven, 1997).

Schaefer-Graf, V. M., Buchanan, T. A., Xiang, A., Songster, G., Montoro, M., & Kjos, S. L. (2000). "Patterns of congenital anomalies and relationship to initial maternal fasting glucose levels in pregnancies complicated by type 2 and gestational diabetes." *American Journal of Obstetrics and Gynecology, 182*, 313-320.

Cancer (Chapter 13)

Colditz, G. A. (1998). "Relationship between estrogen levels, use of hormone replacement therapy, and breast cancer." *Journal of the National Cancer Institute, 90*, 814-823.

Riman, T., Persson, I., & Nilsson, S. (1998). "Hormonal aspects of epithelial ovarian cancer: Review of epidemiological evidence." *Clinical Endocrinology, 49*, 695-707.

Schildkraut, J.M., Schwingl P.J., Bastos E. et al. (1996) "Epithelial ovarian cancer risk among women with polycystic ovary syndrome." *Obstetrics and Gynecology* 88, 4 554-559.

Menopause (Chapter 14)

The North American Menopause Society (1998). *Menopause Guidebook: Helping You Make Informed Healthcare Decisions at Midlife.* USA.

Medical (Chapter 15)

American Association of Clinical Endocrinologists "Medical Guidelines for clinical practice: Diagnosis and treatment of dyslipidemia and prevention of atherogenesis. (2000)." *Endocrine Practice, 6*, 162-213.

Agrawal, R., Sladkevicius, P., Engmann, L., Conway, G. S., Payne, N. N., Bekis, J., Tan, S. L., Campbell, S., & Jacobs, H. S. (1998). "Serum vascular endothelial growth factor concentrations and ovarian stromal blood flow are increased in women with polycystic ovaries." *Human Reproduction, 13*, 651-655.

Cronin, L., Guyatt, G., Griffith, L., Wong, E., Azziz, R., Futterweit, w., Cook, D., & Dunaif, A. (1998). "Development of a health-related quality-of-life questionnaire replacement therapy on the vascular reactivity and endothelial function of healthy individuals and individuals with type 2 diabetes." *The Journal of Clinical Endocrinology & Metabolism, 84*, 4159-4164.

Dahlgren, E., Johansson, S., Lindstedt, G., Knutsson, F., Oden, A., Janson, P. O., Mattson, L. A., Crona, N., & Lundberg, P. A. (1992). "Women with polycystic ovary syndrome wedge resected in 1956 to 1965: A long-term follow-up focusing on natural history and circulating hormones*." *Fertility and Sterility, 57*, 505-513

Deedwania, P. C., guest editor (1998). "Proceedings of a symposium: The cardiovascular dysmetabolic syndrome." *The American Journal of Medicine (reprinted), 105*, 1S-82S.

DesPres, J. P., Lamarche, B., & Mauriege, P., et al. (1996). "Hyperinsulinemia as an independent risk factor for ischemic heart disease." *New England Journal of Medicine, 334*, 952-957.

Di Carlo, C., Shoham, Z., MacDougall, J., Patel, A., Hall, M. L., & Jacobs, H. S. (1992). "Polycystic ovaries as a relative protective factor for bone mineral loss in young women with amenorrhea." *Fertility and Sterility, 57*, 314-319.

Elting, M. W., Korsen, T. J. M., Rekers-Mombarg, L. T. M., & Schoemaker, J. (2000). "Women with polycystic ovary syndrome gain regular menstrual cycles when aging." *Human Reproduction, 15*, 24-28.

Hulley, S., Grady, D., Bush, T., Furberg, C., Herrington, D., Riggs, B., & Vittinghoff, E. (1998). "Randomized trial of estrogen plus progestin for secondary prevention of coronary heart disease in postmenopausal women." *Journal of the American Medical Association, 280*, 605-613

Mather, K. J., Vermal, S., Corenblum, B., & Anderson, T. J. (2000). "Normal endothelial function despite insulin resistance in healthy women with the polycystic ovary syndrome." *The Journal of Clinical Endocrinology & Metabolism, 85*, 1851-1856.

Medical Education Collaborative (1997). "Depressive Disorders in Women: Diagnosis, treatment, and Monitoring."

Shlipak, M. G., Simon, J. A., Vittinghoff, E., Lin, F., Barrett-Connor, E., Knopp, R. H., Levy, R. I., & Hulley, S. B. (2000). "Estrogen and progestin, lipoproteinα, and the risk of recurrent coronary heart disease events after menopause." *Journal of the American*

Medical Association, 283, 1845-1852.

Talbott, E., Clerici, A., Berga, S. L., Kuller, L., Guzick, D., Detre, K., Daniels, T., & Engberg, R. A. (1998). "Adverse lipid and coronary heart disease risk profiles in young women with polycystic ovary syndrome: Results of a case-control study." *Journal of Clinical Epidemiology, 51*, 415-422.

The Sixth Report of the Joint National Committee on Prevention, Detection, Evaluation, and Treatment of High Blood Pressure. National Institutes of Health, National Heart, Lung, and Blood Institute. November 1997.

Visser, M., Bourter, L. M., McQuillan, G. M., Wener, M. H., & Harris, T. B. (1999). "Elevated c-reactive protein levels in overweight and obese adults." *Journal of the American Medical Association, 282*, 2131-2135.

Surviving to Thriving (Chapter 16)

Aronson, Diane, Resolve, The National Infertility Association, *Resolving Infertility: Understanding the Options and Choosing Solutions When You want to Have a Baby,* (Oxford, MD.: Amaranth, 1999).

Burns, Linda Hammer and Covington, Sharon N. *Infertility Counseling: A Comprehensive Handbook for Clinicians,* (New York: Parthenon,1999).

Doress-Worters, Paula and Diana Laskin Siegal, *The New Our selves, Growing Older.*(New York: Touchstone, 1994).

Glahn, Sandra and Cutrer, William. *When Empty Arms Become a Heavy Burden: Encouragement for Couples Facing Infertility,* (Nashville: Broadman and Holman, 1997).

Johnston, Patricia Irwin. *Understanding Infertility: Insights for Family and Friends ,* (Indianapolis: Perspectives Press, 1996).

Sheehy, Gail, *The Silent Passage: Menopause* (New York: Random House 1991).

Internet sites:

http://www.angelfire.com/la/IslamicView

http://www.heartfelt.com/default.html

http://www.desloge/infertile_catholic.html

Therapy (Chapter 17)
Surgery

Campo, S. (1998). "Ovulatory cycles, pregnancy outcome and complications after surgical treatment of polycystic ovary syndrome." *Obstetrical and Gynecological Survey, 53*, 297-305.

Gadir, A. A., Alnaser, H. M. I., Mowafi, R. S., & Shaw, R. W., (1992). "The response of patients with polycystic ovarian disease to human menopausal gonadotropin therapy after ovarian electrocautery or a luteinizing hormone-releasing hormone agonist." *Fertility and Sterility, 87*, 309-313.

Lemieux, S., Lewis, G. F., Ben-Chetrit, A., Steiner, G., & Greenblatt, E. M. (1999). "Correction of hyperandrogenemia by laparoscopic ovarian cautery in women with polycystic ovarian syndrome is not accompanied by improved insulin sensitivity or lipid-lipoprotein levels." *The Journal of Clinical Endocrinology & Metabolism, 84*, 4278-4282.

Medical

Gaspard, U. J., & Lefebvre, P. J. (1990). "Clinical aspects of the relationship between oral contraceptives, abnormalities in carbohydrate metabolism, and the development of cardiovascular disease." *American Journal of Obstetrics and Gynecology, 163*, 334

Garg, S. K., Chase, H. P., Marshall, G., et al. (1994). "Oral contraceptives and renal and retinal complications in young women wit insulin-dependent diabetes mellitus." *Journal of the American Medical Association, 271*, 1099.

Godsland, I. F., & Crook, D. (1994). "Update on the metabolic effects of steroidal contraceptives and their relationship to cardiovascular disease risk." *American Journal of Obstetrics and Gynecology, 170*, 1528-1536.

Korytkowski, M. T., Mokan, M., Horwitz, M. J., et al. (1995). "Metabolic effects of oral contraceptives in women with polycystic ovary syndrome." *The Journal of Clinical Endocrinology & Metabolism, 80*, 3327-3334.

McClure, N., McQuinn, B., McDonald, J., Kovacs, G. T., Healy, D. L., & Burger, H. G. (1992). "Body weight, body mass index, and age: Predictors of menotropin dose and cycle outcome in polycystic ovarian syndrome?" *Fertility and Sterility, 58*, 622-624.

Petersen, K. R., Skouby, S. O., Sidelmann, J., et al. (1994). "Effects of contraceptive steroids on cardiovascular risk factors in women with insulin-dependent diabetes mellitus." *American Journal of Obstetrics and Gynecology, 171*, 400-405.

Nader, S., Riad-Gabriel, M. G., Saad, M. F. (1997). "The effect of a desogestrel-containing oral contraceptive on glucose tolerance and leptin concentrations in hyperandrogenic women." *The Journal of Clinical Endocrinology & Metabolism, 82*, 3074-3077.

Whelan, J. G., & Vlahos, N. F. (2000). "The ovarian hyperstimulation syndrome." *Fertility and Sterility, 73*, 883-896.

Complementary

Blumenthal, M., Goldberg, A., & Brinckmann, J. *Herbal Medicine.* (Newton, MA: Integrative Medicine Communications, 2000).

Jellin, J. M., et al. *Natural Medicines Comprehensive Database.* (Stockton, CA: Therapeutic Research Faculty, 1999).

hair. *See also* hirsutism
    facial, 105, 315, 341
    growth of, 100-01
    loss of, 49, 100, 111-12, 342
    problems with, 111, 341-42
    removal of, 105-07, 341
    sexual, 57-58, 99
hCG. *See* human chorionic gonadotropin
HDL. *See* cholesterol; lipids
headaches. *See also* migraines
    and amphetamines, 369
    and clomiphene citrate, 378
    and flutamide, 366
    and oral contraceptives, 353-54
    and PCOS, 320
    and progesterone, 359
    and prolactin inhibiting agents, 390
    sinus, 307
    tension, 305, 307
Healing Mind, Healthy Body, 320
health care professionals, 425-30. *See also*
        physicians
health insurance, 316-17
    and PCOS, 95-98
    options in, 97-98
Healthy Weight Journal, 170
Heart and Estrogen/Progestin Replacement
        Study, 300
heart
    and atherosclerosis, 292. *See also*
        atherosclerosis
    attack, 291, 355, 368
    disease, 293, 296-97
    and hypertension, 295
HEELP syndrome, 231
Heinberg, Leslie, 168
hemorrhage, 232
herbal remedies, 396-402
    and migraines, 308
    and pregnancy, 402
    and premenstrual stress, 306
heredity, and genes, 41-44
Herman, C. Peter, 172
Herman-Giddens, M. E., 56
HERS. *See* Heart and Estrogen/Progestin
        Replacement Study
hidradenitis suppurativa, 100, 113
Hirschmann, Jane, 174

hirsutism, 99, 327, 341, 364-65. *See*
also hair cause of, 18
    definition of, 103
    and GnRH analogs, 387
    and hormones, 102-03
    idiopathic, 104
    and menopause, 266
    and oral contraceptives, 353
    and PCOS, 320
    and puberty, 324
    quantification of, 104
    treatment of, 108-110, 299, 317
HMG-CoA Reductase Inhibitors, 294-95
HMG-Pergonal, 380
hormone replacement therapy, 266, 275-
        84. *See also* estrogen;progestin
    benefits of, 276
    bleeding in, 284
    and cancer, 278-79
    and cardiovascular disease, 300-01
    and cognitive function, 269, 332
    components of, 280-82
    and gallstones, 304
    and menopause, 331
    and mood, 269, 332
    and osteoporosis, 273-74
    and PCOS, 279
    risks in, 278
hormones. *See also* androgen;
        corticosteroids; Depo-Provera;
        estrogen; oral contraceptives;
        Progestins; steroid hormones
    and aging, 263-64
    and brain development, 52-53
    and cancer, 254
    and depression, 305
    effect on skin, 102, 315
    function of, 17-19
    and glitazones, 376
    and hirsutism, 102-03
    and the immune system, 311
    and lactation, 240-41
    and male infertility, 185-86
    and migraines, 309
    and miscarriage, 49, 234, 236
    and mood, 332
    and ovarian cycle, 26 illus.
    and ovarian surgery, 347

PCOS: The Hidden Epidemic

**has received these early comments from respected
physicians and advocates in the field...**

Dr. Sam Thatcher is a renowned expert in Reproductive Endocrinology. He brings to the field both scientific and clinical expertise. This fine book provides superb explanation, insight, and direction in regards to the polycystic ovary syndrome. In a comprehensive yet easy to read format, Thatcher has provided a text that has all the answers (known at this time) in regards to this complex disease entity — polycystic ovarian syndrome. It is a unique contribution.

Alan DeCherney, M.D.
Editor, *Fertility and Sterility*
Past president, American Society for Reproductive Medicine

As a woman with PCOS, I spent many years searching for answers to the multitude of problems that plagued me: acne, irregular cycles, excess hair, weight problems and infertility. Over the years, as my symptoms increased I felt increasingly stripped of both my physical health and my femininity. Deep down, I thought that there had to be a connection between all of my seemingly disparate problems but neither I nor my doctors were able to recognize that connection. Thankfully, times are changing, in no small part due to doctors like Samuel Thatcher. Dr. Thatcher was one of the earliest advocates for PCOS awareness. He recognized the connections, realizing that this is a syndrome which crosses medical boundaries, and began treating the whole woman rather than the individual symptoms. His knowledge in the fields of gynecology and endocrinology are only surpassed by his depth of understanding and compassion for the women afflicted with this syndrome. He is a true champion of women with PCOS!

Kristin Hellman Rencher
Executive Director, PolyCystic Ovarian Syndrome
Association, Inc.
http://www.pcosupport.org

As an INCIID advisory board member and PCOS Forum moderator on the Internet, Samuel Thatcher, M.D., has helped drag this debilitating syndrome out of the closet and enabled thousands of women to find relief from their symptoms. In his book, *PCOS: The Hidden Epidemic*, Dr. Thatcher takes his distinctive, conversational style, mixed with solid science, and provides the most comprehensive overview of PCOS to date. He gives women the ammunition they need to insist upon appropriate diagnostic testing and the new and successful treatments that can help overcome hormonal disturbances and dramatically improve the quality of their lives.

Theresa Venet Grant
President, INCIID (International Counsel on Infertility
Information Dissemination)
http://www.inciid.org

Polycystic ovary syndrome is a common and complex endocrine disorder. While much has been learned in recent years regarding its causes and treatments, much remains unanswered. For women diagnosed with PCOS, there has not been a single authoritative source of information written with the patient in mind. Now, Dr. Thatcher has filled that gap. This text is an informative, readable, and useful source of information for patients and their families. Dr. Thatcher conveys his expertise in this area to those who need it most. I will recommend this book to anyone who has or is interested in learning more about PCOS.

David Ehrmann, M.D.
University of Chicago, Center for PCOS

Dr. Thatcher provides the reader with understandable and straightforward information about PCOS. This book is a vital and much-needed resource for patients as it empowers them to gain a better understanding of PCOS' life-long issues and take back control back of their lives.

Pamela Madsen
Executive Director, The American Infertility Association
http://www.americaninfertility.org

Perspectives Press:
The Infertility and
Adoption Publisher

http://www.perspectivespress.com

Since 1982 Perspectives Press has focused exclusively on infertility, adoption, and related reproductive health and child welfare issues. Our purpose is to promote understanding of these issues and to educate and sensitize those personally experiencing these life situations, professionals who work in these fields, and the public at large. Our titles are never duplicative or competitive with material already available through other publishers. We seek to find and to fill niches which are empty.

Currently in print titles include

For adults

Perspectives on a Grafted Tree
Understanding Infertility: Insights for Family and
    Friends
Sweet Grapes: How to Stop Being Infertile and
    Start Living Again
A Child's Journey through Placement
Adopting after Infertility
Flight of the Stork: What Children Think and
    When about Sex and Family Building
Taking Charge of Infertility
Looking Back, Looking Forward
Launching a Baby's Adoption
Toddler Adoption: The Weaver's Craft
Choosing Assisted Reproduction
PCOS: The Hidden Epidemic
Inside Transracial Adoption

For Children

The Mulberry Bird
Filling in the Blanks
Lucy's Feet
Two Birthdays for Beth
Let Me Explain

About the Author

Samuel S. Thatcher, M.D., Ph.D. began his career in reproductive science in 1973 when studying the detrimental effects of aging on reproduction. This culminated in a Ph.D. in human anatomy/reproductive biology at West Virginia University, where he simultaneously received his M.D. A year of post doctoral research was spent between Edinburgh and Johns Hopkins Universities. On completion of his residency training in obstetrics and gynecology at Yale/New Haven Hospital, he returned to Edinburgh University as Lecturer in Reproductive Medicine and Medical Director of the IVF program of Edinburgh University and the Royal Infirmary. He completed a fellowship in reproductive endocrinology and served on the faculty in the Division of Reproductive Endocrinology at Yale before returning to East Tennessee. His research interests continue in reproductive aging, ovarian function, assisted reproduction and early human development. He is a member of over 20 national and international societies and has authored numerous medical journal articles.

Dr. Thatcher is an active consumer advocate, serving on the Advisory Board of The American Infertility Association as well as on the Advisory Board of INCIID (the International Council on Infertility Information Dissemination) for which he co-moderates the Polycystic Ovary Syndrome (PCOS) forum on INCIID and writes the Internet column "Thatcher's Thoughts."